COMMENTARY ON THE DOCUMENTS OF VATICAN II

COMMENTARY
ON THE DOCUMENTS OF VATICAN II

GENERAL EDITOR:

Herbert Vorgrimler

EDITORIAL COMMITTEE:

Heinrich Suso Brechter
Bernhard Häring
Josef Höfer
Hubert Jedin
Josef Andreas Jungmann
Klaus Mörsdorf
Karl Rahner
Joseph Ratzinger
Karlheinz Schmidthüs
Johannes Wagner

COMMENTARY
ON THE DOCUMENTS
OF
VATICAN II

Volume V

PASTORAL CONSTITUTION ON THE CHURCH
IN THE MODERN WORLD

HERDER AND HERDER

1969

HERDER AND HERDER NEW YORK
232 Madison Avenue, New York, N. Y. 10016

BURNS & OATES LIMITED
25 Ashley Place, London S. W. 1

Original edition:
"Das Zweite Vatikanische Konzil, Dokumente und Kommentare",
Part III, Herder, Freiburg, 1968 (pp. 241—592)

Translated by
W. J. O'Hara

Library of Congress Catalog Card No. 67-22928
First published in West Germany, © 1969, Herder KG
Printed in West Germany by Herder

CONTENTS

PUBLISHER'S NOTE

The publishers have not given the text of the Council documents in this book, as separate text editions, both in Latin and English, are easily available. All quotations from the English translation of the Council texts in this volume have been taken from *The Documents of Vatican II* (Walter M. Abbott, S. J., General Editor; Joseph Gallagher, Translation Editor), © America Press, published in New York, 1966, by Guild Press, Herder and Herder, and Association Press, and in London, 1966, by Geoffrey Chapman Ltd. Grateful acknowledgment is made herewith for permission to quote from these texts.

ABBREVIATIONS

AAS   *Acta Apostolicae Sedis*

CC   *Il concilio vaticano II* (1965–66)

D   H. Denzinger, *Enchiridion Symbolorum* (32nd edition, 1963)

DC   *Documentation Catholique*

DSAM   M. Viller, ed., *Dictionnaire de Spiritualité ascétique et mystique. Doctrine et Histoire* (1932 ff.)

H   F. Houtart, *Par delà le schéma XIII* (manuscript of a book in preparation)

HTG   H. Fries, ed., *Handbuch theologischer Grundbegriffe*, 2 vols. (1962–63)

K   B. Kloppenburg, *Concilio vaticano II, Prima, segunda, sessão preparação* (1962–64)

L   René Laurentin, *Bilan du Concile*, 4 vols. (1963–66)

LTK   J. Höfer and K. Rahner, eds., *Lexikon für Theologie und Kirche*, 10 vols. and index (2nd edition, 1957–67)

NRT   *Nouvelle Revue Théologique*

R   H. de Riedmatten, *Histoire du schéma XIII* (manuscript of a study in preparation)

T   R. Tucci, "Introduzione storico-dottrinale alla Costituzione pastorale Gaudium et spes", *La Chiesa e il mondo contemporaneo nel Vaticano II* (1966), pp. 17–134

TQ   *Theologische Quartalschrift*

W   A. Wenger, *Vatican II, Chronique de la première . . . seconde . . . troisième . . . quatrième session*, 4 vols. (1963–66)

ZNW   *Zeitschrift für die neutestamentliche Wissenschaft und die Kunde der älteren Kirche*

Pastoral Constitution on the Church in the Modern World

History of the Constitution

by
Charles Moeller

I. THE FIRST TEXT

The announcement of the Council was made in the name of Christian unity. To John XXIII, however, this meant the witness which must be borne throughout the world, and which divisions obscure. A month before the announcement, he had been thinking of a Council like a "shepherd or a pilot in a storm", as Laurentin writes, because of the insoluble problems of the hour. "His diplomatic career had produced this sensitive awareness of world-wide horizons and especially of Eastern Europe, where he had seen the problems of unity take concrete shape. Mgr. Roncalli understood what Rome looks like from Istanbul, the former Constantinople, and what Istanbul looks like from Rome." His life as Patriarch of Venice had taught him to see men's concrete needs. Yet although Pius XI and Pius XII had thought of resuming Vatican I, John XXIII apparently made the decision without reference to documents or the example of his two predecessors.

1. Unity and the world were the two poles of the Pope's thought; they produced extremely varied reactions in the writings of journalists and commentators. The idea of unity in particular amazed and perplexed, as can be seen from Hans Küng's book *Council and Reunion* (1962). Others spoke chiefly of episcopate and laity, the first an essentially internal Church concern, the second at that time a knot of unsolved problems. H. Küng's book *Council in Action* (1963) speaks of problems which, though important, are internal ones — liturgical reform and dogmatic questions. It does indeed touch on the theme of "the Church in this age", but does so from the point of view of the Petrine office, of the need for the Church to be sensitive and open to other cultures at the present time, in the age of ecumenism. Thus one chapter deals with world mission in the age of the ecumenical movement. The chapter about what Christians look for from the Council likewise sees all the problems in the perspective of unity.

From the very beginning, some people, especially in France and Latin America (Brazil), emphasized the importance of the Council in a world which had changed and grown to an enormous extent in the preceding 15 years. From 1962 onwards, Laurentin had been writing pages which already sounded like an anticipation of the Introductory Statement of *Gaudium et Spes*. F. Houtart had become familiar with the situation of the Church during his travels in Latin America. Religious sociology, still a very young science, adopted world-wide perspectives and showed the need for the Church's active "presence" in the world. All the alert minds in Latin America were aware of the urgency of these important problems.[1]

2. Now when we examine the programme of the conciliar preparatory commissions, we discover that out of 70 schemata, only one was devoted to the social order, No. 7, one of the schemata of the Theological Commission. For reasons which still call for close examination, the majority of theologians working for the bishop members of the preparatory commissions had obviously given practical effect to their reserve in regard to the original outlook on "unity and the world". No doubt ecumenism had been entrusted to a secretariat, but it could only gain entry to the conciliar programme through an unguarded back-door. The commissions appointed corresponded to the standard dicasteries of the Curia and had intentionally made it plain that the Council was a domestic affair of the Church.[2]

3. Two commissions were concerned with the social order, the Theological Commission and the Commission for the Apostolate of the Laity. The former had not enough time to complete its work in this respect; the Co-ordinating Commission ordered it to continue it and to present its draft later. This explains why the text only appeared once, in Volume III of the schemata distributed at the First Session (pp. 5–44). A text on international order was likewise planned. In fact the next document in Volume III concerns this topic (pp. 47–56). It belongs to the draft on social order.

The Theological Preparatory Commission had established a subcommission to deal with this schema on social and international order (in the original plan only one schema was envisaged). Sigmond lists its members as: Mgrs. P. Pavan, A. Ferrari-Toniolo, Frs. F. Hürth, G. Grundlach and G. Jarlot, all of the Society of Jesus, A. R. Sigmond, OP; the *relator* for marriage questions was E. Lio, OFM.

[1] *K* I, p. 18; *Wort und Wahrheit*, special number: "Was erwarten Sie vom Konzil?" 16 (1961), pp. 569–718; *Fragen an das Konzil*, Herder-Bücherei 95 (1961); "Vœux pour le Concile", in *Esprit* (December 1961), pp. 673–874; *Qu'attendons-nous du Concile?* in the series *Études pastorales* (1961); H. Küng, *Konzil und Wiedervereinigung* (1960), E. T.: *Council, Reform, and Reunion* (1962). In all these publications the "expectation of the world" aspect is found, but that of openness towards the world is still not very prominent. It is mentioned in connection with the endeavour for unity and, later, with *aggiornamento*. Laurentin's text will be found in *L* I, pp. 109–13.

[2] *L* I, pp. 100–48.

2

The Preparatory Commission for the Apostolate of the Laity for its part was preparing a text on social action. This was more concerned with practical measures but also contained doctrinal elements. The president of the second subcommission was the Bishop of Essen, Mgr. Hengsbach; until almost the end of the Council he remained responsible for supervising the preparation of the chapters on concrete practical applications; in the end he became the *relator* of the second part of Schema 13. Mgr. Pavan was vice-president of this subcommission, to which Mgrs. A. Ferrari-Toniolo and G. Jarlot also belonged.

It is clear that Mgrs. Pavan, Ferrari-Toniolo and G. Jarlot were members of two subcommissions, for theology and the lay apostolate. They were assigned to Fr. Tromp for that part of the texts which concerned practical applications. Tromp, who was Secretary of the Theological Preparatory Commission, quite soon accepted Mgr. Pavan's views — the latter's role in the encyclical *Pacem in Terris* is well-known — and soon made Pavan's perspectives his own. Nevertheless there were a few difficulties which were deeply felt, especially by the three experts from the Commission for the Apostolate of the Laity. The tension that arose from the fact that the same theme was being approached from various sides is very obvious if the text of the Theological Preparatory Commission (*Schemata constitutionum...*, series III a, pp. 5–44 [1962]) is compared with that of the Commission for the Lay Apostolate (*Schemata constitutionum...*, series IV, pp. 137–73). It will be encountered again at all phases of the discussions in preparation for Schema 13. In the end a text was successfully produced which while not too exclusively theological or lacking in direct reference to contemporary problems, was not excessively sociological and theologically pointless. The final text in fact maintained a dynamic balance between the two points of view, and genuine polarity is visible between the first and second part. But the tension is also evident in the fact that Mgr. Garrone, although responsible during the last conciliar session for the whole text, in practice dealt mainly with the first part, while Mgr. Hengsbach, as we have already noted, was chiefly concerned with the second part.

The Theological Subcommission gave the text a rather classical stamp by emphasizing the objective character of the moral order. Later revisions of the theological section obviously did not deny this, but preferred for their own purposes a more biblical, concrete and existential — not Existential — viewpoint. In other words, even though Schema 13 always involved a polarity between the theological viewpoint and that of concrete particular problems, the fundamental character of the theological part changed. It followed the course of development of all the conciliar texts, which moved from a more abstract, conceptual and timeless perspective towards a biblical, patristic, liturgical and conciliar outlook.

These details on the parallel preparation of the two conciliar texts illustrate the dual origin of the schema. Before going further, we must complete the list of members of the subcommission: Mgrs. L. Civardi, L. De Pietro, G. Higgins, W. F. Kekky, L. Ligutti, V. Portier, S. Quadri, and Frs. W. Ferree, J. Géraud, J. B. Hirschmann, J. Ponsioen, V. de Vogelaere. Of these, Mgr. Quadri was to become Auxiliary Bishop of Pinerolo. Fr. Hirschmann, SJ, who took part in the drafting of Schema 13 from the beginning, was for a time specially responsible for the chapter on the dignity of the human person. He finally belonged to the central editorial committee during the Third and Fourth Sessions until the close of the latter. He was one of those who combined close concern for concrete and particularly social realities with equal concern for the most precise theology. [3]

4. On examination, the Theological Subcommission's document *De ordine morali christiano* published in the first volume of schemata and delivered to the fathers in September 1962, displays remarkable ambivalence. The first four chapters bear the mark of the same ideas as the famous earlier schema *De duobus fontibus revelationis*. The first chapter, "De fundamento ordinis moralis christiani", insists on the "indoles obiectiva ordinis moralis", on its "character absolutus", on God as "custos, iudex, vindex ordinis moralis", on the double revelation of the moral order as "lex naturalis" and as "revelatio Dei", on the object of the moral order and, finally, of errors to be rejected. Chapter II speaks of the Christian conscience, defining it as the place where the moral order is manifested. The need for correct formation of the conscience is emphasized. Mention is made of the erroneous conscience, stressing the need to correct it and recalling that its error does not in any way affect the objectivity of the moral order. Criticism is expressed of the "pseudo-conscientia autonoma" and finally it is shown how conscience should be "signata Christi veritate et caritate" (arts. 7–11). In this perspective Chapter III combats the errors of "subjectivism and ethical relativism" (arts. 12–15). Chapter IV speaks of sin, in what sense the "regnum peccati sit destructum". It is recalled that man can commit a sin even when he "explicite Deum contemnere renuat". Attention is drawn to the danger of calling any sin "venial" if it is committed "sub influxu sensibilium virium hominum". In this sense judgment is passed on "falsae theoriae psychologicae". Finally, it is confirmed that the Christian can advance on the path of righteousness as well as having the grave duty of penance; this provides an opportunity for pointing out some new errors in this domain (arts. 16–22).

Chapter V is distinguished by a very different tone, which partly anti-

---

[3] *T*, notes 7, 8. We are very indebted to this masterly study. We have also added a number of details from notes made in the course of the various meetings by the present author, who had the good fortune to take part with Fr. Tucci in the work of preparing each of the successive versions of the schema. Some of the details given in section I, 3, of the present commentary were supplied by Mgr. Glorieux, who also worked on each of the versions as secretary of the commission, with unshakable patience and serene optimism.

cipates that of the future Schema 13. Though the title "De naturali et super-naturali dignitate personae humanae" is still very "classical", the contents are less so. The first chapter in fact expressly links human dignity with the fact that man is made to the image of God: "Humanae personae dignitas in eo sita est, quod homo ad imaginem et similitudinem Dei factus, et natura sua immediate ad Deum ordinatus, rationis lumen, liberae electionis potestatem, amoris flammam, rerumque corporalium dominium a Deo accepit" (art. 23).

This text is indubitably dealing with what will be said later in *Gaudium et Spes,* art. 12, par. 4, directly after mention of man's ability to know and love God. After the introductory statement there is a reference to human' dignity, which is defended by the Church's laws and only shines with its full lustre in those who submit to God "eiusque legatis". The theme of man as the image of God has entered the conciliar text in a context which still to a large extent bears the stamp of an abstract, conceptual outlook, not to say that of a thesis-theology.

Two facts nevertheless stand out. The theme of man made to the image of God appears in the very first version of a document which was not in fact accepted as it stood, but whose essential substance was preserved during the preparation of the second text. The theme of human dignity which was to be the focus of the last three chapters of the second part of the final schema is already contained in this preliminary draft. It is yet another theme which does not appear to be bound up with a conception of natural law and of a natural theology which will always cause difficulties for our Protestant brethren, but with the biblical reality of man made to the image of God.

How exactly did the theme of man as the image of God find its way into the texts of Vatican II? It did so, moreover, precisely in the perspective of man's dominion over the world, which is expressly connected with the divine image which irradiates his countenance. The whole of Article 26 of the preparatory schema — *scientia, artes liberales, technica* — is in fact connected with what the final schema will call culture, and with what it has to say about technology, the sciences and dominion over the world: "Dignitas personae humanae modo prorsus singulari elucet non solum in filiatione divina consortioque divinae naturae, verumetiam in eo, quod a Deo homo constitutus est supra opera manuum suarum, adeoque Angelis paulo minor sit dicendus." The fundamental justification of the attitude of the Church to learning and culture derives from this fact. The passage quoted from *Quadragesimo Anno (D* 2270) mentions the theme, it is true, but in the anti-totalitarian context of the human person, who must give glory to God.[4]

---

[4] It seems to me that the introduction of the theme of the image of God in connection with the presence of the Church in the world is just as important a fact as the adoption of the themes of collegiality and the People of God in *Lumen Gentium.* The present state of documentation does not make it possible to determine the historical origin of the introduction of this theme. That is a task that remains to be done.

5. The text on the "moral order", as it was called, has to be examined in the first version of the second text. The other schema, *De ordine sociali,* also began with the theme of man as the image of God, this time, however, in connection with social life (*Schemata,* Vol. III, p. 5). The link is not so much that social life is as it were transparent to the image of God stamped upon it, but that social life in fact "ex rationalis hominis natura intrinseca manat" (art. 1). The theme of the image of God is stated chiefly in order to recall that the purpose of all social life is the human person.[5] Obviously a correct thesis, but in the definitive version of the Constitution it is taken up again in an even more biblical context of a social life in the form of social solidarity or love intrinsically connected with the fact of creation to the image of God (*Gaudium et Spes,* art. 12, par. 5).

In this respect Chapter II, "De dominio universali humano et de privata proprietate", is also typical. The whole of Article 11 takes up again the theme of the image of God in connection with dominion over the world in a context the clear sense of which is that man is lord of all the goods of this earth. From this point of view the patristic quotations are typical. The articles which follow (12–17) are concerned with private property.

Chapter III, however, "De indole laboris humani", first of all states its "character poenalis" and only later *(insuper)* comes to its connection with the vocation of man made to the image of God, which is described as "complendum opus divinae creationis". Also *(imo)* its connection with the well-being of the whole of mankind and the Church is indicated (art. 18).

These material similarities in very different contexts make it possible to determine clearly the change which took place between Text 1 and Text 2. It is not at all a matter of what is said — for of course the essential theme of the image of God, for example, is already found in the first version — but rather a question of outlook. We move from a timeless, conceptual perspective in the form of theses to a concrete perspective which takes account of the historical moment at which we live.

6. The schema on the Apostolate of the Laity contains a section entitled "De apostolatu laicorum in actione sociali". This takes a more positive view of human action. The theme of man as the image of God only appears marginally, and is not explicitly related to the duty of establishing an "earthly order" in Christ. The authors charged with drafting the second part develop ideas which were then taken up in successive revisions. On the whole it is surprising how little the theological aspect of this activity of the layman is brought out. Certainly it is true that the first schema on the Church contained a dogmatic chapter on the laity, and therefore the authors of the laity schema wanted to avoid unnecessary repetition. Nevertheless the biblical

---

[5] This is the origin of another central idea of *Gaudium et Spes,* that of the connection between human dignity and the biblical truth of man as the image of God.

setting seems very slight; we move in an order of "natural" if essential truths, but no attempt is made to show their connections with biblical and patristic realities. We remain in the realm of social action deliberately presented in a way that may interest non-believers.

This radical difference in outlook, on the one hand theological, even dogmatic but rather negative, on the other hand descriptive, natural and very positive, was, as we have already noted, to characterize all subsequent versions. It extended not only to the difference of attitude and formation of the authors of the first documents, but also to the subject itself. This difficulty — which also included a fruitful tension — was to become even more prominent when the possibility was considered of combining in a single schema both viewpoints, the theological and one based on "social doctrine".

7. Before the need for a single schema on the Church and the world could really be understood, the First Session had to come. Then it was realized that John XXIII from the very beginning had aimed at openness to the world. The account of this question which follows reveals the contrast between the repeatedly expressed wishes of the Holy Father and the extent to which they were carried out in the very diverse schemata produced by the Preparatory Commission. On this point, and in order to make clear the genesis of Text 2, we must return to the original vision of the Council as John XXIII intended it to be.

II. THE ORIGIN OF TEXT 2

1. The speeches

From the beginning John XXIII strove for the Council to be open to the world. As early as his Whitsun sermon on 5 June 1960 he said that "each believer ... as far as he is Catholic, is a citizen of the whole world, just as Christ is the adored redeemer of the whole world".[6]

The Constitution *Humanae Salutis* of 25 December 1961, which announced the Council, devoted an important passage to this problem: "It is a question in fact of bringing the modern world into contact with the vivifying and perennial energies of the gospel." After a short description, John XXIII continues: "This supernatural order must also reflect its efficiency in the other order, the temporal one, which on so many occasions is unfortunately ultimately the only one that occupies and worries man." In this text the expression "i segni dei tempi" ("the signs of the times") occurs in an optimistic context.[7]

---

[6] The whole discourse will be found in *CC* I/1, pp. 187–92.

[7] *CC* I/1, p. 45; *Osservatore Romano* of 26–27 December 1961; *CC* I (1962), pp. 174–5, 176; *K*, pp. 83–9.

The speech of 11 September 1962 mentions the distinction between the Church *ad intra* and *ad extra:* "The Church must be sought as it is both in its internal structure — its vitality *ad intra* — in the act of representing, above all to its sons, the treasures of illuminating faith and of sanctifying grace ... Regarded in relation to its vitality *ad extra,* that is to say the Church in face of the demands and needs of the nations ... feels it must honour its responsibilities by its teaching: *sic transire per bona terrena ut non amittamus aeterna.*" A list follows of some of the problems which will form the essentials *of Gaudium et Spes:* the fundamental equality of all nations in the exercise of their rights and duties; defence of the sanctity of marriage; social responsibility; the underdeveloped countries, where the Church must show itself to be the Church of all, and especially of the poor; disorders of social life; the right to religious freedom; peace between nations.[8]

H. de Riedmatten gives valuable indications on the genesis of this speech. The Archbishop of Malines had addressed a pastoral letter to his diocese in 1962. "In this letter he made clear the intense anxiety which was inescapable to a mind as open to the feelings of his contemporaries as his." By chance John XXIII saw this letter and immediately informed its author that it expressed exactly the Holy Father's ideas about the Council. The same John XXIII then got Cardinal Suenens to produce "a report on the organization and aims of the Council's work". The Cardinal did so and submitted two important memoranda, one on what the Council ought in his opinion not to be and another which approached the problem from the positive side. It is not indiscreet now to state that the allocution of 11 September 1962 largely drew its inspiration from the second of these notes, so much so that John XXIII the next day made the Cardinal a present of one of his books as a sign of his agreement and gratitude. This makes clear the line which leads from the allocution of 11 September to Cardinal Suenens's intervention of 4 December. It is no longer an unfounded hypothesis to affirm that the speech of 4 December was not made in the Council aula without the Pope's prior knowledge, despite the serious state of his health at that time. These precise details are extremely important because they show, as in any case might be surmised, that the very idea of the Pastoral Constitution goes back to John XXIII's fundamental intentions for the Council.

At the opening of the Council on 11 October 1962, the Pope took up the idea again. This is all the more important because we know that John XXIII wrote the entire opening address to the Council himself. "No one stuck his nose in it", he liked to say, in one of those spontaneous confidences of which he had the secret.[9]

A week later a message to the world was published. The original version

[8] *CC* III (1962), pp. 522–23, notes 11–12, 15, 18; *T,* p. 20, notes 3 and 4.
[9] *L* II, p. 14. All this is taken from the study by H. de Riedmatten.

was the work of M.-D. Chenu and Y. Congar, but it was also revised by four French bishops. Using almost the same words as *Gaudium et Spes,* it spoke of the Council which "unites all nations. As we undertake our work, therefore, we would emphasize whatever concerns the dignity of man and whatever contributes to create a genuine community of peoples." [10]

2. The documents

Even if the Pope had foreseen an eventual dialogue between Church and world, he had not measured its full significance. This is shown by the fact that no commission was set up to prepare a text on this topic, and that no schema under this heading was in prospect. Furthermore, the Pope dealt with these problems in his two encyclicals *Mater et Magistra* and *Pacem in Terris* without reference to the work of the Council. Even if, as H. de Riedmatten also thinks, that was providential — for texts of that kind could never have been drawn up by an Ecumenical Council — the fact remains that they tended rather to divert the attention of the fathers of the future Council from these questions. We have already seen in the first part of this outline (see above, I, 2–5), how the texts envisaged by the preparatory commissions fell below what was expressed in the message of 11 September, especially by their tone.

Another index of this unpreparedness is the complete absence of laymen from the preparatory commissions and during the First Session of the Council. They only obtained access to the work on the future Schema 13 on 24 April 1964. According to H. de Riedmatten, Mgr. Guerry argued at length in a paper composed in 1962, that the work of a Council only admits of the "episcopal" type of presence. No doubt Mgr. Glorieux let it be known at the beginning of 1960 that the question of lay participation in Rome had been discussed very early on, but the Pope "explicitly emphasized on 23 January 1962 the private character of the work and studies of priests and laymen on the subject of the Council". In a "very important lecture given in the summer of 1962, the Master of the Sacred Palace, Fr. Ciappi, justified this exclusive participation of the bishops, heads of religious orders, Roman dicasteries and Catholic universities. He said in so many words that the laity had played no part, at least openly, in producing the great mass of documents which had served as basis and source of the preconciliar work. He pointed that out for the sake of truth."

This speech "not only justifies the absence of the laity from the official preparations for the Council, but also explains the fact that the Theological Commission had dealt with themes which later were reserved for the Pastoral Constitution". Here we have a rigorous conception of a General Council as

[10] *L* II, pp. 22, 105–6; *K* II, pp. 84–7.

consisting of bishops advised by theologians. Here, too, a prior decision to exclude the laity had quite clearly been taken as a consequence of the purely canonical concept of Ecumenical Councils. This also involved the difficulty, if not the impossibility, of entering into dialogue with the world as a valid partner. But such a dialogue was the very meaning of the work which led to *Gaudium et Spes*. By bringing laymen into the Commission, Paul VI succeeded in "giving Vatican II its own true character".

The question of the Church and the world had been under discussion in other circles besides those who were preparing the Council. At its Munich meeting in the summer of 1960, the Congress of International Catholic Organizations (OIC) dealt with the perspectives opened up by the Council and created a special commission which in collaboration with COPECIAL (the international preparatory committee for the Congress of the Lay Apostolate) was to collect materials for the use of the Council. From 1960 onwards, this group held a series of meetings on themes such as "Catholic social practice, reorganization of Caritas, the activity of Catholics in world organization, peace, participation in technology, culture — a theme dealt with in 1965 by the Congress in Vienna — the position of women, the problem of the technological world, etc." Documents were distributed to the Council fathers and experts. Some of the future "auditors" and "lay experts" who collaborated on the production of Schema 13 came from OIC.

Then there were the "papers" sent to the bishops, and a speech of Cardinal Montini at the Mendola in the course of the traditional Milan University Week, 1960, in which he "emphasized that the Council was of course devoting special attention to the modern world, with which the Church must increasingly engage in dialogue". That was the beginning.

The *Informations Catholiques Internationales* of January 1961, drew attention to the initiative taken by certain persons and groups to bring the Church face to face with the world of today and thus to work out what should be the main points in achieving a new aggiornamento. The *Informations Catholiques Internationales* also organized on 13 and 14 May 1961 two study sessions on "The Church, the Council and the Others". The prospectus announced: "A glance at the world. What is the present-day world like? What are its hopes and fears? What road are men following and where to? What do they expect of the Church?"[11]

3. The decisive impulse

It was a bishop from Latin America who in fact gave the impulse which led to the decision to produce a schema on the Church in the world. Dom Helder Câmara who at this time was Auxiliary Bishop of Rio de Janeiro, constantly

[11] We owe this to H. de Riedmatten, confirmed by the present author's conversations with persons directly concerned.

discussed with visitors the problem of the Third World. He kept on asking "What ought we to do now?" He spoke of the excessively internal character of the Council discussions. "Are we to spend our whole time discussing internal Church problems while two-thirds of mankind is dying of hunger? What have we to say on the problem of underdevelopment? Will the Council express its concern about the great problems of mankind?" In a lecture in the Domus Mariae he also said: "Is shortage of priests the greatest problem of Latin America? No! Underdevelopment."

A small group, the "Church of the Poor", inspired by Abbé P. Gaulthier, had been studying this problem since 26 October 1962, and a few of its members asked Cardinal Cicognani on 21 November for a secretariat specially devoted to these matters to be set up. Dom Helder Câmara attached himself to this group from the start. He thought its work too exclusively spiritual, but the group had the advantage of actually existing. As secretary of the Brazilian Bishops' Conference, Dom Helder was aware of the importance the episcopal conferences could have for the Council. He called together the secretaries of other bishops' conferences. Soon France (Mgr. Etchegaray), Africa (Mgrs. Zoa, Blomjous), Germany, Holland, Japan, India, Canada and the Congo took part in the meetings, which Mgr. Helder called "ecumenical". He soon made contact with Cardinal Suenens. The two men were very different, but understood one another. The Cardinal of Malines had been surprised by the distinction *ad intra, ad extra* in the 11 September message. On 1 December about 50 bishops, the key figures of various continents, were at a meeting in the Belgian College. In the closing address, Cardinal Suenens spoke of documents which the Council must produce. He also stressed the necessity of a secretariat for these questions; the recently-founded Secretariat for Promoting Christian Unity might serve as a model.[12]

Even during the First Session, cardinals and bishops had written to the Pope pointing out the importance of this theme. Cardinal Léger was among those who expressed themselves most emphatically in this sense. After the meeting in the Belgian College, Cardinals Suenens, Lercaro, Liénart, Léger and also Cardinal Montini came to identical conclusions about introducing some arrangement and interconnection into the conciliar schemata.

On 4 December, Cardinal Suenens made a speech proposing to group the schemata round two poles: *ad intra, ad extra;* this won the approval of the Council fathers. The next day Cardinal Montini emphasized the bond between Christ and the Church and went on to express his own agreement with the proposed schema on the Church and the world. On 6 December, Cardinal Lercaro emphatically insisted on the necessity of speaking about the Church of the poor.

---

[12] *H*, pp. 8–13 (mss.); *T*, n. 11. The "Justitia et Pax" Commission, announced at Christmas 1966, fulfilled this hope.

So the First Session was not restricted solely to internal Church questions. Even at the very start the theme of Church and world proved inescapable.[13] And since Pope John had announced the measures taken for the intersessional period, among others the formation of a Co-ordinating Commission, quick results could confidently be expected.

4. The composition of Text 2 (January–May 1963)

At its first meeting in January 1963, the Co-ordinating Commission arranged the schemata around the central axis: *Ecclesia Christi, lumen gentium.* The last two words, which were to be the introductory words of the Dogmatic Constitution on the Church, were chosen — it must be emphasized — in order to include the two essential aspects of the plan for the conciliar texts as a whole: the Church *ad intra* and the Church *ad extra.* In this sense it was fortunate in the end that *Gaudium et Spes* was a pastoral constitution; as well as giving it doctrinal authority this fact clearly links it with the Dogmatic Constitution on the Church.

The schema devoted to the Church and the world bore the number 17; it was the last of the texts. A new numeration and arrangement of the schemata in July 1964 — except for the first two on the Liturgy and the Instruments of Social Communication — turned the schema on the Church and the World into Schema 13, a name which it has retained, as well as that of Pastoral Constitution.[14]

Cardinal Suenens had first asked the experts he summoned, to follow as far as possible the texts of the preparatory period (Text 1). As it was thought that the Council was not going to last long, they were told to hurry. At the same time he asked for the basic outline of this or that chapter to be sketched to him, when it was possible to rewrite it completely. He called in F. Houtart, Y. Calvez of Action populaire in Paris, who is well-known for an important book on Marxism, Canon Lalande of Pax Christi and H. de Riedmatten, who was responsible for the Office of the International Catholic Organizations in Geneva and was soon to be the representative of the Holy See to international institutions in Geneva.

At the meeting of the Co-ordinating Commission at the end of January 1963, the Cardinal proposed to incorporate as many of the preparatory texts as possible into the schema. He added the important proviso that the whole must form a unity, in six chapters: 1) De admirabili vocatione hominis secundum Deum; 2) De persona humana in societate; 3) De matrimonio,

---

[13] *L* II seems not to have recognized the importance of these days from 4–7 December for Schema 13. They are only mentioned in note 17 (p. 126); similarly in *K* II, p. 556.

[14] *T*, p. 26, n. 13. The Italians like to think that 13 is a lucky number, whereas in northern countries it is considered unlucky.

familia et problemata demographico;[15] 4) De cultura humana; 5) De ordine oeconomico et de iustitia sociali; 6) De communitate gentium et pace. Since for practical reasons it was not possible to set up a completely new episcopal commission to draw up this schema (all the bishops had gone home and an election was impossible), he proposed to form a Mixed Commission in which the members of the Theological Commission and of the Commission for the Apostolate of the Laity would collaborate. That gave the Mixed Commission a total of 60 members and on occasion made its work difficult, but guaranteed a wider outlook. Finally it was proposed to divide the combined schema into two parts, a more theoretical section which would present principles — the most important chapter of this part is Chapter I — and another more pastoral section with a few concrete applications in various domains. This division already foreshadowed the separation between conciliar text and "adnexa" (appendices) which lasted from September 1963 till February 1965. Although this distinction, which threatened to develop into a separation, was not maintained, it nevertheless influenced the final structure of the Pastoral Constitution in other ways. Chapter I, much expanded, became the first part; Chapters 2–6 formed the nucleus of the second part. It was only in this way that its unity was apparent and it became clear that the whole would bear the title of a "pastoral constitution".

The theologians and experts who worked on this Text 2 from 6–10 February were J. Daniélou, Mgrs. Pavan, Ferrari-Toniolo, Ligutti, Ramselaar, Klostermann, Canon Moeller, Frs. Labourdette, Sigmond, de Riedmatten, Tucci. Between February and May 1963, five successive versions were produced.

Concurrently with the work of this Mixed Commission, a few experts from the Theological Commission also worked on certain chapters. For example, Fr. Lio made a revised version of Chapter I, in which he held fast to the objective character of the moral order. And the Secretary of the Theological Commission, Fr. Tromp, proposed a text on culture. These "doublets", which were submitted to the Mixed Commission about 15 May, endeavoured in accordance with the instructions of the Co-ordinating Commission to incorporate the Preparatory Commission's materials into the new schema.

a) The first text prepared by the experts of the Mixed Commission originated in the period from February to March 1963. The first chapter, which we will take as an example since it was to form the kernel of the first dogmatic section of the final schema, was partly composed by Fr. Daniélou. In spite of a few sections expressed in rather scholastic language, it was notable on the whole for its biblical and patristic perspective, its emphasis

---

[15] The previous text (Text 1) had been entitled "De matrimonio, de castitate et de virginitate".

on the creation of man in the image of God (viewed here, it is true, in its very significant connection with participation in the divine life), on the restoration of man in Christ, his glorification, the expectation of the resurrection and the Kingdom. At a moment when efforts were being made to introduce the biblical perspective into the new version of *Lumen Gentium* (which began with the "mystery of the Church"), the same tendency was visible in the outline of the future Schema 13. Part of this first text was examined on 11 March by the Mixed Commission.

b) The second text was drafted between 14 March, the end of the meeting of the Theological Commission, and 24 April. In the meantime the Coordinating Commission had met at the end of March. It could devote only a short time to examining the first draft, as the most important matters for debate were the new Schema on the Church, of which two chapters were ready, and the famous text on "The Sources of Revelation". At the same time the text was sent to the fathers and *periti* with the request to get to work on comments and suggestions. Answers began to come in during the second half of April.

Chapter I preserved practically the substance of the earlier version (arts. 1–14), but a second part was added on the moral order (arts. 15–25), composed no doubt by J. Fuchs, S.J. Labourdette's text on marriage was altered, in the sense that passages which spoke of mutual love in marriage were suppressed. This was done in order to base the doctrinal statements on what were called "more objective" norms. This was the beginning of an argument that was to continue until the end of the Fourth Session.

Meanwhile the encyclical *Pacem in Terris* appeared on 11 April 1963. This of course met with a wide response, even beyond frontiers which encyclicals do not usually cross. This was an instance, as H. de Riedmatten pointed out, of "an important event which intensified the expectation of the nations in regard to the Council's action on these problems; it also put those drafting the texts into a considerable quandary, for they had the feeling that this document had already forestalled a very substantial part of the tasks which had been assigned to them". Some wanted simply to take over the themes of *Pacem in Terris*, others favoured a theological explanation of the document. The first alternative was soon abandoned.[16] In reality John XXIII had published the document — even before the Italian elections of 28 April — because he knew his days were numbered, and he wanted that text to appear at all costs. Furthermore, some of the Pope's actions were being severely criticized, for example the audience granted to Khrushchev's son-in-law. It

---

[16] *R* brings out this point very clearly. The chronicles of the Council (*L, W, K, CC*) have not recognized in *Pacem in Terris* the combination of encouragement and need to seek the deeper sense in which the theme could be incorporated into the schema. We owe the details about the efforts made outside the Council to *R*, pp. 9–11.

was even said in the press that the Communist's gains in the elections were partly due to *Pacem in Terris.*

One of the most difficult problems for those drafting the schema was that of style. *Pacem in Terris* has just proved that language which was not directly theological or biblical, and a treatment which took the description of concrete situations as its starting-point, could arouse enormous interest. Shouldn't the same method be used again now? On the other hand, those who opposed Schema 17 itself once more argued that the very plan of the schema entailed in their view the danger of naturalism and left-wing tendencies.

c) The third text was composed, after consulting some lay people (24–27 April) in accordance with past suggestions, between 28 April and 14 May, when the Mixed Commission met.

Laymen had already taken part in the discussions of the Commission for the Apostolate of the Laity on 26–27 February. Cardinal Cento, who presided with imperturbable optimism over the often muddled and confused discussions of his commission, insisted how useful it would be to have laymen take part in the work of the Mixed Commission. Despite the more than reserved attitude of several bishops of the Theological Commission, 23 laymen were invited, 14 of whom were able to attend; three more were invited as observers, one of them a woman, Miss R. Goldie.[17] The opposition in the commission was shown by the fact that the purely dogmatic chapter was not submitted to them, but was discussed on 27 April by the clerical theologians alone. It was still thought at that time that the meetings of the commission from 24–28 April were not conciliar, because of the presence of the laity. They had only been called in to advise, a high ecclesiastic stated.

In reality the laymen took part in the discussions and suggested numerous amendments, despite such distinctions and despite the difficulty caused by the Latin language. When, for example, some clerical theologians considered it more expedient to omit the chapter on marriage on the grounds that the question was not yet ripe for discussion, it was the laymen who insisted that the subject should be dealt with. In regard to culture, they pointed out that

---

[17] The following is a list of those present: L.-C. Baas, A. Barrère, Prof. B. Colombo, P. Crowley, J.-P. Dubois-Dumée, Prof. A. Ferrari-Toniolo, J. Folliet, J. Larnaud, Prof. G. Lombardi, J. J. Norris, Prof. J. Ruiz Giménez, K. Schmidthüs, Prof. R. Sugranyes de Franch, V. Veronese. The following could not attend: J. de Mierry, Prof. S. Golzio, H. Rollet, R. Salat, C. Santamaria, K. Tanaka, H. S. Taylor, M. Vanistendael, Prof. F. Vito. The following were consulted in writing: Miss R. Goldie, M. de Habicht, Prof. J. Mertens de Wilmars. As a result of a full meeting presided over by Cardinal Cento, subcommissions were set up, one for each chapter. Bishops Kominek and Guano, and the two secretaries S. Tromp and Mgr. Glorieux worked with the laity. There were also the following *periti:* Mgrs. Ferrari-Toniolo, Klostermann, Pavan, Quadri, Ramselaar, Can. Haubtmann, Frs. Daniélou, de Riedmatten, Hirschmann, Lio, Sigmond, Tucci (Résumé of *T,* p. 29, n. 15).

it was better to expand the *description* of the phenomenon rather than attempt an impossible definition. They also drew attention to the excessively literary character of the view of culture presented in the proposed text.

As regards the first chapter, which was revised again on 28 April, though without the laymen, the number of articles was reduced (from 25 to 7) by combining the ideas into groups: natural dignity of the human person, unity and variety of mankind, mystery of the supernatural vocation, moral order founded on the dignity of the person, grace of Christ and moral order, happiness of the eternal Kingdom. In this way the natural law viewpoint was more closely fused with the biblical perspective.

The Preface was condensed from four to three articles. It expressed in a more reserved way the role of the Church in preserving human dignity, the present situation marked by the hopes and fears of the world — this is the seed of the "Introductory Statement" of the final text — and the link with *Lumen Gentium*. This last point is of some importance, for, for the first time, it shows unmistakably that the future Pastoral Constitution must be read in conjunction with the Dogmatic Constitution on the Church. Some criticisms, e.g. that certain theses have been omitted, lose their force if they are examined in this light.

d) Between 20 and 25 May, almost the whole Mixed Commission met several times and discussed the third version. In fact only a few sessions were devoted to these discussions, because of shortage of time; the Theological Commission was occupied at this time in working over Chapters II and IV of *Lumen Gentium*, and the Commission on the Apostolate of the Laity had to prepare its own text. Only the Preface and Chapter I were submitted to detailed examination. As regards the others, discussion was confined to the main lines and was entrusted to the six subcommissions, which were regrouped for this purpose.

The fourth text which was completed in this way on 25 May, is more theological in character and takes better account of the element of sin and fragility, which in previous versions had been rather neglected. In Chapter I, for example, the theme "De imagine Dei peccato obscurata" had a separate article devoted to it. At the same time the structure of the following articles was modified and they were headed "De restauratione imaginis Dei in Christo", instead of "De missione Filii" and "De restauratione imaginis Dei in hominibus". The theme of moral order and the relation of Christ to the moral order which had occupied almost half of Text 3, now appeared only in a short concluding article (7): "Ecclesiae competentia in vita temporali et iure naturali".

It is evident that within the framework of the Council's work at that time this chapter represented a still very novel attempt to compose a Christian doctrine of man on the basis of the biblical truth of the image of God. As of course the theme had already cropped up, but without giving its stamp to the whole, a little "treatise" was set before the fathers of the commission this time.

In reality this structure was due to the united efforts of several theologians. I remember a meeting at Mgr. Garrone's on 15 May. Fathers Congar, Daniélou, Häring and Mgrs. Delhaye and C. Moeller were present. It was emphasized that the schema must be built more closely round this biblical idea, which still seemed new at that time. After a moment's hesitation, Mgr. Garrone gave his enthusiastic consent. The subcommission worked long and regularly.

These details have their importance, for in fact the theological build of the purely dogmatic section was assuming definite shape. Some thought that Chapter I was now composed too much on the lines of a system of speculative theology — this remark was made on 20 May — but this perspective was finally adopted.

In other domains, such as culture, there was a general wish to point out that the Church civilizes by preaching the gospel. It was also suggested that the Constitution *Dei Filius* of Vatican I should be quoted on the two orders and methods of cognition. The two themes thus introduced were maintained to the end.

e) From 25 to 29 May, members of the subcommission still in Rome — a large number of bishops had to leave on urgent diocesan business or because of the feast days — revised the text in the light of the comments received. In response to objections raised by some theologians who were very concerned about the objectivity of the moral law and the natural law, three sections were added in Chapter I to Article 7 on "Munus Ecclesiae in vita temporali": Lex naturalis est obiectiva; Finis legis amor Dei et proximi; De conscientia. This meant a return to Text 2 but in a deeper form, enriched by the biblical and patristic outlook and given greater precision by the perspective of the moral order and the natural law.

Mgr. Garrone had already emphasized this point in his report on 20 May: "Hiatus expleatur inter vocationem supernaturalem et legem naturalem." Since the fathers were of the opinion that Text 4 did not fulfil this promise, the editors had once again incorporated parts of Text 2 in the version which was submitted to the Co-ordinating Commission.

5. Until the Malines text (Interim Text A)

Previous discussions had shown the difficulty of reaching agreement on dogmatic perspectives. However, this was not the most difficult part. The Theological Commission had already faced at least equally difficult problems in regard to collegiality and the text on revelation. The chief dilemma was presented by the extremely concrete questions in Chapters II–IV when envisaged in the framework of a Council. How could the Council's authority be claimed for such questions?

H. de Riedmatten mentions that on Ascension Day, 23 May 1963, a group of *periti* met at Mgr. Charue's and, on account of these difficulties, suggested that the work should be divided into two parts, a doctrinal text and pastoral instructions of less authority on more detailed matters.[18]

In the meantime, the news of John XXIII's state of health became increasingly alarming. The chapter on the call to perfection in *Lumen Gentium* had just been successfully completed on 30 May, when a sudden worsening of the Pope's condition was announced.

When the Co-ordinating Commission met again on 4 July, Paul VI had announced that the Council would continue. The Commission discussed Schema 17, which at this time bore the title: De praesentia efficaci Ecclesiae in mundo hodierno. There were six chapters: 1) De admirabili vocatione hominis; 2) De persona humana in societate; 3) De matrimonio et familia; 4) De culturae progressu rite promovendo; 5) De ordine oeconomico et de iustitia sociali; 6) De communitate gentium et pace.[19] Cardinal Browne

---

[18] *R*, p. 17 (mss.). This fact is not mentioned anywhere else.

[19] The preface stated that after dealing with the mystery of the Church, the Council was now turning to the human family with the aim of presenting to the faithful and to men of good will some aspects of its task of promoting the well-being of contemporary society. Clearly it is not the business of the Church to solve scientific and technical problems which are subject to their own laws. It rather teaches, in virtue of its mission, that no adequate solutions to difficult problems of this kind can be found unless Christian doctrine is taken into account. Chapter I spoke of the dignity of the human person, of man created in the image of God, deformed by sin and restored in Christ, of the natural law and its objective basis, of awareness of the Church's duty to defend, explain and teach the truths which manifest the natural dignity, sacredness and vocation of the human person as an inalienable part of Christian revelation, in relation both to individual and social life, in general principles as well as in concrete applications. Chapter II on the person in society presented a charter of various personal rights, including those of following one's conscience *bona fide informata* and of professing a religion *ad rectam conscientiae suae normam*. It devoted a separate article to women. Then it dealt with the social and finally with the juridical and political community. Chapter III on marriage and the family gave an account of the present situation of the family, going beyond the terminology of primary and secondary ends and placing the emphasis on the generous fecundity of love. Procreation and education were presented as *ordinatio innata et specifica instituti matrimoniali*. The final decision and responsibility for the number of children is said to rest with the married couple, *salva semper lege divina*. Chapter IV on culture began with a descriptive section and then dealt with the relations between culture and person, culture and society, between the Church and the various cultures. It went into the mutual assistance rendered by the Church to culture and by culture to the Church. It closed with a paragraph on the need for competence whether in the domain of secular or of religious culture. Chapter V on economic and social life was the longest, with five chapters on human work, just payment for work, economic contracts, right to earthly goods, responsibility of political authorities in the economic field. Chapter VI on peace had three chapters, on establishing peace, maintenance of peace, duty of the Church and of Christians. Apart from Chapter I, which after much oscillation between "death and transfiguration", was to become the first part of *Gaudium et Spes*, in a completely rewritten form, the other five chapters remained all along the editorial basis

represented the Theological Commission, Cardinal Cento the Commission for the Apostolate of the Laity. Mgr. Glorieux was also present. The *relator,* Cardinal Suenens, indicated the importance of the text and referred to the recent address of Paul VI on the day of his enthronement, in which he had spoken of dialogue with the modern world. He expressed, however, rather an unfavourable opinion of the text. Certainly he accepted the fundamental idea of man as the image of God, but pointed out that it did not sufficiently permeate the six chapters as a whole. He emphasized the lack of synthesis between the natural law elements and the message of the gospel. Moreover, he noted the insufficient distinction drawn between general statements of faith and concrete applications which could not be the object of conciliar pronouncements. He also stressed that delicate questions such as the "fertility of marriage, dignity of labour, the social function of private property" had not been thought out deeply enough. Finally, he criticized the text as being too European in character, and as taking too little account of the developing nations.

This judgment, which for our part we consider too unfavourable, had a double result. It led to the establishment of a commission to draw up a new text expounding the general principles of the relation between Church and world; for this purpose the first chapter of Text 2 could be used. The second result was the formation of subcommissions charged with carrying on the work already begun on Chapters II–VI; they were, however, to call in special experts, both clerical and lay. The Council could adopt the doctrinal "main text" in detail but endorse the texts on special problems only in a general way, and these might be termed "instructions".[20]

6. Ecumenical collaboration

It is important to note that Lukas Vischer of the Faith and Order section of the World Council of Churches wrote a long letter on 18 April to Mgr. Guano, who with Mgrs. Hengsbach and Blomjous was one of the three

---

of what was eventually to be Part II of the Pastoral Constitution (compiled on the basis of *T*, pp. 32–6 and personal notes). The title was "De praesentia efficaci Ecclesiae in mundo hodierno". The opening words were, "Missionem continuans Filii Dei".

[20] *T*, pp. 38–9. The wish was also expressed for religious freedom to be dealt with, if only in one article. It was not known at that time whether there would be a conciliar document on the subject or not. In case it was later added on to the Decree on Ecumenism "like a carriage coupled to a train on the point of departure", there was a desire to ensure that it would play a part in Schema 17 (*T*, n. 23 and personal notes). Later, during the meeting of Faith and Order in Montreal in July 1963, Bishop Newbegin had to explain that the connection between "De libertate religiosa" and "De oecumenismo" was quite a chance one. The text, which fortunately remained in the hands of the Secretariat for Christian Unity, was of course separated from "De oecumenismo" (as was "De habitudine Ecclesiae ad religiones non christianas"), and this helped to clarify matters.

bishops of the Laity Commission who were to deal with Schema 17. This described the way in which Faith and Order would set about producing a "Schema on the Contemporary World", if it were asked to do so. Five long appendices were added, the first on the attitude of the WCC to disarmament; the second reproduced part of the report of the second World Conference of Churches in Evanston 1954 on Christian hope in the world of the present day especially in view of the divisions in the world; the third, also from Evanston, on international relations; the fourth on developing countries and the fifth on religious freedom.

This letter laid great emphasis on a theme on which the WCC had prepared a study after 1956, "Christ's lordship over Church and world". It criticized the ideas of natural law, and set the activity of the Christian in relation to that of the risen Christ. Similarly the letter, for ecumenical reasons, stressed that the bond which unites Christians is their confession of faith in the risen Christ. This, it said, is the basis of the difference between the communion of Christians with one another and the relation which they can have with non-Christians. In this setting Lukas Vischer raised the question of the utility of Christian institutions, which the Churches are all too eager to maintain. The letter then summarized the earlier documents appended and added a characteristic touch, namely the wish for collaboration with Catholics on practical questions such as refugees, not in a narrowly apologetical or denominational, but in a truly ecumenical spirit. Finally, the letter spoke of marriage and emphasized "responsible parenthood"; it concluded by expressing the wish for a chapter on religious freedom.[21]

Mgr. Guano took this document very seriously, had it duplicated and distributed on 17 May 1963 to all who wanted a copy. Cardinal Suenens asked for one.

Lukas Vischer's document had scarcely any influence on Text 2. It did have some influence in February 1964 at the Zurich meeting. Mgr. Guano, Ch. Moeller, B. Häring had in fact had a long talk with Lukas Vischer in Glion at the beginning of February on the contents of his letter. They noted the comments of the theologian of the Reformed Church on Interim Text B, which was due to be discussed at that time.

This clearly dated fact (18 April 1964) initiated a collaboration which was to last until the end. Even though it was not to our mind deep enough, nor regular, it is nevertheless worthy of note. The only proof we need of this is the following fact for which we can vouch. It was Lukas Vischer's letter which made the then editorial committee realize the need to speak about Christ's lordship and to make it a central idea. No doubt other bishops had also said that, but the specifically *paschal* aspect of Christ's lordship,

---

[21] Lukas Vischer gives his final view of the Council in "Überlegungen nach dem Vatikanischen Konzil", *Polis* 26 (1966), pp. 58–73. On religious freedom, see previous note.

and the endeavour not to confuse it with natural law themes, is due to Vischer's influence. [22]

III. INTERIM TEXT A: MALINES (SEPTEMBER 1963)

1. From 6 to 8 September 1963, Cardinal Suenens assembled a small international team in the archiepiscopal palace in Malines, in the very room in which the famous "Malines Conversations" had taken place. The team was composed of Mgrs. Cerfaux, Philips, Prignon, Canons Delhaye, Thils, Dondeyne and Moeller, Frs. Congar, K. Rahner, Rigaux and Tucci. They were to prepare a sketch of the purely dogmatic part of the schema. Several of them had published books and articles on this precise theme or were actually working on such texts. [23]

The first point raised was: To whom is the schema addressed? It was decided to speak to all Christians and to all men of goodwill, with the aim of bringing the light of the Lord to them, so that they may rightly understand the realities of this world, whose Lord has chosen a people for himself and given it the task of spreading his gospel.

After this discussion it was also decided to start with a theological statement on the Church's mission. Those taking part in fact thought it would be impossible to describe the state of the world of today without descending to platitudes. The most important reason, however, was that an "objective" and "neutral" description is impossible. A description must necessarily be based on criteria and it would therefore be better to state them. The final reason was that this would make clear the real purpose of the schema, which was to show the light which the gospel throws on the contemporary world.

In these problems the exegetes expressly insisted on the idea of the new man (B. Rigaux) and on eschatology (Mgr. Cerfaux). They were supported by Mgr. Philips who had himself prepared a basic outline in which he stressed the gospel message. Others placed the main emphasis on religious freedom (Tucci). [24] Others again, for example Canon Dondeyne, also drew

---

[22] It would be very important to compare the texts of the World Conference of Faith and Order in Montreal in July 1963 with those of Vatican II. We ourselves had the opportunity through a private invitation to take part with Canon Rodger and Fr. Baubien in some of the discussions of that conference, and sometimes had the impression that both on the Catholic side and that of the World Council of Churches the rapprochements which had become apparent in Montreal were being lost sight of to some extent. People are beginning to rediscover them by reference back to Vatican II and to this ecumenical Faith and Order meeting, and also because Catholics and the World Council of Churches are discovering the growing importance of the circle of problems concerning Church — world — kingdom of God.

[23] *T*, pp. 39–43 and personal notes written up during the Council.

[24] Cf. note 20 above. The history of "De libertate" was the stormiest. Until the Ariccia

attention to new aspects of men's consciousness of a wider world: for the first time the unification of the world has become possible, there is real solidarity, we can speak of a new humanity, a new experience of society and of love. At the same time there is the problem of class, labour and the poor; there is a will to justice which often becomes a source of atheism. Consequently the Church and Christians must "hear what the world has to say".

Similarly, the duality of the present development of the world was brought out; unification, but also divisions which lead practically to civil war or to actual wars between nations; dominion over this world but also "ensnarement in the elements of this world"; freedom, a privilege of divine origin, but also its abuse, particularly by sin, which is a choice of evil for its own sake.

In this way a double tension was discovered, between the Church as a heavenly structure founded on the word of God, on the one hand, and the world which is developing, growing together and seeking true justice on the other. There is also a tension within the world itself, between positive and negative aspects of its own evolution.

Gradually a synthesis was arrived at. On the one hand, Christians need not accept the world as it is. On the contrary they should build it up in the light of the principles of their faith, for example in accordance with the command to fill the earth and subdue it (K. Rahner). On the other hand, it is "not necessary to reduce the role of humanity to that of a laybrother in a monastery" (Congar). A type of presence of the Church in the world must be achieved which is not one of power and domination but of service. And this kind of presence should also guarantee the principle of free access to the gospel without compulsion of any kind.

Mgr. Philips put forward an idea that met with approval. After a preface, mention should be made of the specific mission of the Church, the present situation of the "building up" of the world should be described, the Church's relation to the contemporary world explained and finally the services performed by the Church for the world should be gone into in greater detail.

The emergence of the idea of service will have been noticed. This was no accident, but the result of collaboration with the separated brethren. The letter of Lukas Vischer already mentioned spoke of the trilogy: communion (koinonia), diaconia and witness. This theme which figures particularly in the documents of the WCC, especially at the Faith and Order meeting in Montreal, July 1963, is certainly a feature of Interim Text A. It was likewise a fundamental characteristic of the Zurich Interim Text B, and remained in subsequent versions until the promulgation. Congar introduced it into a draft for the Malines session to work on; it was accepted and incorporated in the final version.

Text 4, care had always been taken for an article on this theme to be included; the final fate of this text nevertheless remained uncertain until the fourth session.

2. Between 9 and 16 September, Mgr. Philips produced a text which was discussed at a second meeting on 17 September. K. Rahner and Canon Dondeyne could not be present. It was criticized in detail and more emphasis was laid on the greatness of human work. At the same time it was insisted that the ambiguity of the world must be fully maintained, more stress laid on religious liberty — reference was made to the first text of the Secretariat for Christian Unity — and proper mention made of the eschatological transformation which the Church's liturgical presence in the world is preparing.[25] From 18 to 21 September, Mgr. Philips revised the text in accordance with these suggestions, and on 22 September 1963 it was sent to Rome to the conciliar secretariat for distribution to the fathers.

3. Analysis of the Malines Text. It will have been noticed that this document stresses both the transcendent aspect of the gospel message and the enormous importance of the changes which are at present taking place in the world. It emphasizes the ambivalence of these changes and at the same time the need to preserve the freedom of the human person. The point at which these rather opposed lines meet, has the threefold character of community, service and witness. In other words, an approach had been chosen which was Eastern by its concern for eschatology and Western by its detailed description of the changes in the world, while at the same time it was ecumenical because it took up the themes of the WCC (which in any case were biblical ones).

The text included only three of the four parts which had been planned. The fourth part, on the various services which the Church performs for the world, was to be included in the "Instructions" as these were then envisaged. As this text is little known, we shall outline it here. A preface is followed by three parts, each divided into two. I. De ecclesiae propria missione. This part is divided into: A. De evangelisatione mundi, B. De ecclesiae influxu in ipsum ordinem mundi.

The first section speaks in outline: De munere Evangelium proclamandi. The basis of this was the missonary command of Mt 28:18. This is followed (3) by "De libertate fidei", founded on the freedom of man's response. This demands that those who announce the gospel should "spread the light of truth as Christ himself did", "praedicando, exemplum vitae praebendo, benefaciendo, quoscumque amice, prudenter et patienter ad Evangelium perducendo". Then (4) "De pauperum evangelisatione". All this leads to the theme (5) "De homine ut imagine Christi". Here we find again the theme of the

---

[25] In my study of "De Cultura", published in the book *La Chiesa nel mondo di oggi*, edited by G. Baraúna (1967), the text of this Malines article may be found. It survives in the four words "actione sua etiam liturgica" in Article 54 of *Gaudium et Spes*. The title of that version was "Adumbratio schematis XVII de activa praesentia Ecclesiae in mundo aedificando". It comprised 12 (in the last version 17) pages of typescript. Its opening words were "Mysterio intimo Ecclesiae". In this way an attempt was made to express the distinction between *ad intra* and *ad extra*.

image of God but in an ecclesiological context. On this basis the following article (6) "De praesentia Ecclesiae in mundo per suam constitutionem" expounds how the Church by its preaching and its liturgical action contributes to and effects the transfiguration of the world and its restoration in Jesus Christ. Thus the theme of the image of God was presented in the context of an "eschatological humanism" which was of a kind suitable to open a dialogue with the Greek Orthodox in particular but also with the Eastern Churches generally.

The second section B began with an article (7) "Ecclesia ad bonum mundi confert". This recalls how the Church even by its preaching civilizes. This theme had been present from the start, and figures here in the perspective of the two orders which meet, call one another in question, yet should not oppose one another because each in its own way comes from Christ. This is the light in which the article (8) "De fructibus huius laboris" is set. Here it is shown how deeper knowledge of the creation and the world can lead to a fuller knowledge of God. The theme (9) "De dignitate hominis agnoscenda" is treated in a similar way, and also (10) "Bona creata grato animo accipienda". This whole first part closes with an article (11) "Testimonia Scripturae", which speaks of the goodness in which all things were created, and deals with the restoration of all things in Christ by their recapitulation through his victory over sin.

The second part (II) "De mundo aedificando", deals first of all with (A) "De autonomia mundi". In this important section three points of view can be distinguished: (12) "Principium distinctionis statuatur"; this establishes the basis of the independent existence of each order. This theme, further developed, will be found in the final text of the Pastoral Constitution in Chapter III of Part I (art. 36). In the following number (13) "De labore hominum in mundo", it is expressly affirmed that work is not a consequence of original sin but "iam in originali justitia ad officium hominis pertinet": a doctrine which must be recalled, for example, in face of Marxism which has always claimed that in Christian eyes work itself is a punishment for sin. Here, on the contrary, it is stressed that only the burdensome character of work stems from original sin. Finally a new feature of men's present-day experience of their work is dealt with (14) "De mutuo amore".

The second section (B) "De unificatione mundi", presents the positive aspect of the (15) "Nova conscientia unitatis" and of the (16) "Diffusio huius phaenomeni" as well as of the (17) "Significatio huius phaenomeni" and of its ambiguous aspect (18) "De bonorum terrestrium ambiguitate": unity but also divisions and wars; mastery over nature but also the enslavement of millions of men in the technological machine; freedom, but actual inability of the masses concretely to achieve this freedom.

All this leads to a simple conclusion: the radical impossibility of eradicating all roots of disorder from the world; the need to seek salvation.

The third part (III) "De officiis Ecclesiae erga mundum", already fore-shadows the future Chapter IV of the First Part of the final text. The schema first speaks (19) of the "Testimonium pro veritate et vita", then of the light which shines in the teaching of the Church (20) "De intimo rerum sensu", (21) "De hominis sublimi vocatione", (22) "De peccato et redemptione", (23) "De ordine morum". All these articles are based on the first of the themes proposed by the theologians of the WCC: witness.

The second section of the third part (B) is centred on *diaconia (servitium)* and communion *(communio):* (25) "De unica caritate erga Deum et proximum", (26) "De caritate et iustitia" (the first duty of love is justice), (27) "De caritate in vita quotidiana". All this is crowned by an article (28) "De communio cum omnibus" which introduces (29) the concluding section which speaks of the polarity of Church and world which is overcome by the eschatological hope and the *restauratio omnium rerum in Christo.*

4. The period until Interim Text B (29 September 1963 — January 1964). a) At the beginning of the Second Session, Pope Paul VI made practically no reference to Schema 17 except in the very general context of an "answer to the appeal of the world". Apart from Cardinal Gracias, who on 26 November underlined the importance of the problems of the collaboration of all Christians, especially in regard to the developing countries, and Cardinal Florit who referred to Schema 17 when speaking of religious freedom, the fathers did not speak on the schema. They were fully occupied with the debates on collegiality (October), the bishops (beginning of November) and ecumenism (end of November). Cardinal Gracias called for priority for the debate on Schema 17 at the Third Session.[26]

b) The meeting of the Mixed Commission on 29 November 1963. The Malines text had been sent to the members of the Mixed Commission only a week before. The other text of May 1963 (Text 2) was not very well known either. Moreover, by the decision of 21 November, the number of members of the commissions had to be raised to 30, which meant that twice times four new members had to be taken into the Mixed Commission. This also slowed the course of its first meeting during the conciliar session.

Considerable objections were raised to the Malines schema. It was re-garded as a good contribution but its purely theological perspective was crit-icized. Many wanted to follow the style of *Mater et Magistra* and *Pacem in Terris,* so as to gain a hearing from modern humanity. Furthermore it was thought that the Malines text would lose its impact if it did not speak in

---

[26] *T,* p. 45. The same cardinal emphasized (*T,* p. 45, n. 26) the connection between Schema 17 and the Eucharistic Congress which was to take place after the Third Session. Pope Paul went to Bombay, where he pronounced his well-known appeal. It may be questioned whether the very explicit support which Paul VI gave to the Schema on the Church in the World, especially on the eve of the Fourth Session (cf. below, section VI, and note 78), was not partly connected with his journey to Bombay.

concrete terms of concrete things. At the same time at least a few members acknowledged that from the theological point of view this text represented an advance on the old Chapter I of Text 2; instead of a very definite but rather onesided view of man as the image of God, they now had a more open approach to the relations between Church and world.

Practically no one thought of going back to Text 2. A sort of tacit agreement formed in regard to Chapters II–VI which were supposed to become "Instructions" though no one knew exactly what that would mean; at this stage what Duchesne says of the anathemas of Cyrill at Ephesus could be said of these supplementary chapters: "There was to happen to them what God pleased."

Tacit agreement was also reached that Chapter I of Text 2 must be rewritten; it was not possible simply to go back to the text of May 1963. As the Malines text also was not accepted even as an "adumbratio" — psychological factors played a hidden part in this — the Mixed Commission was left in the air, in a sort of no man's land. Hence the idea of a new text (the fourth!) which was to be more pastoral and to incorporate elements of the previous texts.

c) All this was rather confusing. Mgr. Pelletier, the Bishop of Trois-Rivières, had the idea that a select commission should be appointed to direct and co-ordinate the work. Bishops Ancel, McGrath and Schröffer for the Theological Commission, Guano, Hengsbach and Ménager for the Laity Commission, belonged to it, and Mgr. Guano was named President on the grounds of his earlier work and proposals. Mgr. Wright of Pittsburgh was also elected for the Theological Commission and Mgr. Blomjous for the Laity Commission. The latter in fact exercised considerable influence on the texts even though he seldom took part in the meetings between the conciliar sessions. Fr. Bernhard Häring was secretary.

d) On 30 December, a small group of Council fathers and experts of the Central Commission met and reached agreement on the main lines of the new schema. Mgrs. Guano and Blomjous took part, and Frs. Häring, Sigmond and Tucci were present as experts. Suggestions had been sent by Mgrs. Hengsbach, Schröffer, Ménager, Renard, Hien and Ancel. It was decided not to start from a theological draft but from gospel truths which more directly concerned the world to be built. Stress must be laid on dialogue, the reading of the signs of the times (the expression was taken from *Pacem in Terris*),[27] the Church must be presented as the People of God — a theme which had taken shape and form in *Lumen Gentium* in the course of the debate in the Second Session at the beginning of October 1963. The foundations must be laid for the Church to respect earthly realities. The new duties of the

---

[27] Mgr. Ménager submitted a detailed document, and another was put forward by Dom Helder Câmara, Mgr. Hien and Mgr. Renard as a result.

faithful in a pluralist society must also be dealt with. Finally one of the decisive points of the draft must be human dignity, so that religious freedom, marriage and family, social order, the conquest of world hunger, international solidarity and peace could be dealt with.

It was left to the Central Commission which was to meet in Zurich, 1–3 February, to work all this out and also to decide on the famous appendix chapters.

e) In the course of 1964, a new text was drawn up by the committee appointed for this purpose. From the middle of January a first text was in existence, drawn up by Fr. Häring and Fr. Sigmond. In reality a young and brilliant Dominican, Professor of Sociology at the Angelicum, Fr. Dingemans, had produced the nucleus of the new text. Only the first two of the projected five chapters were completed: man's inalienable vocation, the Church in the service of God and the world. Chapter III was to deal with the attitude of the individual and of the Christian community to the modern world. Chapter IV was to speak of the most urgent problems, in a sort of brief sketch of the appendix chapters. Chapter V was to appeal to the separated brethren, to all men of goodwill and to all who worship the one God.

On 21 January an already revised and expanded text was presented for discussion in Zurich by the committee. It is important to realize that this Zurich commission included almost none of the authors of Texts 1 and 2 or of Interim Text A, with the exception of Canon Moeller, R. Tucci and, on occasion, H. de Riedmatten. This clearly indicates the intention to start again from the beginning. It may be wondered, however, whether much time was not lost by this decision and whether what had been achieved in the earlier texts was not in practice forgotten.[28]

IV. INTERIM TEXT B:
ZURICH (1–3 FEBRUARY 1964)

The text was composed in French under the title *La participation active de l'Église à la construction du monde.*

1. The introduction includes five articles: (1) "Solidarity of the Council with mankind". The beginning of this article "Joy and sorrow, hope and anxieties . . ." was to remain in substance in all subsequent revisions, including the final text, whose first words are of course *Gaudium et Spes.* Then follow (2) "Progress and failure of mankind", (3) "Questions to mankind",

---

[28] All the members of the Central Subcommission were present with the exception of Mgr. Blomjous. The others were Frs. de Riedmatten, Häring, Hirschmann, Sigmond, Tucci, and the laymen Prof. Sugranyes de Franch and M. de Habicht.

two articles which were to be incorporated in expanded form in the final version, as the Introductory Statement. In connection with this (4) "Those to whom the schema is addressed and its purpose". After long hesitation it was decided to address the schema to Catholics but in a form which, it was hoped, might also interest all men of goodwill. At the discussions in Zurich it was then decided to add a declaration that the Catholic Church joyfully "acknowledges" all that non-Catholic Christians have achieved in the domain of the questions with which Schema 17 is concerned. This would avoid giving the impression of a rather paternalist appeal, and would recognize what had been done, for example, by the Life and Action section of the WCC. Finally (5) "The Church as the servant of man" approaches the fundamental problems of the whole schema in the perspective of the diaconia which had already been expounded in the Malines text.

2. The first chapter takes up again the earlier Chapter I of Text 2 on man's integral vocation, but in a more biblical and more concrete way. It has five articles (6) "The value of earthly tasks". This does not deal with man as made to the image of God but speaks directly of the earthly life of the incarnate Word who in this way gave theological significance to the activities of this earth. At the same time it shows how man by his work and dedication can actively "share God's care for all mankind without neglecting the fulfilment of any aspiration which God has placed in our nature". In the (7) "Spiritual Dimensions of the Universe", man's divine vocation "to know the Father" is placed in a clear light, particularly by means of texts from the New Testament. On this basis the following article (8) "On not imposing limits on man", shows the short-sightedness of those who try to reduce human life to its earthly dimensions alone. With this the next article (9) "God's care for sinful man", again declares in very biblical style that mankind's failure is not merely a consequence of errors in the organization of society, but the result of a root cause, sin. This theme was increasingly developed in subsequent revisions so as to make it clear that it is an absolutely central feature of the human situation. All this leads to the concluding article (10) "The unity of the human vocation", which shows the connection and also the necessary distinction involved in man's task of dealing with earthly realities as well as with the Kingdom of God.

In regard to Article 7 it was suggested that explicit mention should be made of the resurrection, the new heaven and the new earth over which the faithful "will rule with the Lord". To Article 10 it was proposed to add another article, 10a, on Christ as the light of the world, making use of suggestions put forward by Mgr. Ménager. The purpose of these additions was to ensure a better theological balance. It was proposed also to deal here with the creation of man to the image of God, a theme which had practically disappeared from this Interim Text B, and also with the theme of the creative and enlightening Word.

These additions were not inserted in the text because they were declared to be too dogmatic, in the sense that they presented in a non-historical way themes which are very inaccessible to modern man. A directly biblical and evangelical style was preferred. These are mentioned here because in the end they did find a place in Texts 4, 5 and 6, together with the idea of the Servant of God, and form the dogmatic structure there. A letter of 13 March to Mgr. Guano, who presided over the Zurich meeting, attests that at that time such a structure was in the mind of one of those drafting the schema.

3. Chapter II was entitled "The Church in service of God and the world". The Church referred to here was understood both as the apostolic hierarchy (art. 11): "The specific mission of the disciples", and as the faithful in the world. It dealt in succession with (12) "The distinction between the authority of the Church and that of the world", (13) "Religious freedom", (14) "The world helps the Church", (15) "The Church takes part in building the earthly city".

In this chapter the delicate problem of the Church's relation to temporal things arises. There was a danger either of seeing only a purely evangelical aspect, in accordance with which the Church would have to renounce all support from the earthly order and from secular or Christian institutions, or else of clinging too much to given historical situations, for example in countries where the Church has a special, publicly recognized predominance. This problem will reappear in Chapter III on "The attitude of Christians in the world of today". It was one of the central points of discussion in Zurich.

4. After an introduction (16) in which it is made clear that the conciliar assembly is in question but also all Christians, Chapter III deals with the theme (17): "Not to sin by omission", continued by (18) "True love of the poor and of poverty". There was lively discussion of this last subject. The danger of falling into the style of a charity sermon was noted, so there was insistence on the need for rational solutions. This problem was viewed in connection with that of work and widened in scope so that "cultural values" are to be distributed just as much as "material goods". In particular the spirit of poverty was dealt with, and with suffering borne in hope as a mark of the Christian.

The chapter closed with an article (19) on the spirit of dialogue. The discussion here emphasized the necessity, or at least the great utility, of Christians joining international organizations. As well as personal dialogue there must in fact also be dialogue on the plane of the international organizations, for as one of the two persons who played a large part in the Zurich discussions, H. de Riedmatten, remarked, if individual Christians are not supported by some internationally recognized organization, in practice they are not heard, in fact they get no hearing at all. In this domain everything is a matter of pressure groups. An exaggerated evangelicalism would run the risk that the witness which the Church has to bear to the world would not be heard at all.

It is also well to realize that six months before Paul VI's encyclical *Ecclesiam Suam*, which devotes the whole of its third part to dialogue, this theme was the subject of an explicit article in Interim Text B. It scarcely figured at all in Texts 1 and 2. The Malines text contained it implicitly, though in fact only through Mgr. Dondeyne's collaboration; he had written a book entitled "Faith listens to the world".

5. Chapter IV on "The tasks of Christians" sketches a few themes which, with the exception of culture, economical and social life, had been dealt with in greater detail in the adnexa. Chapter IV was completed, as far as those topics were concerned, at the meeting at the end of April. A more dogmatic outline of principles was given, while their applications were dealt with in detail in the appendix chapters (the former Chapters II–VI of Text 2).

On the theme (20) of "Starving mankind", H. de Riedmatten asked for emphasis to be laid on the permanent economic revolution which two thirds of humanity had to face if they were to reach a human standard of life. He also insisted that the theme must be widened to make it clear that mankind effects its own further development. R. Tucci proposed on this point that Articles 15, 16 and 17 of the Malines text should be taken over.

After the sequence of the articles had been modified, the theme (22) of "Personal dignity of man and the family" was dealt with. Two aspects of the problem were raised, the demographic and the family aspect. The positive sense was also stressed in which legislation must support the right of families to have children, for only too often its only idea is to guarantee a right to have no children. Finally the subject of responsible parenthood was discussed, in the positive sense in which the term was being used.

Next "War and disunity among the nations" (21) was debated. Here, however, a number of concrete points which they did not wish to deal with in such a short and therefore general text were relegated to the appendix chapters (Chapter VI of Text 2) which were already in existence. The chapter ended with (23) "Man's spiritual unrest". This concentrated on the ethical rather than on the economic and social aspects of mankind's endeavours to better its lot. This theme was to be the focus of the chapter on culture in the final text. In addition "the lack of hope and the religious uncertainty of a great number of human beings" was noted; this represents an appeal to our love as heart-rending as their lack of earthly food.

6. The second version of the Conclusion, which was revised in Zurich, so that it should be addressed to all men, Christians, non-Christians and unbelievers, ended with a very fine addition, an appeal to all men of goodwill for a hearing and collaboration. Two quotations concerning hope (Eph 4:13; 3:20–21) introduced this theme at the close of the text.

7. None of those who took part in the Zurich discussions will forget the atmosphere of warmth, trust and gay hope that prevailed. We must add that the fact that these meetings took place in a Central European town most of whose inhabitants were Protestants, raised the question of the presence of the Church in the world from the plane of noble but rather abstract generality directly onto that of lived experience, of "real" knowledge. Even before the idea of the signs of the times which have to be read played any part in the text of the schema, it was brought to the attention of the members of the Central Subcommission.

Agreement had been reached that the schema would be pastoral in character and at the same time that it must not be framed as a message. Similarly there was no thought of composing a theological treatise on earthly realities. The aim was to present a theological interpretation of the world situation at the present day and the tasks it sets Christians. There was no intention of going into much detail.

During the composition of the texts and their discussion, it had become clear that the Church was presented not as standing outside the world but as listening to the world. The most difficult problem, and the one that was longest discussed, was, In what respect is the Church involved in these problems and makes them its own? Two extremes must obviously be excluded; the Church is neither indifferent to them nor so occupied with them as to be totally identified with them. Another aspect of the same question was, Who is meant by the word "we" in the text? Christians? The Council in the sense of the assembled fathers? Hierarchy and laity? The laity alone? This was to be the subject of long debate in subsequent stages until the final solution, which consisted in proposing the People of God as the main "analogon" of the Church in the schema.

The general intention was biblical and sociological in the wide sense of the word. Great mistrust was shown for any attempt to introduce additions regarded as too doctrinal. At the same time there was a sort of incessant swing between a too exclusively evangelical outlook and another which was more concerned with the concrete situations in which the Church actually has to live. The aim was to present the Church less as *of* the world and more as *for* the world, and also to stress its inevitable involvement in a concrete temporal order; an "angelist" outlook tends to minimize this.

The laity expressly insisted on the biblical tone; they had no confidence that the readers to whom the schema was addressed would find any abstract systematic treatment easy to folllow. They proved to be particularly struck by the detailed problems in Chapters II and IV. Journalists questioned by B. Häring also approved the concrete, evangelical style, close to actual problems, employed in the Zurich text. That did not prevent these laymen declaring they were bewildered by the biblical quotations with which at some points the text was liberally strewn. It was suggested that these might be relegated to the footnotes, and this was done, but with the paradoxical result that at the June meeting the lack of biblical references in the exposé was criticized.

8. From the ecumenical point of view, we have already referred to the meetings in Glion, 27–30 January, on "Laity and service". Lukas Vischer had a long talk with Mgr. Guano, R. Tucci and Canon Moeller about the Zurich text, the full version of which he received on 21 January. The notes taken are of such interest that it will be useful to summarize them here. It was emphasized first of all that before an appeal was addressed to the separated brethren, it would be necessary to acknowledge what they had already achieved and were still doing in the domain of international justice, the status of woman and the battle against illiteracy. Furthermore, the wish was even more definitely expressed that where the world has to be met, this should be done jointly. Dialogue with the separated brethren takes place within a dialogue with the world. It must also be realized that there are more differences between Christians and the world (in the double sense of this word) than between Christians themselves. In this domain, it was considered, the image of concentric circles lying increasingly distant from a centre consisting of the Catholic Church, must be abandoned. In fact all Christians find themselves confronted with the same difficult problems.

It is really incredible that even at that time, when it was still questionable whether there would ever be a conciliar text on religious freedom — which is why the Zurich text envisaged an Article 13 on this subject [29] — a *prospective* ecumenism developed, i.e. one which would bring together all Christian denominations in face of the urgent problems set by the world. As well as the retrospective ecumenism which remains important and is concerned with the study of the inner differences between Christians in the past and the present, this prospective ecumenism was to assume increasing importance as the Council went on and Schema 17 took form. [30] Similarly the formula suggested by R. Tucci in this sense — "to meet and enter on common dialogue with the world" — (as well as anticipating in spirit one of the results of the Geneva World Conference for Faith and Society in July 1966) was to serve as a guideline during all the later work in Zurich and until the Third Session.

On Chapter II of the Zurich text the Protestant observer remarked that insufficient account had been taken of the dramatic character of history. It spoke of sin and the conception of nature, but in the New Testament there is Antichrist also. What the Church does in the temporal order is a *sign*, not in virtue of the action itself in which the Church takes part, but by the

---

[29] Cf. note 20 above.

[30] K. Rahner outlined this distinction at the end of a theological study week on Vatican II at Notre Dame University in March 1966.

fact that the Church's temporal action constitutes a sign of its vocation in a world characterized by the conflict between good and evil. The impression must not be given that it has a programme. What the Church can and must do is to bear witness. Rather than speak of failure, we must therefore speak of "the sign of hope", and the proposed text did not do this sufficiently.

In Chapter III Lukas Vischer underlined the need to speak more clearly of the lordship of Christ, for he thought the text gave too much of an impression that the Church has its own knowledge of Christ and looked at the world in order as it were to see its own reflection. Here we recognize one of the sources of the Zurich proposals and of the later incorporation of these themes into the text.

It was suggested that Chapter IV should begin with the dignity of man, and that it should be stated explicitly that the problems referred to, hunger and war, were intended as examples, and that there was something else lying even deeper, that the peasants of Asia and Africa are not waiting for recognition in their fight against hunger, but for something that will help them to develop human dignity.

Finally, as regards the theme of the hidden presence of the Word in the world, Lukas Vischer said he feared that this might lead to underestimating the importance of the proclamation of the word of God. There is a "judgment" *(krisis)* which is already taking place in the world in the name of the incarnation and the redemption. Furthermore, taking up an idea of Karl Barth, he pointed out the danger of speaking too much of this presence of the world in Christ. That might give rise to a terrible misconception which would provide even Nazism with a semblance of justification. On the contrary, they must emphasize the "simul justus et peccator" even for the Church, and speak of the "two Kingdoms".

9. We have laid so much emphasis on this Zurich session firstly because it is very little known, like all the earlier drafts of Schema 17, and secondly because of the importance of the problems with which it was concerned. They were to remain until the end, and the kind of style used also remained essentially the same. In this way the *first* Zurich text, which was discussed from 1 to 3 February, was of great importance.

The spirit of the Zurich meeting left its mark on all who took part. Here they acquired the unshakable conviction that a Schema 17 was necessary, that it was the most difficult but also one of the most important of the conciliar schemata. Whatever the setbacks, they maintained their determination to complete the text.[31]

---

[31] This whole section IV is based on notes made during the Zurich meeting. For the last section cf. also *T*, p. 65.

V. TEXT 3. SECOND ZURICH TEXT, SUBMITTED AT THE THIRD SESSION (FEBRUARY — NOVEMBER 1964)

1. From 4 February till 4 March 1964

A small group of experts (Frs. Sigmond, Häring, Tucci, de Riedmatten) revised the text in accordance with the indications given. At the same time the old subcommissions had been given the task of examining the appendix chapters. The new revised version was ready in the first half of February. A first Latin translation by H. de Riedmatten was finished on 21 February. At the beginning of March a second translation by B. Häring was ready. This was to form the basis of the debates of the Mixed Commission in March.

2. The meeting of the Mixed Commission (4, 9, 12 March 1964)

a) At the first session a vote was taken whether the text could be accepted as a basis for discussion; only six out of 41 votes rejected it. For the first time lay auditors took part in the discussion.

b) The Latin style was criticized by some as too journalistic, too much like a message. All agreed, however, on the need to employ a style which was both doctrinally precise and likely to arouse the interest of people at the present day. It was insisted in particular that those "outside" must be induced to take an interest in spiritual values, while Christians "inside", who often take little interest in the world, should be induced to do so. From this point of view it was regretted that too many biblical quotations had been used "non secundum verba ipsa, sed quoad sensum", i.e. not literally but in substance. Others approved this, stressing what a difficulty literal quotations from the Bible can cause some people nowadays, who find their style quite alien.

c) Discussion was particularly lively on the doctrinal content, and turned on two points. On one hand some particularly insisted that the schema should remain centred on human problems as people actually raise them. Modern literature, for example, describes the destruction of man. Sometimes it magnifies him in optimism, at others it brings him to the ground by the experience of the absurd. Consequently much more detailed treatment would have to be given to gratia sanans. On the other hand it was argued that the text "integrated the temporal into the spiritual far too easily". That is not only an ascetical, but also a dogmatic question. "We must begin by reminding people of the Christian truths", one member of the commission said. "We must not shrink from presenting the paradox of the Christian life. It is not only faith in the Cross which redeems, but also faith in him who rose from the dead." Another stressed very emphatically that it must be shown much more clearly, for example by giving far greater prominence to the texts of Genesis, how the Church takes the riches and values of the world seriously. At the same time, however, the relation between creation and redemption must be expressed more clearly. Practically no theological basis at all was provided on this problem.

d) Agreement was quickly reached that Chapter IV needed to be completely revised so as to give a brief dogmatic survey of all the matters which were to be reincorporated in the appendix chapters. It should also be noted that, despite two very pressing interventions, the Mixed Commission preferred not to make express mention of racialism, Marxism and Communism.

This meeting took place to the accompaniment of the persistent rumour current in Rome at that time, that the Council must end with the Third Session. At the same time there was insistence that this Constitution must be completed, despite the pressure of time, since it corresponded to a perhaps excessive but nevertheless real expectation of the world.

3. The meeting of the Central Subcommission (28–29 April) [32]

a) By the beginning of April the drafting committee had completed the revision of the first three chapters. With R. Tucci [33] we must note that a new theme appears, new at least by its treatment, that of the "signs of the times"; the paragraph devoted to this was new.

The expression comes from *Pacem in Terris*. The suggestion had already been made that it should serve as a guideline for the appendix chapters. It now appeared in the main text intended for presentation to the Council. It had a strange fate. On the one hand it was strongly criticized, particularly by some WCC observers (letter of 29 May 1964), because biblically it has a very special, eschatological meaning, and this almost completely disappears in the context of the new paragraph. This involves, they argued, the danger of reading history in a human way and of indulging in prophetic exegesis of events. In the end the term disappeared completely, emerging only once in the final text (art. 4), where it is made clear that these signs are to be read in the light of the gospel.

On the other hand it soon stimulated considerable effort and concern to provide a description of the state of the world. A Subcommission for the Signs of the Times was formed at the meeting of the select subcommission on 10–12 September, and was to meet each week during the Third Session.

---

[32] Those taking part from 28–29 April were Mgr. Ancel, Hengsbach, Ménager, Schröffer, Glorieux, Canon Moeller, Frs. Congar, Dalos, Häring, Hirschmann, Sigmond, Tucci; the laymen M. de Habicht, Vanistendael, Mgr. Kominek and Prof. Ruiz Giménez had sent in their views (*T*, n. 39).

[33] *T*, p. 58; cf. below, commentary on the Introductory Statement.

It called to a large extent on representative bishops of non-European countries, and asked for the help of many experts. Each meeting was devoted to one part of the world.[34]

b) In the first half of April the draft was examined again, together with a new version of Chapter IV. The revised text bears the date 15 April.

c) On 28 and 29 April the subcommission again revised the text. It is noteworthy what a large part was taken in the discussion by the lay auditors. A Polish bishop, Mgr. Kominek, spoke of the significance of suffering as witness and of the importance of the institutional Church for the problems dealt with in Schema 17. This first participation was to be followed during the drafting of Texts 3, 4, 5 and 6 by very regular collaboration which left its mark on the whole schema and particularly on Chapter IV of the first part which originated almost entirely in the wishes and the work of the bishops of Poland.

d) From 30 April to 2 May a few members of the Subcommission for the Adnexa met in Rome. Those who were working on the chapter on culture were able to revise Article 22, which had been inserted in the text at the beginning of April (see above, b). Two points were brought out: the divorce that in fact has existed since the Middle Ages between the Church and culture, and the position of the Church "which is not bound exclusively to this or that cultural form", a position which involves both a certain link with Hebrew and Greek culture through the text of the Bible and a universal vocation of openness to all cultures.

e) One observer-delegate from the WCC pointed out the need to mention non-Catholic Christians; it was not sufficient that they had been spoken of in the Decree on Ecumenism; all the Council texts should make clear their own ecumenical import. He wanted Schema 17 to avoid any suggestion of an "appeal", but to speak hopefully of ever closer collaboration. This observer also thought the text "too unproblematic", especially in expressions such as "vox temporis, vox Dei". He repeated his doubts whether Christ could be perceived in nature and history, since Christ "has spoken once and for all in a unique way". He regretted that eschatology was largely lacking, and that the theme of God's rule and kingdom and the judgment was practically absent. "It represents a rather meagre belief in progress, such as might just as well be found in non-Christian documents."[35]

---

[34] The dossier contained about 90 pages, and would be worth publishing. Mgr. P. Delhaye acted as an energetic voluntary secretary. He was one of the most active of the Council experts, especially in connection with this schema; he took part later in the discussions on the chapter on marriage and the family. Another secretary was Canon Houtart.

[35] *T*, n. 39, § 2; personal notes and unpublished documents.

4. The meeting of the Mixed Commission (4, 5, 6 June 1964)

a) In the revised text we immediately notice the development that had been asked for in regard to the signs of the times, not only at the beginning in the Preface, but also in each chapter. The Christological orientation is shown, for example, by the addition to the preface of a final paragraph on Christ the light of the world. Human solidarity based on common descent was more clearly distinguished in this way from unity in Christ. The schema takes greater account of the theology of the Cross and the resurrection. The tone is not so paternalistic and admonitory. It is clearly stated that the Church has not always got an answer to every new question. At the same time the function of the hierarchical Church is more clearly distinguished from that of the individual Christian. And the tension which always remains between striving for the Kingdom of God and the building of the earthly city, although harmony has to be aimed at, is clearly indicated.[36]

b) The status of the appendix chapters was also discussed. It was again repeated that these texts would not be debated in the Council aula but were to be distributed to the fathers, who would be asked to send in their comments in writing. They would in due course be published in the revised version of the subcommissions (those of May 1963, which, however, were assuming ever greater proportions), by authority of the Commission, as an official commentary on the schema. In any case they could certainly not be regarded as private documents.[37] The principles inspiring them were expressed in Chapter IV of the conciliar text.

c) At the end of this series of meetings, Cardinal Cento, who with Cardinal Ottaviani was co-president of the Mixed Commission, asked whether they approved the text in its present form and whether it could therefore be submitted to the Co-ordinating Commission after a few suitable emendations. If so, the text plus the appendix chapters might be printed at once and sent to the bishops, for submission to the Council. A vote showed almost complete unanimity in its favour.

5. The distribution of the schema to the Council fathers

a) After hearing the report of Cardinal Urbani on 26 June 1964, the Co-ordinating Commission decided that the text was sufficiently ripe to be sent to the fathers. The Pope gave his approval on 3 July. The text, consisting of 25 articles and a conclusion, was distributed early in July.

b) Henceforward this schema bore the number 13. It will be remembered that the list drawn up by the Co-ordinating Commission between 21 and 27 January 1963 contained 17 schemata, the last of which was the Schema

[36] Summary in *T*, pp. 59–60.
[37] *W* III, pp. 390–2.

on the Church and the World. On the list which was enclosed with documents sent to the fathers in 1964, the schema again came last but the list had been reduced to 13. (The two texts already completed on the Liturgy and the Instruments of Social Communication were not included in this count.) We may add that by the end of the Council there were neither 17 nor 13, but 16 documents.[38]

c) From this point, therefore, people spoke of Schema 13, and the name persisted for a long time, even after the promulgation. Some people spoke of the "famous schema" or "the schema without a name". It is true that the title *De ecclesia in mundo huius temporis,* printed on the green cover of the Council text and the grey cover of the appendix-chapters, was to remain unchanged. But there was no lack of criticism. Someone expressed it in the widely-quoted remark that Schema 13 was the Noah's Ark into which all the themes for which there was no place elsewhere were put for the time being. At the same time the anticipations of those fathers who had some idea of what people at the present day expect, were very high. But they were also afraid, as R. Tucci wrote, that the text had been prepared too exclusively in "a European and clerical kitchen".

d) It may be useful to point out that work was also being done outside the circles of those officially commissioned to draft the text. In Brussels there were meetings at the beginning of March between Denis and Frisque and Houtart to study the Zurich Interim Text A. At that time the second edition of *Bilan du monde* was in preparation. The objections raised during this Brussels meeting inspired Houtart's book *Église et monde. À propos du schéma XVII* (July 1964). He said people expected Schema 17 to echo the hopes and fears of the world and to provide a doctrine which would put an end to the separation of Church and world and guide thought and action in the future. Copies of another small book originating in lectures given at the Marquette University in August 1963 to 150 members of more than 80 religious orders, *The Challenge to Change* (New York 1964) was sent to all the American bishops.[39]

In Poland a group of bishops under the aegis of the Archbishop of Cracow, Mgr. Wojtyla, set to work and prepared a text which after some modifications was included among the texts discussed at Ariccia (Text 4). One of its central ideas was that "the presence of the Church does not consist only in the will of God but also in the will of those who freely belong to it", a clear reference to countries where a different view of religious freedom is held from that of the West.[40]

---

[38] Cf. note 12 above. The appendix chapters were distributed 30 November. Almost immediately it was impossible to obtain copies, for the number printed had been calculated with some care. Until the Council acta are published, this document will remain a rarity for bibliophiles! (Cf. *T,* pp. 71–2 and n. 56.)

[39] *T,* n. 46; *H,* p. 38.   [40] *H,* pp. 43–45.

On the eve of the Third Session, or more exactly at the meeting of the Central Subcommission 10–12 September 1964, "one of the best specialists on questions of international economics and sociology, especially those of the Third World, Fr. Lebret",[41] was coopted.

e) A final factor heightened anticipation on the eve of the Third Session and encouraged the authors of Schema 13, the publication of Paul VI's first encyclical *Ecclesiam Suam* on 6 August 1964. Its third part was devoted to dialogue between the Church and the world in which it lives. The text expressly stated that it did not intend to deal with these questions in detail "in order to leave the Council fathers the task of doing this frankly". The Pope nevertheless examined the deep motives and the method of dialogue with the world. He developed here, in relation to the partners involved, his idea of concentric circles: the circle of unbelievers — in the summer of 1964 he summoned V. Miano and made him responsible for organizing a Secretariat for Non-Believers — the circle of believing non-Christians for whom Paul VI likewise created a secretariat under the direction of Cardinal Marella; the circle of separated Christians whose presence and life had already become perceptible to millions of people through Paul VI's pilgrimage to the Holy Land in January 1964.

6. Meeting of the Central Subcommission (10–12 September 1964)

The wave of efforts and hopes embodied in Schema 13 had been swollen, on the eve of the Third Session, by increasingly precise theological demands and the more and more urgent "expectations of the nations". These two poles, whose connection is not immediately evident, are reflected in the very important decision taken at the session of the Central Subcommittee 10 to 12 September 1964.[42] On the one hand a new theological or dogmatic subcommission was formed under the direction of Mgr. Garrone. With Mgr. Philips as secretary, it was to produce a revised text of Chapter I on man's vocation, completed by 12 September.[43] Only fragments of this were used in

[41] *R*, p. 22. The news of Fr. Lebret's death during the Geneva Church and Society Conference was announced by Prof. A. Philippe with great emotion. He stressed how great a loss this was. These events show what deep repercussions the theme of Church and world or Church and society was having. Experts were making contact, though a day or two before they had scarcely known each other.

[42] The list of those invited ran: Cardinal König, Mgrs. Ancel, Blomjous, Charue, Dearden, Garrone, Guano, Hengsbach, McGrath, Ménager, Roy, Schröffer, Wright. Experts: Mgrs. Ferrari-Toniolo, Glorieux, Pavan, Philips, Can. Thils, Delhaye, Haubtmann, Moeller, Frs. Benoît, Congar, Daniélou, de Riedmatten, Gagnebet, Häring, Hirschmann, Lebret, Medina, K. Rahner, Rigaux, Semmelroth, Sigmond, Thomas, Tucci, the laymen de Habicht, Larnaud, Manzini, Sugranyes de Franch, Vanistendael.

[43] Mgr. Philips had tried to integrate the theme of sin and redemption into the context of "presence in the world". Members: Mgrs. Garrone (president), Philips, Glorieux, Ferrari-

the end, and this cost a good deal of time. On the other hand a Signs of the Times Subcommission was formed, which drafted the important documents which made possible in Ariccia in February 1965 the composition of what was to be the Introductory Statement of the Pastoral Constitution. [44]

In order to forestall a number of objections, the Central Subcommission asked that at the beginning of the Session the Fathers should be sent a list of the amendments to the printed text and also a statement about guidelines for the future revision of the text. All this was delivered on 17 September. [45] What was aimed at was greater clarity and a more logical structure, more precise definition of the terms "world" and "signs of the times", focussing of Chapter II on the tasks of the Church as a whole, including the hierarchy, and of Chapter III on the tasks of Christians generally, the more particular aspect being taken up again in Chapter IV.

This preventive step, unique in the history of conciliar texts, was useful in the end because it saved time, but in many people's view it did not really contribute to making things clearer. It also marked a certain gap which still existed at that time between the bishops and theologians who had prepared Schema 13 on the one hand, and the mass of bishops at the Council on the other. On the one hand there was a growing awareness of the importance and urgency of the schema. In the course of the Third Session, when many circles were debating whether to abandon the schema and replace it by a declaration, they were told in very plain terms that the world would not understand how the bishops could spend three sessions studying their own position in the Church but could not find time for serious study of the problems of two-thirds of mankind. On the other hand, there was very acute realization of the difficulty and risk involved in composing a text which from the point of view of the conciliar theology would be sufficiently precise and solid.

In this light the formation of the two new subcommissions was to prove providential, for without them the goal would certainly not have been

---

Toniolo, Canon Moeller, Frs. Benoît, Congar, Daniélou, Rigaux, K. Rahner, Prof. Sugranyes de Franch.

[44] Members: Mgrs. McGrath, D'Souza, Can. Delhaye (cf. above, n. 33), Frs. Daniélou, Gagnebet, Lebret, Tucci. A number of persons were invited to take part in the work to ensure that the different parts of the world were represented: Mgrs. Blomjous, Zoa (Africa), D'Souza (India), Nagae (Japan), Ayoub (Syria), Helder Câmara (Brazil), Wright (USA), Wojtyla (Poland), Ancel, Ménager (France). Experts: Mgr. Ligutti, Canon Houtart, Canon Moeller, Frs. de Rietmatten, Joblin, Lebret, Galarru, Gregory (Brazil), Galiléa, Medina (Chile), Frs. Dingemans, Gagnebet, Greco, Martelet, Neuner, Pute and the laymen M. de Habicht, Norris, Ruszkowski, Sugranyes de Franch. The secretaries were Can. Delhaye and Houtart. No one who took part in these meetings every Monday evening in St. Martha will ever forget them. The spirit was already almost that of the future Commission for Peace and the International Community.

[45] CC IV, p. 243; W II, p. 389.

reached. It must in fact be noted that each had a mandate for a comprehensive view of the whole schema, one from the theological point of view, the other from its task of ensuring that all the analyses in the text were very universal in scope.

7. The conciliar debates (20 October — 5 November, 9–10 November 1964)

a) The report, considered and approved (with only 3 adverse votes) by the Mixed Commission on 13 October, was read by Mgr. Guano, who had actually presided over the work on Schema 13. The purpose of the text, he said, was to show the Church turning its attention to the great problems of our time in the light of its specific mission of preaching Christ, and its recognition of human values. Mgr. Guano explained the meaning of the terms used. The word "Church" here means the whole People of God, not only the hierarchy, while the "world" is understood in its totality as loved by God but also as affected by sin. Man is viewed in his earthly situation and in his Christian vocation.[46] He pointed out the chief difficulties, especially that of striking a balance between the principles of the gospel and the description of contemporary problems. He referred to the appendix chapters and recalled that they had the full authority of the commission.[47]

b) The general debates were very seriously pursued but remained fragmentary. Cardinal Liénart thought the text was too admonitory and did not distinguish clearly enough between natural and supernatural. Cardinal Lercaro called it too European and added that too much was being expected from this schema; it was certainly good to give an answer to the world but "this answer must be accompanied by self-knowledge and real reform on the part of the Church". Cardinal Léger wanted greater realism. Cardinal Döpfner pointed out how "the theology here is as new as the problems themselves". The intervention of Cardinal Meyer was certainly one of the most important, at least in regard to the theological aim of the schema. "The community of redemption forms the link between Church and world. God offers his glory to the whole man, body and soul, and to the whole created world. The Son has a cosmic mission because, as St. Paul says, it has pleased the Father to reconcile all things in his Son. This work is only completed at the end of time by the resurrection of the body and the mysterious transformation of the world. There will be, Scripture tells us, a new heaven and a new earth. This transformation actually begins with men's work in the world. That work is consequently not merely something profane. Similarly, the course of the world's history is not purely contingent but corresponds to a redemptive plan on the part of God."[48]

[46] W III, pp. 393–4; on the "crisis" at that time cf. H, pp. 57–58.
[47] W III, p. 394 and note; T, pp. 73–75.   [48] W III, p. 397.

This intervention was one of those which had most influence on versions 5 and 6. It continued to dominate the theological horizon. As well as having an anthropological purpose, Text 4 was particularly characterized by a view of Christian cosmology which was due in part to this speech of Cardinal Meyer. From Text 4 to Text 5 this gained in precision (cf. art. 29) but lost in material importance to such an extent that some hasty commentators could not find it in the final text (Text 6).[49]

After a few objections of sometimes painful facetiousness — as an example we may quote Cardinal Heenan's remark which gained a certain notoriety ("Timeo expertos et annexa ferentes") — a vote was taken whether the text was to be approved in principle. It received 1576 votes in its favour to 296 against, out of 1876.

c) Discussion turned chiefly on four points. One was the reason for the relative silence of the text in regard to atheism. The best speech came from Mgr. Guerra, the Auxiliary Bishop of Madrid, who pointed out that the "Marxist ideal is a genuinely humanist one".[50] When the final text was drawn up (Texts 5 and 6), three articles were of course devoted to atheism, emphasizing the need to know the various forms of unbelief and to understand their psychological, sociological and other motives, and to respond to this fact which is one of the most momentous of our century. But Text 6 makes no express mention of Marxism or Communism, because these terms have a social, economic and political meaning which is inextricably bound up with propositions of the philosophical or religious order.[51]

The second question was why the Church should speak about earthly things. It does so neither to attract people nor because it has become untrue to its spiritual mission, but because it "would fail in its eternal task if it neglected earthly things ... The mission of the Church consists wholly and entirely in proclaiming the gospel as *Ecclesiam Suam* points out. Dialogue with the world is founded on revelation. It is primarily evangelical." These words of Mgr. Ancel reinforced those of Cardinal Suenens who had recalled the saying of Pius XI that "the Church civilizes by preaching the gospel". In this connection, however, Cardinal Léger thought that the problem of evil and suffering should receive more emphasis. In this way Chapters II and III provided the Council with an opportunity "to satisfy the wish of the Church, both hierarchy and faithful, to serve mankind in humility and poverty". Thus authority is a form of love, as the Pope had said in his public audience on 4 November while the debates on Schema 13 were in progress.[52]

The third point concerned person and family and whatever affects racial

---

[49] *W* III, p. 409; they are found for example in Article 38 § 1, 39, 57 § 4.
[50] *W* III, pp. 409–10. [51] Cf. below section VII 2 c; VIII 2.
[52] *W* III, pp. 411–17; *L* IV, pp. 184–90; *CC* IV, pp. 296–8.

discrimination in this respect. The debates were very lively, produced by the clash of two very different points of view: the speeches of Cardinals Suenens, Léger, Alfrink and Patriarch Maximos IV etc. on one side, and those of Cardinals Ottaviani, Browne, Ruffini etc. on the other. Mgr. Dearden, the president of the commission responsible for this article of Chapter IV, presented the problem with great wisdom and moderation. "Parents decide the number of their children, but it is not a matter of indifference what means they use" is Fr. Wenger's summary. The debate ended on 30 October at 11:30. It had created an atmosphere of sustained and profound emotion owing to the difficulty and complexity of the subject and its problems. "We feel", Fr. Wenger writes, "that the fathers spoke frankly, but also with the very great respect due to love, family life and the human person." [53]

The fourth point concerned culture, development, peace and atomic weapons. The most important speech on the first of these was that of Cardinal Lercaro who declared that this section must become the core of the whole schema. Culture in fact is a "fundamental medium", a "form" involved in each and every content expressed in words, symbol, ritual or any other means. He also maintained that the Church's "paedeia" is in fact tied to an almost exclusively Western "organon". He concluded that the Church should acknowledge its "poverty" in the cultural domain and realize more clearly that its irreplaceable contribution lies in the realities of Scripture; on this basis a genuine dialogue of the missionary Church could develop with the various cultures and civilizations of the world. This important intervention contributed to having this chapter closely linked in later versions with the first dogmatic part. [54]

The concluding debates chiefly concerned peace, war and the atom bomb. "Make peace, do not just preach it", Cardinal Feltin declared, and Mgr. Ancel, in one of the most remarkable interventions, pointed out the contradiction involved in outlawing war and atomic weapons and at the same time declaring defence against unjust aggression to be legitimate. In order to be effective that defence would have to use the same weapons as the aggressor. Two speakers, one from England and one from the United States, put the question: "But supposing the atom bomb is the means of ensuring peace?" [55]

A certain number of bishops had declared that on a variety of points the appendix chapters contained more precise and better digested materials than the text of the "conciliar Constitution". This argument was quickly to lead to the incorporation of these chapters in the amended text, and they finally

---

[53] *W* III, pp. 419–32; *L* IV, pp. 193–209; *CC* IV, pp. 299–310. The first meeting of the papal commission set up in June 1964 took place in July (*L* V, p. 385, n. 14).

[54] *W* III, p. 434; Mgr. Elchinger asked for the rehabilitation of Galileo. *L* IV, p. 209 expresses himself unusually laconically on this chapter. *CC* IV, pp. 316–22.

[55] *W* III, pp. 432–47; *L* IV, pp. 215–20; *CC* IV, pp. 346–8, 352–6.

formed the second part of Texts 4, 5 and 6. Even if this created some difficulties over calling the schema "a pastoral constitution", since the problems it dealt with were very various, doctrinal in the first part, mixed in the second, it nevertheless saved Schema 13. The division into actual conciliar text and appendix, had had the advantage of compelling the specifically theological point of view to be both deepened and widened. But without the appendix, the text would have been no answer to what the world was expecting. Conversely, if the appendices had remained separate from the text, they would never have attained the authority which they henceforward enjoyed. And this is important for two chapters, for example that on marriage and the family, which obviously contained important doctrinal elements, and for the chapter on the promotion of culture which would otherwise never have had sufficient importance attached to it in connection with the presence of the Church in the world (cf. Article 62 in Text 6).

The division into two parts, conciliar text and appendix, had consequently its pedagogical and pragmatic value, but it is fortunate it was abolished in the last stage of revision. The agreement of numerous bishops permitted the Central Subcommission to incorporate the appendices once more with the rest.[56]

8. The reorganization of the editorial work
(16 November 1964 — 31 January 1965)[57]

a) The Mixed Commission met on 26 October, and on 10 November, the Central Subcommission which had been enlarged on the lines laid down at the 10–12 September session. From this point onwards, laywomen and nuns also took part in the discussions of the commission as auditors, in accordance with a papal decision of 24 September.[58]

b) On 16 January the Mixed Commission met and chose 8 new members of the Central Subcommission: for the Dogmatic Commission, Mgrs. Garrone, Šeper, Poma and Butler; for the Commission for the Apostolate of the Laity, Mgrs. Morris, Larraín, Errázuriz, László, Fernández-Condé. Approval was also given to a proposal of Mgr. Guano that a certain number of fathers should be coopted to speak for various continents which were scarcely represented in the working groups: Mgrs. Fernandes (India), Satoshi Nagae (Japan), Zoa (Africa), González Moralejo (Spain), Wojtyla (Poland), Edelby (Syria) and Quadri (Italy). The Mixed Commission also confirmed the formation of the two subcommissions for doctrine and for "the signs of the

---

[56] Though the appendix chapters had been removed from the body of the schema in Text 2, thus causing something of a stir, they returned quietly without serious opposition — a very curious episode in the history of the schema.

[57] *T*, p. 78; personal notes; *W* IV, pp. 117–21; *L V* gives practically nothing on this period.

[58] *T*, p. 78, n. 64. However, they did not go as far as to allow the women auditors to speak "in aula concilii".

times"; these were to work in close collaboration with the Central Sub-commission. Mgr. Ancel was appointed vice-president. The Central Sub-commission thus acquired, as R. Tucci says, "a breadth and variety com-parable to those of a conciliar commission", even though it always worked in subordination to the Mixed Commission. [59]

c) A full meeting of the subcommission was held on 17 November, and two committees met on 19 and 20 November. Further important decisions were taken on the criteria of the revision. This was to start from the text which had been approved as a basis for discussion, but the oral and written amendments (more than 800 single spaced pages of typescript) were to be taken into account as well as other conciliar texts, in particular *Lumen Gentium* and *De oecumenismo,* which were to be promulgated on 21 Novem-ber. Editorial uniformity was also decided upon.

The form and revision of the texts were, of course, still the responsibility of those fathers who were members of the Central Subcommission. It was nevertheless decided to entrust the co-ordination and direct supervision of the text to a central editorial committee for which Canon P. Haubtmann was responsible. He is well-known for his remarkable studies of Proudhon and *Pacem in Terris* and for the brilliant daily press conferences in which he expounded for French journalists the meaning of the debates in the General Congregations. In March 1963 he had taken part in the work on the docu-ment on economic and social life. Frs. Hirschmann and Tucci and Canon Moeller were members of this Central Committee. B. Häring was secretary-general, and Mgr. Philips, now that he was relieved of responsibility for the Constitution on the Church, declared his willingness to employ part of his time on the final doctrinal supervision before the text was submitted to the Mixed Commission. He also undertook to give the report on the text to that commission. [60]

The two additional subcommissions, for doctrine and for the signs of the times, remained in office. The five other subcommissions, which had drawn up the appendix chapters and the corresponding sections of Chapter IV, were to revise their text once more in the light of the fathers' comments. "Let us note", R. Tucci wrote, "that no one had any further intention of dropping the appendix chapters."

Each subcommission was instructed to divide the work into three parts: description of facts, theological principles, applications. The style was to be accessible to a wide public of believers and non-believers. It was also recom-mended that there should be more comprehensive consultation of competent

---

[59] *T,* pp. 78–79. These decisions contributed to extend the range of problems dealt with by the schema.

[60] Personal notes; *T,* pp. 80–81. He explained very precisely to Can. Haubtmann and Moeller on 20 December 1964 how he envisaged this role.

persons, particularly among the laity, whether directly or by correspondence, especially in view of the meeting planned to take place in February 1965 at Ariccia (near Rome). And the revised texts had to be sent in at latest by 15 May.

In view of the setbacks during the Third Session — some people continued to maintain that Schema 13 would be dropped, at least as a separate conciliar document — the passage in Paul VI's final address in which he spoke of the Church and the world, was a great encouragement. At the same time the period available became shorter, for the same address made it clear that the Fourth Session would be the last. [61]

d) The meeting of the Co-ordinating Commission (30 December 1964) laid down a timetable for the work; the revised version of Schema 13 had to be submitted in March so that after receiving the Pope's approval it could be distributed to the fathers at the beginning of June. They would thus be able to study it seriously and at leisure before the Fourth Session, which was expected to begin early in September. Finally the Co-ordinating Commission decided that the Mixed Commission was to see that everything important in the appendix chapters was incorporated in the schema. [62]

e) On 5 December, Mgr. Guano presided over a meeting in Rome with Frs. Häring and Tucci, Canon Haubtmann and Mgr. Glorieux. A circular on the meetings of 17, 19 and 20 November was drawn up and sent to all the members of the Mixed Central Subcommission. Canon Haubtmann went to Louvain on 28 December to meet Canon Moeller, F. Houtart and Mgr. Philips.

Canon Moeller helped to clarify the method by asking a few questions: Should the document be based on theology, natural law, philosophy or description of facts? Who is speaking? The Church, of course, which says that in virtue of its awareness of what it is, it has something to contribute to the welfare of mankind. Nevertheless it must be made even clearer who is speaking. The hierarchy? Christians? The People of God? The assembled Council? And who is being addressed? What is being said?

As regards the last point: to talk rather unthinkingly of eschatology or the Spirit was somewhat pointless in regard to non-Christians. It would be better to show that revelation also throws light on earthly things. Common ground must be found. The Church must present itself, not hide what it is. What it says interests Christians on an additional, deeper level because of their faith. At the same time what it says should interest non-Christians because they discover there are things they share in common with the Church.

Mgr. Philips also insisted on maintaining continuity with Text 3: "The fathers must be able to recognize the text which they have debated as well as the essential elements of their comments. This is what was done with the Schema *De Ecclesia;* during the Second and Third Sessions it was both the

[61] *T*, pp. 81–82. [62] *T*, pp. 83–84.

same and not the same. For example, the structure of the first part with its three chapters must be maintained."

In regard to the description of the world, he emphasized the fact that there is no such thing as an objective, factual description. There is always a criterion, a fundamental interpretation. Tillich once said that there is an antecedently Christian interpretation of reality, and criticized Barth in this respect because he made revelation fall from heaven like a meteor.

Finally, Mgr. Philips stressed how important it is to show that the schema is not concerned with the Church "in face of" (coram) the world, but "in" the world. [63]

f) On 12 January 1965, Canon Moeller, on his way back from Rome, stopped in Paris and informed Canon Haubtmann of the timetable laid down by the Co-ordinating Commission (cf. above, d). In the course of a working session, they agreed on the basic lines of the comments made by the fathers and how they were to be worked into the revised texts. A certain structure quickly took shape, of which the following were the essential features.

The Church should be presented as the People of God and the various meanings of the word "world" defined. Then the significance of change and development should be shown: the People of God is journeying towards a kingdom and this also involves a historical orientation. In this perspective the Church stands in various relations to civil society. A relation must be found which is appropriate to our time, a relation concerned with dignity, respect, freedom, autonomy and the participation of all. Christians must be treated as adults.

In this line — People of God, world, history — a certain dualistic morality which is still all too powerful, must be overcome. An "ethics of intention" far removed from the healthy realism which characterizes people at the present time, goes hand in hand with a certain dualism in judging the world. The best way to overcome these would be to work out a Christian anthropology; the theme of the image of God might be taken up again, none of the bishops had criticized it. On the other hand, since the continuous transition from the natural to the supernatural order had been censured, these terms should be avoided and the biblical expressions covenant, grace, new creation, participation in divine life, should be employed, in the way they had been expounded by H. Bouillard, for instance, in his article in the H. de Lubac Memorial Volume, L'homme devant Dieu, vol. III. In this connection moral conscience would have to be dealt with and placed in relation to religious freedom.

If the bases of this anthropology were once laid down, they could proceed to deal with the relation between human tasks and the Kingdom of God.

[63] Notes made during the meeting.

That would amount to a fresh view of the classical doctrine on duties of state, which would be seen in conjunction with the two central truths of the presence of the Spirit in the Church and beyond the confines of the visible Church, and of the lordship of Christ, with the main emphasis placed on the Resurrection. All this should lead to eschatology. Just as Cardinal Meyer had emphasized continuity, Cardinal Bea had shown the necessity of manifesting the discontinuity.

Starting from these basic ideas, Canons Haubtmann and Moeller sketched the main lines of the Introductory Statement, taking into account the comments made by the fathers. Most of them had insisted that the text must be addressed to mankind; they must "speak as Christians to the world rather than to Christians about the world". There was a difficulty here, because the commission appeared to address Christians. They had also insisted that the Church must speak with humility, for it too is engaged in inquiry. Events lead the Church to understand its mystery better. Cardinal Spellman clearly expressed this in a remarkable speech. Furthermore, though the text must no doubt be addressed to men's understanding, it must also have human warmth, without falling into the sentimentality which some had criticized.

In this sense it was possible to deal with the *signa temporum*. On this theme there were few comments; the fathers liked facts to be mentioned, but the theologians were reserved. All agreed, however, that the signs of God are to be read in events; this is where the biblical idea of "time", of *kairos*, is apparent. Yet too sociological an outlook must be carefully avoided in describing the facts. Present-day problems are not merely connected with the change in the technical and economic order but also with ethical demands and moral discovery. Behind the problems of Africa and Asia, for example, there is a human problem of secularization. [64]

g) On this basis Cardinal Haubtmann revised the text which was to be submitted in Ariccia. He did not actually use Text 3 in making the revision. He decided on this despite the risk involved, because he considered that the comments and suggestions of the fathers taken as a whole, i.e. taking into account not only the speeches (cf. above 7b, c) but also all the written texts (cf. above 8f), contained so many amendments to the already "accepted" text that it was practically impossible to retain the latter. When Text 4 was submitted to the fathers at the Fourth Session, a concordance of themes and passages for the previous and the present text was included. This was done more for the sake of appearances than anything else, and not many fathers actually used the list.

It is scarcely credible that despite this risk — it was the fifth rewriting ab ovo since the beginning of the Council's work — the definitive text was in fact arrived at. This success must be attributed to the tireless work of the

---

[64] This plan was drawn up during the meeting of 12 January in Paris.

central editorial committee and Mgr. Philips. But it was also due to the fact that certain bishops and experts had had a hand in all the versions and had perpetually kept before their minds all the themes and the structure of the schema. Even if almost nothing of the latter remained,[65] the great themes were salvaged one after the other from every shipwreck, by the careful efforts of men such as Guano, McGrath, Ancel, Hirschmann, Tucci, Glorieux and Philips. This fact inevitably made the history of the "famous schema", as the secretary of the Theological Commission, Fr. Tromp, liked to call it, long and difficult.

VI. TEXT 4: ARICCIA
(31 JANUARY — 14 SEPTEMBER 1965)

1. Meeting of the Central Subcommission
(Ariccia 31 January — 6 February 1965)

a) We give in the notes the composition of the seven subcommissions which shared the work.[66] The atmosphere was marked by prayer, intensive work and collaboration; living together made possible a constant exchange of results between the various sections. The same spirit inspired it, but even more intensely, as a year before in Zurich. "The Ariccia session", R. Tucci wrote, "became for the new text what the Zurich meeting had been for the previous one, with the notable difference that it was very much more representative and the corporate collaboration lasted longer."[67]

b) The basic draft of the dogmatic part comprised in the French version 27 pages and 3 pages of notes,[68] consisting of an introduction and three

---

[65] Cf. below, section IX 1.

[66] Apart from Cardinal Cento, 19 of the 23 Council fathers of the augmented Central Subcommission (Mgrs. Blomjous, Edelby, Morris and Šeper were absent): Mgrs. Charue, Dearden, Franić, Heuschen, van Dodewaard, P. Fernández from the Theological Commission, Mgrs. Castellano, Da Silva, Petit, P. Möhler. Clerical experts were: Mgrs. Ferrari-Toniolo, Géraud, Higgins, Klostermann, Lalande, Prignon, Ramselaar, Thils, Worlock, Can. Haubtmann, Moeller, Dondeyne, Heylen, Houtart, Frs. Calvez, Goggey, Congar, Daniélou, de Riedmatten, Dubarle, Gagnebet, Girardi, Grillmeier, Häring, Hirschmann, Labourdette, Lebret, Lio, Martelet, Mulder, Schillebeeckx, Semmelroth, Sigmond, Tromp, Tucci, Van Leeuwen. Lay experts: Prof. Colombo, M. de Habicht, Prof. De Koninck (whose death shortly after in Rome was a grave loss to the Marriage and Family Subcommission), J. Folliet, Keegan, Prof. Minoli, Ruiz Giménez, M. Scharper, Prof. Swieżawski, M. Vanistendael. Laywomen: Miss Belosillo, Goldie, Monnet, Vendrik. Nuns: Sisters Guillemin, Mary-Luke. Secretaries: Fr. Dalos and Miss Besson (T, notes 73–74).

[67] T, p. 86; W IV, pp. 121–3 (W speaks of "universal forums").

[68] There was also an English and a Latin version. The original was French. This fact does not facilitate understanding of the text, for it was promulgated in Latin.

chapters: a survey of the conditions of life in the world of the present day, man in the universe, man in society.

The Dogmatic Subcommission under Mgr. Garrone soon split up into sub-groups or sub-subcommissions. The first, on atheism, was given the task of fitting a more precise description of this phenomenon into the descriptive part of the schema. It was also to compose a text on the attitude of the Church to this most momentous phenomenon of our time, as Paul VI had called it.

The second was to formulate the text on man himself (the future Part I of Chapter I, but at this time still Chapter I of Part II). The demand had in fact been made that the doctrine of man should be further developed, still in conjunction with the theme of the image of God, but treating in greater detail certain truths such as freedom, reason, aspiration towards God, etc. The aim here was to draw on biblical truths but to select and present them in such a way as to interest non-Christians.

The fourth sub-group was to revise the text on the Church as an institution and its saving significance for the world of today. This chapter had been newly inserted in the schema at the insistence of Mgr. Wojtyla, speaking on behalf of the Polish episcopate. The text of the schema which he proposed took into account the situation of the Churches in Socialist countries. He proposed that the text should speak much more explicitly about atheism and then present the whole of the rest of the text in relation to this fundamental kind of unbelief. It is not simply a question of showing what the Church does for the world by proclaiming true doctrine — that, he thought, was the content of the first three chapters of this part — but of showing that the Church is present and active in the world by what it does as a whole visible institution. It represents a different concrete solution to the other institutions set up in those countries. In particular Mgr. Wojtyla insisted on the Church's doctrine on freedom, which concerns a weak point of Marxist humanism. The Dogmatic Subcommission had decided to accept these considerations and to embody them in the text, without however changing the fundamental orientation of the text put forward at the beginning of the Ariccia session. The solution lay in the revised draft of this Chapter IV. As a result there were no doubt some repetitions, but the theme seemed so important that it was agreed to insert in a sense the content of the old Chapter II of Text 3.[69]

It had also been agreed practically unanimously that the style of the document under examination was at last just what was needed. It was indubitably characterized by solid, vigorous and clear language with texts and

[69] The four subgroups were composed as follows: 1. Mgr. Garrone, Fr. Girardi; 2. Mgr. González Moralejo, Frs. Daniélou, Tromp, Canon Moeller, Miss Goldie, Sister Mary-Luke; 3. Mgr. Wojtyla, Frs. Congar, Grillmeier, Semmelroth. The decisions were submitted at the meeting on 5 February, at which Cardinal Cento was present (based on *T*, n. 77).

quotations in support, bearing the evident stamp of a French style. Later some asked for it to be modified a little in the direction of greater sobriety. An effort was made, however, to maintain the same concrete style throughout, at least in Part I. It did in fact stimulate interest and was aimed both at head and heart.

This point was all the more important as it was quickly decided to address all men directly, though Catholics in the first place, for of course it is only to them that a Council can, strictly speaking, be addressed. But non-Christians and non-believers were also to be spoken to. It had already been decided in Paris on 12 February and confirmed in Ariccia, that terms drawn directly from natural law or philosophy were to be avoided. Instead, biblical language that might appeal to people today would be used.

By the end of the Ariccia meeting, the Dogmatic Subcommission had decided to devote a special chapter of the doctrinal section to man's activity in the world. In this way a total view would progressively be obtained: man, society, world. No doubt this division involved the danger of giving the impression that it was possible to speak of "man as such" without also speaking of his position in society and his action in the world. Yet man in a certain sense is all those things simultaneously. In order to avoid this defect, it was decided to present the essentials of subsequent chapters *in nucleo* from the first paragraphs of Chapter I onwards. The theme of man as the image of God made this unified presentation possible because it includes a relation both to God and to the neighbour and dominion over the world. In addition, this triple subdivision brought out man's total vocation: embodied spirit, existing in a society, situated in a history, in the centre of a universe for which he is responsible as God's viceroy. In this way a return had been made, though in extended form, to the theme that had stood at the beginning of the very first versions (Texts 1 and 2).

Finally, this new chapter removed the objection that the new draft was more a doctrine of man than a theology of the Church's presence in the world. The anthropological aspect was completed by the addition of a Christian cosmology incorporating all that Chapter IV had to say about the Church's place in all this, i.e. to proclaim these truths and to realize them by its activity and presence.

c) The other subcommissions were also at work. The Signs of the Times Subcommission was preparing a revised text of the descriptive section (at this time Part I). It also aimed at bringing out more clearly the ethical origin of modern changes and at the same time to widen the whole perspective so as to give it a less European character.

As the Dogmatic Subcommission was also revising the text of Chapter I and dealing with the same subject, there were some difficulties in harmonizing the two perspectives, for one was concerned more with content, the other with uniformity of style. It would have been better to entrust this part entirely to the Signs of the Times Subcommission. That in fact is what finally happened when the last difficulties arose over this meeting in Rome directly after the Ariccia meeting.[70]

Once the suggestion of the Subcommission for the Dignity of the Human Person, that these themes should be inserted in the chapter on man's vocation, had been accepted, that subcommission was divided up among Subcommission VII (for Peace) and the Subcommission for Political Life. In reality the number of subcommissions was not decreased, since the idea of introducing a chapter on political life was now put into effect.[71] This chapter was composed fairly late and remained one of the least satisfactory of the whole schema; its absence, however, would have left an inexplicable gap.

The Subcommission for Marriage was the largest. Under the chairmanship of Mgr. Dearden and with the collaboration of numerous experts, several of them from Belgium, it composed what, in comparison with the old appendix II of the May 1963 text, was practically a new draft.

The Subcommission for Culture, with Mgr. Guano as chairman, endeavoured to give a clearer structure to the chapter, and especially to insert a more complete description of culture with its tensions and antinomies. For it was considered that this chapter had turned out too idyllic. At this time a division, though a fruitful one, appeared in the commission, between those who stressed external civilization, i.e. its technical elements, and those who stressed wisdom, objective truth, play, the non-utilitarian. Some experts from Poland in particular stressed this latter feature. This dialectical tension continued until the end of the Fourth Session and contributed to enrich the text which finally became one of the most important in the whole Pastoral Constitution, having been regarded as one of the most difficult ever to be dealt with by a Council.[72]

---

[70] *T*, p. 91. There was a very regrettable lack of co-ordination. The version submitted in Rome was found unsatisfactory. Another, prepared by another subcommission, replaced it. A number of elements which had been inserted by the Signs of the Times Subcommission were lost sight of and were not replaced at once. Fortunately from March 1965 onwards the competence of this commission was fully recognized once more. This is the only unpleasant episode in the long history of the schema (see below, commentary on the Introductory Statement).

[71] The authors of this first text were Mgr. Quadri, Fr. Coffey, Prof. Ruiz Giménez. At the meeting of the Mixed Commission at the beginning of April 1965, Mgr. Philips submitted a version based on this first text but with a better arrangement. The addition of the chapter on politics and the insertion of the chapter on the person into Part I established the order of the appendix chapters as it was to remain in the future: I. Marriage and family, II. Culture, III. Economic and social life, IV. Political life, V. International community and peace.

[72] One of the chief "media" in which the world presents itself to the Church is culture. It is also profoundly connected with the proclamation of gospel truth. Furthermore all other realities such as marriage, economic and political life, peace etc., are primarily and thoroughly "cultural" i.e. linked with a language, imagery, etc., in order to manifest

d) At a full session on 6 February the results of the work were gathered; it was possible to submit "De vita oeconomico sociali" and "De dignitate matrimonii et familiae" in their Latin form.

2. The committee meeting (Rome, 8–13 February 1965)

At this session the members of the Central Subcommission and the presidents of the subcommissions met; in addition some experts were present who had directly shared in drafting the text.[73] The chief event of the meeting concerned the descriptive section, which was considered too optimistic, too sociological and too occidental. It was handed over to a small group — Mgr. A. Fernández, J. Folliet, R. Tucci and Miss Goldie.[74]

The subcommission examined the chapters "De vocatione personae humanae", "De homine in communitate humana", "De homine in universo", "De munere Ecclesiae erga hominem". The whole second part bore the title "Ecclesia et conditio humana", which had been suggested by Mgr. Garroni. The second part under the general title "De praecipiis muneribus a christianis nostrae aetatis implendis", contained six chapters, among them the chapter on the dignity of the person, and the recently added chapter on political life.

3. The meeting of the editorial committee (17 February 1965)

"Then", as R. Tucci says, "there began one of those periods of really feverish work which were to be very frequent in the subsequent history of the text."[75] Some idea of this may be formed from a list of the successive versions of the dogmatic part of the schema in Text 4: Text 4 A: Ariccia 31 January to 6 February 1965; Text 4 B: Rome 8–15 February; Text 4 C: Rome 16 to 26 February; Text 4 D: Louvain 11–13 March (Philips revision); Text 4 E: Rome 13–24 March; Text 4 F: Rome, meeting of the Mixed Commission, 29 March — 8 April; Text 4 G: Rome, Paris and Louvain, amended text,

themselves to us. Logically, the chapter on culture should have been placed at the very beginning of Part II. The close connection with the dogmatic part of the schema, which it always retained, would then have been more perceptible. An attentive examination of Text 6 would show that this chapter is one of the richest of the schema.

[73] As well as the members of the augmented Central Subcommission, Mgr. Dearden and Fr. Möhler belonged to it. Clerical experts: Mgrs. Ferrari-Toniolo, Glorieux, Higgins, Klostermann, G. Philips, Prignon, Ramselaar, Thils, Worlock, Canons Haubtmann, Heylen, Moeller, Frs. Houtart, Calvez, Coffey, Congar, Daniélou, de Riedmatten, Gagnebet, Grillmeier, Häring, Hirschmann, Lebret, Schillebeeckx, Semmelroth, Sigmond, Tromp, Tucci. Lay experts: J. Folliet, Prof. Ruiz Giménez, Miss Belosillo, Goldie, Sister Mary-Luke (*T*, n. 81; *W* IV, pp. 121–2, n.).

[74] Mgr. McGrath did not belong to this group. Cf. above, note 66.

[75] *T*, p. 93; *W* IV, p. 122 says nothing about this irritating period.

9 April — 5 May. The same applies by and large to the appendix chapters. At the meeting of the editorial committee the timetable was laid down; this was considered very important. Thus, for example, Mgr. Philips at the beginning of March was to examine the text from the point of view of dogmatic content, Latinity and technical unity. Similarly, the final decision was taken to incorporate the chapter on the human person into the dogmatic part. The chapter on political life was to follow that on economic and social life. An index of the various articles was also approved. The division in three parts was maintained: after an introduction, a first part on "The situation of man in the world of today"; a second part, "The Church and the position of man" in four chapters, the first of which concluded with an article on atheism on the lines of *Ecclesiam Suam;* a third part on some particularly urgent problems, with its four chapters in the order which henceforward remained unchanged: marriage, culture, economic and social life, political life, international relations and peace.[76]

4. Successive revisions: Texts 4 C D E F (18 February — 29 March)

a) It is impossible to deal with the various revisions in detail. The first phase consisted in producing a fair copy of the text that had emerged from the comments at the meeting in Rome, the second in translating certain parts into Latin, and its simultaneous revision by Mgr. Philips in Louvain, either alone (1–11 March) or with a small committee (Canons Haubtmann and Moeller). The third version was then made partly in Paris and Rome on the lines of Philips's revision in accordance with the suggestions discussed in Louvain but which it had not been immediately possible to incorporate in the text (Paris—Rome, 13–24 March).

An example may make this last point clear. It had been requested that the chapter on man and society should be shortened, more lucidly expressed and better arranged, and above all that its theological aim should be made clearer and shown to be the deeper meaning of the purely sociological view. The draft discussed in Louvain and partly revised by Canon Moeller was sent to Paris to Canon Haubtmann and incorporated by him in Text E in yet another modified form.

b) The deadline fixed by the printers for delivery of the text for the meeting of the Mixed Commission was 24 March. The drafting committee will not forget the hours spent day and night on the translation of the sections which had not yet been turned into Latin. Fr. Hirschmann worked one day until 2.30 in the afternoon, the last moment before taking the plane to Frankfort, in order to translate the revised version of Chapter IV. At

[76] *T,* pp. 92–93; W IV, p. 122 does not remark that the chapter on political life had been in preparation since the Ariccia-Rome meetings.

2.30 a.m. on the night of 23–24 March, the text was finished which had to be taken in the morning to St. Martha for printing. All this was done amid the pressure of other duties; on 24 March, Canon Haubtmann had to go to Paris for a meeting of the French episcopate. From 28 to 31 March, R. Tucci and Canon Moeller had to go to an ecumenical meeting in Geneva in preparation for the World Conference on "Church and Society" which was to take place in July 1966. Schema 13 was to be discussed there and compared with the text that the WCC for its part was working on.[77]

This latter fact shows that contact between the editorial committee of Schema 13 and the ecumenical movement was constantly maintained. It will be remembered that it had begun with an exchange of views and documents prepared by Lukas Vischer. It was pursued through contacts with those who were preparing the World Conference and who belonged to the Department of Action of the WCC. This double influence of Faith and Order and the Department of Action, reflects the polarity of Schema 13 and of the preparatory texts for the ecumenical meeting in July 1966, both of which were striving at the same time to be strictly theological and also to face the problems of contemporary mankind.

5. The meeting of the Mixed Commission (Rome 29 March — 8 April)

a) This important session was completely dominated by the personality of Mgr. Philips. "It is certainly his wide theological competence", R. Tucci writes, "his well-known masterly command of the Latin language and above all his conciliar and parliamentary experience, which deserves a large share of the credit for producing a text which nevertheless prompted a good deal of astonishment by its openness and novelty and by the many delicate matters it dealt with; there had not been enough time to consider these deeply and to express them in sufficiently qualified terms. Success in overcoming this difficulty was attained in varying degrees; they set about producing a new version of certain paragraphs in accordance with suggestions made in the debate. This was what was done for example with the section on atheism which had still met with severe criticism. Several fathers asked for a new consideration of the biblical quotations, and renewed endeavour to avoid repetitions and intrinsic as well as terminological inconsistencies. As usual, the chapters on marriage and on peace were the subject of lively discussions. Sometimes work had to continue late into the night preparing

[77] As well as other Catholics, Canon Moeller, Frs. Houtart and Tucci were present in Geneva. It was the first real contact between the groups who were preparing the documents for "Church and Society" and some of those who were working on Schema 13. The discussion among other things turned on two points: man made to the image of God (the meaning of this biblical statement) and the meaning of human "nature" or of the "natural law" for a Protestant theologian.

a new draft on this or that controverted point in order to be able to present next day a version that satisfied the Commission and so escape from a blind alley."[78]

When it is remembered that the proposed text contained 34 large pages of single-spaced typescript, one is amazed that it was possible to bring the discussion to a successful conclusion. Mgr. Philips was able to obtain agreement on an exceptionally strict timetable and a method of discussion which saved an enormous amount of time by combining into one answer the replies to several questions submitted by the fathers. Yet to bear in mind the sometimes very varied if not actually contradictory amendments, to combine them and to contrive to give a concrete positive answer in a few minutes, called for intense concentration. It is due to him that this dangerous reef was negotiated. A clearer idea of the pressure of time will be given by the fact that the concluding section was revised on 4 April and distributed on 7 April for debate the next day.

b) In the meantime, a *relatio* had also been composed which explained the grounds for the new text (4 F) which had emerged from the suggested amendments (to Text 3) made by the fathers during the Third Session. Nor must the work of the subcommissions on the chapters of the third part (the former appendices) be forgotten.

c) Mgr. Philips also suggested at this session that the description of man's situation in the world of today should be entitled "Expositio introductoria", "Introductory Statement". For of course the Council could not commit its authority in the description of facts which in 20 or 30 years may be quite different, in the same way as it could in the doctrinal statements. The word "introductoria" was preferred to "praevia" because this latter expression seemed — wrongly, as a matter of fact — to be compromised by unfortunate memories of the end of the Third Session and the *nota praevia*. The schema was thus composed of two main parts, one doctrinal, the other concerned with applications though at the same time also containing extensive doctrinal sections, for example in the chapters on marriage and on culture.

d) Finally, the question of the literary genus of the document was raised. The term "Constitutio pastoralis", which had been suggested by Mgr. Guano in May 1963 and which had been revived by Canon Moeller, now received a majority vote.[79]

The session concluded with global approval of the text — there was not a single abstention — but nevertheless with the proviso that it should be submitted to further examination, especially as regards the most disputed sections.[80]

---

[78] *T*, p. 95; *W* IV, p. 122.
[79] *T*, p. 55, 89, 97, 98, 103. Cf. below, section VIII 3.
[80] *T*, pp. 95–96; *W* IV, p. 122.

6. The activity of the editorial committee
(Rome, Paris, Louvain 9 April — 5 May)

a) Between 8 and 10 April in Rome, the committee was able to revise the Introduction and Part I, while the other subcommissions introduced the modifications that had been asked for in the second part.

b) After these preliminaries everything had to be revised once more, co-ordinated, and the Latin checked. Some idea may be formed of the modifications required when it is realized that the summary of the amendments proposed at the full session covered 24 pages of written notes. Moreover, Canon Haubtmann had to travel to Louvain twice and Mgr. Guano once. In fact the whole schema had to be revised, prepared for the Co-ordinating Commission and, with its consent, got ready for the Vatican Press. As Mgr. Charue, who since January had been in charge of the chapter on culture, wished someone concerned to go to the OIC Congress in Vienna, Canon Moeller was nominated to be there from 22 to 26 April. As a result, the very interesting conclusions of that Congress could be used, to the advantage of the chapter on culture and of the whole schema, in the final version made in Rome from 26 April onwards and especially during the Council session.[81]

These remarks show how the drafting of the schema was increasingly carried on in association with ecumenical and secular organizations. It must also be added that in the course of successive revisions, the chapter on culture gradually turned out to be most closely connected with the doctrinal part of the schema. Culture is in fact a fundamental factor at the base of all political, economic, social and international realities. Some even wanted to place this chapter at the head of the second part. But it was too late now to alter the order of chapters again.

c) The text was ready by the end of April. It was entitled: "Schema XIII: Constitutio pastoralis De Ecclesia in mundo huius temporis". After the Prooemium (Articles 1–3), it contained an Introduction (Articles 4–9), a first main section, "De Ecclesia et condicione humana" (Articles 10–58), a second main section, "De quibusdam problematis urgentioribus" (Articles 59–103) and a "Conclusion" (Articles 104–106). Including the footnotes, this amounted to 96 large sheets of single-spaced typescript.

The opening words from now on were not "Gaudium et luctus", but "Gaudium et spes".[82] The former no longer seemed to correspond to the funda-

---

[81] On this point *T*, p. 98, must be slightly corrected. The discussions in Vienna led to avoidance in the schema of some rather unclear and dangerous distinctions in the domain of secular sciences in contradistinction to the method of theological knowledge. Article 59 § 3 with its lucid mode of expression could therefore stand.

[82] The opening words of *Gaudium et Luctus* had been criticized because of the juxtaposition of a Christian term with one borrowed from classical humanism. The new opening was obtained simply by regrouping the first four words into two pairs, one expressing joy and Christian hope, the other the grief and anxieties of modern man. Cf. *T*, p. 97.

mental character of the schema. This was now expressed in two words drawn from biblical language but at the same time of a kind that might appeal to the sensibility and outlook of contemporary man.

7. Approval of the schema and translation into modern languages
(5 May — 14 September)

a) On 4 May, the presidents of the Mixed Commission, Cardinals Cento and Ottaviani, transmitted the document to Mgr. Felici for submission to the Co-ordinating Commission, which met on 11 May. Mgr. Guano took part, in his capacity as president of the subcommission. Cardinal Suenens, who had been responsible for the schema from the start, gave a report. After long discussion the text was approved as it stood, including the title "Pastoral Constitution". After receiving the Holy Father's approval on 28 May, it was printed and distributed to the fathers. It comprised 122 pages, 79 for the text itself, which was printed without typographical indications of changes made. Its present version was too new for that to be possible.[83]

b) English, German, Spanish and Italian translations were made during the Council and distributed to the fathers. The French text, which to some extent (Part I and Introductory Statement) was the original, was issued in May and June with the explanatory note that reference might be made to it. But the Latin remained the only official text.

R. Tucci has described the not very optimistic atmosphere that prevailed even among the members of the various subcommissions during the weeks preceding the Fourth Session. They realized better than anyone the faults of the text, which were due to the exceptionally short time available for its preparation. Rumours were also current that the schema might possibly be cancelled or reduced to the status of a less official document, or even entrusted to a post-conciliar commission or handed over to the Pope with a view to an encyclical. Some also thought it would be wiser to drop the title "Pastoral Constitution". On the other hand, the personal interest shown by the Pope on several occasions lessened the anxiety.[84]

VII. TEXT 5. FOURTH SESSION
(14 SEPTEMBER — 12 NOVEMBER 1965)[85]

The Ariccia Text 4 was the subject of study and discussions during the summer at various episcopal congresses, for example at the Fulda Conference and

---

[83] An excellent analysis is given by *W* IV, pp. 123–8; *L* V, pp. 71–104 links an account of the debates with analysis of the content of the text. A concordance table was included in the volume for the Council fathers (pp. 93–95).   [84] *T*, pp. 101–3. Cf. note 26 above.

[85] This refers to the time available for discussion of Text 5. Text 6 was revised on the basis of the *modi*, from 17 November onwards.

at the meeting of the Italian episcopal conference. The latter sent the editorial committee 23 pages of suggestions.

1. This Text 4 was debated at the Council from 21 September (132nd general congregation) to 8 October 1965

a) It was clear from the start that severe criticism would be voiced. This became plain at a meeting on 17 September, when the German bishops strongly disapproved of the first part. They had already done so at Fulda, as Fr. Hirschmann had reported. They contended that the doctrine on man and the world needed supplementing. Attention should be directed more to man's temporal and historical character; the point of view of the text was too static. The doctrine on sin was inadequate, so was the *theologia crucis* and the *theologia eschatologica*. They also reproached the text with naturalism, optimism and oversimplification of some problems. It was not made clear what was contributed by faith, what was the task of the Church through its hierarchy and through the faithful. Insufficient distinction was drawn between principles and practical prescriptions. Insufficient account was taken of the ecumenical point of view in the way the problems were stated. As regards style, too, much more account should have been taken of the mentality of unbelievers, and it ought to have been stated that the text itself was incomplete on many points. Finally, they expressed grave doubts whether it was opportune to call the whole document a "Pastoral Constitution". What was needed as, for example, K. Rahner said, was a theological gnoseology to make it clear what the Church was enunciating as propositions and what it was recommending as directives.

The German bishops present, Volk, Reuss, Hengsbach, concurred. The French and Belgian bishops present, Ancel, Garrone, Musty and Elchinger, defended the text. While readily admitting its imperfections, they pointed to its fundamental purpose, which was not to present the Christian message in its entirety, but to illuminate the problems of civilization in the light of the gospel. To these arguments of Fr. Daniélou, Mgr. Garrone added that the aim had been "to apply a doctrine of man to the problems of the world". They must "speak of the Christian doctrine of man so that the light of faith may become effective for the study of certain very serious problems, such as that of the family". Furthermore, Mgr. Garrone added, "the anthropology of the schema is progressive, but it is not distorted. At the beginning of each chapter we are placed in the light of faith, for example by speaking of man as the image of God. That is then gone into more deeply and leads to the Easter mystery." Fr. Congar likewise stressed the idea that "the chief problem of the present time is the doctrine of man: *sermo de homine, sermo de Deo,* their unity must be sought in Christ". Canon Haubtmann emphasized that in the revision of the text, account had had to be taken of the suggestions made by the fathers at the Third Session. He added that it had had an excellent reception among many laymen in France. He noted in conclusion that seven-tenths of the fathers had wished the starting-point to be truths common to all, not the natural order — a term which for that reason had been avoided in the text — but the biblical presentation of those truths common to all, so that gradually they could move forward to the more profoundly Christian truths, that is, to the crucified and risen Christ.

It is evident that the opposing points of view were quite clear. It was the great merit of Mgr. Elchinger to have organized this meeting, which was decisive for subsequent work on Schema 13. Mgr. Philips suggested a concrete solution. He first recalled how novel a venture Schema 13 was. If, he said, "this attempt is not accepted as a working basis, we shall risk being left empty-handed at the end of the session, which would be a considerable disappointment". He said that he had accepted the task of revision without enthusiasm but with conviction. The problem was, he knew, an extremely difficult one; they had to speak the language of the Church yet in such a way that those who heard could understand and feel that the Church understands their problems. There is disquiet; contact and dialogue are needed. That is what the text attempts. It can be improved but should be accepted as a basis from which to start.

He explained this by declaring that from the start two things needed to be said: the Church speaks yet cannot give a definitive answer to all concrete questions. In other words, we are dealing with a document based on faith, but concerned with its application to problems of actual life. The Church in accordance with its mission, speaks to man as he is, yet in the light of Christ. The method is pedagogical. Of course the text has a different impact when it is read by Germans, French or Americans. Not everyone recognizes himself in it, but this is only natural. The Council must speak a universal language. As far as the more concrete suggestions were concerned, their non-definitive but guiding character must be made clear.

Thanks to this discussion, agreement was reached to accept the text as a basis but to improve it. For this purpose, care would be taken to see that a number of theologians (German-speaking for the most part) who had expressed the severest criticism, should be members of the ten subcommissions when these were appointed next day. As will be seen, each subcommission in fact contained at least one and sometimes several theologians who had been opposed to Text 4. The result of this decision was that the text was once again changed quite considerably — for example Chapter III of Part I was rewritten almost completely — but that the version put to the vote by the fathers before its promulgation represented the consensus of the two main tendencies which had stood confronted since the beginning of work on Schema 13: one a concrete outlook marked by a certain fundamental optimism, the other a dialectical, paradoxical attitude insisting on the polyvalency of the world in which the Church lives.

This little-known episode has been described in detail because of its importance. In fact it was decisive because it meant that all revisions during the last two stages were made on the general lines that a balance must be struck between the opposing tendencies of the two ways of envisaging the problem. At the same time the observer delegates were to express their criticisms; two sessions on 21 and 28 November were devoted to this.

As a consequence, the final text doubtless lost a little of its homogeneity, its continuous forward movement, in favour of a presentation which multiplied contrasts. But it gained in wealth of content and complexity. In short, it acquired a more dialectical character, which the Malines Schema (Interim Text A) had possessed but which had practically diappeared from later versions.[86]

b) Since 14 September, at the express wish of the Pope, Mgr. Garrone had taken the place of Mgr. Guano who was ill. It was a heavy sacrifice for the latter to have to be absent from the session which promulgated the schema which he had supported and worked at from the beginning with flexibility and prudence but also with invincible confidence.

In his *relatio*, which was read and discussed in the Mixed Commission on 18 September and submitted to the fathers on 21 September, Mgr. Garrone emphasized — and the course of the 17 September meeting had shown the deeper meaning of this point — that the central theme and the vital principle of the whole schema was the problem of man. The text aimed at tracing a few essential lines of the Christian anthropology which so many conciliar interventions during the Third Session had demanded.

c) The debate on the schema in general lasted until the 134th general congregation on 23 September. The vote resulted in 2111 for, 44 against, 1 for with reservations, out of 2157. The discussion of the chapters began on 23 September and lasted until the 145th general congregation on 8 October 1965.

The opinions voiced may be summarized as follows. There were very few amendments to the introductory section apart from a wish to see the universe as a whole taken more into account. As regards the word "Church", it should be pointed out that in Part I Chapters I–III it meant the People of God, whereas in Chapter IV it referred to the hierarchy. As regards the word "world" it should be indicated that it means human society in this world but also that that very world itself has fallen into disorder and is under the dominion of the Devil, and will ultimately be restored in its plenitude through Christ's death and resurrection.

This request was granted in the form of the second paragraph of Article 2,

---

[86] Notes made at the meeting on 17 September. The bishops present have already been listed. The experts present were: Frs. K. Rahner, Semmelroth, Hirschmann, Daniélou, Congar, Schillebeeckx, Ratzinger, Haubtmann, Philips, Moeller, Heylen. Cf. W IV, pp. 128–32.

where these three aspects are remarkably well combined. This amendment, suggested by the German theologians, is one of the most important, because by its position in the Preface it makes clear that wherever the word "world" appears in the schema, it is to be understood in this complex sense. Similarly the term "Church" was defined. Although in the Preface the expression "the faithful" is preferred, as a better expression for the presence of Christians in the world of men, the word "Church" most often signifies the People of God, except in Chapter IV, as we have already noted. In this way the fundamental aim of the Zurich text was rediscovered, and some sections of that text might well have been reincorporated in the schema.

In the first part the style was criticized as excessively philosophical, optimistic and static, as lacking the dramatic note which is typical of the present-day conception of man and the history of culture. A more explicit condemnation and also a more finely shaded description of atheism were called for, and an outline of the Church's attitude to it. None of the fathers asked for mention of culpable responsibility and sin on the part of atheists.

These amendments too were accepted by adding a very fine paragraph on Christ at the end of the Preface, thus giving it a Christological, prophetic and paschal character. This was a kerygmatic statement, which was to be regularly repeated at the end of each chapter of the first part, producing an alternation of light and shade which the authors of the text had deliberately aimed at and which was accepted by the fathers. As regards atheism, it was considered that the schema as a whole would itself constitute an answer.

The chief comment on the second part was that its connection with the first part was not entirely clear. The promise was given that this would be corrected, for example by modifying the prologues which preceded each chapter. It was in fact only a question of making clear the connection which was actually there in each case, at all events in the first two chapters, and which had been deliberately established.[87]

2. The revision of the text

a) The oral and written comments filled almost 500 large pages of single-spaced typescript. Thanks to an organization set up by Mgr. Philips, which had stood the test in connection with the Dogmatic Constitutions on the Church and on Revelation, the interventions were all recorded on cards. The desired amendments could thus be classified as follows: general remarks on the schema, on a chapter, on an article, on a line, on a word. A team of about a dozen *periti* and the voluntary helpers, who were often the most active, worked day and night to make these three thousand or so cards. Canon Haubtmann had photostats made so that the president and secretary

---

[87] Good accounts of the discussion in *W* IV, pp. 132–282; *T*, pp. 104–9; *L* V, pp. 71–105.

of each subcommission, as well as the general president and the chief *relator* (Mgr. Garrone and Mgr. Philips) could have them at their disposal.

b) The work was divided among ten subcommissions, one for practically every chapter.[88] The first six had completed their work by 17 October, the other four finished on 19–20 October. The full session of the Mixed Commission was fixed for 20–30 October, with about 12–15 meetings in all.

Work went on doggedly and feverishly day and night. The amendments had to be considered one after the other from a report composed from the cards and the changes submitted at a full session of the Mixed Commission. The further revisions had then to be inserted in a typed copy of the text ready for the Vatican Press.

c) On 12 November the *Textus recognitus* of Part II, and on 13 November that of Part I, was submitted to the fathers, 151 pages in all in two fascicules. On 15 November the voting began at the 161st general congregation and lasted until the 163rd general congregation on 17 November, 33 votes in all being taken.

R. Tucci sums up the main lines of the emendations as follows. Nothing was changed in the substance of the text, not even in the parts which were completely new such as Part I, chapter III; this was yet another example of

---

[88] Subcommission I (Central): Cardinal Browne, Mgrs. Charue, *Garrone*, Hengsbach, Ménager, the presidents of the subcommissions, Mgrs. Glorieux, *Haubtmann*, Philips, Canon Moeller, Frs. Häring, Hirschmann, Tromp, Tucci, Miss Goldie, Sister Mary-Luke.

Subcommission II ("De condicione hodierna"): Mgrs. A. Fernández, Fernández-Condé, *McGrath*, Nagae, Zoa, Frs. Anastasius a S. Rosario, Medina, de Lubac, Prof. Sugranyes de Franch, Vásquez.

Subcommission III ("De homine"): Mgrs. Doumith, Granados, Ménager, Parente, Poma, *Wright*, Frs. Benoît, Congar, Daniélou, Gagnebet, *Kloppenburg*, Nicolau, K. Rahner, *Semmelroth*.

Subcommission IV ("De humana navitate"): Mgrs. Bednorz, González Moralejo, *Garrone*, Volk, Cattauri, Thils, Frs. Balić, B. Lambert, Molinari, *Smulders*.

Subcommission V ("De munere Ecclesiae"): Mgrs. *Ancel*, Pelletier, Spanedda, Wojtyla, Vodopivec, Frs. *Grillmeier*, Ochagavia, Salaverri, Miss Belosillo, Sister Guillemin.

Subcommission VI ("De matrimonio"): Mgrs. C. Colombo, *Dearden*, Heuschen, Morris, Petit, Van Dodewaard, Géraud, Lambruschini, Prignon, Can. Delhaye, *Heylen*, Frs. Schillebeeckx, Van Leeuwen, the laymen Prof. Minoli, Adjakpley, Work.

Subcommission VII ("De cultura"): Mgrs. Charue, Vallopilly, Yü Pin, Frs. Moehler, Granier, Abbot Butler, Mgrs. Klostermann, Ramselaar, Canon Dondeyne, Moeller, Frs. *Rigaux*, Tucci, the laymen Swiezawski, Folliet.

Subcommission VIII ("De vita oeconomica-soc."): Mgrs. de Araujo Sales, Franić, Granier, Gutiérrez, *Hengsbach*, Larraín, Pessôa Câmara, Mgrs. Ferrari-Toniolo, Pavan, Rodhain, Worlock, Frs. Laurentin, *Calvez*, Lio.

Subcommission IX ("De vita politica"): Mgrs. Henriquez, László, Quadri, Frs. *Guglielmi*, Leethan, the laymen Prof. Ruiz Giménez, Veronese.

Subcommission X ("De pace"): Cardinal Šeper, Mgrs. Kominek, Nécsey, *Schröffer*, Fr. Fernandez, Mgr. Schauf, Frs. Alting v. Geusau, *H. de Riedmatten*, *Dubarle*, Labourdette, the laymen de Habicht, Norris.

substantial identity persisting throughout a new version, which was typical of the history of Schema 13.

Another phenomenon unique in the annals of the Council was that the revised text was shorter than its predecessor, 93 paragraphs instead of 106. Such a novelty should have been received with acclaim, but there was too much hurry and the plaudits only came later.

In the Introductory Statement the term "signs of the times" was used once but only in the very general sense which John XXIII had given it. The style was simpler and clearer. Each chapter in Part II began with these signs and then proceeded to principles. After long discussions, a return had been made (at least in the second part and the introduction) to the idea Mgr. Pavan had suggested in May 1963 of starting from concrete situations.

In Part I an even greater effort was made to place the whole exposition in the light of the central mystery of the incarnation and the redemption. Emphasis was laid on sin by introducing into Chapter III a new article (37) "Du humana navitate a peccato corrupta". The section on atheism was likewise completely rewritten so as to add finer shades to the description and also to emphasize possible guilt on the atheist's part. This, it must be noted, had not been mentioned in the aula, but was very insistently called for by some bishop members of the Secretariat for Non-believers who had joined the conciliar subcommission responsible for revising the text. When the Central Subcommission examined this text of Subcommission III (for Chapter I), as it did those of all the subcommissions, it modified the version of article 19 ("Undeniably those who wilfully shut out God from their hearts...") so much, that it no longer corresponds to the Council's general intention to avoid anathemas.

It was also agreed, after very lively discussion in the Mixed Commission, not to mention Marxism and communism by name. The reality was described in Article 20 (on systematic atheism), but the words were nevertheless avoided because of the multiplicity of their possible meanings and also because of potential pressure. This decision was, in the words of Mgr. Garrone in his oral report, "in accord with the pastoral purpose of the Council, as well as with the express will of John XXIII and Paul VI".[89]

In Part II an effort was made to achieve greater balance between general statements and special applications, between a specifically Christian viewpoint and one based on the natural order, between opinions which had not yet received the general approval of the Church and those which are found in every manual, between a concrete and sober mode of expression and a prophetic style.

On this a general observation may be made. While Part I and Chapters I–II of Part II are based more on the biblical idea of man as the image of

---

[89] W IV, p. 133; T, n. 111, who alone mentions the important oral addition in the aula.

God, the last three start from the idea of personal dignity. The connection between this and the creation of man to the image of God is insisted on because, for biblical and ecumenical reasons, they wished to avoid the concepts of "natural law". This point, which was stressed at the Geneva Conference for Church and Society in July 1966,[90] will prove increasingly important.

The very numerous alterations made to the chapter on marriage — this subcommission had by far the most bishops and *periti* — left open all the questions which are still under discussion and which are being dealt with by the papal commission. The objective moral order was more clearly emphasized than in the earlier version, though the term "objective" here is not to be understood in a materially biological way, but in such a way that the attitude of the consciously free human person is itself included in the objective order. More emphasis was also laid on the Church's teaching office. Finally, practically a new article (56) was added on the pastoral aspect of marriage, especially in the world today.

In regard to culture the subcommission endeavoured to bring out even more clearly the dialectical character of this phenomenon, both in its own domain (art. 56) and in relation to the Christian faith (art. 62). In addition, a better arrangement was achieved by combining the various parts (e.g., arts. 60–62) and regrouping them. Mgr. Elchinger, who acted as spokesman of numerous groups of intellectuals and scientists, was invited to take part in the meetings. Similarly the description of culture was also expanded and placed in relation to natural science, history, art and religion; the reference to art was extended in the direction of problematic modern art without excluding this from all connection with the liturgy. The autonomy of culture in its own sphere was once more affirmed. Express mention was made of the position of women, and this time the women auditors accepted this more than honourable mention. It must be said that by the participation of new men such as Fr. Moehler and Abbot Butler, and of men such as Fr. Léger, Mgrs. Ramselaer and Klostermann, who were well acquainted with the present state of thought, this chapter reached a maturity and balance which made it one of the most important and modern in the schema.

As regards social and economic life, the main problem was to avoid vagueness and yet not to fall into the danger of committing the magisterium in fields where not even Catholic specialists themselves are of one mind. Consequently mention is made of the purpose of earthly goods to serve all men, refugee problems, world hunger, agriculture — the stepchild of modern times — automation, workers' participation in industry, strikes; it must be borne in mind the whole time that the special situation in the authoritarian states could not be overlooked.

[90] Cf. Canon Moeller, "L'Église dans le monde d'aujourd'hui", *Documentation Catholique* (4 September 1966), pp. 1500–3. An attempt to deal with this point.

It is well-known that on the themes of peace and international justice controversy continued until the very end of the Council. It is sufficient for our purpose to point out that the pendulum swung strongly between a text which, though it condemned war, nevertheless took some account of actual concrete situations and one which expressed a more "realistic and dynamic view", with "a more evangelical tone with some truly prophetic accents corresponding to what many were looking for in this connection".[91] As regards international society and the duty of Christians to collaborate in international organizations, a completely new paragraph was included on how useful it would be to create an organization of the world-wide Church devoted to promoting progress in underdeveloped areas. The urgent need for such a body was endlessly repeated at the Geneva World Conference for Church and Society. At Christmas 1966, Paul VI announced the setting-up of this commission. A return had thus finally been made to a suggestion put forward by H. de Riedmatten in February 1963 at the Zurich meeting.

At the same time it is extremely regrettable that an amendment suggesting that mention should be made of collaboration with the separated brethren in this very field (art. 90), and which involved nothing more than taking up again a formula already prepared in Zurich, "was lost or mislaid" among the subcommission's papers, and could not be included. The ecumenical aspect of the Pastoral Constitution would have found much better expression if it had been included.[92]

For the Conclusion, the gnoseological suggestion made by K. Rahner at the 17 September meeting was accepted. An amendment was included that the question had quite deliberately been treated in a very general way, and that several of the matters dealt with were left incomplete because of the relative novelty of the material.

3. Voting on the amended text

The fathers expressed their opinion in 33 votes from 15 to 17 November.[93] The most important result was that the *placet juxta modum* never amounted to more than one third of the votes. This made it possible to take into account at the *expensio modorum* only those which made the accepted text clearer, deeper or more complete, and to exclude all those which contradicted the substance of the text. These figures surpassed the expectations even of

---

[91] *T*, p. 120, n. 113; *W* IV, pp. 262–82; *L* V, pp. 96–102, who points out the connection with Paul VI's journey to the United Nations.

[92] *T*, n. 114. The conference in Geneva in July 1966 had given first place to this need.

[93] We give at the end the excellent table from *L* V, pp. 417 ff. The votes marked with an asterisk are those whose results were not announced the same day but at a subsequent session. The figures in brackets refer to the text of the book.

the greatest optimists, and the members of the drafting committee were not among the latter.

As R. Tucci notes, the largest number of *non placet* (74) was reached in Part I in the section on atheism. Otherwise they were fairly uniformly distributed, reaching a peak of 45 in the article concerning man's action corrupted by sin and its relation to the eschatological goal (arts. 35–37). In the second part the greatest number of *non placet* (140) concerned marriage, Articles 54–56 on fertility and harmony between conjugal love and respect for human life. In the last chapter there were 144 *non placet* in regard to the section on peace and war.

All in all the points criticized remained the same from the start, and it is probable that the majority of the *non placet* and the *placet juxta modum* came from those who found the schema too progressive. The fathers who were chiefly concerned that the document should be accepted before it was too late voted in favour even if they were not satisfied with everything. R. Tucci says at the end of his commentary: "It was a case of avoiding irreparable loss of time."[94]

VIII. TEXT 6. FOURTH SESSION
(13 NOVEMBER — 7 DECEMBER)

1. The last hurdle had still to be crossed, that of the *expensio modorum*. There were about 20,000 of them! Even though many were identical, they had to be classified and a report had to be drawn up arranging them according to themes — often one set cancelled another — and they had to be discussed in the subcommission and then by the Mixed Commission. Mgr. Philips had had to leave Rome on 7 November, and his absence was painfully apparent.

The subcommission set to work. It was absolutely necessary to decide to limit the Mixed Commission's examination of amendments to the most important, though each of the fathers had the right to demand that any particular *modus* should be considered. This method prevented the Mixed Commission from dealing with suggestions that were better ignored.[95]

2. The proposed amendments once more centred on three main points. In regard to atheism, the earlier condemnation of communism with a reference in the footnote to papal documents was introduced once more. As regards marriage, there was the penultimate conciliar controversy because of the *modi* sent in by the Holy Father. Some of the more moderate members of the Mixed Commission (some of them were members of the Theological

---

[94] *T*, pp. 123–5.
[95] *T*, p. 121; *W* IV, pp. 164–6.

Commission) did not hesitate to say that this was the most serious crisis of the Council. After long debates, which fortunately took place in the presence of the experts and lay auditors, the essential content of the *modi* was accepted, without, however, altering the substance of the text; it was no longer possible to do so, since it had already been accepted by a majority of two-thirds. Here the famous footnote 14 (Abbott, note 137) of Chapter II was composed, discussed, modified and finally approved, recalling the teaching of the magisterium, especially *Casti Connubii* and Pius XII's Allocution to the Midwives but also mentioning Paul VI's Address to the "porporati" in which he announced the formation of a papal commission for the study of certain problems which the Council had left to the Pope's decision. The note ended with a famous sentence in which the absence of a comma after one word made a very definite difference to the meaning: "Sic stante doctrina magisterii" ("With the doctrine of the magisterium in this state") and not "Sic, stante doctrina magisterii" ("Thus, the doctrine of the magisterium remaining as it is . . ."). This footnote is celebrated because it is unique among all the conciliar texts; all other notes simply contain references to biblical, patristic, scholastic or papal texts.[96]

The third focus of debate was the section on war. The quotation from *Pacem in Terris* which radically condemned all war, was relegated to a footnote, and the schema was less unqualified. But some bishops, especially from the United States, thought that even now there was still danger that some governments who were trying to defend freedom in the world by intervening wherever it is threatened, would be placed in a difficult if not impossible situation. Two North American bishops proposed an amendment at the very last moment. It is true, as one of the experts said, that the Text 4 version was very pacifist on this point, but one wonders why the bishops from the USA did not insist at that juncture on amendments of the kind they wanted. Moreover, they had approved Text 5. It was rather late now, during the voting on Text 6, to question its substance.

Fortunately the crisis which might have prevented the final vote on the whole Pastoral Constitution was overcome by an explanatory note which was proposed by Mgr. Garrone and approved by the Mixed Commission. It showed that the anxiety of the American bishops was unfounded and that the text was less unqualified than it appeared.[97] Consequently, after a final excitement that brought the telephones into action and provoked busy

---

[96] The translation given, for example, by Editions du Centurion is unfortunate. "The doctrine of the Church, which remains as it is . . .". It seems to suppose that the Latin text runs "Sic, stante doctrina magisterii . . ."

[97] The best account is in *W* IV, pp. 276–80; Cf. also the three valuable notes and documents on the problem of the condemnation of atheism (*W* IV, pp. 166–8: Reference to *Divini Redemptoris;* pp. 168–73: Soviet reactions, problems of dialogue, G. Mury and R. Garaudy).

activity among bishops and theologians, it was possible to put the text to the vote. We may note that the more prudent and realistic and at the same time more prophetic tone of the definitive text on this delicate point, derives in part from Paul VI's speech before the United Nations.

3. Vote on the *Expensio Modorum*

The two volumes (256 and 155 pages) were put to the conciliar vote on 4 December. The result was extremely favourable and the contested points were once again the chapters on atheism and marriage (131 and 155 *non placet* respectively).[98] Meanwhile a vote had been taken on the title *Constitutio pastoralis*. 541 fathers had asked for a different title, the most favoured being *Declaratio pastoralis* (217). The amendments covered such a large number of different suggestions that it was obvious that the term *Constitutio pastoralis*, which had been suggested in Zurich by Mgr. Guano, was the most precise. During the last phase of the conciliar session, the difficulties arose not so much because dogmatic weaknesses were criticized in the text, but because of the very varied if not even disparate character of its different parts. It had been proposed to call only the first part a *constitutio* and the second a *declaratio*. But there was an inescapable objection to this, for the chapter on marriage, which was one of the most important on account of the "expectation of the nations" and the essential dogmatic statements that it contained, would have been of less authority. And there was no question of that.

Furthermore, the chapter on culture, contrary to appearances if read superficially, also contained a series of dogmatic statements — for instance a reference to the text of the Constitution *Dei Filius* of Vatican I on the autonomy of secular disciplines in their own sphere. There was no advantage here, either, in breaking the connection between culture and the theological viewpoint which throws light on it and at the same time imposes on theology itself the obligation of respecting culture.

The connection with theological doctrine as such, especially from Chapter III of Part II onwards, assumes a more "analogous" form. Here too, however, it was useful not to classify these texts as *declarationes* for that would have meant weakening the significance within the Church of what was said about international justice, peace and population problems. And it would once again have meant running the risk of seeming to be uninterested in the concrete problems of millions of human beings. It would have given the impression that certain domains are regarded as secondary, although, even if not directly theological, they are none the less important and are

---

[98] Cf. the results of the votes on the *expensio modorum*, according to the table given by *L·V*, pp. 41 ff.

becoming increasingly important. The title *Constitutio pastoralis* was there-fore retained for the whole, it being sufficient to note the analogical applica-tion of that title to its various parts. No further attempt was therefore made to revive *in extremis* the all too famous and fatal division into "conciliar constitution" and "appendix chapters"; heaven alone knows what authority the latter would have enjoyed.

We believe that this vote, which expressed the opinion of the majority, is a sign of the guidance of the Spirit. The further away one moves from the Council, the more one recognizes how important it is that *Gaudium et Spes* is one of the four great conciliar texts with the Dogmatic Constitutions on Revelation and the Church and the Constitution on the Liturgy. That is the very heart of the Council. *Lumen Gentium* is founded on *Dei Verbum; Gaudium et Spes* is rooted in *Lumen Gentium* and, in addition is directed "ad extra", to use Cardinal Suenens's words again, not only beyond the Church but even beyond the sacred domain to that world of men and the created universe for whose salvation the Church is sent. Finally, there is the Liturgical Constitution, which is revelation announced, prayed, lived and conveyed to the People of God in and through the Church.

Those who defended the title *Constitutio pastoralis,* and the author of this survey is one of them, were not always aware themselves what they were doing, and perhaps it was better so.

4. The two final votes and promulgation (6–7 December 1965)

At the 168th and last congregation on 6 December, the vote was taken on the complete text; out of 2373 votes, 2111 were *placet,* 251 *non placet* and 11 invalid.

On 7 December at the ninth public session, which will be always unforget-table "because of the erasion of the mutual excommunications in 1054 from the memories of the Churches of Rome and Constantinople", the last vote took place: out of 2391 votes, 2309 were in favour, 75 against and 7 invalid.

Through five phases in which it had died, and five phases of resurrection, the dogmatic part of the text had overcome an incredible number of obsta-cles. These had arisen from the fact that the text was completely new, contained such a mass of different problems and involved so many members of the Mixed Commission. Only the appendix chapters had victoriously won the day, i.e. preserved their fundamental tendency and a substantial part of their formulation. After a period of obscuration which lasted for two texts (Malines and Zurich), when they were demoted from one moment to the next to the rank of "private texts", they emerged again. Then they were coupled like a row of carriages to the dogmatic train which was on the point of moving forward, and at every station their order was rearranged. One wonders whether it was not in fact precisely these chapters that contributed to salvaging the main text, which became less pretentious, more concrete and simple, while they were raised into the half-light of an important doctrinal statement and sometimes, as with marriage and culture, even into the clear light of revelation.

This success was due to men who carried the schema through the darkest hours: Cardinal Cento in the first place, whose enthusiasm even in the worst crises was disarming, Mgr. Guano who was absent in body at the end but present in spirit, Mgr. Philips who was responsible for the text passing the scrutiny of the Mixed Commission in March and April 1965, H. de Ried-matten whose precise and concrete remarks were a constant inspiration, J. B. Hirschmann, an indefatigable worker, R. Tucci, wise and tireless, Canon Haubtmann, who in the last phase (Texts 4, 5 and 6) managed to overcome the hazard of rewriting the whole text afresh, and finally Cardinal Suenens who, if he was not the first to form the idea, nevertheless managed to formulate it on 6 December 1962 so effectively that it aroused the interest of the Council.

IX. CONCLUSION

1. Themes which appear in all versions

a) Christian anthropology. This is the nucleus which, with the theme of man made to the image of God, was already in the texts of the Preparatory Commission. This theme, new for a conciliar text, was to appear in a number of passages in the Pastoral Constitution and play a part in other conciliar texts. Its acceptance by Vatican II is an important event, for it oriented Vatican II along the axis of this Christian anthropology, the elaboration of which is perhaps the most urgent task of the 20th century.

This anthropology was gradually expanded. From the Malines text onwards it was connected with the theme of Christ's dominion, which also includes another, that of the Servant of God. A fourth theme appeared from Text 3 onwards, that of the creating and enlightening Word. This was very much weakened during the revision between the 4th and the 5th version (chiefly under the influence of German theologians) but it is still clearly recognizable, for example in the chapter on culture (art. 57 §§ 3 and 4).

b) The autonomy of secular activities in their own sphere. This theme which is illustrated by a quotation from Vatican I, played a part in Texts 2, 4, 5 and 6. While it was being developed, the theme of the intrinsic reality and value of earthly things in their own sphere was gradually made clear (from the Malines text until the end).

c) The theme of the Church which "civilizes by evangelizing" appears in Text 2 and is maintained through all the others.

d) The theme of the ambivalence and paradox of the term "world", according to whether it is a question of human society or of human action, was present from the Malines text onwards, in which it played a central part. It disappeared in the Zurich text, reappeared in Text 3, disappeared in Text 4 and was placed in the very centre of Texts 5 and 6, giving them a dialectical character.

2. a) The theme of the Holy Spirit acting in history and recreating and renewing man "in justice and in holiness of truth". This was in the Malines and Zurich texts and in Text 3 and then disappeared without trace.

b) The theme of the Church which in its liturgy "transforms the world". In the Malines schema there was a whole article devoted to this eschatological humanism. It disappeared completely with the exception of a word or two in the chapter on the Church's culture which civilizes "actione sua etiam liturgica".

c) The theme of the "humanism of the Sermon on the Mount", that is to say, of the human values which appear in abundance if one takes as starting-point the Sermon on the Mount as the "charter of the kingdom of God". This theme was in the Malines Text 2. It disappeared completely under the pressure, quite unjustified when as exclusive as this, of mass culture and of an exaggerated fear of flight heavenwards, of escapism.

d) Christian cosmology. A view of history and the universe in the perspective of the plan of salvation. This was present in Malines Text 2 and Text 4, but almost completely disappeared from Texts 5 and 6, through anxiety not to go beyond what is biblically certain in this respect. Any confusion of Schema 13 with Teilhardism is impossible. The text takes up a position beyond systems.

It will be noticed that the four themes that practically disappeared are closely related to Eastern theology. The tendency of the text, however rich it may be, remained too Western. What the Orthodox have to say about it should be very significant.

3. Ecumenical perspectives

a) Collaboration in the realm of the dogmatic treatment from 1963 onwards. This was continued in February 1964 in Zurich and during the Fourth Session, though not so intensely because of lack of time.

b) The wish for practical collaboration was expressed in the Zurich text in February 1964. It was in fact much more explicitly stated there than in any subsequent version. Such collaboration will no doubt assume concrete form in the Commission for International Affairs ("Iustitia et pax").

c) The Pastoral Constitution places all Christians together, in face of the same fundamental problems, a sort of challenge to the Churches by the world in five questions: man, God, Christ, Spirit, meaning of history (eschatology). To find an answer in common to these questions, for example through the work that is being done in the Institute for Ecumenical Studies in Jerusalem *(Mysterium Fidei)*, means to tread the path of a "pro-spective ecumenism" (K. Rahner) which even if it does not replace the other (retro-spective) is nonetheless an essentially new factor in the consciousness of the Churches.

d) The absence of the Eastern Orthodox Church in this dialogue with the "Church of Schema 13" is striking. It shows that "adhuc grandis tibi restat via".

Results of the Votes on the Schema

No.		Date	Number of Votes	Placet	Non Placet	Juxta Modum	Invalid	Subject voted upon (The numbers refer to the old numeration)
		24. Sept.	2157	2111	44		2	Do the fathers wish to proceed to examine the Introduction and the two parts of which it is composed?

Amendments
Preface and Introductory Statement

No.		Date	Number of Votes	Placet	Non Placet	Juxta Modum	Invalid	Subject voted upon
1	(472)	15. Nov.	2187	2009	41	134	3	Art. 10: Man's present situation

FIRST PART:
Chapter I. The Church and Man's Calling

No.		Date	Number of Votes	Placet	Non Placet	Juxta Modum	Invalid	Subject voted upon
2	(473)	15. Nov.	2113	2074	27	(7)	5	Art. 11: Human values
*3	(474)	15. Nov.	2133	2088	35	(8)	2	Arts. 12–18: Creation, sin, freedom, death
*4	(475)	15. Nov.	2144	2057	74	(11)	2	Arts. 19–22: Atheism
*5	(476)	15. Nov.	2149	1672	18	453	6	The whole chapter

Chapter II. The Community of Mankind

No.		Date	Number of Votes	Placet	Non Placet	Juxta Modum	Invalid	Subject voted upon
*6	(477)	15. Nov.	2115	2074	34	(3)	4	Arts. 23–26: Common vocation and the common good.
*7	(478)	15. Nov.	2155	2115	35	(3)	2	Arts. 27–32: Dignity of the person, equality, etc.
8	(479)	16. Nov.	2212	1801	18	388	5	The whole chapter

Chapter III. Man's Activity throughout the World

9	(480)	16. Nov.	2216	2173	33	(8)	2	Arts. 33–36: Value, significance, autonomy
10	(481)	16. Nov.	2227	2169	45	(9)	4	Arts. 37–39: Sin, eschatology
11	(482)	16. Nov.	2223	1727	25	467	4	The whole chapter

Chapter IV. The role of the Church in the modern world

12	(483)	16. Nov.	2227	2107	113	(3)	4	Arts. 40–42: The helpful contribution of the Church
13	(484)	16. Nov.	2222	2095	112	(11)	4	Arts. 43–45: The help which the Church receives. Christ A and Ω
14	(485)	16. Nov.	2202	1817	99	284	2	The whole chapter

SECOND PART: URGENT PROBLEMS

| *15 | (486) | 16. Nov. | 2149 | 2106 | 39 | | 4 | Art. 50: Preface |

Chapter I. Marriage and Family

*16	(487)	16. Nov.	2150	2052	91	(4)	3	Arts. 51–53: Present situation, holiness, love
*17	(488)	16. Nov.	2163	2011	140	(10)	2	Arts. 54–56: Fruitfulness, progress
*18	(489)	16. Nov.	2157	1569	72	484	5	The whole chapter

Chapter II. Culture

*19	(490)	16. Nov.	2158	2102	52	(2)	2	Arts. 57–63: Situation and principles
*20	(491)	16. Nov.	2125	2058	61	(2)	4	Arts. 64–66: Urgent problems
*21	(492)	16. Nov.	2146	1909	144	185	8	The whole chapter

Chapter III. Socio-Economic Life

*22	(493)	16. Nov.	2162	2115	40	(2)	5	Arts. 67–70: Economic progress
23	(494)	17. Nov.	2260	2182	68	(4)	6	Arts. 71–72: The world of work
24	(495)	17. Nov.	2233	2157	68	(3)	5	Arts. 73–76: Property
25	(496)	17. Nov.	2253	1740	41	469	3	The whole chapter

Chapter IV. Political Life

26	(497)	17. Nov.	2261	2188	70		3	Arts. 77–78: Present situation, nature and goal
27	(498)	17. Nov.	2217	2145	66	(5)	1	Arts. 79–80: Participation of Christians
*28	(499)	17. Nov.	2241	1970	54	210	7	The whole chapter

Chapter V. Peace and the Community of Nations

*29	(500)	17. Nov.	2242	2081	144	(12)	5	Arts. 81–86: Peace and war
*30	(501)	17. Nov.	2170	2122	43	(1)	4	Arts. 87–90: The international community
*31	(502)	17. Nov.	2200	2126	65	(3)	6	Arts. 91–94: Continuation of the same theme

CONCLUSION

*32	(503)	17. Nov.	2218	2165	33	(17)	3	Arts. 95–97: Dialogue, building-up and goal of the world
*33	(504)	17. Nov.	2227	1656	45	523	3	The whole chapter and the conclusion

Amendments

1	(528)	4. Dec.	2230	2153	72	(1)	4	Preface. Changes in the world
2	(529)	4. Dec.	2238	2103	131	(3)	1	Chapter I. The dignity of the person
3	(530)	4. Dec.	2236	2166	68	(1)	1	Chapter II. The community of mankind
4	(531)	4. Dec.	2230	2165	62	(1)	2	Chapter III. Man's activity
5	(532)	4. Dec.	2228	2149	75		2	Chapter IV. The Church in the modern world
*6	(533)	4. Dec.	2209	2047	155	(1)	6	Second part. Chapter I. Marriage and Family
*7	(534)	4. Dec.	2226	2137	81		8	Chapter II. Culture
*8	(535)	4. Dec.	2212	2110	98	(1)	3	Chapter III. Socio-economic life

Preface and Introductory Statement

by

Charles Moeller

The literary genus. 1. From the first version submitted to the Mixed Commission (Text 2) onwards, the schema was entitled a "Constitutio". The Malines Interim Text A no longer mentions the term. The same is true of the Zurich Interim Text B. The Central Subcommission at its meetings on 4, 9 and 12 March 1964, put forward a draft which distinguished between the Constitutio conciliaris and the "Adnexa". Text 3, which was discussed at the Third Session, did not bear the title "Constitutio". Mgr. Guano used it twice in his report. He emphasized its pastoral character, but did not use the two terms in conjunction. During the sitting of the Mixed Commission at the beginning of April 1965, the whole text received the title "Constitutio pastoralis", which was first proposed by Mgr. Philips and then accepted by the Co-ordinating Commission at its meeting on 11 May (when the Adnexa were also included in the text). The commission accepted it, without excluding, but also without actually providing for, debate on it at the general congregation.[1]

During the period immediately before the Fourth Session, even the authors of the draft were not very optimistic about the reception it was likely to receive. Among other things, they were afraid it would be downgraded and so become less authoritative. Some thought it would be better to abandon the name "Pastoral Constitution" so as to salvage the substance of the text and prevent its being handed over to the Holy Father for future encyclicals. They thought it would be better to be content with a less important title which would allow the whole schema to be preserved as a conciliar text

---

[1] W IV, p. 129, n. 89. Mgr. Guano's report at the third session uses the two terms. In April 1965 one of the members of the editorial committee in answer to a question put by Mgr. Philips suggested the expression "Pastoral Constitution" and Mgr. Philips immediately accepted it. In 1963 some of the members of the Theological Commission wanted to call the text "Constitutio dogmatica" (*T*, n. 14).

x

rather than to present it as a mere message which, of course, is apt to be very short-lived.

These fears were confirmed at the beginning of the Fourth Session. At a meeting of some German and French bishops on 17 September in the "Mater Dei" House, there was an actual discussion whether to be content with a less ambitious title. The outcome, however, was fortunately very positive, and it was decided to leave the matter of the title to the conciliar debate.

2. In the report presented at the opening of the debates, the title was explained as follows: "Quoad qualificationem documenti, visum est ab eadem Commissione coordinationis, in sessione diei 11 maii 1965 Romae habita, aptiorem titulum esse: 'Constitutio pastoralis'. Scopus enim praecipuus huius schematis non est directe doctrinam praebere, sed potius eius applicationes ad condiciones nostri temporis necnon consectaria pastoralia ostendere et inculcare. Altera parte, schema hoc difficulter posset vocari 'decretum', cum fere nullam contineat praescriptionem. Momentum autem schematis bene exprimi videtur per verbum 'constitutio'. Quae cum ita sint, iure meritoque convenire videtur titulus 'Constitutio pastoralis' per oppositionem ad 'Constitutionem dogmaticam', scilicet De Ecclesia *(Lumen Gentium).*"

The explanation was neither particularly happy nor clear; it obscured an essential aspect of Text 4, namely its dogmatic significance, especially in Part I. It is concerned with something quite different from purely pastoral directives. Even if a style is adopted which makes it possible to address all men, this does not necessarily mean that there is no intention of teaching doctrine and that it is restricted to concrete applications. Similarly, the words "per oppositionem ad 'Constitutionem dogmaticam'" were not very fortunate. Another intention of the authors and the Mixed Commission was lost sight of, which was to continue *Lumen Gentium,* not only in the domain of practical application but also in that of theological doctrine. The intention of the authors had more and more been to select the conciliar and liturgical elements of biblical and patristic doctrine which could be understood by Christians but which might also arouse the interest of non-Christians.

3. The conciliar debate also dealt with the question of the title. Mgr. Garrone, in his report at the end of the debates, also spoke of it in a more than cursory way. He first recalled the considerable difference between this text and that of the Third Session, now that the Adnexa had been incorporated in Part II. This had created a certain difficulty about the character which the whole document was to have. If the Adnexa were omitted, it would become too general, but if they were retained as its second part, the problem once more recurred of how to avoid obliging the Council to deal with too many concrete details in a perspective of dogmatic statements.

Furthermore, the value of the text should not be minimized, for it very definitely intended to make doctrinal statements to throw light on the relation between State and world (hence the title "Constitution"). But it aimed at making these statements in such a way as to throw light on the world at the present day and its problems (this was expressed by the term "pastoral"). Nevertheless, he declared, objections would be taken into account.

As can be seen, this *relatio* expressed the meaning of the title very much better. Furthermore, Mgr. Garrone declared in the report of 15 November on the amended text (Text 5), that is, before the *expensio modorum*, that the fathers must be given the opportunity of voting on the choice of title. He merely added — and the progress in ideas can be measured by this — that: "Sedulo autem attendendum erit ad hoc ut titulus electus in mente omnium auctoritatem schematis *non minuat*, et etiam in luce maneat munus eius complementarium constitutioni 'De Ecclesia' in seipsa considerata: ex ambobus tantum integre perficitur scopus Concilio expresse impositus."[2] The fathers recognized and valued the dogmatic significance of the schema more and more. There is no doubt that this report of Mgr. Garrone greatly contributed to making the real problem visible.

4. When the vote took place, out of 541 fathers, 217 proposed *Declaratio*, 138 *Epistula or Litterae*, 110 *Expositio*, 32 *Nuntium*, 17 *Instructio*, and 12 *Declaratio* for the second part, and 15 voted for various other titles. The majority was therefore positively in favour of retaining "Pastoral Constitution". The fragmentary character of the voting also shows how people were lost and uncertain as soon as they abandoned the proposal accepted by the Co-ordinating Commission and supported by the authors.[3]

It is also as well to point out that for a time some were inclined to a mixed solution, "Pastoral Constitution" for the first part, "Declaration" for the second. This seemed to solve certain difficulties. Members of the Subcommission for Marriage (Part II, Chapter I) realized the danger involved in such a division; it might be thought that the paragraphs on marriage and the family had no great doctrinal authority, which would have been the precise contrary of the intentions of the authors of this chapter. The same thing was felt, though not so consciously, by the Subcommission for Culture. Furthermore, such a division might lead to the further misconception that there is no pastoral element in the first part and no dogmatic element in the second, which is not the case.

The result of the vote is important. It showed clearly that the schema is one of the central quartet of conciliar texts, the four Constitutions, on the Liturgy, Revelation, the Church, and the Church in the Modern World. Since this was very important, especially in view of "the expectation of the nations", it is once again clear how fortunate the result of this vote was.

[2] Text of the *Relatio ad expensionem modorum*, p. 5.
[3] *Relatio*, vol. I, p. 12; *W* IV, p. 124.; *T*, n. 123 and 102–3.

Even a year after the Council, it is scarcely possible to imagine any other title.

At all events the Mixed Commission thought it necessary to compose the explanatory note which is appended to the title, in answer to the 541 fathers who voted against the title. Its essential point is that there are doctrinal elements in the second part and pastoral in the first. It draws attention to the fact that in Part II "the subject matter which is viewed in the light of doctrinal principles is made up of diverse elements. Some elements have a permanent value; others only a transitory one." It is recalled that the text must therefore be interpreted according to the general rules of theological interpretation, taking especially into account the changing circumstances which are involved in the second part.[4]

Title. 1. The title of Text 2 was "De Ecclesiae praesentia et actione in mundo hodierno". The words "et actione" had been included in order to meet the fact that the French term "présence" in its present-day meaning, as frequently used in pastoral literature, is not accurately translated by the Latin "praesentia". Consequently the title suggested for the last version of Text 2 (submitted to the Co-ordinating Commission on 4 May 1963) ran "De praesentia efficaci Ecclesiae in mundo hodierno". The Commission preferred a more Latin expression, "De munere ecclesiae". Unfortunately this more correct Latin had the disadvantage of not keeping the idea of presence in the world. The title of the Malines Interim Text A had also been "De activa praesentia Ecclesiae in mundo aedificando". Interim Text B (Zurich) proposed a slight variant: "De praesentia activa Ecclesiae in mundo aedificando".

With the last version of Interim Text B submitted at the Third Session (i.e. Text 3), the final title appears: "De Ecclesia in mundo huius temporis". The term "présence" was dropped. It does not bear in any other language the sense it has in French. Furthermore, even if the meaning had been clarified by the word "active" or "effective" there would still have been the danger of narrowing the perspective of the document. This would have been detrimental to it precisely when the attempt was being made to go beyond merely pastoral applications and to aim at a doctrine of the Church in the world.

2. It will have been noticed that for a time the words "in building the world" were added. Interim Text A had proposed this in order to avoid ambiguities, in particular the mistaken idea that the whole doctrine of the presence of the Church in the world was included, whereas the intention was to restrict the treatment and merely name certain aspects of the contribution which the Church makes to problems connected with the building of a better world.

[4] *T*, pp. 27, 55, 98 n. 89, 102–3, 107–8, 129, n. 123, 140, n. 124.

The expression "in building the world" was provisionally retained at the meeting of the Central Subcommission on 30 December 1963. Although the Malines text had been rejected, this word "building" should make it clear, it was thought, that it is not the Church as a whole, or the Church alone or chiefly, which establishes the better world. It had to be made clear that this is the task of men in their earthly city. The schema simply aimed at saying what the Church contributes to this independent world which men are building. From Interim Text B (Zurich) onwards, the expression was dropped for the reasons given above. Without seeking to present the whole of Christian doctrine, it did want to deal with more than the Church's contribution to the world under construction.

3. The expression "in" was retained from the first version onwards. It makes clear that it has never been a question of the Church standing opposite to and facing the world, but of presence in it. That is the fundamental fact which must be taken into account all the more because many people (and especially translations) neglect this essential aspect. The Council never in fact used the words which are so often repeated today — "the world is present in the Church, the Church is present in the world" — but right from the start it was never a matter of two opposed realities.

Theologically, that is not something to be taken for granted as a matter of course, for at that time the view of the World Council of Churches, for example, was rather that of an opposition, a "paradoxical tension". The title of the World Conference in Geneva in July 1966 was "Church *and* Society".

4. The term "world" was also retained from the beginning. It, too, was not something that went without saying. Everyone knows the arguments it provoked. What was meant was the world of men. In and through society, men are trying to "make a better world". At least implicitly the authors of the schema were thinking of the universe of creation as such. Without in any way denying the biblical meanings of the term, they did not want to place it in the forefront, for, of course, the Constitution *Lumen Gentium* had already recalled the redemptive mission of the Church in Christ. The discussions led to the word "world" being used with greater attention to shades of meaning, but it was not removed from the title. The reserves, and also the quite different theological position of the Protestants on this point, was shown in the title of the Geneva Conference where the second member of the pair of terms was not "world" but "society". This certainly displays the very characteristic and perfectly legitimate endeavour to stick more closely to biblical vocabulary and to maintain the paradoxical aspect of "God's judgment on the world". We likewise observe Protestant Christianity's instinctive mistrust of any Christian cosmology which, it holds, is always rather presumptuous and premature.[5]

---

[5] It was the speech of Archpriest Borovoi which finally convinced the Geneva assembly

It may be questioned whether everything would not have been clearer if from the beginning the problem of the "sign" had been presented not as a polar opposition, but as a triple reality: Church — world — kingdom of God. But these terms could not have figured in a title because they express the problem rather than outline a conciliar document. That does not alter the fact that in this form they might represent a sort of synthesis of the two points of view.

5. As regards the words "huius temporis" it must be noted that they did not appear until the last version of Interim Text B submitted to the Mixed Commission in March 1964. Previously the phrase used was "in mundo hodierno" (from Text 2 until the first version of Interim Text B with the exception of Interim Text A) or "in mundo aedificando" (cf. above). The objection raised to "in mundo hodierno" was that it seemed to canonize the modern world. In fact some, especially in the Dogmatic Commission, detected behind the Latin word an aroma of suspicious modernity. The words finally decided upon were chosen because they expressed simply the fact of the Church's presence in the world of the present time. Without any semblance of a value judgment, this latter title simply notes the fact: The Church is in the world of today and cannot withdraw from it. This fact gives rise to a series of obligations, responsibilities and questions for the Church.[6] Furthermore, the words "of this time" suggest the biblical theme of the *kairos,* the *hodie,* the "today" which God speaks.

Article 1. *Title.* The title of Text 2 ran "Ecclesia praesens et positione conferens ordini temporali". In Interim Text A the preface consisted of a single paragraph without special title. In Interim Text B the first article was headed: "The Council's solidarity with mankind". The title of Text 3 was "Ecclesia concilio repraesentata quantopere generi humano iuncta sit". This is also found in simplified form in Text 4, clarified and made more precise by the addition of the term "intima" in Texts 5 and 6: "De intima coniunctione Ecclesiae cum tota familia gentium".

Until Interim Text A, the theme was more general: the Church is represented as assisting the world in its work of construction by its whole activity, but especially by the teaching of its magisterium and by its sanctifying action. This conception is particularly clear in the Malines Interim Text A which is quite definitely theological and doctrinal in character.

From Interim Text B onwards, however, the accent changes. It moves to the Church as the People of God in the world of men. Between the Malines

---

and made them vote in favour of a text outlining a theology of the creation of the universe and of man as the image of God. One father had proposed "De Ecclesia huiusce nostrae aetatis" on account of this ambiguity.

[6] *T*, pp. 27, 30, 31, 38, 41, 48, 50, 55, 65–66 and n. 14, 17.

text (September 1963) and that of Zurich (February 1964) lay the Second Session, during which Chapter II of *Lumen Gentium,* devoted to the People of God, was elaborated. We must remember the importance of this "Copernican revolution" in the Dogmatic Constitution. In our view, this was just as important as the rediscovery of the theme of the collegiality of the bishops. Meanwhile the authors of Schema 13 decided to place the theme of the People of God in the forefront of the text in order to make quite plain the mission of this messianic people to the world.

The expressions "human race", "the whole human family" in Interim Text B and Texts 3, 4, 5 and 6 will also be noted: they show a similar change of perspective. Whilst Text 2 speaks of the "temporal order", an expression which corresponds more to an hierarchical view of the Church, from Interim Text B onwards the expression used in this context is "the world of men". This change not only shows the rather sociological purpose of the Zurich text, the first article of which substantially weathered all storms and survived until the end, but also shows that the word "world" primarily signifies the world of men rather than the created universe as such. This perspective widens in subsequent articles and in subsequent versions, but is established in the first article of the Preface.

The Incipit. Every conciliar document goes down in theological history under the first words of the text: *Pastor aeternus* for Vatican I, *Lumen Gentium* for the Constitution on the Church. Schema 13 is no exception. Text 2 in its May 1963 version began with rather colourless words which nevertheless expressed its connection with *Lumen Gentium* and emphasized the profound theological meaning of this document: "Missionem continuans Filii Dei".

After its examination by the Co-ordinating Commission, the same Text 2 began with the words: "Postquam S. Synodus egit de mysterio Ecclesiae", which were rather colourless but aimed at making the logical connection with *Lumen Gentium* even plainer. The Malines text began: "Mysterio intimo Ecclesiae ... declarato, S. Synodus ...".

From Interim Text B onwards, the new atmosphere was apparent in the idea of the Church's solidarity with the joys and sorrows of mankind, and this was retained almost word for word until the Constitution was promulgated. In Zurich the text began in this way: "The joy and grief, hopes and fears of the men of this age, especially of the poor and the suffering, are also the joy and sorrow, hopes and anxieties of this assembly. For we too are men, members of that innumerable people which God created according to his image and likeness (Gen 1:27) which is called to the unity of the children of God in Jesus Christ (Jn 11:52), which permits of no distinction of race, language or nationality (Gal 3:28; Col 3:11; Eph 2:11–22; Acts 5:9), which excludes no human being, not even the sinner (Mk 2:17) and rejects nothing but sin."

We have reproduced the first article in its entirety in order to give an impression of the open and comprehensive sweep which characterizes this first sentence in the Zurich version. A rather general and impersonal dogmatic outlook has been transcended in favour of an existential (but not existentialist) aim of the assembled Council which no doubt speaks with authority but also as an assembly formed of members of the People of God. In these two sentences the transition from one view to the other can even be observed. Text 4 proceeds immediately to address the members of the People of God and omits the mention of the conciliar assembly in the first article.

It will also have been noticed how in this first article of the Zurich document the theme of the People of God immediately continues into that of man created to the image of God and called to the unity of his children. The connection with *Lumen Gentium* which speaks in its first article about the Church "as a kind of sacrament of unity" is thus plain in yet another way.

However that may be, the first words of this article in the Latin translation became: "Gaudium et luctus, spes et angor hominum huius temporis". And they remained so until the end through all vicissitudes, with one important modification. From Text 4 onwards they read: "Gaudium et spes, luctus et angor". This change was made for two reasons. Whilst the word "gaudium" corresponded to biblical usage, "luctus" did not. It suggested quite a different mental climate, too strongly contrasted with the first and too exclusively human to be a good choice as second word. A more logical arrangement of the terms presented itself, with two words expressive of joy and hope followed by a pair expressing grief and anxieties. The Incipit thus admirably combines the biblical motive of joy and hope with the human one of dread and grief. And so the two first words "Gaudium et spes" gave the whole document a note not of superficial human optimism but of divine hope and joy in the love of God. The Incipit of the four Constitutions are mutually complementary: *Sacrosanctum Concilium* with the Liturgy, *Dei Verbum* with Revelation, *Lumen Gentium* with the Church and *Gaudium et Spes* with the Church in the World of Today. "The Sacred Council", "The Word of God", "The Light of the Nations", "Joy and Hope" — the aim proper to Vatican II is immediately apparent: positive, pastoral, yet built on the deep foundation of the Word of God and the theological virtues, and given expression by the conciliar assembly. The whole theology of the Council is shown in this Incipit.[7]

The meaning of the term "Ecclesia". In texts 5 and 6 it only occurs in the title; Text 4 contained it in the second sentence — "Ecclesia enim, seu

---

[7] Other openings were suggested: *T*, pp. 30, 31, 56, 84, 94, 97. At the fourth session, "Hominum huius temporis" and "Signum salutis" were proposed (*Relatio post emendationes, sessio quarta,* 7).

Populus Dei" — and was explained as follows: "Explicite dicitur quod Ecclesia est imprimis *Populus Dei,* etsi semper hierarchicus, ut plurimi Patres rogaverunt. Unus tamen Pater vult ut vox Ecclesia potius citetur in sensum Ecclesiae hierarchicae. Quodcirca, in tribus prioribus capitibus, Ecclesia praesertim ut Populus Dei exhibetur, utique hierarchice constitutus, dum autem in capite quarto de Ecclesia ut communitas hierarchica explicite agitur" (Text 4, 96). This statement applies to the whole first part of the schema and, *mutatis mutandis,* to the second as well; we must therefore bear it in mind in expounding the Preface and the Introductory Statement.

Christi discipulorum. The Zurich text (Text 3) spoke first about the Council, "Concilii sunt angor et spes", and then declared "for we are all human beings, members of that innumerable People created by God . . .". In Text 4 the mention of the Council was transferred to Article 2 and the theme of the Church introduced directly by ". . . grief and anxiety of the members of the People of God" (cf. above the explanation of the meaning of *Ecclesia*). In Text 5 the words "of the members of the People of God" were replaced by ". . . of the disciples of Christ", and this was explained in the *relatio* as follows: "It seems appropriate to avoid speaking of the People of God here because of the all-inclusive range of those whom we are addressing."

The brevity of this explanation is explained by the discussions in the Central Subcommission. The latter wanted to avoid giving the impression of a chosen people cut off from humanity as a whole. It was not that they had forgotten the fundamental election and separation, but they wished to avoid separation being understood as separation from humanity. Christ is "separated" from the world of sin but not from the mass of mankind. In order to avoid this ambiguity, the words "the disciples of Christ" were used in the first article so as to make clearer and more concrete the fundamental fact that the community of the faithful lives like those in the diaspora, in the midst of the world of men.

This change of stress came even more to the fore in the further course of the text. At the point in Text 4 where the next sentence began with the words "For the Church, or People of God", Texts 5 and 6 read "For theirs is a community composed of men" and this is explained in the Relatio: "It is better to avoid the word 'Church' here, lest the text might seem to insist too much on the hierarchical or institutional element." In the same context another proposed emendation had been rejected, which sought to add to the words "People of God", "Body of Christ", "temple of the Spirit".

This *"expensio emendationum"* clearly shows the endeavour to emphasize the fact that the community of the faithful is a part of the community of mankind. The chosen people does not go *to* humanity, it is a community of Christ's followers in the midst of the human family. Furthermore, the words "the followers of Christ" express very well the breadth of the fundamental outlook, for they include all non-Catholic Christians, for they are followers of Christ too. In other words, there is an ecumenical intention here, implicit of course but perhaps for that reason all the deeper. That intention is evident again in Article 2 with the words "All who invoke the name of Christ".

Despite these references, it is a pity that the express mention in the Zurich text of similar concern among non-Catholic Christians disappeared. Article 4 there read, "After our Christian brethren, who confess with us that Jesus is the Saviour of the world (Lk 9:56) and who live by his word, have proved in so many ways that they are filled with this same concern, we are convinced that they will examine with interest our present doctrine about work in common." It was hoped in this way to avoid the style of an appeal to the separated brethren. That would have been quite out of place, for they had been busy working on these problems for many years.

Text 3, Article 3, had read, "But since we are doing the same work, we earnestly wish to be heard also by our dear brethren of the Church communities separated from us, who confess the same Lord and Saviour of the world and who have given not a few proofs of similar concern."

From all this the phrase "of the followers of Christ" survived in Article 1 and "... not only to the sons of the Church and to all who invoke the name of Christ". Their ecumenical intention is plain, but too implicit and, at least in Article 2, not very well-chosen. The sentence seems to say that those "who invoke the name of Christ" are not the "sons of the Church". Certainly if the term "Church" is being taken in the strict sense, the Council is speaking only to the sons of the Church "reapse et simpliciter". Yet the fact that these words "reapse et simpliciter" could find their way back into the text after they had been eliminated from *Lumen Gentium* (arts. 8 and 15) shows that the final revision was not meticulous enough. It is in fact clear that the Orthodox are also sons of the Church, and that all who invoke the name of Christ are on various theological grounds "linked" (*Lumen Gentium*, art. 15, § 1: "baptismo signantur quo Christo coniunguntur"), "incorporated" "in a certain though imperfect communion with the Catholic Church" (Decree on Ecumenism, art. 3: "... in quadam cum Ecclesia catholica communione, etsi non perfecta constituuntur"; "in baptismate, Christo incorporeantur").

No doubt the text of *Gaudium et Spes* did not need to repeat all these details once again since they had already been expressed in other conciliar documents. It must be regretted, however, that the way the participation of the separated brethren in our endeavours was formulated, left the impression that they were not of the Church at all. This weakness is compensated by the text of Article 92, § 3, which deals explicitly and fully with this collaboration. This reads: "fratres nondum nobiscum in plena communione viventes eorumque communitates". But the ambiguity of the text in Article 2 remains no less regrettable because it was due to editorial negligence.

Notes on details. "Gaudium sunt": one father had proposed "gaudium sint". This change was rejected because "this would begin with moralizing and the indicative is intended to convey a true fact". "Nihilque vere": the word "vere" was added at the request of one father. This doubtless rather exaggerated regard for prudence has somewhat obscured the tacit quotation from Terence: "Homo sum et humani nihil a me alienum puto." The expression "ex hominibus coalescit" had been retained in order to make it clear that the followers of Christ are human beings who share the fate, hopes and fears of their fellow human beings. "... Eiusque historia se *revera* intime coniunctam": this was added to meet a desire for the ontological aspect to be given precedence over the gnoseological. The last five lines of Text 4 on the very vivid awareness of unity at the present time, were struck out in Text 5 "because they express an idea which is dealt with several times later".

Commentary on the Article as a whole. The first sentence expresses the theological and human aspect of joy and hope, the human aspect of the griefs and anxieties of human society. Emphasis is placed on the followers of Christ in order to stress their intrinsic connection with the world and the fact that they are a community of men united in Christ and led by the Holy Spirit, on pilgrimage to the kingdom of the Father. This makes clear the Trinitarian aspect (corresponding to *Lumen Gentium*) and the eschatological aspect *(Lumen Gentium,* art. 8). At the same time we are reminded that this community of the faithful has received the message of salvation in order to announce it: "nuntium salutis omnibus proponendum acceperunt". This is a clear reference to Chapter II of *Lumen Gentium* regarding the messianic people which is sent to the world.

All this shows the close link of this community with mankind and its history. The very words indicate that historical aspect of man which contemporary thought denotes by the category of temporality or "historicity". And that also includes another aspect, even though the text does not actually express it or even allude to it in the slightest, that of the "history of salvation".

This first article is thus extremely rich in content. It takes up a series of themes from *Lumen Gentium* in relation to believers in Christ in their diaspora condition within the perspective of human history which, in a mysterious sense manifested by the prophets, is also history of salvation or salvation in history. The tone is marked by resolute acceptance of human joy and sorrow at the same time as all the riches of humanity. The deliberate allusion to Terence is like a foretaste of Chapter II, Part II on culture, but also sets the tone for the whole Pastoral Constitution. And finally, the two opening words, by their double meaning, at once theological and simply human, admirably express the profoundly original character of the whole document.

Article 2. The present title was already included in substantially the same form in Text 3 (though in Article 3): "Those to whom this schema is addressed and what its intention is". In Texts 4, 5, and 6 it became its present: "Ad quosnam Concilium sermonem dirigat". This title entirely suits only the first paragraph of the article. The second paragraph makes plain the meaning of the "world" to which the schema is addressed. At the same time it contains essential dogmatic statements which dominate the whole Constitution. This feature is explained by the history of the article (cf. below). Text 3 contained in Article 2 presented the Church as reading the signs of the times: "Ecclesia perscrutatur signa temporum". That article became the Introductory Statement and consequently disappeared from Text 4 onwards. The schema is addressed to Catholics who are called "sons of the Church", to separated Christians and to all men. Text 3 had spoken more precisely of the wish to collaborate with the separated Christians. The vocabulary of an appeal was avoided. In regard to this theme, our commentary on the expression "the followers of Christ" will be remembered where, since the two ideas go together, we also commented the expression from Article 2, "all who invoke the name of Christ". "Not only to . . . but to the whole of humanity." Text 4 had read "not merely to the sons of the Church but even to all men": this expression was thought too condescending. ". . . Iam non tantum ad Ecclesiae filios . . . sed etiam ad universos homines." "Quomodo Ecclesiae praesentiam . . ." Text 4 read: "Quomodo Populus Dei, Ecclesiae videlicet praesentiam . . ." It insisted rather pedantically on the meaning the word "Ecclesia" bears generally in the schema. "Praesentiam ac navitatem in mundo hodierno." The word "praesentia" appeared from the very beginning of the work on this schema. It is of French origin and since its meaning is not, in itself, particularly clear in other languages, including Latin, the word "navitas" was added: "presence and activity". "Hodierno" was added: on this we must note that the constitution never uses the word "modernus", no doubt on account of its possible associations. "Concipiat": this term is perfectly appropriate to the first three chapters of Part I and for the whole of Part II, but is not so appropriate to Part I, Chapter IV, which speaks of the role of the Church and makes it clear that the Church contributes to the modern world not only by teaching but also by what it is and by its action. This feature is explained by the history of Chapter IV.

Paragraph 2. Text 4 is almost completely new. Text 3 had not developed the theme; that was one of the main objections to it. The second paragraph of Text 4 explained the meaning of the term more clearly but in a different perspective, which was felt to be inadequate. It was made clear that by the word "world" we understand on the one hand "heaven and earth or the totality of things created by God". Here traces were still found of the presentation of the Christian cosmology which Text 4 had introduced. Text 5 on the other hand speaks of the "universe of things" but in relation to man: "Mundum igitur hominum prae oculis habet seu universam familiam humanam cum universitate rerum inter quas vivit." This sentence shows very clearly what the criticism was aimed at and the point of the emendation. Agreement was quite quickly reached in the subcommission that the destiny of the universe of things must be seen in the light of man's vocation. Article 39 was corrected in this sense (it should be compared with Article 38, "De humana navitate in paschali mysterio ad perfectionem adducta"). In this respect, Article 48 of *Lumen Gentium* had laid a certain foundation for Schema 13 by showing that a new heaven and a new earth are brought to fulfilment by man's sanctification through the Church. Text 4 then spoke of the world of men who, though sinners, are loved by God and for whom Christ gave his life. A sentence was also added rather clumsily recalling that the "world" stands "sub signo Maligni", yet is nevertheless loved by God.

Text 5 which has survived here, plainly the same, in Text 6, is incomparably better because it shows in a single Latin sentence the profoundly paradoxical character of the "world" which figures in the title of the constitution. The unity of the sentence expresses very well that the same complex reality is in question from one end to the other. Translations, however, have great difficulty in reproducing this single complex sentence. Numerous objections were raised during the session. They wanted the expression "the dominion of the evil one" explained. Neither the formula "quamvis peccatoris sint" nor "hoc tempore adversatur" found favour on account of the ambiguity of the biblical term "kairos". The lack of a historical outlook was also criticized, "eschatological additions" were called for and a reference to the mystery of the incarnate Word, the crucified and risen Christ.

Since the proposed changes were very varied but all insufficient, the paragraph was completely rewritten. Its first version was drafted by a single writer who took into account the serious reserves expressed by the German bishops in particular. The very complicated question of the terminology of holy Scripture regarding the "world" was omitted, for this was to be dealt with in another passage of the schema. Stress was placed on the anthropological, cosmological and historical aspects of the "world" which is in question here, and the Christian interpretation appropriate to the schema was added.

"Mundum igitur hominum...": this is the anthropological aspect. "Cum universitate rerum...": this is the cosmological aspect. "Mundum, theatrum historiae generis humani": this is the historical aspect which is so prominent nowadays. The deliberately chosen word "theatrum" echoes the "theatrum mundi" of the Middle Ages. It indicates the aspect of comedy, caricature and deception which the stage of this world often presents, and at the same time it shows that the world is always envisaged here in connection with man, since the world "theatre" presupposes actors. "Eiusque industria, cladibus ac victoriis signatum": this expresses the age-old human endeavour to make the world better, and at the same time the mixture of defeats and victories which are equally characteristic of human history. All facile pessimism and complacent optimism was avoided and the ambiguity of this world was noted. It is very important to recall, as the text does, that this becomes clear even in the domain of experience which is not yet Christian. "Mundum, quem Christi fideles...": this shows the Christian conception of the same world spoken of in previous lines. The fact that it is introduced by a semi-colon, very well shows the fact that we are here dealing with what Gabriel Marcel has called an "elucidation": the self-same reality which has been described in terms of what is to be seen at a first examination, now discloses that it has a deeper meaning. "Ex amore creatoris conditum et conservatum": this states the fundamental dogma of creation. "Sub peccati quidem servitute positum": Text 5 read: "peccati regno profunde turbatum". Several fathers asked for the expression "regnum peccati" to be avoided as too complex. It was decided to use the equally biblical expression "sub servitute", which in this context is clearer and which is often used and commented by Protestant theologians. In comparison, the words "profunde turbatum" did not embody any particularly clear statement. Those which were inserted instead touch on an important biblical theme: the "hamartiological" viewpoint. "Sed a Christo crucifixo et resurgente": these words were inserted for an ecumenical reason and with reference to the theology of the Eastern Church; and, let us say, also on theological grounds for, after all, how can the mystery of the crucifixion be separated from the resurrection, from the mystery of salvation?[8] "Fracta potestate Maligni": the mention of the evil one already figured in Text 4. It was retained in this context because it was fundamentally impossible to speak of the world, of sin and the redemption, without mentioning Satan. Not only because today some people incline to a sort of facile and simple psychologizing which must be rejected, but also because the texts of the Bible themselves incessantly speak of victory over "evil"; the liturgy is full of them. Here, of course, the Council was approaching delicate questions which it was not obliged to deal with, but there was also an essential point of faith involved which the Council did have to put in its right place. "Liberatum, ut secundum propositum Dei transformetur et ad consummationem perveniat": the changes in Text 6 were made for reasons of greater clarity. In addition, in this last member of the sentence, the eschatological aspect finds expression and in a text where the transformation of this world is on the point of the final accomplishment. And that transformation is seen throughout in the light of man and his vocation.

As it stands, this second paragraph is one of the most important in the Pastoral Constitution. We must insist that by its construction as a single sentence and by its content, it exhibits the very movement by which an

---

[8] Cf. F. X. Durwell, *Resurrection* (1960).

already complex and paradoxical reality discloses itself in the light of faith to be even more paradoxical and divided, and is shown to be situated in a dramatic dialectical tension. This paragraph was conceived as a preliminary guide to the whole Constitution. Whenever mention is made of the "world", therefore, at least when the context says nothing to the contrary, this description must be borne in mind with its rich content and contrasts. The last lines are radiant with the light of eschatological fulfilment in a sense very close to the tradition of the Eastern Church.[9]

Article 3. *Title.* This is found in precisely the same form in Texts 4, 5 and 6 but is lacking in Text 3. The term "ministerio" is intended to make clear the meaning of diaconia for the whole schema. It was introduced into the first versions of Text 2 under the influence of Lukas Vischer's letter of 18 April 1963. It was found in Interim Text A, Interim Text B and all the versions of Text 3.

Contents. These correspond to Text 3, Article 2, § 3 and a part of Text 3, Article 4. Text 6 amended "Qua propter Concilium ... cui inseritur" for the sake of clarity and to avoid the impression that it is the Council that is "bound up with the entire human family", for of course it is the People of God that is meant. In the last paragraph all the verbs had to be put in the singular because Text 6 replaced "episcopi in communione cum summo pontifice" by "Sacra Synodus". "Cui inseritur": on this the *relatio* remarks: "This makes clear the connection of the People of God with the world, and the impression of distance and false condescension is avoided." "Lumen afferendo ex Evangelio": as opposed to a suggestion to say "revelation", the word "gospel" was retained, because it conveys better the concern to serve in the light of the gospel. "Accipit": instead of "accepit", in order to show that the Church is constantly "open", "hearing" the word of God and imbued with the life of the Spirit. All this is a very compressed repetition of essential themes of *Lumen Gentium* and *Dei Verbum.* "Homo igitur ...": this makes it plainer that the pivot of the whole Pastoral Constitution is man, as Paul VI was to say in his concluding speech. We have also seen (art. 2, § 2, above) that the universe of things is envisaged from the point of view of man. "Man is not a child of this earth", said Rabbi Heschel in Notre Dame in 1966, "the earth was made for him." In any case to turn to man does not mean to turn away from God and succumb to anthropocentrism. The whole Constitution will show this. "Cum corpore et anima": although some Fathers pointed out that this expression is not biblical in origin, it was retained, for after all it is true. In addition it is said that man is "unus et totus". Article 14 takes up the words "corpore et anima unus" and adds "homo per ipsam suam corporalem conditionem". These words were chosen precisely in order to show the concrete unity of man.

[9] An Orthodox view of *Gaudium et Spes* may be found in *Vers l'unité chrétienne* (July—September 1966), pp. 51 f.

The body is no longer merely a "thing" which one has, an instrument which one uses, it is also the means of communication with others, etc. Furthermore, the term "condicio corporalis", which echoes present-day existential vocabulary, aims at linking what is good in this anthropological trend with the revealed doctrine of man as the image of God. In view of the false ideas which flow from the generally far too oversimplified dualistic conception still held by far too many Christians, it is important to note the *relatio* on Text 5 [10] which declares that the aim was "to avoid every kind of dualism". Nevertheless this biblical anthropology was not placed in the very centre of the schema. Yet it could have been without diminishing in the slightest the truth and usefulness of the "body-soul" view. The foundations and elements are there, but the thread is not taken up again. However, this biblical and extremely topical doctrine of man is implicitly present and presupposed in the Chapters on Marriage (art. 49, especially § 4) and Culture (art. 57, §§ 1, 2 and 6).

Paragraph 3. "Quae huic vocatione respondeat": the *relatio* comments, "This avoids giving the impression that a merely natural destiny is in question, and prevents any confusion of the Church's mission with the destiny of men as citizens." Text 4 merely speaks of brotherhood without qualification. "Spiritus Paracliti ductu": Text 5 uses a different style in order to avoid repetitions. Nevertheless the absence of the Holy Spirit is what is most noticeable in this anthropology of Schema 13. The reason for this, according to Mgr. Ziadó, is that pneumatology is only just developing in the Western tradition. [11] "Non ut judicaret": Text 5 retained this more general, very biblical expression which also has a certain ecumenical significance.

Commentary on the article as a whole. (The first sentence expresses in concentrated form the subject of the Introductory Statement, that is, the questions that mankind is raising. The second sentence shows how the Council, which bears witness to the faith of the whole People of God, knows no other means of dealing with these problems than discussion in the light of the gospel and the contribution of the saving resources which the Church constantly receives from its founder.) We may point out in passing the fine expression "witness to the faith of the whole People of God" which is applied to the Council. The following sentences recall that what is in question is man. One might comment by quoting Saint-John Perse, "For ultimately it is a question of man and his bond with the world". Then the theme of service is taken up again and extended by the reminder that the Church has no earthly motive but aims at imitating its founder who did not come to be served but to serve. [12]

---

[10] *Relatio ad expensionem modorum,* I, p. 8.

[11] *W* III, pp. 62–63.

[12] There is something here of the triad suggested by Lukas Vischer: communion, witness, service.

Introductory Statement. *History of the text.* From the beginning there were controversies about how Schema 13 should be introduced. Some, for example Mgr. Pavan, wanted it to begin with a description of the situation of the world at the present day. They thought it advisable to take inspiration from the encyclical *Pacem in Terris.* Others, such as Mgr. Philips, were more in favour of an opening based on essential theological truths, because the Council as such could not commit its authority to the description of contingent facts.

1. Text 2 devoted its first part, or at least Chapters II–VI, to a short description of the present situation before giving a statement of principles. This arrangement was maintained for the second part down to Text 6. In Interim Text A, on the other hand, the opening was purely theological. Only the second section, "De mundo aedificando", contained a part on "De autonomia mundi" and another "De unificatione mundi", which closed with an article "De bonorum terrestrium ambiguitate" (arts. 12–18, that is, 7 out of 29, about a quarter of the whole).

2. In Interim Text A the general tendency was concrete and theological. The descriptive features were distributed along the dogmatic line of thought.

In Text 3, which grew out of the Zurich text, article 2 of the Preface bore the title "Ecclesia perscrutatur 'signa temporum'". The expression was placed in inverted commas to indicate the special sense in which it was to be understood; it had been taken over from John XXIII who had used it in *Pacem in Terris.* It at once attracted attention because it was so well chosen to express the new phenomena which had arisen in the world, and which the Church must "read" in order to discern the opportunity they offer for it to deepen its own teaching.

Text 3 certainly went further, for it applied the word "sign" to "time" and said, "Tempus enim signum et vox est, pro Ecclesia et hominibus, quatenus secumfert praesentiam Dei, vel, infeliciter, absentiam a Deo, necnon hominis magis minusve consciam apud Deum invocationem, Dei magis minusve patentem ad hominem vocem. In voce ergo temporis vocem Dei audire oportet ita ut in luce fidei praesentes opportunitates et miseriae hominum conscientiis concretum caritatis mandatum adumbrent."

This pointed to a theology of "kairos". Time can be the bearer of a religious meaning, the place of divine revelation, of man's approach to God or fall from him. Some elements of the "history of salvation" gave their stamp to this text, especially the sentence "In the voice of time we must hear the voice of God". There was considerable boldness in this acceptance of history, this "historicity" as certain present-day thinkers would say. One of the criticisms made of Text 4 was its lack of historical perspective; Text 3 had not much more, but at least it directed attention to one aspect in this exceptionally pregnant statement.

This sentence disappeared almost completely in the final text and with it the idea that "the voice of time is the voice of God". Text 5 is content with a general statement about the Church reading the signs of the times. The expression is used in the empirical sense of *Pacem in Terris*. "The words 'signs of the times' are used on this single occasion not in a technical but in a general sense, as they are found in several documents of Popes John XXIII and Paul VI", said Mgr. McGrath in the *relatio* before the voting.[13] In fact it had been realized through the comments of some observers and also of some of the fathers, that the expression "signs of the times" has a very precise meaning in the Bible — the eschatological signs of the time — and that, as a consequence, it did not fit into the context of Schema 13. So it was dropped, and in the last versions it only bore the meaning we have just described. Text 4 omitted it completely. Despite this, the special subcommission entrusted with this part of the schema was called throughout the Council "Subcommissio de signis temporum".

3. This Signs of the Times Subcommission was formed at the same time as a Dogmatic Subcommission, at a session of the Central Subcommission from 9 to 12 September 1964. Its purpose was to draft the descriptive part of the schema and to see that this perspective was borne in mind throughout. It met on more than ten evenings during the Third Session. Each of these sessions dealt with a particular part of the world; an account was given of its economic, social, cultural and religious situation, and then there was a discussion. This led to draft and discussion of the ways in which the Christian message can be presented in these conditions. On occasion there were up to 30 people present. The document finally produced contained 87 closely written pages, and its size meant it could obviously not be used in the schema as it stood. Here and there, however, an expression shows the many points it has in common with the schema. A separate commentary would be needed to point them out, however. What is much more important is that a wide horizon of this kind made it possible to work out the main lines of what were to be the articles of the Introductory Statement.[14]

4. At the end of the Third Session it was decided to extend the Signs of the Times Subcommission by coopting bishops from Japan, Africa, India and Spain. It was more difficult to find experts capable of making a really original contribution.

At the same time Mgr. McGrath, the president of the subcommission, called a first meeting to prepare the descriptive part of the schema in which the fathers had asked for more detail. F. Houtart, one of the secretaries of the subcommission, promised to submit a draft of this chapter in January 1965. As a basis he used documents gathered during the session and his recently published book *Église et monde*.[15] In numerous journeys which he

---

[13] *Relatio* on Text 5, 9. [14] *H*, pp. 49–55; *T*, notes 53, 66.
[15] Brussels, Éditions universitaires, 1964.

had made and was to make in connection with international organizations for the sociology of religion, he was able to gather an ever-increasing quantity of information. A first draft was sent to a number of cultural and sociological institutes with a request for their opinions.

5. Meanwhile, Canon Haubtmann had received the draft from Mgr. Philips and Canon Moeller at a meeting in Louvain on 28 December 1964; F. Houtart was also present. On its basis Canon Haubtmann drafted Chapter I of Text 4 in the first, so-called Ariccia, version. He did so because, according to one of the most urgent requests of the fathers and the decisions of the Central Subcommission, unity of style had to be ensured throughout the document. He therefore set about a version based on the facts supplied by the subcommission. The chapter bore the Latin title "Conspectus generalis" and the French title "Vue d'ensemble". It contained 8 articles: The modern world and its origin, Scientific and technical control, Demographic development, Inequality and universality of this development, Some consequences, Changes in the collective psychology of groups and nations, The unorganized character of this development, Present-day questions of mankind. The original was written in French.

6. During the meeting in Ariccia (31 January — 6 February), the Signs of the Times Subcommission met to examine the opinions on F. Houtart's draft which had come in from all sides. Taking account of the need to overcome an outlook that was both too European and too exclusively sociological, and insufficiently ethical and spiritual — the members of the Subcommission De Cultura had insisted on this — the subcommission drew up a largely new text based on Canon Haubtmann's but also on the first draft submitted on 28 December 1964.

The Dogmatic Subcommission which also had to keep watch on the unity of the whole, expressed its agreement with the principles underlying the changes made, and expected that only slight modifications would be needed. In actual fact the Signs of the Times Subcommission altered this first chapter quite radically, using the materials already mentioned. When the text was submitted on 3 February at a common session of the two subcommissions, it was poorly received by the Dogmatic Subcommission, which objected that it was not a case merely of a few emendations, but in places of a new version or even a new structure. The Signs of the Times Subcommission was extremely surprised at this reaction.

Since the beginning of the intersessional period, confusion had been caused because, while the task of collecting facts for the general descriptive part had been given to a subcommission, the latter was not in practice allowed either the time or the right to draft the text, or at least to give it its final revision. At this moment the Dogmatic Subcommission, which was also the Central Subcommission, considered it could deal in the same way with the other chapters of the Adnexa. It worked out a text consisting of a mosaic of new elements proposed by the Signs of the Times Subcommission but introduced into the sequence of thought of its own version.

7. The meeting in Rome (8–13 February 1965). This text was rejected. Thereupon a small commission was formed to which Mgr. McGrath, the chief mover in the earlier drafts, did not belong. Joseph Folliet made an important contribution to the new version, which emphasized the cultural side of the problem and was more homogeneous. It was composed without reference to any prior draft and there was no time to use the material that had been gathered; it lacked all the elements of the earlier versions. Apart from Mgr. Fernández, none of the members of this shadow subcommission, which only lasted one morning, had had any hand in the previous versions. This new text was "approved" at the end of the session without the fathers realizing the loss that had been suffered. [16]

8. Meeting of the Mixed Commission (28 March — 8 April 1965). In fact the Signs of the Times Subcommission resumed its work of revision but with a delay of almost a year caused by the Rome version. This is sufficient to explain the fact that at the beginning of the Fourth Session the same criticisms were made of lack of spiritual perspective and the excessively European character of the text.

During this plenary session, Mgr. Philips succeeded in getting a new arrangement of the schema accepted. Instead of a division into three parts, one on man's situation in the world, one on the Church and man's fundamental condition, a third on some special problems, he suggested a division into two parts, a dogmatic section and a section devoted to a few more urgent problems. He suggested that the previous first part might be called "Expositio Introductoria" — not "praevia", in order to avoid any unpleasant association with the controversial "Nota praevia". This proposal was immediately accepted, and had the advantage of showing clearly that the Council was not combining dogmatic statements and the description of the present situation under the same heading. In a rather more discreet way it ultimately meant opting for a dogmatic presentation and for giving second place to the description of the contemporary situation, at least its more general section. Furthermore, this arrangement made clear the basically bipartite division of the Constitution into general principles and concrete applications.

9. The Fourth Session. Mgr. McGrath's *relatio* (23 September 1965). Mgr. McGrath presented the introductory section to the fathers, recalling that a number of them had asked for a more detailed survey of the present situation with two purposes in mind, firstly so that real account might be taken of the situation on the world at the present time which it was proposed to speak about, and secondly so that dialogue with all men might be easier and more honest. He pointed out the novelty of the proposed schema as a

---

[16] *T*, p. 9, n. 82, which we have slightly modified and completed.

conciliar text, but also recalled that papal documents since Leo XIII had gone into new situations *(Rerum Novarum)*. He referred in particular to the encyclical *Ecclesiam Suam* which called for dialogue with the world. He added that many fathers had asked from the beginning that they should not restrict themselves to the Western world alone and particularly to Europe. In this connection he also recalled the history of the Signs of the Times Subcommission.

He stressed that the description was not exhaustive. From the phenomenological point of view in fact it was no different, objectively speaking, from the descriptions that had been received from all kinds of sources, especially international organizations: the world it speaks about is in fact the same world. He pointed out that the same triple division, description, principles, applications, is found in each chapter of Part II.

After these remarks on the form of presentation, he listed its most important elements. First, the radical transformation which from the beginning had sponsored the Council's own will to renewal. Article 5 presents the reasons and sources of this transformation: scientific thought and technology which alter man's own picture of himself but also gradually bring reality under man's domination. These cultural, intellectual, scientific and technological changes have had profound social, psychological, moral and religious effects on man and society. All this has created tensions within the human person, between individuals, families and social groups, as well as between nations, between the various groups inside the same State and especially between rich and poor (arts. 5–8). Article 9 gives the guiding idea of the whole, which is a view of man and the human situation which sees him as asking himself the ultimate meaning of everything. All this shows how earnestly the Synod desires to bring the light of Christ and his love to all men. But the Constitution does not claim to be able to give a solution to every special problem.

10. Debate. Second *relatio* of Mgr. McGrath. Present-day historians of *Gaudium et Spes* report practically nothing of the debate on the introductory section.[17] It is clear that its outlook was not yet able to affect the circle of questions with which the Council was dealing. The Council was still very far from listening to the world sufficiently.

On 12 November, Mgr. McGrath, in his second report, gave an account of the alterations introduced into the text as a result of the debate. To the objection that it was too superficial and had an almost existentialist air, he replied that it was descriptive and objective. He explained why it is necessary for the Church to scrutinize the signs of the times, and also explained once more the meaning of this expression, which had only been used once, not in its special scriptural sense but with the general meaning it has in

[17] *W* IV, p. 132; *L* V, pp. 75–76; *T*, pp. 106–7.

John XXIII's encyclical. He added that the text had been amended so as to emphasize man's influence on his own historical situation; every kind of determinism had to be avoided. At the same time he said the revision (Text 5) was intended to make the schema a more human and universal document.

The most important alteration was undoubtedly in Article 9, which was now divided into two sections, the first on the "appetitiones" becoming objectively visible, and a second section, henceforth Article 10, dealing with questions which already concern the fundamental interpretation of the problems. The problems of human unrest raised in Article 10 were thus to introduce the first part. Furthermore, he once again showed how difficult the absence of theologians from the Third World and from Latin America had made it to achieve a really universal outlook. He then summed up what he had already said on the methodology and purpose of this part: description and dialogue. [18]

11. Text 6. The last revision on the basis of the *modi* altered the text very little. There were amendments worth mentioning on three points: on the conflict between the generations, particularly as regards youth (art. 7), on the imbalance between specialized work and universal outlook (art. 8), on the existence of realities which remain immutable in the flux of change (art. 10).

The text was accepted on 4 December 1965. Out of 2230 votes there were 2153 *placet*, 7 *non placet*, 1 *juxta modum* and 4 invalid votes.

Article 4. § 1. Text 5 added four lines to clarify three points: the constant need for the Church "dignoscendi signa temporum"; the way in which knowledge of the world is obtained; the problem of the ultimate questions which arise in new forms in every age and which every generation has to solve. In the last sentence of Text 5 a rather pedantic mention of "idonei auctores" was dropped.

§ 2. Text 5 reads "gradatim extenduntur" instead of "progressione quadam extenduntur", in order to mark the steps of the development better and to avoid any appearance of a too superficially favourable judgment. Text 5 also mentions the religious changes; Text 6 adds "etiam" to avoid exclusiveness.

§ 3. Text 5 replaces "potestatem" with "potentiam". Text 6 replaces "cordis intima altius penetrans", which might give the impression that people today penetrate deeper into the secrets of the human heart, by the less absolute phrase "animi intimiora altius penetrare satagens".

§ 4. Text 5 adds a second sentence to Text 4 in order to show that even if the feeling for freedom is more acute, we must also recognize the emergence of new forms of social and psychological slavery. This theme had been

---

[18] *Relatio* on Text 5, p. 10.

treated in great detail in the Malines Interim Text A, which devoted a whole article to it. The third sentence was changed in Text 5 so that the types of human divisions should be mentioned right from the start; one of the fathers wanted racialism to be added. The fourth sentence was added in Text 5 in order to show more clearly the ambiguity of the vocabulary of different ideologies. Text 6 replaced "commercium", which has a quite specific meaning applied to ideas (as can be seen by the fact that a cultural periodical founded by Saint-John Perse and others such as C. du Bos could have the title *Commerce*) by the banal but more easily intelligible word "communicatio". The last sentence, added in Text 5, aims at dealing in a discreet way with the theme of evil and sin by pointing to the disharmony between earthly and spiritual progress. Finally, Text 6 added "et egestate" to the first sentence to describe want. It is a better word to denote the hell of those who do not know whether they will be alive from one day to the next.[19]

§ 5. Text 5 describes a torturing dread, a mingled hope and fear. It recalls a book of Tibor Mende, *Zwischen Furcht und Hoffnung*. It is ultimately rooted in uncertainty about God and the future life.

General commentary. The title "Hope and Anguish" shows in a flash that we live in a period of tensions. The Pastoral Constitution stands beyond condemnation or praise of the present. Our age is marked by what are often dramatic characteristics. This expression is not to be understood in the sense which some people, for example Jean Anouilh give it, distinguishing between "drama" which finally ends happily and "tragedy" where we know from the start of the play that it will end in catastrophe. The expression "dramatica indoles" simply means tension between two poles.

The expression "signa temporum" is used here, the only time it is, and bears John XXIII's sense of the main facts which characterize an age. It is a function (munus) of the Church to read them (officium perscrutandi). Since what St. Paul says (1 Cor 2:15) applies to the Church in the Holy Spirit, it has the gift of "discernment" of the Christian meaning of events. Thus it has some share in the prophetic office.

The essence of the dramatic tension in question consists in a transformation, the crossing of a threshold, which more or less implicitly forces itself on the attention. Man's activity and work has given rise to changes which recoil upon man himself, rather like a boomerang. Sartre has described this phenomenon very well in what he calls "le practico-inerte". *Gaudium et Spes* points out that these consequences of human action affect man's judgment, his individual and collective desires and his way of thinking and acting in relation to things and people. The text adds they have consequences too for religious life.

---

[19] Péguy of course vividly expressed this sense of poverty and destitution in *De Jean Coste*.

This transformation which forms the centre of the Introductory Statement is a commonplace to sociologists.[20] They also say that the unfinished character of the change, the impression felt everywhere that everything is altering, is the characteristic mark of our age. (Changes in the past took place very much more slowly and in a sense were not perceptible to the masses. Today, however, everybody is aware of radical change. There was much more hesitation about accepting the fact of such a remarkable transformation on the part of the Council fathers.) This explains the addition in Article 10 already referred to, concerning many realities "which do not change". (There is an essential task of the Church here, that of distinguishing realities which are really not subject to change from those which do change and must change. It also has to say how these immutable realities fit into the changing world.) On this point in the Pastoral Constitution the Council gives principles rather than concrete illustrations.

§ 3 names some of the crises referred to: greater power and greater enslavement, better knowledge of depth psychology and people's growing uncertainty about themselves, knowledge of the laws of social life and uncertainty about the way to give them direction.

The fourth paragraph indicates some other aspects, this time of the collective order: development of wealth and potentialities and a huge (ingens) part of humanity living in want (egestate); growing awareness of freedom and new forms of social and mental enslavement; discovery of the unity of the world and of the solidarity and dependence of each on all and conflict between the various political, social, economic, racial and ideological forces, entailing the risk of a war of annihilation; ever-increasing exchange of ideas and ambiguity of the most important terms of the various ideologies; finally the disproportion between the earthly order and growth (incrementum) in the spiritual domain.

The last paragraph brings together what has been said in the light of the importance of eternal values for the human person (whose defence is in question) and the "fresh discoveries". This is the root of the tension between hope and fear, and the ultimate reason prompting men to ask questions and, in fact, compelling them to do so.

Article 5. This article attempts to show just how far-reaching the transformation is. Text 6 condensed a text of 8 paragraphs into 3. Paragraphs 1–2 of Text 5 form paragraph 1 of Text 6, concerning the great importance of mathematical sciences today and the consequent growing importance of technology. Paragraphs 3, 4 and 5 of Text 5 become paragraph 2 of Text 6, devoted to the progress of historical knowledge which makes it possible "dilatare intellectum super tempora"; to the advances in biology, psychology and the social sciences which deal with human conditions and finally to the

---

[20] That is the predominant idea in F. Houtart, *Église et monde*, quoted above (cf. note 15).

growth of population which it is daily becoming more possible to plan in advance. Paragraphs 7 and 8 (paragraph 6 of Text 5 was assigned to Article 6) formed paragraph 3 (Latin, § 4 Abbott) of Text 6, which is concerned with the increased rapidity of historical development and therefore with the transition from a more static to a more dynamic view of the world. New possibilities, advance planning and dynamism are the three essential characteristics of the change.

§ 1. Few alterations were made in Text 5 or in Text 6. The insertion of the word "condicio" — Text 4 spoke of "vitae commutatio" — was made in order to use a standard term of modern humanism. André Malraux, for example, had given his novel published in 1933 the title of *La condition humaine*. Text 5 used the more precise expression "spatium ultraterrestre" instead of the perhaps more poetical but vaguer "tractus insidereos" of Text 4. Text 6 replaced the "magis magisque praevaleant" of Text 5, which was not a very happy formula, for it appeared to forget philosophy for example, by "crescens pondus acquirant".

§ 2. Text 4 was simplified. Text 5 is finer-shaded in regard to the influence of biological, psychological and social sciences. It omits reference to the calculus of probabilities and planning. It states the problem of the population explosion better by speaking of the possibility "cogitare de proprio demographico incremento iam praevidendo et ordinando". Text 5 reversed the order of the sentences by putting the second sentence of Text 4 at the end, which makes the sequence more logical. In Text 6 nothing was altered. The last paragraph had been simplified in Text 5 in order to avoid the impression of total mutability. The expression "novae analyses et syntheses" becomes clearer as a result.

General commentary. Paragraph 1 describes the repercussions of the technological forces with which man is shaping the world. The aim was to recognize the full extent of these forces but at the same time not to succumb to a monistic type of explanation tracing everything back to changes of a technological kind, because of course ethical and philosophical, i.e. non-utilitarian, motives also play their part. Paragraph 2 is mainly centred on the factor of "historicity". The great importance of this point is well known; in contemporary thought it is the basis of a really new dimension.[21] Mention is then made of the human sciences and planning. The last paragraph stresses chiefly the acceleration of development and concludes by pointing to the transition from a static to a dynamic view of the universe.

All this, it must be admitted, is not very well put together. The version which was unfortunately rejected in Ariccia had presented a more complex as well as a more logical view, including both technological and ethical change. The concluding sentences bring out yet another essential element. The

[21] A. Dondeyne, *La foi écoute le Monde* (1965), E. T.: *Faith and the World.*

transition from the static vision of the little world of antiquity which was ultimately based on a cyclic view — the "works and days" — to a dynamic view of the developing universe in which man experiences himself from the quantitative point of view as a speck of dust on a tiny ball hurled into space.[22] It is obvious that some spontaneous religious imagery — heaven "above" and hell "beneath", for example — is affected by this.[23] This is what the text means when it speaks of a call for new analyses and syntheses. This theme is taken up again in the chapter on culture (art. 62).

Article 6. The final text regrouped the paragraphs, adding one on means of communication in Article 5. Paragraph 1 of Text 6 corresponds to paragraph 1 of Text 5; paragraph 2 corresponds to paragraphs 2 and 3 of Text 5; paragraph 3 comes from paragraph 5 of Text 5; paragraph 5 corresponds to paragraph 4 of Text 5 and paragraph 6 corresponds to paragraph 5 of Text 5. The sequence of thought is therefore clearer: changes in a small unit of society, clans, tribes, patriarchal groups of families; industrial and urban forms of life; mass media; the problem of shifts of population; socialization and personalization; the scale of these changes, which are clearly perceptible among economically advanced peoples and have positive effects, and which are less visible but eagerly hoped for by the other nations.

Paragraph 1 in Text 5 as in Text 6 takes over the same paragraph of Text 4. We may draw attention to the change of "clani" (Text 4) into "clans" to make the meaning clearer by using the original word.

Little change was made in paragraph 2. Text 5 changed "subvertens" into "transformans" in order to show that it is simply a description and not a value judgment. Text 6 put "a saeculis" instead of "a millenniis", which was rather pompous. Paragraph 3 reproduces Text 5 which had been slightly changed from Text 4, adding before the sentence speaking of the "modi cognoscendi" the phrase "ad eventus cognoscendos". This was a valuable addition focussing attention on the essential, namely, information about events; this must precede the dissemination of what people think and feel about them.

Some change has been made in the position of paragraph 4. Text 6 inserted it at this spot whereas in Text 5 it was at the end, because it was added at the request of the fathers; Text 4 does not mention it. Text 6 also specifies the central problem which this fact implies, the "mutatio rationis vitae".

Paragraph 5 was revised for the sake of greater precision. Text 5 adds "urget" after "multiplicat" in order to show that the age is exerting inescapable pressure and compelling a multiplication of social relationships, whether people like it or not. Text 6 expresses it more precisely: relations

[22] Bertholdt Brecht has expressed this experience notably in *Galileo Galilei*, E. T.: *Life of Galileo* (1963).

[23] D. Dubarle, *Initiation théologique* II (1952), pp. 303–49.

between human beings are multiplied and "socialization" itself brings further ties. There is a sort of reciprocal influence. Furthermore, the second part of this sentence, which corresponds more closely to the preceding sentence (in the English), shows the absence of necessary connection between such socialization and "personalization". These two technical terms are used deliberately for the sake of clarity. At the same time the new version replaced the verb "urget" by the adverb "indesinenter", which is even stronger, for it denotes a lasting impulsion which leaves no rest.

The last paragraph includes an important addition on the developing countries who even more strongly than others desire easier access to the exercise of freedom. (Text 6 clarified the expression by speaking of an "exercitium maturius magisque personale".) This addition was requested by the African bishops, who described Text 4 as too Western. Text 5, on the other hand, says that attachment to ancient traditions — very evident in tribalism, clans and other forms of "sacred" societies — is closely linked with a deep desire for a more mature and personal use of freedom and the opportunity for human development. In this way it becomes clear that one-sided criticism of the phenomenon of socialization hides the fact that for some traditional peoples the attainment of Western forms of socialization can represent something positive. The same thing was repeated in Article 7 at the request of the same African bishops. No one will fail to realize the great importance of these contentions and therefore of this addition. Text 6 reads "commodis" instead of "beneficiis" in order to avoid any appearance of optimistic evaluation and to remain within the limits of pure description.

General commentary. This article is on the lines of one of the youngest academic sciences, sociology. Even 20 years ago it was regarded as a not very serious appendix to legal studies; nowadays in almost all the universities in the world there is a faculty for political and social sciences.

The transformation is most clearly visible in social forms of the most ancient kind. Industrial and urban forms of society are transforming centuries-old structures. To grasp this one only has to think of the city of the future in the Futurama of the New York Exhibition 1964–65.

What is said about the mass media will be taken up again in the chapter on culture. The paragraph on the fact of population shifts, on the other hand, is of great importance. At the Geneva Conference "Church and Society", the fact of these migrations was discussed at length. The "stranger within your gates" of whom the Bible speaks, was often mentioned in this connection, and it is regrettable that the text of *Gaudium et Spes* does not refer to this. Special emphasis must be laid on the changed way of life which results. We only need to think of the Italians living in the north of Europe who have left a world of sun and wine for one of rain and beer!

In the end, *Gaudium et Spes* did not hesitate to take up the now classic terms "socialization" and "personalization" and to Latinize them, despite everything. It also pointed to the permanent influence of this phenomenon and its complexity.

Finally, the gap between the new nations and technologically developed countries is clearly stated. This was one of the points most discussed in Ariccia; and the difference in stage of development between the various parts of the world was made clear. Unfortunately, with the rejection of the Ariccia text, this idea was also pushed into the background, at least in the present context of social changes.

The fact that Article 6, the first which deals with changes in detail, is devoted to social transformations, shows the importance of sociological study; an abundant literature is available on the science itself and on its religious consequences. [24] The arrangement here does not mean, however, that the phenomena dealt with in Article 7 and the following are consequences of social change. One of the main concerns was to avoid sociologism which, like all "isms", all too often produces bad ideologies.

Article 7. The first paragraph of Text 5 and Text 6 corresponds to the first part of the first paragraph of Text 4. The second paragraph is the second part of the first paragraph of Text 4. This division is due to the very much greater importance attributed to the problem of the conflict between the generations in Text 5 and even more in Text 6. The present paragraph 2, which speaks in a more general way of the gap between the "instituta, leges atque modi cogitandi" handed down by the "maiores" and the present-day state of affairs, indicates the scale of the phenomenon which involves more than the conflict between the generations. A peculiar fact must also be mentioned. In Text 4 there was a second paragraph devoted to the passivity shown by the majority of people towards these problems, which it indicated by saying "pauciores certamini non renuntiant". This paragraph disappeared without trace between Text 4 and Text 5. As far as I know, no explanation was given of this, either in the report on Text 5 or in the *expensio modorum* of Text 6. I should like to express the conjecture that this section was simply overlooked when the text was revised during the Fourth Session. Nobody noticed this because of the really inhuman speed with which that revision had to be done. The disappearance of the paragraph is to be regretted. In fact it pointed to one of the gravest aspects of present-day changes, the growing division between a small number of men who decide and a very great number whose fate is decided for them. This is in fact a slavery which contradicts the freedom which Christ has brought us. Roger Mehl spoke

---

[24] F. Houtart founded FERES (University of Louvain), an international organization which groups and co-ordinates centres for religious sociology; cf. also H. Carrier and E. Pin, *Essais de sociologie religieuse* (1966), E. T.: *Sociology of Religious Belonging*.

about the sociological and religious implications of this phenomenon in his Strasbourg lecture of 23 January 1967 on "Church and Society"; he regarded it as a possible basis for the preaching of the Christian kerygma. In view of the topical interest of the theme, it may be useful to reproduce here the passage from Text 4. "Plures passive se gerunt erga transformationem quam dominari non valent, immo quam ne intellegere quidem conantur, praesidium quaerendo in vitae commodis et oblectamentis aut in cuiuscumque generis effugiis. Pauciores tamen certamini non renuntiant et nostra aetatis progressionem valida manu dirigere aggrediuntur" ("Many adopt a passive attitude to the transformation which they cannot control, and do not even try to understand it, seeking a refuge in the comforts and pleasures of life or in various forms of escapism. A very few, however, do not give up the struggle and strive to give firm direction to the progress of our age"). Paragraph 3 of Text 5 and Text 6 corresponds to paragraph 3 of Text 4 (in which two paragraphs had been condensed into one).

The first paragraph was made very much more precise and elaborate between Texts 4 and 5 and Texts 5 and 6. Text 5 had included the topic of necessary changes in education. It also said that some parents are in fact incapable (sic) of fulfilling their duty of upbringing. Text 6 adds the essential idea that the younger generations have become aware of their role in society and wish to take up their place in it as quickly as possible. The last sentence could then extend the problem of the difficulty felt by parents about upbringing, and at the same time qualify the rather too sweeping statement of Text 5. Text 6 also mentions "educators".

The second paragraph simply takes over Text 4 with one slight exception. Text 5 reads "non bene semper aptari videntur" instead of Text 4's "non amplius aptantur". A typical example of the use of the Latin verb "videri" in conciliar texts!

The rest of the article in Text 5 is much subtler and more elaborate than in Text 4. With a view to giving a more accurate description of the fact of atheism and indifference to religion, as well as the relation between atheism and scientific progress, Text 6 points out more clearly with reference to the "sacral" societies, how the kind of changes described make it possible to escape from a "magicus mundi conceptus". We find once again here what was said in Article 6, but now in regard to religion. African bishops in fact expressly observed that changes which in the eyes of Western theologians chiefly suggest unfavourable effects on religious conviction, can actually help to liberate the belief of non-Western societies from a religious sentiment permeated with superstition and inextricably bound up with a magical view of the world. Science and technology make it possible, for example, to develop the concept of causality in the proper sense, and to distinguish it clearly from sacred events. At the same time the additions in Text 5, taken over into Text 6 — as well as a "practice a religione discedunt" instead of "ab usu religionis discedunt" — show that religion is abandoned in practice by many people as a result of all these different changes. As a consequence, the rejection or abandonment of religion is no longer an unusual and isolated fact. We often hear it said nowadays that it is demanded by scientific progress and a certain new humanism. There is also a reference here to the famous Sartre theme "Is atheism a humanism?". Text 6 adds in the final sentence that even the civil laws are affected by atheism and religious indifference.

General commentary. This most important article speaks of the radical questioning of traditional values (bona) which is connected with the change in thought and structures, i.e. with a cause far wider than merely social changes. This finds particular expression in the conflict between the younger and older generations. The text refers more than once to the impatience of young people, even to the "angry young men" ("immo angore rebelles fiunt"). It speaks very well about their awareness of their role in society and of their desire to fulfil it as quickly as possible. This is the key to the increasingly urgent — and presumptuous — demands of young people for participation in the management of university faculties, schools and social organisms. At the same time this creates obvious difficulties for parents and educators. Paragraph 2 links up with this very neatly and shows that the institutions, laws, mode of feeling, sensibility and habits of thought of older people no longer correspond to the present state of affairs. This gives rise to great uncertainty both about norms of action and about how to apply them. We must repeat how absolutely central this fact is. The calling in question which we are living through and which this article attempts to sketch, is very much more radical than at the time of the Reformation. Its consequences for the religious domain are described in the following paragraph. It is a pity that this text did not inspire an article in the first or second part of *Gaudium et Spes,* attempting to provide a few principles and practical examples of this necessary "aggiornamento" of institutions, laws, habits of thought and sensibility. This is the post-conciliar task par excellence, the question which the Church is putting to itself at the present time. The second half of the century will be decisive in this respect.

Certainly the first part of *Gaudium et Spes* with its doctrine of man founded on four important biblical principles — man as the image of God, the Servant of God, the humanity of the risen Christ and the creative and enlightening Word — plus Part II, which builds on this doctrine of man and the idea of human dignity, offer both a theological foundation making use of biblical and patristic sources, and a possibility of dialogue with the present generation which questions everything. But it all remains too general. There is not enough share in the dramatic tension which is perceptible in this Article 7. In other words the dialectical mode of expression of the introductory part is not sufficiently maintained in what follows. Furthermore, no effort was made to supply criteria for the endeavour to find an "aptior modus loquendi" of which Article 62 speaks.

The last paragraph expresses remarkably well the complexity and even the polarity of the religious difficulties and the changes which we are experiencing. On the one hand there is a possibility here, as has already been explained, to distinguish faith more clearly from superstition and a magical view of the world. There is also an opportunity for more active (actuosa) and more personal religious conviction. This theme, which is taken up again in Article 62, is very important. It can never be pointed out sufficiently how every effort must be made to avoid making Paul Valéry's remark seem plausible: "Some pious people make me think that God is stupid." *Gaudium et Spes* speaks, on the contrary, of possible access "ad vividiorem Dei sensum".

The text also points out that this change leads a certain number of people to abandon the practice of religion. We only need think of what has been called "purely sociological Catholicism", which evaporates as soon as the believer is torn from his social milieu, to grasp the gravity of this phenomenon, especially if it is viewed in conjunction with the shifts in population mentioned in Article 6.

The text then makes an observation which it formulates unhesitatingly, very courageously and very fairly. Whereas for example in the Middle Ages faith was a universal fact, unbelief was rare and limited to isolated individuals, today almost the opposite is the case. One thinks of Julien Green's words, "Today we live in a world in which doubt has become public opinion." *Gaudium et Spes,* however, goes even further and says that quite often nowadays a connection is made between scientific progress and a certain kind of new humanism, unbelief and absence of religion. Here we are dealing with what Jean Lacroix calls "scientific atheism" and "moral atheism".

The end of this paragraph is concerned with the atheism which is widespread not only in philosophy but also in literature, the arts, the interpretation of the humanities and of history. Nothing in fact has to be taken more seriously than this kind of tacit, unspoken atheism, which is nevertheless taken for granted all the time and profoundly marks an enormous quantity of publications, films and modes of thought. The text then says that even the civil laws of some countries are affected by this atheism, thus touching on the political atheism of which Jean Lacroix also speaks.[25]

This paragraph expresses no value-judgment but simply describes. It is extremely regrettable that the authors and revisers of Articles 19–21 did not take sufficiently into account the description given in this Article 7. If they

[25] J. Lacroix, *Le sens de l'athéisme moderne* (1958), E. T.: *Meaning of Modern Atheism* (1965).

had, it would have given more precision and authority to their text. Above all, they would have preserved an important idea which also expresses a key-situation of our age, namely, the radical questioning to which reference has been made, the tremendous interest in religion which is also apparent and the process of deepening and purifying religious conviction which is also taking place at the same time as a result. Similarly the political atheism of Article 7 also very clearly includes other forms in addition to the examples in the socialist countries. Even though Articles 19–21 go into great detail, they lack the balance and authority of Article 7.

Article 8. The title of Texts 5 and 6 ("De inaequilibriis in mundo hodierno") replaces the words "De disruptis aequilibriis" which is better Latin but not very clear.

§ 1. Text 5 clarifies by speaking of an "acrior conscientia" of the disturbed balance. Text 6 writes "mutatio . . . progrediens" instead of "progressus", which might have been taken for a value-judgment, which this Introductory Statement avoids.

§ 2. Text 5 simplifies and shortens Text 4, though in doing so omits the theme of "imprisonment in the suburbs". "In ipsa densissima turba cum acerbiore animi dolore solitudinem suam persentit." Text 6 adds at the end of the penultimate sentence a reference to contemplation. It likewise mentions the imbalance between specialized activity and a comprehensive view of reality. This last point is taken up in Article 61.

§ 3. Text 6 replaces "ex conflictu" by "ex difficultatibus", no doubt in order to achieve a more universal outlook, for the *expensio modorum* gives no explanation of the change. Text 6 makes the Latin clearer by adding "ex surgentibus" and puts "viros et mulieres" in the plural in order to move from the abstract to the concrete.

§ 4. Text 5 condenses four paragraphs of Text 4, the first two of which were only one line long.

§ 5. Texts 5 and 6 are identical with Text 4. In any case it is a banal conclusion that might well have been omitted.

General commentary. ⟨The rapid changes are experienced with an ever more sensitive awareness. They produce or intensify disharmony and contradictions.⟩ This imbalance exists within the human person between the practical reason which is so developed nowadays and the theoretical mode of thought, and no synthesis seems possible to attain. There are contradictions between the collective mode of life and the needs of personal reflection and contemplation. Finally there is the conflict between specialized activity and a universal outlook. All this is taken up again and developed in the chapter on culture.

In the family, the equilibrium is destroyed by demographic, economic and social conditions or by difficulties between successive generations. The tempo has become quicker here and a generation now consists of about five years.

Finally there are problems created by the new relation between men and women. We only need here to recall the two signs of the times referred to by John XXIII in *Pacem in Terris:* the emancipation of youth and of women, to measure the significance of this rather banal reference to them in *Gaudium et Spes.* The participation of women in social life, their personal freedom in the relation of conjugal love, recent studies of female sexuality [26] which show even more clearly the tension between activity and passivity and also its essential role in a relation of genuine service and generous love, the problem of careers for women, who have to harmonize them with their role as wife and mother, all this has to find its place and full rights in the thought and action of Christians.

Disharmony between races and between the various classes of society, between rich and poor nations, between the work for peace of the international organizations inspired by the desire of the nations themselves for peace, and the ambition to propagate one's own ideology and, even graver, the collective lusts of nations and groups. In all this man is both author and victim of his own activity.

Article 9. In Text 4 what are now Articles 9 and 10 formed a single article, which has thus been almost completely rewritten. The theme had been divided, the better to express the double aspect of desires and questions which underlie the social, psychological and religious changes described. In fact these two last articles form one section. They are intended to present quite clearly the non-utilitarian, ethical origin of the transformation which we are living through. Article 9 takes up the sociological considerations again but progressively widens them. Article 10 then concerns itself with man's deeper questions. Similarly, Texts 5 and 6 replaced the title of Text 4 "De appetitionibus et interrogationibus profundioribus et in dies universalioribus generis humani" by the wider title "De appetitionibus universalioribus generis humani" and Article 10 got the title "De profundioribus interrogationibus generis humani".

§ 1. Text 5 adds "in dies magis roborare" and replaces "personalitatem" by "dignitatem sibi propriam".

§ 2. Text 5 makes it clearer that it is appealing to justice by inserting "per iniustam vel non aequam distributionem". At the express request of some fathers, Text 5 inserted into the second sentence "nationes in via progressus sicut vel recenter". Text 6 will say even more clearly "sicut illae recenter..." for there are nations which, though they have long achieved independence, are still at the same stage of development as those which only achieved it recently.

In the same sentence Text 6 speaks of "bona civilisationis" where Text 5 read "bona culturae". No explanation is given. We must suppose that the

---

[26] A congress on this theme took place in May 1966 at the University of Louvain.

text aimed at saying more precisely that what is meant are the fundamental benefits of civilization of which Article 60, § 1, speaks, and that some of these are distinct from "culture", a term to which they give a wider meaning. Nevertheless, the expression "cultura" is used in the same way as in Article 60, and the ultimate reason for the change in this passage is not clear. In the same sentence we read: "distantia simul ac persaepe dependentia etiam oeconomica", for the gap and interdependence exist simultaneously and not only in the economic sphere. This point, which was not mentioned in Text 4, was added to Text 5 at the request of the fathers and more clearly expressed in Text 6. Then, despite a demand that it should be stated that women should remain in the sphere "qui ei competit", Text 6 spoke unambiguously of "paritatem de iure et de facto" which is even clearer than Text 5 "aequalitatem iuris et facti". The fifth sentence in Text 5 was supplemented by an important reference to the "ruricolas" and the whole sentence completed by the three words "sociali, oeconomica et culturali". This emphasized admirably the agrarian problem, not only from the economic point of view but also from that of the developing human dignity of the rural population. This is one of the most serious defects of present-day civilization. Article 60 takes up this question again. The expression "universi populi" was added in Text 6 to express the universality of this endeavour to develop culture for all.

At the express request of the fathers, Text 5 inserted the last sentence on the need for an international community. Text 6 clarified this by adding "plenam atque liberam vitam" thus displaying two different but complementary aspects. The last paragraph in Text 5 made it clearer that men have come to realize that they themselves have unleashed the forces which now threaten to turn against them. The last sentence introduces Article 10.

General commentary. The central idea is the awareness that man is not called only to master the material world, but that he is also responsible for making the political, social and economic order increasingly serve all and each.

This explains the feeling of collective frustration which two-thirds of mankind harbour because of an unjust, unfair distribution of material goods. The slight they feel, and their dependence, are still increasing, especially among starving peoples. The text then speaks about women whose position in two-thirds of the world is still inhuman;[27] about agricultural workers, who have not yet really been adopted by any kind of Marxism, so that here, too, two-thirds of mankind are perishing through what should give life; about industrial workers, whose lot must not too quickly be supposed to have improved everywhere. All this is comprised in the widespread conviction that the nations of the earth without exception should share in the same way in the benefits of culture.

---

[27] We may refer to the researches of Madeleine Barot of the World Council of Churches.

The following paragraph then describes a deeper aspiration which lies at the root of these facts, the striving for a full and free life, worthy of man. In this way the absolute necessity of creating a world society is felt. Paul VI gave powerful expression to it in his UNO speech.

The last paragraph takes up again a theme that had been treated in more detail in Interim Text A: The world is both too weak and too strong; human endeavours are ambiguous; the need for moral decisions if a catastrophe is to be avoided is more and more apparent.

Article 10. This article appeared afresh in Text 5. It will be best to quote the *relatio*. "Hic numerus confectus est ad vota plurium Patrum implenda, de mandato Subcommissionis centralis. Intentio textus est quod ultra descriptionem sociologicam perveniatur ad intimum cor hominis, in quo problema fundamentale ponitur. Homo enim, licet sit creatura limitata, ad vitam aeternam vocatur. Homo, insuper, indesinenter exponitur peccato, de quo hic tantum *descriptivo modo agitur*, dum postea de eius profunditate theologica tractabitur (in parte I, cap. I). Denique Ecclesia seipsam *ut respondentem praesentat*, non ut pro omni problemate completam solutionem praebeat, sed ut, omnibus cooperantibus, ad solutionem perducat: quod fieri nequit nisi sub luce Christi. Ita *transitus* obtinetur ad *expositionem doctrinalem* partis primae" ("This article has been composed to meet the wishes of several fathers at the command of the Central Subcommission. The text aims at going beyond sociological description to the very heart of man, where the fundamental problem arises. For though man is a finite creature, he is called to eternal life. He is also constantly exposed to sin which is here dealt with in a purely descriptive way, its theological depth being dealt with later [in Part I, Chapter I]. Then the Church presents itself as replying, not in order to provide a complete solution to every problem, but so that if all co-operate in helping, a solution may be found; and this cannot be done except in the light of Christ. This provides a transition to the doctrinal exposition of the first part").

A second reason must also be mentioned. It was thought possible to solve the problem of giving a purely descriptive exposition which nevertheless employed quite definite criteria. In fact everybody always uses criteria in this kind of inquiry, whether believers or not; there has never been such a thing as pure description. Consequently the religious criterion operative had to be indicated.

Finally, the significance of the ethical factors in these changes had to be mentioned. They are indubitably connected with religious decisions but have their own intrinsic consistency, and it is to be regretted that the Text 5 version practically equated ethics with religion. Text 4 had not done so. Text 5 could not completely avoid the danger of presenting the Church as a kind of *deus ex machina*.

At the same time version 5 was characterized by very fine spiritual, religious, Christian and ecclesiological breadth. It also succeeded in bringing out the connection of the descriptive part of the schema with the dogmatic exposition. Since theologians are only too accustomed to prescind from concrete existential situations, there was willingness to pay for that connection at the cost of a rather awkward short circuit.

Since Text 5 was new, there is no point in comparing it with Text 4. Text 6 adds a few precisions. The word "quorum" was added to the phrase "plurimum vita", and by the additions to the sentence "existentiam humanam *omnis* significationis propriae expertem existimantes, ei *totam* significationem ex *solo* proprio ingenio conferre nituntur", made it clearer that men sometimes find a meaning for their own existence. This avoided a dangerous oversimplification, that of opposing the "all" of the religious explanation to the "nothing" of the human explanation; what in itself is primary is not necessarily so in regard to us. Text 6 reads "quamquam tantus progressus factus est" instead of "non obstante tanto progressu" of Text 5, which is not so clear.

In the last paragraph, Text 5 inserted the lines "affirmat ... saecula" so that "mention might also be made of immutable realities". The remarks made above on Article 4 may be recalled; nevertheless it will be observed that the immutabilia are well connected up with the person of Christ "qui est heri, hodie, ipse et in saecula". Here, whether one will have it so or not, is a criterion of the very first importance, which is illustrated by Aquinas' remark about dogmatic formulas: "Actus fidei non terminatur ad enunciabile sed ad rem." Text 6 added the words "ad cooperandum ... veniendam" in order to arrive at a version more in correspondence with the *relatio*.

General commentary. It is first said that the imbalances under which the modern world labours are connected with a more fundamental loss of balance in the human heart. Man is experienced both as finite and also as oriented towards a limitless, higher vocation. He is solicited on all sides and does not know what to choose. He is also weak and a sinner. This point is presented here in such a way that man can recognize that he is a sinner even though he does not believe in God. Depth psychology and an abundance of literary works provide ample illustration of this.[28] Consequently a man experiences a division in himself and in society; the text echoes Euripides and the 7th chapter of the Letter to the Romans.[29]

Certainly some adherents of practical materialism do not think of this, and others are so poor and wretched that they no longer have even the strength to think of it. Others again content themselves with accepting the interpretation that is offered them, without reflecting in the slightest about it.

[28] A. Vergote, *La psychologie religieuse* (1966).
[29] H. Carrier, *Essais de psychologie religieuse*, chapter on the sociological significance of collective sin, pp. 167–92.

Some look to human effort for everything, including the satisfaction of all the desires of their hearts. The text here succumbs to the temptation of allowing language to triumph over reality, and of listing antitheses, for in fact there is no system of this type, promising the satisfaction of all desires. Marxism, for example, is well aware that there will always be death. The psychoanalysts also know that man's greatness lies in his acceptance of his limits. And the meaning of the existentialism of Heidegger, for example, consists in the contention that it is impossible to overcome contingence in any way whatsoever. Here there is a clear contrast to all forms of German Idealism.

While some think that human endeavour can create an earthly paradise, others despair of any meaning in life, and praise those who are bold enough to say that human existence has no deeper sense and who strive to give it a total meaning on the basis of human ideas alone (solo ingenio). This brings out the tone of voluntary risk, difficulty and discomfort, and the description here is much juster than the previous one but must be correctly understood. There must be no illusions about the word "despair", for in this perspective, hope can in fact only arise on the other side of despair. We must avoid contrasting the faithful who hope, with unbelievers who do not hope; that would be far too much of an oversimplification. The controversy in this context is between an unlimited and a more limited form of hope.

The text then lists the eternal questions of mankind, omitting, however, a very superfluous: "Ad quid haec omnia?" The Council rightly returns to these questions, which also play an important part in the Declaration on the Relationship of the Church to Non-Christian Religions. There is an element here which unites men despite the differences of their belief, namely, the unity of their questions — that is a notable idea in the Declaration on Non-Christian Religions — and also an immutable fundamental fact which will still remain, even after the disappearance of present-day prejudices which claim that it is a sign of weakness to raise these questions.

The last section speaks of the Church. It is important, however, to point out and explain that the Church is primarily represented here as a Church which is proclaiming the crucified and risen Christ, bringing light and strength to man by the Holy Spirit and announcing that the key to all human history lies in the Lord. It is enormously important to stress this fact. What the Church brings is in fact not one system, an ideology, as people say, among others, but the proclamation and the action of Jesus.

The word "master" then introduces another statement about the Church, saying that there are immutable things but which once again have their foundation in Christ.

All this concludes with reference to the light of Christ, "the image of the invisible God", "the first-born of every creature". This is the truth of the mystery of man. In a flash, this reveals the profoundly biblical and Christological perspective which characterizes the first part and the first two chapters of the second part of *Gaudium et Spes*.

By stating (in Text 5) that the Council is turning to all in the name of this light but also in order to collaborate in working out a solution to the main problems of the world at the present day, it also recalls another aspect. Even if the Church has no ready-made solutions to a number of concrete earthly problems, it at least wants to collaborate in constructing the world to which men are devoting themselves with so much hope. That is implied in Part I, Chapter IV, and also in the last three chapters of Part II, though it must not be overlooked that this double viewpoint of the light of Christ and of collaboration permeates the whole of *Gaudium et Spes*. This final section thus places the whole Pastoral Constitution in the perspective of Christ and the Church, which is obviously the specific contribution of a General Council.

This Introductory Statement might be summarized by saying that it endeavours to sketch the situation of man at this time (giving the expression "this time" the biblical sense of the "kairos", the "hodie", the "today", which God speaks), in order the better to grasp man's vocation. This situation is described in detail by the following features: upheaval, consciousness of changes, which involves loss of equilibrium, and desires. The latter are ethical in nature, but also include ultimate questions and finally, therefore, religious problems. The Church is then presented as witness to the light of Christ, the image of the invisible God. It is ready to collaborate in making the better world of justice and solidarity which men are striving to build.

[30] Cf. our study in *A la lumière du concile* (1966), pp. 21–30.

PART I

The Church and Man's Calling

The Dignity of the Human Person

by
Joseph Ratzinger

Article 11. In this article the Constitution endeavours to make clear the theological context and justification of its own undertaking — dialogue between the Church and the world of today. The Zurich Text (art. 2) had attempted to provide this justification by means of the concept of "signs of the times" based on Mt 16:3 (Lk 12:56). It regarded time as a sign and a voice to the extent that it involves God's presence or absence; consequently the voice of the age must be regarded as the voice of God. In this form the idea was sharply attacked. To link the Roman proverb on time as the voice of God with Jesus' eschatological warning against the blindness of his nation which, though on the look-out for signs, was not able to interpret him, God's eschatological sign to that age, or his message, was considered not only exegetically unacceptable but of doubtful validity in itself. Since Christ is the real "sign of the time", is he not the actual antithesis to the authority of *chronos* expressed in the proverb "vox temporis vox Dei"? The Ariccia text consequently gave a more cautious version of the idea, and this was refined and further moderated in Text 5, but without abandoning the initial basic and guiding conception. It was now said that in the events, needs and aims of the age the Church must detect indications of God's presence. The whole was now given a strong pneumatological emphasis in the context of a Trinitarian outline of history. The Church as the People of God united by the Father, must endure in hope in Christ the redeemer and is guided in this by the Holy Spirit "who fills all things and blows where he wills". In support of this, Wisdom 1:7, the Church's Pentecostal liturgy and Jn 3:8 were quoted. Of course in the debate one was once again conscious of the problems of how to apply Scripture in a way appropriate to the age, and of the dilemma presented on the one side by historical precision which withdraws Scripture into the past and keeps it there, and on the other by the conviction that Scripture is also concerned with the present day and can be assimilated today. It became plain, as so often in the debate on the Pastoral Constitution,

115

that we still have no rules of kerygmatic hermeneutics. Consequently it was necessary to follow the exigencies of historical exegesis which, if taken radically, would ultimately forbid any contemporary application of Scripture. But the schema was concerned precisely with the presence of Christianity. Consequently what was fundamentally mirrored in the argument over the possibility of scriptural quotations, was the deeper dilemma of the schema generally, and of the Church at the present time. By appealing to the testimony of Scripture, does it necessarily belong to the past, or can it, without being unfaithful to itself, be the Church of the present? Perhaps after all Auguste Comte was right when he diagnosed the past as the age of the Church and the present and future as the age of Positivism? Doesn't the Church itself confirm its dismissal to the past by affirming that that past was the decisive time? When we recall this background, it is not difficult to see that in reality the debate on method which we have immediately encountered decided the problem of the Pastoral Constitution itself, i.e. the question of the presence of Christianity, of faith, "in the world of today".

The definitive text (scarcely altered after Text 5) seeks an escape route. The pneumatological reference of Wis 1:7 (the Introit of Pentecost) was left, but was no longer given explicitly as a quotation. The Trinitarian outline fell victim to the tendency to simplify. Furthermore, the idea was treated more critically by replacing "animadvertere" by "discernere"; in the events of the age the signs of the divine will are not simply to be "detected" but "distinguished". This must be considered a felicitous touch, for it drew from the spiritual tradition of the Church into the framework of the conciliar text the idea of discretio spirituum, the discernment of spirits. This happily completes the Council's novel enterprise and marks the historical context in which it in fact stands, revealing under what, at first glance, seems its secular aim, a spiritual purpose and depth. The meaning of the conciliar text as a whole may be taken to be that, as opposed to a onesided, purely Christological and "chronological" outlook, it brings to the fore the pneumatological and "kairological" aspect, and as it were finds the point at which this is anchored. Certainly the Church is tied to what was once and for all, the origin in Jesus of Nazareth, and in this sense it is obliged "chronologically" to continuity with him and the testimony of the beginning. But because "the Lord is the Spirit" (2 Cor 3:17) and remains present through the Spirit, the Church has not only the chronological line with its obligation of continuity and identity, it has also the moment, the kairos, in which it must interpret and accomplish the work of the Lord as present. The Church is not the petrification of what once was, but its living presence in every age. The Church's dimension is therefore the present and the future no less than the past. Its obedience to the Lord precisely as such must be obedience to him as pneuma, as summons today; it must be accomplished with discernment of spirits and must accept the risk of submitting at all times to such discernment. That is of course necessary in order that the moment of the Holy Spirit may not imperceptibly change into the momentary spirit of the age, and what is done under the appearance of obedience to the pneuma may not in fact be submission to the dictates of fashion and apostasy from the Lord. This shows the intrinsic connection between holiness and aggiornamento. As acceptance of the kairos it must at the same time be the dia-krisis of the spirits of the age, on the firm basis of the one Spirit of the Lord. In this dual yet single sense it is a task for the Church, the necessary pneumatological complement of Christological obedience.[1]

As well as this line in the contents of our text, we must note its formal structure, which is determined by the idea of dialogue. For a dialogue to be possible, certain conditions are of course required: there must be two partners with a certain difference or even opposition between them which the discussion seeks to overcome, but at the same time there must be a minimum of agreement for the conversation to take place at all. This is not the place to reflect on the nature of dialogue and its various historical kinds (Platonic, biblical). We will simply pursue the last idea, that of the unity postulated by dialogue, a little further, because it concerns one factor which is perhaps taken into consideration too little at present. If we consider Jesus' dialogues or the early Christian missionary preaching as the form of dialogue with non-Christians of that period, it is evident that that dialogue was not addressed to total strangers at all. It was carried on within a common intellectual climate without which it would not have been possible. Jesus' controversies take place within a common recognition of the Old Testament as the binding Word of God and on that basis aim at determining the meaning and import of Jesus' claim. Similarly, the early Christian mission, including that of Paul, with its maxim "first to the Jews" maintained this fundamental common element and, even when that limit was crossed, found its immediate sphere of work among the "fearers of God" who were already influenced by the faith of Israel and consequently offered a point of contact for the Christian dialogue. The Council could not directly appeal to any such "preamble" to Christianity. It expressed its point of contact in a double statement: first in agreement with John XXIII, by the idea of "homines bonae voluntatis" (e.g. art. 22) and secondly in the idea of "humanitas" (already clear in art. 3 and repeatedly recurring). Goodwill, of course, establishes a purely formal criterion in place of a definite content. As regards the second concept, it is remarkable that in contrast to the essentially theological starting-point of the early Christians ("the fearers of God") an anthropological theme now comes to the fore. This anthropocentrism, which

[1] On the spiritual roots of John XXIII's concept of *aggiornamento*, see F. M. Willam, *Vom jungen Angelo Roncalli 1903–1907 zum Papst Johannes XXIII. 1958–1963* (1967), pp. 32 ff. and 146 ff.; cf. my detailed review in *TQ* 148 (1968).

determines the whole theological conception of the text, probably represents its most characteristic option. It was already plainly apparent in the *relatio* in which Bishop Guano presented Text 3 on 20 October 1964: "In hanc quaestionem centralem de homine quae semper maximi momenti manet, confluunt problemata humana nostri temporis" ("In this central question of man which still remains of the greatest importance, all the human problems of our time converge"). Even more incisively, Archbishop Garrone expressed the same point of view on 21 September 1964, when introducing Text 6: "Ut ex tabula rerum videre est, totus Schematis prospectus in hominem et in conditionem humanam quasi contrahitur; haec est vere veluti anima Schematis" ("As may be seen from the list of contents, the whole scope of the schema is summed up as it were in man and the human condition; this is the real soul of the schema").

In the present article this point of view finds expression at the end of the first and third paragraphs. The purpose of the Council's discernment of spirits is said to be to lead to "fully human solutions". Then it is said even more explicitly that the Council's pronouncements will show that the Church's mission is "religious and by that very fact supremely human in character". What is to be demonstrated, therefore, is that precisely by Christian faith in God, true humanism, i.e. man's full development as man, is attained, and that consequently the idea of humanism which present-day atheism opposes to faith can serve as the hinge of the discussion and a means of dialogue. The problem of God is approached in the mirror of the idea of full human development, and consequently atheism too is examined from the standpoint of humanism. The whole Pastoral Constitution might therefore be described in this light as a discussion between Christian and unbeliever on the question who and what man really is.

The problem of an inner principle of dialogue, of the element of unity which makes dialogue possible, may be said on the whole to have been approached successfully, but the way the partners in the discussion are described is much less satisfactory. Even in the present brief article we find three terms designating one of the partners, but no reflection on the nature of the distinction between these terms and no reason given for the change from one to the other: "populus Dei" — "Concilium" — "Ecclesia". It is obvious that Council and Church are not identical. On the other hand, the *expensio modorum* on Text 6 in answer to the suggestion made by two fathers that "Ecclesia" only should be used, and "populus Dei" omitted, observed that both mean the same, namely the whole Church. But the way "People of God" is thus turned into a sort of empirical term, can only be regarded as extremely questionable. We can only agree with G. Alberigo that this way of speaking of the Church involves no small danger of sinking once more into a purely sociological and even ideological view of the Church through ignoring the essential insights of the Constitution on the Liturgy and the Constitution on the Church and by oversimplifying, externalizing and making a catchword of a term which can only keep its meaning if it is used in a genuinely theological context.[2]

The use of the term "genus humanum" to denote the other partner is also quite unsatisfactory. For we must obviously object (as, of course, was repeatedly done at the Council) that the Church itself is part of the genus humanum and cannot therefore be contradistinguished from it. When proposed amendments to Text 6 were dealt with, it was stated that the reason for retaining this expression was that it was indispensable; a certain distinction has to be made between Church and human race for dialogue to be possible at all (*modus* 13). But this missed the point. The Church meets its vis-à-vis *in* the human race, for example in non-Christians, unbelievers, etc. But it cannot stand outside the human race, and even for reasons of dialogue it cannot exclude itself from the human race and then artificially create a solidarity which in any case is the Church's lot. The lack of understanding shown in this matter by those who drafted the text can probably only be attributed to the deeply-rooted extrinsicism of ecclesiastical thought, to long acquaintance with the Church's exclusion from the general course of development and to retreat into a special little ecclesiastical world from which an attempt is then made to speak to the rest of the world.

Article 12. The text of this article was particularly hotly disputed, precisely because it involved a decision about the whole theological approach and therefore the structure of the entire schema. General approval was given to the fact that no attempt was made to give a static philosophical doctrine of man on the lines of the neo-scholastic tradition, that the body-soul pattern had not been employed, and that, without any attempt at a complete and systematic doctrine of man, a mosaic of basic statements had been assembled which in conjunction formed a dynamic account of man, stressing history and essentially based on biblical data. Nevertheless it seemed to many people, especially theologians from German-speaking countries, that there was not a radical enough rejection of a doctrine of man divided into philosophy and theology. They were convinced that fundamentally the text was still based on a schematic representation of nature and the supernatural viewed far too much as merely juxtaposed. To their mind it took as its starting-point the fiction that it is possible to construct a rational philosophical picture of man intelligible to all and on which all men of goodwill can agree, the actual Christian doctrines being added to this as a sort of crowning conclusion. The latter then tends to appear as a sort of special possession of Christians, which others ought not to make a bone of contention but which at bottom can be ignored. This was the real reason for

---

[2] G. Alberigo, "Die Konstitution in Beziehung zur gesamten Lehre des Konzils", in G. Baraúna, ed., *Die Kirche in der Welt von heute* (1967), pp. 49–76, especially pp. 69, 71. This contribution in its entirety is one of the best pieces of critical writing so far on the problems of the Pastoral Constitution.

the protest against the "optimism" of the schema (all these objections refer to Text 4). It was not a question of imposing a pessimistic view of man or of constructing an exaggerated theology of sin because of a certain correspondence with some forms of Lutheran thought. The text as it stood itself prompted the question why exactly the reasonable and perfectly free human being described in the first articles was suddenly burdened with the story of Christ. The latter might well appear to be a rather unintelligible addition to a picture that was already quite complete in itself. Consequently the text was blamed for only apparently choosing a theological starting-point in the idea of man as the image of God, whereas in reality it still had a theistically-coloured and to a large extent non-historical view. As opposed to this, it was urged that the starting-point should be Christ, the second Adam, from whom alone the Christian picture of man can be correctly developed. Advocates of this position could point to the fictitious character of a supposedly rational picture of man and therefore say that the only realistic picture must start from the actual Christian creed which, precisely as a confession of faith, can and must manifest its own intelligibility and rationality. To this it was objected that dialogue demands a gradual advance, which alone can open out some access to the centre of belief. Ultimately the whole question of the relation between faith and understanding comes up for debate here. It can hardly be disputed that as a consequence of the division between philosophy and theology established by the Thomists, a juxtaposition has gradually been established which no longer appears adequate. There is, and must be, a human reason *in* faith; yet conversely, every human reason is conditioned by a historical standpoint so that reason pure and simple does not exist. On the other hand, it must be admitted that the various concrete forms of dialogue can take place in a number of ways and that here there is much to be said for an advance from outside inwards. Despite all opposition, this finally prevailed in the conciliar text. The preparatory work and models for any other were simply not there, of course.

However, as a result of these objections, an attempt was made to frame the text with much more regard for history. This was shown above all by the insertion of a separate article on sin, and also by a more elaborate version of the present article. It no longer simply begins with a reference to man as made to the image of God and man's consequent greatness, but shows by a more phenomenological method the tremendous tension in the human being between greatness and baseness, between his highest aspiration and an abyss that may be one of despair. In the background here, there is not only the thought of the actual contradictions in modern thought and in the attempts made in all ages to construct a doctrine of man, but also of Pascal's saying about the mysterious polarity of man between "grandeur" and "misère". Article 13 finally comes back to the dialectic of "sublimis vocatio" and "profunda miseria", and shows in Pascal's sense that biblical revelation gives the interpretative key to this contradictory state of affairs. In contrast to the one-sided and excessively static optimism of the Ariccia text, this gives a very much more wide-ranging view of man and includes not only the polarity of his being but the tension of his history and the dynamism of the biblical picture of history which can only be understood on that basis.

The problems involved in starting from the idea of man as the image of God spring from the fact that in the Old Testament (leaving out of account the special view expressed in Wis 2:23) this idea is left quite indeterminate in content. It only receives its full meaning from the fact that in the New Testament the Adam-figure and the doctrine of man as the image of God are transferred to Christ as the definitive Adam. Consequently this idea not only has its origin in the theology of creation, it becomes an eschatological theme, concerned less with the origin than with the future of man. It therefore appears less as a static endowment than as the dynamism of a promise located above man. It was implicit in the logic of the starting-point, once this was chosen, that its authors wanted to introduce Christology at the end and were not ready to admit it here, even though it forces itself on the attention here as an indispensable component of a Christian anthropology. Consequently the perspective remained exclusively that of the theology of creation, but one which is not even adequate to the wealth of a Christian theology of creation, for this is only intelligible in eschatology; the Alpha is only truly to be understood in the light of the Omega. At bottom, the very verses of Ps 8:5–7 quoted in the text should have prompted a widening of the perspective. These Old Testament statements about man were interpreted messianically within the Old Testament and then Christologically within the New Testament, so that the link between Adam and Christ, anthropology and Christology, presented itself here quite inescapably. It would also have been in complete accord with making the central idea of the Pastoral Constitution that of "humanitas" and with its attempt to show that true "humanitas" is something that can only be achieved theologically.

In view of the exclusion of the New Testament, the statements which remain in the text seem rather lustreless and colourless, although they have been enriched and animated from patrology as opposed to traditional neo-scholastic manuals. With Augustine (De Trinitate, XIV, 8, 11) the image of God is interpreted as capacity for God, qualification to know and love God. That is what for Augustine gives the idea of man as the image of God its dynamic aspect; man is the image of God to the extent in which he directs himself to God; man disfigures his likeness to God by turning away from God. Our text displays another rather different aspect by presenting man's claim to dominion over the world as a consequence of his likeness to God. Nevertheless the Augustinian line remains, for dominion over the world is only the consequence, not the content, of likeness to God, and consequently points beyond itself back again to the image of God. That dominion must ultimately consist in bringing things into man's glorification of God. In this way an important prior decision is being taken here in regard to the fundamental question of the whole Constitution, that of the significance of work. Work is not purely and simply likeness to God, even if it must be regarded as closely bound up with it. The clearly stated difference between content and consequence of man's creation to the image of God implies an affirmation which has not been sufficiently taken into account in post-conciliar discussion. Ultimately it is the basis of the intrinsic justification of worship, and explains the impossibility of simply identifying man's secular service with the service of God.

The conciliar text does not accept Karl Barth's well-known theory that the image and likeness of God consists in the relation between man and wife and is therefore a pure "analogia relationis" (Augustine reaches a similar conclusion in a much more subtle way). It does, however, bring the existence of humanity as man and woman into undefined connection with human likeness to God. And on that basis it describes man as a social being who essentially exists in relationships. It is evident that an attempt is being made here to introduce the modern philosophy of the human person, for example the dialogue principle of F. Ebner and M. Buber. At the same time, even here it is a question of laying a foundation for a theology of the sexes and a theology of marriage built upon it, and of indicating that the sexual differentiation of mankind into man and woman is much more than a purely biological fact for the purpose of procreation but unconnected with what is truly human in mankind. In it there is accomplished that intrinsic relation of the human being to a Thou, which inherently constitutes him or her as human.[3] If, of course, G. Baum in this connection means that man is constituted as a person by the interpersonal relationship as such,[4] the state of affairs is only roughly expressed, because (as in the case of work already mentioned) the likeness to God in sexuality is prior to sexuality, not identical with it. It is because the human being is capable of the absolute Thou that he is an I who can become a Thou for another I. The capacity for the absolute Thou is the ground of the possibility and necessity of the human partner. Here too, therefore, it is most important to pay attention to the difference between content and consequence. Previously it excluded any simple identification of secular service with the service of God, and here it makes it impossible to identify religion with human solidarity. Yet that would be the case if the human person were constituted solely in relation to the human partner. On the contrary, the circle of human solidarity is open

[3] Cf. P. Delhaye, "Die Würde der menschlichen Person", in Baraúna, *op. cit.*, pp. 154–78, especially p. 160, n. 10.
[4] G. Baum, "Der Mensch in seiner Welt", in J. C. Hampe, ed., *Die Autorität der Freiheit* III (1967), pp. 68–86, especially p. 76.

to a third, who is wholly other, God. And that, for the Council, is the content of the doctrine that man is made to the image of God. Man stands in immediate relation to God, he does not merely have to do with God indirectly through his work and his relations with his fellow-men. He can know and love God himself.

Article 13. In the Ariccia text, sin was only referred to indirectly; it was not expressly the subject of a single sentence at any point of the present chapter.[5] Various reasons can be given for this almost total absence of an essential theme of the biblical doctrine of man. The first reason may have been the optimistic view of the world and of man with which John XXIII in his opening speech sent the Council on its way, as it were, and which he opposed to the "prophets of doom" who can see nothing but constant decline from bad to worse. The intention that inspired Pope John really pointed, of course, in quite a different direction. He was opposed to a mentality which clung to the Middle Ages as the sole ideal embodiment of the Church and really wanted to see them restored. He, on the contrary, maintained that each age offers the Church new opportunities; the Church can work through the possibilities of any particular age and must respond to them.[6] His optimism essentially consisted in rejecting the romantic nostalgia for the Middle Ages which makes people forget that every age belongs to God and can and must stand open, each in its own time, to God's eternal present. At all events, the basically optimistic atmosphere which was given to the Council by this affirmation of the present, must have combined in the authors of the draft with a view of the world rather akin to that of Teilhard de Chardin, though endeavours were made to keep specifically Teilhardian ideas out of the conciliar text.[7] Finally, there was the fact that the strong stress, deriving from Luther, on the theme of sin, was alien to the mainly French authors of the schema, whose theological presuppositions were quite different. Their thought

---

[5] Cf. the Council speech of Bishop H. Volk on 24 September 1965, reproduced in Hampe, *op. cit.,* pp. 31 ff. The bishop's statement that "the word 'sin' does not occur in any of the 106 pages of the schema" is not in fact quite correct; the word appeared for example in no. 11, pp. 13, 21; no. 15, pp. 15, 27; no. 17, pp. 16, 20; no. 20, pp. 18, 30. The reality itself was referred to quite often, but was never treated explicitly in itself.

[6] See the text of the speech in the official edition: *Constitutiones — Decreta — Declarationes* (1966), pp. 854–72, especially p. 859: "Hi enim ... dicitant nostra tempora, si cum elapsis saeculis comparentur, prorsus in peius abiise ..."; p. 860: "... Nemo tamen negare potest, has novas inductas rerum condiciones, id saltem commodi habere, ut e medio innumera illa impedimenta iam auferantur, quibus olim saeculi filii liberam Ecclesiae actionem praepedire consueverant..." Cf. also in Willam, pp. 131 f., material from the Venetian period.

[7] Cf. on the question of Teilhard de Chardin and the Pastoral Constitution the contributions of O. Spülbeck in Hampe, *op. cit.,* III, pp. 86–97, and S. M. Daecke, *ibid.,* pp. 98–112. In regard to the actual importance of Teilhard de Chardin for the conciliar text, Daecke presents a more accurate picture than Spülbeck, whose article aims too much at harmoni-

probably sprang from a theological attitude which was Thomistic in tendency and also influenced by the Greek Fathers. This position does not ignore sin but is influenced more by the thought of creation and the knowledge that redemption has already taken place. It is not at all prepared to make sin the centre of the theological edifice. In view of Christ's triumph it is considered mistaken "to persist in this consciousness of guilt and to resign oneself to it".[8]

The addition of Article 13 in Text 5 removed the onesidedness of the Ariccia text, but retained its fundamental outlook, which was essentially specified by a redemption which has already taken place. The mysterious character of sin is fully acknowledged, but it does not determine the outlook as it does in Lutheran theology or even in Catholic Augustinianism since the Reformation. It is worth noting that in discussions since the Council, voices have been raised from the Lutheran camp in precisely the same sense. Thus S. M. Daecke quotes a remark attributed to Teilhard de Chardin, "You are all hypnotized by evil", and then continues, "Isn't he right with his sovereign disdain for sin and evil, with his will to see the world as a good creation, to regard it positively and not to overestimate what is negative? In his conviction that evil is not a power opposed to God but something that is always already overcome, Teilhard is in agreement with Karl Barth . . . Even for the Bible, sin is not the central idea to the extent it is for Teilhard de Chardin's critics. For Paul himself, to whom they appeal, sin has been overcome in Christ and has lost its domination; it belongs to the old aeon which is past."[9] Now the Council did not show a sovereign disdain for sin and evil and there is really no reason to do so, either from the Bible or our own experience (especially of the present century). The Council did in fact decide for a theological view which does not allow itself to be hypnotized by the theme of sin, but adopts an entirely positive basis. It is noteworthy in this connection that Text 6 once again toned down this section as compared with Text 5, sometimes in a way which may easily tend to give a slightly semipelagian impression. One change is to be welcomed, however; in the description of the partners in the "luctatio dramatica", the pair of opposites "inter Malignum et Deum" was struck out. In Scripture the devil nowhere appears as God's vis-à-vis; God does not need to fight, he is a sovereign power against whom no one can fight. A view which sets the devil on a level with God rouses the suspicion of a dualism which is alien to biblical tradition.

A number of *modi* asked for express mention to be made of the sin of

zation. On the other hand Daecke interprets Teilhard in terms of a post-conciliar kind of thought which was certainly quite alien to him. On the controversy at the Council about the questions raised by Teilhard de Chardin, see also J. Ratzinger, *Die letzte Sitzungsperiode des Konzils* (1966), pp. 39 ff.

[8] P. Delhaye in Baraúna, *op. cit.*, p. 162, and especially p. 161.

[9] In Hampe, *op. cit.*, III, p. 110.

man's first parents, of their original condition and of the raising of man to the supernatural order. The pair of concepts nature—supernatural was nevertheless avoided here as in the whole Constitution, though of course the reality they designate was maintained. Nevertheless the way was deliberately left open for a new consideration of that whole subject. There was not to be any further hardening of the representational schema previously used. Similarly, in view of recent debates on questions connected with the original state of man and original sin, explicit treatment of this topic was avoided. Here, too, there was agreement that the essential content of Trent cannot be abandoned, but that theology must be left free to inquire afresh precisely what that essential content really is. Consequently, in accordance with biblical usage in speaking of Adam, they were content to speak of "man", not in a narrowly individual sense but in an essentially collective and at the same time quite fundamental way, as having placed himself against God and as seeking to reach his goal without God. Likewise, specific mention of the moment of the Fall was avoided, and instead it was simply affirmed that "from the very dawn of history" man revolted against God. Consequently the biblical reference chosen was not the text from Rom 5, the interpretation of which has been firmly established by the history of dogma, but Rom 1:12 ff. Here Paul is certainly unfolding the theme of universal sinfulness and the universal need for redemption, but not on the basis of principle, the theology of Adam, but on the factual basis of man's constant revolt against his Creator. This is a more concrete presentation of universal sinfulness as compared with the standard kind of neo-scholastic teaching on original sin, and in accordance with the perspective opened out by Rom 1:21 ff., it at once makes it possible to turn to man's situation as he experiences it, with his divisions, abysses and disorder. The text of the Pastoral Constitution is therefore much closer to Pascal than to Scheeben. One is immediately reminded of Fragment 434 of the Pensées: "The knot of our condition draws its twists and turns from this abyss, so that man is more inconceivable without this mystery (i.e. of original sin) than this mystery is for man."[10] Scheeben rather acidly remarked on this: "... Examined in the light of this assumption, no mystery remains ... At all events it could only be called a mystery because of the incomprehensibility of its nature, which in that theory is really so great that it arises not so much from the weakness of our reason as from the absurdity of the thing itself ...".[11] The conciliar text, of course, does not go into the problem of the theory of original sin and consequently decides nothing. But it nevertheless takes for granted that the general sinfulness of man of which Scripture speaks is also confirmed by

[10] E. Brunschvicg, p. 532.

[11] M. J. Scheeben, *Die Mysterien des Christentums* (4th ed., 1925), p. 171, E. T.: *Mysteries of Christianity* (1953).

125

our experience of man as he is and his history. It assumes that this factor and the actual concrete fact of man's sin cannot be separated too far from that revolt against God which has determined the drama between man and his Creator from the very start of history. That the connection between human experience and the message of faith is important for the Council is once again shown in the last sentences of Article 13. These take up a theme already touched upon in Article 12, that of the polarity in man between "grandeur" and "misère". They affirm that this fact, which is first drawn to our attention by phenomenology, can be "read" and interpreted in the light of the Bible. The linking of experience with faith, or the insight that faith provides the key to the meaning of our human experience, is of course a presupposition of dialogue between faith and unbelief. Only if faith throws light on experience and proves to be the answer to our experiences, can talk about man's humanity lead to talk about God and with God. To that extent the linking of experience with faith, and the turning to Pascal's view, were implicit from the start in the very meaning of the Pastoral Constitution and formed the very basis of its possibility. At the same time, it must be remembered that Pascal was not of course elaborating a theory of experience merely at random; it imposed itself upon him because the *Pensées* were in fact planned as a dialogue with unbelievers. They are therefore one of the few texts in modern theology which anticipate or foreshadow what the Pastoral Constitution attempts to do.

Reference to experience is also constantly maintained in the second part of this article. This explains the recourse to Rom 7:13–25, the second passage from the Letter to the Romans in which the theme of sin is approached from the angle of experience. It is noteworthy that with Rom 1 and 7 the text circles round the problem of Rom 5, while at the same time there is a perceptible attempt to make full use of those two texts in such a way as to loosen too rigid an interpretation of the Adam-Christ passage and to make it more accessible by fitting it into a wider and more concrete context. Furthermore, the preeminence of the Christ theme over that of sin is maintained, while at the same time the fundamental optimism of the whole schema is confirmed, for with Jn 12:31 it recalls that Christ's victory has already taken place. This general tenor was even emphasized in the final version, for instead of "in servitute peccati retinet" we now have "retinebat", so that the slavery of sin is no longer characterized as present but, in relation to Christ, as already past. The commission gave purely grammatical reasons for the change (*modus* 17) but at the same time it was acting on a whole intellectual attitude which in this case cannot be regarded as entirely above question.

Article 14. The whole article originally dealt solely with "the dignity of the human body", and the following article concerned "the dignity of the soul and particularly of the human intellect" (Text 4). In Text 5 this division was suppressed and the whole constitution of man was included in Article 14 in order to oppose as much as possible any kind of dualism and to emphasize human unity even in this external way. That unity is so complete that man can only be described as simultaneously body and soul, each in the other, not separate from it.

Whereas the second part of the article chiefly deals with man's soul, the first part attempts to present something like a theology of the body. The first words, "Corpore et anima unus" go beyond the purely methodical division, and are intended to express the fundamental theme of the text: the inseparable corporeal-spiritual unity of man. The fact that the aim was to avoid technical theological terms as far as possible and yet not to leave room for any ambiguity, set clearly recognizable limits here to the Council's attempt to state a convincing anti-dualist doctrine of man. Consequently it had to renounce the use of the possibilities offered by the Thomist formula: "anima unica forma corporis". On its basis, for example, K. Rahner and J. B. Metz define the body as "the soul's making itself present in the world, soul as it were in a certain 'aggregate condition'", and can say that man does not really consist of two realities ("partial substances") but is the one and constantly total reality of the anima "inasmuch as it is only really itself in real being-outside-itself . . . and as body".[12] Similarly the biblical distinction between σῶμα and σάρξ is not mentioned and there is no explanation of the antithesis between σάξρ and πνεῦμα. It is consequently not apparent that the Bible always regards man as a totality and does not draw its distinctions from constitutive metaphysical parts of man but from the directions of his historical decisions. "Flesh" is not the same thing as body. "Body" (like "soul") simply denotes the whole human being as he appears to our experience as a living unity, and just as he comes from God's hands, as one single creature. "Flesh" denotes man as wilful, rejecting the divine claim. It also means man under the divine mercy which meets him in the Pneuma and causes him to become wholly a pneumatic existence (πὲν νεῦμα with the Lord: 1 Cor 6:17). Even G. Marcel's helpful distinction between "avoir — possession" and "avoir — implication" is not used in the text, though it makes it possible to distinguish "I have a body" from any other kind of having. It is only to the body that we can apply an "I have" which "on account of its interiority can also be an 'I am'."[13]

The only attempt to go beyond the mere schematism of the body-soul dualism and arrive at a new way of speaking adequate to the unity of the human being, consists in the concept of "interioritas", which introduces the

---

[12] J. B. Metz, "Leiblichkeit", HTG, II, pp. 30–37, quotation, p. 33.
[13] Cf. on this F. Böckle, "Zum Personenverständnis in der Moraltheologie", in J. Speck, Das Personenverständnis in der Pädagogik und ihren Nachbarwissenschaften (1966), pp. 172–88, especially p. 174.

second part of Article 14. Some Council fathers indeed thought that the word "smacks of Protestant pietism" (*modus* 6 on Article 14). The Commission rejected this objection, and rightly so, because the context points to a completely different origin. In the first place one is reminded of Teilhard de Chardin's "intériorité" which may very well have been the immediate occasion of this locution. For him it means that inner side of things which of course does not appear in the objects of physics and chemistry but is nevertheless a fundamental principle of all reality, without which one cannot ultimately understand anything of reality as a whole.[14] It is hardly necessary to say that the Council did not incorporate this view of the two-sided structure of the whole universe into its statements, but it probably drew partly on Teilhard's idea of "intériorité" in order to suggest a sort of intuitive representation of what "interiority" in man, his mind and spirit, means and is. A stronger influence on the content of the concept here is probably that of Pascal; the impress of the great Fragment 793, with its account of the orders of reality, is clearly perceptible. When it is said that by his interiority man transcends the whole universe of things, it is impossible not to notice the close resemblance to Pascal's words: "All bodies, the firmament, the stars, the earth and its kingdoms do not equal the least of the spirits; for the latter know all those things, whereas bodies know nothing."[15] And, finally, Augustine's theology of the interior life is perceptible behind the mention of "conversio ad cor", and of the depths where God awaits man. We hear the echoes of Augustine's spiritual experience that "intimum" and "summum" coincide, that the distant God is a God who is most near to man, nearer than man is to himself, that man is only far from God because he is far from himself, that man finds himself and God by accomplishing a pilgrimage to himself, into his own inner depths, away from self-estrangement among things. Thus our text is influenced by two fundamental concepts of Augustinian thought, by which the great Father of the Church aimed at a synthesis of biblical anthropology, more historical in tendency, with the metaphysical conception of antiquity. The first is the distinction between the "homo interior" and "exterior". As compared with the corpus-anima schema, this introduces a greater element of personal responsibility and decision regarding the direction of life. It therefore analyses man more on historical and dynamic than on metaphysical lines. The second is the concept of the "philosophia cordis", the biblical concept of the heart which for Augustine expresses the unity of interior life and corporeality. This again becomes a key concept with Pascal[16] and here enters the conciliar text, bringing

---

[14] *The Phenomenon of Man*, pp. 56–57.
[15] E. Brunschvicg, p. 697; cf. R. Guardini, *Christliches Bewusstsein* (2nd ed., 1950), pp. 40–46, 101 ff.
[16] Cf. Guardini, *op. cit.*, pp. 185–96.

with it by implication a good deal of what Karl Rahner and Gabriel Marcel have had to say on other grounds and from other angles.

Perhaps we may regard these concepts of heart and interiority, with all they imply and the mental horizons they open out, as the real theology of the body presented by this section. For theology of the body cannot ultimately consist of a purely regional theology concerning the body in contradistinction to the soul, and listing the merits of the body. Its function must be to understand the body as a human body, describing it in its humanity as the corporeal embodiment of mind and spirit, the way in which the human spirit has concrete existence. It must therefore be a theology of the unity of man as spirit in body and body in spirit, so that a genuine theology of the body will be achieved in proportion as the "cor" is spoken of as spirit "to the extent that it has come close to the blood" and therefore no longer merely spirit but embodied and therefore human.[17]

This context alone gives meaning to the various statements assembled in the brief encomium on the body which constitutes the first part of Article 14. Man, corporeal and spiritual, is, to use K. Rahner's phrase, "Spirit in world", i.e. through the body he gathers the whole world into the spirit and thus at the same time draws it into adoration. In him as the point of contact and compenetration of matter and spirit, matter adores its Creator. Here too various conceptual elements are perceptible. The very important neo-Platonic idea of "reductio" introduced into theology by Pseudo-Dionysius appears, i.e. the idea that man represents the terminus of the cosmic movement and brings it from the "emanatio" back again into the self-diffusive divine love.[18] The idea of the microcosm is present, but links up with Teilhard de Chardin's visions of adoration through matter, for his forceful language seems to be echoed here, though muted.[19] This gives the static conception of the microcosm a dynamic tendency. Man is not simply a reflection of the universe and its manifold composition, but is the point where its movement is transformed into adoration. What is expressed in the first sentences of this article in a great cosmic perspective is given a more individual and ethical sense in the last, with reference to 1 Cor 6:20. Man's body must serve to glorify God, not self-seeking. But it is probably correct to interpret this lesson in the light of the opening sentence; it thus regards St Paul's precept in a new light and adapts it to the circumstances of our time. Between the two there is a sort of short history of the body in the economy of redemption. Its components are creation — promise (resurrection) — responsibility. The mystery of the Alpha and the Omega, origin from the creative might of God and

---

[17] *Ibid.*, p. 187.

[18] On the historical background, cf. J. Ratzinger, *Die Geschichtstheologie des heiligen Bonaventura* (1959), pp. 140–8.

[19] Cf. Teilhard de Chardin, *Hymne de l'Univers* (1961), E. T.: *Hymn of the Universe*.

future in the Lord's redemptive love, constitute the present situation in which the body can be either a means of adoration or an instrument of rebellion. In the centre between origin and future, is the summons to decision.

At the request of one of the Council fathers, an explicit statement was inserted at the end of the article on the spirituality and immortality of the soul.[20] This decides nothing about the "anima separata" or the way in which immortality may be explained philosophically and theologically (in terms of nature, or dialogically, etc.). But it does exclude the dissolution of man into mere matter; for then survival could only be regarded as a pure miracle, a resurrection which would be a completely new creation. That would inevitably give rise to an insoluble paradox. What would continuity with the previous creature, a particular human being, consist in? Without continuity, the idea of resurrection from the dead is meaningless. The fact that the Council opposed the kind of intellectually woolly theories which are sometimes put forward nowadays as the results of once more taking biblical anthropology seriously, but which should really be regarded as products of intellectual inertia, is wholeheartedly to be welcomed. The language employed for the purpose, however, may be thought rather negligent and open to misconception. The conciliar statement obviously has another purpose also, that of pointing to the fact that man only attains the real truth of being when he goes beyond the zone of what is merely verified to be correct. The soul cannot be found in the realm of purely observable facts. Anyone who restricts himself to the latter may come to regard the soul as an abstract collective term for a multiplicity of elements which can be accounted for as the reflex of physical (biological) and social factors. In fact to reject metaphysical statements on principle in this way, posits an anti-metaphysics, it makes a principle out of the methodological renunciation of truth in the exact sciences, which have to be positivist and therefore restricted to what can be correctly established. Consequently it does the most inhuman and destructive thing possible; it robs man in principle of the capacity to attain truth. Our text, on the other hand, sees the affirmation of the soul (i.e. man's spirituality) as an affirmation of metaphysics and therefore as the affirmation of man's capacity for truth, man's openness to truth. And contact with truth is not only possible to man, it is as necessary as love. Truth is the bread without which the mind cannot live.

Article 15. The three following articles (15–17) expound what human spirituality is under three aspects: as intellect (i.e. as man's capacity for truth), as conscience (i.e. as man's capacity for good), and as freedom. It is noticeable that the phenomenon of intersubjectivity, man's essential ordination to love, is not mentioned. Thus not only the modern philosophy of the

[20] Cf. *Relatio* on Text 5, p. 29.

person but even the term "person" plays no part. Yet modern Christian anthropology regards this term as its centre and as a specifically Christian insight into man. The concept of the person is a product of theology i.e. of the compenetration of biblical faith and Greek philosophy. It was formed in the endeavour to elaborate the Christian conception of God (in Trinitarian doctrine and Christology), and apart from those contexts it is neither possible nor intelligible.[21] For the same reason it constitutes the link between doctrine about God and doctrine about man. The Christological controversies of the ancient Church were just as much concerned with God as with man, and it was through them that it became clear that the question about God can be expressed as the question about man, in the way the Pastoral Constitution does, and that, conversely, the question about man can only be carried to its conclusion as a theological question. The fact that this article does not deal with the I-Thou relationship or with the human spirit as love, is probably to be explained by the method of composition, which assigned the social phenomenon as a whole to Chapter II. In Text 5 Article 12, for example, sentences describing in rather greater detail the implication of the doctrine of the image of God for man's relations with others were deleted for that reason.[22] The disadvantage of this arrangement is that the philosophy of love, the whole set of I-Thou questions, are practically absent from the doctrine of man laid down as a basis. Consequently the constitutive character of these realities for human existence does not stand out as clearly as it could have done. The concept of the personal factor is thus almost completely lacking, although isolated elements are found in Chapters I and II.

The first sentence takes up again the Pascalian idea of the superiority of mind in comparison with the whole universe, but now applies specifically to the intellect what was previously said about "interiority" generally. This is entirely in line with Pascal, who also locates the superiority of mind in its capacity for knowledge. At the same time there is an echo of the medieval Augustinian tradition. When the intellect is described as a participation in the light of the divine mind, we hear an echo of the medieval doctrine of illumination, derived from Augustine, in its thomistically domesticated form, it is true.[23] And the idea of participation is another fundamental concept of a Christian metaphysics drawing its inspiration from Plato.[24] Both elements,

---

[21] J. Ratzinger, "Zum Personenverständnis in der Dogmatik", in J. Speck, op. cit., pp. 157–171; C. Andresen, "Zur Entstehung und Geschichte des trinitarischen Personbegriffs" ZNW 52 (1961), pp. 1–38.

[22] Relatio, B, p. 28.

[23] On the doctrine of illumination, cf. especially É. Gilson, La philosophie de saint Bonaventure (2nd ed., 1943), pp. 274–346, E. T.: Philosophy of Bonaventure; J. Ratzinger, "Licht", HTG, II, pp. 44–54, especially pp. 51 f.

[24] On this see in particular the penetrating study of G. Söhngen, "Thomas von Aquin über Teilhabe durch Berührung", Die Einheit in der Theologie (1952), pp. 107–39; W. Pesch and R. Schlette, "Teilhabe", HTG II, pp. 630–41 (with bibliography).

the metaphysics of light and the ontology of participation, are only mentioned, not developed further. But they indicate the background of Augustinian tradition which the authors of the text had in mind. They are therefore of some importance for the interpretation of the Pastoral Constitution, and for placing it in its intellectual context. Despite the inspiration of Teilhard de Chardin's progressive views and of other elements of modern thought, the tradition of Christian metaphysics forms the real intellectual background of the text.

This is also clearly apparent in the pair of terms "scientia-sapientia", on which the present article is built. Full recognition is given to the important advances achieved by the human mind in the field of science and technology in making the material world serviceable to mankind. But it asserts no less emphatically that science is only one form of activity of the human mind, which does not exhaust its capacity and even omits the specifically human element, which only finds scope in wisdom. It is interesting to note here how the concept of science formulated by Augustine as the opposite pole to wisdom, closely resembles the present-day conception of science. *Scientia* in Augustine's sense deals with the *mundus sensibilis;* it makes the latter capable of manipulation by *ars* (τέχνη). In this way it makes possible the practical use *(uti)* of the world, but it is limited to the phenomenal, to appearances, which is what is meant by sensible things in contradistinction to non-phenomenal, non-sensible, genuine reality. It is therefore useful to man *(uti — usus)*, but does not give him truth. So it remains ambivalent, because it does not indicate what use man actually puts his technique to. Indeed it is dangerous if it takes itself to be ultimate and exhaustive, for then instead of "use" it becomes "enjoyment" *(frui)*, which holds man back from the genuine.[25] This Platonically-inspired conception of science as knowledge of phenomena, is very close to the view held in the natural sciences, with its necessary methodological positivism and its exclusion of the question of ontological truth. This Augustinian concept gave the authors of this article the opportunity to insist once again today on the need for *sapientia*. Augustine defines it as the possibility of advancing from the visible to the invisible and of going beyond phenomena to the "intelligible reality" which is capable of giving man true certainty. These statements recall the formulas of Vatican I on the possibility of attaining with certainty a knowledge of God by reason. In both cases it is also admitted that as a result of sin man has been obscured and weakened. In fact the theme of the two Councils is ultimately the same; the question of metaphysics and the question of God are fundamentally the same. The problem of God is not a supplementary section of metaphysics, but is posited simultaneously with the question of being itself, while con-

---

[25] Cf. G. Söhngen, "Wissenschaft und Weisheit im augustinischen Gedankengefüge", *Die Einheit in der Theologie* (1952), pp. 101–6.

versely, the question of being implies the question of God. Consequently the present text simply deepens the statements of Vatican I by inserting the problems connected with the question of God into the context of the relation between *scientia* and *sapientia*. In this way it exhibits the specific form of knowledge of God in contradistinction to the world of modern science. At the same time the reference to sin as endangering knowledge of God only assumes its full meaning in this light, for purely objective, demonstrative knowledge is of course not hindered by sin. With *sapientia*, on the other hand, what is involved is man's very humanity, and this is hampered by his tendency to be inhuman or less than human. Only where he is light can he see the real light; but since so often he is darkness and aversion from the light, he sees nothing. The dynamic character of the metaphysics of light, in which knowing and being are inseparable and both are envisaged as vital activities, makes plain the demands made on man in his totality by knowledge of God (and by the knowledge of "truth" generally). The affirmation of metaphysics which Articles 14 and 15 formulate with regard to the question of man and of God, is one of the fundamental positions of the schema. Where the metaphysical question is definitely rejected, the "death of God" is the inescapable consequence. But equally inescapable is the mutilation of man of the dimension of wisdom, and any theology which survives is inconsequential chatter.

By employing the "scientia-sapientia" framework, the text also arrives once more at its chief guiding idea, that of "humanum", and this makes it possible to carry out the programme of discernment which the Pastoral Constitution set itself. Critical distinctions can now be drawn on this basis in the concept of progress. The advance of science and of the techniques which it makes possible, brings no certain assurance of man's future, which continues to be threatened if a lack of wisdom runs parallel with the growth of knowledge. What is new, the discoveries of the human mind, is not automatically something intrinsically more humane; it has first to be humanized by wisdom. The humanization of man is not accomplished by science alone. Whether or not scientific advances actually represent human progress is determined in each instance by man himself. Here therefore, all mechanical faith in science and hope in the liberating force of technological progress is called in question by the principle of "wisdom" as what is essentially human. At the same time there is a possibility on this basis of doing justice to the nations and cultures referred to as "developing countries", that is, which are only at the beginning of technical progress, but through their unbroken continuity in wisdom can make a contribution to the human family as a whole no less valuable than the industrial achievements of economically more advanced nations.

The concluding reference to the wisdom of faith gives a certain impression of having been added from outside. Behind it is an attempt to keep the natural and supernatural orders separate, and this tends to make both appear rather questionable. Augustine's idea of *sapientia,* on the other hand, expresses a conception in which the two were still envisaged in inseparable unity, as man's one openness to truth. This indeed involves a hierarchy according to the measure of man's light or darkness, but it cannot be cut up into two domains.

Article 16. Since Newman and Kierkegaard, conscience has occupied with new urgency the centre of Christian anthropology. The work of both also represented in an unprecedented way the discovery of the individual who is called directly by God and who, in a world which scarcely makes God known any more, is able to become directly certain of God through the voice of conscience. At the same time, for Newman, conscience represents the inner complement and limit of the Church principle. Over the pope as the expression of the binding claim of ecclesiastical authority there still stands one's own conscience, which must be obeyed before all else, if necessary even against the requirement of ecclesiastical authority.[26] This emphasis on the individual, whose conscience confronts him with a supreme and ultimate tribunal, and one which in the last resort is beyond the claim of external social groups, even of the official Church, also establishes a principle in opposition to increasing totalitarianism. Genuine ecclesiastical obedience is distinguished from any totalitarian claim which cannot accept any ultimate obligation of this kind beyond the reach of its dominating will.

For its purposes our text, of course, does not go into such problems directly but simply presents the general outline of a Christian doctrine of conscience. But merely by the weight it attributes to the subject of conscience within the framework of its doctrine of man, it takes its place in the line of thought deriving from Newman. As opposed to any purely sociological or psychoanalytic interpretation of conscience, it affirms its transcendent character; it is the "law written in the heart by God", the holy place in which man is alone with God and hears God's voice in his innermost centre. This, of course, simplifies the problem, passes over the epistemological question and excludes the psychological and sociological factors which cannot in fact be left out of account in considering conscience as it actually is. How conscience can err if God's call is directly to be heard in it, is unexplained. As in previous articles, we cannot but observe at this point the inadequate use made of the insights of modern philosophy and allied disciplines, which here makes it particularly difficult to avoid an impression of pre-critical thought. Modern thought for the most part supplied only the general impulse, in the present case the intention to do justice to the individual and his conscience, in Newman's sense. On the other hand, the specific findings to which those modern tendencies have led, are scarcely touched on. What prevails is a

[26] See the texts in A. Läpple, *Der Einzelne in der Kirche* (1962), p. 262.

scholastic tradition freed from the framework of the schools and looser in structure.[27]

As well as the transcendence of conscience, its non-arbitrary character and objectivity are emphasized. The fathers were obviously anxious (as, of course, was repeatedly shown in the debate on religious freedom also) not to allow an ethics of conscience to be transformed into the domination of subjectivism, and not to canonize a limitless situation ethics under the guise of conscience. On the contrary, the conciliar text implies that obedience to conscience means an end to subjectivism, a turning aside from blind arbitrariness, and produces conformity with the objective norms of moral action. Conscience is made the principle of objectivity, in the conviction that careful attention to its claim discloses the fundamental common values of human existence. The epistemological optimism which once again finds expression here is only qualified by the final observation that negligence in the search for the values of truth and goodness and the habit of sin can dull and practically blind the conscience. This passage was inserted in Text 5 in order, as the *relatio* said, to express the "pessimistic aspect" on which many fathers insisted. Yet it is significant that here too the problem is not examined in the light of principles but only factually. Blindness to values is presented as a danger to individuals who remain too much in the darkness. But that general crisis of the human mind in regard to moral good, which so deeply disturbed Luther's thought, does not come into the field of vision of the conciliar text. Certainly it can quote Rom 2:14 ff. with some justification for its view. Paul shows there that he was convinced that there is a law written in men's hearts which even among sinful mankind makes it possible for every individual to know the essential will of God.

With Paul the content of this unwritten law remains indeterminate. The present article attempts to specify it more precisely from the New Testament as a whole, by means of the Christian epitomization of the Law in the double precept of love of God and the neighbour. Though it is impossible to affirm that an explicit reference was intended, this recalls the beginning of the *Decretum Gratiani:* "Ius naturale est, quod in lege et evangelio continetur, quo quisque iubetur alii facere, quod sibi vult fieri et prohibetur alii inferre, quod sibi nolit fieri." In this important text, the natural law is identified with the Golden Rule and thereby equated with the kernel of the gospel. By pursuing the same idea, the present article arrives once more at the essential leitmotiv of the whole Constitution. For if the simple voice of conscience, which discloses the whole will of God, consists in the precept of love, then what it commands is ultimately man's "humanity" — being

[27] On the history of the problem and the present state of the question in regard to conscience, see J. Stelzenberger in *HTG* I, pp. 519–28.

human in the full sense. At the same time it is clear what the content of "humanity" actually involves in the field of action. Even the formal definition of good will takes on definite content. A good will is a will which is in accordance with conscience, a consent to the love which makes man human. This gives concreteness to the statement of the Constitution on the Church that life according to conscience leads to salvation. Ultimately conscience does not concern merely a law, even less does it represent the purely formal imperative that action must conform to particular existing religious and national ordinances. With its summons to humanity as consisting in that double love, it concerns at the same time the kernel of the gospel. Above all, however, conscience is presented as the meeting-point and common ground of Christians and non-Christians and consequently as the real hinge on which dialogue turns. Fidelity to conscience unites Christians and non-Christians and permits them to work together to solve the moral tasks of mankind, just as it compels them both to humble and open inquiry into truth. In this essential kernel the "objectivism" of the schema is certainly right and not vulnerable to critical thought. What is unsatisfactory is simply the way the concrete form of the claim of conscience is dealt with, the inadequate view of the facts of experience and the insufficient account taken of the limits of conscience.

As regards the binding force of erroneous conscience, the text employs a rather evasive formula. It merely says that such a conscience does not lose its dignity. We must note here that the thesis emphatically asserted by J. B. Metz in particular, that Aquinas was the first definitely to teach the obligatory force of an erroneous conscience, is historically and objectively the case only to a certain extent and with considerable qualifications. Historically speaking, Aquinas here is following Aristotelian intellectualism, according to which only what is presented to the will by reason can be its object; and the will is always in the wrong if it deviates from reason. It cannot once again control the reason, it has to follow it; it is consequently bad if it contradicts reason, even if reason is in error. In reality, Aquinas's thesis is nullified by the fact that he is convinced that error is culpable. Consequently guilt lies not so much in the will which has to carry out the precept laid upon it by reason, but in reason itself, which *must* know about God's law.[28] The doctrine of the binding force of an erroneous conscience in the form in which it is propounded nowadays, belongs entirely to the thought of modern times.

Article 17. The section on freedom, in which the Constitution deliberately takes up a theme of modern thought, is one of the least satisfactory in the

[28] *Summa Theologica*, 1a 2ae, q. 19, a. 5, 6; *Quaes. disp. de veritate* q. 17, a. 3 corp. and ad 4, ad 5, 8. J. B. Metz had presented his thesis in his book *Christliche Anthropozentrik* (1962), p. 60, and based on it his contention that the "anthropological turning-point" occurred with Aquinas.

whole document. The entire New Testament doctrine of freedom was completely excluded after Text 5, and as a result the standpoint adopted is, for the Christian, quite simply an unreal one. The omission of Christology from the doctrine of the image and likeness of God, with which the idea of freedom is linked here, once again imposes its consequences. The attempt to lead up to the Christian doctrine of man from outside, and thus to render what faith affirms about Christ gradually accessible, has led to the mistaken decision to leave aside for the present what essentially belongs to the Christian faith, as being supposedly less susceptible of dialogue. In reality this approach would only have had point if it had really led step by step to the kernel of the New Testament message, disclosing this in the midst of what is human, and so had manifestly opened out the perspective onto Christ. It was not wise to remain as far as possible in what is pre-Christian and then bring in Christ without preparation at the end. The Council fathers had rightly criticized Text 4 for confusing the New Testament saving gift of freedom conferred in Christ with the purely philosophical idea of freedom of choice. It can scarcely have been those speakers' intention that as a consequence the specifically Christian statements should be to a large extent struck out.

The choice of the two biblical texts quoted in this article is characteristic (Ecclus 15:14 and 2 Cor 5:10). The tribunal of Christ, of which Paul speaks, has tacitly become the judgment-seat of God. This transfers the text from the perspective of faith to that of natural theology, which is also that of the Sirach passage. Through the latter, recourse had been had to that trend in late Jewish wisdom theology which was marked by ethical optimism. It developed something resembling a *theologia naturalis,* or, even more, an *ethica naturalis.* This, however, must be read in the light of the critical wisdom theology of Job and Ecclesiastes, which both (Job quite explicitly) criticize the optimistic wisdom doctrine. It should also have been taken into account that Ecclus 15:14 is a moralizing and individualistic reinterpretation of Deut 11:26 ff., which in Jer 21:8 undergoes a striking pragmatic modification, and stands at the starting-point of the Jewish ethical doctrine of the two ways. If Jer 21:8 is rooted in the concrete situation of beleaguered Jerusalem, the statement of Deut 11:26 is entirely determined by the theology of the Covenant. The Thou who is addressed is Israel, which in God's offer of the Covenant receives the choice between life and death. Consequently in using such texts the Christian cannot leave out of account the actual history of the Covenant, cannot exclude the fact that Israel — representing mankind — was not in a position to carry out what the Covenant offered, but inevitably experienced the Law as a yoke "which neither our fathers nor we have been able to bear" (Acts 15:10). It is impossible to prescind from the fact that the promised life ultimately came not from freedom in fulfilling the Law but from the death of him who allowed himself in accordance with the Law to hang on the tree as a transgressor of the Law (Gal 3:12 ff.). To tear Ecclus 15:14 from these contexts in the history of revelation and to use it in support of a colourless philosophical doctrine of freedom, represents not only an unhistorical reading of Scripture but also an unhistorical and therefore unreal view of man. The general doctrine of freedom developed in the conciliar text cannot therefore stand up either to theological or to philosophical criticism. Philosophically speaking, it by-passes the whole modern discussion on freedom. It simply takes no account of that overshadowing of freedom of which psychology and sociology at the present time inform us in such a disturbing way. Consequently it shuts itself out from the factual situation of man whose freedom only comes into effect through a lattice of determining factors. Theologically speaking, it leaves aside the whole complex of problems which Luther, with polemical onesidedness, comprised in the term "servum arbitrium". The whole text gives scarcely a hint of the discord which runs through man and which is described so dramatically in Rom 7:13-25. It even falls into downright Pelagian terminology when it speaks of man "sese ab omni passionum captivitate liberans finem suum persequitur et apta subsidia . . . procurat". That is not balanced by the following sentence, which logically is scarcely linked with it and which speaks of a wound inflicted by sin but regards grace only as a help to make the will once more "plene actuosam". The extent of the human dilemma, which is not constituted by the modest difference between "plene actuosus" and "actuosus", but calls man in question to his very depths and makes him unfree, is not taken even roughly into account here. Fundamentally, the formula "plene actuosus" means that an at all events semi-Pelagian representational pattern has been retained. One cannot escape the impression that here the theologically quite justifiable will to optimism which dominates the whole text has been misinterpreted and has led to anodyne formulas which it need not necessarily have given rise to at all. If optimism in John XXIII's sense means readiness for today and tomorrow, if it means abandoning nostalgia for the past for a spirituality of hope in the midst of each particular present moment, then it does not in any way impose the platitudes of an ethics modelled on that of the Stoa. Here it would have been possible to learn from Marxism about the extent of human alienation and decadence. Not to take them seriously does not mean to think highly of man, but to deceive him about the gravity of his situation.

The fact that the problems of human freedom were not really raised, also meant that only freedom of choice was dealt with, and the full extent of the theme of liberty was not perceived. The actual ontological content of the idea of freedom, the capacity to accept one's own nature and to become identified with it, is just as little realized as the dialogue character of human freedom, which is only brought to the full possibilities of its realization by that appeal of love which can never be forced upon it. But only on this basis would it have been possible to show that God's summons, under which man stands, is not in opposition to his freedom but makes it truly possible; that human freedom does not consist in abstract selection between different possibilities of behaviour, but by its very nature lives in the presence of God and can only be really understood in relation to this vis-à-vis. Only on this basis would it also be possible to explain the perfect fulfilment of Christian freedom in the "freedom of the children of God", whereas the conciliar text is incapable of opening any access to its significance.

Despite all the objections that can be brought against the text in this way, it is important also to consider its positive intentions. It is primarily concerned to make a positive affirmation of the value of freedom expressly on the basis of faith; for modern man experiences that value more and more explicitly, even though the idea of freedom is becoming progressively more problematic. Of course here — once again because of the structure of the text — it is not intended to extend that affirmation to the whole range of the idea of freedom, social or political for example, but only to the psychological plane. Nevertheless it is done with the intention of establishing the starting-point for the concept of freedom and on that basis to affirm man as the free being who must himself decide to be himself and who may not be subjected either to external coercion or to the compulsion of instinct (which nowadays offers the real lever for the social manipulation of man). On the other side, the Council was concerned to oppose that confusion of freedom with absence of commitment which is beginning to a considerable extent to represent the guiding idea of public opinion today, and which is used precisely as a means to manipulate mankind. With the help of this fallacious image of freedom, people are robbed of their freedom and put at the disposition of powers which anonymously control the intellectual and economic market.[29] Finally, the conciliar text is concerned to state man's moral responsibility in opposition to any kind of determinism. In the background a paradox of our present intellectual situation is also perceptible. On the one hand this is determined wholly by the demand for freedom and is opposed to any tie; on the other hand, as opposed to the phenomenon of morality, it stresses the discoveries of determinism. It endeavours to transfer to man the results of researches into animal behaviour, and insists on the inescapability of statistical laws of behaviour. In opposition to this, the text professes man's moral freedom and also opposes it, with complete biblical justification, to any theological determinism. However much the New Testament, as we indicated above, may speak of the decadence and impotence of man, it nevertheless always expressly affirms the moral responsibility of all men; despite the important aspects calling for consideration which it expresses, Luther's "servum arbitrium" cannot be maintained on New

[9] Cf. the important study of W. Dreier, *Funktion und Ethos der Konsumwerbung* (1965).

Testament grounds. All these intentions would doubtless have been more effectual if they had been more critically explicated. But even so they remain significant and important, and represent an important positive contribution which the text can make, despite its weaknesses, to the controversy about man.

Article 18. The introduction of the problem of death into the outline doctrine of man given in the Pastoral Constitution, involved the transition from a purely essentialist treatment to a presentation taking into consideration the plane of existence. It is certainly no accident that it is only here, in a fragment of existential analysis, that Christological themes find expression (apart from the newly incorporated Article 13, which is likewise concerned with the existential plane). The structure of the text is not uniform, it is true; three levels can readily be distinguished. There is first an attempt to view the whole question of being human on the basis of the fundamental phenomenon of death. This is rather like the analysis of a fundamental constitutive feature of human life. Then there is the ontological level of thought, in the sense of traditional metaphysics. Finally we move on to the theological plane of the history of salvation, the Christological plane.

The text therefore begins by showing that death is not merely an extrinsic moment at the end of a life unaffected by it, nor merely a biological process which fundamentally has nothing to do with what is really human, but that it is a constant determining aspect of human life. In the process of dissolution and in the phenomenon of pain, it is constantly present in life itself. As the dread of nothingness it permeates man's whole existence. Man continually experiences death as in contradiction to being, showing his own existence to be beyond his own control. The possibility of death, which is beyond his power to manipulate, shows him that existence is his and yet not his. All his planning and calculation comes up against the limit set by what cannot be planned, and encounters the phenomenon of limit as such, the power of what is simply other than himself. The text emphasizes this aspect by showing the non-naturalness, the existential absurdity of death. Man's being cries out for self-possession, for certainty about itself, for eternity; it is identical as it were with a will to exist always. At the same time, however, it is characterized by the presence of nothingness, of the end, which thus as dread (timor — abhorret — respuit) gives man's existence its typical form. Within the framework of an official pronouncement of the magisterium which offers points of view but could not aim at giving a developed philosophy or theology of death, it was doubtless not possible to extend this line of thought and so present the intrinsic unity of the various levels of the theme more clearly than was actually done. Otherwise the question of the desire for immortality would have had to be specified more clearly. In fact people nowadays often object to the assertion that they want to live for ever. They say they know nothing about it and are quite reconciled to their transitoriness. To this it may be replied in the first place that such statements mostly spring from a situation in which man has not yet really been face to face with the question of death. Man only really becomes aware of his own contradiction to the phenomenon of the end when he has become aware of, and experienced, the end as a reality, as an intrinsic constituent of himself. Conversely it must also be taken seriously into consideration that man does not in fact wish for an endless prolongation of his present reality. The real form of his desire for eternity is better expressed by Nietzsche's words, "All pleasure wants eternity". It is only the moments in which man attains or thinks he attains authentic life, that he does not want to see pass away; in them the inauthenticity of his ordinary life becomes palpable to him; in the light of such moments it does not really seem like life at all. At the same time, of course, he realizes that an authentic life would have to be eternal and that the passing away of what is authentic is like a wound, a contradiction within himself. On the basis of this phenomenon of absurdity, shown above all in dread, as well as on that of the difference between authentic and inauthentic life, it would have been possible to make clearer the meaning of the statement which appears rather disconnected in the latter half of the article, to the effect that man would have been immune from bodily death if he had not sinned. This thesis in its classical dogmatic form is scarcely intelligible to present-day thought, but could be made so by means of an existential analysis of the constitutive features of human life which established a distinction between death as a natural phenomenon and death as seen in the personal categories proper to human life. It is clear that the authors were at all events conscious of these questions, because they rejected the various proposed alterations asking for mention to be made in this context of the preternatural gifts.[30] The problems connected with this "natural" terminology were deliberately kept out of the text. The same caution was evident in the careful procedure followed in Article 13 in regard to original sin and man's original condition. To a certain extent, the ideas we have just outlined are perceptible in the text. It explicitly says that technical improvements are no answer to the phenomenon of dread (as mirroring the nothingness which dwells in existence because of the line drawn by death). It points out that biological lengthening of life, made possible by modern medicine, has nothing to do with the demand for eternity implicit in human existence. What man needs is not as lengthy as possible a prolongation from day to day, even on a less intense level, of a life threatened by death (quite apart from the problems created for mankind as a whole by such a biological extension of life), but the authentic life which he seldom comes in contact with but to which all his longing is directed.

The classical philosophical doctrine of immortality finds only brief ex-

---

[30] *Modi* 8 and 9, Text 6, p. 170.

pression by implication, when it is said that man bears within him a seed of immortality which cannot be reduced to mere matter. This statement is not harmonized with the Christological soteriology of the latter part of the article. This does not start with enduring ontological components — transitory matter, non-transitory, non-material being — but regards the necessity of death and the promise of immortality historically: Death comes from sin, eternity from the saving work of Jesus Christ. Every attempt to explain the relation between the two statements, and between the ontological and the Christological viewpoints, fails. This is probably due to the fact that the authors were determined not to use traditional terms such as "nature", "preternatural", "supernatural", but did not find it possible to describe the coordination of ontology and history without the nature-supernatural framework. In this respect there is a striking difference of stress between Articles 14 and 18. The first uses as a matter of course the classical terminology of "anima spiritualis et immortalis"; in the second, all the emphasis falls on the historical consideration that eternal life is made possible by the saving work of the Lord. Philosophical thought only intervenes indirectly, when it is said that faith, linked with solid arguments, provides man with an answer to his anxiety. The trust in arguments referred to here, is astonishing. It is probably to be explained in the first place by scholastic tradition and its habit of linking *fides* and *praeambula fidei* or *fides* and *argumenta*. On the other hand, it certainly springs from the endeavour to make the Pastoral Constitution a dialogue with unbelievers. They have to be shown not only what faith promises, but also its reasonableness. At the same time it ought to be clear that statements like that about man's eternal life, can by their very nature only be statements of faith. Their rationality must be exhibited as the reasonableness of faith and as such, of course, is to be demanded.

In a positive sense, the Christological promise is expounded in three directions: as a promise of eternal community of man with God, as a promise of the new communication of men with one another in Christ, and finally as a reference to Christ's community with us in death, which at the same time guarantees and includes our communion of life with him. Here for the first time the Easter mystery appears as the centre of Christology and as the centre of Christian personal life as such. Archbishop Garrone had expressly referred to this point of view in his *relatio* to Text 4 on 21 September 1965. He declared that the analysis should have started in the depth of faith, especially in belief in creation and in the paschal mystery. In view of previous Catholic theology, and especially with the Christological renewal which had taken place in Germany between the wars and which was generally perceptible in connection with the Chalcedon celebrations, that may seem rather surprising. Catholic theology in fact from the time of the Greek Fathers, and again with Aquinas and once again with new urgency in the last few decades, has viewed Christology entirely in the perspective of the Incarnation. That the design of the Pastoral Constitution names creation and Easter as the two foci of the theological ellipse, probably also points to the impulse received from Teilhard de Chardin, and to the strange confirmation which his life was given when he was granted his wish to die at Easter — with eyes fixed on Christ whom he, thinking in paschal terms, had known much more as Omega than as Alpha.

Article 19. The Zurich text (Text 3) discussed by the Council in the autumn of 1964 contained no section on atheism. On the other hand the encyclical *Ecclesiam Suam,* published on 6 August 1964, dealt with it in some detail, though it still identified atheism largely with communism and considered dialogue with it to be scarcely possible: "In these circumstances dialogue is very difficult, not to say impossible ... Instead of dialogue, therefore, there is silence ... How can a dialogue be conducted in such circumstances as these, even if we embarked upon it? It would be but 'a voice crying in the wilderness'." It nevertheless prescribed the specific task of discovering the hidden causes which confuse men and lead them to deny God. In the case of atheists who as scientists are pursuing rigorous logical thought, it is suggested that they should be helped not to stop prematurely on the road of thought but to push it forward right to the primordial truth itself. And when they are working on practical assistance for men's life in the world, their action should be led back to its Christian sources.[31] No doubt this text was not without influence on the conciliar debate, where the encyclical was repeatedly quoted. But even apart from this, the subject of atheism must inevitably have presented itself in the Council's attempt to pursue discussion between faith and the modern world. In fact in the general debate as well as in the debate on Chapter I, the theme was constantly mentioned in a great variety of ways. As far as I can ascertain, the first speaker to deal with it, and he raised it at once to a very high plane, was Cardinal Silva Henríquez of Santiago (Chile) on 20 October 1964. He pointed out the humanist character of modern atheism, which cannot be met by a mere condemnation but can only be given a Christian answer in terms of Christ as the new man. True Christian anthropology lies in the mystery of Christ, "which is not only the epiphany of God but also the epiphany of man in his plenitude".[32] This showed the decisive point from which a maeutic of belief in God can start, taking present-day mentality into account. It pointed the way for a new conciliar text on the theme of atheism as a question about man which would show Christian faith in God to be the answer to the question about man. Furthermore, the Cardinal had correctly seen the fundamental spiritual direction to follow, for he declared

---

[31] Vatican Edition 1964, pp. 48 f.
[32] Quoted from L. A. Dorn and G. Denzler, *Tagebuch des Konzils* III (1965), p. 208.

that one task of the schema would be to outline an eschatology on the basis of the risen Christ. He thus recognized that modern man's orientation towards the future presents a problem for the Church's proclamation of the faith. He therefore called for eschatology to be centred in a personalist way in Christology, and Christology itself in the Easter mystery. On the very next day atheism was dealt with by a series of speakers, especially Cardinal Suenens who (in contrast to Silva) first spoke against the militant forms of present-day atheism but, like him, demanded that the phenomenon be taken seriously instead of merely condemned. He developed the idea, which has also found place in the text, that many people who deny God are merely rejecting a caricature of God and do not know the living God of faith at all. In following days two opposite tendencies emerged among speakers on atheism. One group demanded a condemnation of communism, in particular Franić of Split, Yü Pin of Formosa, formerly Nanking, Bolatti of Rosario, Argentine, and, in substance, Stimpfle of Augsburg. On the other side stood the line begun by Cardinal Silva, which once again found a well-informed spokesman in the person of the Auxiliary Bishop of Madrid, Guerra Campos. In the course of his Council speech, he attempted to clarify the problems of Marxist atheism and thereby provided some valuable suggestions regarding the form of discussion with atheism.[33] Cardinal Alfrink returned to the theme on 5 November 1964, associating himself with this positive tendency.[34]

In accordance with these suggestions, the Ariccia text (Text 4) was given a separate and fairly detailed section on atheism, and the fundamental structure and tendency of this were retained in the final version. On 26–27 September 1965, there was another significant and urgent debate on the problem of atheism, and the two schools of thought clashed even more sharply and insistently than the previous year. The highlights were the speeches of Cardinals König and Šeper and of Patriarch Maximos Saigh. Šeper pointed expressly to the partial responsibility of Christians for the spread of atheism, and the need for a new attitude on their part. König above all traced the roots of atheism in the history of ideas. Maximos called for a thorough examination of conscience by the Church. "Some have asked for the schema to affirm the sin of the world. But the great and enormous sin of the world which Jesus constantly scourges in the gospels is egotism and exploitation of man by man. Some have asked for the text to speak chiefly of the need to bear the cross ... But who in fact bears a heavier cross than the working masses of the poor who try to better their lot by work, solidarity and socialization? ... Isn't it the egotism of certain Christians which has chiefly caused and is causing the atheism of the masses? Let us therefore have the courage to restore the moral values of solidarity, fraternity, socialization to

[33] Text in Hampe, *op. cit.*, III, pp. 576–80.
[34] Text *ibid.*, p. 580 f.

their roots, which are Christian roots. Let us show that true socialism is Christianity when it is lived to the full by the just distribution of goods and the fundamental equality of all ... If we had lived and preached the gospel to the full, we would have spared the world atheistic communism. Instead of sending the world of work a banal condemnation with which it has long been familiar, let us send more and more priests and laymen, to share the life of toil and the social effort of the men of our time ..."[35] On the other side there was a forceful speech from Bishop Hnilica, originally from Czechoslovakia, who has himself suffered imprisonment and who spoke of the mystery of Satan which must be opposed by the mystery of love. Even more emphatic were the speeches of the exiled Ukrainian Rusnack and the Ruthenian Niclos Elko, who lives in the USA and who described dialectical materialism as the real dragon of our time, an armada of the anti-Christians and the plague of modern society, which cannot be met with anything but a solemn condemnation.[36] Cardinals Florit and Slipyi spoke in a more conciliatory sense, though the latter it is true tacitly criticized Patriarch Maximos by remarking that at all events the Marxists themselves would not confirm his diagnosis of the reasons for their success. In their opinion, Marxism does not owe its success among the working masses to the faults of Christians, but to its intrinsic correctness. A militant programme of action was developed by the General of the Society of Jesus, Arrupe, who regarded a central strategy of the Church's work, directed by the Pope, as the correct counter-measure to Marxism and atheism.

Cardinal König, who between the third and fourth sessions had been appointed President of the Secretariat for Non-believers, offered to draw up with the help of experts a new text on the problem of atheism. This proposal was accepted. A small subcommission was formed with König and Šeper as Council fathers and the Jesuits H. de Lubac and J. Daniélou as experts. In essentials the new text is based on their work. Three bishops from the Secretariat for Non-believers were added to the subcommission: Aufderbeck (Erfurt), Hnilica (Rome) and Kominek (Breslau); the same secretariat supplied the *periti* Frs. Miano and Girardi. In arrangement the text follows the proposal put forward by Cardinal König in his speech. It deals first with the forms and roots of atheism, then with its refutation and remedies. In view of the extremely many-sided problems, it is not surprising that the text that emerged was general and summary in character. A learned analysis, after all, was not the business of a Council. On the whole a balanced and well-founded statement had resulted from the thorough debate, and it may be counted among the most important pronouncements of Vatican II.

[35] From A. Wenger, *Vatican II, Chronique de la 4e session* (1966), pp. 151 f.
[36] L. A. Dorn and W. Seibel, *Tagebuch des Konzils* IV (1966), pp. 78 f. Cf. on the whole question the material in Wenger, *op. cit.*, pp. 149–63.

Its location is important in the first place. At first sight this may seem surprising, and in fact it was largely a result of chance. Nevertheless it is not without deeper justification. Very deliberately the question of atheism is dealt with in the framework of the question of man. This makes it clear that it does not simply express a metaphysical failure or a breakdown in epistemology, but draws its inspiration from an authentic desire for a true humanism. It must therefore be answered on the anthropological plane. Is God merely a projection of man or is it God who makes it possible for man to be human?

Its close proximity to the problem of death and thereby to the existential aspect of the Council's teaching on man is also important. Atheism is a question which can only be understood on the level of existence; a philosophy of pure essences cannot cope with it. Moreover, atheism comes up against its limit in the problem of death, to which it can give no answer. Finally, it is also important that the section on atheism is followed by the Christological article of the Pastoral Constitution. In answer to the denial of God for the sake of man, the Church professes its faith in the God who became man. To alleged self-projection of man, which is said to create God, it opposes the God who empties himself of what belongs to him in order to lead man to what is most his own. This adopts the line indicated by Cardinal Silva: in Christology, Christian faith in God shows itself to be a humanism of the new man, Jesus.[37]

It is probably merely chance that Article 19 begins with precisely the same words as the Declaration on Religious Freedom: "Dignitatis humanae..." At all events the link thus created is full of meaning. Only a faith which is grounded entirely on man's freedom and on respect for that freedom can meet the humanist promise made by present-day atheism, by advocating a better humanism. At the same time this opening (which also recalls the prayer at the addition of water to the wine in the Roman Mass, "... humanae substantiae dignitatem") foreshadows the contents of the whole. The faith that man is a partner speaking with God, called to enter into a community of love, created to see and love him, guarantees man a dignity which no one else can give him. It does not lower him but says the highest about him that could possibly be conceived.

In the next section the extraordinary variety of the phenomenon of atheism is described. Its various species are indicated in broad outline: sceptical, agnostic, positivist atheism, atheism for lack of religious experience — the problem of man's "incapacity for God", of the man who does not need to deny God at all but simply lives in the absence of God and scarcely seems to be aware at all of the question which this raises. The positive kind of

[37] Cf. on this H. Gollwitzer, "Das Gespräch des Konzils mit dem Atheismus des Ostens", in Hampe, *op. cit.*, III, pp. 596–603, especially p. 597.

atheism is also indicated which consists more in siding with man than against God ("magis ... ad affirmationem hominis quam ad Dei negationem"), a revolt against the inhumanity of the world and also, of course, a rebellion against the injustice, suffering and distress of this world generally: Job's question, but now transformed into the gesture of Prometheus.[38] This also touches on the causes of atheism: the theodicy problem to which Cardinal Florit had referred. Cardinal König's reference to the history of ideas has also been incorporated. The form of present-day civilization, the man-made world of technology, does not seem to open out any perspective on God any more in any way. Man everywhere encounters himself alone.[39] And of course, the obscuration of the idea of God is also mentioned. The God whom atheism denies is frequently merely an idol, a caricature of God. It has never learnt to know the true God, the face of the Father of Jesus Christ. This introduces a further cause, the guilt of Christians who have often hidden rather than revealed the face of God. In fact, it is surely terrible to realize, as Cardinal König pointed out in his conciliar speech, that atheism has its roots in the Western world, not in Asia or Africa: in other words that it has sprung up precisely where Christianity has been preached for 2,000 years. Every mere condemnation of others ends with this realization, and we must agree with Gollwitzer that a declaration on atheism is Christian only to the extent "that it is ready to do penance".[40] Only in the spirit of penance can Christians speak rightly about atheism today, for it is their fault too, and to that extent their affair, not simply that of others who can be contrasted with the good, and condemned.

Article 20. Separate from the sketch of the various kinds of atheism, a special article is devoted to two forms of atheism which are of particular importance for the intellectual situation at the present time. The first section of the article deals with "postulatory" atheism, the second with Marxist atheism. This was clearly intended to juxtapose the atheism widespread in the Western world and the atheism associated with communism, thus making it quite plain once more that the absence and denial of God are most definitely not limited to the communist countries. The free world has its own form of godlessness which very deeply affects its intellectual and spiritual character. In accord with the actual situation, the description of Western atheism is less specific, vaguer; we might most probably be led to think of N. Hartmann's reversal of Kant's postulates of the practical reason: human dignity and freedom no longer postulate that there is a God, but that there cannot be a God.[41] The authors, however, more likely had Sartre's existentialism in

---

[38] Gollwitzer, *ibid.*

[39] Cf. J. Frings, *Das Konzil und die moderne Gedankenwelt* (1962), pp. 17 ff.; J. Ratzinger, "Neuheidentum", *LTK* VII, cols. 907 ff.

[40] *Op. cit.*, p. 601.   [41] G. Söhngen, "Postulatstheologie", *LTK* VIII, cols. 644 f.

mind, which deliberately persists in a desert of pride without God: "Even if there were a valid proof of God's existence, no flight to transcendence would be allowed to man, for the sake of his dignity and humanity: no court of appeal in another world could free him from his freedom." [42] In addition there is the general mentality of people who are dazzled and fulfilled by technical progress and who therefore hope for man's redemption solely from more science, more action. They do not look for a saving God, for such expectation — waiting for Godot (S. Beckett) — to them is a meaningless and absurd gesture.

Understandably, the Council's attention was more engaged by the pronouncements on Marxism, which had a rather stormy passage. In connection with the debate on the first part of Schema 13 (Text 4), 22–28 September 1965, a group of bishops close to the Coetus Internationalis Patrum sent a proposed amendment to the General Secretary of the Council asking for an explicit condemnation of communism to be included. By an oversight of the Secretary of the Mixed Commission, Mgr. Glorieux, these *emendationes* did not reach the relevant subcommission, and the *relatio* on the revised text made no mention of them. It simply noted under heading B to Article 20 (p. 30) that two Fathers had asked for Marxist atheism to be mentioned by name at this point. "But the Commission did not think it should." Those who had signed the amendment were extremely indignant that their request had simply been passed over. The Steyl Press service, which was under the influence of Archbishop Sigaud, one of the heads of the Coetus Internationalis, expressed its indignation, and this was echoed by one section of the press. There was talk of 450 fathers having signed the petition. The matter was brought before the conciliar tribunal, and it turned out that the number who had signed was 334, 297 of whom had sent in their request at the proper time. As, however, no blame could be proved to lie with Mgr. Glorieux, who in those days was exceptionally burdened with proposed amendments, the démarche led to nothing. In any case the opinion in the commission was that the decision would have been negative, even if the petition had been brought to its notice, because it concerned the spirit and structure of the text, and this, after the generally favourable conciliar vote, could no longer be modified. The direction in which the commission would have made its decision was stated in a masterly way by Archbishop Garrone in his *relatio* on the *Textus emendatus*, 15 November 1965. "... ad hoc tendit textus, ut, si ab aliquo atheo legatur, nihil in expositione non verum inveniat; ut inde etiam Ecclesiae clamorem percipiat, de filiis oppressis et de mutilato homine 'sine Deo' crudeliter dolentis; sed nihilominus sciat et sentiat se ab Ecclesia vera et invincibili dilectione diligi." This took into account the

---

[42] Quoted from G. Flügel, "Der atheistische Marxismus als Frage an die Christen", in Hampe, *op. cit.*, III, pp. 604–15, quotation, p. 613.

essential aim of the 334 Council fathers and at the same time was in harmony with the spirit of the whole debate which had shown mere condemnation to be inadequate and had called for a new attitude. This attitude would in no way diminish the Church's profession of faith or its protest against injustice, violence and persecution. Nevertheless, even in the atheist it would recognize the human being who is the Church's responsibility and for whom it must endeavour to open a path to the gospel of Jesus Christ.

The vote which took place on the same day on the new text (5) of Chapter I, nevertheless confronted the commission once again with the problem which it had previously only been spared by chance. 220 fathers asked not only for express mention of communism but also that in addition to atheism "all its errors" should be condemned. They also wanted this part to deal exclusively with communism "as the chief error of the present day", and this must be done in detail. Ten fathers also supported the first of these three wishes (that communism be named) and four others wanted at least Marxism to be mentioned by name. One suggested quoting the passage from Paul VI's encyclical *Ecclesiam Suam*. In reply to these proposals as well as to another of similar tendency (listed as *modus* 12 in the *expensio modorum*) the commission declared that they would represent a substantial alteration of the text, which was no longer permissible. Furthermore, "communism" also comprises political and economic views which were not in debate here or which were positively dealt with in other passages of the schema. "Marxism" signifies a philosophical system requiring a far-ranging interpretation, consequently the word was better avoided here. The commission took this opportunity to explain what had happened about the 334 petitions of 29 September which had not been taken into account (see above)[43] and pointed out that the answer now given to the 220 also met the wishes expressed at that time. A small concession was nevertheless made to that group. In Article 21 the words "omni firmitate reprobet" (first paragraph) were extended by "sicut et antehac reprobavit". In addition there was a new footnote, 16 (Abbott 47), listing earlier condemnations of communism. The real purpose of the petitioners was not of course satisfied by this, especially as what for them was the decisive text was not included in the note, i.e. the Holy Office's decree of excommunication of 1 July 1949. Moreover, a text of John

---

[43] This declaration has been misunderstood by G. A. Wetter ("Konzil und Kommunismus", in Hampe, *op. cit.*, III, pp. 590–96, in particular p. 593) as though at the vote on 15 November 1965, 220 + 334 amendments had been handed in and 334 of these had not been forwarded and as though this was a separate event from the disregarded petition of 29 September, the number of signatories of which, according to Wetter, was "never known" (p. 592, n. 1). My account is based directly on the conciliar *Acta*; cf. also A. Wenger, *Vatican II, Chronique de la 4e session* (1966), pp. 164 ff.

XXIII (from *Mater et Magistra*) and of Paul VI (from *Ecclesiam Suam*) were added, thus indicating once again even in this note, that the question is in movement and that individual texts must each be read and understood in their own historical context. The procedure of the commission here recalls to some extent what was done in the mattter of birth control, where in a similar fashion the direct repetition of the norms of *Casti Connubii*, which was what was finally desired by the Pope himself, was avoided by a foot-note (14 on Part II, Chapter I) in which they insisted on mentioning in addition to the documents of Pius XI and Pius XII, Paul VI's allocution of 23 June 1964, thus once again, at least by implication, inserting the texts in a line of developing thought.

To the question whether the Council made a correct decision by refusing to name communism and condemn it afresh, divergent answers will be given according to people's differing standpoints. G. A. Wetter thinks that this silence is strange and regrettable; only the last-minute mood of the final session makes him feel that possibly the way chosen was the best way out, after all.[44] He points out that events in the contemporary world are "at least equally determined by the conflict with communism as by the population explosion, famine and the danger of atomic war". One must ask, he says, whether the short statements on atheism in general, only a small part of which concern communist atheism in particular, would offer the faithful the necessary assistance for them to get their bearings in these difficult questions.[45] H. Gollwitzer, on the other hand, says that "one must be very thankful for the basic tenor of these three sections".[46] And P. Delhaye expresses a similar opinion.[47] In fact we may say that the weapon of condemnation had been tried to the limit of possibility by the decree of 1 July 1949, and that it is no longer possible to deal with the problem in that way now. It is clear that the Church cannot but reject atheism and must oppose quite universally not only the persecution of the faithful but also the attack on human freedom generally. It is no less clear, however, that in addition it must reflect on its own share in the whole question of Marxism and the defectiveness of its own "humanism", and so accept the comprehensive question represented by Marxism as also concerning the Church itself. That the Church in Council decided on this step is the real drama behind Article 20, and makes it stand out like a milestone in the Church history of our century. It is scarcely less important than the decision represented by the Declaration on Religious Freedom. A new attitude is attained which will be fundamental for the possibility of announcing the faith within the structures

[44] G. A. Wetter, *op. cit.*, p. 596.
[45] *Ibid.*, pp. 590 and 595 f.
[46] Hampe, *op. cit.*, III, p. 599.
[47] P. Delhaye, "Die Würde der menschlichen Person", in Baraúna, *op. cit.*, pp. 170–7.

ind conditions of the present century. The examination of conscience prompted by this passage (from what it does not say even more than from what it does say), the shock to the habit of identifying what is Christian with the Western world, and the spur it gives to regard the suffering of the poor and the distress of the disinherited as a Christian task because Christianity must prove itself to be a humanism in order to subsist — this examination of conscience will provide more guidance in coming discussions than any elaborate presentation of communism and new condemnation could have offered.

Article 21. After presenting the various forms of atheism and its causes, Article 21 endeavours to formulate the answer of the Church to the challenge which is thus presented to it. The first two paragraphs of the article give the two sides of this answer. The Church can only say No to atheism as a thesis and reject it, but at the same time it must allow itself to be questioned by atheism. Atheism compels it to understand its own message more deeply by searching out the roots of atheism. For the latter could not have gained such a powerful hold over mankind if in its present form it did not correspond to a human question and to a dissatisfaction left in people by Christian preaching in the form it actually assumed. Since the Church exists for human beings and is hard-pressed by the duty of expounding the gospel to mankind, it must seek new ways to reach men. It must not "break a bruised reed or quench a smouldering wick" (Mt 12:20), but must allow itself to be led and impelled by the love of Christ which it owes to all men without exception. The service of evangelization to which the Church is called thus produces the two sides of its answer. On one hand it means that confession of the one God is opposed to the denial of God, but it likewise implies the obligation of ever renewed concern for human beings in order to understand them and so to be able to make itself understood.

Some details of these first two paragraphs also deserve to be mentioned. In the first place it is to be noticed that the No to atheism is not expressed by the word "damnat" ("condemn") but with "reprobat" ("reject"). In accordance with Pope John's wish that the Council should renounce condemnations, it avoided the word "damnare" on principle, even when it had to draw the line. The only text in which for a certain length of time the word "damnare" figured, was the Declaration on the Relationship of the Church to Non-Christian Religions, where anti-Semitism was "condemned". The fact that this too was changed to "reprobare" has of course frequently been regarded as an inexcusable weakening of the attitude adopted by the Council to the question of Israel. In reality it corresponds simply to a general terminological rule which we come across again here in regard to atheism, for of course there cannot be any doubt that it is decisively repudiated by the Church. The essential has already been said, in dealing with Article 20, about the extension of this "reprobatio" by the addition of footnote 16 (Abbott 47). At all stages of the text there was dispute about the formula which stated that the teachings and actions of atheism "contradict reason and common experience". The optimism in regard to the possibility of knowing God, which echoes in these words in a surprisingly unqualified way, occurs three times more in our text. At the end of the fourth paragraph it is said that God alone "fully and most certainly" provides an answer to the question of the enigma of man. At the beginning of the fifth paragraph it is said that the remedy for atheism is, among other things, to be sought from "a proper presentation of the Church's teaching". The same theme is scarcely recognizable in the last version of the text at the end of the penultimate paragraph, where the atheists are invited to examine the gospel of Christ without prejudice. The present passage certainly represents the central formulation of the idea. That a theologian of Karl Barth's school, H. Gollwitzer, scarcely knows what to make of this passage will not surprise anyone. "After all, God is not an object lying in front of the eyes of everyone, unseen only by people without sound common sense. (This is certainly affirmed by the Council when at the beginning of Article 21 it says that atheism contradicts 'reason and common human experience'; I am conscious that in my criticism I am speaking from the point of view of Protestant theology, but I am nevertheless very surprised that in the year 1965, after the long discussions about the rational knowledge of God, since Vatican I, the Council thinks it can speak in such an unqualified and undifferentiated way."[48])

Before we form a judgment on the text, let us try to examine rather more closely its prehistory and what it is in fact intended to affirm. The first form of the article on atheism (Text 4) had said that the doctrines and modes of action of atheism contradict universal human experience. Conversely, the atheists were invited to consider whether they could support their opposition to God with valid reasons not open to objection ("rationibus validis atque puris fulcire"). Here, therefore, the impossibility of demonstrating atheism was affirmed, and the opinion was expressed that the atheist who begins thoroughly to verify the speculative grounds of his position will come up against the insecure basis of his denial of God. At the same time the conviction was formulated that atheism contradicts the whole experience of mankind and that belief in God therefore imposes itself as necessary on grounds of human experience. The only qualification that the text admitted, consisted in the fact that it did not positively teach the demonstrability of God's existence but the indefensibility and irrationality of atheism. It took the latter for granted in a way that we cannot but describe as uncritical. The invitation to the atheists to convince themselves of the indefensibility of

---

[48] H. Gollwitzer, "Das Gespräch des Konzils mit dem Atheismus des Ostens", in Hampe, *op. cit.,* III, pp. 602 f.

their thesis was not in Text 5, although its starting-point was perhaps a better one. The non-demonstrability of atheism can really be affirmed, or at all events much more readily than the "demonstrability" of God. On that basis, too, it would have been possible to make it plain that the question of God both positively and negatively stands outside the realm of demonstrative thought; the special plane of decision which the question of God demands could have been indicated, and then on these lines, as the case demands, atheism could have been stripped of the illusion of being scientific and rational in character. Instead, the first sentence remained, though some fathers, who (because of Modernism) still thought concern for experience in theology sounded suspicious (as had also been shown very clearly in the debate on Revelation), rejected the exclusive appeal to experience which to them seemed more like evasion of the full claim of reason. So different does a text sound according to the standpoint from which it is heard. In order to appease them, the words "rationi et" were added, and the "universalis experientia" was muted into a "communis experientia". The intention of this new version is clear. The term "ratio" was simply meant to recall in abbreviated form the well-known definitions of Vatican I, and by the addition or retention of "experientia" the aim was to limit the neo-scholastic rationalism contained in the formula of 1870 and to place its over-static idea of "ratio naturalis" in a more historical perspective. The text indicates (these were obviously the lines on which they had been thinking in Ariccia) that the possibilities of reason in regard to knowledge of God should be thought of less in the form of a non-historical syllogism of the philosophia perennis than simply as the concrete fact that man throughout his whole history has known himself confronted with God and consequently in virtue of his own history finds himself in relation with God as an inescapable feature of his own existence. The background which the text thus adds to Vatican I is not so much the history of philosophy as the history of religion. In order to find confirmation for the thesis of Vatican I, one must not ask whether there were philosophers before the time of Christ who worked out an incontestable monotheistic conception of God, but rather whether mankind knew about God or not. It knew about him even when God encountered mankind obscured by the form of the gods.

When the vote was taken on Text 5 the problem had obviously become clear to the fathers. A considerable number of amendments were concerned with the question, and representatives of both the opposing tendencies expressed their wishes. Only the most important can be mentioned here. Once again it was chiefly the "communis experientia" which was the stumbling-block. Some wanted it replaced by "fides", others by the "experientia sanctorum". The reasons were of various kinds. As before, some regarded "experientia" as weaker than "ratio", as an evasion of the rigorous idea of God's demonstrability which they had formed. Others had in mind the ambiguity of human experience. The commission did not accept these wishes, declaring that "tota humana historia" bore testimony to the "factum religiosum". Certainly the level of the claim implied in this answer is considerably more modest than that of the conciliar text; it speaks only of testimony to the "factum religiosum", but this need not directly of itself bear witness to God or against atheism. Mere fact decides nothing in regard to truth. In that respect the commission's answer complicates rather than solves the question. The experience of history leads only to the "factum" and not to the "veritas". That is the real reason why in theology, shifting the argument from reason to experience has fallen into discredit, however much it may correspond to the general movement of thought. But it is of course precisely this movement of withdrawal to experience and mere fact which has led man into crisis in the question of truth and the question of God. [49]

A further group of *modi* declared that atheism has its origin in the critical philosophy of Kant and Hegel. In face of this, they said, the validity of the principles of "sound philosophy" must be emphatically asserted and the definition of Vatican I regarding natural knowledge of God must be reaffirmed. The other side wanted it said that atheism, though always rejected by the Church, nevertheless offers the faithful an occasion to purify themselves from every trace of idolatry; for despite his revelation in Christ, God remains inaccessible, and no man in his pilgrim state can intellectually see God in his essence. As ground for their request, the two fathers who sent in this *modus* urged that, after the condemnation of agnosticism, the divine transcendence must also be acknowledged. The commission's answer is as unintelligible as it is unsatisfactory: "Locus non est ut de hac disputata quaestione tractetur. Unde modus non accipitur" (*modus* 21, Text 6, p. 183). How the affirmation of the divine transcendence, emphasis on the fact that even when revealed God remains hidden, in short the element of *theologia negativa*, is supposed to be a controverted question, is absolutely impossible to comprehend. Certainly the two fathers had given the commission a certain excuse for this answer by their clumsy formula that God by the "viator intellectu per essentiam videri non potest", but fundamentally there can be no dispute even about this statement. Whatever judgment is passed on the expression, the *modus* did raise a question which should not have been pushed aside so easily. After all, an exposition which attempts to understand atheism simply must take into account God's invisibility; it cannot be taken seriously if it acts as if reason and revelation present a smooth, plain certainty accessible to everyone; in that case atheism could only be a matter of evil will. In that case, too, the atheist could not consider that he was being taken seriously. He would feel little inclination to engage in discussion when his cause is declared from the start to be contrary to plain reason and he is

---

[49] Cf. J. Ratzinger, *Einführung in das Christentum* (1968), especially ch. I.

treated merely as a sick man worthy of pity, the causes of whose malady are being inquired into so that he may be cured.

A rather peculiar answer was given to *modus* 8 (p. 181), which asked for a statement of Text 4 to be included once more, inviting atheists to verify the validity of their reasons for atheism; the reply is that the proposal has been accepted. Reference is made to the last sentence of the penultimate paragraph (which originated in *modus* 34), i.e. the invitation to atheists to examine the gospel with an open mind. In itself that is certainly a meaningful statement, but it is something quite different. In view of the strong emphasis on reason which is already evident in the text, it was probably wise not to return to the formula of the Ariccia text.

Taken as a whole, our text does not represent any positive advance in regard to the problem raised by Vatican I. The mere addition of "experientia" to "ratio" is not sufficient to do so. The new intellectual situation is taken into account as little as the intensive theological discussion of this question which has been pursued especially since Karl Barth's criticism of the *analogia entis*. The Council passed over the essentials of the *theologia negativa*. It took no account of Augustine's epistemology, which is much deeper than that of Aquinas, for it is well aware that the organ by which God can be seen cannot be a non-historical "ratio naturalis" which just does not exist, but only the *ratio pura*, i.e. *purificata* or, as Augustine expresses it echoing the gospel, the *cor purum* ("Blessed are the pure in heart, for they shall see God"). Augustine also knows that the necessary purification of sight takes place through faith (Acts 15:9) and through love, at all events not as a result of reflection alone and not at all by man's own power. By ignoring these approaches, the opportunity was lost of manifesting the positive service to faith performed by atheism. In face of an all too affirmative theology, it must time and again assume the role of negative theology and thus contribute to the purification of faith and of the idea of God. Despite such criticism of the article, its positive content must not, of course, be overlooked. It endeavours to show that atheism cannot justly claim to be the outcome of science. Furthermore, it is convinced, even against Barth, that faith in God does not mean pure paradox for human knowledge, that ultimately it cannot remain inaccessible to a reason which is ready to listen, to allow itself to be led and to go to the root of things.

After the first two paragraphs have expressed refusal of atheism as a doctrine but acceptance of dialogue with atheists, the next paragraphs attempt to indicate the main course of such a dialogue. The guiding-line is provided by the idea of the *humanum*, what is human, which here receives its special colouring from the reference to postulatory atheism and Marxism. On the basis of these two tendencies (dealt with in Article 20), two positive statements are made, firstly that faith in God does not alienate man from himself but, on the contrary, grounds and strengthens human dignity, for it

155

is only man's direct relation to God which perfectly assures his freedom and his claim to truth. Secondly, it is said that eschatological hope does not lessen the importance of earthly tasks but provides new motives for them. Then the two points are reinforced by a negative view of the matter. Man without hope of eternity finds his dignity called in question and abandoned to the onset of collective forces; from an end, man easily becomes a means. And without hope in the next world man will inevitably regard his existence, torn with suffering and threatened with death, as an unanswerable riddle and absurdity. Abandonment of Christian hope logically leads to despair. Here existentialism and Marxism are played off against one another, not without skill. The existentialists' desire to free man from God in order to make him really free at last, finds its corrective in Marxism, in which liberation from God is carried through rigorously, and precisely thereby the individual human being becomes a mere function of the collectivity. Marxism again, which turns man's gaze away from another world in order to gain him entirely for the tasks of this world, is viewed in the light of existentialism with its conception of "l'homme absurde" who has nothing left but despair and for whom the earthly task becomes, as for Camus, the labour of Sisyphus — only the joyful meaninglessness which Camus ascribed to his Sisyphus is not convincing. In justice it would, of course, have to be admitted that in actual fact Christian hope has frequently tended to weaken the will to work at earthly tasks. Christian "contempt for the world" has resulted ultimately, in modern times, in the humanist impulse of Christianity having to be pursued in opposition to official Christianity.[50] If this is not said, the assertion that Christian hope does not lessen the energy of earthly commitment, but strengthens it, appears an empty assertion, contradicted by facts. Here, too, a deeper examination of conscience was therefore needed, and it should have been admitted that at bottom, after all, we owe it to the atheists' attack that we have become properly aware once more of our own duties.

The next paragraph attempts to open a way of access to God by pointing to the enigma of man and declaring that there are extreme situations in which no one can totally avoid the question of transcendence. One is reminded of the beautiful words of Schleiermacher: "In the relation of man to this world, there are certain transitions to the infinite, perspectives opened out, to which everyone is led, so that his mind may find the way to the universe..."[51] This reference to extreme situations must not be taken to

---

[50] Cf. P. Delhaye, *op. cit.*, p. 175, n. 47, with reference to M. Bultot, *La doctrine du mépris du monde au moyen-âge* (1964 and 1965); cf. also A. Auer, "Gestaltwandel des christlichen Weltverständnisses", *Gott in Welt (Festgabe K. Rahner)* I (1964), pp. 333–65, especially pp. 333–8.

[51] F. Schleiermacher, *Über die Religion. Reden an die Gebildeten unter ihren Verächtern* (1958), p. 85, in the 1799 edition, pp. 153 f., E. T.: *On Religion: Speeches to its Cultured Despisers.*

mean that God (as Bonhoeffer rightly seeks to prevent) is made a stop-gap for human failure. The way these situations bring man before God by leading him out of everyday superficiality into the authentic depths of his human existence, has nothing to do with the attempt to bring God down to the level of a *Deus ex machina* who becomes superfluous through the advance in man's own capacity. The "plene et omni certitudine" was inserted once again into Text 5 to appease certain fathers who wanted to see "every appearance of agnosticism" avoided.

The same fear also influenced the wording of the first sentence of the next paragraph. Text 5 had said that the remedy against atheism was to be looked for "non solum a doctrina sed etiam ab ... Ecclesiae vita". As opposed to this, one of the fathers wanted it positively stated that a form of evangelization appropriate to the age is a remedy against atheism. The commission shifted this quite intelligible aim onto the same level as the objection just mentioned, apparently confusing intellectual proof with evangelization and, "in order not to lessen the significance of the intellectual aspect of refutation", framed the present formulation which thus fits the rather rationalistic trend of the whole article and also continues to leave out of account the kerygmatic problem to which the father in question had directed attention (cf. *modus* 23, Text 6, p. 138). The second member of the sentence ("tum ab ... Ecclesiae vita") had quite a stormy history. It had been inserted in Text 5 because "many fathers declared that the essential remedy against atheism is the renewal of the Church" (*relatio* on Text 5, p. 31). In the vote on the *modi*, the opposing view was voiced, urging that it is erroneous to affirm that the whole Church must perpetually purify itself. The Church itself is holy, the task of purification only applies to its members (*modus 24*, p. 183). The commission rejected this objection with a reference to *Lumen Gentium*, although it speaks, in fact, explicitly only of the sinfulness of the members of the Church and therefore in reality only speaks directly about the need of its members for purification. It is important that the purely intellectual level was thus radically transcended. The real answer to atheism is the life of the Church, which must manifest the face of God by showing its own face of unity and love. Conversely this includes the admission that the disunity of Christians and their consent to systems of social injustice, hide the face of God. It also implies the realization that knowing God is not a question of pure reason alone, that there is an obscuration of God in the world produced by guilt, which can only be removed by penance and conversion. It is also important to notice the two main elements indicated as the content of Christian witness: justice and love, especially for those in distress. This raises the problem of social justice, though perhaps not explicitly and incisively enough, the need for a love which does not evade justice by almsgiving but takes justice seriously as a form and condition of love and is thus essentially related to the social structures and institutional orders of this world. Only then is brotherly love mentioned. It is probably to be understood here as that love of Christians for one another which is a sign, which has to make the Christians a "signum unitatis" in a world divided but striving for unity. It would obviously have been possible to mention here the division of Christendom as an element of Christian guilt which hides God from men and extinguishes the "sign of unity". Even if that was not done, such an idea is certainly in line with the intention of the text.[52] It should not be overlooked that martyrdom is also mentioned as a sign of Christian life; the theology of the Cross consequently keeps its place in contrast to any onesided activism. The attempt to win over atheists must not lead to suppressing faith, which attains its strongest power to convince precisely by contradiction, by the radical testimony of self-sacrifice.

Since the next (penultimate) paragraph contains the most concrete statements, it is understandable that it was particularly fought over. The text proclaims the collaboration of believers and unbelievers in the joint construction of this world. It recognizes that a condition of this is mutual discussion. It consequently approves "sincere and prudent dialogue". In face of the situation which existed for example in Pius XII's time, this is undoubtedly an important and courageous step. The demand for discussion with atheists which here appears for the first time in an official document of the magisterium, was introduced in Text 5 at the wish of "several fathers" (*relatio*, p. 31). When a vote was taken, various reserves were expressed. Three fathers declared that it must be made clear that dialogue involves as a minimum condition the recognition of the fundamental principles of the natural law (*modus* 29). Two fathers wanted to strike out entirely the reference to dialogue, three wanted it stated that grave obstacles are placed in its way by diametrically opposed fundamental views and by the restrictions placed on the freedom of Christians in atheistic countries. There were also suggested emendations of a more stylistic character, mostly restrictive in tendency (*modus* 30). The commission declared that both aims had already been taken into account in the text. The essential point aimed at by the demand for agreement on natural law was already contained in the word "recte" (rightful), while the other guarantees asked for were in principle summed up in the word "prudenti". This indubitably lent additional weight to these words. It is important that the fathers avoided laying down a strictly defined condition in terms of the controverted concept of natural law, which in its concrete form remains inaccessible to many, even where the reality itself is affirmed. Instead, they restricted themselves to the quite open

---

[52] L. Vischer, "Die Bedeutung der Konstitution für die ökumenische Bewegung", in Baraúna, *op. cit.*, pp. 484–8, in particular p. 485, regrets the lack of such pronouncements, but at the same time deals expressly with the ecumenical importance of the Pastoral Constitution.

word "recte" which leaves much more room for discussion. In any case, the demand for Christians to be freed from measures of State coercion, which in fact must remain a fundamental condition of meaningful dialogue, is clearly enough expressed. It would be absurd, and unjust to the sufferings of the persecuted, to say nothing about this condition.

In the last paragraph the vote on the amendments produced another real improvement. Text 5 had said that the Church knows that it is in harmony with the innermost desires of the human heart. *Modus* 32 (18 fathers) pointed out that the Church has not to commend itself but the Word of God. Thereupon the word "se" was replaced by "nuntium suum" (its message), thus giving the required pointer via the Church to its message. The conclusion once again returns to the essence of the article and its discussion with humanistic atheism. Faith does not diminish man but leads him in the direction in which alone the endless restlessness which impels him can find satisfaction. Man's measure is infinity, everything else is too little for him. Consequently only God can be man's measure.

Article 22. In accordance with the whole composition of the text, the chapter on the dignity of man culminates in Christ who is now presented as the true answer to the question of being human, and therefore to the questions of true humanism and of atheism. Article 22 thus returns to the starting-point, Article 12, and presents Christ as the eschatological Adam to whom the first Adam already pointed; as the true image of God which transforms man once more into likeness to God. The attempt to pursue discussion with non-believers on the basis of the idea of "humanitas", here culminates in the endeavour to interpret being human Christologically and so attain the "resolutio in theologiam" which, it is true, also means "resolutio in hominem" (provided the sense of "homo" is understood deeply enough). We are probably justified in saying that here for the first time in an official document of the magisterium, a new type of completely Christocentric theology appears. On the basis of Christ this dares to present theology as anthropology and only becomes radically theological by including man in discourse about God by way of Christ, thus manifesting the deepest unity of theology. The generally theologically reserved text of the Pastoral Constitution here attains very lofty heights and points the way to theological reflection in our present situation.

The fact that the term "similitudo" is used here for the restoration of the image of God in sinful man, is probably an echo of Irenaeus. By his distinction between "imago" and "similitudo", he anticipated the later distinction between the "natural" and "supernatural" image of God. It certainly seems strange that the "similitudo" is only mentioned as "deformata"; in the classical doctrine the "similitudo" is lost but the "imago" is wounded. By this mode of expression, which from the point of view of scholastic terminology must be described as imprecise, it is once more evident what little intention the Council had of going into these technical scholastic details and how concerned it was to express what is fundamental and common to all. Another reference to the text may be in place here. One father had objected to the expression "Adam primus homo" as prejudging the question whether "Adam" is to be understood as a single individual at the beginning of the history of mankind; the words "primus homo" should therefore be omitted. The commission answered that there was no such prejudgment and that the text could therefore stand (*modus* 3). As in Article 13, discussion about the original state of man and original sin is left quite open.

After the fundamental idea has been presented — Christ the new Adam, the eschatological image of God — the composition of the text follows the three fundamental mysteries of Christology, incarnation, cross, resurrection. The idea of the "assumptio hominis" is first touched upon in its full ontological depth. The human nature of all men is one; Christ's taking to himself the one human nature of man is an event which affects every human being; consequently human nature in every human being is henceforward Christologically characterized. This idea is then extended to the real plane of actual concrete human existence. Human action, thought, willing and loving have become the instrument of the Logos; what is first present on the plane of being also gives new significance to the plane of action, to the actual accomplishment of human personal life.

This outlook is probably also important because it opens a bridge between the theology of the incarnation and that of the cross. A theology of the incarnation situated too much on the level of essence, may be tempted to be satisfied with the ontological phenomenon: God's being and man's have been conjoined. This appears as the real turning-point, and in comparison with it the factual life of Jesus and his death are secondary, as it were the realization of a principle which ultimately adds nothing to the principle itself. But since it is made clear that man's being is not that of a pure essence, and that he only attains his reality by his activity, it is at once evident that we cannot rest content with a purely essentialist outlook. Man's being must therefore be examined precisely in its activities. If this is done, the concept of the "novus homo" takes concrete shape in that of the "agnus innocens". It then becomes apparent that Jesus' concrete reality is "pro me" (and "pro nobis") and for this very reason is a self-sacrificing existence in the mystery of the cross. This alone shows the wholly personal relationship to Christ, for Christ is not a great super-ego into which the I-monads are organized, but a most individual human being who looks at me personally. His relation to me is not that of a great corporate personality. He enters into a personal conversation of love; he has something to say to me alone, which no one else knows (cf. Rev 2:17). Pascal's intense piety which made him place in the Lord's mouth the words: "In my agony I thought of you; I shed these drops of blood for you", is biblically entirely justified in view of the Pauline "pro me".[53] Thus Christ no longer appears as a merely general form to which human existences are conformed. His exemplarity means the concrete summons to follow him, and this gives meaning to man's cross; it calls him to share in the "pro me" of Jesus Christ in a Christian "pro invicem" based on the "cum Christo". To endure in the cross, as the expression of abiding in the "pro me" of Jesus Christ, is thus a concrete result of the way human nature is ontologically affected by the incarnation. Just as, from the point of view of the theology of the cross, the ontological idea takes concrete form in Christ, so also the ontological affirmation that by the incarnation all human reality is affected, must now be understood as a statement concerning personal life. Its concrete meaning is the claim made on me and the consent to its being made on me by the "pro me" of Jesus Christ, and this expresses the concrete spiritual reality of the doctrine of the two natures. Thus the foundation laid by a theology of the incarnation necessarily leads to a spirituality of the cross. For the latter, it is of course important that the incorporation of human suffering into the "pro me" of Jesus Christ is at the same time its incorporation into the promise of resurrection, that is, into an existence under the sign of hope, which lives with a view to the "redemptio corporis".

The clear statement of the *mysterium paschale* as the centre of personal existence and human history, certainly poses a problem which is particularly grave in a document intended to promote discussion with non-believers. If salvation is thus Christologically determined, doesn't Christian faith necessarily exclude non-Christians from salvation? Does it not inevitably appear as a sectarianism which divides mankind into the saved and the lost? Does it remain true to its aim of making true humanism possible? The Council could refer in principle here to the answer which had been worked out in the Constitution on the Church (Chapter II, art. 16). This had tried to combine affirmation of the universal possibility of salvation with that of the obligatory character of the call to faith. The gravity of the problem, which that statement could not eliminate, makes it understandable that the formulation of the present article once more demanded a laborious struggle. Text 4 had expressed the matter surprisingly well: "Because, however, Christ died for all men, we may also believe that the Spirit in a way known to himself gives all the possibility of conforming themselves to this mystery." This stated the universal possibility of salvation, but left the way it is realized to God. Thus all useless investigation into that way, which, after all, ultimately nothing can elucidate, was avoided. At bottom it would have been possible simply to leave it at this. In the debate on that text, however, some insisted that it must be stated that salvation comes to non-Christians through the power of

---

[53] On the problems and limits of the "Pro me" cf. P. Hacker, *Das Ich im Glauben bei Martin Luther* (1966), pp. 21–37.

the Holy Spirit (though in reality this was already expressed by the "pro omnibus"). Thereupon in Text 5 this section was composed, which, with a few modifications, remained in the final version. And with the idea of the unity of the "vocatio" a further reason for the universality of salvation was added and an attempt was made to describe more clearly the meaning of the "omnes": "non tantum pro credentibus in Deum ... sed et pro omnibus hominibus bonae voluntatis." This repeated once more what *Lumen Gentium* had already said, namely that, contrary to a widespread dogmatic opinion, the possibility of salvation must not be restricted to explicit recognition of God. As a result, the *modi* frequently called for even closer reference to *Lumen Gentium*. Instead, a proposal was accepted to name as the counterpart to "all men of goodwill", not those who believe in God, but believers in Christ. Once again, therefore, a more cautious shade of meaning was brought into the text; men of goodwill no longer appear as the antithesis to believers in God, and the question how goodwill must actually be expressed is again left more open. In substance the change is not really important, for the intention of remaining as close to *Lumen Gentium* as possible was probably the motive inspiring all the amendments we have mentioned. Thus all these additions really only amplified the verbal expression and gained practically nothing to set in comparison with the precise and pregnant sentence of the Ariccia text. Really important, on the other hand, is a small alteration in the last word of the paragraph. The active "se consocient" was changed into the passive "consocientur", thus making it clear that the real agent here can only be God. We cannot bring about the paschal mystery for ourselves; as the mystery of death and resurrection, by its very nature it can only be received.

In regard to the whole article it may be observed that, despite less satisfactory elements, it represents an advance over *Lumen Gentium*. The latter lays too much emphasis on man's activity. The search for God and the endeavour to live a life expressed in conscientious action, are named as the central factors of salvation outside the Church. God's activity is reduced to the "influxus gratiae", man appears as the active subject of the saving process and the latter in essentials is described in the categories of natural ethics. Here on the contrary it is decisively acknowledged that the way of salvation is God's affair and cannot be defined by us. Man no longer appears as the agent of the process with his "quaerere, adimplere, conari, posse" and "niti" (these are the very significant words which *Lumen Gentium* uses in this connection). It is God or his Holy Spirit who offers his salvation to man and associates him with it. Finally, its essential content is not determined by the categories of good will (a very questionable formula which can easily border on Pelagianism), but by the paschal mystery, that is, by the very centre of Christology. Salvation is not a "work" of man. Wherever it occurs, it must ultimately be a sharing in the Easter mystery of cross and resurrection. In this way, at the last moment, as it were, the Council gave a re-reading of its own statements and replaced the extremely unsatisfactory expressions of *Lumen Gentium,* art. 16, by better ones. If one is dealing with the views of Vatican II on the question of the salvation of the many, it would be better in future to start from this passage of *Gaudium et Spes* rather than from the Constitution on the Church, whose less fortunate approach has been considerably improved.

The final paragraph returns once more to the enigma of sorrow and death repeatedly referred to in Articles 19—21. It thus takes up the theodicy problem, and that of man's impenetrability to himself, and leads both the question which seems to revolt against God and the extreme situation which leads to him, back to the Christological centre. It ends with the thought of our incorporation into Christ by which we become sons in the Son. The idea of fraternity appears and another central concern of our age is seen in its Christian fulfilment; at the same time, however, it is manifest that fraternity presupposes the Father and achieves its fulfilment by making it possible to say in common Abba — Father. A text which to some appears at first far too humanist in tendency, thus culminates in the idea of adoration. Christ truly shows himself, even from the theological point of view, as the way and the mediator who in the end brings men before the face of the Father. Thereby finally the Pauline form of Christocentrism finds expression, characterized by the little word "per"; it knows Christ to be the centre and has its goal in the Father. Precisely this culmination in adoration, in theo-logy in the strictest sense of the term, justifies the anthropological endeavour of our chapter, which does not lead to an unacceptable form of anthropocentrism but, by taking man seriously, recognizes him as the being who is constituted to be not merely in himself, but above and beyond himself, and who is only in full possession of himself when he has gone forth from himself: Abba, Father.

The Community of Mankind

by

Otto Semmelroth

In a fortnight's work in Ariccia and Rome from 1 to 13 February 1965, the relevant commission[1] worked the theme of the social aspect of human life, as an integral part of a Christian doctrine of man, into Schema 13, as the second chapter of its first part devoted to theological principles. Account had to be taken of a number of written amendments to the chapter, as well as those expressed orally in the aula. When these suggestions were incorporated, the chapter assumed a considerably different form from the text which had been sent to the Council fathers dated 28 March 1965. In particular, the frequently expressed wish for a much shorter version had been fulfilled, and the division into two sections, one on fundamental principles, the other on ways and means, was dropped. The remarkable difference between this chapter and the others in the first part did, however, remain; in Articles 27 and 28 a list of concrete practical applications was given. Some sections concerning social matters were taken from the first chapter into the second to improve the composition. Place was also found here for a more serious treatment of sin and its effects on human social life and, in conjunction with it, the significance of Christ's cross for the healing of society. A wish had also been expressed for the social character of human life to be based on the biblical account of creation. A cautious linking up of human social life with the community of the three persons of the Trinity was also inserted, not of course as an object of faith but of Catholic doctrine. Finally, the connection of the structure of society with the well-being of human persons themselves was more clearly brought out.

On 15–16 November 1965, a conciliar vote was taken on the revised articles of this chapter, in two stages (arts. 23–26, 27–32), as well as a vote on the whole chapter. In the partial votes, in which *placet juxta modum* was not yet possible, the first produced 2074 *placet*, 34 *non placet* out of 2115

[1] On the history of this chapter, cf. the survey in the work of R. Tucci quoted in Chapter II of Part II.

voters, the second 2115 *placet* and 35 *non placet* out of 2155, while there were 7 invalid votes in the first and 2 in the second. At the total vote, 1801 voted *placet*, 18 *non placet* and 388 *placet juxta modum* out of 2212. Consequently there was a large number of *modi* to be dealt with and, together with the *modi* of the first chapter, they were entrusted to a subcommission. Because of their great number this divided into three working groups, one of which dealt with the *modi* to Chapter II.

It will be best to open the exposition of Chapter II by referring to the sequence of chapters in the first main section of the Constitution. These four chapters are not simply juxtaposed, as might at first sight be thought, but are to be grouped in two sections, Chapters I–III and then Chapter IV, which treats a second theme. The two themes are named in the title of the Constitution. Chapters I–III speak of the world in which the Church is to be present in order to carry out its mission, and Chapter IV speaks expressly about the latter.

But do the first three chapters really deal with the world? This is an urgent question precisely at this point, at the transition from Chapter I to the rest. In fact the first three chapters seem to be concerned with man, whereas "the world" usually means the material things of the world around us in which man finds himself and which he has to deal with. But Chapters I–III are not concerned with man in himself but with the three dimensions of his life as a person. Chapter I speaks about man more as an individual, Chapter II about his relations with the society of his fellow-men, Chapter III about the material world in which he has to act in order to develop his humanity. These three chapters therefore concern man in his world. Conversely, by "world" we do not mean material things in themselves. The "world" means, rather, the totality of realities in which man finds himself and has to act. The "world" means a total network of relations, each related to all the others and above all to man. To that extent, therefore, it is true that Chapters I–III deal with the world with which Chapter IV contrasts the Church as having something to say to it, and as having a mission to fulfil in it.

Chapters I–III should therefore be regarded as a unity and we should resist the temptation to juxtapose them independently under the headings of anthropology (Ch. I), sociology (Ch. II) and cosmology (Ch. III). In reality all three chapters are anthropology, for all three concern man and his behaviour, though, of course, in three dimensions of his life. If Chapter I described man in his individuality, Chapter II presents his relation to the society of his fellow-men while Chapter III describes him with his activities dealing with and in the universe of things. And it must be noted that all three are concerned with describing the human person. The features of the human person sketched in Chapter I have to develop in encounter with the community.

Article 23. This introductory article points out the peculiar fact that present-day technology itself is capable of making a special contribution to the central point of Christian life. In many spheres modern technology links men; means of communication and transport have brought humanity into closer contact. Of course, modern armaments have increased the possibility of mutual destruction. But this observation is immediately followed by another. Solidarity based on technology does not itself mean the perfection of human society. Technology can be of assistance if men use it to aid their mutual contacts. This is precisely what relates technical progress to Christian faith. The latter does not reject technical means of human communication but makes it plain that they are instruments which can also be perverted and abused. Technology can neither decrease nor replace responsible personal activity in social life. It can, however, be taken into the service of that life.

In this connection the Council aims in this chapter at recalling a few main truths without attempting to be complete, since the social documents of recent Popes have already dealt with many of these matters.

Article 24. In this article the corporate character of man's vocation is given its theological basis. Three features of human life, each different and yet intrinsically connected, are considered. These are really only three different aspects of one and the same reality. Its vertical dimension shows that all form a community in God's sight. This must lead in practice to community on the horizontal plane, that is to say, in the relations of men to one another. A third aspect shows how closely both dimensions are actually linked in the unity and mysterious complexity of human existence.

The first of these features means that the multitude of men are all made to the image of God. However the content of man's likeness to God is defined, it is the formal element which is mainly in question here. All men, despite all differences between them, have this in common, that they are created in God's image. This, of course, stands in the forefront of the biblical account of man's creation, for immediately after the statement that God created man to his image and likeness there follows the statement: man and woman he created them. This is intended to stress that different though men and women are, they are both in God's image. Consequently no other difference, racial, national or individual can destroy this fundamental community of likeness to God. At the same time it is implied that all have a common goal. They are all created for God. That may at first sight seem a parallel equality, but there derives from it an essential community which links men together in a family and demands a fraternal spirit between them.

This community in relation to God must produce effects in the behaviour of men to one another. Or, as we should rather say, the one must be realized in the other. The remarkable fact is pointed out that love of God must not only not be separated from love of the neighbour, but that in the New Testament both seem to be so fused that the one almost seems to be identified with the other. In fact, express exhortation to love God appears very seldom in the New Testament, though it is presupposed as a matter of course and clearly appears as what must be the life and soul of all other Christian behaviour. Explicit admonitions to love of the neighbour are, however, very frequent; love of God has to find its concrete and most appropriate realization in it. Love of the neighbour must therefore animate the growing interdependence which is imposed on people in our time but which would inevitably become an intolerable tyranny if it were not to experience the redemptive power of brotherly love.

The third point of this article gives the essentially Christian interpretation of the unity of love of God and the neighbour, and thereby explains how the vertical and horizontal dimensions are linked. For, of course, we are not dealing with the dimensions of a material edifice but with the unity of a life representing and participating in the very life of the triune God. Man's likeness to God does not found a community solely because all individuals are created in God's image, but because mankind, multitude in unity, is an image, even if an imperfect one, of the one God in three persons. The fact that the human person, although or because he is a self-contained creature loved by God for his own sake, can only truly find himself by meeting and giving himself to others, has its deepest ground in the fact that his Creator himself subsists in three persons who are constituted by their mutual relationships. Just as if the impenetrability of the mystery of the triune God were to be made perceptible to man, he discovers again and again how much the individual's own independence can endanger the community of all, and to what an extent devotion to the community can endanger personal independence. What in the triune God is wholly a matter of course, has to be achieved by mankind laboriously and attentively again and again in imperfect imitation: personally independent individuals have to realize dedication to others in such a way that mankind may suggest "a certain likeness between the union of the divine persons and the union of the children of God in truth and charity".

Article 25. In what follows, extraordinarily important statements are made about the relation between man's personal existence and society. This dialectical unity pervades all the articles of this chapter. In Article 25 the emphasis lies on the unity and interconnection of persons and society. When we speak of the relation of the two to one another, the impression is given that we are assuming that the personal existence of an individual on one hand and of society on the other, involves two separate subjects related to one another in a certain way. That, however, only really belongs to the logic of the statement, not to real life, where they both belong so closely together that they intrinsically determine one another. Without its social component, the nature of the human person can be given an abstract metaphysical definition but cannot be described as it actually and really exists. The nature of man is social and, conversely, men's common life in society is realized by consciously and deliberately leading a common life. Social life is not something adventitious for man. Man cannot first exist as an individual and then in addition endeavour to form social relationships. The fact is, rather, that the realization and development of his personal life require mutual relations with others in the mutual interaction of life in society.

It is true that the second section of this article points out that not all existing forms of social life are equally necessary and decisive for a person's mode of existence. There are forms of society which are prior to the life of the individual and which are absolutely required if the existence of the individual is to be possible, and which then permanently affect his individual life, though not always in the same way or with the same intensity, the family and political society for example. The latter is not meant in the sense of a particular kind of political life, for that, of course, can differ. What is meant is the fact that no human person can exist except in an actual community organized as a State. These forms of society make the individual acutely aware that he would nullify himself if he did not accept society and be willing to live in it. Other social structures depend on the free decisions of individuals associating for particular purposes or joining groups that already exist. These make people realize that society needs the personal decision of its members in order genuinely to fulfil its purpose. Person and society therefore stand in constant mutual interaction which results from the nature of each.

In the last sentence of the second paragraph, attention was drawn to the great advantages of increasing socialization, even where it is planned and freely accepted over and above the forms of society instituted by nature. The Latin word "socialisatio" used here does not of course mean socialization in the economic sense.[2] It refers to the increasing complexity of social relations produced by organic growth or conscious organization and planning, and which is intended to support and assist the individual in his various vital needs. As well as the help which comes to the person from the growing complexity of social life, attention is also drawn here to dangers to which it may give rise in regard to the genuine development of the human person.

This ambivalence of social life is the express theme of the second section of this article. Care must be taken to avoid the danger of a short-sighted and superficial interpretation of the relation between the individual and society. For if naturally existing or consciously elaborated and developed

[2] Cf. on this O. von Nell-Breuning in his commentaries on Part II, Chapters III and IV of this Constitution.

forms of socialization are depicted as providing definite advantages for human life, the impression is easily given that social solidarity is only a kind of instrument, a means which man can use or not, according as he finds it helpful or not. That, however, would be a misconception of man's social life as well as of the Council's meaning, which clearly implies that existence in society is an intrinsic characteristic of human life, even prior to any concrete association for a particular purpose.

Although a certain ambivalence is attributed here to the social side of human existence, what is primarily stressed is its positive value for the individual. Certainly the advantages of social life and activity for the human person are not emphasized without reserve or even a certain reluctance, which is explained by the painful experiences which everyone has with their human surroundings and which the Church has also had to live through in the course of its history. Certainly it is recognized that socialization in many departments of life "brings with it many advantages with respect to consolidating and increasing the qualities of the human person and safeguarding his rights". This positive statement is, however, introduced with a remark that socialization "is obviously not without dangers". The optimism about the world and ignoring of sin which were often complained of during the work of preparing the Pastoral Constitution, and which have even sometimes been criticized in the finished document, are therefore not really so very marked.

As regards the advantages of social life and its deliberately planned development, the last sentence of this second paragraph merits attention. Life in society is not a second reality juxtaposed with the personal life of the individual and serving the latter. The case is rather that if someone makes his mind up to serve the development of society, this brings an enrichment and development in his own personal life. For the advantages of social life consist precisely in furthering personal qualities; the latter are encouraged to develop when a person opens himself to serve the community. That is more important than the other advantage which also, of course, results from social development, namely, the help which life in an ordered society provides for the safeguard of personal rights.

The third paragraph of the article warns of the dangers which can result from the human social order. The emphasis on the advantages of social life was introduced by a concessive reference to its dangers, and now the reference to its dangers begins by pointing out the advantages which the intensification of social relationships entails for the human person. Advantages and disadvantages, services and dangers, are in fact inseparably connected in the real world, precisely because power for good and liability to evil are themselves so closely linked in man. The world of things, of course, in itself is neither morally good nor morally bad. Man can use the world of things for good service or for evil revolt against God. Consequently this world can either help men to develop or tempt them to evil. The social order, of course, is not simply a world of things, but as a structure which is prior to the individual and his decision, it too is determined by the dual possibility. Its ambivalence for good or evil works itself out in a specific way, because the social structure is not a morally indifferent world of things. As a society of men it is much more directly affected by human decisions for good or evil. In the social structure, sin is much more directly at work than in the world of things. Consequently the difficulties which arise from the network of human social relationships are not to be traced back solely to causes of an economic, political and social kind which human inadequacy and lack of experience have not yet been able to overcome. They are largely due to moral inadequacies, human pride and self-seeking, which tragically interact with the disintegration of the social order which they bring about. The order of things is disturbed by human sin. Affected by the consequences of sin, disorder in its turn exercises a seductive fascination on man's susceptibility to sin. Here there is no hope for man if he does not seek strength beyond his own powers from the helpful influence of grace. This reminder should assume special significance in view of the almost missionary awareness of human social endeavours.

Here it is evident how difficult it is to distinguish the genuine autonomy of secular domains from what falls within the competence of the Church, and consequently how difficult it is for both world and Church to pursue their own activities without exceeding the limits of their competence and trespassing on each other's domain. The laws of social life are indubitably to a large extent the objects of secular sociology, political science and economics. But the knowledge which these provide sets men tasks which they can only fulfil in moral responsibility before God, if they realize that in these structures which they have come to know, God himself makes known his will to men. There, however, the Church is competent with its prophetic voice and sanctifying grace.

Article 26. In this article, subtitled "Promoting the Common Good", the human person receives considerable emphasis. At first sight the two seem to stand to some extent in opposition. Yet experience shows that human beings who know how to look after themselves mostly do so at the expense of the common good, while, conversely, those who promote the common good all too easily favour the dubious principle that the common interest takes precedence over the interests of the individual. The former confuse promotion of the person with individualistic self-interest, the latter want the individual to merge anonymously with the collectivity. Reality demands mastery of the polarity between the two, so that the development of the person is not ruined by service of the common good but is promoted precisely by social service.

The common good is defined in the first paragraph as the sum of those social conditions which help individuals and groups to achieve their own fulfilment. The larger social group therefore has a genuine function of service to smaller groups and above all to the human person. That is only realized, however, by reciprocal activity. Society only serves the fulfilment of the individual if the latter and the smaller group keep their eyes open to the greater society which is perpetually extending and has in fact already become world-wide, and if they acknowledge their duties to the whole human race.

It is no accident that the dignity of the human person is evoked in immediate connection with this reference to service of the great society. It is not only in relation to the world of things that the human person has an exalted dignity. Society, too, must be ready to serve; it must not absorb the human person in itself but realize that society only lives by personal development. Society is not a compulsory collectivity with human beings like things that form part of a whole; it is the freely accepted common life of persons who in conjunction promote the physical and mental well-being of its members. Of course these admonitions are once again addressed to individuals when society is reminded of its duty to see that everything which is necessary for a truly human life should be made available. For if this possibility is to be provided for every individual, every individual will also have to be ready to make his contribution. We must remember that individuals and society are not really partners on an equal footing. The individual must rather be ready to devote himself to the community as its member so that through the community all its members may have what is necessary for human life. For its part, however, society must not endanger the independence, privacy and just freedom of the individual.

It is emphasized that social order must constantly advance and develop both in various forms of socialization and in special functions. But it must never imagine that its perfection consists in becoming an end in itself; it must always regard as its genuine purpose the well-being of the human person. Even though the individual cannot justly refuse to serve the community, the right perspective is, nevertheless, that the social order exists for the sake of persons, and not vice versa. The very service which a person performs for society in fact promotes his own development. It does so not only in the sense that the social order built up by common service will be useful to each individual member, but even more in the sense that the individual's unselfish service of the social order is precisely what develops his own person and increases his dignity.

Here, too, the paragraph ends with a reminder of the need for the divine strength, which is available, if the difficult work of building a social order which really serves human persons is to be successful. The most important feature of the world is human social order, and this must be shaped by the Spirit of God. For it is his gospel which has awakened men to awareness of

171

their personal dignity. His divine power must therefore help to create harmony between society, which has to ask for unselfishness from the individual, and the development of the individual, who is only too inclined to shut himself up in himself. This once again gives the Church a wide range of functions in this apparently so secular domain.

Article 27. A second part of the chapter, which so far has been concerned mainly with principles, begins with this article. Now some concrete conclusions are indicated. This is in marked contrast to all the other articles in Part I and almost gives the impression that it is anticipating Part II, for which, of course, the more practical and concrete statements are reserved. There is a reason for this anticipation, which we shall point out later.

At the beginning, however, another principle is enunciated. In view of the danger created by modern talk of social obligation, of thinking that new insights are involved which, like a new gospel, might supersede Christ's message, we are reminded that all social duties and obligations must draw their life from the central Christian commandment of love of the neighbour. Certainly each powerfully completes the other. The believing Christian may easily regard the New Testament admonition to love his neighbour as himself and to see his neighbour in everyone, especially those in need, as a completely creative personal achievement by which he brings into existence new relationships which did not exist before. But present-day social consciousness shows that love of the neighbour must to a large extent find expression in the free and conscious affirmation of existing relationships. The warning that all men must regard their neighbour as "another self" points to the fact that the attitude of mutual service, the accomplishment of brotherly love, is not creative in the sense that the free personal attitude of men creates for the first time a mutual solidarity which did not previously exist. The human ego never exists in isolation but is always linked with others in such a way that these others belong in some way to one's own ego. Christian love affirms this bond and now regards the other as another self, acknowledges, in other words, that one's own ego cannot live without others. Christian love and social behaviour contribute to developing one's own self. Its contrary "defiles those who are actively responsible for injustice much more than those who are its victims", the end of this article points out.

The two following paragraphs present the more practical points of view positively and negatively. Love of the neighbour, it is said, is not exercised, because the human beings whom it concerns are not yet really our neighbours at all. The faithful in general are not sufficiently aware how much Christian love of the neighbour shares in the creative nature of God's love for us men. God's love, of course, does not turn to men because they are lovable in his eyes; men only become lovable in his eyes because God turns to them with love. God's love is absolutely spontaneous and creative. He creates the partners of his love for himself by turning to them in love, creation and grace. Christian love of the neighbour must rise above all mere humanism by not waiting until someone shows himself to be lovable, and by recognizing the binding obligation to consider each of his neighbours as another self. Where the creative effect of such love begins, whether a man makes himself a neighbour to others or the others become his neighbours, makes no great difference. But the effect of this creative power is double; by turning lovingly to persons he makes them his neighbours and makes himself theirs.

It is also emphasized that love of the neighbour must be an active service and not a mere emotion that binds one to nothing. This is shown by the next lines, which name very concrete situations where love of the neighbour must be exercised if it is to be the Christian inspiration of all social endeavour. That is probably the real reason why, as we have already said, this article anticipates Part II which is more concerned with concrete matters. It is not really an anticipation but the necessary concrete embodiment of an attitude which it is quite easy to affirm to be fundamentally Christian but is far too often left vague and ineffectual. For that reason, concrete applications are pointed out here by which Christian love of the neighbour is to be exercised as an active service. Even Christians quite often set severe limits to their love of their neighbour and their willingness to serve, in dealing nowadays with foreign workers, refugees, illegitimate children and the hungry.

The positive aspect, in which social goodwill inspired by love of the neighbour is at the service of respect for the human person, is completed by a glance at the negative side. It is true that genuine charity not only gives positive service but avoids violating the personal dignity of others. Nevertheless, experience shows that even when a positive attempt is made to show willingness to serve in certain self-chosen spheres, this may be accompanied by violation of personal dignity in other spheres. Consequently this paragraph warns especially against anything which"violates personal integrity... whatever offends human dignity". Here, too, attention is drawn to actual domains in which these violations take place at the present time.

These things are not presented as abominable only because they subvert the common-sense social order of modern humanity. It is important to realize that they cause havoc in various different dimensions simultaneously. This is to some extent a counter-proof that the various aspects of human existence form a unity. These things are a disgrace to human civilization but at the same time they dishonour the personal dignity of those who commit them, and represent an affront to the honour of the Creator who made men to his own image.

Article 28. The subtitle of this article merits attention when compared with the text itself. The theme is stated to be "Respect and Love for Enemies" (*adversarii*) whereas the text speaks of those "who think or act differently from us in social, political and also religious matters". We might ask, are those who think and act differently from us immediately to be regarded as enemies? Certainly not in essence. But the experience of life confirms the realism of this expression. For there are not many who succeed in not at once regarding as their opponents those who think and act differently in social, political and religious questions. Usually we have laboriously to achieve the realization that it is very often possible to think and act differently in these questions, even to a large extent in religious matters, when the question of truth is taken seriously, that one view cannot claim correctness for itself alone, and that in fact the various ways of thinking and acting may fruitfully supplement one another. Far too often those who think differently are opposed as if they were enemies.

Perhaps it is even necessary to some extent that the various ways of thinking should be felt as antithetical or opposed or at least that they should stand in a relation of tension to each other, because it is only in this way that mutual discussion is carried on. For even if a discussion is begun only out of a certain dogmatism or in a polemic confrontation, this is at all events better than acting in complete isolation without any contact at all. True dialogue demands respect and even love; this causes the other to be taken seriously as a partner. With the concept of personal discussion or dialogue, the Church has adopted an idea which permits it to modify the modes of thought of earlier times in a way that our age demands, without actually compromising earlier attitudes of the Church. Dialogue involves a partner and therefore difference, but does not exclude profession of the truth of one's own belief. It does, however, require us to turn to one another with sufficient respect and love for us to be able to speak together and to be as ready to receive as to give. Readiness to receive from one another is very often more difficult than to give to one another.

The text of this article also expressly includes religious matters within the scope of communication of this kind. Ultimately, of course, religious truth belongs more than any other human thing to the life-giving and binding force of society. The second paragraph of the article now says something which also holds good in other spheres of human communication but appears particularly urgent in that of religion and religious truth. Whatever readiness there may be to respect the good in others, discussion with them must not mistakenly identify the predominant importance of love with an uncritical affirmation of everything that the other asserts. In discussion, the true and the good are sought in common, to the extent that they are not already possessed. Consequently, the very purpose of discussion forbids indifference to truth and goodness. On the other hand, it must always be remembered that truth itself cannot be the partner in the discussion and the object of love, but only the person with whom one is speaking and in common with whom one is seeking truth. It is not truth as such which is the subject of right, respect and love, but the human being who is concerned with truth.

Now the attitude in which he seeks the truth and is ready to follow it can be right, even if what he takes to be truth is erroneous. The will to truth may be operative, even in the (involuntary) affirmation of what is objectively false. This certainly demands that truth should be sought and striven for by common discussion. But "we must distinguish between error, which is always to be rejected, and the person in error, who always retains his personal dignity even though he has false or inaccurate religious ideas". If, of course, someone culpably follows error and misses truth, it may certainly be said that he has lost his claim to respect. But even in this case the Council is reserved. Who, except God, is already in a position to judge whether and to what extent a person in error is culpably missing the truth? Finally the Council also reminds us that even in the case of culpable error and a hostile attitude, other people should always meet with forgiveness and love from us.

Two things are therefore to be avoided. Willingness for discussion with people who think differently must not spring from deliberate indifference to truth and goodness, nor should discussion be inspired by the aggressive dogmatism which assumes from the start that what is good and true is only found in oneself.

Article 29. The essential equality of all men and the recognition of this equality in an endeavour to achieve social justice are dealt with in three clearly distinct steps. First the principle of the essential equality of all men is deduced from two premises. The second longer section explains this equality even in the face of certain undeniable differences between human beings. Finally, the last section appeals as a consequence to all institutions to make a common effort to achieve increasing recognition for the equal personal dignity of all men.

The fact that "fundamental equality" is spoken of, means that equality does not exclude considerable differences between groups and individuals. Nor do factual differences call in question the abiding fundamental equality. All human beings are fundamentally equal in two features. They are created by God as persons with a rational soul in God's image. They are therefore intrinsically akin because they possess the same nature and origin. Furthermore, they are all redeemed by Christ and so have the same supernatural vocation to eternal salvation. In view of this fundamental equality, all differences, however considerable, and though they may be the occasion of quarrels, dissension and conflict, are in reality unimportant. Yet in everyday life they force themselves so much to the fore that the Council finds itself obliged soberly to conclude its statement on fundamental equality with the remark that this "fundamental equality of all men must be more and more acknowledged". It is still a goal which has to be patiently aimed at. Furthermore, the Council considers it necessary to justify fundamental equality against two different opposing groups.

Certain ineradicable differences may give the impression that it is not possible to speak of the fundamental equality of all men. Other differences, on the other hand, can be overcome by human effort, though not easily. Differences in physical capacity and intellectual and moral abilities by which human beings are not all on the same footing, are largely due to physical and unchangeable differences of a racial, sexual, national, linguistic and religious kind. They also certainly involve not a few historical and therefore changeable factors which could be overcome by human effort. At all events these objective differences give no right to any kind of discrimination when they are unchangeable, physically stable and consequently make for enduring differences in mode of life and behaviour. That is stressed particularly in regard to the position of women. Freedom and equality of opportunity for women in the choice of husband or state of life and education is insisted on. This must, of course, be a special and fundamental concern of the Church, for the biblical account of creation represents the beginning of human existence as an equality of man and woman, both of whom are made to the image of God (Gen 1:28).

Differences of living conditions are, by comparison, much more directly a matter of efforts to achieve factual equality among men. Equal personal dignity demands a common endeavour for equal living conditions, that is, the overcoming of economic and social inequalities. Precisely because the contradiction between equality of personal dignity and inequality in actual conditions is so immediately perceptible in these domains, social and economic inequality inevitably gives rise to revolt and discontent. The horror of a perpetual threat of war has perhaps at least this good side to it, that it drives the nations to seek agreement in the social and economic domain.

Consequently the article ends with an appeal to private and public institutions, whatever the difference in their immediate tasks, to join in their various ways in a common struggle for social and political freedom and the defence of fundamental rights. Even differences of political regime should not ignore the equality of personal dignity. The article finally observes that the struggle to achieve an order corresponding to the dignity of the human person will be a long one. That is not meant as passive resignation but as a summons to a combative attitude, for without this it is impossible to struggle to mould public life more humanely. The obstacles are considerable, and the most exhausting of all is the way the goal seems to recede further and further into the distance.

Article 30. Acceptance of social involvement encounters, even in the practice of religion, the opposition of a centuries-old attitude, one which many even feel to be quite essential to the domain of conscience, namely, individualism. The Council was very concerned to exhibit the social domain as an essential element of a Christian doctrine of man in harmony with revelation. Precisely for that reason, it had to make a stand against an individualistic ethics which quite often tends to colour the religious life of the faithful.

What this article has to say is best taken as falling into four parts. In the first lines it is clearly admitted that a one-sided development towards increasing individualism can be observed in theology and piety since the later Middle Ages. Individualistic preoccupation with salvation has adversely affected the Church's doctrine in the eyes of the public and is also to some extent strongly opposed to Christian affirmation of the social domain. A purely individualistic ethics is treated in the conciliar text as prevalent to a large extent, but as something to which we must not remain attached. This applies to the individual who has to overcome the indolence which imprisons him in his own ego. But, reading between the lines, we can see that it also applies to the general mentality of Christians. This cannot continue to be tied to the individualistic attitude which has dominated the life of faith and piety in the last few centuries. That an individualistic legacy from history of this kind has to be overcome, is shown by the reason given for the urgency of the admonition: "profound and rapid change". History is the Church's teacher, by bringing to the fore new and different aspects of the total life of man and of the total truth of creation and revelation. It thus supplements attitudes which correspond to the feeling of one age with aspects which always belonged to the whole but did not in fact equally influence reality.

Secondly, we are now called upon to accept a certain institutionalization of the social domain. Individualism must first be overcome by a more open individual ethical attitude to social realities. In our age, however, that would not be sufficient, even if it led to a genuine active contribution to the common good. In harmony with our highly administered world, readiness for social commitment must also lead to collaboration with private and public institutions which serve to improve living conditions. The jealous vigilance over respect for the human person which the Council often enough affirms as its aim, must not be regarded as hostile to institutional realities. In our organized world, social commitment cannot be effective unless it takes concrete institutional form. Rightly understood, institutions as such are not opposed to personal development and to personal action; they are concerned with order among persons and their planned activity. Consequently they stand in a fruitful tension with the human person. This is threatened from two sides, however, by the individualism which affirms the person at the expense of the community and the institutionalism which attributes absolute value to organized society at the cost of the person.

A third section points out certain failures to overcome individualistic ethics. Two forms are mentioned. It is insufficient to side with the community and social duty merely by magniloquent denunciation of individualism, if one's own life is very little marked by concern for the needs of society. Since social order has to be planned and realized among human beings, the language in which programmes are expounded is certainly very important. But such programmes are intended for purposeful activity and practical action. Anyone who merely makes plans and talks about them contradicts himself if he does not prove their validity and utility in his own practical life. A second failure consists in putting the proposed programme into effect in one's general attitude of life and in a few actions that are to one's own particular taste, but ignoring them on other points of special importance at the present time. Taxes and similar contributions without which society cannot fulfil its purpose, regulations for safeguarding health and the life of all, among which even the Highway Code may be included, are expressly raised from a purely secular perspective into a religious moral obligation. It is one of the calamitous results of what has been called the two-tier theory of the relations between nature and grace, to exclude the socially organized domain of the State from that of supernatural, religious obligations, no less calamitous than the contrary error of so-called integrism which sought to regulate the contents of that domain directly on the basis of faith and consequently wanted to attribute to the Church a direct regulative authority over it.

Finally, in the fourth paragraph it is positively stated that social necessities are to be counted among the chief duties of all, and therefore of Christians, at the present day. It is in fact very important to realize that when the Church turns to the world as the Council has done, it means that its members will be concerned with their solidarity with the present destiny and tasks of the world. Social obligations are pointed out as duties before God, as material in which to embody an attitude to God. That is a task for the community, yet has to be carried out by individuals. The smaller groups which give human society its structure must not be overlooked, but individualism often predominates in them even more than in individuals.

Article 31. Institutions which were recommended in the previous article on social commitment serve personal life because, like a ready-made road, they spare the individual perpetually repeated planned and free decisions in many matters of private as well as social life. Forms of life based on custom or institutions need not harm personal life but can in fact leave room for the important personal decisions which at special points determine a life's direction. Consequently the previous article insisted on readiness to develop social commitment in favour of the institutions which actually serve it.

Equally urgently this has to be accompanied by genuine cultivation of the soul and formation of the conscience, if life in the framework of institutionally organized society is to remain a human one. Human life is based on responsibility. Trust in institutions must not eliminate vigilance of conscience, alertness of mind, cultivation of the soul. The more mankind grows together in a network of social relationships, and the more perfectly its social life is institutionalized and organized, the more need it will have of careful education for all, culture, spiritual greatness and the development of man's whole being.

Such a task, however, must not be viewed idealistically without regard for reality. The Council is very soberly aware how very dependent a sense of responsibility is on external conditions of life. How can a human being be conscious of his personal dignity if his living conditions are practically those of an animal? How can he maintain a vivid awareness of his personal dignity if the comfort which surrounds him scarcely leaves him any sense of the need for free decisions and if, enclosed in the world of his own ego, he feels no responsibility for society? Social life must liberate such people from their selfishness with salutary force, so that they meet the needs of social life.

The article concludes with a glance at the life of the State in which men's social involvement finds its most tangible and effective expression. No plea is made for any particular form of constitution, but in the interests of the human person preference is nevertheless given to those regimes in which "the largest possible number of citizens take part in public affairs with genuine freedom". The democratic form of society is, after all, the form of State which best combines personal independence and social responsibility.[3] But "democracy" is not laid down as a norm for the life of the State without qualification, not only because democracy itself can assume very different forms, but even more because this kind of public life presupposes a mature condition of society, which is only found in very different degrees in the various nations or is not yet present at all. The structure of the State is not something to be determined from outside by violent revolution or dictatorial edict. The citizens of a nation will only be ready for responsible collaboration in public life — for this form of social obligation often meets with hesitation or refusal, even from people who are vividly conscious of their social duties — if they find in the various groups of the social body incentives to social service. This is finally expressed in a general maxim of social action. What has to be done is to provide reasons for living in hope if there is to be any success in modifying or contributing to modify men's lot. It is very remarkable how strongly the Pastoral Constitution is attuned to hope. It begins and ends with the word hope. And at this point, where it is a question of showing how necessary it is for the individual to break out of his encapsulation in his own ego and to open himself to others, hope once again appears as the basic force leading him to values and benefits outside himself. By hope, he turns away from himself towards them. Then social

---

[3] Cf. the commentary by O. von Nell-Breuning on Chapter IV of Part II.

service of others will spring from this power of hope to break down isolation.

Article 32. All the chapters of Part I end with an article linking one particular aspect of the Church's relation to the world with Christ and showing that it is fulfilled in him. There are two reasons for this. First to avoid the misconception that the Church wants a link with the world at the expense of its union with Christ. At the same time it has to be shown in a positive way that all domains of human life have been raised in Christ into living unity with God: not only the soul but the body; not only the individual body and soul but also social duty, which also is wholly included in that divinization by which alone human reality attains the fulfilment intended for it by God.

In the social domain itself, Christ's work stands in complete continuity with the foundation that the Creator laid in the work of creation. Christ's work of redemption is certainly a "correction" of the creation in the sense that the disorder brought into created reality by men's sin was eliminated by redemption. Its effects remain, but the disorder is nevertheless overcome so that man can incorporate the goodness of creation into his participation in divine sonship and can make use of the burdensome elements of creation to overcome sin and its consequences by resolute and therefore penitential endurance. The fulfilment and perfecting of the creation by Christ's saving work also takes place through social involvement. That God "did not create man for life in isolation but for the formation of social unity" is a truth clearly expressed in the Bible by the fact that it uses (though not in the same passages) the word Adam, which primarily means the human species, as the individual name of the first man. Man is meant by his Creator in his individuality, in which God "has called him by name". But precisely as such he is meant as member of the whole. Since the beginning of the history of salvation, God has chosen men as members of a redeemed community. Vatican II has very insistently and officially expressed this awareness that God's real partner in sacred history is the People of God and the individual only to the extent that he belongs to this people.

The corporate character of redemption is shown by a few concrete features of Christ's work. The family is to some extent in the foreground as the basic cell of human social life in which every individual human existence begins, so that a social relation is part of his very entity from the beginning, but other references to society in Christ's words and works are not omitted.

Christ's message, being one of love, entails the affirmation of human society and demands its realization through unselfish devotion. The apostles were sent out to gather humanity together into the unity of God's family, whose law is fulfilled by love. Now Christ founded the Church as a sacramental sign and pledge of God's universal saving will, i.e. of the fact that Christ is the first-born of many brothers. By the foundation of the Church as a mysterious body in which all members are interrelated and their unity is not diminished by hierarchical and personal differences, man's social solidarity is confirmed and sacramentally represented on the plane of salvation.

But even in the Christian order of salvation the solidarity of a freely accepted community is not assured once and for all. It has to grow and be preserved against perpetual threat until it reaches its fulfilment. And the latter is not a heaven of many individuals, but perfect corporate glorification of God. The last sentences of the article should not be regarded as pious flourishes but as a renewed reminder that God is not glorified where solidarity with other human beings is neglected. To achieve this solidarity by service, is an indispensable form of glorifying God.

Man's Activity throughout the World

by

Alfons Auer

This chapter gradually developed from its beginnings in social philosophy, via two intermediate forms, one theological and systematic, the other biblical and expressed in terms of redemptive history, into the ultimate pastoral form in which it was finally adopted by the Council.*

The first two versions were based on classical Catholic social metaphysics and social ethics. They envisaged human work in the context of social and economic problems. The schema "De ordine sociali" produced by a sub-commission of the Preparatory Theological Commission consisted of Chapter III, "De indole laboris humani" (nature and dignity of work; duty and right to work; conditions of work, etc.), and Chapter IV, "De iusta laboris remuneratione" (criteria of just wage; relation between economic growth and social progress; welfare and security for the workers; right to strike, etc.). The second version, "Constitutio de Ecclesiae presentia et actione in mundo", drafted by the Mixed Commission specially set up for the purpose, presents practically the same themes in Chapter V, "De ordine oeconomico et de iustitia sociali". All that was new was Article 63 on women at work. Texts 1 and 2 were kept rather abstract and didactic, very much in the same style as the social teaching of the Church in the papal social encyclicals since Leo XIII. What K. Rahner in a *longus sermo* criticized in the schema as a whole also applies to this chapter. What is said about man's creation to the image of God, the relations between nature and grace, Christ's saving work and original sin, is inadequate. At the same time a certain triumphalism

---

* Preliminary note. The historical part of the commentary on Chapter III is based in substance on the article of R.-A. Sigmond, "Unterlagen zur Geschichte der pastoralen Konstitution über die Kirche in der Welt von heute", *IDOC* (International Documentation Centre), Bulletin nos. 66–2 and 66–3 (referred to as Sigmond I and II respectively).

is evident in it, because the Church speaks as if it had ready at hand a solution for every evil.[1]

The philosophical social doctrine about work developed in detail in Texts 1 and 2, was of course not abandoned in later drafts but it was condensed into a single section. Text 3 brought it into Adnexa IV, Article II, Texts 4 and 5 into Chapter III, "De vita oeconomica-sociali", Article 79 or 67.

The Malines text (Interim A), produced on the initiative of Cardinal Suenens, represented a strictly theological but no less didactic version. Article 14, "De labore hominis in mundo", presented in short outline a theology of work. This sketch, it is true, was set in a broad theological framework. After speaking of the specific mission of the Church, Chapter II dealt with the building up of the world and in particular with the autonomy of earthly domains, with the new awareness of the unity of mankind, the ambiguity which this presents and which has to be overcome. We note that the section on work comes in the middle of the statements on the autonomy of the world. It is quite clear that the resolutely theological approach in the Malines text produced an entirely new intellectual atmosphere. Although the draft bore the provocative title "Adumbratio Schematis XVII de activa praesentia ecclesiae in mundo aedificando" and began directly with a dissertation on the specific mission of the Church, it was able to create an atmosphere in which it seemed quite convincing to talk of the Church respecting the autonomy of the world. But the text could not be used because it was written in the ambitious style of a highly compressed theological treatise.

The Zurich version (Text 3) once again introduced an entirely different approach. The doctrine drawn from social philosophy, "De praestantia laboris humani et de eius obliteratione", was, as has been noted, relegated to the appendices (IV, 11). The main conciliar text itself also dealt with the question of human activity in the world, but from the comprehensive point of view "De integra hominis vocatione" (Chapter I). Articles 6 and 7 of Interim Text B, drawn up in French by Fr. R.-A. Sigmond, assisted by Fr. Dingemans, OP ("Valeur des tâches terrestres" and "Dimensions spirituelles de l'univers"), are condensed in Text 3 into the one Article 6 "De valore rerum et munerum terrestrium". After the philosophical disquisitions of the first two versions and the lofty theological speculation of the Malines text, the Zurich draft is biblical in outlook. We would not be far wrong in describing this text with its biblical foundation, inner coherence and stylistic homogeneity, as the most unmixed success in the whole history of the Pastoral Constitution. (This applies particularly to the first draft of the Zurich text made by Fr. Sigmond.) Recourse to the Bible had made it possible to give the whole schema a Christological orientation. Christ is the last end of man's

---

[1] Cf. *Acta commissionis de doctrina fidei et morum*, p. 17 (report by the secretary on the meeting of Subcommissions II and V, 20 March 1963).

natural and supernatural vocation (Chapter I); the Church seeks to bring him to all humanity (Chapter II); spiritual union with him enables Christians to serve effectively in the various domains of the world (Chapters III and IV). Fr. Sigmond brings out clearly the new element in the Zurich text as a whole, not only in regard to our immediate theme of the vocation of work and its integration into the fundamental human and Christian vocation, into the "integra hominis vocatio": "The text endeavours to bring together things which in appearance stand in diametrical opposition — to speak to the world directly and to use a language which the world can understand, without falling into platitudinous moralizing; to expound doctrine about the vocation of man and the position of the Church in the modern world without adopting a pedagogical tone; to express an optimistic view about people of the present time and to announce the Church's willingness for genuine collaboration in creating a more humane world without losing sight of the difference that exists between the world and the Church's essentially supernatural function. In this sense a new attempt was made in an entirely new direction. But because of the ambiguity entailed, it aroused not only great enthusiasm but also sharp criticism. Consequently it could not serve as the definitive text."[2] Probably here and there there were fears that because of its radically biblical line the draft might sound to many people too "Protestant", although this feature in fact considerably increased the possibilities of ecumenical dialogue.

The Ariccia version, Text 4, combined the two parts of the Zurich version (schema and adnexa) into a "Constitutio pastoralis de ecclesia in mundo huius temporis". The material on social philosophy is again found in an abbreviated form in Part II (Article 79); but in Part I the question of the significance of human activity throughout the world is treated in a separate chapter, Chapter III: "Quid significat humana navitas in universo mundo?" At the *sessio plenaria mixta* in Rome, 29 March — 7 April 1965, this question appeared explicitly for the first time, though at first the word "activitas" was used instead of "navitas".[3] The Ariccia text in no way repudiates its predecessors, the theological Malines text and the biblical Zurich text, not even in our Chapter III. It attempts rather to combine the two and by explicit analyses of the contemporary situation, as well as by an accessible style, to adapt itself as far as possible to the pastoral aim in view. It is true that Chapter III in the Ariccia version is not as coherent in structure or as lucid as Chapter I of the Zurich draft. And it also deals in greater detail with a larger number of questions.

Text 5 presents considerable modification and substantial shortening of

---

[2] Sigmond I, p. 3.
[3] Cf. *Acta commissionis de doctrina fidei et* morum, pp. 14–16 (Introduction to the secretary's report).

Chapter III of Text 4.[4] No essentially new points of view are added, but existing ones are given greater precision and clarity by the new, more concise form. The pastoral purpose is well served by the fact that Text 5 moves inductively from below upwards. "The exposition begins with a description of the present situation of mankind, goes on to deal with human problems in the light both of the natural law and of divine revelation, and culminates by pointing to the mystery of Christ in whom man is renewed and reaches the ultimate goal of his pilgrimage through the centuries."[5] Text 5 met on the whole with so much approval from the Council that only those *modi* were accepted which did not alter the line it had taken. After the last amendments had been incorporated, the schema was finally approved in the general congregation as follows:

	Votes	*Placet*	*Non placet*	*Placet juxta modum*	*Invalid*
1st Vote					
arts. 33–36	2216	2173	33	—	10
arts. 37–39	2227	2169	45	—	13
Chapter III					
as a whole	2223	1727	25	467	4
2nd Vote	2230	2165	62		3

Article 33. *Statement of the problem.* The question of the meaning of human activity is not suggested by the Church and theology but is forced on people's attention by the most urgent realities of contemporary life. The text mentions two facts, first the emergence of *homo faber,* in other words of man who by the application of scientific thought and technical skill has extended and is perpetually extending "his mastery over almost the whole of nature". Secondly there is the fact of "socialization", by which "the human family is gradually establishing itself as a world-wide community" and at the same time is becoming conscious of itself as such. These two facts imply, though this of course is not expressly stated in the text, two important intellectual developments, the formation of a dynamic view of the world and the experience of man's temporal, historical character. Both come about in proportion as man achieves his own self-realization by creative interaction with the world. Finally our text points to the consequence that follows from technical domination of the world and the increasing socialization of the whole of humanity. Many benefits which in earlier ages men used to expect "chiefly from higher powers", they now obtain for themselves

[4] The number of articles was reduced from 11 to 7, that of pages from 6 to 4.
[5] Sigmond II, p. 2.

by their own industry. This immense enterprise of mankind itself impels people to question its meaning. What values are inherent in this development? In what direction is it leading? How can it continue to serve the well-being of the human person and of human society? Whenever the question of meaning and purpose is raised, the Church has something to offer. The Council does not appeal here too hastily and in the usual manner to the traditional patterns of natural law doctrine. It does not claim at all that the Church can arrive at binding decisions even in questions of natural morality by infallible pronouncements of its magisterium. The Church of Vatican II appeals rather to "the deposit of God's word" which it holds. From this it can indeed derive "principia in ordine religioso et morali" but not ready-made answers to all the detailed questions which arise. It has the honest wish to combine the light of revelation with universal human knowledge and experience ("lumen revelationis cum omnium peritia coniungere"). That is not a claim to a monologue of proclamation, but the spirit of dialogue which Paul VI evoked so strikingly in his encyclical *Ecclesiam Suam* (6 August 1964).[6]

In this sense the *relatio generalis* on Chapter III had already formulated the aim of the chapter as: "quaestio de valore navitatis humanae, quae praecipue intelligitur externa (scientiae naturales, technica), coram fide; et ab altera parte, quid fides afferat huic conamini."[7] Several fathers, it is true, wanted the Council to speak about technology in greater detail because it is the "soul of the modern world" and because its progress strongly influences the present situation of mankind.[8]

However, no change was made in the schema. Even the request of 16 fathers that the emphasis should not be onesidedly placed on technical enterprise but that more account should be taken of *navitas spiritualis*, was refused, and so was another father's criticism of the idealistic unrealism of this chapter (Chapter III, *modus* 1). The final text, like its predecessors, the Malines text (Articles 20 and 21) and Text 3 (Article 2), stressed the two facts of growth of technology and of socialization. The statement that earlier generations looked mainly to higher powers ("a supernis viribus praesertim") for many benefits which people obtain by their own efforts, was introduced in response to a request from 45 fathers. Instead of "a supernis viribus" it at first had "a natura". The *modus* was accepted on the grounds that in the primitive religions men did not in fact look to nature for these benefits but to supernatural powers, or at least to nature understood in a more or less magical or religious way (Chapter III, *modus* 2b).

---

[6] As well as a whole series of definitions of the term "dialogue", we also find here the formula: "divinas cum hominum cogitationibus coniungere".

[7] *Textus recognitus et relationes* I (1965), p. 48.

[8] Cf. Text 4, 99.

Of course the Council was not primarily concerned with facts but with the meaning which arises from them for man himself. In his *relatio generalis*,[9] Archbishop Garrone, in the absence of Bishop Guano, emphasized precisely the great importance of this chapter from this point of view: "Hic enim problemata tanguntur ex iis quae maxime conscientiam humanam hodie pungere et premere constat: quid de rebus terrenis censendum? Quem ipsis valorem agnoscit Ecclesia? Quid de rerum terrenarum autonomia? Ecclesia iis rebus consistentiam propriam agnoscit an non? Quid de progressiva evolutione mundi, quid de victoriis quibus mundus hodie gloriari posse credit? Haec omnia putatne Ecclesia grave quid et serium esse? Quid tandem omnia haec respectu promissionum caelestium et Regni? Graves omnino questiones quae ad imum hominum hodiernorum pertingunt et simul puncta difficilima et minime explicita revelationis christianae respiciunt." Precisely the fact that very difficult questions are involved which revelation hardly deals with at all explicitly, imposes on the Church that prudent reserve which was described as the "spirit of dialogue". Article 33 of the *Textus recognitus* (1965) still included the words: "Ecclesia, quae responsa universaliora possidet..." One Council father gave the warning that a more modest expression than "Ecclesia responsa possidet" would be more appropriate to the dialogue that was to be undertaken; forty-six others asked for the deletion of this sentence (Chapter III, *modus* 5). The final formulation was the result of examining a whole series of emendations.

Chapter III is therefore concerned with the question of the "value of human activity, especially external (science and technology) in the light of faith and also with the contribution of faith to this enterprise" (*relatio generalis* on Chapter III). The chapter handles the question by outlining a view of work in the theological perspective of the history of salvation:

Articles 34–36 human activity in the light of the mystery of creation

> 37 human activity in the shadow of the mystery of sin
> 38 human activity in the light of the mystery of Christ
> 39 human activity in the light of the mystery of perfect fulfilment.

Article 34. *The value of human activity.* The belief in creation provides a first partial answer to the question of the value of human activity, that is to say, of that tremendous effort extending over centuries, undertaken by individuals and by the whole of society, to improve the material and intellectual conditions of their life. This immense enterprise, considered in itself, is in accordance with the divine plan. That plan assigns to man a double vocation. As God's image he is to bring the whole earth under his

---

[9] Text 4, 8.

dominion and exercise that dominion in justice and holiness. But he must also refer himself and all the things which he has subjected to himself, to the Creator. That really only means that he must consciously put into effect the intrinsic relation which links him and things to God. The subjection of things to man is a condition of the glorification of God on this earth. The Council considers it important to note that this interpretation of human endeavour also enhances the significance of commonplace everyday tasks. Article 38 in Text 4 had explicitly referred to the services rendered by particular occupations (the mother in the home, the workman, the scientist, farmer, baker, office-worker, engineer) but this concrete detail had to be sacrificed later to the need for brevity. At all events the final text still observes that all who employ their energies to provide for themselves, their families and society advance (evolvere) the work of God in the course of history. Mankind's universal enterprise of world-development in no sense stands in opposition to God, and those engaged in it are anything but God's rivals. Clearly the Council was not afraid that to describe man as collaborating with God or as completing the work of the Creator might attribute too much independence and creative activity to man to the detriment of God's transcendence.[10] From the triumphs of the human race it looks, rather, for an increasingly striking manifestation of divine greatness, and at the same time a growing awareness of human responsibility. Belief in the Creator does not undermine the Christian's resolute involvement in the world but mobilizes his capacities to the utmost.

Text 4 had also emphasized that this observation also applies to "those creations of the human mind which fill us with amazement at the present time, e.g. the manned machines which he is building to send through measureless and unimaginable space". This sentence was fortunately omitted in Text 5.[11]

An improvement of this article as compared with Text 4 may also be seen in the fact that the presentation is more clearly centred on the doctrine of man's creation to the image of God. This is the real reason why man must bring material things under his dominion and refer himself and the whole material world to the Creator.[12] A proposal of 194 fathers was not accepted which suggested that even at this point it should be emphasized that man must direct the employment of earthly things not only to his natural but

---

[10] A different viewpoint will be found in K. Barth, *Kirchliche Dogmatik* III/4, p. 596, E. T.: *Church Dogmatics* (1961).

[11] K. Rahner, *Anmerkungen zum Schema "De Ecclesia in mundo huius temporis"* (unpublished expert opinion on Text 4), p. 9: "Laus harum machinarum astronauticarum satis indiscreta potius omittatur." Rahner rightly asks whether what is later said about nuclear weapons does not also apply to these technical inventions. It is plain that the schema gives no "norms governing the evolution and active transformation of the world as such".

[12] Cf. *Textus recognitus et relationes* I (1965), p. 48.

also to his supernatural end (Chapter III, *modus* 7).[13] Eighteen fathers requested the omission of the words "si recte ordinatur" (Text 4) and "in seipso consideratum" (Text 5), because these expressions seem to speak of the "rectitudo moralis" (Chapter III, *modus* 6).[14] In fact this was one of the most important of Karl Rahner's criticisms of Text 4.[15] The improvement of social conditions ("condiciones vitae sociales meliores reddere" or "in melius mutare"), he remarked, must be regarded as a direct moral obligation. But it ought to be indicated what standard is to be employed to decide between the various possibilities of improvement. There are, he continued, significant values, norms and directions in active transformation of the world. On the other hand there are norms of moral activity. Finally there is a religious meaning to this transformation. These are very different things, K. Rahner insisted, yet the schema does not clearly distinguish between intrinsic value or autonomy on the one hand and moral obligation and religious orientation on the other. But that is precisely the issue today, for we no longer live in a static, but in a dynamic world. Expressions such as "creatoris opus peragere" (Text 4) or "opus creatoris evolvere" (*Textus recognitus* and final text) are in fact too vague. The schema ought not, as K. Rahner said, to engage in direct moral teaching, but should first make clear the intrinsic value of human activity before it presents its moral and religious finality. The things of this world are more than mere material for moral and religious probation, more than merely "occasiones moralitatis sive pietatis", as the Middle Ages used to say. People nowadays no longer wish their dealings with the world to be purely meditative or philosophical, they want to shape the world for their own use and get the best out of it. Perhaps ecclesiastical thought is still to a large extent too dominated by Platonic idealism or Aristotelian intellectualism for it to be able fully to appreciate natural science and technology. An influence of that kind easily leads to the kind of moralism which readily provokes aversion in people today.[16] Of course it is not a primary function of the Church to expound the intrinsic value of earthly domains and their significance for human existence. It can only take cognizance of what insights are offered by phenomenology and the philosophical doctrine of man in conjunction with human experience.

Article 35. *The regulation of human activity.* In the light of belief in creation, human activity appears as human participation in the unfolding of the divine plan in the world. Now man is set in the midst of the entire

---

[13] In the answer it is said that this insertion would mean a "substantial addition" and that in any case it is expressly dealt with subsequently.

[14] The *Responsio* confirms that it is the ontological goodness of human endeavour which is meant here, while moral goodness is not dealt with until the next two articles.

[15] Cf. Rahner, *op. cit.,* pp. 2 f., 9.

[16] *Ibid.,* p. 3: "Normae et exhortationes morales 'idealisticae' etiam verissimae abundanter prolatae facile nauseam movent."

cosmos and its development as an all-embracing principle of organization. Man is a person and his personality develops in the social and the material sphere. The regulation of human activity can therefore only consist of bringing man's powers into action on all three planes of his life. Consequently the fundamental regulation of human activity in the world aims at developing personality, at integration into social life and at shaping material things. More important than things and than technical progress in mastering them, is man himself and the universal fraternity of all men. And this has to lead to a more human regulation of social relationships. Advancing technical command of matter does not *ipso facto* mean progressive humanization; it represents merely the raw material of human advance which can and must be achieved through it. The final sentence of Article 35 summarizes these statements and integrates them into the divine plan and will for the world. "The norm of human activity is therefore that, in accord with the divine plan and will, it should harmonize with the genuine good of the human race and allow men as individuals and as members of society to pursue their total vocation and fulfil it."

Text 4 had included the substance of this statement in Article 39, "De fide christiana et humanis victoriis". There it was also expressly given a Christocentric orientation, as the context suggested. When the passage was placed earlier, this Christocentric orientation disappeared. It seemed more important to the Council fathers to make clear from the very beginning the hierarchy of earthly values, i.e. their culmination in man and his orientation towards transcendence.[17] Many of them nevertheless thought the present article lacked a clear distinction between the "ontological" and the "moral value" of human activity. If they regarded their moral worth as consisting in the "ordination of human activity towards God",[18] the confusion of ideas becomes even more evident. For the moral value of human activity lies precisely in realizing human potentialities in their three dimensions, while its religious significance and value consists in relating that activity to God. Sixteen fathers would have liked to term the orientation of human activity towards the common welfare of man its "prima", "universalis" or "proxima norma", and only then introduce the "divina norma". The final decision was different, however: "Mentio consilii divini obtineat locum magis eminentem." As a result the final version of the closing sentence of the chapter already quoted was drawn up (cf. Chapter III, *modus* 14).

Article 36. *The rightful independence of earthly affairs.* At this point the Council seeks to remove a deep-seated resentment felt by people today. In the previous articles the value and order of human activity are referred back to the Creator. Now there is no doubt that any close linking of human

[17] Cf. *Textus recognitus et relationes* I (1965), p. 49.
[18] Cf. *ibid.*

activity with religion suggests to many of our contemporaries that great danger may ensue for the autonomy of man, social structures and scientific work. That is certainly not difficult to understand. At one time there was indubitably a doctrine of the "potestas directa ecclesiae in temporalia". To be sure it was later softened into the doctrine of the "potestas indirecta". But not a few people are of the opinion that the traditional natural law doctrine is ultimately nothing but an ideological formula — adapted under the pressure of necessity to secular feeling — with the help of which the Church tries to maintain the *potestas indirecta in temporalia* in a different historical epoch. For that reason the Council was well-advised strongly to emphasize in this article the doctrine of the autonomy of the various secular spheres. This has been proclaimed for a century, but it is still far from having prevailed everywhere in the Church. The Pastoral Constitution acknowledges this autonomy wholly and entirely. Autonomy is entirely justified, if by autonomy we understand "that created things and societies themselves enjoy their own laws and values which must be gradually deciphered, put to use and regulated by man". The theological interpretation regards this autonomy as based on the "word" of creation. Because the world was created through the "word", all things are endowed with their own ontological consistence, truth, goodness, their own laws and orderly structure ("propria firmitate, veritate, bonitate propriisque legibus ac ordine"). The rationality of the whole world, i.e. all the laws of the physical, biological, mathematical and logical realms of reality, as well as those of the world of artistic significance and those of personal existence and of man's social solidarity originate in the "word" of creation. The Pastoral Constitution draws clear conclusions from this insight, two concerning principles and one concerning the historical point of view. It is first noted that the intelligible values and laws of the various domains must be discovered and employed usefully in human life by applying "the methods proper to each of the sciences and techniques". Then it is said with welcome serenity that scientific research, if "conducted in a genuinely scientific manner and in accord with moral norms", cannot conflict with faith, because the rationality of the world and the message of faith both have their origin in the same God.[19] Finally the Council sincerely regrets that even among Christians the autonomy of the secular domains was not always sufficiently acknowledged and that as a consequence there were occasionally quarrels and controversies. The last part of this article once again expressly rejects the false conception of autonomy which denies that things have their root in the divine will of the Creator and so abandons their use to the arbitrary will of man. This is said totally to overlook the fact that creatures are nothing without the Creator, that their true pattern is obscured

---

[19] At this point the Council refers to the corresponding statements of Vatican I (*D* 1785 f. [3004 f.]).

by forgetfulness of the Creator and that by this, men place themselves out-side the community of all believers of all religions.

Article 36 certainly does not bring anything new. But its acknowledgment of the intrinsic value of the world will certainly not fail to produce its effect. It testifies that the Church is determined to abandon the medieval confis-cation of the world in a single unitary order and to set the world free into what is intrinsically its own. The road to the recognition of the "duality of the ecclesiastical and the secular order" (Y. Congar) is open.[20] Articles 38 and 39 will show that this duality only attains its full truth through the integration of the world in the reality of redemption.

A few points only will be noted from the earlier history of the text. Even in the discussion of Text 2 and in particular of Chapter IV "De cultura et progressu", one *peritus*, Bonet, had remarked that the chapter smacked of clericalism ("redolere clericalismo") and that a declaration must be made about the autonomy of science. Y. Congar completed this remark by point-ing out that civilization had formerly borne an ecclesiastical and clerical stamp, whereas today as a result of scientific progress, a gulf had opened between civilization and Church.[21] It has already been indicated that the Malines text (Interim Text A) very definitely took into account what these *periti* said, by placing the idea of autonomy at the head of Article 2 "De mundo aedificando". In this version we probably have the most decided definition of the term autonomy: "Mundus ... propria viget consistentia et suis regitur principiis ac legibus, quas Ecclesia libenter et sincere agnoscit, non quidem tanquam suas (!), sed tamen a Deo, auctore naturae, statutas" (art. 13). Similarly, Text 4 had a special section devoted to autonomy, though this section is described in the *relatio generalis* as an "appendix" to the doctrine of man as the image of God and of the creation. The *relator* does not seem quite to have realized that what is involved is so fundamental and essential a part of the doctrine of creation that it simply cannot be omitted in this context.

Originally the present article had begun in Text 4 with the words "Pro credente igitur omnia ultimatim vim religiosam induunt ..." This introduc-tory sentence was then omitted, however, perhaps because of the sharp criticism to which K. Rahner had subjected it.[22]

The concept of autonomy was no longer so clearly formulated in Text 4.

---

[20] Cf. Interim Text A, arts. 8 and 11.

[21] Cf. *Acta commissionis de doctrina fidei et morum*, p. 26 (report of the meeting on 24 May 1963).

[22] Cf. Rahner, *op. cit.*, p. 9. Rahner asks what this "ultimatim" actually means for in-stance in regard to the building of spacecraft or the abstention from building them. In any case he did not see why this *vis religiosa*, if it is to be found everywhere, should only concern the believer.

In Text 5 it came out better again.[23] The polemical, apologetical tone in Text 4 which even persisted in Text 5 was strongly criticized and finally removed.[24] The remarks on the relation between faith and science, as well as on earlier errors that had crept in, were shortened in Text 5.[25] There were several discussions of the case of Galileo. Some considered that only some general reference should be made to it. Others thought that a special statement ought to be made about it, in the interests of the scientific world; the laity especially expected this. Of course it was pointed out that the case would have to be presented in its historical context. Luther, too, had opposed the thesis Galileo had maintained.[26] Two fathers argued against any statement on the matter because it would simply reveal an inferiority complex. Another wished the Church's services to science to be emphasized (Chapter III, *modus* 18a). A suggestion made by 46 fathers explains why the text speaks not only of laws but also of values (Chapter III, *modus* 15b: "Nam non agitur de solis legibus, sed et de valoribus realitatis profanae"). At the point where autonomy is given its basis in the will of the Creator, 14 fathers would have liked to insert: autonomia "cum Creatoris voluntate congruit, quia est conditio participationis in opere creationis et sic quaevis interpretatio magica mundi evacuatur" (Chapter III, *modus* 16). In the reply, the connection between the striving for autonomy and secularization is conceded, but the commission regarded the matter as too complex to express in a few words.

Article 37. *Human activity as infected by sin.* Having considered human activity in the light of the mystery of creation, the chapter comes to speak of the effects of sin. The experience of the centuries and the statements of Scripture agree that the achievements of human progress are not solely positive in character. Sinful human beings, whether as individuals or collectively, primarily seek themselves, have no concern for the hierarchy of values, mingle good with evil and not only prevent the growth of true brotherhood but even threaten the survival of the human race through their continually increasing power. The whole of history testifies to the unceasing struggle against the powers of darkness. The task of the Church in view of this situation is double. Despite its trust in God's creative will for the world, it must not close its eyes to the disorder which deforms the working world, and must summon men to struggle against vanity and malice, so that what is intended to be a blessing will not be transformed into an instrument of sin. It must also confess that the corruption of human activity needs the

---

[23] Cf. *Textus recognitus et relationes* I (1965), p. 49.
[24] Cf. *ibid.* and the *Expensio modorum*, Cap. III, *modus* 15 a.
[25] Cf. *Textus recognitus et relationes* I, p. 49.
[26] Cf. *Acta commissionis de doctrina fidei et morum*, pp. 11, 26 (reports of the meetings on 11 February and 1 April 1965).

purifying and perfecting power of Christ's cross and resurrection. In the communion with Christ effected by the Holy Spirit, man can love the things of the world in the right way. He is "brought into true possession of the world 'as having nothing yet possessing all'". The article ends with a reference to 1 Cor 3:22f.: "... all are yours, and you are Christ's, and Christ is God's."

Naturally all earlier texts had mentioned the disorder introduced into human activity by sin. Text 3 (Article 8; Interim Text B, Article 9), strongly marked by biblical theology, dealt with this theme in a separate article. In Text 4, however, there was no mention of it in the chapter headings. K. Rahner noted this specifically in his criticism. General lamentations over human immorality are fruitless, he pointed out, if they only express everyday experience; the schema lacks a correct theology of sin. "The depth of sin, which cannot be eradicated from the world, is not made clear ... it is not said what follows from the recognition that sin cannot be overcome (before Christ's second coming), for the concrete mode of action." Instead of the legitimate and necessary "pessimism which Christians need to profess, the schema contains in fact the ideology of a better or even of an excellent world".[27] From other quarters, too, a more detailed treatment of the world's sin was called for.[28] One father appealed to Teilhard de Chardin in a positive sense. Two others, on the contrary, warned against his type of optimism. In a similar strain, six Council fathers maintained that man's salvation consists solely *(unice)* in flight from the world *(fuga mundi)*. This is so, they said, because there is an "absoluta incompatibilitas inter Christum et mundum qui totus in maligno positus est".[29] Consequently, Article 37 was once more recast in Text 5, but even so it did not meet with approval. 203 fathers wanted more precise statements about the sin of the angels, the first sin and original sin, because the text seemed to regard sin as something more like a "cosmic cataclysm" than a moral action (Chapter III, *modus* 22b). Some account of this was taken in the final text. Other fathers stressed that the process of man's higher development cannot come to fulfilment without the cross of Christ. This was how the reference to the purifying and perfecting power of Christ's cross and resurrection came into the text (Chapter III, *modus* 24).[30]

Article 38. *Human activity finds perfection in the paschal mystery.* Human activity, from a theological point of view, is a partnership with the

[27] Cf. Rahner, *op. cit.*, p. 3.
[28] Cf. *Textus recognitus et relationes* I (1965), p. 49; Méouchi; German Bishops' Conference; Marafini; Seitz; Corboy; Indonesian Bishops' Conference; Zambian Bishops' Conference; De Provenchères.
[29] Cf. on this Text 4, *Relationes particulares*, p. 98.
[30] Cf. also *Textus recognitus et relationes* I (1965), p. 49, on the relation between faith in the dependence of things on God and a right understanding of poverty.

divine creative will in developing the world throughout history (arts. 34–36). Human activity means partnership with the divine will to order, in conflict with the powers of destruction unleashed by sin (art. 37). But human partnership with God also extends into a quite different dimension; it is a partnership in building up the body of Christ. Article 38 begins with an extremely important statement: "For God's Word, through whom all things were made, was himself made flesh and dwelt on the earth of men (Jn 1:3, 14). Thus he entered the world's history as a perfect man, taking that history up into himself and summarizing it (Eph 1:10)." In his incarnation the eternal Word took the whole of humanity and the whole cosmos, with its being and its historical development, as his body; all realities, all values and all orders are joined into one in him. This interconnection is the ontological condition which makes it possible for the Lord's death and resurrection to become the events which save the world.

By the Lord's incarnation it has been made plain that God is love, that love is the fundamental law of human perfection and of the transformation of the world, that it is the way to universal brotherhood and that such love must be aimed at even in the small things of daily life, as Christ's example makes strikingly clear.

Then the Pastoral Constitution comes to speak of the saving power of the resurrection. The exalted Lord, to whom all power on heaven and earth is given, is active by his Spirit in the hearts of men. He awakens longing for the world to come (which is already a reality in the Lord on high, who is its centre). But he also prompts the generous aspiration which impels men to shape the world in a more humane way. The gifts of the Spirit are no doubt various. Some people have to bear direct witness to the world to come by the whole pattern of their life, and have to keep the memory of that world alive in the public mind. Others have to place themselves at man's service and "by their ministry create the conditions for the kingdom of heaven (materiam regni caelestis parantes)".

As "a pledge of this hope and as food for the journey", the Lord left the holy Eucharist to those who are his. In bread and wine as figures of the cosmos the whole universe and human activity in it are linked more and more closely with the head. The form of the meal represents that fraternity into which men grow in a mystical way more and more by the celebration of the Eucharist. The perfect order of the Lord's love and peace which is celebrated eternally in the heavenly banquet, is already a mystical reality in the Eucharist. The mysterious renovation of all creation is not only announced here in advance but is already realized inchoatively. In the Eucharist men and world come nearer to their head, they are more and more taken into the possession of Christ as his Body and thus are brought further on the road to fulfilment. This sets the great goal of all efforts to establish order in human society and of all cultivation of earthly things. It is a question of bringing about in history what is already a reality in the Eucharist as the sacramental centre of the world. In a single sentence the Pastoral Constitution briefly but plainly expresses these essential aspects of the Eucharist (the cosmic, the social and the eschatological).

The statements in Text 3 about integrating the conception of human activity in the mystery of Christ did not seem explicit enough. It was decided to speak at greater length about the work of redemption — from incarnation to fulfilment.[31] That was done in Text 5, but not lucidly enough. A new version was expected to take the following into account: the sanctification of the world and its history through the incarnation of the Word; the fundamental law of love and its connection with daily work; the saving power of the resurrection; the dominion of Christ; the operation of the Holy Spirit; contemplation and renunciation of the world; the liturgical aspect; the celebration of the Lord's Day.[32] These wishes were to a large extent realized in Text 5, where the article expresses both Christ's operation and the norms of human action.[33] Particular importance was attached to establishing that not only man but the whole cosmos has received a new ontological dignity. One Council father, it is true, held that only the spiritual creature can be raised to the supernatural order, even though the whole creation is extrinsically referred and oriented to Christ ("tota creatio extrinsice ordinetur ad Christum"). Most of the fathers, however, emphasized that by reason of the essential connection of the cosmos with man as the created centre of its meaning, all creatures are raised to a new dignity in him.[34] It has already been noted that a few fathers objected to "Teilhardian optimism" and that six fathers saw the way to salvation solely in flight from the world, on account of the "absoluta incompatibilitas inter Christum et mundum qui totus in maligno positus est". Yet nearly all the fathers emphatically wanted the bases of a theology of earthly values to be worked out. The real focus of many of their speeches was the question of the ultimate meaning and value of earthly activity, and its relation to the kingdom of God is part of this. Only if earthly values are subjected to theological consideration is it possible to overcome the "false dualism between a merely natural order and the supernatural goal".[35] Consequently they demanded the elaboration of a "Christian cosmology", in which "the incorporation into Christ does not appear to be an alienation from the world but is shown to ennoble secular

---

[31] Cf. *Acta commissionis de doctrina fidei et morum*, p. 27 (report of the meeting on 2 April 1965).

[32] Cf. *Textus recognitus et relationes* I (1965), p. 49 ad n. 38.

[33] *Ibid.* German Bishops' Conference.

[34] Text 4, *Relationes particulares*, pp. 98 f.; one Council father referred to St. Thomas Aquinas.

[35] Text 4, *Relationes particulares*, p. 98.

values".[36] Finally, five fathers tried to have the word "assumens" in the first sentence of this article struck out, on the grounds that Eph 1:2 (presumably Eph 1:10 was meant) does not mention "assumptio" but only "recapitulatio" and because in any case the idea of a "cosmic incarnation" is still theologically disputed. The answer was brief and to the point: "The modus is rejected because the idea of the assumption of history is entirely traditional, biblical and patristic. Nothing is said here about a cosmic incarnation" (Chapter III, *modus* 28).

Article 39. *A new earth and a new heaven.* This final section of Chapter III deals with the eschatological consummation. Human activity prepares the final state of the world which the Lord will bring about on his return. The text does not speak of things of which we are ignorant (time of the consummation and nature and manner of the transformation). In faith we know that the shape of this world distorted by sin will pass away, but that God "is preparing a new dwelling place and a new earth where justice will abide and whose blessedness will answer and surpass ... man's longings for peace". The Constitution does not restrict itself to this general statement, however, but applies it specifically to human activity: "While charity and its fruits will endure, all that creation which God made on man's account will be unchained from the bondage of vanity." Not only charity but also the works performed in charity will survive destruction and will be comprised within the last saving action of the Lord. Certainly not every single professional action of man, not every work he produces will be expressly eternalized. But if man is to rise again with his concrete personal, social and material reality, then his activity in the world must also find eternal expression. H. Rondet rightly asks in his book on the theology of work: "What would the risen Gutenberg be with a body which is identical with his earthly body of flesh, but without any relation to the discovery for which he is famous? What would a Christian painter be without his work, a musician without his symphonies, a poet without his poems? And is nothing to remain of the tremendous efforts of modern industry, of engineers and workmen? Do we have to continue to say with medieval theology: 'solvet saeculum in favilla'?"[37] The Pastoral Constitution makes it clear that the Christian who believes in the resurrection of the body and the transfiguration of the world, may also believe in the consummation of technical achievement in the transformed world and in the fulfilment, in the communion of saints, of the socialization brought about by technology.

What consequences follow from this for human action? Naturally it profits a man nothing if he gains the whole world but in doing so loses his soul.

---

[36] Text 4, *Relationes particulares,* p. 99: cosmologia christiana "in qua incorporatio ad Christum appareat non ut abalienatio a mundo, sed ut elevatio valorum mundi".
[37] *La théologie du travail.*

But attention to the end and fulfilment in no way weakens the will to engagement in the world itself, in fact it acts rather as a spur. For a better order of human society and of material things has a real significance for the Kingdom of God. It removes obstacles, brings about a pattern of the world which creates better conditions for the coming of the kingdom. The growing body of the new human family represents as it were an adumbration of the world to come. Of course the Pastoral Constitution rightly rejects any identification of earthly progress with the growth of the Kingdom of God. Human activity in the world cannot directly achieve salvation or even transmit it. But it brings about the conditions which make it possible and which encourage the growth and establishment of the salvation which appeared in Christ. If we are not afraid to believe that Christ has assumed the whole universe, including matter, as his body, then all human activity appears explicitly as collaboration in building up the body of Christ. It completes and unfolds that figure of Christ, and so contributes to his glorification. It certainly does not effect salvation but makes things open and transparent to the kingdom by discovering the potentialities they contain. The article ends with a precise theological statement. "On this earth that kingdom is already present in mystery (*in mysterio*, that is, in the sacrament). When the Lord returns, it will be brought into full flower." Thus once more the idea of the Eucharist finally appears as the world's road to fulfilment.

However valuable this last article may be thought, it did not satisfy all expectations. R.-A. Sigmond considers that it leaves the question of the relation between secular and spiritual activity open. The Christian integration of secular activity is not solved here, he thinks, whereas in Text 3 it was. There great emphasis was laid on man's "total vocation" and the fulfilment of man's vocation to work. In Article 43 the question does in fact arise again. "It is almost as if an uneasy conscience kept prompting the authors to rethink the problem."[38] One can agree with R.-A. Sigmond without overlooking how difficult the question is. K. Rahner also criticized Text 4 severely. According to him it does not show that the Christian theology of history teaches that conflict is inevitable between the world entangled in evil and Christ's followers, and that this conflict becomes more intense the farther time advances. The schema is silent on the consequences of this for concrete action. It also omits any confrontation or dialogue with a profane, secularized eschatology such as Marxism proclaims.[39] Nothing was done in this respect, even in the final text. In any case some fathers took the view that work is only a source of natural fulfilment and that exaggerated optimism ought therefore to be avoided. By far the greater number, however, insisted that work has theological significance and value. This, they considered, con-

---

[38] Sigmond II, pp. 5 f.
[39] Cf. Rahner, *op. cit.*, p. 3.

sists not only in personal sanctification or in a right intention but in the fulfilment of a function conferred by God. In this sense we must say that "Labor hominis constituit partem integralem oeconomiae salutis quia suo labore homo praeparat illam consummationem qua Deus mundum transformabit".[40] To 21 fathers the text almost gave the impression that there is no damnation and no hell. "Textus de iudicio et reprobatione silere nequit, ne christiani et non christiani falsa imbuantur spe." This request was refused on the grounds that there was no intention at this point of presenting a treatise on the Last Things (Chapter III, *modus* 37a).

Evaluation of the chapter on man's activity throughout the world. The chapter must certainly be considered a good theological text. It deals with the essential problems in an open, dynamic and forward-looking way. In order to form a just opinion, it must be remembered that until very recently individualism and moralism prevailed in the way books on moral theology dealt with the theme. Thomas Aquinas had spoken of a fourfold purpose of work: to obtain a livelihood, to avoid the capital sin of sloth, to mortify the perpetual rebellion of the flesh and finally to make alms-giving possible.[41] In theology and preaching the Genesis command to subdue the earth was not of course forgotten but what was predominant was the admonition that work should be done in a spirit of penance and atonement and that the example of Jesus should be kept in mind, working in a poor workshop and dying for us on the cross. The Pastoral Constitution leaves this negative atmosphere behind. It does not quote only those passages of Scripture which speak of the toil and transitoriness of all human effort. It is not content to point to the ascetical, charitable and pedagogical significance of work. It sketches a theology of human work, a convincing one because it moves forward in the perspective of the history of salvation.

The text has succeeded in striking the happy medium which preserves it from three possible misinterpretations. It cannot be quoted in support of the superficial and sometimes even boisterously expressed view that real, positive Christianity is nothing but fulfilment of duty in the service of the world and at work. It also stands in clear contrast to the dualistic-eschatological view which cannot see any connection between earthly work and Christ's coming. (True Christianity cannot be limited to interiority, because Christ is not only a principle of sanctification for the world in the specifically Christian sense but also a principle of order and healing in the sphere of what itself is natural.) Finally the text avoids the ambiguous and dangerous approach to the evolutionistic-incarnational view of the development of humanity according to which a directly Christian value, a saving value in the strict sense,

---

[40] Text 4, *Relationes particulares*, p. 99.
[41] *Summa Theologica*, 2a 2ae, q. 187, a. 3. Other quite different aspects can of course be found in the works of Aquinas.

must be ascribed to earthly activity. (It is well-known that Teilhard de Chardin did not always avoid this third mistaken view of secular enterprise.)

It has already been noted that Chapter III did not entirely succeed in integrating earthly activity into the vocation to saving communion with Christ. But perhaps such an integration has not yet been theologically achieved anywhere in a satisfactory manner. At all events, in the actual concrete context of this chapter, a reference to the charismata would have been desirable; which can be bestowed on any Christians, including the laity.[42] The Holy Spirit awakens charismata within the Church at times when its credibility has to be manifested to the world. We know the striking phenomena of the life of the primitive Christian community. The Church needed this in order to direct men's attention to the reality of the salvation that had appeared in Christ. Today the Church above all needs charismatic lay people in science, technology, journalism, politics, art and so on, so that authentic Christian personal life may be lived in the midst of the world in an exemplary way, widely visible to all. In our age, charismatic achievements of Christian service to the world must make it clear what the saving reality of salvation means for the true pattern of human society and for the accomplishment of its work in the world.

Perhaps the chapter would have had greater inner coherence if the fundamental formula of the three planes of human existence which are brought into activity by work had not only been dealt with in Article 35 but had been more expressly developed and pursued through all the sections which follow. That would have meant inquiring into the significance of the mystery of sin, the mystery of salvation and the mystery of the consummation, for the development of the personality, for its insertion into social relationships and for the domination and organization of material things. The section on sin especially does not go beyond a few far too general remarks.

The basic statements of the chapter, that human activity is a partnership in developing God's creation, in overcoming the disorder due to sin, in building up the Body of Christ and in preparing the pattern of the world of final fulfilment, would perhaps stand out even more clearly if the text had not merely accepted a more dynamic view of the world, but had expressly accepted a more dynamic way of thinking about God. The creator God is not the God of deism who after performing his work retires to an eternal repose. By his Word, he set in motion the whole process of evolution; he perpetually maintains this in movement by the power of that Word and impels it towards its goal of perfect accomplishment. But this whole process is also underpinned by the saving power of the Lord, who in the sacraments of the Church, especially the Eucharist, incorporates the powerful advance of world history more and more into his order of love and peace. The Lord

[42] Cf. *Lumen Gentium*, II, 13.

on high is not a powerless inactive outsider to the world. He is its permanent mover, the incessant promoter of its development, who has established himself in the depth of the world and now constitutes its ontological impulse towards accomplishment, the real *promotor mundi*. This radical and extremely dynamic theocentrism and Christocentrism is the first and decisive reason why there is history and why man is occupied, throughout history, to fill the earth.

The second basis of any theology of activity is the anthropocentric character of the world. Recent philosophical doctrines of man have clearly shown that the cosmos has to be shaped in relation to man, that it is ultimately an extension of his own corporeality and that it therefore has a thoroughly personal relevance. Man can only develop and fulfil himself if at the same time he develops and brings to fulfilment the world which in him is comprised in unity.

It is apparent that this anthropocentric, theocentric and Christocentric basis of human activity will have to be worked out very much more clearly by theology. Only then will it be really clear what valuable starting-points the chapter on human activity in the world contains. [43]

[43] On the whole question see A. Auer, *Christsein im Beruf* (1966). This presents the fundamental ideas of our Chapter in a systematic way.

The Role of the Church in the Modern World

by

Yves Congar

The present Chapter IV originated in a draft in French composed by Mgr. P. Haubtmann when the versions submitted during the third session were completely recast. After translation into Latin, it was presented to the Council fathers with the whole schema at the beginning of the Fourth Session in September 1965.

The first debate on the chapter took place on the occasion of the general debate on Part I of Schema 13 on 21, 22, 23 and 24 September 1965. At this stage, Chapter IV was only expressly mentioned once, on 22 September, when Cardinal König expressed the wish for it to be placed first in the schema, before the chapters on man (Chapters I–III).

On 24 September the Council voted by 2111 votes to 144 to close the general debate and to proceed to separate discussion of each chapter. In fact, however, all four chapters were dealt with without distinction, so that we cannot speak of any real discussion of Chapter IV as such. Nevertheless, on that same day notable speeches were made specifically concerning this Chapter IV on the role of the Church in the modern world. The first contribution was made by Mgr. Cantero, Archbishop of Saragossa, who expressed the views of all the Spanish bishops and asked whether the Church was not here occupying itself with temporal problems for which it has neither the authority nor the necessary special knowledge. Archbishop Cantero concluded with the words, "The activity of the Church among men is regarded as an answer to their questions and as sharing in their joys and anxieties, whereas it flows above all from the Church's own nature as an instrument of salvation for men."

A second viewpoint was expressed by Mgr. Elchinger, Bishop-Coadjutor of Strasbourg.[1] "The schema speaks at some length of what the world has

---

[1] *DC* (7 November 1965), 1864–6. Cf. A. Wenger, *Vatican II, Chronique de la 4ᵉ session*, pp. 140 f.; H. Fesquet, *Le journal du Concile*, p. 878.

to do, and says very little about what the Church is proposing to do in order to make contact with the world and form a true estimate of it. People nowadays pay more attention to deeds than to words and they would like to know how the Church can reform itself in its relations with the world."

This was the total outcome of the conciliar debate. The text of Chapter IV was voted on after the first three chapters on 16 November 1965, with the following results:

	Votes	Placet	Non placet	Placet juxta modum	Invalid
Articles 40–42	2227	2107	113	(3)	4
Articles 43–45	2222	2095	112	(11)	4
Chapter as a whole	2202	1817	99	284	2

The vote on the *modi* on 4 December was as follows:

	Votes	Placet	Non placet		Invalid
	2228	2149	75		4

a) The position of Chapter IV in the Pastoral Constitution

Surprise may be felt at the position assigned to this chapter. It formulates doctrinal statements which have already been presupposed and concretely applied in the three previous chapters. That is in fact the case. The order chosen is, however, expressly explained both in the introduction to Part I (art. 11) and at the beginning of this Chapter IV (art. 40). What the Council has said about the dignity of the human person, the life of men in society and the significance of their earthly activity, represents the immediate reasons for the relation between Church and world and provides the basis of their mutual dialogue. Because the Church has something to say on these three themes of a comprehensive doctrine of man, it has a function (*munus*) in relation to the world. It is therefore possible throughout the Pastoral Constitution to consider the Church, not in itself (as in *Lumen Gentium*), but in its life and action in the world.

The first duty of the Church in regard to the world clearly consists in converting it to the gospel. That is its mission (and explains the missions). In other words, it teaches men to become sons of Abraham and members of the People of God (cf. the Dogmatic Constitution on the Church, art. 17, and, above all, the Decree on the Church's Missionary Activity). As a result, the world becomes Church. But there is another domain in the Church's mission, another activity of the Church in regard to the world, namely the function it exercises in the world and for the world in the latter's own structures and activities, but leaving the world as world in its own order. The Pastoral Constitution is concerned with this domain of activity. Practically nothing is said about the relation which must be established between these two activities of the Church which taken together form its total mission. It is all the more important to emphasize that this relation is very close and that in the realization of the Church's mission it is impossible to separate work for the welfare of mankind from the preaching of the gospel.

It is true that this could have been said at the beginning of *Gaudium et Spes* in the form of a doctrinal thesis. But in accordance with the inductive method employed in this first part of the Pastoral Constitution, a mere statement to the effect that the Church has a function for the world as such, in regard to its actual life as world, was not wanted; the aim was to show that this is so. At the end of each chapter Christ is shown as the key to what has been said; this is not simply affirmed but is shown to be so. Similarly, at the end of the three chapters devoted to man and human life, the Church is presented as having a contribution to make to the world.

The context into which this chapter was fitted seems to have yet another significance. It might be said that the Church acts in the world and intervenes in its life only to the extent that it spiritually transforms men. Certainly by Easter, Christ renewed everything. Does the activity in the Church in the world therefore consist purely and simply in preparing the transfiguration of the cosmos by spreading the grace of Easter throughout the world, in virtue of Pentecost, through preaching and the celebration of the sacraments? It seems that the tradition of the Eastern Church has developed on these lines.[2] Such a conception is clearly an integral part of Christian tradition, and the Pastoral Constitution takes it into account, at least by implication, in the first three chapters. But these also contain something else, and the Constitution has a whole second part with five chapters devoted to social doctrine. Certainly it could be shown that this doctrine merely defines in specific detail some of the demands made on the new man who is born at Easter. But it goes beyond the purely transfiguring activity of celebrating the sacred mysteries and the life of Christian asceticism; it already in fact does so in Chapters I–III of Part I. It obliges men to action and even to a programme of action. As regards the nature of its mode of expression, it addresses and concerns people quite apart from their formal membership of Christ and his ecclesiastical body. Chapter IV presents the reason for this undertaking and forms the link between the previous anthropological chapters and the long second part devoted to the problems of the contemporary world.

[2] Cf. C. Lialine, "L'action de l'Orthodoxie", *Qu'est-ce que l'Orthodoxie? Vues catholiques* (1945). Cf. the statement of Mgr. Ziadé at the Council in 1963 in Y. Congar, H. Küng and D. O'Hanlon eds., E.T.: *Council Speeches of Vatican II* (1964). Cf. also, *Chrétiens en dialogue* (1964), pp. 273, 285.

What justification does it offer for this activity of the Church which goes beyond the work of conveying to the faithful the Easter grace of renewal?

b) The basis of this function of the Church

The decisive foundation is theological and Christological. In the Old Testament God's intervention in history is regarded as based on the fact that he is the Creator and therefore the lord of all things (cf. Is 40:21–26; 42:5 f., and many prayers which introduce this motive). In the New Testament, especially with Paul, sovereignty is attributed to Christ who is the head (κεφαλή) both of the Church (Eph 1:18, 22) and of all things (Eph 1:22; Col 1:15–18; cf. 2:10). Thus two domains are marked out, one absolutely universal in scope, comprising the whole of creation, the other formed of men who accept the gospel and which is, properly speaking, the Church: two concentric circles, as it were, which coincide by their common dependence on the same head, the same supreme authority, Christ.[3] The latter pursues a single purpose which embraces the whole of creation by means of that part of mankind from which he has formed his Body by faith and the grace of the sacraments. For this reason, the realization of the Covenant relation which constitutes the People of God, the body of Christ and the temple of the Holy Spirit, has consequences for the world and the whole cosmos. Already in the Old Testament, social duties were deduced from the demands of the Covenant, and the realization of messianic righteousness, that is to say of God's rule, was conceived in a way which connected it with a restoration of order in the whole cosmos. Christ fulfilled this promise, eschatologically, it is true, but the end of the ages has already begun, for the foundation of the restoration of all things has already been laid in Jesus Christ. This fact imposes on Christians the duty of working in the world to establish an order in harmony with the gift of truth and grace which they have received in Jesus Christ.[4] Paul did not proclaim the abolition of slavery, but when he sent back the runaway slave Onesimus to his master Philemon, he suggested to the latter that he should consider Onesimus as his companion in the service of the gospel, thus showing that Christ has provided the basis for new relations between men.

The Pastoral Constitution obviously does not disregard this theological and Christological foundation. In fact it expressly refers to it on occasion

---

[3] Cf. O. Cullmann, *La royauté de Jésus-Christ et l'Église dans le N.T.* (1941); id., *Christus und die Zeit*, E.T.: *Christ and Time* (rev. ed., 1964); Y. Congar, *Lay People in the Church* (1964), ch. III; id. *Jésus-Christ, notre médiateur, notre Seigneur* (1965).

[4] Cf. Y. Congar, *Jésus-Christ*, pp. 215 f., E.T.: *Jesus Christ*, on the realization of Christ's rule over the world, and Y. Congar, *Sacerdoce et laïcat devant leurs tâches d'évangélisation et de civilisation* (1962), pp. 357 f., E.T.: *Priest and Layman*, on temporal work and gospel message.

(art. 42 towards the end, in a very strange way, almost as a difficulty; art. 45); it several times states that our eschatological vocation in no way diverts people from their earthly tasks but rather imposes an obligation on them to perform them (arts. 34, 39, 42, 43, 57). This is perfectly correct, but on grounds of historical truth we must admit that this was not always fully recognized. The consciousness of our eschatological vocation long favoured a certain "contempt for the world" which hardly encouraged dedication to earthly tasks. In this respect, the 1965 text no longer deserves the criticism directed against the 1964 text, and the new text expressly admits the many faulty attitudes of clerics and laity (art. 43). Nevertheless it also sometimes speaks as if these mistaken attitudes had never influenced certain points of doctrine which are receiving emphasis today: for instance, Article 41 on despising the body, or its final paragraph on the rights of man and the dynamic meaning of human planning. It would have been of advantage if a few sentences rather more in harmony with historical reality had been added. But Vatican II made even less room for historians than it did for exegetes.

The Pastoral Constitution does, of course, clearly say that Christ is the centre and lord of history (arts. 10, 45). But on the whole it represents Christ more as the revealer of the truth about man (cf. arts. 10, 22, 38). Similarly the Church, following Christ, reveals the truth about man (art. 41). It is true that these and other texts (arts. 40, 45) link the aspect of revelation and that of effective communication. Above all it is true that the Holy Spirit has really effected what Christ revealed (arts. 1, 10, 22, 38, 45). We should also have to indicate here the pneumatology which is scattered throughout the Pastoral Constitution and other texts of Vatican II. This would clearly show that the Council does not deserve the reproach frequently brought by some observers, that it was lacking in pneumatology. Nevertheless it remains true that the Pastoral Constitution does not markedly develop the Christological foundation of the relations between the Church and the world. In our opinion, this is due to the fact that it seeks to address all men, Christians and non-Christians, believers and unbelievers (cf. art. 2); it did not want to give first place to statements which presuppose faith. In general, therefore, it employs an inductive method which advances from what is better known to what is less known. This is why the Christological statements are found at the end of each chapter.

What then is the basis of the relations between the Church and the world? The basis is man, the fact that Christianity concerns man and that the articles of faith affect him. That is made clear from the start. The Church is inserted into the history of men because it is formed of men (art. 1); therefore the world is both the scene of human history and the realization of God's saving plan (art. 2). It is a matter of saving man; man asks himself the question to which the gospel has an answer (art. 3); faith throws light on man's destiny (arts. 11 and 21). The Preface could therefore declare: "Hence the pivotal point of our whole presentation is man himself whole and entire, body and soul, heart and conscience, mind and will" (art. 3).

That is the reason why Chapter IV begins by repeating a statement which had already appeared at the beginning of Part I (art. 11), "Everything we have said about the dignity of the human person and about the human community and the profound meaning of human activity lays the foundation for the relationship between the Church and the world and provides the basis for dialogue between them" (art. 40). Because Christianity concerns man, it has, taken all in all, the same material to work on and the same goal as the world: to make man's future a success. But there is something in man which transcends what is merely earthly; this is what the Pastoral Constitution understands as man's integral vocation, and this something declares its presence even on the plane of observable facts. Thus humanity proves to be religious, just as religion proves to be human.[5] It is on this common subject-matter, represented by man himself, that the Pastoral Constitution bases what it has to say about the task of the Church in the world of today.

c) A new attitude and a new line in the question of Church and temporal society

The Preparatory Theological Commission set up by John XXIII had composed eleven chapters De Ecclesia; the ninth bore the title "On the relations between Church and State".[6] This document amounted to a summary of the doctrines of Popes liberally referred to in the footnotes, from Benedict XIV, Pius VI, Gregory XVI and Pius IX down to Pius XII (and even John XXIII, who is quoted once), while Leo XIII, Pius X and Pius XI were passed over. The Church and earthly society, each with full powers and authority to exercise them,[7] are here viewed in relation to the last, supernatural end of man. Earthly society, though free in domains for which the divine law does not legislate, must frame its laws in such a way that man's access to the spiritual benefits conveyed by the Church is facilitated; it must also keep out of its legislation anything which the Church considers an obstacle to the attainment of eternal life. The only new element in what was in fact classical doctrine, was the mention (inspired by Taparelli d'Azeglio)

[5] Cf. Art. 11; cf. K. Rahner at the discussions of the Paulus-Gesellschaft between Christians and Marxists, Herrenchiemsee, April–May 1966: "Mankind in its entirety is religious, and religion in its entirety is human."

[6] The text of the schema was published by C. Falconi, Documents secrets du Concile, Première session (1965), pp. 51–128. Chapter IX, ibid., pp. 105–13.

[7] "Each of the two societies was endowed with the faculties necessary to fulfil its own mission according to its norms; furthermore each of them is perfect, i.e. in its sphere it is supreme and consequently is not subordinated to any other, and is endowed with legislative, judicial and executive power" (no. 40): Falconi, op. cit., p. 105.

of a condition for the fulfilment of these requirements, namely, that the people, from whom earthly power derives, should itself be composed entirely of believers (art. 43; Falconi edition, p. 107).

There was little debate on this document (beginning of December 1962), just enough for the conclusion to be arrived at that the question must be framed and thought out in relation to the present, not the past, with less talk of authorities and subordination and more use of the language of apostolic responsibility. Subsequently the question of the relations between the Church and secular society was removed from the schema De Ecclesia,[8] in fact it was practically excluded from the Council's discussions. It is indeed mentioned in our Chapter IV, principally in Article 42, but in a quite different perspective from the 1962 text. Nothing is more characteristic for the change which Vatican II underwent, than the difference between the two ways in which this question was approached. This must therefore be gone into more closely.

In full agreement with the Dogmatic Constitution Lumen Gentium,[9] Gaudium et Spes has a profoundly different outlook on the relations between the spiritual and the temporal to the one which the Middle Ages bequeathed and which prevailed in classical doctrine down to Chapter IX of the schema De Ecclesia of the Preparatory Theological Commission. It is clear that what was involved was not so much a contradiction as a development; the problem itself had altered, by moving from the juridical and political plane to the anthropological plane of personal belief.

As the result of a long history, which it is impossible to retrace here, the Middle Ages dealt with the question of the spiritual and temporal in the framework of the distinction between two authorities, the Sacerdotium with its summit in the Pope on the one hand and the princes on the other. By that fact, however, the question was propounded on the juridical plane, where the issue could only be one of equality or of subordination and dominion. Since there was no question of equality — for there can only be one caput here, and the soul is superior to the body — only subordination was left. The assertion of this inevitably led to frequent rivalry. Furthermore, the distinction was only envisaged in an earthly framework; here on earth kings rule over men's bodies, priests over their souls. Temporalia and saecularia did not denote the totality of earthly activity which is ultimately bound up with eschatology, they meant the lower realm subordinate to the spiritualia or coelestia which anticipate eternity, and which formed the privileged domain of monks and clerics. This view of the domain proper to monks certainly led to a certain disregard for earthly activity, even if the

---

[8] Cf. ibid., p. 240 (October or November 1963).

[9] Cf. on this the remarkable study of G. Martelet, "Die Kirche und das Zeitliche. Auf dem Wege zu einer neuen Auffassung", in G. Baraúna, ed., De Ecclesia I (1966), pp. 474–93.

historic theme of "contempt for the world" should not be viewed in an over-simplified way.[10] What was in question, therefore, was the domain proper to clerics and priestly authority. At a certain moment, which must be sought in the context of the Gregorian reform, the theme of Christian anthropology which is expressed in 1 Cor 3:15, "Homo spiritualis iudicat omnia et ipse a nemine iudicatur", was given a juridical and political sense and used to justify the assertion that the Pope judges kings and that there is no appeal from his judgment. In this line, 1 Cor 6:2–3 was often added to 3:15, "Angelus iudicabimus. Quanto magis saecularia![11]

In this medieval perspective, little active service was expected from the ordinary laity. They had primarily to obey and live according to the laws. The princes were expected to enact laws in harmony with the law of God, as expounded by the priests, and to place their sword at the service of the faith.

The situation, and with it the perspectives and ideas, have profoundly changed. Pius XII affirmed this with regard to Boniface VIII,[12] and Paul VI has also expressed it recently.[13] It may be said that, by documents like the Pastoral Constitution and the Declaration on Religious Freedom, Vatican II has finally turned the page on the Middle Ages. The perspectives of *Gaudium et Spes* are in fact very different, as is immediately apparent from the vocabulary and the categories it employs. Of course the word *Ecclesia* is the one most often used. Generally it denotes the organized society which originated from the incarnation and revelation of Jesus Christ and was entrusted with the faithful preservation of the gospel and the mission of preaching it.[14] When doctrine about these realities is expounded, it is the

---

[10] See M. Bultot, *La doctrine du Mépris du Monde* IV, Parts I and 2 (1963) and his historical account, which has been vigorously criticized in various articles; cf. also his reply in *Revue d'ascétique et de mystique* (1964), pp. 481 f.; *La Vie spirituelle* (March 1966), pp. 313 f. See also J. C. Guy and others, *Le Mépris du Monde (Problème de vie religieuse 22)* (1965); J. Daniélou, "Mépris du monde et valeurs terrestres d'après Vatican II", *ibid.*, pp. 189–96.

[11] We have assembled abundant documentary material on this and hope to publish a study of this history.

[12] Address to the members of the Tenth International Congress of Historical Studies 7 September 1955 (*AAS* 47 [1955], pp. 678 f.); cf. the address to the pilgrims at the canonization of St. Nicholas of Flüe on 16 May 1947 (*AAS* 39 [1947], pp. 369 f.): "A return to the Middle Ages? No one has any idea of that!"

[13] Address to the Diplomatic Corps, 8 January 1966: "The Church shows itself free of every temporal interest ... Does this mean that the Church withdraws into the desert and leaves the world to its fate, fortunate or unfortunate? Quite the contrary. It only frees itself from the interests of this world so as to be in a better position to permeate society, to place itself at the service of the common good, to offer its help and means of salvation to all — and there is a new feature of this Council which has often been stressed: the Church is doing so in a way which is partly in contradiction to the attitude which marks many passages of its history."

[14] Cf. the excursus on the use of the term "Church" in *Gaudium et Spes,* below, pp. 222–3.

Ecclesia which speaks, or, as it says in Article 43, "Ecclesia per christianos", the Church through Christians. But when it comes to carrying into effect the relations between the spiritual and temporal, it is the Church as the People of God which is brought in. This is clearly shown in Article 11, which serves as introduction to the whole of Part I: "Populus Dei . . . Exinde apparebit Populum Dei et genus humanum cui ille inseritur, servitium sibi mutuo praestare . . ." The same thing is certainly meant by the term *Ecclesia* at the beginning of Chapter IV, in Article 20. It may seem surprising that "People of God", though it appears here and there,[15] is on the whole used very little. There are two reasons for this. Firstly, what is in question is the mission received from Christ, and consequently the Constitution uses the word *Ecclesia*. Secondly, the intention was to avoid the impression which might be given by too frequent a use of the expression "People of God", of a chosen people cut off from the rest of men and the world. The aim was in fact quite the contrary, namely to point to a people of believers in the midst of mankind, and quite often scattered throughout the world in a diaspora situation. This is what is expressed in the passage of Article 11 quoted above, and in Article 40 by the word "Church" and in Article 42 by "family of God's sons"; the latter phrase is placed in relation to "the human family", an expression which is often used as equivalent to "mankind".[16] This draws attention to the way in which the temporal is envisaged and described.

The word "State" is not used here any more than it is in any document of Vatican II, if we are not mistaken. Rulers are mentioned,[17] but the term usually used is "political (or civil) society" or "community".[18] The question has moved from the plane of relations between authority and authority, constitution and constitution, to that of relations between the Christian faith professed by the Ecclesia or the "ecclesial community" (art. 44) and the human society, the family of mankind, or mankind. The problem of the spiritual and temporal is here the problem of the relations between faith and history, gospel and civilization. In this much wider frame, the special question of the relations between the Church and the political community is taken up later in Article 76, in an atmosphere of respect for the autonomy of the two spheres and of the apostolic freedom of the Church.

[15] Arts. 3, 32, 44, 45, 88, 92, where it is said that it includes "pastores et fideles". Our references do not claim to be exhaustive.

[16] The human family: arts. 2, 24, 29, 33, 37, 39, 42, 57. Humanity: arts. 4, 9, and in general the Introduction, where "mankind" is used alternately with "world of today"; arts. 11 (chief reference), 40, 42, 45.

[17] Reipublicae moderatores: art. 75; populorum moderatores: arts. 79; 82; auctoritas publica: arts. 75, 79, 87 (or civilis: art. 76).

[18] Arts. 25, 74, 75, 76. Also humana societas (arts. 40, 47, 59), societas temporalis (art. 50), vita socialis (art. 25), communitas personarum (art. 23).

The Church which is in question in Chapter IV is therefore the People of God characterized by the following features: 1. It is not separate from the world but exists in the midst of the world, living and acting with it. 2. It is sanctified as a whole (cf. Chapter II of *Lumen Gentium)* but this does not turn it from its earthly tasks. 3. It has a structure composed of shepherds and simple believers (cf. footnote 11). The world in question is the totality of men's earthly activities and could be just as well called civilization or history, provided earthly values or realities are understood to be included. The Church recognizes the positive value and autonomy of this world; it does not reduce the world to the role of a mere means of getting to heaven. [19] Of course it seeks to sanctify and even consecrate the world, but not by removing elements from their place in the structure of the world and from secular use — except perhaps by way of example or for instruction, as first fruits, or in order to express an intention symbolically. It respects their true nature and sanctifies them through the actual use made of them in harmony with the transcendental purposes of salvation. [20] Certainly the Church's magisterium is competent to declare what these transcendent ends involve, and even to command or forbid its faithful certain courses of action. But the Middle Ages are over; it is no longer a question of subordinating the temporal domain to the Church but of relating it to the Last Things.

This does not diminish man in his genuine earthly nature, because (1) the eschata are transcendent; they can give meaning to different cultures and activities at different places and times; [21] (2) because the eschata are the meaning of the earthly things and historical activities themselves (cf. above, Chapter III). Although they come from above as a gift, they will not come as a violent breach in things or in life, because they will, of course, come about precisely with the attainment of the goal. The eschata, or salvation (it is all one), are inclusive in regard to nature and history; they mean fulfilment and transfiguration. They are not something external and foreign. Consequently, if Christians direct their actions and life towards the eschata, they do not have to renounce earthly activity, nor may they betray it; they give it its ultimate integrity and realize their integral vocation as human beings. [22]

---

[19] Cf. arts. 36, 42, 56 (on culture), 76 (the political community). Cf. *Lumen Gentium,* art. 36; *Apostolicam actuositatem,* art. 7.

[20] Cf. on this the very important studies of M.-D. Chenu, "Consecratio mundi", *NRT* 96 (1964), pp. 608–18; "Die Laien und die 'consecratio mundi'", in G. Baraúna, ed., *De Ecclesia* II, pp. 289–307.

[21] Cf. what is said about catholicity or the gospel in *Lumen Gentium,* art. 13, and in the Decree on the Church's Missionary Activity, art. 8, and also *Gaudium et Spes,* art. 42.

[22] Consequently *Gaudium et Spes* says several times that our vocation from above does not divert us from earthly activity but makes our duty to take part in it all the more urgent: arts. 34, 39, 42, 43, 57. Cf. John XXIII, *Mater et Magistra,* art. 255.

All this has various other implications and consequences. We should like to point out three of the more important.

1. This conception involves a theology of the relations between nature and grace or the supernatural. This question, which for centuries has been of such great and inalienable importance, is now propounded in quite a new way. It has become clear that the two realities were separated from one another too much as a consequence of a mistaken interpretation of St Thomas which derives from Cajetan and Suárez.[23] Of course, the absolute gratuitousness of our vocation to become children of God must be maintained, but this vocation was intended by God from the beginning as the goal of man whom he created to his image and likeness. That involves for man's nature an ordination which, according to the point of view, means capacity, openness and vocation, a condition in which the destiny of each individual must be fulfilled. This theology forms the basis of what *Gaudium et Spes* has to say on man's integral vocation, on the wound which atheism makes in his very nature itself, and on the ultimate significance of earthly activity (art. 41). On this basis it is not sufficient to regard the Church and the world as two powers which do not overlap but are merely juxtaposed (or placed one above the other). The "world" is not simply the power of the State, it is mankind at work; it is capable of becoming Church and is called by the Church, if the Church is understood to be what reveals to the world its own ultimate meaning.[24]

2. Seen in its concrete existential situation, the world is therefore not so much an opponent in competition with the Church as the material of the Church itself, capable of becoming Church and at least ontologically or secretly called by the Church. *Gaudium et Spes* repeatedly shows how the world is marked by the hidden presence of Christ or of his Holy Spirit (art. 57 on the Word; arts. 22, 26, 38, 41 on the Holy Spirit). This being

---

[23] The works of H. de Lubac are very important on this: *Surnaturel. Études historiques* (1947); *Augustinisme et Théologie moderne* and *Le Mystère du surnaturel* (1965). Cf. also K. Rahner, "Nature and Grace", *Theological Investigations* IV (1966), pp. 165–88; L. Scheffczyk, "Die Idee der Einheit von Schöpfung und Erlösung", *TQ* 140 (1960), pp. 19–37; on the biblical viewpoint, A. Feuillet, *Le Christ Sagesse de Dieu d'après les Épîtres pauliniennes* (1966), and the Council speech of Cardinal Meyer, 20 October 1964.

[24] Cf. also what is said in art. 45 on the Church as the "universal sacrament of salvation". The way missionary activity is spoken about is in accordance with this. The schema of the Theological Preparatory Commission contained a Chapter X on the duty of the Church to announce the gospel to all nations everywhere in the world (Falconi, *op. cit.*, pp. 114–18); what was chiefly in question was the Church's right freely to preach the gospel. This right has natural and supernatural foundations and is also claimed in the Declaration on Religious Freedom (art. 13). But the Decree on the Church's Missionary Activity which also of course refers to this right, expresses in a more positive way the intrinsic connection between missionary activity and the world. "By manifesting Christ, the Church reveals to men the real truth about their condition and their total vocation" (art. 8).

so — and it is also affirmed from the point of view of missionary activity in the Decree on the Church's Missionary Activity (art. 9) — a certain dialogue character necessarily ensues for the relations between the Church and the world. This will come up for consideration again in Article 44.

3. (The role or function of the Church in regard to the world (its *munus*) is not based only on the positive divine realities,) such as the will of God, the mission received from Christ, the grace which the Church serves, (but also on man and the human conscience to whose appeal that service and mission have the answer.) This viewpoint, which was particularly advocated by the Polish bishops, was very influential in *Gaudium et Spes* (cf. arts. 11 and 40), which, as we have seen, does not take the Christ-event as its starting-point.

The Church's function comprises everything human; it reveals and produces its third aspect, namely, its meaning for God. Consequently the Church must not be restricted to a "religious" domain, identical in practice with public worship. That, of course, is the tendency of all more or less totalitarian political régimes. They try to attach and subject to themselves the whole of man's effectual life. That involves a misconception of the transcendence of faith, which makes a general claim to illuminate and motivate the whole of life, but at the same time includes the possibility of doing so without coming into conflict on the same plane with political, economic or cultural realities. This idea that all that exists (apart from sin) can bear the stamp of living faith, as well as the corresponding doctrine of *Lumen Gentium* on spiritual sacrifice (art. 34), also provides the principle of a sound criticism of the distinction between a sacred and a profane domain, because this distinction can create a sort of believers' laicism. The distinction can have a valid meaning, but needs to be precisely delimited; it would be false and disastrous if it were to lead to a material separation of the two domains in the life of mankind. In this respect everything can be sacred to the Christian; the only profane thing is what he has profaned by his own sin.

(Like Jesus Christ, the Church is not content merely to reveal or announce saving truth, but carries it into effect in action. The People of God is not something cut off, isolated between heaven and earth, it lives the life of other men and does so with them (cf. art. 40), but it endeavours to direct that life to God and in harmony with God.) *Gaudium et Spes* draws the main lines of such an orientation for a few particularly important domains. Several times, however, as well as by its whole tone, the Constitution stresses collaboration with other Christians and with all men of goodwill.[25] The action

---

[25] *Gaudium et Spes* does not determine more precisely the conditions for such collaboration. Cf. Y. Congar, "Les conditions théologiques d'un pluralisme", *Sacerdoce et laïcat* (1962), pp. 401–35.

of Catholics therefore extends far beyond the work which they are able to do within the framework or by means of Catholic organizations, however useful these may be.

Gaudium et Spes must be read in connection with the other conciliar texts, the Decree on the Apostolate of the Laity (itself based on the Constitution on the Church);[26] the Declaration on Religious Freedom, that on Christian Education, which envisages the Christian school in the framework of the Church's task of forming Christian human beings, finally the encyclical *Ecclesiam Suam* and the whole work of Paul VI. These texts are not a defence against laicism, such as was first attempted in the 19th century, by strengthening clericalism and by creating protected areas or denominational structures against, or side by side with, the ordinary social structures. They are on the same lines as the Catholic Action inaugurated by Pius XI. This involves no claim to power over society, but endeavours to act in society, to undertake that kind of non-violent action which we call influence, the chief instrument of which is bearing witness. As regards the various theological theories formerly current, we are very far here from the theory of direct power, and even further from the very unfortunately named "directing power" as well as from the also fundamentally ambiguous "indirect power".[27] We have seen that "Church" here means the social body which owes its origin to the incarnation and which has received a mission for the world; but what is active in the world is the People of God in the midst of all humanity.[28]

Certainly this People of God has a structure; there are ordinary believers and believers who guide and direct. The 1964 text (Text 3) was criticized for trying to speak in two separate chapters and as a result, "primo loco de servitio Pastorum Ecclesiae erga mundum, deinde de toto Populo Dei . . ., speciatim autem de laicis". This order was criticized because it was different from that followed in *Lumen Gentium*. It was also noticed that it was not in fact consistently followed, and that statements were made about the pastors which had much wider application. The text finally adopted speaks throughout the chapter of the Church as the whole People of God (cf. footnote 28). Where a distinction is introduced, as in Article 43 first the laity

---

[26] In this passage, "apostolate" is taken in the widest sense, as "every activity of the Mystical Body" which is directed to this goal of "spreading to the honour of God the Father the rule of Christ over the whole earth . . . to relate the whole world to Christ" (art. 2).

[27] Cf. Y. Congar, "Église et État", *Catholicisme* III (1952), pp. 1430–41, reprinted in *Sainte Église* (1963), pp. 393–410. Cf. on the other hand A. de la Hera, "Posibilidades actuales de la teoría de la potestad indirecta", *Revista española de Derecho Canónico* 19 (1964), pp. 775–800.

[28] Cf. above. In his *relatio* of 20 October 1964, which introduced the debate, Mgr. Guano referred expressly to this point: "non solum agitur de hierarchia sed de toto populo Dei" (art. 42).

are spoken of *(Christiani, laici)*, then bishops and priests, the text is perfectly clear.

Unfortunately we find that *Gaudium et Spes* has not taken up the expression "messianic people" which is twice employed in *Lumen Gentium* (art. 9). We think we know the reason for this. There was hesitation about representing Christians as a people different from other peoples, but the rich content, the appropriateness and, if we may so express it, the classical origin of the term "messianic people" are so great that the advantages would, to our mind, have immeasurably outweighed any misunderstandings that might have arisen. What does "messianic" mean? A dictionary answers: pertaining to the Messiah.[29] But the Messiah was essentially the bearer of a hope for Israel and for mankind. Anyone who speaks of messianism means a promise of salvation and therefore a hope for men. This hope is borne by a people, it is announced and explained by prophets, and concerns a renewal of human conditions in the sense of liberation and victory. That is why the term messianism was transferred in the 19th century to political movements and social ideologies, e.g., Polish, Slav or socialist messianism. Would it not have been appropriate, especially in a document in which the Church is formulating its teaching on the great problems disturbing mankind, for the Church to present itself as the bearer of true messianism, and to claim for itself the honourable and magnificent title of "messianic people"?

In our view, the adoption of this title would have involved a corresponding development in the anthropology formulated in Chapter I. We are absolutely in agreement with the importance it attaches to the theme of the image of God. This is not only a very unifying view common to Eastern and Western tradition, but is also in its perfectly correct place here, for it explains the openness of human nature to the supernatural and the continuity between the appeal of that nature and the answer of grace. We ourselves in fact contributed to making it the basic idea of the doctrine of man in the May 1963 version of the schema. But however rich it may be, it does not express a historical dimension, which is not only an integral part of human reality but is linked with the idea in Scripture. The historical economy of biblical revelation shows how men endeavour to achieve certain values: knowledge, power, justice, the fullness of life which they lack, harmony or peace in many forms with others and with themselves in the face of many painful confusions and conflicts. These five great endeavours characterize humanity and constitute the dynamism of the slow conquest which fills

---

[29] This is probably the meaning of the expression in Paul VI's address of 28 October 1965: "The Church lives, the Church thinks, the Church speaks, the Church grows, the Church builds itself up. We must realize this astonishing phenomenon; we must grasp its messianic aspect" *(DC,* col. 1951). The Decree on the Apostolate of the Laity likewise speaks of charity as sign of Christ's messianic mission (art. 8). Cf. M. D. Chenu, "Un peuple messianique", in *NRT* 89 (1967), pp. 164–82.

human history. Man is not only the image of God, he is mankind engaged in the difficult quest for these values. The Pastoral Constitution does not overlook this aspect, which is in fact referred to from the start, but it plays scarcely any part in the anthropology of Chapter I. Now the Messiah Jesus Christ stood in a quite specific relation to these endeavours. As prophet he has an answer to our desire for knowledge, as king he makes us understand the truth of power, as priest he transmits righteousness and holiness to us, as redeemer he brings community, peace and fullness of life and guarantees that this will triumph over all the consequences of death. Christ's spiritual messianism is not only eschatological, it is operative in the earthly history of man, which is permeated and animated by the endeavours we have been describing. Perhaps that could have been briefly said in Chapters I, II and IV of this main part and so given its full meaning to the title of "messianic people" used in Lumen Gentium.

d) The structure of Chapter IV

The structure of Chapter IV is very simple. Article 40 links the chapter with what precedes by showing the function of the Church in the various matters discussed in Chapters I–III, and also points out a certain mutual influence in the relations between Church and world. Articles 41, 42 and 43 take up again the subject-matter of Chapters I, II and III from the point of view of the contribution the Church can make. Article 44 explains the help which the world can give the Church, because there is a mutual exchange between them. Article 45 concludes with a Christological perspective in accordance with the method used in Part I.

Article 40. The first paragraphs link up with what Lumen Gentium had to say about the Church, and carry it further. After the theme of the Church in itself, we here deal with the Church with the world and for the world, in the sense explained above. The Trinitarian pattern — from the Father to the Father through the Son in the Holy Spirit — is one of the theological motives most frequently used in Vatican II. The Trinitarian idea pervades Lumen Gentium,[1] just as it dominates the great description of God's saving plan in Ephesians 1:10–14 (referred to in a footnote to art. 40). The central part of the article touches on the situation peculiar to the New Testament: the Last Things are already present and operative, but not yet complete and manifest. We possess the earnest of the Spirit, but in the flesh. Only faith, "the assurance of things hoped for, the conviction of things not seen" (Heb 11:1), makes possible for us an experience of a dimension of present reality which lies beyond what is accessible to the senses. An essential feature of

---

[1] Cf. M. Philipon, "Die Heiligste Dreifaltigkeit und die Kirche", in G. Baraúna, ed., De Ecclesia I, pp. 252–75.

Vatican II was the recognition of the reality of "others"; it abandoned the fictions in which some had long shut themselves up. The Council looked at other Christians and the world in a positive light. The Decree on Ecumenism did this in regard to other Christians. And the Declaration on Religious Freedom also stated: "In addition it comes within the meaning of religious freedom that religious bodies should not be prohibited from freely undertaking to show the special value of their doctrine in what concerns the organization of society and the inspiration of the whole of human activity" (art. 4). This declaration and that of the Pastoral Constitution create for the future, possibilities of collaboration on the specifically Christian plane in the social domain; this is repeatedly emphasized in the Decree on the Apostolate of the Laity. Moreover, valid assistance on the part of the world, the immense activity of individuals and societies, is presented as a possible "praeparatio evangelica". The expression goes back to Eusebius, but the idea is found in the Apologists, in Irenaeus, Clement of Alexandria, Origen, etc.[2] It is taken up in *Lumen Gentium* (art. 16) and in the Decree on the Church's Missionary Activity (art. 3). The present passage does not deal with the religious aspect as such, that is, with conversion to God; it is concerned with order, of which the principle in earthly life is the gospel. Consequently the theme of preparation for the gospel does not seem to figure here with its full theological import. What is in question is an approach to the gospel, inasmuch as the latter, in accordance with God's plan, brings human nature to its fulfilment. At all events the "preparations for the gospel" are important for the realization of God's saving plan, because this includes the well-being and final succes of the world and cannot be reduced to a decree of salvation in regard to some individual human beings as such, taking no account of the world.

Article 41. Because the mystery of God as such without distinction, is the goal to which man's endeavours tend, the Church with its function of proclaiming the mystery of God can offer something to man. "Something": nothing other and nothing more than the ultimate meaning, the definitive meaning, of what he is as spirit and as person. Here it is apparent that faith and Church lie on a different plane from science and technology. This is very important for avoiding conflicts between them. The conciliar text can only allude, without detailed justification and analyses, to what is elaborated in the philosophical analyses of Maurice Blondel or Karl Rahner: man's openness to what is transcendent, the insufficiency of his own answers to his own questions.

[2] Eusebius of Caesarea, *Praeparatio evangelica* I, 1: *PG* XXII, 28 AB. Cf. R. Holte, "Logos spermatikos. Christianity and Ancient Philosophy according to St. Justin's Apologies", *Studia Theologica* 12 (1958), pp. 109—68; W. Bierbaum, "Geschichte als Paidagogia Theou. Die Heilsgeschichtslehre des Klemens von Alexandrien", *Münchener Theologische Zeitschrift* 5 (1954), pp. 246–72; H. Butterfield, *Christianity and History* (1949); A. Luneau, *L'Histoire du salut chez les Pères de l'Église. La doctrine des âges du monde* (1964).

What the Church can contribute, essentially concerns the dignity of the human person and, precisely for that reason, factors which serve the liberation of man. This liberation must be distinguished and preserved from a false autonomy which would cut man off from any higher law, as well as from the freedom of the flesh in the Pauline sense of the term (cf. Gal 5:1, 13).

Article 42. The help which the Church can offer society as such, is above all concerned with unity. The unity of the Church is supernatural, just as its mission is of the religious order (we do not say "purely spiritual" because this expression is ambiguous). If, however, the religious element is what concerns the living God, it includes the whole destiny of man. In this connection the Church at the very moment in which it is least *of* the world, can be most *for* the world. When Pius IX possessed and defended a temporal power, he was in conflict with many earthly powers. Paul VI, who has only a minimum, as it were a symbolic temporal sovereignty, and no ambition to enter into competition with any temporal power, can offer himself disinterestedly, with humility and love,[3] for service to the cause of man, and in particular to the cause of bringing about unity among men. The Church in the first place approves all that is already being done in the world in this sense, but adds a higher principle, that of love. This text is one of those which proclaim love as a social and political principle. It is in its place there, if it is true that peace does not originate in the domain of things but in that of personal relationships. According to Aquinas, peace is a result of love (*Summa Theologica,* 1 a, 2 ae, q. 29). The present chapter adds that the Church itself is an element of unity, standing as it does, in virtue of the principles which make it what it is, above the realities which divide men. That is indeed true, but it might be remembered also that the opposition between East and West would not be what it is today if there had not been a breach in communion between Eastern and Western Christendom on the ecclesiastical plane. Not only the unity achieved in the Church is important for the unification of mankind, but also the unity sought and hoped for in the ecumenical movement.

Article 43. The text speaks for itself, but three points deserve special mention.

1. The extreme care with which any separation of religious life from earthly duties is avoided. The second commandment is like the first, if indeed one can really say that there are two, for one and the same love is realized in each. "We conceive the virtues in the love of God and give birth to them in love of the neighbour" (Catherine of Siena). The earthly duties aspect

---

[3] Cf. Paul VI's speech to the United Nations, 4 October 1965. Cf. also note 13 above, and the words F. Rolfe puts into the mouth of his Hadrian VII: "The world longs for the Church, but will never admit it as long as the Church appears to be its rival."

must be specially emphasized in a world which is so little interested in the strictly theological aspect. It is a fact that the last few Popes, especially Pius XII, have pointed with increasing emphasis to the need to enter boldly into the movement of the world and to collaborate freely with other men.[4]

2. Stress is laid on the conditions on which the faithful can and must preserve unity among themselves despite their legitimate differences of opinion in political, economic, cultural and other questions.[5] They are invited not to attribute to their own views the absolute character of a dogma of the Church, and to remain open to dialogue with others. Cf. later Article 75.

3. The last paragraph contains an admission of the faults and weaknesses of the members of the People of God. *Gaudium et Spes* had already referred to certain cases of historical errors (art. 36, with footnote 7 [Abbott, note 100], in reference to the condemnation of Galileo). The Constitution on the Church had provided the doctrinal foundation for this, not only in the passage from Article 15 quoted here, but also in Articles 8 and 9; the Decree on Ecumenism (arts. 3 and 7) and the Declaration on Religious Freedom (art. 12) likewise contain discreet but clear admissions of our historical mistakes and omissions.

Article 44. The Church has probably never before uttered such official and solemn confessions of guilt, never before acknowledged so plainly that it too receives from the world. This is admitted in the present article. Because of its richness of content and relative novelty, it calls for a more detailed commentary. Four domains are listed in which the Church receives from the world.

1. The treasures of culture, especially in regard to man's self-knowledge and the opening up of new ways of access to truth.

2. The different cultures, to the extent that they possess a language which the Church can use to speak to the world and announce the gospel to it. This point, which is taken up later (art. 58), touches on the limitless subject of the relation between culture and language. That the Council understands by language something other and more than a mere means of expression — and that in itself is no small thing! — is evident from the fact that all the faithful and especially pastors and theologians, are invited to study and listen

---

[4] Cf. the texts collected in Y. Congar, *Lay People in the Church* (1964); and *Sacerdoce et laïcat*, pp. 414–17 and 434 f.; T. Suavet, *Libération de l'homme* (1946), towards the end; A. Auer, *Weltoffener Christ? Grundsätzliches und Geschichtliches zur Laienfrömmigkeit* (2nd ed., 1962), E. T.: *Open to the world.*

[5] Cf. the pastoral letter of Cardinal Feltin on unity in the Church: *DC* 49 (1952), pp. 401–16; Y. Congar, *Lay People in the Church* (1964); id., *Sacerdoce et laïcat*, pp. 437–40; *Cahiers universitaires catholiques*, April–June 1955 (contributions of A.-J. Maydieu and P. Dabosville), and the supplement to no. 3, December 1955: the unity of Catholics.

to the numerous languages of our time. It is therefore a matter of all the modes of expression of the immeasurable researches and discoveries of the human mind throughout time and space. Even more explicit mention might have been made of the questions which frequently inflict wounds on the Church, but necessary and fortunate wounds through which blood flows which must nourish and save.[6] They are questions which fertilize the mind and bring to light the half-buried treasures of its life.

3. If the Church is a factor of unity for the world (art. 42), the world does not present the mere material of the Church's unity but prepares the actual structures of that unity, because it creates unity in the domain of families, culture, economy, in the social, national and international political domains. It is well-known that the unity of the Roman Empire was favourable to the spread of Christianity.[7] In subsequent ages the Church's organization took its line from secular organization. We recognize better today the importance of factors other than political ones in the life of human society. We realize the pastoral importance of natural social elements.

4. The Church even admits that it owes something to the contradiction of its enemies and persecutors; their opposition is not purely negative. It also represents questions put to the Church, liberating it by fire, destructions and tears, freeing it from the weight of its superficialities and the fetters of its illusions. The deportation and exile had a purifying effect on Israel. But one hesitates of course to pursue this theme further when one lives oneself in a peaceful situation without oppression.

On the other hand we must go briefly into the question of what the possibility of receiving from the world in this way means for the Church. In the first place it means that its dialogue with the world cannot simply consist of the conversation between doctor and patient, of which the encyclical *Ecclesiam Suam* speaks (*AAS* 56 [1964], pp. 638f.). It is a question of a dialogue, and this involves reciprocity; the world has something to contribute. Here the theology of catholicity comes into play. It is quite certain that this catholicity has a source from above, namely Christ's "pleroma" but it also has a source as it were from below, namely, the indefinite power of human nature.[8] The Church is the actualization of the mystery of Christ

---

[6] We are using an image of Origen (cf. H. U. von Balthasar, *Parole et mystère chez Origène* [1957], p. 130, n. 25), which was rediscovered by Paul Claudel (discourse on his reception into the French Academy: *DC* [1947], p. 441).

[7] Eusebius, *Theophania* III, 1–2; Ambrose, *In Ps.* 45, 24; Prudentius, *Contra Symmachum* 582–91; Augustine; Paul Orosius, *Hist.* VII, 1; Prosper of Aquitaine; Leo the Great, etc. and of course, Charles Péguy, *Eve.*

[8] Cf. Y. Congar, *Chrétiens désunis* (1937), ch. III; id. *Sainte Église* (1963), pp. 155–61 id., "Über die Katholizität", in J. Feiner and M. Löhrer, eds., *Mysterium Salutis* (with bibliography); H. de Lubac, *Catholicism. A Study of Dogma in Relation to the Corporate Destiny of Mankind* (1950); M.-J. Guillou, *Le Christ et l'Église. Théologie du Mystère* (1963). On the

in mankind. It is therefore called — and this is a source of its essential missionary character — to meet what is in Christ for mankind and for the world, and what is in mankind and in the world for Christ. It is a traditional doctrine that the unity of the Mystical Body also has a first basis in the unity of human nature which was, of course, formed by God with a view to Christ; the unity of men in Christ consequently realizes on a higher plane the longing for unity which is implanted in man's nature:[9] "God has raised to a supernatural perfection the unity which men possess among themselves by their very nature."[10] This structure of the divine action is the reason for the Church's having to receive from the world, and lends the accomplishment of its mission a certain dialogue character of which missionaries today are very conscious. This goes further than (but only after it has accepted) the idea of apostolic "adaptation" which was developed particularly between 1920 and 1935.

Article 45. The task of the Church in this, in the full sense Catholic, realization of the "mystery", is here expressed in a Christological perspective by means of a favourite idea of *Lumen Gentium* (arts. 1, 8, 15 and 17): the Church is the "universal sacrament of salvation". The Church is the historical, social, visible and public form assumed by God's comprehensive, salvific will.[11] This character belongs to the Church because Christ is the principal centre and goal of the universe and of human history. He was sent into the midst of this history as a new ontological principle, by which the creation can achieve its ultimate meaning and so attain fulfilment. The whole function

---

"pleroma Christi" aspect, cf. J. Witte, "Die Katholizität der Kirche. Eine neue Interpretation ,nach alter Tradition", *Gregorianum* 42 (1961), pp. 193–241. On the philosophical implications of a full understanding of man's contribution, cf. Testis (M. Blondel), "La Semaine sociale de Bordeaux et le Monophorisme", reprinted from the *Annales de Philosophie chrétienne* (1910). The same ideas could be added if one were to start with the theme of wisdom, which is linked with the ideas of the Pleroma, the "mystery" of Christ, creation and the universe, and which occupies an important place in the Christology of the New Testament, especially with Paul; cf. A. Feuillet, *Le Christ Sagesse de Dieu d'après des Épîtres pauliniennes* (1966).

[9] Cf. the texts in H. de Lubac, *Catholicism;* E. Mersch, *Le Corps mystique du Christ. Études de théologie historique* (2nd ed., 1936) I, p. 450, n.; II, p. 37, n.; id., *Théologie du Corps mystique* (1944) I, pp. 301, 382 f., II, pp. 85, 374, E.T.: *Theology of the Mystical Body* (1951). Of the moderns: Pilgram, Staudenmeier, Pius XII (*AAS* 50 [1958], pp. 163 f., 172 f., 215, 263, 321 f.).

[10] E. Mersch, *Théologie du Corps mystique* II, p. 374; *DSAM* II, 2380.

[11] Studies on this idea: O. Semmelroth, "Die Kirche als 'sichtbare Gestalt der unsichtbaren Gnade'", *Scholastik* 18 (1953), pp. 23–39; id., *Die Kirche als Ursakrament* (1953), E.T.: *Church and Sacrament* (1965); B. Willems, "Der sakramentale Kirchenbegriff", *Freiburger Zeitschrift für Philosophie und Theologie* 5 (1958), pp. 274–96; K. Rahner, *The Church and the Sacraments,* Quaestiones Disputatae 9 (1963); Y. M.-J. Congar, "L'Église, sacrament universel du salut", *Église vivante* 17 (1965), pp. 339–55; P. Smulders, "Die Kirche als Sakrament des Heils", in G. Baraúna, ed., *De Ecclesia* I, pp. 289–312.

(munus) of the Church is to serve this saving plan. Once more we meet the New Testament and traditional doctrine of the relations between nature and grace, creation and redemption. Finally, a Christological light is thrown on this. We find ourselves here at the meeting-point of the biblical ideas of Wisdom, of the "mystery" (Paul), of a theology of history, of earthly realities, of the comprehensive mission of the Church, which is much wider than its mission to proclaim the gospel, and finally of the doctrine regarding the specific role of the laity in the exercise of this mission. "Where does our path start? What course should it follow? What goal must be set?... Three essential questions, in all simplicity. There is only a single answer to them...: Christ. Christ our principle; Christ our way and our leader; Christ our hope and our goal." [12]

Excursus on the use of the word "Church"

Is a word usually employed in theology to designate the Church in its mysterious aspect deliberately avoided? *Gaudium et Spes* only speaks once of the body of Christ (art. 32), and does so to stress the idea that men are members of one another, thus presenting the Church as an example of unity and solidarity. As we have already observed, the expression "People of God" is not used very often, although it accurately expresses the content of the word "Church" in the Pastoral Constitution. It was feared that if it were used too often it might give the impression that the Church is a people or nation side by side with other peoples, a sort of *tertium genus* in the sociological and not in the purely religious sense. The word *Ecclesia*, on the other hand, had the advantage of being generally accepted, and raised no problems. It seems to us, however, that in *Gaudium et Spes* it generally means the original community founded by Christ which watches over the deposit of faith of the gospel and has the task of communicating it to the world. The following list is not intended to be exhaustive, but may provide some indications.

Article 4: The Church has the duty of scrutinizing the signs of the times.

Article 10: The Church believes, the Church says.

Article 11: What the Church thinks about man.

Article 18: The Church, taught by divine revelation, says ...

Article 21: In its devotion to God and men, the Church ... must repudiate atheism. The Church holds that ... (throughout the article).

Article 33: The Church which guards the heritage of God's Word ... desires to add the light of revealed truth to experience.

Article 37: The Church of Christ, to which the heritage of the World is entrusted, must proclaim ...

[12] Paul VI, Speech at the opening of the Second Session of the Council, 29 September, 1963

Chapter IV, title and Article 40. The word "Church" is used a dozen times. It is said that the Church springs from the love of the eternal Father, is founded by Christ and united by the Holy Spirit, that it has as purpose ... and as mission ...

Article 41: The Church was entrusted with the task of revealing the mystery of God and also of preaching the gospel. The Church knows ...

Article 42: The mission which Christ has entrusted to the Church (several times).

Article 47: The Church's doctrine.

Article 63: The Church has worked out a social doctrine.

Article 76: "The political community and the Church."

Article 76: The Church, founded on the Redeemer's love.

Article 89: The Church must be present in the community of nations.

Article 92: The Church by virtue of its mission.

If *Ecclesia* designates the whole People of God as founded and charged with a mission, and does not signify merely the hierarchy, as was so often the case in official documents before Vatican II, we must find a more discriminating terminology to denote on one hand the leaders or hierarchical bearers of office, and simple believers on the other. In this respect the following are important:

Article 21: On the whole life of the Church and its members.

Article 23: The documents of the Church's teaching authority; similarly Articles 43, 50, 51.

The disciples of Christ: art. 28.

Christians: arts. 34, 43, 72, 88, 90, 93.

Believers: arts. 34, 36.

Believers in Christ: art. 43, 89.

Laymen: art. 43.

Article 42: The Church draws its children's attention to ...; cf. arts. 44, 51.

Article 43: The Church, through Christians.

Article 43: The Church is well aware that among its members, clerical and lay ...

The bishops: Article 43.

Pastors: Article 43, twice.

PART II

Some Problems of Special Urgency

CHAPTER I

Fostering the Nobility of Marriage and the Family

by

Bernhard Häring

Before the Council, the bishops had been sent a schema on "Marriage, Family and Chastity". Taken as a whole it was timeless and unproblematic. It was intended to perpetuate the negative and rigorist casuistry of the standard textbooks. The events of the First Session of the Council made it perfectly clear that this schema could expect no better fate than the almost equally bad schema on the "Sources of Revelation". The Council was spared a discussion. Towards the end of the First Session a document on the Church in the world was projected and the commission immediately realized that marriage and the family, the most burning problem of our time, could not be evaded in such a document. Work on a draft gave rise to vigorous argument in the subcommission, which was composed of members of the Theological Commission and of the Commission for the Lay Apostolate. The conservative group, supported by Cardinal Ottaviani and Fr. S. Tromp, S.J., made every effort to salvage the structure and spirit of the schema on Marriage, Family and Chastity and to incorporate it in the new schema. The subcommission had perpetually to deal with drafts in this sense composed by Fr. E. Lio, O.F.M. These were rejected by the open-minded bishops of the subcommission as not worth discussing. A dramatic clash finally occurred when Bishop McGrath in a letter to the Mixed Commission expressed a strong protest against Fr. Lio, who himself retorted with a letter accusing Bishop McGrath. The text finally arrived at a typical compromise. Its basis, however, was already that of marriage as a covenant of love, the family as a loving and sacred community.

This chapter was probably one of the reasons why the Central Commission did not consider the draft of the whole schema (known at that time as Schema 17) worthy of discussion in the Council aula. Men such as Cardinals Suenens and Döpfner had the impression that this text was no answer to the signs of the times, despite the considerable progress it indubitably represented over the pre-conciliar text. After a Central Subcommission had been set up to draft the whole schema (now known as Schema 13), the text was further revised between the Second and Third Sessions of the Council. It was more consciously, or rather it was expressly, placed in whole perspective of "signs of the times", of novel questions and of discrimination between the eternal and changing forms. This improved draft, however, only achieved the status of an appendix. It was distributed to the Council fathers but was not submitted to discussion in the assembly. The new elements in this text on marriage probably provided one of the chief grounds for Archbishop Heenan's biting remark in the aula (during the debate in the Third Session): "Timeo peritos annexa ferentes". During the working session in Zurich, the Central Subcommission decided to draw up a short document (about a page of print) in addition to the longer text of the appendix, for the schema which was to be presented to the Council for discussion. Because of shortage of time, the Central Subcommission was chiefly responsible for this short but essentially more courageous text, and not the Mixed Subcommission which had previously done the decisive work on marriage questions. This short text, and not the longer appendix on marriage, was then accepted (with a certain amount of excitement) by an astonishingly large majority of the whole Mixed Commission for transmission to the Central Commission. While Cardinal Ottaviani's supporters concentrated their opposition chiefly on this short text and on the theologian whom they regarded as the chief offender, its statements, which were few, but realistically faced the problems of the present time, provided grounds for several progressive theologians to support the whole schema even though they could not raise much enthusiasm for it otherwise. The strength and weakness of the text was obviously that, while it had the courage openly to state the problems involved in responsible parenthood, and the danger of a short-circuit if continence were presented as the sole solution, it did so without attempting to offer a solution; instead of a solution there was an appeal for humble and courageous study. This text, which came up for discussion during the Third Session, was retained in substance, with many details of expression and with its fundamentally open attitude on controverted questions, in the Constitution finally approved by the Council. It was also, however, enriched, qualified, and here and there slightly weakened.

After the Central Commission and the Pope had judged Schema 13 worthy of submission to the Council fathers, its 600 or so words on marriage and the family were once again one of the chief grounds for the attempt of a powerful minority to get the whole schema rejected without debate in the Council. In the general congregation itself the attacks of the minority (among others Cardinal Ruffini and Archbishop Heenan) concentrated on this section. The spirited interventions of Patriarch Maximos, Cardinals Alfrink, Léger and Suenens on this chapter, were highlights of a Council prepared for new theological reflection and pastoral renewal.

The appendix on marriage and family disappeared from view with the end of the debate during the Third Session. A little of Schema 13 was worked into the expanded text (now Chapter I of Part II). Some courageous suggestions of the appendix were disregarded, for example a carefully-worded proposal whereby divorced persons living in good faith in a new marriage might in certain circumstances enjoy the *favor iuris* if they were in good faith about their present union up to the time of their conversion. As condition of conversion — only conversion to the Catholic Church was meant in the first place, but the intention obviously covered any conversion — termination of conjugal life would not be demanded if this would only involve greater moral and human distress on the one hand, and if on the other there was not a positive moral certainty or very high probability of the validity of the earlier marriage. It is a pity that Patriarchal Vicar Zoghby did not link his intervention (during the Fourth Session) on the toleration of re-marriage of the abandoned partner in the Eastern Churches, with this suggestion in the appendix on marriage and the family. In that way the pastoral character of the whole question would have been made more evident and its compatibility with dogmatic positions easier to grasp.

After the Third Session a subcommission worked on the text under the extremely circumspect direction of Archbishop Dearden, and with the assistance of new theologians such as Canon Heylen and E. Schillebeeckx and of many lay people. Some of the theologians of the Papal Commission for Population Problems known to be more conservative were also invited. Among the bishops of the subcommission, Ireland, England, Italy and Portugal were permanently represented.

The same subcommission worked over the texts again after the first debate in the Fourth Session, without making any substantial alterations. The new version was then debated again, and on 11 November 1965 was submitted for the first time to a detailed vote. Despite the strong warning by Cardinal Ottaviani that the principle of responsible parenthood is incompatible with the faith, only 91 fathers (as against 2052 *placet*) voted against Articles 51 to 53 and only 140 (as against 2011 *placet*) against the critical Articles 54 to 56. On the chapter as a whole, together with the preface to Part II, 1596 fathers out of 2157 voted *placet*, 72 *non placet* and 484 *placet juxta modum*, and there were 5 spoiled votes. Among the 484 who voted *placet juxta modum* there were perhaps as many who wanted to keep the text even more open as wanted to introduce more guarantees or the "old" modes of expression. The subcommission performed an unbelievable amount of work day and night, considering and judging thousands of detailed suggestions. For the work of drafting the final text, the theologians — not the laymen — from the Papal Commission for Population Problems in the subcommission were also called in, and this time, all who were within reach.

All that can be reported of the dramatic events of the end of November is what has already been made public. A series of *modi* were pressed by the Secretary of State of the Holy See; these would quite clearly have altered the text, which had already been accepted by a two-thirds majority, in the direction desired by a small minority. Acceptance of the *modi* would either have made the Council, and especially the relevant commission, quite unconvincing, or would have provoked a massive *non placet* from the open-minded majority of the Council. The Council was being asked to slam the door, by a snap decision, on a question which had been more or less withdrawn from explicit discussion by the Council. Those persons on the commission (cardinals, one bishop and some theologians) who wanted the very solution which was implied in the *modi*, attempted to get them accepted without discussion "in holy obedience". When this failed, at least the theologians and laity were to be excluded from the discussion. The majority in the commission acted with a wisdom and dignity worthy of the admiration of posterity. They first of all ensured their essential freedom by inquiring whether it was a question of giving consideration to the *modi* in accordance with conciliar procedure, or of an order from the Pope. When a clear answer in the sense of freedom and maintenance of the fundamental rules of the Council had been received, account was taken of the *modi* with the greatest conscientiousness and freedom. That is to say, pastoral safeguards against misunderstanding were introduced, while at the same time the line adopted in the text by the majority was faithfully maintained. The clearest proof that those who claimed that the *modi* were an order from the Pope were wrong, was the fact that Paul VI approved the commission's answer on the very same day.[1]

Article 46. It is of decisive importance that the various statements of the chapter on marriage and the family are always envisaged and interpreted in the perspective of the Constitution as a whole. The whole Pastoral Constitution deliberately avoids a one-sidedly analytical mode of statement. It aims at giving a unified view, in order to counteract loss of balance. For this reason it allows itself numerous repetitions, which are irksome to the analytic mode of thought.

Article 46 recalls the outlook which dominates Part I, that of the dignity of the human person, its irreplaceable uniqueness and its essentially social vocation which extends to the whole world. It is also said that the points of view of the gospel and of human experience have to be combined. It is clear that "the gospel" here does not mean a mere repetition of biblical statements but rather a light in which human experience finds its true meaning. What is in question, therefore, is a specifically Christian conception of the history of

---

[1] The main lines of the history of the chapter and a bibliography are given by R. Tucci, "Introduzione storico-pastorale alla Costituzione Pastorale 'Gaudium et spes'", *La Chiesa e il mondo contemporaneo nel Vaticano II* (1966).

redemption. God's action still continues. It becomes visible in human experience when this is examined in the light of the gospel. We are here approaching a new way of proclaiming the "law of nature" or the ordinances and the abiding operation of the Creator, expressly in the light of the gospel. In this way the natural moral law is viewed more realistically and historically, incorporated into the actual history of salvation, and in that way it is enriched and verified. "On each of these may there shine the radiant ideals proclaimed by Christ. By these ideals may Christians be led, and all mankind enlightened, as they search for answers to questions of such complexity."

There is no trace here of the self-assurance of the deductive philosophical way of thinking about natural law which appeared to arrive by its syllogisms at absolutely certain metaphysical solutions and so failed to understand the problems raised by a new age and its new difficulties.

Marriage and the family are mentioned first among the burning questions of our time. How momentous a decision it was to deal with marriage and the family in this perspective — that of the world of today — can be seen very clearly if comparison is made with *Casti Connubii,* and even more with the Schema on Marriage, Family and Chastity which emerged from the laboratory of the Preparatory Commission and was sent to all the Council fathers before the First Session. That text was "timeless". In fact it adopted a hostile attitude to all the questions of our time. It will be all the more interesting when the first drafts are published from the archives. When these were first laid on the table of the Preparatory Commission, a moderate conservative advised me not to propose any amendments. He was convinced that a text of that kind would give the Council a very salutary shock. The hundreds of small improvements which we were able to make did not prevent the shock produced by the draft. It was very soon clear that present-day humanity and its problems have to be taken seriously if we are to expect people to take the message of the Council seriously.

It is to be noticed that in the first sentence of Article 46, in accordance with the official reply (cf. *Expensio modorum* 6), we are to read "sive individuale sive commune" ("whether individually or in common") instead of "sive individuale sive sociale", on the grounds, it is stated, that the word "commune" is preferable to "sociale" to express more comprehensively the reference to the community in all its aspects.

Article 47. In the introduction a fundamental principle of pastoral work and social action is stated. Marriage and family are more decisive than anything for personal well-being and for that of human society and the Christian community. This is not laid down, however, with the didactic air of an ethics of mere imperatives, but with a clear awareness of the importance of social action in general and of social pastoral action in particular. This is shown in more detail in Article 52.

From the social point of view it follows that here too Christians should be conscious of their solidarity with all men. The esteem felt for the family community by non-Christians forms a link between us. The positive aspect of the present hour of salvation is mentioned with joy before reference is made to contemporary dangers. Social change, "progress", will, if men use their freedom properly, promote this community of love and foster life. Marriage and family are intentionally described in this introduction as a "community of love". The diminution or loss of many secondary functions of the family of former times has made people in general more conscious of the central function of marriage and family, namely to be a community of love. Similarly the family is assisted in "fostering life" ("in vita colenda") by the new situation. In the patriarchal family the children were centred on the family, they were useful and even necessary to the family unit. In modern society the family is orientated towards the child. It can and must do much more for the upbringing and education of the children, yet without expecting economic advantages for the family group in exchange. If these opportunities are clearly realized and made use of, rich blessings can be looked for. Here the basic structure of this Pastoral Constitution is clearly visible, in the perspective of Ephesians 5:16: "Use to the full the present hour of salvation." The days are evil for those who are only prophets of woe and who, while lamenting over evil, lose sight of favourable opportunities or do not use them.

The predominantly optimistic note is essentially an expression of faith in the age of salvation between the first and second coming of the Lord, and does not allow of any ostrich policy. Those who see and profit by the positive possibilities, also face up frankly to the dangers. These are presented in the text in relation to the dignity of marriage and the family. The first evil is that many do not acknowledge this dignity. It is profoundly obscured by polygamy, divorce, so-called free love and other disfigurements. These are aberrations which falsify the very institution of marriage. Divorce here means successive polygamy, that is, divorce followed by marriage during the lifetime of the legitimate spouse.

Those who drew up the *modi* which were forwarded by the Secretary of State to the commission and wanted to insert on a par with polygamy and divorce "artes anti-conceptionales" (contraceptive procedures, literally "arts"), failed to observe in the first place that the text already approved by the conciliar majority is dealing in this sentence with things which falsify the very essence of marriage, and secondly, that by using a simplifying expression they were condemning particularly harshly the methods ("artes") which were intended to make periodic continence a more reliable method of regulating births. Consequently the commission firmly refused either to introduce the question of contraception at this point or to use the proposed expression. In response to the *modus* the problem of contraception was inserted in the following sentence, which deals with faults against conjugal love. This decision is characteristic of the spirit in which the question of the methods of birth regulation was propounded in the Council. What is directly involved here is therefore not the attitude of being averse from having children, which is unmasked in Article 50, but practices ("usus") which are inadmissible because they are contrary to the dignity and specific character of married love.

This position, firmly adopted by the commission and approved by the Pope and the general congregation, is a milestone in the handling of this difficult question. The following seems to me to stem from it. 1. Regulation of births is not, like polygamy and free love, contrary to the institutional character of matrimony (as is of course absolutely clear from Article 50). 2. It is not the artificial character as such ("artes") which is to be condemned, nor the efficacy of a method of rational regulation of births. 3. The question of methods has limits set to it by regard for the authenticity and dignity of conjugal love. It is not until Article 51 that we are positively reminded that in solving this question sufficient scope must be left for the cultivation of intimate conjugal love.

Many difficulties of married and family life are caused by a structure of economic life which is either directly hostile to the family or at least does not correspond to the fundamental position of the family and to the changes which history has brought. As a consequence of this, and far more important than the automatic effects of economic causation are the social and psychological conditions, a decisive factor which makes demands on personal and group responsibility. Here the influence of public opinion is certainly meant, though not only that. The word "civiles" which follows does not designate "social" circumstances in general but the structure of the life of the State.

Although the problem of the rapid growth of population in some parts of the world is not dealt with until Article 87, in connection with world peace, it had of course to be mentioned here, because population problems are reflected on the plane of marriage and family life.

The Council recognizes that, while all the circumstances referred to indubitably present many consciences with complex problems and not infrequently confuse and perplex them, they nevertheless contribute on the whole to a clearer view of the essentials of marriage and the family. Social change itself is of such a nature that the immutable elements in human experience stand out more clearly as a result of it.

The final paragraph of Article 47 underlines the pastoral purpose of the exposition which follows. Yet nothing would be more false than to conclude that the Church's doctrine is not to be found here, but solely in older, "purely doctrinal" pronouncements of the magisterium. If anything became clear in Vatican II, it was something which John XXIII had pointed out to the Council fathers: The Church's magisterium is pastoral through and through. To speak of purely doctrinal documents of the magisterium without pastoral purpose is largely to devalue them. It is always a question of saving truth. And this can only be correctly presented if the mode of its presentation is such as to enlighten and strengthen men here and now, so that there is hope that the fruits of genuinely Christian action will follow from it.

It is a new thing for the Church to address "all men" with such a specifically Christian doctrine as that of marriage, and to invite them as well as Christians "to defend and to foster the natural dignity of the married state, and its sublime sacred value". The choice of the term "sacred value" instead of "sacrament" is explained by the intention of addressing not only Christians but also those who, though they do not know the sacramental character of matrimony, nevertheless regard it as a sacred sphere, that is, one very closely linked with religion.

Article 48. Before dealing with sanctification and salvation, the text states what it is that is regarded as holy: "the intimate partnership of married life and love". The explicit emphasis on love as belonging to the essence of marriage was maintained here, as elsewhere, despite the *modi*. These asserted that the pre-eminent role attributed to love contradicts earlier pronouncements of the magisterium and makes it seem as if marriage can be dissolved as soon as love is extinguished (cf. *Modi generales ad num.* 47–52). The answer is plain. The objective meaning of matrimonial consent is an acceptance of marriage as a community of love; if, therefore, love becomes extinct, the partners have to do everything to re-learn it. In any case, the chapter repeatedly makes it clear that merely emotional love is not what is meant. What is in question is a community, the purpose and nature of which is not subject to man's arbitrary discretion. That is expressed in the words "established by the Creator and endowed with its own (intrinsic) laws". The word "legibus" in this context cannot be understood as a moral law simply imposed or added. Even "lawfulness" does not render the full meaning. "Laws of essence" or "structure" is nearest to the meaning.

This community of life and love established by God is designated as the "marriage covenant". It is rooted in "the irrevocable consent of the persons". The insertion of the word "contractus" (contract) instead of "foedus" (covenant) was rejected by the commission despite repeated numerous petitions and 190 *modi*. There are many reasons for this. The relation between Christ and the Church is not a contract but a covenant. Historically speaking, the "marriage contract" was often something bargained for by the two families and frequently obscured the genuine nature of the marriage covenant which is a community of love. People nowadays think of a contract as an agreement whose content can be determined by the contracting parties themselves and which can later be revoked by mutual consent. A contract concerns things, services and rights which in one way or another can be separated from the person. 34 Council fathers wished to revert to a more juridical concept, not only by using the word "contract" but also by defining its meaning as "the mutual transfer of specific rights and duties". In reply, the Commission insisted that more is involved than mere rights, namely, a covenant between persons, "traditio personae" (cf. Encyclical *Casti Connubii: ASS* 22 [1930], p. 553), two persons' mutual self-giving with a view to an exclusive community of life and love. 190 fathers wished to insert the impersonal definition of the code of canon law: "ius in corpus, perpetuum et exclusivum in ordine ad actos per se aptos ad prolis generationem". The Commission pointed out laconically that juridical language of that kind is neither pastoral nor conducive to discussion with the world. We can only hope that such humiliating language will also disappear from canon law. "Right to the body" comes down from a time when the wife was still listed with the husband's possessions. Merely to emphasize its mutual character scarcely improves matters. Moreover, if it were merely a question of a right to purposeful acts of procreation, we should nowadays have to exclude from the "marriage contract" not only the marriage of the sterile but also intercourse during the unfertile periods. The idea of a "covenant", which the Council fought so resolutely to maintain, corresponds to an understanding of marital intercourse as mutual self-giving. In the text at this point, however, it is not the single act but the whole community of life and love which is viewed as mutual self-giving. The stability of the covenant is explained by the "divine ordination", which is more than a merely factual arrangement. Its counterpart is the divinely-willed stability and irrevocability of the consent. The phrase "and in the eyes of society too" emphasizes that the stability of the marriage covenant is also of concern to society. Marriage is a personal association but at the same time redounds to the well-being or detriment of the whole of society. Society therefore has to protect and promote it. The well-being of all, married people, children and society, demands that the stability of the marriage covenant should not be at the mercy of men's whims. The expression "vinculum sacrum", "sacred bond", indicates that ultimately God is its guarantor.

Mention is then made of the blessings and purposes of marriage. The context makes it perfectly clear that this has nothing to do with the Augustinian doctrine of the benefits of marriage which were put forward as "reasons excusing" marital intercourse. It is simply a matter of the wealth with which God has intrinsically endowed marriage itself, in view of the perpetuation of the human race and the temporal and eternal well-being of the partners and the children. It is significant that no attempt is made to subordinate these purposes or benefits to any one of them. The Commission refused a request to do this on the grounds that the hierarchy of values can be regarded from various points of view (*Responsum* 15 and 19b).

233

The emphasis that marriage and conjugal love are intrinsically directed towards procreation and the upbringing of children and, as it were, find their peak or crown in this, cannot be regarded as confirming the theory which considered conjugal love as a purely secondary, non-essential purpose and benefit of marriage. The 10 Council fathers who wished the phrase "quasi fastigio" to be used, so that by undue stress on procreation the impression should not be given that the childless marriage is lacking in an essential element, received the reply that "That is exactly what is meant by the world 'veluti'" (*Responsum* 23 c). But the text makes it equally plain that procreation and upbringing are not incidental.

The word "itaque" (and so, and thus) which in fact is difficult to understand in the present text as it stands — in an earlier version it was more logically linked with the stability of the marriage covenant — was probably the reason why 16 fathers asked for it to be replaced by "insuper" (moreover). Another 11 fathers asked that instead of merely stressing the covenant of love, the even stronger expression "this pre-eminent covenant of love" should be used, to avoid giving the impression that marriage was established solely for the sake of fertility. The Commission overlooked that the word "itaque" was being criticized, and answered, "The formula 'vir insuper...' is to be retained", but did not correct the text and retained "itaque", which is obscure and in my opinion, in view of the commission's answer (*Responsum* 24 b), should be replaced by "insuper". At all events it is clear that from this "itaque", which only remained in the text through an oversight, it cannot be inferred that marriage was instituted and the community of love itself exists for the sole purpose of fertility. The Commission stated that "the text does not suggest this in any way".

It is clear from the context that the "mutuum adiutorium" is not meant as a secondary purpose side by side with a purely or primarily purposeful view of the marriage act as means to procreation. Growing unity and mutual perfecting in genuine love, a love prompt to mutual service, are presented here with their own intrinsic significance; they are not subordinated one-sidedly to the purpose of procreation and upbringing. An essential feature of marriage, even of a childless marriage, is in question.

The total fidelity and indissoluble unity of marriage are similarly grounded on the intrinsic nature of this community of love itself and not, as in many old natural law treatises, on the *bonum prolis,* the blessing of children. Love itself — not as a sentimental affair but as a genuine disposition and vocation — demands fidelity and indissolubility. The repetition of the expression "the mutual gift of two persons" is significant. Here again 161 fathers demanded that "self-giving by persons" should be replaced by the bestowal "of rights and duties". The Commission pointed out that, in the opposite sense, 11 fathers were asking for an alteration in order to emphasize even more strongly that it is not simply a question of rights and duties. These 11 fathers were told that the text already makes its meaning quite plain (*Responsum* 25 c and d).

The first paragraph of Article 48 describes the conjugal covenant of love as something sacred, and does so in a way accessible to all men of whatever religious conviction. Then the specifically Christian element is introduced. It is characteristic that the expression "this many-faceted love, welling up as it does from the fountain of divine love" forms the link with the previous paragraph. The synthesis is therefore ultimately sought by reference to God who is love. This idea is then deepened by reference to the covenant of love between Christ and the Church. Already in the Dogmatic Constitution on the Church (arts. 11, 35 and 41), in regard to the mystery of the Church, the essential theological connection between love and fruitfulness is observed. The love which the Church receives from Christ and gives him in return is not a subsidiary purpose juxtaposed with the apostolate. The Church by its love and in proportion to its love is the mother of the living. Accordingly the "abundant blessing" which Christ bestows on marriage is introduced as a blessing on the covenant of love, not merely as a blessing of fecundity. The sacramental nature of marriage is here described in very personalist terms, as a meeting with Christ. He abides with the couple who in his name have become an indissoluble unity. The purpose of his abiding presence, which is understood dynamically, is to make their love increasingly resemble his own love for the Church, so that it will truly become mutual dedication in absolutely faithful love. Marital love itself in its entirety becomes more genuine and richer through the sacrament, because it is more closely united to the primal source of all love. Here, too, one of the Council fathers wanted to introduce instead of the blessing on love, a blessing on the "contract". 148 fathers wanted to speak of the blessing only in regard to "fruitful union". But the Commission could appeal to the Council of Trent: DS 1799 (*Responsum* 26 d).

The outcome of the abundant blessing on mutual self-giving is both the personal sanctification of the married couple — they come closer to God — and the proper fulfilment of their vocation as parents. It is therefore clear that sanctification and successful upbringing of children are not simply juxtaposed with conjugal love and unrelated to it. The more genuine and redeemed the love of the married couple, the more marriage becomes a way of salvation and children a real blessing. The second part of the sentence, "so that the married couple are helped and strengthened in their sublime office of being a father or a mother", was in fact added in the final version at the request of six Council fathers. They wanted it inserted "so that the intrinsic connection of genuine conjugal love with the vocation of father and mother should be mentioned". On the other hand the 151 fathers who wished to teach that conjugal love is taken up into divine love "by fecundity", were not followed. It is noteworthy that they did not even receive an answer here.

Their perpetually repeated amendments onesidedly stressing fecundity were frequently answered by reference to the unqualified worth of a childless marriage when there is a right attitude in other respects.

After such a long and detailed treatment of the sanctification of the covenant of love, there is certainly no moralism if express mention is now made of "duties of state", particularly as this is done in the perspective of sacramental strengthening and consecration. The rather moralistic sequence whereby duties are mentioned before dignity ("ad sui status officia et dignitatem") was explained by the Commission in a reply to suggested amendments (*Responsum* 29) as simply due to quotation from *Casti Connubii*; no principle is involved. Yet since it is not a literal quotation, and since the whole Constitution does not derive dignity from duties but rather moral requirements from dignity, the Commission ought to have remained logically consistent. The next sentence too is moralistic, in structure at least, if not in its deepest intention. In a long complex sentence, the following are listed as the fruits of the sacrament: (1) fulfilment of the duties of their state; (2) being filled with the spirit of Christ; (3) permeation of their whole life with faith, hope and love; (4) help for mutual perfection; (5) glorification of God in common. Certainly to place the climax in the worship of God is good, but the Christian mode of fulfilment of duty ought to have been set out more clearly even in the structure of the sentence, as the result of being filled with the spirit of Christ and of a life imbued with faith, hope and love. In that way the "law of faith" and life under the rule of grace would be clearer, and the true source of Christian morals would be unmistakably plain. Yet the Council was certainly far from any intention of maintaining a moralism which on principle put fulfilment of the law before being filled with the Spirit. This isolated sentence must therefore be understood in the light of the whole paragraph.

Family prayer in common corresponds to the nature of the family as a sacred community worshipping God together. At the request of 57 Council fathers the word "humanitas" ("human maturity") was inserted before "salvation and holiness". As the Commission remarked (*Responsum* 33), that is already implied by the statement regarding salvation, yet it is right to emphasize it, so that the link between holiness and human maturity will not be overlooked. Similarly the whole humane education of children is mentioned here in connection with religious education. As in *Lumen Gentium* (art. 11) the fundamental responsibility of the family for religious education is stressed. And so religion remains wholly linked with life and the family with religion.

The solidarity of parents and children in regard to salvation is mutual. Children's contribution to their parents' sanctification is made in close connection with the attitudes naturally appropriate to them (cf. *Responsum* 36). The noble reference to widowhood was added in the final version and is to some extent foreign to the context. Four Council fathers had proposed a longer text on the relation between virginity and the sanctity of marriage, and as a sequel to this had stressed the holiness of the state of widowhood in relation to marriage and celibacy (cf. *Responsum* 41). The sanctity of the family is described as a sharing in the mystery of the covenant of love between Christ and the Church. Sanctity means the radiance, communication, attestation of the sanctifying presence of Christ. The Christian family is called to manifest to the world the true nature of love, fecundity, unity, fidelity, solidarity. At the same time it contributes to making it easier for the true nature of the Church to be more easily recognized. This positive view of the apostolate and of witness replaces the structure of the schema "De castitate, matrimonio et familia", which included at the end of each article a paragraph headed "Condemnation of false doctrines".

Article 49. The older teaching about the "ends of marriage" usually dealt with procreation first and then with conjugal love in a more or less subsidiary way, but the Council decided after long discussion to describe first the fundamental nature of marriage as a covenant of love, thus making it clear that love is not a merely subjective supplement to the objective, divinely established "ends" but is, as it were, the root or stem from which truly human, generous fecundity is to be expected. Conjugal love is a value in itself. The Council's starting-point was chosen with reference to biblical thought and to psychological and pastoral needs. That is especially stressed.

Article 49 attempts a phenomenology of conjugal love, in order to defend it against possible misunderstandings current today, and in order to clear away old prejudices. Conjugal love is fully human, personal, total. The whole human being expresses himself or herself in it, with will and heart responsive to the beloved partner in willing self-giving. The bodily element is not considered solely in teleological categories but shares in the personal mode of existence in speech and love. Conjugal love is not regarded one-sidedly as limited to the marital act, but as pervading the whole of life. But marital intercourse is a culminating expression of that love and of its continual development. The word "perficitur" here does not mean "accomplished for the first time", but implies an advance towards greater perfection. By the sacrament of matrimony this total love is healed, perfected and raised to greater dignity.

In Western theology until the time of St. Alphonsus Liguori, the Augustinian view prevailed that in fallen humanity the marriage act as such requires a "cohonestatio", that is to say, a special motive giving it moral character. It was generally considered that the explicit intention to procreate, or the fulfilment of marital duty if the other partner requested it, constituted such a motive. Alphonsus adopted the minority view that the marriage act as such is morally good ("honestus ex natura sua": *Theol. moralis lib.*, VI, tr. VI, n. 927), and stressed that as an expression of conjugal love (of the "mutua traditio") it remains good even if the couple have good reasons for not wishing a new pregnancy to ensue. The discussion in the general congregation (e.g. Cardinal M. Browne) showed that the Augustinian view still finds support, though only among a minority. The Council has perfectly plainly put an end to the controversy. Marital intercourse is morally good and has its own special dignity as an expression of genuine conjugal love. As such it enriches the married couple. It is a means to maintain their mutual love. This does not settle the current controversy about ways of responsible birth regulation, but it puts an end to the possibility of one form of argument. It can no longer be claimed that marital intercourse becomes meaningless if for a time — even on compelling grounds — the couple wish to avoid a new pregnancy. In practice the Church has always taken this line, not just by permitting choice of time as a means of birth regulation, but in its unqualified recognition of sterile marriages, and of marital intercourse during pregnancy. Previously, of course, it was possible for the rigorist school to maintain even in these cases that marital intercourse at infertile times was only morally justified if in practice it was the only way to avoid sins against chastity.

The conciliar text deals in this perspective with marital fidelity, indissolubility of marriage, and the consequently reprehensible character of adultery and divorce (i.e. divorce followed by subsequent remarriage). Those who held the view that the immorality of adultery and divorce can only be maintained if the sexual act is defined solely and strictly as the procreative act, will have difficulties with this article. The Council's view, which states so explicitly the moral goodness and dignity of loving conjugal intercourse, offers a much better and more intelligible basis and motive for the whole of sexual morality than the Augustinian opinion which depreciates the marriage act as something inferior unless it is explicitly willed as procreative or as accomplishing a duty in response to the request of the other partner. If young people today can realize that the marriage act essentially expresses irrevocable mutual self-giving and unity, they will also understand that pre-marital sexual intercourse is contradictory and profoundly false and inauthentic, because it expresses complete unity, "being one body", when such a unity of persons does not exist.

The opinion which regarded the marriage act onesidedly or even exclusively as procreative led, in conjunction with the mistaken biological idea that the man alone supplies the elements of life, to a momentous underestimation of the woman's role. Full recognition of the marriage act as a mutual self-giving and union of persons in a reverent and loving mutual relation, contributes more to the full acknowledgment of the dignity of woman than the modern discovery of the significance of the female ovum in copulation. The text therefore rightly speaks at this point of the equal dignity of women.

The reference to the great demands made by conjugal love and the consequent need for notable virtue, including self-sacrifice, may calm the anxiety of those who think that all safeguards are disappearing when the Council attributes such importance to conjugal love and the marriage act, without subordinating everything to the purpose of procreation.

Article 49 ends as Article 48 did, with the idea of bearing witness. The family has a noble mission to show the world what true love is. As well as fidelity and harmony, mention is also made here of the influence of conjugal love on the careful upbringing of children. Fundamental as good example is, and the influence which inevitably radiates from it, we must not under-estimate the quite deliberate and purposeful exertion of influence on public opinion, and the improvement of environmental conditions. This paragraph shows clearly that in singing the Song of Songs of conjugal love the Council had not in mind an idyll of self-sufficient solitude à deux or a self-centred marriage and family. What is in question all along is the salvation of the world. In view of the increasingly evident interrelation between family and environment, it is impossible honestly to accept the high vocation of the Christian family without taking part in pastoral work and in social and cultural action.

Not without reason the Council deals with well-timed instruction in pre-marital and marital chastity at this point, that is, in the perspective of conjugal love. In this way education in sexual matters receives its decisive orientation from the mystery of love.

Article 50. In answer to the numerous proposals from the minority who wanted Article 49 to teach in one form or another that every marital act is ordained towards procreation, the Commission replied, "Non enim omnes actus ad generationem tendunt" (*Responsum* 56 d). To a suggested amend-ment asking for it "to be clearly stated that conjugal love does not justify the marriage act independently of the will to procreate", the reply was given, "This assertion is incompatible with the doctrine adopted" (*Responsum* 67). On the other hand, the Council teaches extremely clearly in the first sentence of Article 50 that marriage and married love, *regarded as a whole*, are essentially and intrinsically ordained to the creation of life. This turning away from a narrow and at the same time incorrect analysis of the marriage act to a view of the married vocation as a whole is momentous. It is funda-mental for the understanding of responsible parenthood. Some representa-tives of the older view, which was based on a onesided analysis of the marriage act, considered that such a high estimation of married love and its bodily expression might entail the conclusion that procreation is something secondary in marriage. The Council has obviated this erroneous inference with all possible emphasis. The Commission willingly inserted here, at the last minute, so to speak, the sentence which well summarizes the contents of Article 50. "Children are really the supreme gift of marriage and contribute very substantially to the welfare of their parents." Earlier proposals to replace "donum" by the traditional expression "praestantissimum bonum" did not obtain a majority, because such a formulation could easily have been misunderstood as a continuation of the Augustinian doctrine of the threefold good of matrimony. The difference of opinion in no way concerned high esteem for the blessing of children; it simply turned on whether the individual instance of the conjugal union of love must receive its moral "justification" from other "goods" of marriage. The biblical quotations from Genesis and Matthew are intended to emphasize once more the mutual relationship between the personal attachment of the married couple and the vocation to parenthood.

Texts 3 and 4, which served as basis for discussion in the third and at the beginning of the fourth session, stated that "the proper cultivation of married love and the whole mode of family life arising from it have the aim of disposing married people to co-operate firmly and willingly with the love of the Creator and Redeemer . . ." At the beginning of the Fourth Session, very strong objection had been raised to this in the aula. The text seemed once again onesidedly to orientate marital love towards the procreation and upbringing of children, and in practice, despite all that had been said in the previous article, to sanction a hierarchy of "ends" of matrimony. The commission bowed to the criticism and inserted an "etiam", but emphasized in the *relatio* before the vote in November 1965 (p. 18) that this insertion was not to be regarded as taking up sides in the controverted question of the hierarchy of the ends of marriage. The rather vague "etiam", however, did not meet with much approval. More than 100 Council fathers criticized it. 117 wanted it replaced by "praecipue" which would have suggested one particular point of view regarding the doctrine of the ends of marriage. A *modus* put forward by the Secretary of State asked for its simple deletion. The Commission preferred to replace "etiam" by the much clearer text "non posthabitis ceteris matrimonii finibus". This makes it perfectly clear that the Council opposed the opinion which holds that high esteem for the blessing of children can only be maintained if all else is reduced to a merely secondary end.

The idea of responsible parenthood is introduced in the phrase "interpreters of God's creative love". This is probably the most expressive renunciation of an attitude which identified trust in divine providence with a blind or at least unreflecting abandonment to chance or the functioning of biological laws. Man trusts God's providence in the way most worthy of a human being by attempting to read the will of God from the given facts and by adopting an attitude of response to the gifts of God and the needs of the neighbour, and then of course also accepts the risk of decision. The word "veluti" ("so to speak") is not without its importance. Man can never have a complete grasp of everything. His service as interpreter cannot go beyond the range of his knowledge. But this is much greater today than in past ages.

Responsible parenthood has nothing in common with arrogant planning or birth-control inspired by unwillingness to have children. The Christian attitude is one of "docile reverence", and basic to it are respect for the gifts and possibilities bestowed by God, and mutual regard of the married couple for one another. The phrase "the interests of civil society" includes population problems, which can mean under-population as well as over-population. Practically speaking, a family which brings up its children well in every respect fulfils its obligations in this respect. For demographic problems arise principally because of the lack of capable people or as a result of the presence of a large number of people who lack appropriate training and education.

The principle that "ultimately the married couple themselves must make this judgment" emphasizes the maturity of the Christian conscience, whether in relation to the confessor or in refusing undue regimentation by State authorities. At the *expensio modorum,* the emphatic addition "and no one else" was deleted, in order to avoid an unnecessarily acrimonious tone. The Commission stressed, nevertheless, that by this deletion the meaning of the sentence, namely "the exclusion of any undue interference", was not altered in any way. Consequently even the confessor may not presume to dictate his own opinion about the desirable number of children or the time at which a married couple should wish for another child. He can nevertheless, if the occasion arises, admonish penitents — even in the form of sacramental penance — to pray for knowledge of God's will.

In complete agreement with the fundamental idea of *Gaudium et Spes,* it is emphasized that the interpretation of the divine law takes place "in the light of the gospel". This assigns its due place and limits to thinking in terms of natural law, which must always be examined and expounded in the light of the gospel.

The reference to married love being protected by the divine law is not alien to the subject-matter of this article on the fecundity of marriage. In the first place it is becoming increasingly evident that in the new circumstances of the present day only genuine conjugal love can ensure joy in having children, because the economic and social motives which formerly prompted people to have large families are disappearing one after the other. Furthermore, the decision responsibly to regulate births at once raises the problem how, when a new pregnancy is not desired, conjugal love is to be fostered in such a way that the readiness to further, responsible parenthood will be encouraged.

Many Council fathers asked for explicit praise to be given to the large family, when it carries out in exemplary fashion the duty of bringing up the children. Once again a clear distinction is thus drawn between the principle of responsible parenthood and the kind of propaganda for birth-control which on principle wants all families to be kept small.

Unenlightened zeal has sometimes praised large families in a way that offended married people who quite inculpably had no children or only one or two. The impression was even given that the childless marriage has essentially failed to attain the meaning and purpose of marriage. The child itself cannot be loved for its own dignity as a person, if an unfertile partner is not loved for his or for her own sake as husband or wife and is therefore dismissed as soon as his or her sterility is known. In view of the Church's constant teaching on the indissolubility of the childless marriage, the Council's attitude is more pastoral than the opinion which regarded conjugal love merely as a secondary end wholly subordinated to the purpose of procreation.

Article 51. The subtitle of Article 51 expresses clearly and frankly a problem which is still largely unsolved. How is the harmonious cultivation of conjugal love to be meaningfully reconciled with responsible regulation of births? The Council had the courage frankly to state the difficulties and even the dangers of an over-simplified solution. A long period of continence in marriage, even if undertaken by mutual agreement, can represent a danger to marital fidelity, as the apostle of the gentiles himself pointed out (1 Cor 7:5). It quite often involves a very real psychological "sterilization". We only need think of the case where a young mother gives every mark of affection to her first or second child but avoids any conjugal expression of tenderness for her husband so as to be sure of remaining continent. She may, for example, do so as a result of rigorist views on sexual matters which forbade as "actus impudici" anything which might possibly be the occasion of sexual satisfaction. The fostering of conjugal affection certainly involves self-control. But self-control must not allow specifically conjugal love to atrophy, but must protect it. That statement, of course, is not directly present here in the conciliar text. For as footnote 14 of the Latin text (Abbott, n. 174) says, no immediately concrete solutions are proposed. The Council states the essence of the problem and then marks out its scope with general principles. In the first place, the worst solution of all, an immoral one, is excluded, i.e. infanticide or abortion. It is then said that there can be no contradiction between the divine laws governing the service of life and those which concern the fostering of genuine conjugal love. The Council, however, certainly did not mean to claim that the Church always knows those divine laws so perfectly that even when faced with new difficulties the Church can show at once how the two are compatible in all cases. The Church is seeking a way of harmonizing them, and consequently limited itself at the Council to stating those general principles which are beyond all doubt.

The apparently very abstract principle that the noble function of transmitting and preserving life has to be carried out in a way worthy of human beings, can be rich in consequences if we take into account what the first part of *Gaudium et Spes* has to say about the dignity of the human person. Preservation of human life is one of the highest principles of natural law and is clearly confirmed by revelation. Parents have a pre-eminent rôle in this respect. The Commission chose the expression "from the moment of its conception", in order not to have to go into the difficult question of the moment at which the soul is infused (*Responsum* 101 a). At all events it is clear that in case of doubt whether a real human life is yet present, nothing may be done which might possibly put an end to a human being.

The request of three Council fathers for a precise definition of "abortus" was not granted (*Responsum* 101 c). There are in fact marginal cases where no unanimity as yet prevails whether an "abortus" is involved or not, e.g. when the foetus certainly has no further prospect of life, while the mother's life can still be saved. It may be disputed whether in a particular case an attack on a human life is involved. But there is absolute agreement with the Council that an attack on an innocent life — and the foetus is always an innocent life — is a serious crime.

Any false biological views which overlook or underestimate the immense difference between merely animal structure and human sexuality is most expressly excluded. The norm of moral action must preserve the specific character and dignity of human sexuality. The starting-point of the doctrine of natural law is not that of biological laws regarded as inviolable, but the essence ("natura") of the person and of personal actions. The actual structure of the sentence itself places the accent on "personae" ("obiectis criteriis ex personae eiusdemque actuum natura desumptis"). And in order to link the word "actuum" very closely with the personal perspective, the conjunction "et" was not used, but the particle "-que" attached to "eiusdem" was chosen, because it forms a closer link. The personalist viewpoint provides the decisive criterion of the Council's teaching on natural law. The Commission observed in answer to the *modi* which prompted the expression of the doctrine in these very plainly personalist terms: "These words mean that the acts are not to be judged solely by their biological aspect but as acts proper to the human person, and the latter is to be fully envisaged in its total reality" (*Responsum* 104 c and f). As the text itself states in the first part of the sentence, the personalist perspective in no way implies a subjective morality in which a good intention justifies anything and everything. But neither does the expression "objective standards" sanction reified thinking which attributes no more value to the human person and personal relationships than to mere relations between things or to biological functions. The "objective standards" mean above all that in the question of birth control and its methods, care is to be taken that the full meaning of the marriage act as "mutual self-giving" is preserved, as well as the full meaning of "human procreation in the context ('in contextu') of true love". This lays down two clear guidelines for all further discussions on methods of birth control. In accordance with a *modus* sent by the Secretary of State, the Commission inserted at this point the admonition that "This cannot be done unless the virtue of married chastity is sincerely cultivated". In this way married chastity is once again expressly presented as an intrinsic and essential requirement of the conjugal love the fostering of which is in question. And because such chastity protects the spiritual climate of genuine married love, it also serves the dignity of human procreation. The Secretariat of State had suggested that its sentence should be inserted in the first paragraph of Article 51. The Commission, however, did not approve of this, because a reference to the virtue of chastity in that context could have been misunderstood by some to mean that only chastity in the sense of renunciation of any intimate conjugal manifestation of love, or protracted continence, was being offered as *the* solution (cf. *Responsum* 98 c).

The admonition to obedience to the Church's teaching authority was somewhat sharpened because of a *modus* sent by the Secretariat of State. The text presented for vote in November 1965 had "ne ineant" where the present text reads "inire non licet". Is this a general admonition to obey the magisterium, or are quite definite instructions inculcated? The words "his principiis innixis" in themselves would indicate that the fundamental principles previously expressed, and which are an interpretation of the divine law ("in lege divina explicanda") are to be observed in practice. That would not add anything new, because it is obvious that the Council intended to enlighten and therefore bind people's consciences by these principles. Does the sentence mean that earlier pronouncements of the magisterium, which on the one hand were interpretations of the divine law in general and on the other hand gave an answer to the questions of a past age expressed in the language and on the basis of the knowledge of a past age, must be interpreted and followed in substantial agreement with the principles previously laid down in this Article 51? Footnote 14 (Abbott, n. 173) points the way, for it indicates a dynamic conception of the Church's teaching on the question of birth control. The reference to *Casti Connubii* stands in conjunction with Pius XII's Address to Italian Midwives in 1951 in which for the first time the idea of consciously responsible procreation clearly appeared in a pronouncement of the magisterium. Both texts must also be understood in the light of Paul VI's address of June 1964, according to which certain questions were to be submitted to thorough study in view of the new situation and new scientific knowledge. The magisterium is viewed as functioning within the history of redemption. This also points to an understanding of natural law which more consciously takes into account the temporal, historical character of man than was done by the purely static doctrine of natural law which prevailed with the advent of rationalism.

Article 52. The emphasis on education to deeper humanity and on the dialogue and collaboration of married people, is in the general line of *Gaudium et Spes* and recalls Paul VI's encyclical *Ecclesiam Suam*.

As opposed to onesided older tendencies to describe the role of the wife exclusively as that of housewife and mother, stress is laid on the presence of the father and his importance for the children's upbringing, as well as on the legitimate social progress of women. The goal of education is presented as a person able and willing to assume responsibility and ready to take his or her place in society. The family must be conscious of its social responsibility, and society and the State must make it their business to organize social life in ways which further the family. Onesided individualistic morality and pastoral care are less capable than ever at the present day of solving questions of marital and family morality.

Mention is made of the art of "distinguishing eternal realities from their changing expressions" as a condition of the effective presence of Christians in the world, able to influence public opinion and shape social life in a way favourable to marriage and the family. Unenlightened Christians who cling stubbornly to past modes of life and fight doggedly for secondary matters which are often not specifically Christian but only things of the day before yesterday, have no influence on the course of history. A union of forces is needed to solve the grave problems which threaten marriage and the family today. The Council appeals simultaneously to the Christian sense of the People of God, to the sound moral conscience of all men and to the efforts of theologians. The special appeal addressed to the representatives of modern sciences which bear on questions of marriage and the family, shows that the teaching Church is willing to learn.

Priests are reminded of the importance of family pastoral work and of the preparation this entails. The aim is radiantly happy families. Harsh practice in the confessional would be incompatible with this paragraph.

The various family associations, movements and similar organizations merit honourable mention. Care for proper preparation for marriage and for young families are pointed out as their special field of work.

The final paragraph once again sums up everything in the great perspective of the mystery of love. By its life and what it expresses, the family is to proclaim to the world the living and loving God.

See below, *Excursus on Humanae Vitae,* pp. 397–402.

The Proper Development of Culture

by

Roberto Tucci

Unlike other chapters of the second part of the Pastoral Constitution, Chapter II did not really have any prehistory during the preparatory phase of the Council. Among numerous schemata drafted by the various commissions, none dealt expressly with the relations between Church and culture. The need for one on this theme had, however, become apparent in the Commission for the Lay Apostolate which, for lack of time, had devoted only an appendix to it: "Inter humanas res longe mirabilior omnium, hac nostra aetate, culturae profectus in omnibus suis coetibus ac saeptis, praesertim sub scientifico ac technico respectu, procul dubio censeri debet. Permagni tamen interest ut haec doctrina vere sincera atque ingenua sit, scilicet quoquoversus humana atque christianis principiis ac moribus adaperta ac praenuncia, quin immo vere christiana sit oportet, evangelicis veritatibus ac legibus consona." A few brief indications followed on the action which cultivated lay people can undertake in this field and on the necessary conditions for a fruitful cultural apostolate.[1]

---

[1] *Schema Constitutionis de apostolatu laicorum,* Pars II: *De apostolatu laicorum in actione ad regnum Christi directe provehendum* (1962), pp. 47 f.; after revision by the Central Commission: *Schemata Constitutionum et Decretorum ex quibus argumenta in Concilio disceptanda seligentur,* Series quarta (1963), pp. 118 f. Since this text is not very accessible, we reproduce it here in full:

Alia insuper argumenta, hac nostra aetate valde urgentia, Membra Commissionis voluntatem habebant profundius investigandi ac tractandi, prouti "cultura", "publici mores", "communicationis socialis instrumenta", "ludicra certamina" (sport), "peregrinationes ac itinera relaxationis et instructionis gratia suscepta (tourism)".

Ad severiorem tamen investigationem, prout opus erat, tempus defuit (Notandum vere est Secretariatum de Prelo et Spectaculis unum ex dictis argumentis optime pertractasse, Commissionem autem de Episcopis ac Dioeceseon regimine integrum caput argumento "De peregrinatorum seu turistarum cura" dicasse). Sed coetus romanus Commissionis voluit saltem praecipua seu summa lineamenta eorum quae a Commissione non definitive apparata sunt hic tradere. Sicut in caeteris studiis nostris, uti patet, etiam his in quaestionibus, quae

Reference is made to the problems of civilization in the Message of the Council Fathers to All Men (20 October 1962), where the hope is expressed that from the work of the Council will come a spiritual renewal "from which will also flow a happy impulse on behalf of human values such as scientific discoveries, technological advances, and a wider diffusion of knowledge".[2]

It is all the more surprising, therefore, to find no mention of this viewpoint

---

universam Ecclesiam respiciunt, iis, quae apostolatum laicorum eorumque in Ecclesia responsabilitatem tangunt, potissimum locum fecimus.

1 — De cultura. Inter humanas res longe mirabilior omnium, hac nostra aetate, culturae profectus in omnibus suis coetibus ac saeptis, praesertim sub scientifico ac technico respectu, procul dubio censeri debet. Permagni tamen interest ut haec doctrina vere sincera atque ingenua sit, scilicet quoquoversus humana atque christianis principiis ac moribus adaperta ac praenuncia, quin immo vere christiana sit oportet, evangelicis legibus consona.

Ad hanc efficiendam culturam, laicorum actio perurgens est.

A — Exculti laici quadruplici praecipue sensu actionem operamque suam dare possunt:

a) ad culturam genuinam et christianam pro omnibus effingendam adlaborare;

b) ad culturam in proprium coetum apud collegas, apud sibi subditos et clientes afferendam;

c) ad disciplinarum humanarum diligentem investigationem quae profectui scientiae theologicae deservire possint (philosophia, historia, archaeologia, etc.); ad regimen Ecclesiae, ad ipsius etiam administrationem fovendam (disciplinae iuridicae et oeconomicae); ad cultum liturgicum provehendum (artes, praesertim architectura);

d) ad diversa culturae saepta mutuo componenda et ad unum redigenda; ad recte aestimandos varios gentium humanos civilesque cultus ac ea quae in eis bona sunt aperto animo amplectanda; ad commercia cum culturis nondum christianis ineunda.

B — Peculiaria culturae munera ac saepta.

Curetur christiana cultura laicorum qui munera directiva habent, in primis circa singulorum professionem. Novae professiones, quae saepe in campo scientifico et technico evolvuntur, cultura vere humana et christiana imbuantur.

Apostolatum vero exerceant in coetibus altioris et culturae, praesertim in coetibus universitatis inter professores et alumnos, saeptis scientificis peculiari modo prae oculis habitis.

C — Ad apte apostolatum culturalem exercendum, in primis scientificae methodi exigentiae debite observentur. In singulis culturae saeptis augeatur peculiaris peritia et novissimae notitiae sedule acquirantur.

Praecipuis doctrinis theologicis laicus excultus carere non potest, ut sciat res sensu theologico diiudicare et interpretari utque theologia et vita mutuo proprius accedant.

Commercia inter excultos viros catholicos ineantur et foveantur. Vitam proprii culturalis coetus unusquisque scienter et intime vivat, relationibus tamen cum suo ambitu sociali diligenter servatis.

Magni momenti est, praesertim pro excultis laicis, vitae commercia cum clero statuere.

Ad haec omnia facilius consequenda necesse est ut sacerdotes peculiari cura et ratione praeparentur.

In Part IV of the same schema. "De apostolatu laicorum in actione sociali" (1962), pp. 37–40, and in the volume already quoted, pp. 165–7, there are also two small chapters entitled "De scientiis et arte" and "De ordine artium technicarum". These treat briefly the themes eventually dealt with in *Gaudium et Spes*, Part II, ch. II.

[2] *L'Osservatore Romano*, 22/23 October 1962.

in the well-known speech of Cardinal Suenens (4 December 1962) in which he suggested the methodical reorganization of the various matters to be dealt with by the Council and put forward a plan of dealing with the problems of the *Ecclesia ad extra,* that is, of the Church inasmuch as it is undertaking a dialogue with the world. On the other hand, in the draft schema "De Ecclesiae principiis et actione ad bonum societatis", submitted by the same cardinal to the Co-ordinating Commission (21 January 1963), the fourth chapter was entitled "De cultura humana". In the first months of 1963, various versions of that chapter were prepared; the one examined by the Co-ordinating Commission on 29 March 1963 contained the following headings: 1. De cultura humana; 2. Ecclesia et culturae diversae; 3. Extensio culturae hodiernae; 4. Character culturae hodiernae; 5. Cultura et persona; 6. Cultura et gloria Dei; 7. Collatio Ecclesiae ad vitam culturalem; 8. Collatio culturae ad vitam Ecclesiae; 9. Cura Ecclesiae de culturae saeptis. This amounted to three typed pages in all. Further elaboration of the following points was requested: the nature and importance of culture for man; the relations of mutual assistance between the life of the Church and the world of culture. It was also noted that almost nothing had been said on the recapitulation of all things in Christ, and on the relations between cultural values and the reign of God, and that something should be said on the special duties of the laity in this field.

Between March and May 1963, the text was rewritten several times, with the collaboration of laymen. Chapter IV of the schema, discussed at the plenary session of the Mixed Commission on 24 May 1963 and emended according to the observations made on that occasion, now bore the title "De culturae progressu rite promovendo" and was subdivided as follows: 1. Condiciones culturae in mundo hodierno describuntur; 2. Cultura et persona; 3. Cultura et communitas; 4. Cultura et gloria Dei; 5. Ecclesia et cultura; 6. Ecclesia et culturae diversae; 7. Quid Ecclesia ad culturam conferre possit; 8. Quid cultura ad vitam Ecclesiae conferre possit; 9. Cura Ecclesiae de culturae campis; 10. Peritiae in cultura sive profana sive religiosa necessitas. This text runs to eight typed pages.[3]

---

[3] For a well-informed account of the history of the text, cf. C. Moeller, "La promozione della cultura" in G. Baraúna, ed., *La Chiesa nel mondo d'oggi* (1966), pp. 372–83. On the above-mentioned version he writes: "Text 1, 5 constitutes in substance the basis for the successive versions... Up to that point a number of themes were introduced, and these though successively clarified, transposed and modified, remained on the whole the same. Finally the chapter on culture was practically the only one which was composed with the aim of maintaining in view the theme of man created to the image of God, and with the idea of the transformation of the world which culture helps to prepare, etc.; the other chapters were in fact very much more disconnected and lacked a sufficiently clear link with the themes of anthropology, cosmology and biblical eschatology which had now appeared in Chapter I" (p. 374).

In the "Adumbratio schematis XVII De activa praesentia Ecclesiae in mundo aedificanda", prepared in Malines in September 1963 by an international team of theologians invited by Cardinal Suenens, there was no special section devoted to culture. For this and the other themes which figured in Chapters II–VI of the previous text, it was proposed there should be "instructions" or, as they were subsequently called, "adnexa" ("appendices"), which were not to be laid before the Council for discussion. Some reference was in fact made to culture, but in a general theological context concerning the ensemble of human values in relation to the Church's mission in the world.[4]

The first half of 1964 produced a new draft of an actual conciliar text, known as the Zurich text. Its fourth and last chapter dealt briefly with the most important tasks of Christians at the present time. At first something was said about problems of culture in one or other article of this chapter, for example, on promoting the dignity of the human person, and on marriage and the family. Later, between April and May 1964, it was decided to devote a separate article to culture, based on materials from the corresponding chapter of the schema which had been discussed and amended at the plenary session of May 1963. In the final version, debated and amended by the Mixed Commission at the meeting at the beginning of June 1964 and finally sent to the Council fathers at the end of July 1964, the special paragraph on culture was no. 22 and was entitled: "De cultura rite promovenda". One and a half small pages in all, somewhat meagre, and showing signs of rather hasty composition.[5]

---

[4] C. Moeller, *loc. cit.*, p. 374.

[5] *Schema De Ecclesia in mundo huius temporis* (1964), pp. 24 ff. We give a brief summary here:

The developments of science, technology, mass-media, etc., offer an ever increasing number of people the possibility of access to the benefits of a higher and wider culture. Although distinct, religion and culture have many points of contact; Christians should encourage these and co-operate with other men in the development of true culture.

1) By devoting ourselves to human activities, we follow God's command which gave man dominion over the earth. At the same time we contribute to enhancing the dignity of the human person.

2) It is clear that spiritual values occupy the first place in the hierarchy of values. Even if in certain circumstances the work of providing material goods necessarily takes precedence of all else, the development of truly human living conditions means that higher values are promoted and that opportunity and means are offered to all to make them their own.

3) The meeting of cultures initiates a dialogue which requires above all mutual respect.

4) In carrying out its mission, the Church also exercises a cultural function, as is shown by the vast number of works of art which Christian doctrine has inspired. The Church came into existence in a particular historical and geographical environment, it is true, but it is not tied exclusively to any particular culture; it takes root in all in a vital exchange, giving and receiving. If this dialogue is to be fruitful for both sides, the messengers of the gospel must know the values of the two cultures, and the intellectual élite must come to

In the meantime, a special subcommission had been working since April 1964[6] on the revision of the chapter of the May 1963 schema, in order to prepare a special appendix on culture.

The directives issued by the Central Subcommission for this revision, from the end of February 1964, drew attention to the following points: The theological bases of the exposition should be brought out more clearly, by showing the connection between culture and salvation, sin and redemption, yet without reducing culture to a mere means of evangelization; the text should manifest that specifically Christian spirituality which regards all valid expressions of the various cultures as gifts of God, in the perspective of the mystery of the incarnation and of Easter. Furthermore, it stressed the need for collaboration of laymen qualified in the various branches of culture, if a sound revision of the text was to be made.

The definitive text of the appendix "De culturae progressu rite promovendo" (the third after the chapter on the human person in society and matrimony and the family) was ready at the beginning of July 1964. Together with the other adnexa it was distributed to the Council fathers at the beginning of the Third Session (30 September 1964).[7]

In substance the text of this appendix corresponds to that of the chapter on culture in the schema of May 1963, with the same articles, except Article 10, which had been incorporated into Article 9 with an only slightly modified title, "Sollicitudo Ecclesiae ad culturam fovendam". Emendations, apart from purely stylistic ones, or additions of any importance, are not numerous in the first seven articles: a more positive introduction to Article 4 (Cultura et gloria Dei) and Article 5 (Ecclesia et cultura), the mention of the contribution of the Church to the progress of culture even by its liturgical and pastoral activity and not merely by preaching the gospel, in Article 7 (Quid Ecclesia ad culturam conferre possit). In Article 8 (Quid cultura ad vitam Ecclesiae conferre possit) on the other hand, there is an obvious attempt to develop more fully the themes which are just indicated briefly. Especially noticeable is the addition on the contribution which the cultivated Christian can make to the apostolic work of the Church by the influence which he can have on the formation of public opinion, through the authority he enjoys. For this it will be necessary to ensure him "illa filiorum Dei libertas sive cogitandi sive suam mentem aperiendi circa ea quae ad ecclesiasticae communitatis bona pertinent, quae christianum in fide adultum decet, dummodo ipse

appreciate the riches of faith. Consequently all, especially the laity, must esteem and cultivate in the light of Christ the arts and sciences in which they are skilled. Similarly those who are engaged in the apostolate, especially pastors and theologians, should learn to present revealed truth in the language of the cultural milieu in which they are working.

[6] At that time the following took part: Cardinal Léger, Bishops Charue, Doumith, Yü Pin, Larraín Errázuriz, De Vet and Guano, assisted by a group of experts.

[7] *Schema de Ecclesia in mundo huius temporis. Adnexa* (1964), pp. 26–33.

christiana prudentia, veracitate, humilitate, fortitudine et caritate ducatur. Proinde, cum de doctrinae quaestionibus vel de rebus in Ecclesia agendis habeantur variae opiniones, quae sua gaudent probabilitate, necdum a competenti auctoritate decisio facta sit, nemo scientiae cultor impediendus est, quominus id quod sentit libere exponat..." Article 9 is almost completely recast and much extended, to provide pastoral guidelines for the action of Christians in the domain of culture. A certain verbosity and especially a lack of coherence is evident in the list of concrete tasks with which the chapter ends. On the other hand, this final paragraph lends the appendix on culture a less abstract and more practical character in comparison with Article 22 of the conciliar text itself, which is almost devoid of practical elements.

The conciliar debate on Article 22 during the Third Session was quite rich in interventions and interesting reactions. It began at the 113th general congregation (30 October 1964) and was continued at the 114th (4 November) with a supplementary speech at the 119th general congregation (10 November). In all, fourteen fathers spoke on this paragraph. Others were content to present their comments in writing. The secretariat of the commission collected 53 closely printed pages of oral and written interventions. In a brief summary of these comments, it may be said that the following aspects in particular were stressed: The Church's ability to permeate and make use of all cultures, since it is not indissolubly tied to any; the Church's duty to achieve in the field of ecclesiastical culture, the poverty demanded of it by the gospel, i.e. the Church must have the courage, if necessary, to renounce certain riches of a glorious but perhaps anachronistic past, or at least not to presume too much on them, since they may prevent it from welcoming the true values of a new culture or of ancient non-Christian cultures, and limit the universality of the Church's language, divide instead of unite, and present an obstacle to its true mission, which is to bring a biblical spirit to all forms of culture.[8] Also stressed was the need to renew the educational system of seminaries; the tragic fact that two-thirds of humanity are practically barred from access to the benefits of culture; the need for mutual respect between Church and culture, if the possibility of any repetition of the Galileo case is to be excluded; the urgent need to establish more clearly a just hierarchy of values in this domain.[9] In general it may be said that the judgment which emerged from these speeches was favourable in tendency. They expressed a wish that this article should be completed and improved by making use of the further elements contained in the corresponding appendix.

[8] This is the essential content of an important and very critical intervention by Cardinal Lercaro, fully reported in *La Civiltà Cattolica* (1965) II, pp. 485–7, and in G. Caprile, ed., *Il Concilio Vaticano II* IV (1965), pp. 318–20.

[9] Cf. *La Civiltà Cattolica* (1965) II, pp. 483–9; III, p. 62, and *Il Concilio Vaticano II* IV (1965), pp. 316–22, 353.

Since the Ariccia meeting (February 1965), that appendix had in fact been used as a basis for the work of drafting a text on culture. This was now destined, in the new plan, to form a separate chapter in the second part of the schema of the "Constitution on the Church in the world of today". [10]

The diffuse treatment had to be condensed, the connection with the doctrinal section made clear, a less "Western" text composed, one more open to forms of culture other than the scientific and technical culture of economically highly developed countries, due prominence given to the values of wisdom and contemplation. The outcome was six tightly packed pages composed as follows.

Under the title "De culturae progressu rite promovendo", the chapter had three parts. The first described the cultural situation at the present day (the "signs of the times"), emphasizing the factors which have contributed to modify it. It stressed the more acute consciousness which people possess nowadays of being the makers of their own culture and that of the society to which they belong, the difficulties met with in this sector because of the transformations that have occurred (need to put an end to illiteracy, relations between a culture of the humanist and of the scientific and technical type, danger that modern civilization may destroy the authentic values of the ancient civilizations, temptation of a purely earthly humanism).

The second part laid down a few fundamental principles for the proper promotion of culture. A first article deals with culture in the light of faith, showing how it is in accordance with the will of the Creator and predisposes men to recognize the Word incarnate. It then speaks of the manifold relations between the good news announced by Christ and culture, taking up again the ideas already developed in the adnexum on the mutual help which Church and culture can give each other. The third article illustrates the various aspects that have to be present for a truly integral human culture and its indispensable conditions, in particular respect for legitimate independence and liberty.

The third part is devoted to some particularly urgent duties of Christians today in this domain. Successive articles deal with the recognition of the right of all to equal participation in the benefits of culture, and the duty to ensure that this right can in fact be realized; the task of educating to a really integral culture; the endeavour to achieve wider and deeper harmony between human culture and Christian education, between secular disciplines and ecclesiastical studies, whether in the training of the laity or of the clergy. Some references are also made to the inclusion of artistic values.

[10] In Ariccia the working group on culture consisted of Bishops Charue, Guano, Zoa, Fr. Möhler, S.A.C., Mgrs. Klostermann and Ramselaar, Canon Dondeyne, Fr. Tucci, S.J., Professors Minoli and Swieżawski and Mr. Folliet. They had before them not only the *animadversiones* of the Council fathers, but also an ample documentation of other criticisms and emendations, some of them from lay people.

This text, discussed on 9 February by the augmented Central Subcommission, revised in accordance with emendations suggested on that occasion, then slightly shortened by the editorial committee under its chairman, Mgr. Haubtmann, and by the editor-in-chief, Mgr. Philips, was examined by the Mixed Commission at a full meeting on 3 April 1965. It formed Chapter II of the part of the schema devoted to the most urgent problems of the contemporary world, and comprised Articles 65–74. Revised again as a result of the suggestions made by the Mixed Commission, and enriched with some new elements, it was sent with the rest of the schema to the Council secretariat at the beginning of May. In the schema sent to the fathers in the first half of June 1965, it bore the slightly revised Latin title "De cultus humani progressu rite promovendo". It was arranged in the same three sections with ten articles in all, and was accompanied by a report explaining the reasons for the various changes made in comparison with section 22 of the schema debated during the previous session.[11]

For the further history of the text, we shall deal with only a few points, because there will be occasion in the commentary to indicate the most important changes made during the final stages. In the new conciliar debate during the Fourth Session, the chapter on culture was discussed at the 140th and 141st general congregations (1 and 4 October 1965), with 12 interventions in all.[12] The comments received by the secretariat of the Mixed Commission on this specific theme amounted to about 30 typed pages. The text was revised by the relevant subcommission between 12–18 October.[13] It was then discussed by a full meeting of the Mixed Commission 26–27 October,[14] again revised on the basis of the suggestions made on that occasion,[15] and

---

[11] Constitutio pastoralis de Ecclesia in mundo huius temporis, Pars II (1965), cap. II, nn. 65–74, pp. 52–59; Relatio, pp. 108–12. As for other parts of the schema, this relatio indicates the interventions and criticisms of the fathers during the Third Session which determined the arrangement of the various parts of the chapter.

Henceforward this fascicule is referred to as Text 4, 1.

It may be noted that the use of "cultus humanus" instead of "cultura" in the chapter-heading, in various subtitles and in many passages of the text, had been introduced during the revision of the Latin version after the text had actually been distributed by the Mixed Commission. The Council debate was later to show that this change displeased many of the Fathers.

[12] Cf. La Civiltà Cattolica (1966), I, pp. 169–76; the well-known speech by the newly appointed Archbishop of Turin is reported in full on pp. 170–2. See also C. Moeller, loc. cit., p. 374.

[13] The chairman was Fr. Möhler, S.A.C. Those taking part were: Bishops Charue, Elchinger, Vallopilly, Yü Pin, Abbot Butler; the periti Mgrs. Klostermann, Ramselaar, Canons Dondeyne and Moeller, Frs. Dupont, O.S.B., Liégé, O.P., Rigaux, O.F.M., Prof. Swieżawski.

[14] The relator was Fr. Rigaux, while Canon Moeller answered the requests for clarification and the objections.

[15] By 3 November Mgr. Philips presented a new version of the more controversial points of the third part of the chapter, at a meeting of the Central Subcommission.

finally sent to the printers. On 12 November the fathers received the *Textus recognitus* of Part II of the schema with the reports on the various chapters.[16] As regards our chapter, it may be noted that the first article of the first section now forms an introduction to the whole, with notable additions intended to give a fuller description of what is meant by culture. A better account is given of the relations between culture and the sciences, art and religion, and also more attention is given to historical research. The problem of legitimate autonomy receives more emphasis. The role of women in cultural life is stressed. An effort is made to remain on a truly universal plane of values. As regards form, we note the resumption of the use of the term "cultura", which is now preferred to "cultus humanus" starting with the title which once again reads "De culturae progressu rite promovendo".

The result of the vote on the chapter on culture, taken on 16 November, was as follows: Articles 57–63 (= 53–59): 2158 votes, 2102 *placet*, 52 *non placet*, 4 invalid. Articles 64–66 (= 60–62): 2125 votes, 2058 *placet*, 61 *non placet*, 6 invalid. On the chapter as a whole, 2146 votes, 1909 *placet*, 44 *non placet*, 185 *placet juxta modum*, 8 invalid. We note that only the vote on the Preface and the Introductory Statement produced a smaller number of *placet juxta modum*, i.e. 134.

Once more the relevant subcommission set to work to classify and consider the various *modi* and to prepare answers to the various suggestions (slightly fewer than 150).[17]

This was completed by the Mixed Commission at its plenary sessions of 25 and 26 November. Few changes of any importance were made at this stage. The two fascicules containing this final revision were distributed on 2–3 December.[18] On the *Textus denuo recognitus* of the chapter on culture, a conciliar vote was once again taken on 4 December with the following results: Articles 53–62: 2226 votes, 2137 *placet*, 81 *non placet*, 8 invalid. Once again our chapter was one of those which received relatively the smallest number of adverse votes.

---

[16] *Schema de Ecclesia in mundo huius temporis. Textus recognitus et relationes*, Pars II (1965), cap. II, nn. 57–66 (corresponding in the promulgated text to Articles 53–62), pp. 22–30; *Relatio*, pp. 31–37. Henceforward this fascicule is referred to as Text 4, 2.

[17] Chairman: Fr. Möhler; Members: Bishops Charue, Pulido Méndez, Yü Pin, Abbot Butler; *Periti:* Mgrs. Klostermann, Ramselaar, Canons Dondeyne, Moeller, Frs. Dupont (secretary), Liégé, Rigaux *(relator)*, Prof. Swieżawski, Mr. Folliet.

[18] *Schema de Ecclesia in mundo huius temporis. Textus et correctiones admissae necnon expensio modorum Partis Primae* (1965), text of the chapter on culture, Articles 53–62, pp. 50–8; *correctiones admissae*, pp. 110–12; *Expensio modorum Partis Secundae* (1965), cap. II, pp. 45–67. Henceforward these fascicules are referred to as Text 4, 3 A and 3 B. Cf. the interesting summary by C. Moeller on variants and invariants in the revision of this chapter from its first to its last version (pp. 377–8).

Article 53. This answers the question raised during the first conciliar debate (cf. Text 4, 1, *Relatio*, p. 109) as to what is meant by "culture" and "civilization". It was not easy to give a definition, and not merely because of the special difficulties caused by Latin terminology. Even among philosophers, sociologists, anthropologists and ethnologists there is considerable difference of opinion.[1] In fact the Council was content to give a description, which was considerably extended in Text 4, as a result of the specific questions raised during the second conciliar debate (*Relatio*, pp. 31–32). That revision not only reintroduced the word "cultura" as being more readily intelligible, but also underlined the close connection between nature and culture. This was intended to eliminate from the start any misconception that the term bore a restricted meaning valid only for those who have received an elaborate education, i.e. "cultivated persons" in the sense of the Latin "humanus civilisque cultus": "quia caput agit non tantum de culturis elevatis, sed de omni humana cultura" ("because the chapter concerns not merely higher cultures, but all human culture") says the *Relatio* (p. 32). Etymologically, culture (from *colere:* to till the fields and, by extension, man's mind and mental faculties) signifies the activity by which man, acting on and transforming the world around him, develops and transforms himself. (Man is a being with physiological, emotional and spiritual needs,) food, clothing, shelter, procreation, ties of affection with his fellow-men, thirst for knowledge, beauty, power. (To satisfy these, man,) unlike the animals, (must transform the world around him.) The animal finds what it needs ready-made; it only has to search, collect, or, as the case may be, hoard. (Man,) on the other hand, (has to make what he needs by means of the specifically human activity which we call "work". "Nature" is the material and object of man's work; man applies mind and hand to it and adapts it to himself, transforms it according to his requirements, makes it provide what he needs. But while acting upon nature, man also transforms himself. Thus culture is an immediately evident and essential feature of human life,) a universal fact: "Man is by nature a cultural entity. Wherever there is man, there is culture."[2] Equally clear is the pointlessness of a "Marxist criticism of culture understood solely as the byproduct of an infrastructure of wealth and idleness; on the contrary, man's 'working' activity constitutes an essential element of culture".[3]

---

[1] Cf. R. van Kets, "The Church and Culture", *IDOC*, n. 162 (1965), pp. 1–7; V. Mathieu, "Cultura", *Enciclopedia filosofica* I (1957), cols. 1369–71; R. Scherer and O. Köhler, "Kultur", *Staatslexikon* V (1960), cols. 164–78; R. Hauser, "Kultur", *LTK* VI (1961), cols. 669–672. All these works include extensive bibliographies.

[2] A. Dondeyne, *loc. cit.*, p. 174; cf. J. Maritain, *Religion et culture* (1930), ch. I: "Nature et culture", pp. 11–26.

[3] C. Moeller, *loc. cit.*, p. 379.

Text 4, 2 adds to this rapid ontological consideration, a phenomenological description of culture in its anthropological aspect. The *Relatio* notes (p. 32): "Homo vitam animalem transcendit, quia (a) cognitione et labore orbem terrarum in suam potestatem redigit; (b) vita sociali, familiari et politica mores institutionesque humaniores reddit; (c) experientias spirituales et aspirationes suas in operibus exprimit et conservat." The only variant of any importance in Text 4, 3 consisted in the substitution of "vitam socialem tam familiarem quam politicam" by "vitam socialem, tam *in familia* quam in *tota consortione sociali*", which widens the sense. This paragraph, which does not claim to be exhaustive, is intended to indicate how by culture man puts a human stamp on the most characteristic expressions of his life in his relations with himself, the external world and his fellows.

The beginning of the next paragraph (also added in Text 4, 2) introduces the description of culture in its historical and social aspects, and this brings out its sociological and ethnological meaning, thus explaining how it is possible to speak of a plurality of cultures. A brief description follows, which had already figured in Text 4, 1, of how "diversae communes condiciones vivendi et diversae formae componendi bona vitae" are formed, i.e. the various cultural patrimonies which constitute the concrete historical environment in which every individual is situated and from which he obtains the means of promoting his own culture and that of his social group. This explains the fact that the culture or civilization of a social group is never identical with that of another group. For although man is fundamentally identical in nature, his action is conditioned by innumerable external factors which deeply affect him even in the emotional and intellectual sphere. He is conditioned in particular by history and geography; it is not a matter of indifference for a man or a group to live at this or that moment of history or at this or that place on the earth. That means that time and space determine the rhythm of human civilizations and give them different features and forms. No mention is made of the various means which make possible the preservation and transmission of the different cultural heritages to new generations and which themselves influence the character of any particular civilization: transmission by predominantly oral tradition, by writing, or by writing plus modern audio-visual media.[4] At all events the introduction to the chapter has the merit of having gone beyond a purely aristocratic conception of culture, by clearly rejecting the idea of "uncivilized nations".

Although the risk of giving a perhaps questionable definition was avoided, the description of the essential elements of culture is sufficiently complete,

---

[4] Cf. the recent discussions in the popular press on the ideas of Marshall McLuhan; cf. *Understanding Media: The Extension of Man* (1964); in collaboration with Q. Fiore, *The Medium is the Message* (1967).

and certainly constitutes a novelty in comparison with earlier pronouncements of the magisterium dealing with the question in any respect. For while
remaining on the descriptive plane, and therefore abstaining from a formal
value judgment, it nevertheless implies a favourable attitude to cultural
pluralism and the researches of cultural anthropology and ethnology. This
was prompted, among other things, by the desire to face the problem of how
Christianity can be embodied in non-Western cultures, as is plainly stated in
the *Relatio* of Text 4, 1.

Article 54. The first lines, added in Text 4, 2, are intended to underline its
connection with the Introductory Statement at the beginning of the Pastoral
Constitution, to which explicit reference is made in note 1 (Abbott, note 180)
rather than in the text itself, in answer to a *modus* (Text 4, 3 B, p. 47). Again
in this addition it is stated that *it is possible* to speak of "a new age of
human history": this was to relieve the anxiety of those fathers who
regarded such an assertion as naive or presumptuous or even perhaps inspired by a dangerous optimism of an evolutionary kind, on the lines of
Teilhard de Chardin. With the above-mentioned qualification, the text
already seemed quite sufficiently cautious. Consequently a *modus* was rejected
which asked for the insertion of "*aliquo modo* loqui liceat" (*Relatio*, p. 47).
In any case this article, too, remains on the plane of description and factual
observation. After reference to the main factors which have largely determined cultural change — new means of perfecting and diffusing culture —
it proceeds to describe their effects on contemporary culture. The latter in
fact owes some of its own characteristics to these transforming factors. In
this way, less of an impression is given that the noteworthy advances in
natural and human sciences, technology and the instruments of social communication are to be regarded merely as instruments of culture, whereas in
fact the very object of culture is also in question, for it would be more exact
to speak of their "reciprocal action".[5]

The chief features of contemporary culture, produced by the deep and
extensive process of transformation briefly described above, were indicated
in greater detail from Text 4, 2 onwards, "ut amplior et accuratior fiat
descriptio phaenomenologica eorum quae culturam hodiernam constituunt"
as the *Relatio* observes (p. 33). The chief additions concern the "critical judgment" developed chiefly by the exact sciences and the particular awareness of
the mutability and development in human affairs encouraged by historical
studies. The intervention of Mgr. Pellegrino already referred to above, was
decisive for this last addition. He drew the attention of the fathers to the
incontestable fact that "historical science is of the greatest importance in the
culture of our time". He recalled how much importance springs from the fact
that "its direct and immediate object is man himself, whose nature, customs,

---

[5] C. Moeller, p. 384.

aspirations, efforts and weaknesses appear both similar and yet diverse at all periods". As for the opportuneness of mentioning this in the conciliar text, he insisted especially on the close connection between historical research and knowledge of the history of salvation, and he regarded the latter as "the centre of all theological learning". As an additional reason he gave in conclusion the following: "Learned men who everywhere devote themselves to the study of history will be glad to see such a recognition of their labours, especially those who pursue historical research in the various fields (Bible, Church history, patristics and archaeology) which more closely concern the history of salvation." [6]

Another significant addition concerned such typical phenomena as industrialization and urbanization considered not merely as factors producing a certain uniformity, but also as promoting community life, and of "new forms of culture" of the kind summed up as "mass-culture". Notwithstanding the tendency of more than one father, even in the Mixed Commission, to regard that phenomenon mainly in an unfavourable light, the conciliar text, while remaining on the descriptive, neutral plane, seems to emphasize chiefly its positive aspect as an "authentic but contemporary cultural creation". [7]

In Text 4, 2, deliberate stress was placed on "the unity of mankind in the progress of culture, so that the universality of culture might clearly stand out" (*Relatio*, p. 33). The previous version in Text 4, 1, had merely said "Aucta simul commercia inter varias gentes societatisque coetus thesauros

---

[6] Cf. *La Civiltà Cattolica* (1966), I, p. 171; Mgr. Pellegrino has published a more extensive version of this speech: "The Importance of Historical Research and the Need for Freedom", *IDOC*, doss. 67–17 (May 1967).

C. Moeller justly remarks, with reference to what is lacking in the conciliar text: "As regards the historical dimension, the Constitution limits itself to mentioning the aspect of mutability and change, and makes no reference to the important function of temporal *duration* in the new anthropology. The text here must be completed — as indeed is quite legitimate — because this aspect is in fact implied by depth psychology, which is expressly mentioned. Time can appear to man engaged in cultural endeavour either as an eternal return, or as a place of birth, growth and maturation, open to the future, to hope and expectation. It is sufficient to recall the significance of time in the economy of salvation from Genesis to the Apocalypse, to realize the rich possibilities of dialogue between Christian thought and that dimension of historical and psychological duration which is so essential to the new anthropology referred to in the text of the Pastoral Constitution" (p. 386).

[7] A. Dondeyne, *loc. cit.*, p. 178: "The democratization of culture has not merely encouraged a certain uniformity; it has also created new forms of culture, among them what modern literature calls 'mass culture'. Under the influence of the aristocratic cultural ideal of former times, this is very superficially dismissed as cultural decadence, whereas in reality it is a genuine contemporary cultural creation" (cf. J. Folliet, *A toi Caliban: le peuple et la culture* [1965]).

diversarum cultus humani formarum omnibus et singulis latius aperiunt, et sic universaliorem provehunt cultus ingenii rationem" (p. 52). The endeavour is immediately apparent here to present the ideal of a more universal human culture, not as a kind of levelling down into uniformity with impoverishment as its result, but as a growth of unity in diversity, i.e. as an even more comprehensive "catholicity". The latter would be capable of opening itself to an ever more universal outlook by knowledge of, and respect for, particular values, which would thus be consolidated rather than dissolved and oppressed.

We can also note that in examining the *modi,* the commission refused to accept the suggestion that they should add a restrictive phrase at the beginning of the passage describing contemporary culture: "quae est technica (vel: scientifica)". The reason given for the refusal is worth mentioning: "It is not accepted because the addition would make nonsense of what follows, which does not deal solely with technical or scientific culture" (Text 4, 3 B, p. 48).

In conclusion, it is to be noticed that in Article 54 the phenomenon of "socialization" which had taken its place in the Church's official pronouncements with John XXIII's *Mater et Magistra,* is considered not only, or principally, under the phenomenological or existential aspect, but chiefly under the very much more fundamental and essential aspect of the actual causes of socio-cultural development: "What constitutes man's mastery of a certain part of his destiny?" Hence the difficulty of relating this chapter on culture to papal documents anterior to it: "For the first time, it seems, the Church has been led to envisage social and cultural life as a whole, at the central meeting-point of all its problems, economic, political, domestic, philosophical, religious, etc." [8]

Article 55. The *Relatio* of Text 4, 1 noted (p. 109) that the aim of this article was to bring out right from the start the correct hierarchy of values, in which "*homo* simul auctor et finis est culturae". In the next revision, however, the article received its final stamp, which is more in harmony with the purpose of the first part of the chapter, for this is mainly devoted to describing the features of contemporary culture. It is consequently a matter of stressing more clearly "the increased awareness which men are acquiring of their autonomy and responsibility and the importance of this awareness for the spiritual and moral maturity of the human race" (Text 4, 2, p. 33; cf. also Text 4, 3 B, pp. 49–50; reply to *modus* 25).

The central idea of the text is that in a world which is increasingly unified by scientific and technical progress, men are simultaneously discovering themselves as independently and communally responsible for making a more human world, because for the first time they are in a position to

---

[8] *Constitution pastorale "Gaudium et Spes"* ... *par l'Action populaire,* p. 214, n. 101.

act effectively on the world as a whole which has now become much less remote.

It is indubitable that this shows a very favourable conception of one absolutely decisive aspect of contemporary culture, which after starting with Faustian or Promethean pride, is gradually being inspired by an increased sense of responsibility and universal solidarity. "Man who is the author of culture" becomes a synonym for man capable of making a better world on the ethical plane itself, i.e. in truth and justice, and consequently capable of a new humanism characterized precisely by moral commitment through corporate responsibility of all for each.[9] Precisely because of this initial favourable judgment, the text met with opposition from various fathers who detected in it an exaggerated and dangerous optimism. Criticisms were directed in particular against the two expressions "new world" and "new humanism", and they were voiced at the presentation of the *modi* and when the latter were discussed by the full Mixed Commission. The decision finally made was to accept only the *modus* which called for a change in the *Textus recognitus* from "novum aedificemus mundum" to "mundum instauremus"; at the same time, however, the word "novum" was changed to "meliorem". Other emendations were refused which suggested that "novum humanismum" should be replaced by "auctores sumus plenioris humanismi promovendi" in order to lessen the ambiguity of the term "humanism", and which wanted "new humanism" to be struck out entirely (cf. Text 4, 3 B, pp. 50–51; reply to *modi* 31–32).[10]

Article 56. The optimism of the previous article is quickly reduced to just proportions by consideration of the many contradictions which confront modern man in his project of achieving a "new humanism" fraught with great hopes. But even here the positive note is the stronger, for the contradictions are not regarded as insuperable obstacles, but as pointers to cor-

---

[9] Cf. C. Moeller, pp. 388 f. A. Dondeyne quotes a very pertinent passage of A. de Saint-Exupéry from *Terre des Hommes:* "Etre homme, c'est précisément être responsable. C'est connaître la honte en face d'une misère qui ne semblait pas dépendre de soi. C'est être fier d'une victoire que les camarades ont remportée. C'est sentir, en posant sa pierre, que l'on contribue à bâtir un monde." Dondeyne rightly concludes: "To define man by his responsibility for his fellows and for history means that he is primarily a moral being" (p. 180).

[10] It can be seen that even when the *Textus recognitus* was being discussed, some fathers of the Mixed Commission were not satisfied with the expression "novus mundus". It was at this meeting that the expressions "novus humanismus" or "nova humanitas" were suggested. The outcome was, however, that at the end of the discussion on this point at the full meeting on 26 October 1965, Mgr. C. Moeller's proposal was accepted, "novus mundus" was retained and "novus humanismus" was added.

The reason given for the gradual elimination of the word "novum" in the phrase "novum aedificemus mundum" may be found interesting: "because 'novus mundus' is an expression which belongs to the eschatological terminology of holy Scripture" (Text 4, 3 B, p. 50, *modus* 31).

responding moral obligations which present themselves to the conscience of people today who want to be lucidly responsible for their task of building a truly human culture, i.e. that of "developing the whole human person harmoniously and at the same time assisting men in those duties which men, especially Christians, are called to fulfil in the fraternal unity of the one human family", to use the final words of Article 56, added for the most part in Text 4, 2.

The description of the contradictions which beset the cultural sector is inspired by the same demand for lucidity which dominated the composition of Text 4, 1 from the Ariccia meeting onwards, and which led to the addition of the Introductory Statement and above all of Article 8 to the schema as a whole. The fundamental aim was to show how, although more frequent and closer contacts between nations now make the creation of a universal culture appear possible, there is also the danger of the loss of "traditional wisdom" and of the threat of "a purely earthly humanism" (*Relatio* of Text 4, 1, pp. 109–110). In the revision which produced the *Textus recognitus* and took into account the opinions expressed during the second conciliar debate, emphasis was also laid on the anxiety with which these numerous contradictions are regarded, and it was decided to express them by means of a series of questions. Among the more important additions or modifications, we note the following. Mention is made of "true and faithful dialogue" on the model of the encyclical *Ecclesiam Suam*; in dealing with the problem of harmonizing fidelity to the traditional cultural patrimony with the new culture, it is also said that this is especially urgent in regard to the antinomy between a scientific and technological culture and "classical" (instead of "humanist") traditions (in order to underline that it is not merely the culture of Western Europe which is intended); attention is drawn to the need for a synthesis of the results of the various special branches of knowledge, which may lead to dispersion, as well as the need to safeguard in contemporary man the capacity for contemplation and admiration which lead to wisdom;[11] greater emphasis is laid on the necessity of making cultural values effectively accessible to all men (cf. the *Relatio* of Text 4, 2, p. 33).

No important changes were introduced as a result of the *modi,* only some stylistic improvements. It is therefore of some interest to note that in reply to one father who would have preferred the suppression of the interrogative form used in the *Textus recognitus* for the various contradictions, the Commission explained that the use of questions makes dialogue easier and avoids dogmatism (cf. Text 4, 3 B, p. 51, *modus* 36). Another who wanted the ex-

---

[11] This met the wish of some lay auditors, especially the Polish professor S. Swieżawski, who was supported by the Polish bishops (cf. *Relatio* of Text 4, 2, p. 33). He had written a book on the subject in collaboration with J. Kalinovski which was published between the Third and Fourth Sessions: *La philosophie à l'heure du Concile* (1965).

pression "especially Christians" in the last paragraph to be struck out, was told that "These words are to be kept because the text here is chiefly intended for Christians" (pp. 52–53, *modus* 45).

In regard to Article 56 as a whole, we may conclude with Dondeyne: "It would be mistaken to regard this catalogue of difficulties and dangers as a kind of jeremiad. Pessimism and optimism are out of place here, since both are a flight from harsh reality. Only by having the courage to place oneself in the midst of these contradictions can we meet the cultural task of the present day." [12]

Article 57. Section 2, which deals with "Some principles for the proper advancement of culture" was intended to meet the wishes of many fathers expressed in the first conciliar debate during the Third Session. They wanted culture to be considered more definitely "in the light of faith" so as to show "what contribution the Church can make to culture and how culture can assist the Church in its task" (*Relatio* of Text 4, 1, p. 110).

The chief difficulty experienced by those drafting the text was to give specific principles for cultural activity which had not already been dealt with in the first part of the schema, especially in Chapters III and IV. This was all the more difficult once it had been decided to consider "culture" in the widest sense of the term as covering practically the whole "humanizing" activity of man in this world. So much so that in face of the Co-ordinating Commission's request to shorten the text considerably, there was even a proposal to omit the chapter on culture and include it in the general part, as was to be done with the chapter on the dignity and rights of the human person. At all events this section must be read and supplemented in the light of the more general doctrinal principles stated in the first part of the Constitution.

The fundamental purpose of Article 57 is to help in discovering the full meaning of cultural activity and its place in man's integral vocation in the light of the mystery of the Christian faith: "De cultu humano sub lumine fidei", as the title of Text 4, 1 expressed it. From the very beginning of the article this aim is clearly visible. It is the same aim which inspires the whole Pastoral Constitution, the desire to show that man's heavenly vocation does not turn him from his duty of sharing in the construction of a more human world, but adds new and deeper force to that compelling motive by incorporating it in a wider view of the destinies of mankind: the "religion of heaven" is not opposed to the "religion of the earth", to use a favourite expression of Teilhard de Chardin; the heavenly hopes of Christianity do not contradict earthly hopes but, on the contrary, are destined intrinsically to support and assimilate them in order to divinize them.

The final version preferred to follow a method of composition which

[12] A. Dondeyne, *loc. cit.*, p. 180.

might be described as one of "convergence", i.e. it points out how cultural endeavour (whether considered in its more immediate aspect of making the world habitable or in the more elevated one of spiritual creation in its various forms) enters into God's primordial plan for man. It therefore possesses an intrinsic value and constitutes genuine co-operation with the work of divine creation, and disposes men to open themselves to the sublime realities of the world of grace by a profound harmony or connaturality which is rooted in the unity of the work of creation and the revelation of grace, and which has its ultimate roots in the Logos in whom all is recapitulated.

In the first paragraphs of Article 57 we note the following variants in the final text as compared with Text 4, 1. From Text 4, 2 onwards, it was emphasized that the orientation of Christians towards the heavenly city not only does not diminish their earthly duty but rather increases the importance of this obligation; in this the mystery of the Christian faith provides them with incentives and helps "of great value" ("praestantia" instead of the more colourless "haud pauca"), enabling them to carry out that task more energetically. The social aspect of the work of making the world habitable is underlined by substituting for the expression "a dwelling worthy of man" the phrase "a dwelling worthy of the whole human family"; with deliberate reference to Genesis 1:28, it is said that the divine plan is that man should "subdue the earth". With the same aim of giving greater emphasis to the social dimension, Text 4, 3 added the phrase "and when he consciously takes part in the life of social groups", but suppressed the in itself fine statement that man carries out the divine plan "signa spiritualia rebus imprimendo", in favour of "and develops himself". In Text 4, 2, mention is made of mathematics, natural science and history at the beginning of the third paragraph; Text 4, 3 B (cf. p. 54, *modus* 59) rearranges the list so as to give philosophy the first place. In the *Textus recognitus* there also appears the more emphatic "can contribute in the highest degree", though the text submitted to the Mixed Commission simply read "maxime confert". Also in the third paragraph, Text 4, 3 B (cf. pp. 54–55, *modus* 60) contains the addition "to a judgment of universal scope", as requested by some fathers. In the fourth paragraph, Text 4, 2 inserts explicit mention of the "Creator" ("ad ipsum Creatoris cultum" instead of "ad ipsum Dei cultum") and of "contemplation".

After these first four paragraphs, which testify to the esteem which the Church has for culture in the light of the mystery of Christian faith, attention is also drawn to the dangers and temptations to which modern progress in science and technology is exposed. The same concern for lucidity is evinced as in Article 56, but good care is taken to avoid suggesting that immanentism is a necessary consequence of the method of investigation which made the progress possible. To remove all doubts, it is immediately added: "These unfortunate results, however, do not necessarily follow from the culture of today." The last paragraphs, devoted to indicating first the temptations, then the positive values of contemporary culture, with the final reference to the "praeparatio evangelica", underwent notable amplification and improvement in Text 4, 2. New is the express mention of the danger of "a certain exclusive emphasis on observable data" and the reference to the limits of the sciences which "by virtue of their methods cannot penetrate to ultimate ontological grounds" (in Text 4, 3 it was preferred to replace "ad intimas *essendi* rationes" by "ad intimas *rerum* rationes"). These sciences are exposed to the immanentist temptation precisely if they do not recognize the limits of their methods and "wrongly consider them to be the supreme rule for discovering the whole truth". Paragraph five on the positive values of contemporary culture is entirely new, apart from the last lines which were also considerably modified.[13] We may also note that the final text reintroduced the phrase "especially for those who are deprived of the opportunity to exercise responsibility or who are culturally poor". This had been approved by the plenary session of the Mixed Commission when revising the *Textus recognitus,* but had then been omitted, probably by an oversight (cf. Text 4, 3 B, p. 69, *modus* 69).

Having justified the position of culture in man's total vocation in the light of faith, without, however, minimizing the ambiguous character which culture may have in relation to religious faith, because it is always liable to succumb to the temptation of claiming to say the last word on human life, Article 57 ends with a very positive outlook. Culture and grace mutually require one another: culture in fact needs grace because it only finds its own fulfilment in grace; but grace also calls for culture, because this constitutes the normal point of insertion of grace in human life. And this explains why evangelization normally demands a minimum of cultural life and development and why it always brings cultural development with it.[14]

---

[13] As regards pronouncements of the papal magisterium from Pius XI to Paul VI drawing attention to the real dangers involved in a certain attitude of mind in scientific research and the invasion of technology, cf. the Action populaire commentary already mentioned, which comes to the following conclusion: "Ultimately the Church believes with all the strength of its supernatural faith that there cannot be any permanent conflict between true science and faith itself; that any momentary oppositions that may appear must be resolved by deeper and honest research on both sides; that the spirit of inquiry which inspires scientists involves very positive human values; that scientific and technical progress can be beneficial if accomplished in conformity with a true morality which tends to the total development of man and his life in society" (p. 220).

[14] A. Dondeyne points out, not without reason: "These few considerations on the significance of culture in the light of faith do not exhaust the theological problems; in fact we have not yet penetrated to the kernel of the real problem, i.e. the position which culture occupies in the mystery of Christ inasmuch as this includes the whole cosmos and will only fully reveal its essence and meaning at the end of time. In the conciliar text all eschatolog-

Article 58. The starting-point of this article was a theme included in the very first version of the schema (cf. Text 3, p. 25, no. 4; adnexa p. 29, no. 7). It was centred on an idea derived from a remark of Pius XI, which the final text refers to in footnote 7 (Abbott, n. 192). At the first conciliar debate during the Third Session, there was a demand that that idea should be stressed, but without lingering over the historical merits of the Church in the domain of culture, for this might sound like a not very convincing apologia (Text 3, p. 25: "Ecclesia proprium implendo munus, id est evangelizando, iam eo ipso ad humanum civilemque cultum impellit et confert. Ceterum, historia teste, religio et cultura multimodis inter se connectuntur. Omnes fere artes in ambitu religionis ortae sunt et floruerunt. Etsi finis religionis per se non sit cultura, sed Dei glorificatio et hominis salus aeterna, tamen religione neglecta, etiam cultura humana dilabitur"). Referring to certain interventions (that of Cardinal Lercaro in particular) which had recalled the contribution of many bishops and especially of the saints to the development of spiritual culture, the *relatio* of Text 4, 1, lays down the following principle. The Church "must spread in the world the plenitude of the humanity of Christ the head"; in that way a true doctrine of man can be safeguarded without falling into anthropocentrism and the false optimism which denies the presence of evil and suffering in the world. This is the sense in which we must understand the idea that the Church, by fulfilling its own function of evangelization, makes its contribution to the advance of civilization. In the second place, the same report quotes the interventions which asked for an emphatic statement that the Church "can and must be open to many forms of culture". It also recalled the warning of other Council fathers who insisted on the difficulty of achieving such openness and on the danger of a "certain relativism" which can insinuate itself into the "humanist vision" or into the theological formula which is to inspire "the new paideia". The *relatio* concluded, however, with a reference to the interventions which had stressed the help which the Church receives from culture in carrying out its essential task of preaching the good news (*Relatio,* p. 110).

Article 58 was in fact built round these two fundamental ideas from Text 4, 1, onwards. The theme of the specifically spiritual contribution to

ical speculation has deliberately been avoided, for two reasons, on the one hand so as not to repeat what has already been said in Part I, Articles 38–39, on the other to leave theologians free over the whole field of eschatology. This domain is in fact so new that it would be premature for the Church to take up a position already on problems about which revelation says very little because it employs symbolic and apocalyptic language. That is certainly not the language of our time and could easily lead to new and useless mystifications dangerous to faith, just as mediaeval speculations about the original condition of man in the Garden of Eden were" (pp. 182 f.). It is also remarkable that the theme of man as the image of God was not expressly taken up again in this article, probably in order to avoid repetitions (cf. in Part I, arts. 12, 22, 24, 29, 34, 41).

culture made by bishops and saints was however dropped, probably in order to avoid any apologetic tone. The text did not undergo many changes in the various versions.

From the very beginning, Article 58 moves on the plane of historical reflection. Revelation itself assumed the form of expression of the type of culture proper to the various epochs at which it occurred. Thus God spoke to the ancient Hebrews in the forms characteristic of Semitic culture. Jesus spoke to men in the cultural forms of later Judaism. Hellenistic culture was the background of the apostles' teaching. In the first paragraph, which sums up this idea, only one emendation of any substance was made at the *expensio modorum*. The phrase "nam Deus, *per revelationem suam, inde a primordiis* usque ad plen*iorem* sui manifestationem" became "nam Deus, *populo suo sese revelans,* usque ad plen*am* sui manifestationem" (cf. Text 4, 3 B, p. 57, *modus* 75).

If this can be said of revelation itself, it is clear that the same principle of incarnation will also apply to the preaching of the Church, which is addressed to all nations. Consequently "the cultural adaptation of the message of salvation is not a form of relativism but a mark of genuine catholicity".[15] Even more significant in this connection is the mention in the second paragraph of the liturgy. This had been included in Text 1 but was then dropped in Text 3 (but not in the Adnexa). Its purpose is to underline "the reality of Christian humanism which overflows from sacramental life",[16] a thought dear to Eastern tradition. It may be noted that to a proposed amendment calling for the suppression in the second paragraph of the words "etiam liturgica" as "otiose", the commission replied "They should remain, because these words refer to the Eastern tradition" (Text 4, 3 B, p. 58, *modus* 85).

The third paragraph which also starts from the universal mission of the Church, is intended to harmonize two principles, that of embodiment of the message of salvation, and the equally important principle of the transcendence of that message in relation to any particular culture. This principle,

---

[15] A. Dondeyne, *loc. cit.,* p. 184. He summarizes the guiding idea of Article 58 as follows: "Although the Christian message is not tied to any particular culture, because it is founded on the universality of the Word of God, it nevertheless always needs a cultural expression, for otherwise it would not be a message, which after all is a special characteristic of the Word of God. God's speech is not a magical event. God speaks to men through men who occupy a historical situation and who necessarily belong to this or that cultural world."

On this whole problem, cf. also: Fr. Arrupe, "Culture et mission", *Christus* 13 (1966), pp. 397–405; "Pluralismo delle culture e cristianesimo", *Sapienza* 20 (1967), pp. 7–16, also published in the collective work *La Chiesa e la cultura* (1967); L. J. Luzbetak, "L'Église et les cultures": *Lumen Vitae* 22 (1967), pp. 29–42; A. R. Sigmond, "Cultura e culture alla luce della 'Gaudium et spes'", *Sapienza* 20 (1967), pp. 17–29; J. Hamer, "Il pluralismo culturale e la Chiesa", *ibid.* 19 (1966), pp. 24–33.

[16] C. Moeller, *loc. cit.,* p. 394.

already present in Text 1 (art. 6), was much debated in the Commission and in the Council aula during all phases of the composition of the schema, but few modifications were made, except the addition of "indissolubly", from Text 4, 1, onwards. In the final version we may note the omission of "constant" from the phrase "Faithful to its own tradition" and the addition of "and at the same time conscious of its universal mission" (cf. Text 4, 3 B, pp. 57–8, *modus* 78). The intervention of Cardinal Lercaro was of decisive importance during the first conciliar debate on the schema. "Above all the Church must acknowledge itself to be culturally 'poor'; it must therefore wish to be more and more poor. I am not speaking here of material poverty but of a particular consequence of evangelical poverty precisely in the domain of ecclesiastical culture. In this field too, as in that of institutions and Church property, the Church preserves certain riches of a glorious but perhaps anachronistic past (scholastic system in philosophy and theology, educational and academic institutions, methods of university teaching and research). The Church must have the courage, if need be, to renounce these riches or at least not to presume on them too much, not to pride itself on them and to be more and more cautious of trusting to them. For in fact they do not always put on the stand the lamp of the gospel message but often hide it under a bushel. They may prevent the Church from opening itself to the true values of modern culture or of ancient non-Christian cultures; they may limit the universality of the Church's language, divide rather than unite, repel many more men than they attract and convince. I do not wish, of course, to set up a purely negative theological and cultural poverty as an ideal for the Church. In the field of culture too, there is a valid distinction between evangelical and subhuman poverty. The latter is not the ideal, not ignorance or wretchedness but sobriety and sense of limits and at the same time the adaptability, magnanimity and courage to try new ways even if this involves risk; modesty and intellectual humility, which is true and very rich supernatural wisdom, as well as a sense of the present and genuine historical realism. Such renunciation of the cultural patrimony is not an end in itself but a way to acquire new riches and, humanly speaking, greater intellectual acumen and a more rigorous critical sense."[17]

In contradistinction to the two tendencies either to exaggerate the Church's contribution to culture or, with Cardinal Lercaro, to stress the "poverty" of the Church in the cultural field, the conciliar text endeavours to maintain a certain balance. This is apparent in the phrase the Church "can enter into communion with various cultural modes, to its own enrichment and theirs

---

[17] Cf. the text of the intervention in *La Civiltà Cattolica* (1965), II, pp. 485–7, or in G. Caprile, ed., *Il Concilio Vaticano II* IV (1965), pp. 318 ff. Other similar speeches on this aspect were made during the Fourth Session by Mgrs. L. A. Elchinger, C. Padin, L. Bettazzi (cf. *La Civiltà Cattolica* [1966], I, pp. 169, 173, 175 ff.).

too". But the essential and difficult problem is not faced, that of distinguishing in the gospel message between what by its very nature is immutable truth and what can be regarded as its "contingent, historico-cultural garb".[18] Cardinal Lercaro's speech had raised the problem but without going into it deeply. "The Church has always said it did not want to identify itself or its doctrine with any particular system, with a certain philosophy or theology. Until now, however, that distinction has been drawn in theory rather than in practice. The time has come to separate more and more in actual fact the Church and its essential message from a particular cultural system, the universality and perennity of which many Churchmen still maintain in far too complacent and possessive a spirit." But he had already introduced into the debate an idea which might have received greater emphasis in the third paragraph of Article 58: "To open itself to genuine dialogue with contemporary culture, the Church must concentrate its culture more and more on the absolute wealth of sacred Scripture, of biblical thought and language. It must not be afraid on this account of not being understood or of disappointing people; at bottom they do not want anything else but this from the Church. And then the Church's culture will no longer give the impression, as it sometimes has, of being a rationalism or scientism of secular origin; it will appear as a very powerful religious force, capable of leavening any culture whatsoever, present or future".[19] The fourth paragraph is devoted to describing the essential contribution of the message of salvation to human cultural endeavour: Christian purification, renewal, stimulus and vivification. Though it takes its inspiration from these words, it has not succeeded, in our view, in clearly expressing the central idea. In the course of composition of the whole Article 58, however, place was found in the text itself, from Text 4, 2, onwards, for the thought of Pius XI referred to in note 7 (Abbott, n. 192): "Thus by the fulfilment of its own mission the Church stimulates and advances human and civic culture." It may be noted that here the term used is not "cultura" but "humanum civilemque cultum" which in Latin is a better rendering of the word "civilization".

Article 59. After expressing the Church's profound esteem for culture and recalling their mutual relations, the text recalls some principles which must preside over the development of an authentically human culture. Here as in the other domains and more urgent problems which are dealt with in Part II of *Gaudium et Spes,* the fundamental principle which justifies the Church's contribution in a domain which at first sight might seem alien to

[18] A. Dondeyne, *loc. cit.,* p. 184.
[19] Cf. *La Civiltà Cattolica* (1965), II, p. 486. Cf. also the interesting remarks of Mgr. J. B. Zoa in one of his speeches during the first conciliar debate on the problems created by the meeting of different cultures, *ibid.,* p. 488. On this complex question, which nowadays is denoted by the neologism "acculturation", cf. A. Dupront, *L'acculturazione, Storia e scienze humane* (1966).

its religious purposes, is the defence of the human person in its entirety: "For the aforementioned reasons, the Church recalls to the mind of all, that culture must aim at the integral perfection of the human person, and the good of the community and of the whole of society." This statement with its various elements was already found in Text 1 (art. 2: Culture and person; art. 3: Culture and the community). In Text 4, however, it was reduced to its nucleus which then remained substantially unchanged. The guidelines which immediately follow are related to this basic principle as its chief applications or consequences: (1) Development of the powers of wonder, insight and contemplation, the capacity of forming a personal judgment, of cultivating the religious moral and social sense, in short, the endeavours to preserve and develop what might be called man's metaphysical powers, which are easily obscured in a world witnessing the prodigious success of the positive sciences and technology and experiencing their undeniable fascination. (2) Safeguard of freedom to promote culture on the basis of the principle that culture, since it springs from man's rational and social nature, needs for its development a proper measure of freedom and recognition of legitimate possibilities for its autonomous exercise. This is all the more urgent in a world which is becoming more and more socially complex and organized and in which as a consequence the scope of public authorities is continually extending, with the obvious danger of massification, depersonalization and state coercion.

Article 59 is largely devoted to developing this second theme of liberty. The *relatio* of Text 4, 1, insists with specific reference to the speeches during the first Council debate, on the need to give due emphasis to "healthy freedom of culture" and for the Church to recognize its legitimate autonomy in its own order. Quoting one of the speeches it says, "The times are past when the entire control and judgment of culture was the province of the Church." Hence the conclusion that the Council "must emphatically make a special and explicit declaration about the full liberty and autonomy of scientific research when carried out wisely" (*Relatio* to Text 4, 1, p. 110). The *relatio* of Text 4, 2, expressly states that it had been thought well to shorten the introductory portion of the article in order "citius pervenitur ad essentiam huius articuli, qui *libertatem* respicit in cultura colenda, sed etiam officium servandi *duplicem* ordinem cognitionis distinctum, fidei nempe et rationis" (p. 34).

The second paragraph forcefully states that culture needs freedom, and demands respect for this essential condition. Few changes were made in this paragraph during successive revisions. We might simply note that Text 4, 2, stated, perhaps more forcefully "Ius ergo habet ad reverentiam" ("It therefore has a right to respect"), whereas Text 4, 3 B states, "Iure merito ergo postulat..." ("Rightly therefore it demands respect...") (*Relatio*, p. 59, *modus* 89). Among the suggestions which were not accepted, we may note the following: the proposal to strike out the term "immediately" from the first sentence of the paragraph, "because the close link between man's nature and culture must be underlined here"; the proposal to add at the end of the chapter, after the words "within the context of the common good", the following sentence: "for their part, learned men, especially scientists, should be conscious of their responsibility for the common good"; this was rejected on the grounds that nothing should be added which has already been said (*Relatio*, p. 59, *modus* 88, 90).

The following paragraph once again reaffirms the autonomy of culture in its own order, referring to a text of Vatican I which had already been used in Text 1 (art. 5: Church and culture), together with a quotation from *Quadragesimo Anno*. The latter had acknowledged that economic theory and morality each depend on their own principles in their own order, but recalls that it would be false to assert that the economic and the moral orders are so different that the first does not depend on the second at all. The only variant of any importance occurs in Text 4, 2, which adds the word "especially" to underline the legitimate autonomy of the sciences. We may note that a suggestion of a rather restrictive kind was refused. This proposed to add to the end of the paragraph the following: "Attamen cum illa principia et illae methodi non sint eiusdem generis in scientiis naturae materialis et in scientiis 'de homine' (specialiter in illis scientiis quae de sanitate, moribus et ethica hominis tractant), Sancta Synodus agnoscit et affirmat iustam hanc libertatem, rite servatis natura et principiis cuiusque scientiae, et optat ut haec legitima libertas vigeat in omnibus campis cultus humani" (Text 4, 3 B, pp. 59–60, *modus* 92). It was not desired to introduce a qualification which suggests a scale of autonomy, or at least a hierarchy based on the object of the various sciences rather than on their method. [20]

The fourth paragraph deals with a few essential aspects of the liberty which has just been claimed and justified: liberty of research, expression and information. These lines were previously placed in the next article of Text 4, 1 (art. 72 in the numeration of that version). In Text 4, 2 they found their final position here and rightly so, because they round off what is said on cultural liberty. Someone wanted freedom of research and expression inside the Church to be dealt with in this context, but it was preferred to gather all the matter on this topic in the last article of the chapter. At all events it is certain that the principles expounded are also valid in the life of the Church; they are affirmed without restriction to any particular communities and justified by appeal to an inborn right of the human person.

Having affirmed the autonomy of culture in relation to faith, and unfolded the essential content of that autonomy, the last paragraph goes on to

[20] Cf. C. Moeller, *loc. cit.*, p. 406.

vindicate the independence of culture in the face of political and economic power. The Council fathers realized that these are the forces which quite frequently aim at bringing culture into their service, by more or less camouflaged but effective coercion or by money. Implicitly rejecting the typical claim of all totalitarian states to create a culture of their own, or to dictate its norms and laws, the Council clearly establishes what should be the functions of public authorities in this matter. In response to the request of 20 fathers, Text 4, 2, added the phrase on the rights of cultural minorities (cf. *Relatio*, p. 34). It was not, however, considered opportune to include in the next version a *modus* from another 20 fathers calling for mention not only of national, but also of religious minorities, the motive being "to avoid controversy about the nature of minorities" (Text 4, 3 B, p. 60, *modus* 94). On the other hand, a proposal was accepted to refer in a footnote to the two documents of John XXIII and Pius XII mentioned in footnote 10 of the final text (Abbott, n. 197) and which deal precisely with the problem of ethnic minorities.[21] And knowing that economic forces or pressure-groups increasingly condition cultural life at the present time,[22] exacting, mostly in disguised ways, submission and service in return for the economic subsidies which they alone are able to give, the Council insists that culture should not be diverted from its proper purpose, which is the integral development of the human person, not the promotion of the sectional interests of economic and political groups.

In conclusion it may be said that Article 59 makes some excellent declarations, especially in regard to liberty. These, however, are completed by what is more fully stated in the first part of the Pastoral Constitution itself, particularly as regards the legitimate autonomy of earthly realities (cf. art. 36), and also by the Declaration on Religious Freedom, and the remarks on cultural liberty within the Church itself contained in the final article of the present chapter. It is evident, however, that the title of the article does not quite correspond to its contents, since it speaks of harmonizing the forms of culture, whereas with the exception of the first paragraph, it actually deals with certain fundamental requirements which flow from the above-mentioned principles, above all the just liberty and autonomy of culture.

Article 60. The Council did not want merely to state general principles which explain the value of cultural life and which should guide its development. Addressing Christians mainly, though not exclusively, it also indicates what needs to be done for the progress of culture in close association with all other men engaged in this great enterprise of our age. Though not lacking

[21] During the discussion of the *Textus recognitus* at a full meeting of the Mixed Commission, a Spanish bishop asked for the addition of the limitation "iuxta limites boni communis" in regard to the respect to be shown for the culture of ethnic minorities; this proposal was not accepted.

[22] Cf. H. Marcuse, *One-Dimensional Man* (1964).

in statements of principle, this third section is dominated by the practical concern for effective action and by pastoral solicitude for the most urgent needs of present-day humanity, grouped round three main points: to make the access of all men to culture really possible, to ensure education to a truly integral culture, which takes account of all the dimensions and values of human life; to achieve a better balance between culture and Christian formation on the various levels.

One of the aspects most frequently stressed from the first conciliar debate on this schema during the Third Session onwards, was indubitably the fact that, as the *relatio* of Text 4, 1, says, although cultural benefits are more widely available, thanks to the means of social communication, we are still very far from making access to them actually possible to all. It is therefore urgent to make every effort to ensure that this as it were abstract availability should become a concrete possibility for the still considerable part of humanity which is deprived of them (*Relatio*, p. 111, where we learn that a request in this sense was presented by more than 70 fathers). Article 60 is mainly devoted to illustrating this theme.

At the beginning of the first paragraph, ignorance is presented as a kind of spiritual penury analogous to material want, which diminishes the personal dignity of its victims. At the same time a clear declaration is made of the right of all to a degree of culture worthy of the dignity of the human person, without any discrimination on the grounds of race, sex, nationality or social status. Later, an amendment was accepted calling for the inclusion of religion among the kinds of discrimination to be proscribed (cf. Text 4, 3 B, p. 61, *modus* 103, presented by 19 fathers). Then mention is made of a fact which makes the duty of working to get that right recognized in practice, even more stringent and urgent: the possibility that really exists of freeing one's fellow-men from such misery. Mention of the instruments of social communication among the causes of this new situation (*Relatio* of Text 4, 2, p. 35) was omitted, though requested by various fathers, on the grounds that they are dealt with elsewhere. Similarly the final text dropped the reference to the fact that humanity is in this situation "for the first time" (Text 4, 3 B, p 60, *modus* 99). But there remains the consciousness of a special possibility "today", of a "sign of the times" which imposes the duty today more than ever "especially for Christians". Objections were made to this latter phrase, but they were rejected on the grounds that the text is addressed mainly to Christians and, above all, that this third section of the chapter deals precisely with the duties of Christians (cf. Text 4, 3 B, p. 61, *modus* 100).

In order not to remain too general, Text 4, 2, accepted an amendment which points out more exactly the line of action to follow in order to get effective recognition for the right to the benefits of culture: "strenua adlaborare, ut ferantur decisiones fundamentales tam in re oeconomica quam in re politica, tam in campo nationali quam internationali..." It is not clear why it was preferred to accept a *modus* which substituted for "decisiones" the vaguer term "iudicia" (cf. Text 4, 3 B, p. 61, *modus* 101). It is significant, on the other hand, that clear refusal was given to a *modus* which proposed to substitute for the quite precise term "ius" the vaguer and weaker term "postulatio"; the reason for the rejection could not be more explicit: "because a real right is involved" (Text 4, 3 B, p. 61, *modus* 102). It was more difficult, however, to determine the content of that right. To avoid too general expressions, it was emphasized that the "sufficient provision of cultural benefits" which must be made available to all, includes "especially those which constitute so-called basic culture". In Text 4, 2 the mention of illiteracy as a cause of an abnormal and therefore inhuman situation for those who are not able to collaborate in a truly human way for the sake of the common good, is completed by reference to "lack of responsible action" consequent upon ignorance. These first two paragraphs clearly reveal the Council's realization "that the benefits of culture are as essential to human life as 'material' goods and this is a new way of showing that culture is not a luxury superstructure, something for superior people or even a useless and rather scandalous leisure pastime, but an essential part of life".[23]

The next paragraph goes on to recommend intensive action to open out access to higher studies, but the text appears too cautious because of its numerous qualifications and because it does not speak of a true right in this matter. The request of various fathers that it should do so was rejected on the grounds that "ius illud determinandum foret" (*Relatio* of Text 4, 2, p. 35). Yet these same fathers, though advocating mention of a "right" to higher studies, had proposed to add "as far as objective conditions permit" (*ibid.*). In our view, the conciliar text would have gained if more serious account had been taken of these suggestions. We may also note that in Text 4, 2, the word "servitia" and the expression "omnis homo" were put before "coetus sociales" (and on stylistic grounds became "quilibet homo" in the final text).

At all events it is stated quite clearly that everyone with the necessary ability should have access to the higher studies without which individuals and social groups cannot achieve the full development of their cultural life. It might perhaps have been as well to say clearly that this access to higher studies must not be available solely on account of the services which the individual can render to society and with the implicit proviso that the public authorities will assign the task to be performed. That would mean that the human person exists for the State, and can be used as a means to an end.

[23] C. Moeller, *loc. cit.*, p. 410; Mgr. Proaño had said in the aula that in view of the immensity of the problem of illiteracy in Latin America, "this problem is as serious as lack of food" (cf. *La Civiltà Cattolica* [1965], II, p. 484).

The lack of elementary education and also cultural poverty caused by lack of the effective possibility of developing one's faculties by higher studies, are not viewed by the Pastoral Constitution solely or mainly in an economical and utilitarian perspective as a "waste of intelligence", but chiefly or even exclusively as a permanent offence to human dignity; for man is a human person before he is a producer of goods and services. This is a very positive aspect of the text. It might perhaps have been possible to add here that, from the religious and Christian point of view, illiteracy is an obstacle to the acceptance of faith itself and religious values, for it is quite frequently associated, both as cause and as effect, with the crude materialism which has no place for spiritual need. Consequently the fight against illiteracy is for the Christian a fight on behalf of man and for spiritual and religious values.[24]

Culture, however, is not primarily a right but a duty; in fact it is only a right because it is a fundamental duty. Precisely because man has the duty of cultivating himself, of developing all his powers and capacities, he has also the right to what he needs to fulfil that duty. And for that reason it is of the greatest importance that everyone should be aware both of "his right to culture and of the duty he has to develop himself culturally", as is said at the beginning of the fourth paragraph. In Text 4, 2 the social dimension is added by the phrase "and to assist others".[25] At this point, at the request of various fathers, an addition made in Text 4, 2 (cf. Relatio, p. 35) recognized that "existing conditions of life and work sometimes thwart the cultural strivings of men and destroy in them the desire for self-improvement". This is especially true of country people and labourers. In regard to them some fathers had proposed an amendment affirming their "right to secure conditions of work which would not impede but encourage their cultural life". The reply may seem to many people much too timid: "This is a concrete case where it seems difficult purely and simply to affirm a right; the emendation is therefore rejected" (Text 4, 3 B, p. 61, modus 108).

Article 60 concludes with a concrete observation added in Text 4, 2, on the participation of women in cultural life. This had been requested by one Council father[26] and the auditors (cf. Relatio, p. 35). When the full Mixed

---

[24] Cf. F. Russo, "L'alfabetizzazione degli adulti", La Civiltà Cattolica (1967), III, pp. 37–48; R. de Montvalon, Un miliardo di analfabeti (1966); A. Lorenzetto, La scoperta dell'adulto (1966).

[25] Cf. J. Folliet, A toi, Caliban: le peuple et la culture (1965).

[26] Cf. La Civiltà Cattolica (1966), I, p. 174, which reports the substance of the intervention of Mgr. Frotz: "The schema states that men are becoming increasingly aware that they make and shape their own culture and that of the community. It is clear that something should also be said about women, who not only share with men a fundamental equality as persons, and the right to higher education, but equally with men have their own specific function in the field of human culture. It is of fundamental importance that this should be made clear, because the complementarity of man and woman is not limited to matrimony

Commission was revising the *Textus recognitus,* a rather unfortunate phrase was criticized and struck out; it spoke of "mulieres genio masculino imbutae". It is interesting to note that the text refers to woman's own characteristic disposition, which must be respected in order to ensure her specific participation in cultural life. On the other hand, it avoids setting limits to this on the basis of a certain traditional mentality. In fact, a *modus* which asked for woman's disposition to be specified by the addition of the phrase "that is, in her home and family", was rejected because the amendment "affert limitationem inopportunam" (Text 4, 3 B, p. 62, *modus* 110).

Article 61. The pivot of this article is its first paragraph which aims at expressing anxiety at the centrifugal tendencies at work in contemporary culture, and at indicating the fundamental principle for overcoming this problem. Once again this consists in an appeal to respect for the whole human person, which demands a balanced development of the various human faculties in accordance with a just hierarchy of values, permitting both the enrichment of knowledge and the integration of this increased information in a unifying process which brings a personal growth and true cultivation. In this perspective the increased opportunities offered by the present situation for "integral" culture, are viewed in substance optimistically.

In Text 4, 1, the introduction to the whole article was as follows: "Germana educatio ad cultum humanum in omni eius gradu institutionem in variis disciplinis artibusque et multiplicem eruditionem ad unum reducere sataget. Qua synthesi persona humana ad rectam rerum aestimationem ascendit et ad congruum iudicium de rationibus vitae et eventibus ferendum, fundatum super universalem intelligentiam et veram hominum sapientiam." This paragraph appeared to various fathers to be too superficial and abstract, and consequently it was decided to rewrite it completely in Text 4, 2 (cf. *Relatio*, p. 35). At the full meeting of the Commission, the discussion concentrated on the actual concept of "integral culture", which is increasingly needed, as distinct from the idea of "general culture" which is increasingly unattainable by modern man. This distinction was intended to answer the objection of some Council fathers in the Commission who thought it was going too far to speak of the disappearance of the Renaissance ideal of the "universal man". This term was retained in the final version as the technical expression for the idea of the "man of universal culture" (cf. Text 4, 3 B, p. 63, *modus* 114). Though not abandoning the ideal of vast information and comprehensive and "organic" (this word was added in the final version) harmonization of the increasingly numerous and diverse cultural materials, the Council recognizes that such an ideal normally exceeds the capacity of

alone, but extends to all spheres of human life. It is not sufficient to proclaim the equality of man and woman, we must ask whether the present situation allows women to make their proper contribution to the life of the community."

the individual and implicitly regards it as a social undertaking. Its attention is directed to the integration of increasingly specialized branches of knowledge (not to speak of their greater or less increase in quantity), into a wider and more comprehensive view of reality. That view must be open to the great problems of human existence, so that knowledge and action, to whatever sector they belong, may become wisdom in the deepest and most vital sense. That is why it insists again here on the so-called totalizing or integrating faculties. Some may perhaps think that in this context something should have been said on what has been called the problem of the two cultures, i.e. the harmonization of the classical culture of the humanities with technological and scientific culture.[27]

The three following paragraphs, as had been projected in the *Relatio* to Text 4, 1 (p. 111), deal with education to integral culture in the family and with the special opportunities offered by the increase of leisure. There were no amendments of any importance as regards the first aspect, but for the second a wish was expressed for special mention to be made of the new means of social communication which can promote general culture. A less superficial treatment of the problem of leisure was also asked for (*Relatio*, p. 111). In particular Mgr. L. Lebrun spoke on behalf of 41 bishops and asked for mention of the importance of sport in the world of today.[28]

---

[27] C. P. Snow, *The Two Cultures;* Fr. Borgomeo, "'Le due culture' di C. P. Snow e un nuovo umanesimo", *La Civiltà Cattolica* (1965), II, pp. 359–64; C. W., "Zur Situation des Naturwissenschaftlers in der Kirche", *Orientierung* (1966), pp. 214–16; D. Galtier, *Peut-on évangéliser des techniciens?* (1966); A. G. M. Van Melsen, "Wissenschaft und Christentum", *Wort und Wahrheit* 21 (1966), pp. 121–32; L. Morren, "La Constitution Pastorale 'L'Église dans le monde d'aujourd'hui' et la science", *NRT* 88 (1966), pp. 830–47; L. Ruggiu, "Il cristianesimo di fronte a scienza, cultura e tecnica", *Questitalia* 9 (1966), pp. 304–21; F. Russo, "Concezione cristiana e umanistica della tecnica", *La Civiltà Cattolica* (1967), I, pp. 339–352; M. Vigano, "Venti anni di riflessione su 'Scienza e fede'", *ibid.* (1967), II, pp. 157–166. It is still stimulating to read L. Mumford, *Technics and Civilization* (1934) and, from the Christian point of view, C. Dawson, *The Crisis of Western Education* (1961), especially chs. X, XI, XII.

[28] Cf. *La Civiltà Cattolica* (1966), I, pp. 169 f.: "It would be well to underline the importance of sport in the world of today, because no social class is untouched by it. By means of the mass media, sporting events are followed by an enormous and continually increasing number of spectators. And those directly engaged in sport are also increasing in numbers and range. There is no doubt, therefore, that the sporting spirit is a characteristic element in the mentality of modern man. We must realize the considerable place occupied by the phenomenon in people's lives, and reflect on its fundamental values, strength, health, harmony of the human body, which all mirror the strength and beauty of the Creator; command of the spirit over the body, which is bound up with the abnegation, stamina, courage needed in contests; development of certain personal qualities useful to the common good: team spirit, quick and accurate reactions, rapidity of decision, endurance, etc. This sporting activity, which combines so many physical and spiritual elements, is a genuine expression of charity towards oneself and one's neighbour. The social aspect of sport must

Text 4, 2, met these requests, despite some reserves expressed in the plenary session of the Mixed Commission, especially as regards the suitability of speaking of sport and tourism as collective cultural activities to be imbued with humane and Christian spirit. These reserves were overcome by reference to the allocutions of Pius XII on the subject.

At the *expensio modorum,* seven fathers requested that some mention should be made among the cultural features of our time of the vast circulation of books and of the importance of this phenomenon for the spread of culture. The seven authors of the amendment suggested two formulas to choose from; both mentioned books and the press, the second and longer also mentioned lending libraries. The Mixed Commission accepted the following addition: "thanks especially to the increased circulation of books and to the new means ("instrumentis" instead of "mediis") of cultural and social communication" (cf. Text 4, 3B, p. 63, *modus* 116).[29] On the other hand it rejected the suggestion of one father that "some kinds of sporting activity such as boxing, bull-fights and the like, would seem to be contrary to the dignity of the human person and its rights and duties". By the reply that "it is not necessary to descend into too great detail" (*Relatio,* p. 63, *modus* 119), boxing and bull fights were spared, perhaps to the relief of quite a few Council fathers.

The closing phrase of Article 61 had been added in Text 4, 2, to satisfy various fathers who wanted something said "on the deep meaning of culture for the human person" (*Relatio,* p. 35). The whole article, which might seem rather disconnected and over-detailed, thus takes up the initial idea which inspired it and acquires a more organic unity. C. Moeller states that the word "interrogatio" ("deep thought to what ... mean") "was deliberately chosen in order to recall at the end of this chapter the problematic character of culture, which in fact has been emphasized from the start. Present-day culture is both question and answer. It could even be said that the path leads from reply to question, returning to the starting-point from which all culture springs, i.e. to the question which man himself is. This question in a certain sense constitutes man, who becomes aware of this only in the gravest moments of his existence. Precisely then, however, the question proves to be the source of greatness as well as of defeat in the theatre of this world. The

---

also be considered: the bringing together of enormous crowds, the fraternization between individuals of different social classes and nationalities, etc. Consequently there should be added to the text a sentence or two to recommend this beneficial activity."

[29] Cf. C. Moeller, *loc. cit.,* p. 417, who remarks that by the expression "new instruments of cultural communication", the commission meant above all "to refer to audio-visual reproduction", as well as people's colleges, exhibitions and travelling libraries. The explicit reference to these means was suppressed in the final version, in order to avoid "descending into too many details and also in order not to run the risk of omitting this or that important institution".

theme is taken up here in a more positive sense, that of a forward-looking search, a constant inquiry into the depths of the person. If in fact in the ultimate resort the religious destiny of man cannot be perceived from his 'intentionality', it will never be possible to attain a certain cultural integration." [30]

Article 62. This final article groups a number of at first sight rather disparate directives, which are to guide the various organizations and authorities in the community of the Church in their arduous but indispensable search for a harmony between culture and Christian education and for a more fruitful dialogue between Church and culture in view of their mutual enrichment. The deepest reason for such a search is not so much concern for a more efficacious presence of the Church in the world of culture, as the renewed consciousness of the very close relations between the message of salvation and human culture which had already been expressed, especially in Article 58 of the present chapter. As A. Dondeyne rightly remarks, "To say that Christianity is a saving message which comes from God does not mean that Christianity is a magic power which acts upon humanity by force from outside. Message means speech (logos) and speech means culture. All genuine speech by which reality is brought forth and made public and thus becomes truth which makes humanity free, is a cultural event." [31]

In the *relatio* of Text 4, 1, the aims of this article are summarized as follows. Above all to recognize the fact that in the course of history there have not infrequently been difficulties in the relations between Church and culture, not only because of a false secularism which has frequently created hostility between culture and the Church, but also because the latter has not escaped the danger of a certain "segregation" from the culture of the age. Furthermore, "it is a historical fact that the development of culture has sometimes taken place through emancipation *(affranchissement)* from certain sociological forms of religion". Consequently, the *relatio* proposed to avoid "facile apologetics" and try, rather, to discover even in certain atheistic tendencies a *modus veritatis* acknowledging that even such conflicts and resistances can contribute to a better understanding of the Church's preaching. These considerations, which led to the composition of the opening paragraphs, make it more urgently necessary than ever today that the benefits of culture should be made available to all by promoting both secular

---

[30] C. Moeller, *loc. cit.*, p. 419; in a footnote (n. 144), he reports that this last chapter was drawn up in its present form in answer to a request from the German bishops: "It corresponds on this point to the general tendency of their observations on Schema 13, which was shown by the very great emphasis which these bishops placed on the paradoxical and antinomian character of man's situation in a world which is at one and the same time the world of man, the created world, and a world which has fallen under the domination of sin. The text thus acquired a more biblical and existential dimension."

[31] A. Dondeyne, *loc. cit.*, p. 189; cf. also pp. 190 f.

and theological learning. The laity in particular must be encouraged to undertake theological studies on a really scientific level ("investigationes vera dignitate scientifica pollentes in theologicis disciplinis") and to distinguish themselves in secular disciplines also in order to "infuse a Christian spirit into them". The *relatio* finally notes the insistence of not a few fathers that true liberty should be accorded to artists, so that artistic expression may manifest man's innermost problems. Some fathers had also asked for new artistic forms to be accepted into places of worship ("in ipso sanctuario"), so that the Church may show itself more open to all in its cultural life (Text 4, 1, p. 111).

These first paragraphs express awareness of difficulties experienced in the relations between the Church and culture, but without indulging either in facile apologetics or self-denigration. In Text 4, 1, the article had begun with the simple affirmation that the harmonization between culture and Christian education, though of the greatest importance, is not easy to achieve; it then recognized as a fact of historical experience that, not infrequently, opposition and a certain dissension had arisen between the Church's dogmatic mode of thought and the progress of the sciences, and between the applications of Christian moral doctrine and certain demands of contemporary man. It concluded that such difficulties can nevertheless stimulate the mind to a more accurate and more profound knowledge of the faith. The duty of Christians therefore, is to learn how to harmonize the new science, the new doctrine and the knowledge of the most recent discoveries, with morality and Christian thought. The request to have a special mention of the case of Galileo inserted here was refused after long and animated discussions in the commission, on the grounds that the notorious condemnation had not been pronounced by a Council and above all because they did not wish to restrict the problems examined in the schema to this single case, however wide its bearings. [32]

Many objections were made to Text 4, 1, and these led to substantial modifications in Text 4, 2. In particular the request to mention the merits of the Church in the cultural field was accepted, and at the same time a clearer distinction was drawn between the *quaestio iuris* and the *quaestio facti* in regard to the difficulties in relations between Church and culture; this is why the expression "for contingent reasons" was added. On the other hand, the

---

[32] On this discussion, cf. C. Moeller, *loc. cit.*, pp. 419 f., note 145. Article 36 of *Gaudium et Spes* also contains a more explicit passage on the legitimate independence of earthly realities: "Consequently we cannot but deplore certain habits of mind, sometimes found too among Christians, which do not sufficiently attend to the rightful independence of science. The arguments and controversies which they spark off, lead many minds to conclude that faith and science are mutually opposed." It is significant that at the end of this passage, reference is made in a footnote to the fundamental work of Pio Paschini, *Vita e opere di Galileo Galilei*.

passage relating to the cleft between the Church's dogmatic mode of thought and scientific progress, etc. was omitted because it was considered ambiguous (cf. *Relatio* of Text 4, 2, p. 36). Then, after the phrase which points out quite generally the positive sense which such difficulties can have in deepening faith, mention was added of the recent historical and philosophical researches which, together with scientific discoveries, give rise to new problems. It is also stated that these problems involve "consequences even for practical life". Since in addition, recent studies and new discoveries raise problems not only for theologians but also for those who engage in these studies, the word "also" was added in regard to the new researches demanded of theologians. The text emended in this way seemed to meet the requirements of those fathers who had observed that not all the acquisitions of science raise real problems, since there are also ambiguous acquisitions; there cannot be any true conflict between theology and science if in their respective fields they stick to what is certain and do not present mere hypotheses as certain and definitive results. Despite a wide discussion in the Mixed Commission on the true nature of theology and its method, it was not considered that this was the appropriate place to deal with it. We may note that among the many reasons which led to dropping the expression "dogmatic mode of thought", was the fact that theological method is not solely deductive, but also and primarily inductive; its starting-point is holy Scripture and the history of the Church. Moreover, a theology which does not remain in contact with science, ends by losing its vitality. Another objection was that the "dogmatic mode of thought" would have been interpreted in countries under communist rule as support for the idea that religious thought is essentially magical and superstitious.

A new item is the passage which goes from "Praeterea theologi" to "maturiorem fidei vitam ducantur" added in Text 4, 2. The mention of John XXIII's famous phrase in his speech at the opening of the Council had been expressly requested by various fathers (cf. *Relatio* of Text 4, 2, p. 36); in the Mixed Commission some wanted it quoted in full, that is, including the expression "eodem tamen sensu eademque sententia". In the definitive text the phrase "servatis propriis scientiae theologicae methodis et exigentiis" was inserted. When the *modi* were examined, however, the proposed suppression of the phrase "in the first place of psychology and sociology", which emphasized the contribution which these sciences can make to up-to-date methods of pastoral care, was rejected. No better reception was given to the emendation which specified that it was a question of "imprimis *sanae et verae* psychologiae, necnon sociologiae *christianae*", or to another which suggested "imprimis psychologiae et *certis sociologiae repertis*" on the grounds that it is not certain that sociology is a genuine science (cf. Text 4, 3 B, p. 65, *modus* 128).

The next paragraphs summarize what Text 4, 1 had said on the Christian estimate of the various forms of artistic expression, which were confined to the end of the article and therefore at the end of the whole chapter. In Text 4, 2, the phrase "Literature and the arts are also, in their own way, of great importance to the life of the Church" was added to bring out more clearly, as the *Relatio* says (p. 36), that "even the arts ... contribute to manifest the activity of the Church in the world, especially as regards its mode of expression (language)". There was also a new sentence which included among the functions of the arts that of "revealing man's place in history and the world, illustrating his miseries and joys, his needs and strength", while in Text 4, 3 B, the expression was added "and to foreshadow a better life for man", to satisfy the request of 8 fathers who suggested it should read "necnon prolusionem quandam sortis felicioris efformant" (*Relatio*, p. 65, *modus* 131). Many discussions were caused in the Mixed Commission at successive editorial stages by the passage on the attitude which the Church should adopt towards artists, and above all about readiness to find a place for their works in places of worship. One wanted to point out the divorce that has come about between art and the Church, partly through the fault of ecclesiastics, in recent times, especially in the last century (cf. *Relatio* of Text 4, 2, p. 36). Another on the contrary displayed to the end strong suspicion of new artistic forms, criticizing the text for excessive optimism and suggesting that it should at least be specified that such forms must undergo severe scrutiny and only be received "pro merito quod habere possunt" or to the extent they are "true" art (cf. Text IV, 3 b, pp. 65 f., *modi* 133–4). In reality the majority of the fathers of the commission inclined to a favourable attitude. In Text 4, 2, the sentence which expressed artists' need to feel they are understood by the Church, was strengthened by the phrase "consequently energetic efforts must be made" and a recommendation is also made to recognize even new art-forms ("agnoscantur") even in places of worship, though with the due reserve indicated by the added mention of conformity with liturgical requirements. In the final version it is made even clearer that it is not merely a matter of giving due recognition to new tendencies but also of "introducing them into" places of worship if they fulfil the necessary conditions (cf. Text IV, 3 b, p. 66, *modus* 135). On the other hand, a request was refused that artists should be invited to acquire an appropriate knowledge of the mysteries of the Catholic faith (*Relatio*, p. 65, *modus* 133) on the grounds that the addition was superfluous and out of keeping with the context. To those who were most preoccupied with abuses, it was pointed out that the reference to the Constitution on the Liturgy and to Paul VI's Address to Roman artists (note 13 in the final Latin text, note 202 in Abbott), was a sufficient guarantee; and furthermore, there was no question here of dealing further with a theme which had already been explicitly treated in another conciliar document (*Relatio*, pp. 65 f., *modus* 134). The reference to Paul VI's discourse also served to satisfy those who wanted a franker acknowledgment of the divorce between art and Church in recent times for which the Church is partly responsible.[33] The importance of this paragraph is considerable. It shows the intention to reestablish fruitful dialogue with the artistic creation of our time and a clear awareness that "the lack of a modern Christian art, widely recognized in ecclesiastical circles, diminishes the Church's influence".[34] This is expressly admitted, though not exclusively in regard to artists, in the brief paragraph which follows, "In this way the knowledge of God . . ." which confirms the deep connection between culture and religion, if not exclusively in regard to artists.[35]

The following section is also quite important. It invites the faithful to live "in very close union" with the men of their time. In substance this was already contained in Text 4, 1, and withstood the objection that it showed an excessively liberal attitude, brought against it even by some members of the Commission. At all events this paragraph is one of the most characteristic expressions of the new attitude of the Council to culture and the contemporary world generally. Someone requested that the words "vel reprobare et respuere" should be added to the concluding phrase. It was pointed out, however, that the term "probare" implies the possibility of approving or rejecting, as in the Pauline text "Omnia probate, quod bonum est tenete" (1 Thess 5:21; cf. Text 4, 3 B p. 66, *modus* 138).

But the Council did not wish to rest content with enunciating the general principles which should guide the attitude of the faithful to the various manifestations of contemporary culture. It also descended to some concrete applications which more directly concern the education of priests. In this connection we also find some valuable indications on the conditions of a fruitful development of theological research. The last paragraphs of Article 62 include an invitation to collaboration between those who are engaged in theological sciences in seminaries and universities, and specialists in other sciences. This is a clear acknowledgment of the importance of interdisciplinary research even for the theological sector.[36] And it is worth noting that

[33] Cf. V. Fagone, "La Chiesa e l'arte contemporanea. Le condizioni di un incontro", *La Civiltà Cattolica* (1964), II, pp. 468–80.

[34] C. Moeller, *loc. cit.,* p. 424; cf. also the basic work of P. Regamey, *La crise de l'art sacré au XXe siècle* (1939), E.T.: *Religious Art in the Twentieth Century.*

[35] Cf. Cardinal König, "La religion et la culture", *DC,* 16 May 1965, cols. 901–12, which reproduces the text of a paper dealing expressly with the relations between Church and culture, read at the Conference of Catholic International Organizations in April 1965, and intended as a contribution to the composition of the chapter on culture in the Pastoral Constitution. Cf. also G. Colombo, *Prospettive della cultura nella luce del Concilio Ecumenico Vaticano II* (1966).

[36] Cardinal G. Colombo remarks in the work referred to in the previous note (pp. 42 f.) on this: "Convinced of the mutual connections of theology and culture, Newman in his old age, and a cardinal, once asked himself with a touch of humour what he would do if he were elected Pope at the next conclave. His answer was that he would at once set

in Text 4, 1, the passage began with the words "Qui theologis *vel philosophicis* disciplinis in Seminariis...". The reference to philosophers was suppressed in the subsequent version, on the grounds that the Church does not wish to express a judgment on the aim of philosophy, and also in order to avoid any sort of clericalism in this matter. At the same time the suppression of the phrase emphasized the specific character of theological research. For the same reason the mention of philosophy was also struck out at the beginning of the next sentence (cf. *Relatio* of Text 4, 2, p. 37). On the other hand, to the principle that theological research must not lose contact with its own age, Text 4, 2, added another essential principle of such research, namely that it seeks deeper knowledge of revealed truth. In this way the two poles of theological development are pointed out; for by its very nature it involves a constant tension between inquiry in faith into the content of revelation and a constant renewal of its questions and language, if it is really to fulfil its function in the Church, i.e. service of the Word in the community of the People of God which feels its close solidarity with the human race and its history, and which has the permanent duty of scrutinizing the signs of the times and of interpreting them in the light of the gospel (cf. arts. 1 and 4).

The need to bring theological scholarship out of a closed world of its own which often offers no access at all to contemporary culture, had been strongly emphasized in various conciliar speeches on the Schema on Priestly Formation. These encouraged the insertion of some substantial reference in the chapter on culture. What Cardinal Lercaro said in the Council debate received attention: "The Church's culture must be given a new direction, especially in the institutions devoted to the formation of its students and to learned research. This is the essential point of our schema. What hope can there be of lasting and promising dialogue if those who speak in the name of the Church, priests and faithful, are educated on a programme of studies which is completely out of date? If the learned language in which they have to think, for all its merits, is now dead, if it is no longer universal and is incapable of expressing the new ideas which are current everywhere in the world? The very heart of the schema, its theses themselves, show in what sense the reforms must be made ... without which no one will believe that

up a mixed commission of learned clerics and laymen for the purpose of studying the findings of the sciences, in order to compare them with Catholic doctrines... This idea of Newman's was in advance of his time. Today, however, it is current in the Church's hierarchy itself, which wants to see mutual respect, mutual relations and continual exchanges between theology and the multifarious forms and expressions of culture. Both would profit by this, and as a consequence, so would the whole of mankind." Cf. also on this: *Universität und Christ. Evangelische und katholische Besinnung zum 500jährigen Bestehen der Universität Basel* (1960); J. Coulson, ed., *Theology and the University. An Ecumenical Investigation* (1964); *Recherches et culture. Tâches d'une université catholique. Études publiées par N. A. Lutyen* (1965).

our intentions are sincere and that we can respect the exigences and genuine achievements of the culture of our age." [37] We should like to risk the assertion that the few sentences on the subject in Article 62 of *Gaudium et Spes* meet such demands more decisively than the Decree on Priestly Formation. It might be noted, however, that they were composed with a view to renewing theological language so as to make it more comprehensible to the mentality of our contemporaries, rather than in order actually to develop knowledge of the inexhaustible religious truth. [38] It may be noted in passing that one father complained that this passage in Article 62 did not pay due heed to the dangers which threaten young seminarians from modern culture. The Commission replied that the text refers to the professors, and indicates precisely how to safeguard effectively the young men entrusted to them from

[37] Cf. *La Civiltà Cattolica* (1965), II, p. 486. Mention should be made of the important conciliar speech by Mgr. M. Pellegrino on renewal in the education of priests, with special reference to the need for the scientific study of theology and auxiliary disciplines, especially history, *ibid.* (1966), II, pp. 180 f.

[38] There are interesting reflections on this in the work of Cardinal Colombo already referred to (pp. 27–30): "The first reason for uncertainty was the attitude to truth as 'possessed' by the Church, but always as 'having to be sought' by modern culture. In this regard, the actual course of Vatican II can show how the Church understands that possession of truth which constitutes its essence. The conciliar debates, which have lasted four long years and have sometimes been marked by very sharp contrasts, unmistakably show that the possession of truth in the Church is not something dead, rigid, static, not a reason for comfortable repose, but a ceaseless, inexhaustible search, struggle and endeavour for renewal.

"This relation of the Church to truth might seem contradictory, for on the one hand the Church is certain of possessing the truth yet on the other hand it is still seeking it. The explanation lies in the fact that the truth which the Church possesses is transcendent and consequently demands to be more deeply grasped and concretely applied. Consequently it can never be convicted of error in its assured conquests, nor yet exhausted in its further development. The very possession of eternal religious truth drives the Church incessantly to search for truth, in order to free it from any obscuration by what is not truth, to discover new depths and new possibilities of its application, and to find new methods for its transmission which correspond more closely to the psychological, technical and intellectual progress of individuals and societies.

"It follows that there is no contradiction but even agreement in many respects between the attitude of the Church and that of culture in regard to truth.

"To describe this relation we might perhaps with profit modify the formula which has led to the erroneous opinion that the Church represents a dogmatism hostile to culture. Instead of repeating perpetually that the Church is in possession of the truth, we should say that the Church is possessed by the truth ... This would destroy the onesided and painfully distressing prejudice that the Church arbitrarily disposes of truth as though it were its own property, and the dependence of the Church on truth and its unquenchable longing for it would be placed in a clear light. Growth in knowledge and love of truth is the basis and inner law of the continued existence of the Church in time. The day on which this growth reached its utmost limit would, according to the Church's firm conviction, be the last day of history; if history were to continue nevertheless, it would no longer have any meaning."

such dangers (cf. Text 4, 3 B, p. 66, *modus* 139). And another father's objection was certainly not accepted; he thought the co-operation recommended would be useful in the universities, but not in seminaries.

Equally important in this final section of the chapter is the recommendation that lay people should be able to share in theological culture on a larger scale. This was in Text 4, 1, and was maintained unchanged by request. Here again it is worth recalling a section of Cardinal Lercaro's speech already referred to, in which he expresses very well the aims of the last paragraphs of Article 62. "There will really be something new in ecclesiastical culture if we open to our lay people not minor roads, that is, theological schools of a secondary kind, if we do not merely admit some of them to the clerical theological faculties, but if we open to them the royal road of genuinely learned research institutes under their own direction, in their own way — naturally under the guidance of the hierarchy. Only then will the theological schools and the formation of clerics discover new paths, and the Church's cultural institutes be profoundly renewed. Then the Church's pedagogy will become more dynamic, its central government will see a new dawn, and all, both priests and laity, will be educated to understand the world. The sons of the Church themselves who, as the schema wishes, are intensively pursuing the sciences of man, will be given more effective assistance to infuse a Christian inspiration into the culture of our time. Then all cultivated people — naturally and spontaneously, as it were — will discover the theology which is the wisdom of God." [39]

Moeller for his part remarks on this, "Until ecclesiastical circles have overcome the 'horror laici docentis', the Church will always lack one dimension of theological discourse". Even if the text we are commenting does not go as far as it might in this direction, it nevertheless moves resolutely along that line. And this is a fact of far-reaching importance.

From Text 4, 1, onwards, we find another noteworthy statement on the need for "christiana libertas inquirendi, cogitandi necnon mentem suam in humilitate et fortitudine aperiendi in iis in quibus competentia gaudent" if there is a real wish for the faithful to contribute to the development of theological studies. As a result of the conciliar speech of Mgr. M. Pellegrino on this chapter, the explanatory phrase was added that liberty of that kind must be allowed to the faithful "sive clericis, sive laicis". In view of the considerable repercussions in the aula and outside, of this part of the speech, we think it well to reproduce it in full: [40] "In a praiseworthy way the right to liberty in the search for truth and in the expression and publication of

---

[39] Cf. *La Civiltà Cattolica* (1965), II, p. 487.

[40] Cf. *ibid.* (1966), I, pp. 171 f. On the same theme, cf. K. Rahner, "Dialog in der Kirche", *Schriften zur Theologie* VIII (1968), pp. 426–44; id., "Lehramt und Theologie nach dem Konzil", *ibid.*, pp. 111–32.

one's own opinion is affirmed here. Nevertheless at the end chapter words are used which, contrary to the intention of the authors of this schema, could, I think, dangerously restrict this right. These words are: 'Furthermore, it is to be hoped that many laymen will receive an appropriate formation in the sacred sciences, and that some will develop and deepen these studies by their own labours. In order that such persons may fulfil their proper function, let it be recognized that all the faithful, clerical and lay, possess a lawful freedom of inquiry and of thought, and the freedom to express their minds humbly and courageously about those matters in which they enjoy competence.'

"I humbly ask: Who are the faithful to whom such a Christian freedom of research and thought is conceded? Anyone would say that all Christians, even priests and bishops, are to be counted among the faithful. But I doubt whether this is a common mode of expression, especially since, immediately before, mention has been made of the laity. No doubt it is the right and duty of authority to watch more carefully over priests, because their errors are more dangerous. Nevertheless that should always be done with due respect for the dignity of the human person, and to this there also belongs the liberty of inquiry which is acknowledged to be everyone's right. And do not let us think that there is no danger in this matter: we are all very grateful to the supreme authority of the Church which stamped out in its time the destructive error of Modernism. But who would dare to assert that in that necessary repression the personal rights and dignity of priests were always duly respected, whether it was a case of priests acting with exuberant youthful zeal, of bishops or even of cardinals of the Holy Roman Church? Lest anyone think that these and such like things only concern the past, I should merely like to recall that a few years ago I knew a religious who was living in exile, certainly not voluntarily, because he had expressed opinions which today we are glad to find in papal and conciliar documents. And we all know that this is not an isolated case.

"It is scarcely necessary to point out that even in the theological disciplines there are things which may have been accepted without question for a long time, but which as a result of the progress of scholarship are seen to require revision, and that the scope for freedom of opinion is perhaps much wider than is thought by those who are not experts in the arduous and sometimes dangerous labour of this kind of research.

"Only on condition that all Catholics are acknowledged to have freedom of inquiry into truth can a dialogue develop inside the Church of the kind described by Pope Paul in *Ecclesiam Suam:* 'frequent and familiar dialogue ... ready to listen to the various voices of the men of our time, of a kind to make Catholics good, wise, just and strong'. I should like to add that if everyone knew that he could express his opinion with healthy freedom as befits his competence, he would do so with that truthfulness and honesty which ought always to mark the Church of God. Otherwise it is scarcely possible to avoid the abominable plague of lying and hypocrisy.

"Here therefore are the four innocent words which I propose should be inserted into the text of the schema: 'In order that the faithful may fulfil their function, let it be recognized that Christian freedom of inquiry is accorded to them *sive clericis sive laicis*'."

It is appropriate to note here that in Text 4, 2, the words "christiana libertas" were replaced by "iusta libertas" in order to satisfy one father in the Mixed Commission who insisted that the "recta significatio" of this liberty must be more clearly stated (cf. *Relatio*, p. 37). When the amendments were examined, however, a refusal was given to those *modi* — in fact suggested by very few fathers — which called for the complete suppression of the whole of this last sentence or at least of the phrase "sive clericis sive laicis" (cf. Text 4, 3 B, p. 67, *modus* 142, 144). On the other hand the commission considered it superfluous to add another phrase to specify the subjects of such liberty, with special reference to religious: "sive clericis, tam saecularibus quam regularibus iusta libertas, ita ut nulli Superiori vel Capitulo religioso hanc libertatem, a sancta Matre et Magistra Ecclesia omnibus concessa, suis subditis negare liceat" (cf. Text 4, 3 B, p. 67, *modus* 143). Finally, an amendment was not accepted which proposed to suppress the mention of "courage" in expressing one's own opinion; the reason given for refusal was that in such a context, "fortitudo non est inutilis" (cf. Text 4, 3 B, p. 67, *modus* 145).

This noble invitation to recognize the close connection between culture and liberty even in the life of the Church, concludes a chapter in which the Council examined some of the most important aspects of the problem of the relations between the Church and contemporary culture. Many questions remain open or at least still require further investigation. The guidelines laid down by the Council are an invitation to Christians to reflect and act in order to find a solution in harmony with the new spirit which the Council has introduced into the Church. In the field of culture, as in others, it is true that the Council did not mark the end of a journey but the opening of new roads by which Christians must courageously travel, in a spirit of initiative and invention, in a climate of fruitful liberty, with humility and courage.

Socio-Economic Life

History of the Text by Herbert Vorgrimler
Commentary by Oswald von Nell-Breuning

History of the Text. The history of this chapter will be dealt with very briefly here, since its chief stages have already been traced by C. Moeller in his chapter on the History of the Pastoral Constitution.

Various elements of Christian social teaching were scattered in the preparatory schemata. But an actual chapter "De ordine oeconomico et de iustitia sociali" only came into existence in the second half of January 1963, when it was decided to produce Schema 17 and to entrust its drafting to a Mixed Commission formed of members of the Theological Commission and of the Commission for the Lay Apostolate.[1] At the plenary meeting of this Mixed Commission from 20 to 25 May 1963, A. Ferrari Tonioli presented the *relatio* concerning this chapter which at that time was the fifth in Schema 17.[2] Together with the whole draft it was sent on 4 July 1963 for general revision by Cardinal Suenens in the name of the Co-ordinating Commission. The meetings in Malines for the revision of the text produced no results as regards this Chapter V.[3] After the formation of a Central Subcommission from the Mixed Commission at the end of November 1963, with B. Häring, C.S.S.R., as secretary, the idea emerged at a meeting of a few of its experts on 30 December 1963 that particular concrete problems might be dealt with in appendices.[4] This plan was confirmed at the plenary session of the Central Subcommission in Zurich, 1–3 February 1964, as well as the principle that the *adnexa* or pastoral instructions should not be discussed by the Council.[5]

---

[1] The history of this chapter is also dealt with by R. Tucci, "Introduzione storico-dottrinale alle Costituzione Pastorale 'Gaudium et Spes'", *La Chiesa e il mondo contemporaneo nel Vaticano II* (1966), pp. 17–134. Some chronological details are also given in the Action Populaire edition of the Constitution (Paris 1966), pp. 27 f., 39, 41, 45.

[2] A short list of the contents of this fifth and longest chapter in Tucci, *op. cit.,* pp. 34 f.

[3] *Ibid.,* p. 40.   [4] *Ibid.,* p. 49.

[5] *Ibid.,* pp. 52, 54 f., 56, n. 37.

After the plenary session of the Mixed Commission in the first half of March 1964, five subcommissions were formed for preparing the appendices. The members of the subcommission for the present chapter were: F. Hengsbach (chairman), A. Ancel, J. Blomjous, F. Franić, A. Herrera y Oría, J. Ménager, H. Pessôa Câmara, S. Quadri and A. Fernández, O.P. [6]

It was decided, however, to incorporate the main ideas of the appendices into the fourth chapter of the schema proper. For the textual history of this chapter, therefore, not only the text of the *adnexum* is of importance but also the text of the then Chapter IV, completed on 5 May 1964. [7]

Two appendices were completed at the meetings of the Mixed Commission, 4–6 June 1964. One of these was on economic and social life. The text was in French, the secretary of the subcommission being J.-Y. Calvez, S.J. The fascicle with the appendices was distributed to the Council fathers on 30 September 1964. On 13 October 1964 they were invited by the Mixed Commission to submit opinions on the *adnexa* in writing. [8]

The Council discussed the new schema during 20 October — 5 November and 9–10 November 1964. The *relatio* on the whole Chapter IV was presented by Bishop J. Wright. No special *relatio*, however, was given on Article 23 concerning economic and social life. [9] The observations of the Council fathers (7 speeches) on this article were "not very productive". [10] After the general acceptance of the schema by the Council on 23 October 1964, a new editorial committee of the Central Subcommission was formed in November with Canon Haubtmann at its head. The letter of the Cardinal Secretary of State, A. G. Cicognani, on 2 January 1965 to the presidents of the Mixed Commission, asked that the most important items should be taken out of the *adnexa* into the schema. [11] Thus the chapter on economics was first intended to be Chapter IV of Part II of the new schema. At the Ariccia meeting of the Central Subcommission, 31 January — 6 February 1965, the chapter was not yet completed. The entire new text, in which it had become Part II, Chapter III, was presented by G. Philips to the Mixed Commission when it met from 29 March to 7 April 1965. After amendments had been incorporated, Cardinal Suenens presented the *relatio* to the Co-ordinating Commission on 11 May 1965. The printed text was distributed to the Council fathers in the middle of June.

The Council debate on the schema began on 21 September 1965. Bishop F. Hengsbach presented the *relatio* on Part II on 29 September 1965. This

[6] *Ibid.*, p. 56, n. 37.
[7] *Ibid.*, p. 58 and n. 38.   [8] *Ibid.*, p. 74.
[9] *Ibid.*, p. 76, n. 61, and bibliography.
[10] Cf. the summary with a list of speakers, *Herder Korrespondenz* 19 (1965), pp. 176 f.
[11] Tucci, *op. cit.*, p. 84, n. 72.
[12] *Ibid.*, p. 109, n. 102 with bibliography; cf. also the report in *Herder Korrespondenz* 19 (1965), pp. 685 f.

time 21 fathers took part in the debate on the economics chapter.[12] A new subcommission was formed to revise it: Hengsbach (chairman), de Aráujo Sales, Franić, Granier, Gutiérrez, Larraín, Pessôa Câmara, Ferrari Tonioli, Pavan, Rodhain, Worlock, Laurentin, with J.-Y. Calvez, S.J., and E. Lio, O.F.M., as secretaries. After discussion in the Central Subcommission, the new text was distributed to the Council fathers on 12 November 1965.[13] A supplement with a fresh *relatio* by Bishop F. Hengsbach on Part II was distributed on 15 November 1965.[14] The results of the vote on 16 and 17 November 1965 were as follows:

	Votes	Yes	No	Yes with reservations	Invalid
Articles 67–70	2162	2115	40	—	7
71–72	2260	2182	68	—	10
73–76	2233	2157	68	—	8
Chapter III as a whole	2253	1740	41	469	3

The *modi* were examined during 22–27 November 1965 by the Mixed Commission (presentation and *relatio* of Chapter III, F. Hengsbach and E. Lio). One *modus* was sent in by "higher authority", asking for the words "formis lege admissis" to be added regarding employees' freedom of association; this was rejected by the Mixed Commission.[15] The final text was ready on 1 December 1965. The results of the vote on the *expensio modorum* on Chapter III on 4 December 1965 were as follows:

Votes	Yes	No	Invalid
2212	2110	98	4

On the final votes, see above, the chapter on the History of the Pastoral Constitution by C. Moeller.

Commentary. The section on economic life (art. 63–72) originated in a French draft. Imperfect though it may be, it is a definite improvement on that draft, which was criticized for lack of what is usually a great merit of the Latin mind, namely lucid arrangement and clear terminology. The same fault is less apparent in the final version, but has certainly not been eradicated.

[13] Tucci, *op. cit.*, pp. 110–13.
[14] *Ibid.*, pp. 113–25. The numbers of the text voted upon do not correspond to the final numeration, because arts. 46–49 did not yet exist.
[15] *Ibid.*, p. 128, n. 122.

The title, which in Latin runs "De vita oeconomico-sociali", no doubt means what we should call economic life as a social process, not the house-keeping of private individuals or the actions of the various economic agents (households, business concerns), but the social economy, the interaction of all that these individuals do and cause to be done and of all the ways in which they mutually affect one another.

It is ultimately only a question of linguistic usage that French, like other Romance languages, forms the adjective *économico-social* in order to single out the economic aspect from the whole social process. German uses the adjective *sozialökonomisch* and English would probably speak of "socio-economic life" to deal with the particular aspect of the economy which concerns the relationships which enter into play within the whole economy, in contradistinction to the choices of ends and means made by individuals and the actions or omissions which derive from them. Between *économico-social*, *sozialökonomisch* and *socio-economic* there is therefore a difference in the *modus significandi* but identity in what is designated.[1]

Article 63. This part of the Pastoral Constitution is introduced by an attempted characterization of the present-day economy. Its dynamism and expansion are celebrated in glowing terms. It is therefore all the more odd that the key-figure in this economy, the *entrepreneur*, is not mentioned in any way, either here or at any other point, not even when the business enter-prise and its proper organization are in question (art. 68). Certainly there is nothing to prevent entrepreneurs deriving satisfaction from the praise which Article 64 lavishes on technical progress. But even "eagerness to create and expand enterprises" is not made an attribute of the entrepreneur in any exclusive sense. For projects of this kind to be carried out also decisively depends on the willingness of others, investors, for example. What actually constitutes the function of the entrepreneur is not even hinted at anywhere in the Pastoral Constitution. Since this omission does not make itself felt only at this point, we must draw attention to it at once. However regrettable

---

[1] It is much more difficult with the word "social" used by itself, for then it is often doubtful whether it is to be taken as meaning "concerning society, company" (German *gesellschaftlich*) or "concerning social welfare" (German *social*). In one particular domain, it is possible to use German terms, or the one English word without specifying its meaning; in other contexts a choice has to be made in German (and *sozial* will bear its special mean-ing) and the meaning has to be made explicit in English. The French *social* and the Latin *socialis* are sometimes equivalent to both domains, and it is impossible to translate without paraphrasing. It is certainly to be welcomed that *Gaudium et Spes* attributed great im-portance to recalling frequently that man is not simply an individual but equally essen-tially an "ens sociale" and must therefore act, and act well, as a social being. But this is several times done by means of expressions which are available in the Romance languages but which German, for example, does not possess. We mean quite different things by behaviour in company and behaviour of benefit to the community's welfare. The fact that we are "social beings" is the common source of both.

the omission is, it does not lessen the really liberating effect of what is said on "Some Aspects of Economic Life" (art. 63). There is no trace here of that sceptical, critical attitude to economic life, so frequently found in ascetical writings and in official ecclesiastial pronouncements, which asserts that it diverts men's minds from higher things and attaches them to lower things. The optimistic attitude of John XXIII (*Mater et Magistra*, arts. 246, 254 ff.) has prevailed. Of course, economic life in this fallen world presents a darker side, faults and weaknesses as well as benefits. What is pointed out as an essential fault, again in agreement with John XXIII (*Mater et Magistra*, art. 122), is the tension or contrast between rapidly advancing and relatively backward branches of the economy, regions and whole countries (industrially highly developed countries and underdeveloped countries now spoken of as "developing" or "emergent countries"). This is taken up again and dealt with in several passages. But it is never clearly and unambiguously stated what exactly is regrettable or blameworthy in such differences. An effort must be made to investigate the matter.

The technical vocabulary of economics includes the term "imbalance". The conciliar text contains its linguistic equivalent: "disaequilibrium". But obviously the meanings are not identical. We speak of imbalance, or of disequilibrium ("fundamental disequilibrium", e.g. in the statute of the World Monetary Fund). If a national economy shows constant excess or deficiency in its balance of production, it imposes a strain on international economic relations and, in particular, disorganizes the international balance of payments. Here it is clear why the disequilibrium is harmful and why it must be remedied. Disequilibrium can also mean a wrong relation between different branches of production, for example, a broad development of manufacturing industries on too narrow a basis of raw materials production or vice versa. Here too it is clear why this is not beneficial and what must be done to eliminate it. In other cases economic science cannot fully succeed in establishing clearly what it means by disequilibrium. Thus, for example, it distinguishes between balanced and unbalanced growth and of course prefers the balanced kind. But it cannot say precisely whether in fact growth does not really need a certain amount of imbalance because perfect equilibrium would lead to a condition of perfect rest where nothing further would happen at all and therefore nothing would grow. However that may be, and leaving such marginal cases out of account, economic science knows very well what it means by equilibrium or disequilibrium. But what does the Council mean?

In several passages the Council speaks not of disequilibrium but quite simply of inequality. This inequality can apply to the income of individuals or of whole circles of the population, to the standard of living and to its effects on the mode of life in different regions or countries. It can refer to differences in the tempo of economic advance, which mean that those who have already made an advance continue to do so, thus increasing their lead even more and intensifying the existing inequality. But even this does not make it clear what the Council really regards as a drawback or even as an injustice, and therefore wants to see remedied.

Leo XIII taught that inequalities in the economic and social situation are unavoidable because authority and subordination are indispensable, an integral part of the divinely-willed order of things, and have to be borne with submission ("Ferenda humana condicio": *Rerum Novarum*, art. 14). Are things supposed to be different now? We cannot impute rigid egalitarianism to the Council. What is the norm by which it determines which differences are to be approved and maintained and which are to be blamed and abolished? One criterion is named. While some lack the necessities of life, others have a superfluity of possessions and squander them. That is a question of plain fact. What is reprehensible about it, however, is not the inequality as such but the fact that some have absolutely (not merely relatively) too little and that those who have more than they need do not make the right use of it.

Is it possible to set a limit somewhere or somehow, beyond which inequality is inadmissible even if nobody lacks necessities? That inevitably raises the question whether inequality, even though not *malum in se seu intrinsecus malum,* needs some reason to justify it, and if so, what that justifying reason is, and what precisely it justifies. Usually it is said that there are natural inequalities which cannot be abolished and for precisely that reason require no justification. Inequalities which are not due to nature, however, are only to be acknowledged as justified, it is said, if they are based on some performance *(causa efficiens)* or encourage achievement *(causa finalis).* But they should be rejected, it is said, when they are arbitrary and likely to provoke resentment and produce socially unacceptable conflicts. There is no sound reason for thinking the Council was envisaging the incentive factor; it is quite plainly concerned with the arbitrary element. Expressions like "discrimen" show that discrimination is what is objected to. By discrimination we mean difference of treatment without any justification for the difference, which is precisely what makes it arbitrary. Justice commands that equals should be treated equally, that is, without arbitrary inequality, and unequals in accordance with the difference between them (principle of equity). Clearly the authors of the French draft were inspired by the *égalité* in the famous triad *liberté, égalité, fraternité,* and understood this *égalité* as non-discrimination.

Some of the demands laid down, however, go far beyond mere non-discrimination and appeal to the generosity of the more fortunate, asking them to be more liberal and open-handed to the less fortunate. It is impossible to determine by reference to the conciliar text where the demands of justice end and how far there is another domain in which obligations of general philanthropy or Christian brotherly love are binding and where it is a case of desirable works of supererogation insistently recommended by the Council. Perhaps there is no great harm in this. A precise delimitation of concepts of that sort could not in any case be translated directly into practice, for in practice limits are blurred and can scarcely ever be sharply drawn. If more is done than is strictly due in justice and charity or in charity alone, certainly no harm is done, and it will not be possible to prevent less being done by strict conceptual definition of the extent of the obligation.

We may therefore conclude that there are inequalities (examples of disequilibrium or disproportion, defective complementarity) which are detrimental to economic progress and which in particular make it impossible or more difficult, at least in the foreseeable future, to attain the goal of providing even necessities for present-day humanity, and even more for humanity with its growing numbers. Since, however, this goal is a binding obligation, we have the duty of removing as far as we can any obstacles that stand in the way.

The Council obviously goes further and adopts a definitely critical attitude to economic and social inequalities. In its view, or so at least it seems, there is a presumption of law (though open to refutation) against them. As regards the exact content of this presumption and what is capable of refuting it in any particular case, it is possible to derive some indications from the Council's remarks, but nothing more. At all events we can say that even from Article 69, in which it is dealing in detail with the thesis that earthly goods are intended for all men, and is envisaging these goods from the point of view of distributive policy, the Council does not draw the plainly foolish conclusion that the same quantity is intended by the Creator for all men.[2]

Obviously the description of the present-day economy given by the Council does not claim to be complete. It simply chooses two features which serve as pegs on which to hang statements and demands which the Council considers particularly important.

This chapter of the Constitution divides into two subsections, the first dealing with economic progress (arts. 64–66), while the more extensive second part expounds a few of the principles which govern the whole of social and economic life (arts. 67–72).

Articles 64–66. For two reasons, economic progress, and therefore all that contributes to it, is more needed than ever today. The number of people to be provided for is increasing, an evident and compelling reason. Secondly,

---

[2] The meaning of *égalité* in French thought would probably throw greater light on what is criticized here (as in *Mater et Magistra*) as disequilibrium or inequality. It is not fully accessible to anyone who is not perfectly familiar with French mentality. The same applies to the term *socialisation*, which plays an important part in *Mater et Magistra* (arts. 59–67), and figures in several passages of *Gaudium et Spes*. One Council father pertinently remarked that only a Frenchman could fully understand it.

men make greater demands; in a conciliar text this is certainly a surprising reason, and one which is characteristic of the progressive attitude of the Council and of what we might call its optimism about civilization. Of course, it does not fail to emphasize strongly that man must always remain master of economic and technical progress. Neither production as such nor the abundance of goods produced is an end in itself. More abundant and better supplies have to serve the intellectual, moral, spiritual and religious needs of man, not of some circle of privileged persons but everyone without distinction. The conclusion which is drawn from this, namely that economic activity must be exercised in such a way that God's intentions for man are fulfilled, contains two noteworthy phrases. One acknowledges the autonomy of economic life and the other completes it by linking it with moral order. The connection of all domains of civilization, and therefore of economic life, with the moral law, is often expressed in official ecclesiastical pronouncements. The acknowledgment of its relative autonomy[3] which is clearly formulated for the first time in *Quadragesimo Anno* (art. 42) is seldom found. But it is an absolutely indispensable condition of dialogue with those engaged in it, that is, in this context, with men engaged in economic activities and with representatives of the economic sciences.

When the Council speaks of man having to be and remain the master of economic progress, it is notable that this is not said of man in the abstract but of men in the concrete. This dominion is to be exercised not by a few, but as many as possible on all levels are to share in it. This already prepares the way for what the Council later has to say about what we in England call "workers' participation" or "partnership in industry". Here the idea is employed in two ways, first against the theoretical model of *laissez-faire* liberalism which regards the whole economic process as subject to the operation of necessary and automatic processes and therefore wants to abandon it to them. On the other hand it is directed against a centrally controlled totalitarian economy which leaves no scope for the initiative of individuals and groups. It is striking how often the Constitution mentions associations or groups as well as individuals. Clearly it is concerned to emphasize their fundamental justification in contrast to the axiom proclaimed by the French Revolution that between the individual and the State there can be no *corps intermédiaires* and certainly no *pouvoirs intermédiaires*. But nothing further is said about the function of these structures and how they must be constituted in order to fulfil it.

Particularly for the economically less-developed countries,[4] the Council

---

[3] Cf. the present writer's "'Lege artis', Sachlichkeit und Sittlichkeit in der Wirtschaft", in F. Böckle and F. Gröner, eds., *Moral zwischen Anspruch und Verantwortung (Festschrift W. Schöllgen)* (1964), pp. 379–94.

[4] The Pastoral Constitution always uses this rather roundabout expression and so avoids

considers progress to be so urgently required that all available forces are to be mobilized to achieve it. Consequently the natives of these countries are reminded of their civic duty, and at the same time of their civil right freely to employ their own capacity and their own material resources responsibly for this purpose. In order nevertheless not to countenance in any way the abuse of totalitarian states which forbid their citizens to emigrate, the specific proviso is made that the individual has the personal right to emigrate. At the same time it is left to the individual conscience — this is presumably how we must interpret it in order to avoid contradiction — to judge whether his duties towards his native country impose on him the obligation to remain and to work for its economic and cultural advance, whether he can leave his country without detriment to it, whether he may even serve his country better, if it is suffering from over-population and lack of opportunities for work, by earning his living somewhere else, or, finally, whether compelling considerations of conscience force him to leave his country because it makes it impossible for him freely and responsibly to provide for the temporal welfare and eternal salvation of himself and his family.

The next article once again expresses the demand for the rapid abolition of the differences of economic and social level which are described as "huge" (*ingentes*). The Council therefore sees the existing differences not merely as big but as intolerably big and as crying out to be remedied.[5] Clauses are carefully added with the aim of preventing unenlightened zeal abolishing not only these inequalities but also the differences or special features of the cultures, traditions, etc., peculiar to the various nations. There has to be a reasonable similarity of level but no imposed uniformity or schematization. In this connection, mention is also made of the flexibility ("mobility" in the technical economic sense of the term) without which no development and therefore no growth is possible. This includes, for example, the willingness but also the objective possibility of changing the place of work, a chosen and favourite occupation, and in certain cases even a dwelling-place, to undertake re-training, to get used to completely different living conditions, etc. But human beings, and certainly the family, need a certain amount of stability. Consequently mobility involves risk. A balance has therefore to be struck between mobility and stability. Pius XII had already drawn attention to this in a very striking way (Address of 20 February 1946 [Utz-Groner, 4108]). The Pastoral Constitution chooses an important instance at the present day, the condition of foreign workers who take jobs abroad because their own country does not offer sufficient opportunities. They above all

---

both "underdeveloped countries", a term which Spain, for example, and other countries resented as insulting, and the polite term "developing countries" which is now customary.

[5] In Article 83, existing political tensions which endanger peace are explained among other things "ex nimiis inaequalitatibus oeconomicis". Here the inequalities are described in so many words not only as enormous (*ingentes*), but as excessive (*nimiae*).

should not be exposed to unfair discrimination. It would certainly be better, instead of bringing men to the work, to bring the work to the men by creating opportunities for work for these men in their own countries. Considerable demands, of a different kind it is true, are made on mobility by increasing automation. Here, too, forethought and preparation must be made in good time to ensure that not only the elementary needs of life but also human dignity is in all circumstances respected.

Articles 67–72. The second section deals with a few principles which hold good for the whole economic sphere.

The first two articles deal with labour. Placed at the beginning, and consequently clearly meant to indicate the direction of the considerations which follow, is the statement that human labour takes precedence over any of the other elements which play a part in economic life, because all the latter have a purely instrumental character. This lays the foundation and gives the bearings of all further statements regarding the relations between labour and property ("capital"). That a really fundamental line is in question here is clear not only because this line is followed consistently in the whole section, but perhaps even more clearly because of a lapidary statement in Part I, Chapter II: "De hominum communitate": "The disposition of things should be at the service of persons and not vice versa."[6] The higher metaphysical rank of human labour was, of course, recognized in earlier documents on Catholic social teaching, but was far from being as prominent or as rich in practical applications as it was for the first time in *Mater et Magistra* and is again here. In the face of the attack of Marxist socialism, the Church found itself obliged to defend the institution of property with great determination (Leo XIII, *Rerum Novarum*). As opposed to misinterpretations of Leo XIII's teaching on property in the direction of liberalism, Pius XI was obliged once again in *Quadragesimo Anno* to deal thoroughly with the question of property in order to make clear its two aspects, individual and social, both equally important. He had to stress its subordination to the perpetually changing demands of the common good, which explains the competence of the State to determine the concrete shape and pattern of property as an institution (and not merely to regulate the use of property!). This perspective still unfortunately gave the impression that the Church was more concerned with defending the supposed sanctity of property, as understood by the

---

[6] "Rerum ordinatio ordini personarum subicienda est et non e converso" (art. 26). The Latin formulation achieves a fine shade of meaning by using the rather passive "ordinatio" for the order imposed on things, but the more active "ordo" for the establishment of order by persons; things (material goods, property) are set in order and can then serve as instruments of order. Persons create order in themselves and in things. The same applies to competition; as a principle of order it would be inadequate, but it does useful service if employed as an instrument to achieve order (cf. *Quadragesimo Anno*, arts. 88, 110).

French Revolution, than with the God-given and God-willed human and Christian dignity of the worker. This false perspective has since been corrected by *Mater et Magistra*. Accordingly the Pastoral Constitution here deals first with labour and mentions briefly the duty to work and the right to work. The latter is understood as a right which implies on the part of society a duty to provide as far as possible the opportunity for its exercise. A single sentence condenses the doctrine of earlier papal documents, in particular *Quadragesimo Anno* (arts. 63–75) on the just wage. The Council's effort not to argue solely in terms of natural law, but to make genuinely theological affirmations, is evident in the statement that labour not only contributes to perfecting the work of creation but even shares in the redemptive work of Jesus Christ, if it is offered to God in the right way. With great earnestness the Council criticizes any kind of abuse detrimental to the working man. As well as familiar matters, a new idea appears: the monotony of work should be compensated to some extent by giving people an opportunity to develop capacities which have no outlet in their work and which therefore tend to atrophy.

The next article, Article 68, especially its first paragraph, was the subject of intense controversy from the start. Unfortunately there is some question about the translation of the Latin sub-title, precisely in relation to the very controversial first paragraph (§§ 1–2 in Abbott). The Latin title speaks of participation in enterprises, and only mentions participation in organization *(dispositione)* in connection with the economic system as a whole ("De participatione in inceptis et in universa rei oeconomicae dispositione, et de conflictibus in labore"). It thus draws a perfectly clear distinction between participation in enterprises in which business is carried on and whose right administration is in question, and participation in the ordering of the economy as a whole, that is to say, participation in economic policy. Sentences 1 and 2 (of the Latin text, Abbott, § 1) deal with the business enterprise, and sentence 3 (Abbott, § 2) deals with the sphere of economic policy.

The Latin "participatione in inceptis" means more than merely taking part in the "curatione inceptorum" — share in responsibility for administering or running a business. The question it raises is, who is actually engaged in the enterprise? In other words, who actually belongs to it? The sentence answers precisely this question. The enterprise is not, as frequently appears in the descriptions given in economics or commercial law, merely the assets and liabilities listed in the balance-sheet. Nor is it to be identified with those who possess legal claims and obligations and bear the consequent risk (chance of success or failure). The enterprise consists in the first place of the human beings who work in it; it essentially consists of them, in association. The French draft had asked that wherever possible, enterprises should *become* "communities of persons" ("communautés de personnes"). The Council text, however, avoided this expression, which would have been open to very different interpretations in different countries, and replaced the demand by an observation. Rightly understood, a business enterprise is always and without exception an association of persons and cannot be anything else. That is the Council's fundamental statement about economic enterprises.

There is a conflict between two current views of the economic enterprise. According to one, it is the sum-total of the objective factors in production, in which the owner employs man-power for a purpose determined by his interests (and usually assumed to be the purpose of making maximum profit). This is a monistic view of the interests involved. The other conception regards the business enterprise as an association of persons who co-operate in production by contributions of different kinds, especially by employing their person ("labour") or property ("capital"); the result (yield or return) of this production is intended to serve the various interests of all those involved. This is a pluralist conception of the interests involved. The Pastoral Constitution unambiguously decides for the second of these views. It is a question of giving this business association, as we say nowadays, the right structure, organization, constitution or whatever term we choose. That is what has to be promoted. We use the term "business association" in order to make it clear that it is not the capital assets or funds shown in the balance-sheet which are referred to but the living business enterprise, that is, the people who are engaged in some corporate undertaking and the undertaking itself. By reference to the triad of "intellectus, res, opera" (e.g. *Quadragesimo Anno*, art. 69) which Pius XI liked to use, for he himself came from a business man's family, a deeper understanding of the economic enterprise could easily have been attained. To match the Council's terminology it would only have been necessary to change the order to "intellectus, opera, res". Without question *intellectus* comes first, that is, the initiative and enterprise of management, in personal terms therefore the directors, the top management, whose function is to combine the productive factors, labour and capital, and to get them to co-operate effectively.[7] Since the Pastoral Constitution does not go further into this triadic conception put forward by Pius XI, it remains tied to the traditional but inadequate dual model of property and labour which, it is true, it inverts into labour and property, and this of course certainly represents a considerable advance.

Obviously people's correct position in an enterprise will be determined by their function; consequently an attempt is made to deal with the various functions. Unfortunately these were not listed, only the persons who exercise them. The entrepreneur and his function, however, are omitted; it cannot be

---

[7] It is said that this had not been overlooked, but that because of the pressure of time, no supporting references could be found. Consequently the idea was dropped. This is a pity, for the entrepreneurs have good reason to complain that they and their particular contribution have not been given due recognition.

fitted into the dual model. Attention is focussed on human beings, who are therefore regarded in the tangible form of their occupation rather than in what for the outsider is the abstract, and therefore schematic-seeming, economic enterprise. The following bearers of functions are mentioned: owners, employers, managers and workers. This list presents several puzzles. The omission of the entrepreneur is difficult to understand. But it also seems strange that, contrary to the rule usually strictly observed by the Council of listing labour first as the personal factor and material means (property, capital) second as the instrumental factor, owners suddenly appear here in the first place. It is not clear, either, who are meant by employers. As things are at present, the employer-function is one of the functions of proprietors, in other words, proprietors and employers are one and the same (physical or juridical) person. If we try to remove this discrepancy by taking the employer to mean executives entrusted with functions similar to those of an employer, new confusion is caused, because the distinction between "employers" and "managers" disappears.

It is unfortunate that bearers of functions and not the functions themselves are listed, not least because the greatest difficulties for the correct ordering or organization of business enterprises derive precisely from the fact that, particularly in numerous small and medium enterprises, one and the same person exercises several functions. On the other hand, in the majority of big enterprises the function of proprietor (and of employer) is not exercised by physical persons but by juridical persons. The text only speaks of the former and describes them as "free, independently responsible human beings created in God's image". It is useless objecting that behind the screen of juridical persons stand the physical persons who own shares. Very often the share-holders themselves are juridical persons, and at least in the corporate foundations referred to specially by Pius XII (Utz-Groner, 3348 f.), it is impossible by definition to point to physical persons as owners.

From the way the Pastoral Constitution came into existence, we know that this list of bearers of functions, which did not figure in the French draft, was only drawn up in the final meetings of the editorial committee by an ad hoc subcommittee and was inserted into the text without further examination. So we must take into consideration that in the last days of the Council no time was available for mature reflection. [8]

At the wish of a few worried Council fathers, a self-evident and therefore in itself superfluous proviso was inserted: unity of direction must be assured.

Another clause, which was added subsequently, observes that the partici-

---

[8] The conciliar text shows that economic enterprise and works or business are treated as more or less equivalent. But they are essentially different. As a consequence questions arising in the daily life of works and firms are not sufficiently distinguished from those which concern the running and management of an enterprise.

pation should be exercised in "appropriately determined ways". At first sight this may seem banal, yet it has real significance. It makes it clear in the first place that the Council is not thinking merely of the atmosphere of a business (human relations) or matters of that kind, but has institutional measures in mind, secondly that it is refraining from any judgment about concrete solutions or attempted solutions. What any suggested solution offers or promises, can and should be measured by the conciliar principles; they are intended as criteria for that purpose only. Detailed juridical and technical solutions are beyond the knowledge and judgment of an Ecumenical Council.

The three additions mentioned are scars, as it were, left from the fierce battles fought in the commission or drafting committee.[9] The conciliar text speaks of "actuosa participatio in curatione". Previously the word *administratio* had been used, but this was replaced by *curatio* in order to satisfy the objections of those bishops who regarded "administratio" as too technical or too definite (i.e. far-reaching). This was obviously done so as to be less specific and so leave greater scope for interpretation. In fact "curatio", as the Latin dictionary will show, has a remarkable range of meanings extending from care or tutelage to supreme charge. Interpretation has accordingly been busy profiting by this wide range of meanings, especially in the direction of weakening its meaning until it is innocuous: "concern for the business" — as though every employee were not obliged to conscientious "concern for the business" on the ground of his contract of employment, and as if he must not expect immediate dismissal if he fails to show it. The Council certainly did not need to try to safeguard the right of everyone belonging to a firm to share in concern for the business. Quite apart from the fact that the Latin word *inceptum* (French *entreprise*) used constantly and exclusively, in accordance with the terminology of *Mater et Magistra,* denotes the business enterprise.[10] Furthermore, as we shall show later, it expressly refers to economic decisions, in other words those which concern the actual running of the business.

Note 7 (Abbott 219) gives an important indication for the correct interpretation of what is to be understood by *curatio*. The expression is taken from the Latin text of *Quadragesimo Anno* (art. 65). Consequently it is at least hermeneutically legitimate to take it as having the same meaning as in the source, in which Pius XI recommended in very cautious terms that the status of the wage contract should be raised by some modification of company

---

[9] "On devait ... âprement discuter les formules sur la participation des travailleurs à la vie et la gestion des entreprises", it is said in the introduction to the Action Populaire edition of *Gaudium et Spes* composed by one of those chiefly concerned, p. 45.

[10] The lack of a clear distinction between the sphere of the actual business or works and that of economic enterprise as such, which was criticized in note 8 above, does not alter the fact that the statements in the conciliar text clearly refer to management and decision-taking.

law; in this way, he suggests, employees would achieve "co-property or co-management" or some kind of "profit-sharing". The Latin text reads "consortes fiunt dominii vel curationis aut de lucris perceptis aliqua ratione participant". This brings out clearly the precedence of "participation by association or co-partnership" in ownership or in management over mere profit-sharing. Pius XI, therefore, understood the *consortium* whether *dominii* or *curationis* as an element of company law built into the mere wage nexus. This participation, whether in ownership or in running a business, does not suppress the wage contract but introduces an element of company law into the wage contract which persists as before. "Participation by association", whether in ownership or in the *decisions* traditionally reserved to owners alone, is what is meant in *Quadragesimo Anno.*

The reference in footnote 7 (Abbott 219) to *Quadragesimo Anno* is, however, significant in another respect. At the time some surprise was felt in certain circles that Pius XII in his address of 3 June 1950 (Ut-Groner, 3266) dismissed this passage of *Quadragesimo Anno* as an incidental remark. Since the Council has returned precisely to the passage and borrowed a technical term to express what it has in mind, the passage has not only been given increased importance, it has become the locus classicus for co-determination, responsibility-sharing, co-partnership, workers' participation. *Curatio* must therefore be understood in the full sense that it bears in the relevant passage of *Quadragesimo Anno.*[11] If, as we may suppose, it was the intention of the drafting committee to weaken the force of the statement by replacing *administratio* by *curatio*, it mistook the means and produced the contrary effect. By the reference to *Quadragesimo Anno*, the statement stands out in higher relief. In substance, what the Council advocates is not new and unheard-of at all. All that is new is the greater decisiveness ("promoveatur") in comparison with the more reserved and cautious recommendation of Pius XI.

It may be possible to dispute whether sentence 2 in its final version at least permits of an interpretation in the minimizing sense aimed at by one group

---

[11] It is rather amusing to remember how the opponents of partnership in industry understood and tried to interpret this passage in *Quadragesimo Anno* earlier. They pointed out that it reads "consortes fiunt dominii *vel* curationis", but "aut ... participant". The change from the weak "vel" to the strong "aut" shows, according to them, that *consortium dominii* and *consortium curationis* are not two different things but merely two different expressions for the same reality. "Curatio" was unambiguously understood as authority to take decisions, which is a direct consequence of the right of ownership and in fact practically equivalent to it; the only person who can be *consors curationis* is one who is *consors dominii*. Now, however, on the contrary, "curatio" is devalued and held to mean merely concern, and "participatio in curatione" is alleged merely to mean a share in concern, and not about management either, but merely about the details of the business. The French draft spoke of "gestion", and the French re-translation of the Latin text has retained this expression.

in the drafting committee, but sentence 3 (Abbott, § 2) excludes all controversy on this point; it rigorously excludes such an interpretation.[12] It states that decisions concerning *economic* and social matters of vital importance to the workers are very often taken, not inside the individual enterprises themselves but by institutions on a higher level ("superioris ordinis institutis"). From this it draws the conclusion that workers ought to have a share in these too. This means economic and social co-determination even on the higher level of economic and social policy — a higher plane than that of particular business enterprises. The thought is clear. If decisions vital to the workers in economic and social matters were all taken in the business enterprises themselves, it would be sufficient to establish economic and social co-determination in these enterprises. But since many of these decisions are taken on a higher level, economic and social co-determination must also extend to these.[13] And such decision-sharing can only be realized "also" on this higher

[12] One cannot avoid the impression that the argument about sentence 2, which led to its being burdened with three insertions and the replacement of "administratio" by "curatio", so monopolized the attention that sentence 3 was completely lost sight of. It was quite overlooked that what they had wanted to leave open in sentence 2 follows as an inescapable consequence from sentence 3. Taken in conjunction with sentence 3, the meaning of sentence 2 is perfectly plain.

[13] Obviously the opponents of partnership in management cannot shut their eyes to the fact that this inference is conclusive and that it would be attributing a downright contradiction to the Council if they tried to make it say that it wanted to concede employees a share in the decisions which are taken on the higher plane of economic and social policy and which are vital to them, whilst at the same time it intended to refuse them any such participation in decisions concerning the actual running of the business where their own livelihood is at stake. Consequently they are obliged to interpret the whole sentence in a different sense. According to this, "in his statuendis" means participation not in decisions but in the establishment or development of the "superioris ordinis instituta". The latter should therefore not be translated as "on a higher level" but "by superior institutions". If this was what was meant, the Latinist must have made a mistake in his choice of the demonstrative pronoun, for according to the rules of Latin grammar, "in his" must refer to the nearest noun ("the latter"). Furthermore, the verb "statuere" is scarcely appropriate to the establishment of institutions, whereas it is aptly applied to decisions about conditions. If for instance we distinguish between "having a say in", "collaborating in" and "co-determining" then "statuere" clearly denotes a genuine share in control, i.e. co-determination. Moreover, a statement about the development or establishment of institutions would be quite out of place in the context, whereas one about workers' additional share in decisions taken on a higher level is in line with the sequence of thought and brings it to a conclusion. That the German and English translations really render what the sentence was intended to mean is also shown by comparison with the French original and the translation of the promulgated text produced under the auspices of the French episcopate — for which the French bishops appear to have taken a greater measure of responsibility than the German bishops did for the version they were instructed to produce. Quite plainly the conciliar text has reproduced the French original. But whilst it is said that the workers should "aussi y avoir part et même participer à l'organisation du développement économique dans son ensemble", the Latin text uses the brief phrase "etiam in his statuendis", which the French have re-

level if in the first place ("similarly", in the French translation "également"), it exists on the level of the enterprise itself.

We may regret this decision of the Council in favour of the *economic* co-determination in business enterprises which has been the subject of such controversy in Germany; doubts may be cast on the technical competence of the Council fathers in this matter; [14] we may contest their recommendation of economic co-determination in the enterprise on valid grounds; one thing, however, is not possible, it cannot be argued out of existence.

Partnership in industry or co-determination may be practised directly or indirectly through representatives. Sentence 3 (Abbott, § 2) returns to this. The French text had pointed out that representation would no doubt be needed for decisions of economic and social policy on the higher level. The conciliar text lists both as equal possibilities; what it is concerned with is the free choice of representatives who must not be imposed by either side. Because the context has caused mention of the possibility of representation to be made only in regard to the higher level, it may be inferred that on the level of the enterprise direct participation is preferred, but not that no other kind is permissible. [15]

The Pastoral Constitution makes no specific pronouncement on the participation of trade unions in decision-taking. If one wished, one could go a step further and say it is excluded. It would probably be scarcely possible to say anything universally valid on the matter. The trade unions of different countries are far too different, both in structure and in the way they regard themselves; American labour unions, for example, think and act in this question in a completely different way from German trade unions.

The next paragraph deals with trade unions. The right to found them

translated "également participer à ces décisions". "Également": it is impossible to express more clearly what is meant by "etiam" (also). When the German version renders "in his statuendis" briefly by "daran" instead of by "an diesen Entscheidungen", this is in accordance with the rule taught in school: when translating into Latin, add a participle or verbal adjective, but in translating from Latin, omit it, because it is superfluous in German. The French have done well in their translation to make the meaning of "in his" quite explicit by using "à ces décisions".

[14] There is no doubt that the question was an entirely new one to the overwhelming majority of the Council fathers. Only a very few bishops can have been in any way familiar with the state of the question. The idea that the Council was taking a decision like a committee of experts about the forms of co-partnership in industry which exist in the German Federal Republic, is too absurd to be taken seriously.

[15] The circumstance that delegated decision-taking is only spoken of in relation to the higher level, strengthens the impression that those who wrote the text did not have in mind vast world-wide concerns, but were thinking of the local works, factory or business, where each worker can himself take part in a meeting of all the employees. But even if the personnel only rises to a few hundreds, direct participation of all in the decisions is no longer possible. All that is left, as in any association of some size, is the possibility, and therefore the problems, of representation.

freely is almost passionately proclaimed and it is emphasized that to take part in the activity of a union must be "sine ultionis periculo", i.e. must involve no sanctions either from employers or the State. In conditions such as ours, employers will scarcely be tempted to blacklist workers who are active in their unions, but in authoritarian and completely or semi-Fascist states, coercive measures by the State authorities against active trade-unionists are still the order of the day. The optimism of the Council regarding the activity and anticipated future development of trade unions, especially their growth to ever greater responsibility, is perhaps wishful thinking, and is in remarkable contrast to the pessimism of some Catholic sociologists and theorists regarding the state and future prospects of trade unionism.

The last paragraph of this article deals with industrial disputes or, to be exact, with strikes, for the weapon of the other side, the lock-out, is not mentioned. It was a long disputed point in Catholic social doctrine whether strikes in general can be justified, on what conditions and within what limits. To the end the question remained open whether only a defensive strike or whether the offensive strike is permissible, though perhaps on more stringent conditions. The Council does recognize the latter variety, though, of course, only as a last resort, as a means of obtaining really justified demands after all other possibilities have been exhausted. The phrase "in present-day circumstances" is worth noting. This seems to suggest that strikes might perhaps become obsolete one day, but clearly states that the need for recourse to them in the extreme case still exists, generally speaking, today. All the statements on strikes are linked with admonitions to reasonable and peaceful agreement.

Such is the content of the two articles devoted to labour. In retrospect one asks what labour is actually meant? When it is said (as *Rerum Novarum*, art. 8. had done) that work puts the stamp of man on matter, and when mention is made of the work that the Son of God did with his own hands in Nazareth and by which he sanctified labour, what is directly meant can only be the work of the craftsman or artisan, which transforms material supplied by nature. The man at the console of an automated assembly line or the man programming a computer, does not put the stamp of his personality on matter. He is not dealing with matter but with technical apparatus which sometimes manipulates matter (e.g. a rolling mill which laminates steel) but sometimes merely supplies signs or signals of some kind, for example, the results of calculations, on which man then bases his decisions. When work in economic enterprises is mentioned, it is clearly a question of the activity formerly exercised by slaves, then by serfs and now by politically free men under legally free wage-contract, non-independent and mostly subordinate activity, i.e. work done under instructions and for pay. This activity is sometimes predominantly physical, sometimes more mental. In the Pastoral Constitution itself, directing and executive activity are distinguished ("dirigentium", "operariorum") and the Latin text does not make it clear whether "dirigere" is counted with "labour" or contrasted with it. There is some reason to think the latter, especially because of the identity of this linguistic usage with that of Italian and French,[16] but there is no proof. Our business men, in particular small and medium independent employers, rightly say that they work on the whole more, and not infrequently very much more, than the "workers" they employ. But on the larger and even on the gigantic scale, businessmen resent the imputation that they are "capitalists", raking in profit without trouble, and want the activity they perform to be recognized. At all events it is no less an outcome of human personality than the activity of the industrial or white-collar worker. From the point of view of social philosophy and the doctrine of man, it can therefore claim the same metaphysical dignity as theirs. Consequently, by the words "labour" and "workers" ("labor", "operarii") *Gaudium et Spes* selects various sectors from the whole domain of human work. The reader has to gather from the context which sector is meant in each case. There is no harm in that, but there is a danger if the reader overlooks the fact that some of the statements made only apply to one precise sector, that he may generalize them unjustifiably.

Three further articles (69–71) deal with property. It is very much to be welcomed that the very beginning of *Article 69* states the purpose of earthly goods, the fact that they are intended for mankind, not for individual human beings. This powerfully underlines the frequently blurred distinction between "usus communis" and "administratio et dispensatio particularis" (*Summa Theologica*, 2a, 2ae, q. 66). The "usus communis" is prior to any property rights. The right to property is the technical instrument to make it practicable, that is to say, to regulate it reasonably and peacefully. It is only in a very much later passage that reference is made to Pius XI's doctrine of the two aspects of property, individual and social ("indoles individualis et socialis", *Quadragesimo Anno*, arts. 45, 49), with the rather colourless phrase that it also "has a social character" ("et indolem socialem natura sua habet quae in communis destinationis bonorum lege fundatur").[17] In fact what is essential to the social function of property, namely that it be used *productively* and so satisfy the needs of other individuals, whether a few, indefinitely many or all, is only expressed by the very general phrase "ut non sibi tantum sed etiam aliis prodesse queant" ("accrue to the benefit not only of himself but also of others") (art. 69). But the context indicates no other

---

[16] Cf. UCID = Unione Cristiana Imprenditori e Dirigenti, in which obviously the dirigenti appear either as appointed directors side by side with the independent entrepreneurs, or, as executives of the independent or appointed directors in co-ordination with them.

[17] Article 71. The only references given are to Pius XII's Whitsun message, 1941, and to *Mater et Magistra* (arts. 111–14).

way of benefiting others than that of giving away property to others. Consequently we are left with the distributive aspect: so that all may have what is necessary and suitable, people should readily give things away, thus helping those in need.

The question inescapably arises, what is the extent of the duty of giving away (i.e. almsgiving, in the language of moral theology); what limits are to be set to it? Moralists usually restrict it to "superflua", in the sense that in general one need only give *of* one's *superflua*. The doctrine of the Fathers, however, indubitably was that *the superflua* had to be given away, that one had to dispossess oneself of them in favour of the poor. Pius XI settled the question by praising as a morally good action the use of what in certain circumstances may be very considerable revenues which are available, i.e. not required for the maintenance of a suitable and worthy standard of life, to create large-scale opportunities for work and earnings, provided the work serves to produce really worthwhile goods (*Quadragesimo Anno,* arts. 50–51). This clearly means that providing employment in this way absolves from the duty of giving away this income as alms, and is even to be preferred to almsgiving.[18] The Pastoral Constitution envisages only the distributive aspect, however, and so cannot avoid the question of the duty of giving away. Rather surprisingly it answers it by saying that the Fathers and doctors of the Church had extended the duty even further, teaching that men are obliged to help the poor "not merely out of their superfluous goods". The Council does not, of course, make this thesis entirely its own, but obviously recommends it as worth remembering.[19]

The latter part of this article makes a noteworthy reference to customs which guarantee social assistance in many primitive societies. These should not simply disappear with economic progress, leaving nothing to replace them, but should be adapted to new situations and needs. As their counterpart in developed societies we have the State welfare organizations of national social insurance, health service, etc. By these the destination of

---

[18] Even in Article 70 which deals with investments, *Gaudium et Spes* does not return to this idea. It does not go into the obvious question of where the investor gets the funds to invest. They are assumed to be available.

[19] On the question of what is to be regarded as "superfluous" in present-day conditions, note 10 to Article 69 (Abbott, n. 223), refers us to a television message of John XXIII. All he says in it, however, is that one should reckon superfluity in one's own possessions by the measure of the needs of others. But this presupposes that we already know what is superfluous, for not everything we possess in excess of other people's needs is by that very fact superfluous to us. Furthermore, John XXIII in this matter refers precisely to the point which has been inadequately treated here, the right *productive* use of goods: "See to it that the administration and distribution of created goods is put to the advantage of all." Here "distribution" clearly means, not the act of dividing up and giving away, but the existing state of distribution, which may favour the utilization of earthly goods to the benefit of all but may also seriously hamper or frustrate it.

earthly goods for all is to some extent assured, though once again only under the distributive aspect.

Article 70 deals relatively briefly and in very general terms with investment and the monetary question. Investment policy, both of private investors and public authorities, must observe the golden mean, neither satisfying present needs to excess at the cost of future generations, nor sacrificing the present generation and its happiness in order to build the foundations of a powerful and splendid future. The needs of developing countries also have to be taken into account. This probably refers particularly to what are called "direct investments" in these countries (development help is dealt with in detail in Part II, Chapter V).

The two brief sentences on monetary policy say practically nothing. "In re monetaria", care is to be taken not to harm one's own or other nations. The economically weak ought not to suffer detriment (losses) unjustly from variations in the value of money. In its time, it had been regretted by serious and well-meaning people that *Mater et Magistra* says nothing about decline in the value of money (inflation). This was not even correct, for something is said, though in a very out of the way place. Measures of agricultural policy (planned market for agricultural products, etc.) are said to contribute "to maintain the purchasing power of money, one of the most important requirements if economic growth is to be maintained on a steady course" (*Mater et Magistra*, art. 129). Whilst *Mater et Magistra* thus attributes great importance to the stability in the value of money precisely in regard to orderly growth (which in the context means one which does not lead to new imbalances), Article 70 here leaves it quite open whether economic calculation or even justice should impose a policy of stability in the value of money, or, on the other hand, on what conditions it may appear justifiable to sacrifice the stable value of money to other purposes which from the point of view of the common good are even more urgent quite apart from the favouring of the economically strong and the detriment of the economically weak which this unavoidably entails. The Council quite clearly reached a limit here where it found itself obliged to stop for lack of specialist knowledge and competence. Since money itself has no intrinsic value, a stable currency is likewise only a means to an end. If it contributes to promote well-being, or to distribute advantages and burdens fairly, it is good and there is a duty to strive for it. To the extent that it could only be achieved at an exorbitant price, e.g. mass unemployment, it could and must be abandoned. The Council here was not in possession of any special competence and had no knowledge of existing circumstances, relation of cause and effect, etc. All German specialists would unanimously have informed the Council that inflation is always economic quackery. But the economic and political "experts" of countries accustomed to inflation would assure it that without the constant assistance of injections of inflation, or even of allowing the value of the currency to decline, no economic growth is possible, at least in their circumstances, and that therefore the luxury of a pharisaical, rigidly virtuous monetary policy must be left to economically strong countries; economically weak countries cannot indulge in it. No judgment can be formed on this question by philosophical and theological means. The Council drew its own conclusion, and contented itself with inserting two little sentences which appear to say something but really say nothing. By confessing its ignorance more openly, by admitting that for lack of sufficient knowledge of the subject-matter and the special questions it raises it could not form any judgment or apply ethical principles to it, it would perhaps have done itself more honour and certainly would not have compromised its dignity.

Article 71. With this article the Pastoral Constitution returns to the principle that material goods are intended for all (art. 69) and draws the conclusion that all should have access to them and share in them. The article has a striking title: "De accessione ad proprietatem et dominium privatum bonorum; et de latifundiis". The distinction between ownership and property, *proprietas* and *dominium privatum bonorum,* which is maintained in the text, though not always uniformly, is probably to be regarded as an attempt to clarify terminology and to reserve the term ownership *(proprietas)* for what originally was alone regarded as property, namely, control over a thing, i.e. authority to have at one's disposal a spatially limited portion of the material world to the exclusion of anyone else. All our traditional statements about ownership and in particular our traditional arguments in support of private property concern ownership in this sense. Only such material goods can be said to have been created by God for the utility of all, yet are to be put to use by the individuals entitled to do so in each case. Even the rights of ownership which are becoming increasingly important at the present time (partnerships, business, artistic and literary copyrights, cartel quotas and the like, legal claims to insurance benefits, etc.) ultimately stand in some relation to the use of material things. They are of human origin, however, and, like the particular form given to the right of ownership, are creations of "industria hominum" (*Rerum Novarum,* art. 7, *Quadragesimo Anno,* art. 49). In certain circumstances they can therefore be open to question and criticism. The Pastoral Constitution intends its statements to refer to ownership in the wider sense, i.e. not only legal ownership of things, but ownership rights generally, and in the third paragraph of this Article 71 it specially calls attention to the increasingly diversified forms which ownership in this sense is assuming. The expression "non obstantibus fundis socialibus, iuribus et ministeriis a societate procuratis" makes it less clear, however, whether this very wide concept of ownership also includes legal property rights to benefits of the various social security organizations (e.g. pension rights) or whether these form an antithesis to them (cf. also *Mater et Magistra,* arts. 105, 106). Here it is no longer a matter of mere terminology but an important question about reality. Respected representatives of Catholic social doctrine regard ownership as an institution which strengthens the position of the individual and the family in face of claims of State authority to omnipotence. In contradiction to this view, there is now not only the legal claim to National Assistance which, according to present legal conceptions is a fundamental right, but also the legal claim against the State (or corporation set up by the State) to a pension, acquired by contributions and capable of being calculated precisely. These consequently lack the independence in face of the superior power of State authorities and their arbitrary will which has been ascribed to ownership. Perhaps nowadays, by bitter experience — not only with totalitarian States — people are no longer as firmly convinced as they used to be that "ownership" (my home is my castle) provides any such independence. Consequently they no longer see such a great difference between property on the one hand and claims on the Welfare State on the other. *Mater et Magistra* and these articles of the Pastoral Constitution consequently mark a change, but obviously wish to avoid plain rejection of the traditional view.

It is a matter for satisfaction that unfortunate expressions about property being an extension of the personality into the world of things, and others of that kind, have not found their way into *Gaudium et Spes*.

Possession of property in the wide sense has the following advantages according to the Pastoral Constitution: It contributes to the development of the personality and makes it possible for a man to take his place in society and economic life; it provides an area of freedom indispensable to personal life and even more to family life, and is therefore to be regarded as an extension of human freedom; consequently it is a condition of civil freedom. Despite the organization of social security (see above), the function of property as an insurance still remains important. This statement, however, is immediately qualified by the indubitably correct observation, also found in *Mater et Magistra* (art. 106), that the same thing applies to non-material goods, e.g. professional qualifications (which, though this is not actually said, can also assume a "material" form, e.g. in diplomas acquired by success in examinations). The practical conclusion is that all should be owners.

The brief paragraph which follows notes that public, or common ownership, as well as private, can justify its existence. In connection with this it is recalled that public authorities have to prevent the abuse of private property to the public detriment; this links up with the statement already dealt with above (art. 69) on the social aspect which property "also" possesses.

The sixth paragraph (Abbott, §§ 6–8), almost equal in length to the five which precede it, is, from the point of view of its practical political importance, the most significant, not only of these articles and of all that is said on the question of property or of this whole chapter, but even of the whole Pastoral Constitution. It deals with latifundia.

In a number of countries, the greater part of the arable land is in the hands of a numerically extremely small but powerful upper class which does not cultivate the land as it could be cultivated and as it urgently needs to be if the population is to be fed. Great expanses are used extensively in a way which is practically equivalent to allowing them to lie fallow. When the owners lease their land to tenants, the farms are much too small and the terms of the leases are too harsh. If the owners farm some of the land themselves, their labourers are given quite inadequate conditions of work and wages. This is exploitation crying to heaven for vengeance. It is not, as in the 19th century liberal capitalism of Western Europe or, as at the present day in the countries of the Eastern bloc, exploitation in the service of an enforced drive for economic development; it is the result of thoughtlessness and irresponsibility supporting the inertia and luxury of an upper class. As long as conditions of penury and hopelessness prevail in the country, conditions in the few industrial centres cannot rise much above them. If the evil is not attacked at the root, by abolishing these latifundia completely and replacing them by a rational use of the land which will ensure sufficient food and a life worthy of human beings for the inhabitants of these countries, which are not lacking in the necessary natural resources, it is impossible to see how they can be prevented from succumbing to communism. Not least among them are Catholic countries whose population probably amounts to almost half the Catholics in the world, and in view of their rate of population growth, which is far above the average, they will constitute in the foreseeable future the majority of all Catholics. Consequently the Church is doubly involved and committed. A large part, which will soon be the majority, of its own children are suffering under these conditions and exposed to this danger. It is a social upper class almost exclusively composed of Catholic Christians which, with a few honourable exceptions, has profited by these abuses and opposes their abolition obstinately and uncomprehendingly. The liberal capitalism which in its time raged mainly in Protestant countries, has long since been tamed. The agrarian feudalism of these Catholic countries is the great scandal of the present time. The practical measures indicated by the Council are not particularly interesting. They offer nothing new, simply describing the necessary conditions if success is to be attained in any agrarian reform, and if the failures which have occurred in agrarian revolutions and in ill-considered agrarian reforms are to be avoided. The Council's merit does not consist in the wise balance of these proposals, but in the courage it shows in addressing these extremely urgent demands for social reform to those concerned, i.e. the powerful Catholic upper class on which the Church of these countries knows it is in many respects dependent, economically, socially, politically. The bishops of some of these countries have already taken courageous steps in the direction of reform. Now the bishops of the whole world assembled in the Council have made that demand their own. This gives it incomparably greater impact. Whether this will be sufficient or whether only the brutal violence of a revolutionary upheaval will succeed in bringing a change, will be of decisive importance, not only for the destinies of these countries and of the Catholic Church there, but also for the destinies of the world and, as a consequence, of the Church everywhere. The Council has played its part.

Article 72. This brief final article deals with the connection between economic life and Christ's kingdom. The first sentence goes no further than what John XXIII had already said. Christians should not have a bad conscience if they are active in economic life and contribute to economic progress. On the contrary, they should be convinced that if it is guided by justice and love, such activity contributes to the well-being of their fellows and to the maintenance of world peace. Furthermore, Christians should not only take part, they should be outstanding by their good example. They should acquire the requisite knowledge and experience, arrange their various secular activities rightly, in faithfulness to Christ and his gospel, so that their whole life ("vita tam individualis quam socialis") may be filled with the spirit of the Beatitudes, especially poverty.

It is not entirely easy to decide what the Pastoral Constitution intends by "vita individualis et socialis". The French text "l'esprit des Béatitudes doit inspirer leur vie personelle aussi bien que collective" distinguished between the life of the individual and that of the community. The actions which are attributed to society as such are to be pervaded by the ethos of the Sermon on the Mount. It seems doubtful whether the Latin "vita socialis" is intended to mean this. "Vita individualis" = the extremely personal interior life, in other words, the Christian in his relation to God and to himself. "Vita socialis" = everything which goes beyond the domain of personal interior life and extends in any way perceptibly and with perceptible effects into the outside world and therefore into society, which for man is an outside world.

The spirit of the Beatitudes presents no difficulty of interpretation. It is quite understandable that special prominence is given to the beatitude of poverty,[20] because the Christian engaged in the economic domain is particularly exposed to the danger of setting his heart on material things and material success. Consequently he has to take special care to avoid this. He has to strive to possess and use temporal goods as though he did not possess and use them (1 Cor 7:30; 2 Cor 6:10). As, however, the Council endeavoured to deal with the theology of poverty in another passage, we may see a reference to that endeavour in the mention of this particular beatitude at this point. If all the scattered references of the Council on the theme of

---

[20] This addition is lacking in the French source. This fact also supports the contention that "vita socialis" in the Latin text does not mean the same as the "vie collective" of the French source. Can a collectivity really exercise poverty of spirit?

poverty were collected, it would perhaps be possible to draw from them a richer and deeper meaning.

A final, hard nut to crack is presented by the brief concluding paragraph, but only in its Latin version. A glance at the French source document explains it: "Quiconque, à l'exemple du Christ, cherche d'abord le Royaume de Dieu, y trouvera un amour plus fort et plus pur pour aider ses frères et pour accomplir ainsi une œuvre de justice, sous l'impulsion de l'amour." The Latin translator rendered the first "amour" by "amor", the second by "caritas". Consequently the reader looks for some difference between them, such as a crescendo perhaps from moral virtue to the theological virtue of charity. This is mistaken, however; the meaning is the same each time. The Latinist and, after him, the French translation from the Latin, dropped the "ainsi", thus creating the misleading impression that two things are involved, firstly help for the brethren, and secondly the *opus iustitiae*, which must be brought to completion and perfection ("perficiendum"). What is meant, however, is that help for the brethren is itself a work of justice inspired by love. In scholastic terms, the content of the sentence is, therefore, that with those who as true followers of Christ seek first the kingdom of God, the socio-economic activity which benefits all their fellow-men (brethren) is at the same time an *actus elicitus virtutis iustitiae* and an *actus imperatus virtutis caritatis*.

The brevity of this article testifies that it is not easy to outline and enrich a *theology* of economics.

An all-round appreciation of this Chapter III of Part II would require it to be placed in the context of the whole Pastoral Constitution and would have to bring in all that is said in a different connection in other passages (e.g. arts. 6, 8, 9, 52, 56, 57, 60, 73, 75, 83, 85 ff., 88), but which is also important for the economic domain dealt with here.

The Life of the Political Community

History of the Text by Herbert Vorgrimler
Commentary by Oswald von Nell-Breuning

History of the Text. The various *adnexa* to the schema of this Constitution have been dealt with by C. Moeller in his introduction to this commentary. No appendix on political questions was envisaged at first. At the plenary session of the Mixed Commission in June 1964, however, B. Häring, C.S.S.R. urged that an *adnexum* should be drawn up on political life.[1] The new draft, produced on the initiative of P. Haubtmann for the meeting in Ariccia from 31 January to 6 February 1965, provided in Part II for a Chapter V on political and international life.[2] The text of this chapter, entitled "De vita politica", was composed by S. Quadri, J. E. Coffey, S.J., and J. Ruiz Giménez Cortés, and its Latin version was distributed in Rome on 8 February 1965.[3] A separate subcommission under Mgr. László, Bishop of Eisenstadt, was then appointed. After the full meeting of the Mixed Commission in Rome from 29 March to 7 April 1965, Chapter IV of Part II, as it now was, under the title of "The life of the political community", was revised, given general approval by the Co-ordinating Commission on 11 May after Cardinal Suenens's *relatio,* and accepted as a whole by a conciliar vote on 23 September. Bishop Hengsbach reported on Part II of the schema on 29 September.[4] In the debate there were only four speeches.[5] To revise the chapter a new subcommission was set up under Bishop László: Henríquez, Quadri, A. Guglielmi (secretary), Leethan, Ruiz Giménez and Veronese (the two latter were laymen).[6] The new version was distributed to the Council fathers on 12 November, and on 15 November a fascicule with a *relatio* by Bishop Hengsbach on Part II of the schema. It is worthy of note that the revision could profit by the debate on religious freedom.[7] The conciliar vote on this chapter on 17 November produced the following results:

[1] Tucci, *op. cit.,* p. 90, n. 79.   [2] *Ibid.,* pp. 86 f.   [3] *Ibid.,* p. 90, n. 79, 80.   [4] *Ibid.,* p. 106 f.
[5] A summary is given in *Herder Korrespondenz* 19 (1965), p. 673.
[6] Tucci, *op. cit.,* p. 110, n. 103.   [7] *Ibid.,* p. 119.

	Votes	Yes	No	Yes with reservations	Invalid
Articles 77–78	2261	2188	70	—	3
79–80	2217	2145	66	—	6
Chapter IV as a whole	2241	1970	54	210	7

The *modi* were dealt with from 22 to 27 November. A *modus* from "higher authority" was rejected;[8] it had asked for the addition of "ubi de iure sunt" to the passage on the range of duties of political parties. The presentation and report on the *modi* were in the hands of Bishop László and A. Guglielmi.[9] The result of the vote on 4 December on what were henceforward Articles 73–76 was: Votes 2214; Yes 2086; No 121; Invalid 7.

Commentary. The last two main sections of Part II of the Pastoral Constitution, Chapter IV, "De vita communitatis politicae", and Chapter V, "De pace fovenda et de communitate gentium promovenda", concern the political domain. Since Chapter V obviously deals with international relations and with supra-national life, it seems probable that "communitas politica" in the title of Chapter IV means the State. For even at the present time States regard themselves as political structures in the highest and strictest sense of the term, and their activities as identical with politics as such. Anyone who, with *Pacem in Terris*,[1] has abandoned this conception as out of date today, and who regards the individual States as elements in the totality of mankind, will regard this interpretation of "communitas politica" as a lamentably retrograde step, or perhaps it would be better to say, as a probably unavoidable concession to the existing or at least still influential state of affairs. There can be no doubt, however, that the conciliar text understands "communitas politica" in this traditional, not to say "classical" sense. That is also clear from the fact that the terms "communitas politica" and "communitas civilis" (and in one passage "res publica" [art. 73] and in another, "civitas terrena" [art. 76]) are used interchangeably, and those who belong to these structures are called "cives", citizens. Consequently "auctoritas publica" must mean the State authority. Of course the Council has no intention of attributing to the individual States either internally or externally that god-like sovereignty which the nation-States arrogated to themselves before the First World War. Nor are they spoken of any more as "societates perfectae et completae", i.e., perfect and complete corporate structures satisfying all men's temporal needs. Nevertheless, echoes of this definition (which ulti-

[8] *Ibid.*, p. 128, n. 122.   [9] *Ibid.*, p. 126, n. 119.
[1] It is remarkable how seldom *Pacem in Terris* is quoted in *Gaudium et Spes*, particularly in this part: twice in Chapter IV (art. 70, n. 5 and 6), three times in Chapter V on war and peace (art. 80, n. 1 and 2; art. 82, n. 3), and not at all in Chapter V, 2.

mately derives from Aristotle) can still be heard (especially in Article 74, § 1). In fact the Church still regards the individual State as its partner, and consequently the Pastoral Constitution discusses the Church's attitude and relations with it (art. 76), whereas the Church is satisfied, at least at first, with an "active presence" in the "communitas internationalis" (art. 89).

The *vita publica*, public life, of which this chapter speaks, does not, therefore, extend beyond the plane of the individual States, the actual or potential members of UNO. The lower dividing line is not so clear. Is there any "public life" below the level of the national State, for instance in the sense of *Quadragesimo Anno*, which recognizes local authorities and professional corporations or guilds as having a juridically public character? Or is everything which lies below the plane of the State private in character, so that to the extent that it fulfils public functions, it receives its authority by delegation from the State? Is all so-called self-government in reality State-delegated administration, not fundamentally independent but a sphere of action delegated by the State?

If I am not mistaken, the conciliar text does not necessarily exclude genuine public life below the level of the State, but it does not take it into consideration at all. The authors of the text quite obviously live and move consciously or unconsciously in the atmosphere of Roman jurisprudence. The text is quite untouched by Germanic juridical thought, which, after all, is not entirely alien to canon law. Germanic jurisprudence did not place *ius publicum* and *ius privatum* in contradictory, but in contrary opposition, and recognized no sharp division between them. And the text is very far indeed from English and American ideas of law, to which the *ius publicum — ius privatum* antithesis is quite foreign. In fact, that antithesis envisages the relation between community and State in precisely the opposite way to the way we do.

It is a pity that the much-talked-of pluralism is not much in evidence at this point. On the other hand it should not be forgotten that the Council was very conscious that it was not uttering prophecy, but trying to produce a pastoral constitution which, in order to influence actual practice, has to adapt itself to the current mode of thought and speech. This does not mean it has to make a doctrinal decision or go back on progress already made on the highest level, or bar the door to further progress. The Pastoral Constitution does not speak the specialized technical language of constitutional law, but the language which our politicians and also our pastors are accustomed to hear and speak. It is the most appropriate language in which to address them in order to be understood.

Be that as it may, "communitas politica" in the heading of Chapter IV means the State as it still, rightly or wrongly, exists today. "Vita politica" or "publica" or "civilis" means political life in the sense of the activity of the State, and politics in the sense of the life of citizens as citizens.

Article 73. *Modern politics.* 1. The starting-point and basis of what the article has to say is the observation that cultural, economic and social development has resulted in a change in the structure of the State, with far-ranging effects on political life. Nowadays all citizens enjoy civic freedoms and exercise of the rights and duties which they imply and all share in what is called the common good. And the legal relationships of citizens among themselves and to the State authorities have changed. It is clear that the text acknowledges all this with satisfaction.

2. The keener awareness of human dignity — a concept of particular importance to the Council — impels men to create constitutional conditions which will safeguard personal rights and freedoms. As examples, the right of assembly, of association, of free expression of opinion and of religious profession are mentioned. Only if personal rights are adequately protected can the citizens as individuals or in groups take an active part in the life and government of the State. "Groups" probably means associations ranging from the political debating society to the political party, but organization representing particular interests cannot be excluded. This "actuose participare in rei publicae moderamine" is obviously regarded by the Council as just as desirable and worthy of encouragement as the "omnium actuosa participatio in inceptorum curatione", the "active participation of everyone" in decision-making and the running of economic enterprises (art. 68).

3. The cultural, economic and social progress already mentioned in the first paragraph awakens in wide circles a demand for greater influence in political life. The following are obviously regarded as particularly satisfactory and praiseworthy. a) Efforts to protect national minorities without minimizing the duties of the latter towards the whole. b) Growing tolerance towards those who think and believe differently. c) Increasing co-operation which results in all members of a State, not just a few as in former times, being actually able to enjoy their personal rights. It is strange that neither here nor in later passages which speak of the participation of all in political life (Article 75 in particular) is any mention made of women. The Pastoral Constitution lags behind *Pacem in Terris,* which congratulated Christian nations on being in advance of non-Christian peoples in their recognition of the human dignity of women and their equality of rights. *Pacem in Terris* also expressly advocated equal political rights for women on the ground of their human dignity ("in civitate iura et officia humana persona digna", art. 41).

4. Although the Council sought to avoid condemnations, here it could not avoid expressly condemning political systems — without naming them — which infringe civil and religious liberties, pervert the course of justice as a means of political coercion and, instead of promoting the common good, serve the private advantage of those who hold power.

5. As the best means of humanizing political life, the Council recommends

the cultivation of an inner sense of justice, benevolence and service of the common good, and the promotion of correct views of the nature and function of the political community. The Council turns immediately to this task.

Article 74. *Nature and goal of politics.* 1. The commentary on *Gaudium et Spes* by Action Populaire pertinently remarks that the Council refers here to Aristotle's definition of the State. The insufficiency of small social units (among which Aristotle includes the local or village community) causes people to join together in a more comprehensive association, the *communitas politica.* This public community exists for the sake of the common good which constitutes its purpose and justification. What is this common good? The term is used in two senses, as a value in itself and as a means to an end. As a value in itself (as in Article 63), it is a comprehensive term for all the values which belong to fully-developed humanity, the full exercise and realization of all the potentialities and faculties inherent in man in society; as a relative value and means to an end, it is the sum of all the general presuppositions or conditions which the individual cannot provide for himself and which must be already available for him if he is to develop in a fully human way, at all, or without too much difficulty. When ecclesiastical pronouncements give a definition of the common good, it usually concerns this second and subordinate sense. This is the case here with reference to John XXIII (*Mater et Magistra,* art. 65). On the other hand, if mention is simply made of the common good, the term primarily denotes or implies the value in itself. The common good in the secondary and instrumental sense is, of course, only of interest for the sake of the common good itself. Furthermore, in general usage and not only in that of official Church pronouncements, the common good usually means exclusively or principally the common good of political society, the State. In fact, however, every social group has its own common good. It was the great merit of John XXIII in *Mater et Magistra* and once again in *Pacem in Terris* to have taken us beyond Aristotle's range of vision and emphasized the common good of the whole of humanity. This shifts the common good of the State from its position as the end and completion of human perfection to that of a mere stage in an ascent on many levels. Practical politics, however, is still guided by the true or supposed common good of the individual State. Consequently the Council too speaks of the common good in that sense. It regards the "communitas internationalis" as an edifice which has still to be constructed; for the moment, therefore, its common good is only an ideal, not a reality. If I am not mistaken, the whole section of Chapter V, "De communitate internationali aedificanda", does not once refer at any point to its common good.[2]

---

[2] In an earlier passage, Part I, Chapter II: "De hominum communitate" (art. 26), the text had referred to the "bonum totius familiae humanae" and had cited the two encyclicals of John XXIII.

2. Because people may legitimately have different opinions, the political community needs an authoritative power to ensure unified co-operation with a view to the common good; it must not do this "mechanically or despotically", but as a moral authority which is addressed to the free but conscientious will.

3. In complete accordance with the traditional line and appealing to Romans 13:1–5, the Council describes the *communitas politica* as grounded in human nature and therefore as belonging to the divine order of the world. The State is a "natural society" and to that extent comparable with the family. Precisely at this point it is important not to limit what is said to the one plane of the State, but to keep it open for all the various social structures in addition to the family which in the course of human history have proved indispensable to the full development of the capacities inherent in man's nature. Consequently not only the form of government and the choice of persons to rule the State, but also the building up of the whole community of mankind on all its levels and with all its structures, is a binding obligation imposed on man by the Creator, though the way in which he fulfils it is left to his own free invention and disposition.

4. As a further consequence, the Council indicates that public authority has to serve the realization of the common good while remaining within the limits of the moral order and preserving the juridical order which exists or which is being created; a phrase inserted in passing describes this as "dynamically conceived". Perhaps we should regard this as an allusion to the dynamism of present-day economy which received such high praise in Chapter III because it leads to increasing prosperity and permits a richer development of cultural life. At all events reactionary tendencies and nostalgia for the past receive no quarter from the Council. Within the limits indicated, the citizens owe obedience. At the same time the responsibility, worth and dignity of those who govern are made clear.

5. But what if the public authority exceeds the limits of its competence, and unjustly oppresses its subjects? Even then the obligation remains of doing everything which the common good demands; on the other hand, the citizens have the right to defend their own rights and those of their fellow-citizens. There is therefore a *right* of resistance; the Council does not say whether there is also a *duty* of resistance. But to the question what measures are justified by the right of resistance, whether only passive or also active resistance can be offered, for example, we receive merely the very general indication "within the limits of natural law and the gospel". The expression "delineat" used by the Council, is one which suggests well-defined limits, a blue-print, so to speak, in which these limits are marked clearly and precisely and from which they need only to be read off. But we are not issued with such a blue-print, and so we find ourselves thrown back on what "probati auctores" have to say, but which they usually prefer cautiously

to keep to themselves. Even the Council was extremely loath to grasp this nettle.

6. The final paragraph of this article recalls once again that the possible structures which may be chosen are of many kinds, but that the only ones which have a right to exist are those which are likely to promote genuine civilization, morality, love of peace and general well-being "to the advantage of the whole human family".

Article 75. *Political participation.* 1. When Pius XII in his Christmas message in 1944[3] praised the advantages of democracy, people tended to regard this merely as reflecting the world situation created by the imminent victory of the democratic powers. In fact, the official Church had long shown great reserve in regard to democracy. It is sufficient to read Leo XIII's encyclicals on the State to realize that the Pope is not addressing the people (except to exhort them to obedience) but the princes, whom Leo XIII in a certain sense treats as his equals. On the other hand, Catholic theologians, in particular the great Spanish scholastics (Vitoria, Suárez, etc.) as early as the 16th century, maintained the principle of the sovereignty of the people, if properly understood. In their time, however, there was no universal schooling and no mass-media, and in these circumstances the whole population was not yet in a position to exercise popular sovereignty itself but had to content itself with being represented by the social upper class, "people of rank". This ancient and venerable doctrine of the sovereignty of the people was suspected for a time of being incompatible with Leo XIII's doctrine of the State, and was not extolled as the Church's official teaching on the State even by Pius XII in his famous address to the Roman Rota on 2 October 1945,[4] though he showed himself very well-disposed towards it, which at all events was a big step forward. Until then, the tendency was to assimilate the structure of the secular State authority as closely as possible to the divinely-appointed hierarchical structure of the Church, thus exhibiting State and Church as closely akin in social structure, and mutually complementary. Pius XII, on the contrary, pointed out that the doctrine of sovereignty of the people has the particular merit of bringing out clearly the fundamentally different structure of authority in State and Church. Authority in the State flows, so to speak, from below upwards; issuing from the people, it extends to the government as the highest *organ* of the State. In the Church, it flows from above downwards, from Jesus Christ to his visible representative, the Pope, who does not receive his office and authority from the members of the Church but simply and solely from Christ whose vicar on earth he is. This contrasted structure of authority makes the essential dif-

---

[3] A. F. Utz and J. F. Groner, eds., *Aufbau und Entfaltung des gesellschaftlichen Lebens. Soziale Summe Pius' XII.* (1954), 3467 ff.

[4] *Ibid.*, 2702, especially 2715.

ference between Church and State particularly clear. *Gaudium et Spes* does not go as far as formerly in endorsing the doctrine of the sovereignty of the people or, to put it in another way, the principle of the intrinsically democratic structure of the State. But it tacitly assumes that principle as a starting-point which it takes for granted as a matter of course. It says that it is simply in accordance with human nature to create juridical and political structures which offer all citizens the real possibility of sharing more fully and actively, without discrimination or hindrance, in establishing and developing the constitution, in dealing with government affairs, in the various branches of administration, etc., and not least in choosing office-holders. Shortly before (art. 74), the Council had observed that the State and its authority are grounded in human nature. This indicates the weight that should be attached to this praise of the democratic form of State as corresponding fully to human nature ("plene congruit"). Certainly the Council is clear that the establishment of democracy (like that of partnership in industry [art. 68]) demands conditions which are not fulfilled everywhere and have therefore first to be created. The changes mentioned at the very beginning of the chapter (art. 73) are far from having advanced to the same extent everywhere. Consequently the Council certainly does not want to impose, with impetuous zeal, juridical and political structures on peoples among whom the necessary conditions for their functioning have yet to be created. Equally certainly, however, it is the mind of the Council that an all-out serious effort must be made to create these conditions. A small sentence recalls that the civil rights of citizens imply civil duties, and that the vote has to be used to serve the common good. In an even shorter sentence, the Council expresses its recognition of politicians, i.e. those who place themselves professionally at the service of the common good and so shoulder a burden which is sometimes not at all a light one; it is clearly not the view of the Council that politics necessarily corrupts.

2. A democratic community needs a number of institutions, in the first place a clear and positive system of law. It is a civic duty to meet all the obligations, whether of personal service or material contribution, imposed for the sake of the common good. Particular examples such as military service, service in labour corps, duty to pay taxes, are not gone into; a book would not be sufficient to deal with all the questions arising. The public authority is warned not to monopolize everything, but to leave room for free initiative. The citizens — not merely individuals but also their associations — are admonished not to leave all the burdens to the State or to expect everything to be provided by the State, but to fend for themselves to the best of their ability.

3. The next section is concerned with the fact already observed by Pius XI in *Quadragesimo Anno* (art. 79) that modern conditions make State intervention increasingly necessary. In addition there is the phenomenon which

Mater et Magistra (arts. 59–67) deals with extensively under the term "socialization", which is familiar enough in French now but less well-known in English. One Council father wanted the expression avoided; he considered that only a Frenchman could grasp all the shades of meaning that the French manage to pack into this word. There is no doubt something in this, but the Council has in fact used the French term. In the sociological sense (in psychology the word has a different meaning) "socialization" essentially means what we usually describe as the network of social relationships and their perpetual multiplication and complication, with the consequent ever-increasing involvement of human beings in this network. Socialization has advanced to a different extent in different parts of the world, but everywhere it is inescapable. It has its advantages but also its dangers; on balance, *Mater et Magistra* judges it favourably, but the Council does not express an opinion; it is, however, obviously concerned about possible dangers. If a state of exceptional emergency requires civil freedoms to be restricted, the restrictions must be removed as soon as they can be dispensed with. Degeneration of the power of the State into totalitarian and other forms injurious to the rights of individual citizens or their organizations is inhuman and therefore contradicts the aim expressed at the end of Article 73, of giving public life a truly human character. This also makes it clear which forms of the State the earlier, anonymous condemnation (art. 43) actually applies to.

4. Citizens in general are recommended to cultivate "pietas erga patriam", that is, the virtue by which we owe love, reverence and obedience to God, our parents and our native country; this *pietas erga patriam* is not a narrow-minded patriotism, but generously takes into account the well-being of the whole human family.

5. The Council reminds all Christians in public life that they have a special duty to give an example of conscientious devotion to the common good. They can thus show how authority and freedom, initiative and solidarity, efficient uniformity and beneficial diversity are complementary. As regards the management of earthly affairs, in other words throughout the realm of practical politics, different and even opposed opinions can legitimately exist, for example in the programmes of different political parties; differing opinions and those who hold them should be treated with respect. This admonition is specifically addressed by the Council to Christians, though it is framed in general terms. The commentary of the French Action Populaire gives a not very flattering, but convincing, reason for this. Catholics in particular, it says, have often been guilty of political intolerance, and have tried to impose monolithic unanimity by force. This remark no doubt applies to France, but not only to France. The Council impresses on political parties the duty of fostering what they honestly believe to be necessary for the common good. But on no account may they or anyone prefer sectional interests to the common good.

6. The last paragraph calls for training in political activity which is urgently necessary for all, but especially for young people. In addition, those who are fitted for it, who already possess the necessary aptitude or can acquire it, are invited to prepare themselves for politics as a profession and to practise it unselfishly and honestly. The profession of politics is described as difficult but honourable (eminent, distinguished). The praise already given to politicians at the beginning of the article is thus echoed at the end. Similarly *Gaudium et Spes* here returns to the fight against tyrannical oppression, whether exercised by a single tyrant or a political party. The politician is to oppose it with honesty and shrewdness. Here at any rate one might think there is a reference to a duty of resistance (cf. art. 74), but here again we find no further indications how far the honest statesman or citizen can take his resistance. The text turns immediately to the positive side and demands sincere and well-balanced devotion to the welfare of all, based on two virtues which the Council regards as vital to political life: "caritas et fortitudo politica". *Fortitudo politica:* It is self-evident that politics demands courage and endurance, so that it obviously makes good sense to speak of "political courage". But "caritas politica"? We quite often speak of "social justice", but "social love" is unusual. Outside official ecclesiastical documents such as *Quadragesimo Anno* which discusses it probably for the first time (art. 88, 126, 137) and *Mater et Magistra* (art. 39), it is scarcely ever met with. And yet the life of human society has to be pervaded by charity, which must at least contribute to shape it. But the political domain? If we understand this in Carl Schmitt's sense as the domain of the friend-foe relationship, then genuinely unselfish love has no place in it, only the will to self-assertion and the will to destroy the adversary. The Council has a different conception of politics and the politician. The ideal politician does not aim at favouring individuals or some group with which he has close ties and whose interests are linked with his; he is concerned with the good of the whole. Certainly this whole is primarily his own political community, his nation and country, but the perspective is also that of the whole human family. Understood in this way, his work flows from a specific and benevolent intention which can certainly be called "caritas politica".

Article 76. *Politics and the Church.* 1. We are accustomed to the phrase Church and State, but here we must read State and Church, because the whole chapter deals with the State, and at this point its relation to the Church is examined. When Leo XIII dealt with the relation between the two, he assumed that the State was Christian or, more precisely, a Catholic denominational State. What variations ensue if the State does not correspond to this conception, one has to work out on one's own responsibility; Leo XIII did not discuss this situation which, ideally, should not exist, nor the consequences to be drawn from it. His successors also remained, in all essentials true to that line, Pius XII, for example, in his teaching on tolerance: As such and by rights, the State professes the Catholic faith as the State religion and therefore promotes and supports the Catholic Church and defends it against the incursion of other religious denominations and, of course, of non-religious ideologies; where this condition is unfortunately not realized, it may be appropriate for the sake of the common good for the State to permit non-Catholic religious societies and non-religious ideological associations on its territory and to grant them protection. The Council starts from a fundamentally different assumption. It accepts the ideologically pluralistic society not as the ideal case but as normal in present-day conditions. The first statement that it makes about the relation between Church and State therefore applies chiefly, though not solely, to pluralistic society. The Council considers it particularly important in this case for the relation between State and Church — perhaps it would even be better to speak of the relation of the State *to* the Church — to be rightly understood, and for a clear distinction to be drawn between what the members of the Church, as individuals or in association, do or do not do under the inspiration of their own Christian conscience, and the enterprises they undertake in the name of the Church and in union with their ecclesiastical pastors. One might detect here an echo of the well-known though by no means universally recognized distinction between the action of Catholics and Catholic Action. This, however, is probably mistaken. At least one cannot say that the Council has sanctioned this disputed distinction, and still less that it makes use of it here. On the contrary, the dividing line does not seem to fall in precisely the same place. The aim here in fact is to make clear to the ideologically pluralistic State what the Church as such is responsible for. The State will then know what it can hold the Church responsible for and what not. For the Catholic denominational State, which recognizes the Church for what it is and for what it understands itself to be, there is no difficulty in classifying and evaluating the actions of its citizens who take their bearings from Catholic doctrine on faith and morals, and the actions and measures which are those of the Church as such. The ideologically pluralistic State, however, which cannot share the Church's view of itself, has difficulties in doing this. In order to spare it mistakes, it should be given a clear indication when it is dealing with the Church as such and when it is a case of the action of Catholic citizens undertaken on their own responsibility. Of course, the spheres of responsibility cannot be traced with perfect distinctness, and the Church is, at least indirectly, responsible for what Catholics do "christiana conscientia ducti". For the Church has formed that conscience, provided it with the criteria for its decisions or has failed to offer adequate and suitable assistance in forming it. Vatican II itself, of course, shows the vast leeway that had to be made up precisely in questions of political ethics.

The following paragraphs are concerned to draw a clear distinction between Church and State and also with their nature, function and means of action. A few expressions in *Mater et Magistra,* especially in the introduction (arts. 1–4), were liable to give the misleading impression that that encyclical wanted to abolish or blur the traditional clear distinction between Church and State, between the Church's supernatural goal, man's eternal salvation, and the function of the State which is concerned with earthly welfare. It also seemed to make men's earthly well-being a function of the Church.[5] *Gaudium et Spes* restores complete clarity if any confusion was in fact caused by the defective verbal expression of *Mater et Magistra* and the excessive zeal with which John XXIII in the kindness of his heart presented his dear farmers, as a Swiss author, J. Bless, so nicely puts it, with a whole bouquet of technical advice on agricultural policy.

2. The function and competence of the Church are completely different from those of the State ("nullo modo confunditur"). But the Church has no elective affinity with any political system. (It has already been said earlier [arts. 74, 75] that it has to reject certain political systems because of their inhumanity.) It is difficult to interpret the statement that the Church is, and understands itself to be, the sign and safeguard of the transcendence of the human person. Since it is concerned with the relation of Church and State, this statement must mean that the Church makes it plain (tangible, evident) that man belongs to the State *totus* (as a whole), but *non totaliter* (not wholly and in every respect); at the same time it offers the citizen the guarantee that at all events the Church, as an institution outside and above the State, takes seriously, recognizes and defends his transcendence, not only of the particular State of which he is citizen, but of the plane of the State as such and earthly society generally.

3. Leo XIII had affirmed that Church and State are sovereign, each in its own sphere ("utraque in suo genere maxima" *[Immortale Dei]*). It is true of course that individual States still endeavour to maintain their sovereignty, and in present-day international politics they still act as though they were sovereign and are treated as sovereign, but this sovereignty is increasingly

---

[5] What was particularly misleading, was the expression "ante omnia" (in Italian: "abbia innanzitutto il compito" [*Mater et Magistra*, art. 3]). Taken literally, this clearly attributed to the Church a main function, which logically implies that it also has a secondary function. The text, however, ignores this logical consequence. Side by side with what, according to the authentic Latin text is "ante omnia" the Church's function ("Ecclesiae est"), or, according to the Italian text, what the Church *has* as its main function, it does not place what is incumbent on the Church as ex supposito its additional secondary function; it speaks of what the Church as a matter of fact is concerned about ("tamen sollicita est"; "essa è tuttavia sollecita"). And it would be surprising if *Mater et Magistra* had wanted to depart from tradition, especially after Leo XIII had introduced his encyclical *Immortale Dei* with the statement that what the Church has done for men's earthly well-being is so great that it could not be greater if it had been founded for that express purpose. Moreover, Pius XI in *Quadragesimo Anno* (arts. 41 ff.) had drawn the limits of the Church's competence with extreme precision.

eroded; it has been called in question. To repeat Leo XIII's formula, especially after *Pacem in Terris*, would be an anachronism. Consequently the Council uses a more cautious formula and simply says that State and Church are mutually independent and autonomous each in its own sphere ("in proprio campo").

Since State and Church deal with the same human beings, harmonious cooperation in accordance with the particular circumstances will contribute to the effectiveness of each. The expression "attentis locorum temporumque adiunctis" leaves open the whole range of possibilities, especially the systems of friendly and benevolent separation of Church and State preferred and advocated by Americans from experience of the United States. This is no doubt the most obvious and perhaps the only system that is logically workable in relation to the pluralist State. The next sentences explain how cooperation is possible and meaningful, despite the fundamental difference between State and Church. One and the same human being has an earthly and historical existence and an eternal vocation. By its preaching and the good example of Christians — would to God it were always so! — the Church protects and promotes political freedom and civic responsibility.

4. A separate paragraph serves to make it clear that the apostles, their successors (that is, the bishops) and the latters' collaborators (priests are principally meant) do not base their apostolic activity on secular power but depend on God, who often reveals the power of the gospel through the weakness of those who preach it. Service of the Word of God must use the ways and means proper to the gospel. In the main ("in pluribus") these differ from those of the State; this indicates that the Church's preaching will in fact use some of the means which the State uses for its purposes, for example in present-day conditions, the mass media which modern technology has made available.

5. This idea is pursued more deeply in the next section. Despite their essential difference, there is a close connection between this world and the next; consequently the Church also needs material means to fulfil its function. But here a very definite turning-point is passed, not so much in doctrine as in practice. The Council proclaims that the Church does not put its trust in privileges granted by the State; on the contrary, to the extent that it enjoys such privileges, it intends to examine them, and if it must admit that the acceptance of such privileges detracts from its credibility, it will renounce them and endeavour to reach a settlement of its relations with the State more appropriate to present circumstances. This is a declaration of intent which with full justification can be ranked with the Council's pronouncement on the latifundia question (art. 71), which has rightly been praised as the culmination of the chapter on economic life (see above). If that pronouncement is a challenge to the powerful and rich upper class of Catholic countries, this declaration is a challenge to the Church itself. There

is one minimum requirement which the Church must maintain; it must be free, not only to proclaim the truths of revelation and its own social doctrine, but also to pass moral judgment on political affairs, at least when this seems necessary for the defence of human rights or the salvation of souls. Today the Church knows what harm was done by its close links with the upper classes of society and particularly with the State (alliance of Throne and Altar) to its credibility in the eyes of the broad masses of the population, the less fortunate, the oppressed and the exploited. Much too late, only after the Church had long lost the greater part of the workers, has this realization prevailed; everything will depend now on translating it into practice. The Council has drawn a cheque; it must be honoured.

6. It might be regretted that the Pastoral Constitution did not conclude this chapter with the proclamation of this change of attitude, one might almost say, this change of front. Clearly, however, a transition was wanted to link up with the following chapter, the first part of which concerns the question of peace. Consequently a passage of *Lumen Gentium* is quoted to recall that, by promoting all that is true, good and beautiful in human society and raising it to a higher plane, the Church consolidates peace among men to the glory of God.[6]

[6] The Latin text uses the same phrase, "Ecclesia cuius est", as *Mater et Magistra* (art. 3). From the purely grammatical point of view, this could be understood, in both cases, as a statement about the function and purpose for which the Church exists. This would then formally ascribe a dual function to the Church, firstly that of promoting all that is true, good and beautiful, and secondly that of raising it from the natural order to which it radically belongs, into the supernatural order of salvation. If that were so, to preserve the meaning, the first of these would have to be interpreted as a subordinate or auxiliary function, i.e. in order to raise these values into the order of salvation, the Church must first interest itself in them in general, more or less as Bishop Ketteler used to say that in order to make people good Christians, we must first make it possible for them to lead lives worthy of human beings. Such an interpretation, however, is completely alien to the relevant text of *Lumen Gentium* (art. 13); consequently, although linguistically possible and perhaps even the most obvious, this interpretation must in fact be excluded. It is noteworthy that the French translation renders "cuius est" by "à qui il appartient"; the "cuius est" thus denotes a "proprium" of the Church, not its function or goal. Cf. on this, Pius XI's remark quoted by the Council in Part II, Chapter II (n. 7, Abbott, n. 192): "Il ne faut jamais perdre de vue que l'objectif de l'Église est d'évangéliser et non de civiliser. Si elle civilise, c'est par l'évangélisation" (*Semaines Sociales de France* [1936], pp. 461 f.).

The Fostering of Peace and the Promotion of a Community of Nations

History of the Text by Willem J. Schuijt
Commentary by René Coste

History of the Text. The problems of peace and the international community were insufficiently represented in the two schemata distributed to the Council fathers at the beginning of the first session in 1962, under the titles "De ordine morali et sociali" and "De communitate gentium". These originated in the Theological Commission, which had approved the first of them, while the second had been composed by an eminent specialist, at the express wish of the Pope.[1] Neither seems to have attracted any particular attention.[2] The intellectual source of Schema 13 is rather to be found in the message broadcast by John XXIII on 11 September 1962. The Pope spoke first about the peace of the world and then about social justice. The Council showed its full agreement with this, for its first solemn act was to address a message to all men,[3] taking up again these two ideas. The draft of this text was composed by the eminent French theologian, M.-D. Chenu, O.P.

That message is a very moving one: "We carry in our hearts the hardships, the bodily and mental distress, the sorrows and hopes of all peoples entrusted to us. We are attentive to the problems which assail them." In regard to the problems of peace and war, the message says that, by the gospel and the hope bestowed by Christ, it wants to help a world which is "still far from the peace it desires, because of the threats arising from the very progress of science, marvellous though it be, but not always responsive to the higher law of morality". Unfortunately this message did not receive the attention it deserved, because the international situation was dominated at that moment by the world-wide anxieties aroused by the Cuba crisis, the first serious confrontation between two nuclear powers since the War.

---

[1] H. de Riedmatten, "Histoire de la Constitution pastorale", *L'Église dans le monde de ce temps* (1967).
[2] *Ibid.*
[3] *Osservatore Romano*, 22/23 October 1962.

On 4 December 1962 in Rome, Cardinal Suenens made conciliar history by appealing to the Church to open a dialogue with the world, observing that "the world is asking the Church some extremely serious questions and expects an answer to them".[4] This gave the signal to start. It was decided to prepare a text, and this was entrusted to a Mixed Commission composed of members of the Theological Commission and of the Commission for the Apostolate of the Laity, with the assistance of a few specialists on questions of war and peace, Frs. Dubarle and Lebret; Mgr. Pavan, one of the draftsmen of *Pacem in Terris* also collaborated. Fr. Lebret later observed, "That was obviously a bad start, for the Theological Commission was overtaxed with other very important schemas, and the Commission for the Apostolate of the Laity by definition was concerned with less far-reaching questions than the presence of the Church in the world."[5] During the preparation of this schema on "the presence of the Church in the world of today", the encyclical *Pacem in Terris* appeared on 11 April 1963; its main concern was the promotion of peace. The world-wide interest aroused by this encyclical was a fact which the fathers and above all those composing a new schema could not overlook. Since the encyclical was published during a Council, the peoples of the world had a right to expect that the Council was likewise going to follow the same path and give its views on the problems of international life and peace. Some raised the objection that the encyclical had already dealt with the essential questions which might be expected to figure in a conciliar text, but others answered that since these questions were of vital importance, the authority of the encyclical should be reinforced by the even greater authority of a conciliar pronouncement. Paul VI immediately emphasized his intention of continuing the work of his predecessor.

The version of Schema 13 drawn up after the Malines text had been rejected, contained an Article 24 dealing with "the promotion of solidarity in the family of nations" and an Article 25 on "the consolidation of peace". Five appendices were added. The fifth was headed "Community of the nations and peace" and was divided as follows: Introduction. 1. Signs of the times. 2. Christ, the prince of peace. A. Work for peace. 3. Universal brotherhood of nations. 4. Basis and purpose of the international community. 5. Promotion of the fundamental rights of the human person in the international community. 6. Fundamental rights of political communities in the international community. 7. Chief duty of the political communities in the international community. 8. Patriotism. 9. Co-operation between developed and underdeveloped territories. 10. International co-operation in the field of population growth. B. Maintenance of peace. 11. Essential conditions of

[4] Cf. H. de Riedmann, *op. cit.*
[5] L. J. Lebret, "La vie économique et sociale et la promotion de la communauté des nations", *L'Église dans le monde de ce temps* (1967).

peace. 12. Means of consolidating peace. 13. Mission of the Church in regard to the international community. 14. Active presence of the Church in the international community. 15. Christians' share in international institutions. Conclusion.

It is to be noted that the Commission had not had an opportunity of studying the five *adnexa* in this text submitted to the Council fathers.[6]

At the 105th general congregation on 20 October 1964, the schema appeared on the agenda and was presented by Cardinal F. Cento, who also spoke on behalf of Cardinal Ottaviani, president of the commission.

At the beginning, the debate seemed to be dominated by a more or less traditional conception of peace, regarded negatively as the absence of war. It was only in the final phase that a more positive and dynamic idea of peace and international society was achieved. Article 78 shows this clearly.

Our mother, the Church, said Cardinal Cento,[7] is aware that it cannot remain indifferent to the fear of an apocalyptic conflict. Have we in any way responded to the trust placed in us, do our proposals and solutions correspond to the magnitude of the needs... so that at the end of so many struggles a happy and stable balance finally rules among the nations? In conclusion he expressed the hope that this text would be a message of hope for a better future, in which with the help of God's goodness not the right of force but the force of right would prevail, not hate but love, not war but the lasting and long-desired peace of Christ in the realm of Christ.

Mgr. E. Guano of the Central Subcommission reported on the schema. In his remarkable speech the following section is of special importance: "Many people expect from this schema a ready-made answer to all problems. And in fact something must be said which can really serve as a signpost and correspond to what the world has a right to expect. Nevertheless, honesty and discretion recognize limits and know how to remain within those imposed by the very nature of things and by historical circumstances."

The presentation of the schema was followed by a debate which chiefly concerned problems of a general character. It must be noted, however, that Cardinal P. Léger (Montreal) asked for the laity to be heard in the conciliar aula, especially on problems of hunger, the family and peace.

On the other hand it is not without interest to mention Cardinal Ruffini's attack on the schema. He drew attention to features in it which seemed to indicate approval of situation ethics. "When it is said that the Church has not always a ready answer drawn from the application of valid doctrinal principles to the changing circumstances of life, this amounts to maintaining that the faithful must act on their own responsibility in accordance with the

---

[6] Cf. H. de Riedmatten, *op. cit.*, p. 74.
[7] For the summaries of the conciliar speeches, I have used the reports published in the *Katholiek Archief* (1962–67).

dictates of their conscience, guided by Christian prudence, the truth of the gospel and the moral doctrine of the Church." No doubt these words were inspired by the marriage question, but they could also apply to the problem of conscientious objection.

The debate on the whole schema was continued on 21 October 1964 (106th general congregation). Cardinal Suenens (Malines), the spiritual father of the schema, emphasized that the Church is and remains an important instrument for peace in the world, not only directly by its diplomatic activity (one immediately thinks of the diplomacy of the Vatican through the Secretariat of State), but also by its very nature. Its whole doctrine is concerned with bringing human beings together. By its ecumenical activity the Church collaborates in the promotion of peace, and similarly by its dialogue with all non-Christians. The Church is therefore a valuable instrument of peace for mankind, since it offers the basis of peace, namely Christ the prince of peace.

Mgr. D. Hurley of Durban discovered an inconsistency in the schema, which speaks of the legitimacy of defensive war and at the same time stigmatizes the use of nuclear weapons as illegitimate, without making it clear whether they may be used in a defensive war.

To the inquiry of the secretariat whether after this general debate the schema could be accepted as a basis for further discussion, 1579 out of 1876 fathers answered Yes, 296 No and there was one invalid vote.

Before the debate on Article 25, which did not in fact begin until 10 November 1964, Cardinal Feltin (Paris), honorary president of the international Catholic movement for peace "Pax Christi", anticipated the discussion of this article by expressing a few ideas on it after the debate on Article 20 on 20 October 1964. Man has a radical longing for peace. Public opinion hoped that the Council would follow the main lines and spirit of *Pacem in Terris*. People expected a condemnation of war, because of atomic terror, and in particular a renewed condemnation of ABC weapons (atomic, biological, chemical), the effects of which cannot be controlled. On the other hand it is not enough to talk about peace, it must be striven for. Peace is both a gift of God and a work of men. As a gift of God it is obtained by prayer, as a human work it can be promoted in three ways: 1. Disarmament: general, progressive and supervised. 2. Development: by working for the equilibrium of justice. Another name for peace today is development. This formula had been a favourite one of Mgr. Larraïn, who until his death was president of CELAM. It was taken up again by Paul VI in 1967 in his encyclical *Populorum progressio*. We shall return to it later.[8] 3. International institutions: Christians must support the United Nations and help to improve its organization. Peace must be brought into pastoral practice, for peace is the sub-

[8] See note 21.

stance of the Church's doctrine. Peace, patriotism and the universal common good must be preached. If this is not done, there is a risk of possessing a doctrine of peace but no practice of peace and no corresponding mentality. There can be an apostolate of peace, a dialogue of peace, provided that it is carried out in accordance with *Pacem in Terris* and *Ecclesiam suam*. Finally, the Cardinal advocated the creation of a commission of theologians and experts to follow closely the development of the questions treated in Schema 13.

The debates on Articles 24 and 25 of Chapter IV of Schema 13 on the Church in the World, started on 9 November 1964 at the 118th general congregation. Article 24 was entitled: "The promotion of solidarity in the family of nations", Article 25 "The consolidation of peace".

In regard to Article 24, Cardinal Rugambwa of Bukoba (Tanganyika) repeated the classical principle that the doctrinal basis of this solidarity is the fact that mankind constitutes one great family. That was God's will in his plan of creation and redemption. That is how the world today understands it. Economic and cultural relations between the nations lead to the conclusion that material possessions must be at the service of the whole human family and not merely in the service of private interests.

Cardinal Richaud (Bordeaux) spoke on behalf of 70 Council fathers and of Cardinal Silva Henríquez. He recalled the origin and activities of "Caritas Internationalis", of which he is president. The radiance of charity must be the root of international solidarity. He agreed with Cardinal Frings in his desire to see a secretariat established to educate Christians in personal responsibility in this domain, to train personel, to exchange information and experiences, to collaborate with other Churches and with international organizations. Mgr. Šeper (Zagreb) regarded the problem of political and social emigrants as the touchstone of international solidarity. Each country must recognize their rights. This problem had to be envisaged in the light of the common good of all nations.

The American Bishop F. Begin of Oakland tried to outline an economic system, *iure divino*, as a remedy against unjust distribution of possessions; this system would be based on the collection of tithes and first-fruits!

Much more interesting was the intervention of Fr. Mahon of Mill Hill. He observed that two years before Vatican I *Das Kapital* of Karl Marx had been published. Yet Vatican I had not had a word to say on social justice, or on the distress of the working classes. There was a real time-lag. What interest could the definition of papal infallibility have for hungry people? Vatican II had already been debating the internal affairs of the Church for two years and a half. Fortunately it was not passing over in silence the difficult problems of justice and international order. This was a great advance, for what was important for social classes in 1870 is important today for poor nations. Finally, Fr. Mahon strongly emphasized the need to pronounce clearly and concretely on this problem so that the nations would not be able to say: We asked for bread and received a schema.

Mgr. A. Ancel of Lyons began the speeches on Article 25: "The consolidation of peace". He pointed out a contradiction in the text. On the one hand it explicitly condemned war, especially nuclear war; on the other hand it recognized the legitimacy of defence against an unjust attack. But the right of defence would seem to include the right to manufacture nuclear weapons. This is the reason why, despite the general will to peace, no progress is made and the armaments race continues. The Council should help to abolish this contradiction, not by offering political and technical solutions, but by telling the world what, from the moral point of view, the only conditions for safeguarding peace really are. These can be expressed in two theses: In the present situation the common good requires all nations finally and completely to renounce the right to war, and consequently to everything needed for waging war; nations must only have the means necessary to guarantee internal order. Secondly, the international organizations should have armed forces at their command to prevent war. That would not diminish national sovereignty, but would put an end to imperialism or to fear of it. If the Council could create a public opinion in this sense, it would do great service to statesmen. The authority of the State had once put an end to war between towns; international authority must now put an end to wars between nations. Mgr. Guilhem of Laval (France) said that no moral principle could justify the use of scientific weapons, which he described as a crime against God and humanity. The Council should condemn such a massacre. They must extirpate the error that peace is bound up with military equilibrium and mutual fear of atomic weapons, whereas peace is founded primarily on mutual understanding and dialogue. It must be stressed that all men, not merely governments, can and should contribute to the renunciation of atomic weapons which swallow up a lot of money which could with benefit be used elsewhere.

Mgr. Ntuyahaga of Usambara (Burundi) emphasized the importance of charity as a basis for solidarity between nations. Cardinal B. Alfrink of Utrecht, who on 20 October 1964 had succeeded Cardinal Feltin as international president of "Pax Christi", the international Catholic movement for peace, began his speech by associating himself with the ideas expressed by Cardinal Feltin on 29 October. He added that the Council could not say less than John XXIII had said in *Pacem in Terris*. He thought the schema was less realistic than *Pacem in Terris* as regards the ban on scientific weapons, and as regards the arms race (art. 25, § 3). The Council disapproves of the arms race as a crime against humanity; *Pacem in Terris* says that armaments must be cut down simultaneously on both sides.[9] There are there-

---

[9] *Pacem in Terris*, art. 112.

fore two conditions for the reduction of armaments; *Pacem in Terris* adds a third: mutual and effective inspection. The Council ought to follow this positive approach so as not to appear to lag behind *Pacem in Terris*. Then Cardinal Alfrink pointed out the dangerous way in which the schema spoke of scientific weapons; it argues that the effect of these weapons is beyond human control. People might conclude from this that the Council was only speaking about the "dirty" bomb and would not condemn the "clean" bomb, which was already known to exist. Finally, Cardinal Alfrink discussed the theory of the just war. The question which is occupying people's minds is not whether an atomic war can be just or unjust, but intense concern that an atomic war should never break out. The cardinal quoted *Pacem in Terris* with Kennedy's words, "If we do not destroy the weapons, the weapons will destroy us."[10] With reference to paragraph 1 of Article 25, he questioned whether they ought not to mention the close link between the gospel of Christ and the Church's mission of promoting peace. The arguments used by the schema are humanity's dread, the fear of extermination of the human race and the cruelty of war waged with the new weapons. The Church's concern for promoting peace should spring from its religious mission rather than from its social work for humanity.

At the 119th general congregation, 10 November 1964, Patriarch Maximos IV Saigh of Antioch uttered a passionate cry of alarm or, rather, of despair. Everything must be done to forestall disaster. The course of history must be changed. Is it still possible to speak of a just war? If human beings are going to disappear, what is the use of working out methods of pastoral care at the Council? The Council could not be silent. John XXIII had spoken. A solemn, clear and radical declaration on nuclear war was needed, to the effect that the sums saved on armaments would be devoted to alleviating hunger in the world.

Mgr. Hengsbach of Essen (Germany) had helped to draft the schema. He thought that an international authority must be aimed at, but the danger of an atomic war had to be averted even now. The best means is dialogue. He noted that until now peace conferences have not succeeded because those taking part had different conceptions of war and peace, or because the dialogue took place between people who did not all have the necessary competence and authority, or because politicians and military men argued from different premises. Consequently dialogue was needed between competent people. Christians needed a moral doctrine for this purpose. All aspects of the problem of war and peace must be viewed as a whole, and the moral aspect integrated into it.

Mgr. P. Hannan of Washington dealt with the problem of justice and

---

[10] Kennedy's words were: "Mankind must put an end to war or war will put an end to mankind."

liberty without which peace is unthinkable. He wanted the text to contain a definition of the rights and duties which the defence of freedom imposes. He maintained it was mere rhetoric to say that all nuclear weapons are uncontrollable. There are small ones with limited effect. In his opinion, the schema was too strict in speaking of general neglect of disarmament and peace. This was insulting to certain nations and responsible persons who have devoted themselves to the defence of freedom and have made great sacrifices for it. They must emphasize the defence of freedom, for dialogue is inconceivable in slavery.

Reserves about the schema's treatment of nuclear weapons were also expressed by Mgr. G. Beck of Liverpool, who maintained that there can be legitimate grounds for the use of atomic weapons. For example they could be used against an aggressor as a defence against rockets and satellites. If every use of atomic weapons is condemned, encouragement is given to extreme pacifism and to political trends which call for unilateral disarmament. It would therefore be unjust if the schema were to blame the balance of terror, which alone has enabled countries to maintain peace. The really important thing is to work for a juridical international order as the only means of solving national conflicts.

Mgr. R. Arrieta Villalobos of Costa Rica considered that the State should restrict its military expenditure, in favour of education. The Costa Rican constitution forbade the existence of an army. An intervention which helped to de-Westernize the character of the schema came from Mgr. M. Nguyen-Kac-Ngu of Long-Xuyen (Vietnam) who spoke particularly of international co-operation. "We need help", he said, "but we do not want this help to compromise our cultural values through the imposition of a technological and scientific civilization. We do not refuse the help of the UN provided it respects our dignity. We reject the materialism of the developed nations. On the other hand, they can learn something from us about the value of the family, respect for life and the virtues of contemplation and meditation."

Mgr. M. Rigaud of Pamiers (France) asked for greater emphasis on international organizations. These should not work solely on the economic level, which makes the rich richer and the poor poorer. Christians should be taught to take an interest in them.

Mgr. G. Hakim of Acre insisted that it should be made quite clear that the Church is not tied to any economic system. Even if Marxism is condemned, not all more or less socialist régimes should be.

One of the lay auditors, Juan Vásquez of Argentine, President of the International Young Men's Federation, stressed the world-wide scope of a whole series of very grave problems, for instance the population explosion and that of access to the international community by nations who until now have lived on its periphery; the problem of supra-national organization, which is new in history and raises the question of how to safeguard the specific culture and spiritual independence of States; the problem of hunger in a world, some parts of which live in luxury; the problem of spiritual hunger; that of lack of freedom to exercise fundamental human rights; that of the spiritual emptiness of modern man; that of failure to recognize the position of women. Giving his opinion on the schema, he pointed out that it showed the lack of genuine collaboration with men and women experts in the various fields. Unfortunately he only spoke in general terms on this, without descending to details.

Mgr. E. Guano ended the debate and promised that account would be taken of what had been said in the aula. In particular, Chapter IV on the problems of solidarity among nations and on peace would be extended by means of appendices. More experts would also be called in during the revision of the text.

After this first debate the commission had to set to work again. It had become evident that the five appendices to the schema would have to be incorporated in the text, as Mgr. Guano had advocated. 29 Council fathers, 38 *periti* or their equivalents and a score of lay people completed this work in the spring of 1965. On 11 May 1965 the fathers received the new text.

The general discussion of the new text of Schema 13 in September 1965 had produced strong criticism but at the same time much approval of its general line; the problems of the international community and of peace were only touched upon cursorily. On 21 September 1965 at the 132nd general congregation, Cardinal Spellman of New York expressed reservations which he was to define more fully later. The values of obedience and authority should be more strongly emphasized. He instanced the reference to military service as though it were not obligatory. This topic should be avoided, because it was beyond the competence of the Council.

On 23 September at the 134th general congregation, the Polish Bishop B. Kominek of Breslau declared that everything said about peace must be in harmony with John XXIII's words in *Pacem in Terris*. He raised the general question which dominated the whole debate: Is it still possible to speak of a just war?

After this general discussion, 2,111 fathers out of 2157 voted to continue the examination of Schema 13. Only 44 did not want to proceed with it. When this number is compared with the 296 who did not wish to continue with this schema after the Third Session, it indicates the ground covered by the Council in this respect.

The 142nd general congregation on 5 October 1965 began the debate on the last part of Schema 13, entitled "The community of nations and the promotion of peace" (arts. 90–103).

The first speaker was Bishop O. McCann of Cape Town. He urged the creation of a secretariat to investigate whether it was humanly possible to achieve a just distribution of all material goods; it should also study the international imbalances which endanger peace.

After him, Cardinal B. Alfrink of Utrecht made a notable speech on the background of these articles. As regards Article 100 in particular, he noted the distinction drawn in the text between the use and possession of modern weapons: "The possession of these weapons for the exclusive purpose of deterring an adversary equipped with the same weapons, cannot be considered intrinsically illegitimate." [11] It is true that in the present situation such an opinion has a certain limited justification, he pointed out, but it is to be feared that every nation, believing it must share in this balance of terror, will draw arguments from this pronouncement to justify its own manufacture and possession of atomic weapons. In his view the only means of escaping from the balance of terror lies in reducing and abolishing these weapons, as Popes Pius XII and John XXIII had clearly stated. But if the literal tenour of the schema were followed, nothing would be done in this direction. Consequently the Church was getting involved in very complex political questions. The Cardinal here was touching on the problem of the non-proliferation of atomic weapons, which at that time was already being discussed in the Disarmament Committee of 18 at the United Nations in Geneva. In the following years this fundamental modern problem dominated public opinion in national and international politics more and more. Cardinal Alfrink was alive to this problem and suggested the suppression of the last two sentences in Article 100. He also suggested that the second sentence of Article 101 should be struck out. This read, "When there is no evident violation of the divine law, the presumption is that the competent authority is right, and its orders must be obeyed." [12] As argument the draft referred to the abuses experienced in totalitarian States. But this text would not help the human conscience. At the same time, the Archbishop of Utrecht pleaded for the next sentence on conscientious objectors to be retained. He also asked the Church to encourage men of learning who are studying the problems of peace within the framework of the new science of "polemology", and that mention be made of the modern institutes of "peace research". He pointed out that war is contrary to the spirit of the gospel, and questioned whether in present conditions it is still possible to talk of a just war. Finally, he found fault with Article 95 on international co-operation in the economic field because, though the word "charity" appeared frequently, the word "justice" was not used once.

These introductory and fundamental remarks were followed by three French and one English interventions on this important theme.

Cardinal Liénart of Lille introduced another aspect of the question of war. Since at the present time there are weapons capable of annihilating the world, the classical distinction between a just and an unjust war is no

---

[11] Original text of Schema 13 as it stood in December 1965.
[12] Original text of Schema 13 as it stood in December 1965.

longer valid. The machinery of war has become inhuman. In this new situation men must no longer think of humanizing the effects of war, nor of
armed defence of their rights; they must aim at eliminating the injustice
which produces war.

The same idea was expressed by Cardinal Léger of Montreal who also
referred to *Pacem in Terris* and called for an energetic and brief declaration
that war at the present time is "alienum a ratione". As regards the passage
on the need for an international authority, he proposed an appeal to governments to avoid the anachronistic cult of State autonomy, collective egotism
and contempt for the international community. As regards conscientious
objectors, the Council should state clearly that conscientious objection can
be inspired by love and the evangelical spirit of peace.

Cardinal Duval of Algiers pointed out that a new kind of thought, a
change of mental attitude (metanoia), and a new line of policy were called
for, as well as a reform of existing economic relations. Racialist policy must
be more strongly disapproved. The Council must appeal to political and
business leaders to think internationally, not merely nationally. There must
be a clearer condemnation of total war. His speech focussed on the problem
of the widening gap between rich and poor countries.

Abbot C. Butler, O.S.B., raised the same objections as Cardinal Alfrink to
the section on the possession of nuclear weapons. They must avoid giving
the impression that the conciliar text could be interpreted as sanctioning the
balance of terror. In regard to conscientious objection, he too opposed the
idea of a "praesumptio iuris", especially as we still had no world-wide
authority. There can be conscientious objectors among us of a prophetic kind
who exemplify a very pure evangelical morality.

The Bishop of Toulouse, Mgr. G. Garonne, who was later to introduce the
new text of Schema 13, observed that war can only be averted if justice has
previously been established.

Mgr. Castán Lacoma of Sigüenza (Spain) took a different view of nuclear
weapons. Whilst emphasizing the benefit of a universal and simultaneous
destruction of these weapons, he considered that it is legitimate to defend
oneself with nuclear weapons against a nuclear attack.

Mgr. Rusch of Innsbruck clearly supported a ban on aggressive war because of the very nature of nuclear weapons. He apparently wanted a similar
ban on preventive and ideological war, but was less specific in regard to
defensive war.

The Bishop of Eger (Hungary), P. Brézanoczy, asked for a solemn, clear,
serious and absolute prohibition of total war, whether conventional or nuclear; this was what mankind expected of the Church.

Bishop Wheeler of Middlesborough approved of the creation of a secretariat for international justice and progress, whilst Bishop C. Grant of
Northampton advocated a peace-corps.

More notable speeches followed on 7 October at the 144th general congregation. The Bishop of Saragossa, Mgr. Cantero Cuadrado, wanted the passage on limited wars to mention revolutionary wars; these not only lead to civil war but also provoke international conflicts.

Mgr. Klepacz of Łódź (Poland) pointed out the need to reform human beings and social institutions if peace were to be obtained.

The Bishop of Rennes, Mgr. P. Gouyon, for several years president of the French section of "Pax Christi", argued that the distinction between total war and limited war cannot be maintained, for war is not a means to restore violated rights.

The same anxiety was expressed by Mgr. Martin of Rouen. He went even further: "The distinctions between defensive, just and unjust wars are obsolete today. War must disappear from the vocabulary of humanity."

The great event of the day was Cardinal Ottaviani's speech. To those who were not familiar with his works on the public law of the Church, in which he had always adopted a progressive attitude to the traditional doctrine of the just war, this speech came as a revelation.[13] He declared his full agreement with the text as it stood. He also agreed with the condemnation of war which had been proposed by several fathers, but added that the schema must say more about the means and steps to safeguard peace and achieve peaceful solutions of possible international conflicts. He put forward two suggestions in regard to education: Encourage the willingness of citizens and governments to co-operate internationally (and for children, no toys that might develop aggressiveness); plus education in fraternity among the nations so as to make class conflicts and political or economic colonialism impossible. Nations must be taught to make sacrifices for the common good of humanity. Totalitarian régimes are one of the main causes of wars and must be condemned. So must guerrillas and ideological war. The Cardinal referred to the *De regimine principum* of Aquinas, who says: "The representatives of the people and even the people itself can get rid of their own government if they see that it wants to throw the nation into the adventure of a war."[14] On the other hand, trust in international arbitration and international organizations must be strengthened (International Court of Justice at The Hague and the UN); the decisions of these bodies ought to bind governments in a special way. The Council should stimulate the formation of a worldwide federation of States in which all nations of the world would form part of a single community *(res publica universalis)*. This speech was characteristic of a man who has devoted himself for years to the problems of the international community. It displayed a world-wide outlook matched with expert knowledge. It placed Cardinal Ottaviani, often regarded as conserva-

---

[13] A. Ottaviani, *Institutiones iuris publici ecclesiastici* (4th ed., 1958).
[14] Translated from the author's own rendering of Thomas.

tive, among the progressives in regard to these vital problems. This resounding intervention by Ottaviani completely eclipsed the preceding remarks of Mgr. G. Beck of Liverpool, who wanted to insist, as he had the year before, on the legitimacy of the possession of nuclear weapons in certain cases.

Cardinal Ottaviani's speech was also in strong contrast to that of Mgr. L. Carli of Segni (Italy). In the circumstances, it was inevitable that the bishop would choose the theme of conscientious objection.[15] As we have devoted ample space to the views of those who defended Schema 13, equal attention must be given to representatives of the opposite opinion, and Mgr. Carli may be regarded as their spokesman. His contention was that Schema 13 dealt with questions that are not yet ripe. He rejected the argument that the conciliar debate itself brings such questions to the requisite maturity. In his view this conflicted with the virtue of prudence. One of the problems that is not yet ripe is that of conscientious objection to military service, which is bound up with the problem of the legitimacy or illegitimacy of war. These questions are under public discussion. In this situation the problem should either be solved quickly and definitively, or a prudent silence maintained. The schema, however, he claimed, did neither. He thought silence was preferable, for then the highest authorities of the Council would not be obliged to deal with a problem which apparently no longer meets with the same unanimity from theologians as it used to. He summarized the teaching of "grave theologians" as follows. 1. In the atomic age a just war is possible. 2. Military service is therefore legitimate in a just war. Consequently it is not morally permissible to refuse military service on conscientious grounds. 3. Since military service is legitimate, to refuse to perform it is illegitimate even in peace-time, that is to say, before or apart from any warlike action. His arguments stressed four main points: (a) In times of peace no acts of violence are committed during military service. (b) It is not certain beforehand whether a war will be just or unjust. (c) If the possibility of a just war is admitted, the legal authority has not only the possibility but the duty here and now of preparing military defence in order to be able to meet any unjust aggression. (d) Military service is necessary for the effective support of international organizations whose noble duty it is to safeguard international peace by means of a common military force.

---

[15] On this we must notice that in the religious life of Italy at that time the attitude of certain Church dignitaries to the question of conscientious objection to military service was the subject of vigorous controversy. There was the case of Don Milani who at a meeting of army chaplains had defended the moral legitimacy of conscientious objection. His bishop, Mgr. Florit, publicly contradicted him in the name of the Church's teaching. When opinions were expressed at the Council which were quite different from those of the majority of Italian bishops, Don Milani and other priests wrote an open letter to Mgr. Florit. Despite the tension which had long existed between Mgr. Florit and his clergy, he was made a cardinal.

Although Mgr. Carli had no doubts about the cogency of these arguments, he nevertheless admitted that, since the appearance of the atomic bomb, voices had been raised which cannot be ignored. But he claimed that the schema was lacking in logic. It first affirms that nobody may give or follow orders which are manifestly contrary to divine law. Then it says that when the violation of God's law is not self-evident, the "praesumptio iuris" must stand in favour of the competent authority. One would rightly expect the schema to proceed to the sphere of practical applications by answering the question, frequently raised even in the civil courts, whether refusal of military service is to be considered contrary to the law of God. But it does not answer this crucial question. On the contrary, it proceeds in an illogical way to recommend support for conscientious objectors through special legal provisions to be adopted by the civil authority. Bishop Carli's conclusion was that the authors of the schema regard conscientious objection as morally admissible, which is contrary to received theological opinion. He went even further and maintained that the recommendation sometimes made that the civil authority should renounce its rights in favour of conscientious objectors should be regarded as interference in other people's business. Mgr. Carli passed the following judgment on the schema's conciliatory attitude on morality and politics. In the moral domain, it is not very logical to question the moral desirability of something before it has been decided whether any moral duty exists in the matter. In the moral order, the Church can give advice to its children on what is desirable yet outside the range of precept in the strict sense. But the Church cannot give such advice to the civil authority, which is the highest authority in its own sphere, except in the case of a moral duty indubitably deriving from the divine law, the natural law or positive law. The Church is not competent to judge whether a particular measure affecting conscientious objection to military service is politically desirable or not. Furthermore, each particular civil authority as such is alone competent to judge this. The whole section on conscientious objection should therefore be struck out of the schema.

The following day, 8 October 1965, at the 145th general congregation, five Council fathers spoke on behalf of 70 others. The great problems of the previous session were not taken up again. There was one exception: Mgr. B. Bouillon of Verdun declared himself a supporter of complete disarmament, observing that peace does not depend on international organizations alone, but on the formation of a public opinion favourable to justice and non-violence. He pointed to an example of non-violent testimony by 20 women in Rome at that moment, who were fasting; he read out a declaration they had made.[16]

---

[16] This fast had been organized by the "Non-violence Movement". Joseph Pyronnet has written a book on this with a preface by Abbé Louis Rétif.

Bishop Ancel of Lyons drew a comparison between world-citizenship and patriotism; sacrifices must be made on behalf of a world-wide federation, which has to have armed forces, just as much as on behalf of one's own country.

Mgr. J. Rupp of Monaco spoke about the right of emigration from over-populated countries. Mgr. L. Faveri (Italy) spoke of love as a basis of peace, while the Bishop of Down (Ireland), W. Philbin, thought the spirit and force of the gospel was lacking to the whole of Schema 13.

In the margin of the problems directly concerned with war and peace and international life, speeches were also made on birth control by F. Simmons, Bishop of Indore (India), and Mgr. J. Marling of Jefferson City (U.S.A.). The former wanted inquiry made into the question whether the number of mouths to be fed might be diminished, the latter stressed the need to increase food production. Mgr. Gaviola of Cebanatuan (Philippines) dealt at length with the problem of birth control, drawing attention to serious physical, psychological, social and moral consequences.

This ended the debate on Chapter V. Mgr. G. Garonne declared in the name of the commission that a new version would be proposed, taking account of the remarks and criticisms of the fathers. He promised that Part II would consist of a precise application of the principles elaborated in Part I. It would be based on the dignity, spiritual nature and divine vocation of the human person.

Twenty-seven speeches on this chapter went more deeply into questions of the just war and conscientious objection. On both sides quite radical views were expressed.

Before taking the vote on Schema 13, Mgr. Garonne presented the amendments on 15 November 1965. He said that three chapters had caused special difficulties; atheism, the family and war. On war and peace they had stated briefly and clearly what is true and certain; they had also indicated the progress made. Mgr. Hengsbach presented Part II before the vote. He summarized the views of the fathers as follows. Some were of the opinion that the Council was exceeding its competence in the matter of the international community. Others thought that the schema had Western conditions of life in view and neglected the new nations and those living under Marxist régimes. The text had been fundamentally revised. Special attention had been devoted to the theme of peace. They had borne in mind the mass of innumerable victims, but also the conscientious anxieties of politicians and soldiers who have the duty of defending the rights of their nation and at the same time of avoiding world-wide fratricidal war. They had tried to avoid casuistical and merely emotional treatment, as well as over-simplification. The Council had not wanted to give an impression that it was in possession of prefabricated ready-made solutions. The guideline had been the concept of peace. Non-violence had been approved, while at the same time the dangers of any misconception had been avoided, for in fact other methods are admitted. Appeal was made to the law of nations. Crimes were condemned. Prominence was given to the development of positive law rather than to military matters, and in this context the suggestion was made for juridical provision for cases of sincere conscientious objection. On the basis of papal pronouncements, total war was condemned and the arms race was denounced as a real scourge. With reference to *Pacem in Terris* it was reaffirmed that it is no longer reasonable to regard war as an adequate means of restoring violated rights. Ways of avoiding conflicts were indicated and appropriate international institutions promoted. A new organization in the Church to encourage international order and to stimulate international co-operation by Catholics was also advocated. An invitation was addressed to Christians to co-operate with all who seek peace in an ecumenical spirit inspired by the principles expressed in the Pope's United Nations speech.

The result of the vote on 17 November 1965 was as follows.

	Yes	No
Articles 81–86	2081	144
Articles 87–90	2122	43
Articles 91–94	2126	65
Articles 95–97	2165	33

On the chapter as a whole, out of 2227, 1656 voted Yes, 523 Yes with reservations, 45 No, with 3 invalid votes.

On 2 December 1965 at the 166th general congregation, Mgr. G. Garonne introduced the *modi* which in Chapter V chiefly concerned the first section on the avoidance of war. The passage on conscientious objection had been revised in such a way that the Council does not make any judgment on its moral character and does not expressly recognize it as a right. It simply says that the case of conscientious objection should be settled in a humane manner. Another amendment emphasized that total war exceeds the limits of legitimate defence. In the passage on immense destruction, the term "indiscriminate" must not be overlooked, or the additional footnotes. The article on the arms race had been changed so that it is not possible to say that the Council had any particular nation in view. [17]

On 4 December 1965, at the 167th general congregation, voting took place on Chapter V (Articles 77–90). In the interval between 17 November and 4 December 1965, the numeration seems to have been revised, for on 17 November 1965 Chapter V plus the Conclusion comprised Articles 81–97,

---

[17] Traces of such reference (cf. art. 79) are found in the recognition of the good intentions of politicians and military men and of the legitimacy of armies provided that they are not employed to subjugate other nations or to maintain national egotism.

whereas on 4 December it consisted of Articles 77–93. The most important alterations were as follows. An insertion had been made in Article 78: One should abstain from the use of violence if this can be done without detriment to the rights or duties of others or the community. In Article 79 mention is made of the crime of destroying an ethnic minority. Conscientious objection is treated with more reserve. The right to legitimate defence is expressed with greater precision. Article 80 on total war has received the addition that indiscriminate destruction far exceeds the measure of permissible defence. The footnote refers to several papal documents, not only to Pius XII's Allocution of 30 September 1954. In Article 81 on the arms race, the polemical tone in referring to rich nations has been moderated. An addition has been made to Article 82 saying that disarmament must take place gradually, simultaneously and with effective guarantees, not unilaterally.

Of the 2201 fathers present, 1710 accepted the new text, 483 opposed it and there were 8 invalid votes. On 5 December 1965, voting took place on the whole of Schema 13, now entitled "Pastoral Constitution". Out of 2373 fathers, 2111 voted for, 251 against, with 11 invalid votes. There were some almost dramatic events in the days preceding this vote. In journalistic circles there was talk that an American atom bomb had been planted under Chapter V. On 25 November 1965, Archbishop Hannan of New Orleans had published a statement violently criticizing Chapter V, which he described as "not ripe and full of errors". He opposed the condemnation of every use of atomic weapons, and accepted the possibility of a just war. He said military experts should be consulted before the conciliar text was promulgated.

After the appearance of the revised, more carefully phrased text, the Council fathers received a letter signed by 10 prelates: Cardinal F. Spellman, Archbishop of New York; Cardinal L. Shehan, Archbishop of Baltimore; Mgr. P. O'Boyle, Archbishop of Washington; Mgr. P. Hannan, Archbishop of New Orleans; Mgr. M. Miranda y Gómez, Archbishop of Mexico; Mgr. G. Clyde Young, Archbishop of Hobart (Australia); Mgr. D. Hurley, Archbishop of Durban (South Africa); Mgr. A. Tortolo, Archbishop of Paraná (Argentine); Mgr. J. Khoury, Maronite Bishop of Tyre (Lebanon); Mgr. F. Cueto González, Bishop of Tlalnepantla (Mexico). These bishops asked for a vote rejecting Chapter V and eventually rejecting the whole of Schema 13. Their chief arguments were that by stigmatizing the use of nuclear weapons as immoral, the chapter ignored the fact that the possession of such weapons had safeguarded the freedom of a large part of the world, as well as the fact that the causes of wars are dissensions and injustices, not the possession of scientific weapons; there is no logic in saying that the police force in a town is the cause of riots. They also claimed that there was a contradiction between the passage on nuclear weapons and the right to defence, for defence is impossible for larger nations unless they have nuclear weapons. Finally, the letter denied that recent Popes had condemned total war.

Finally, a number of American bishops wanted to explain the vote on 5 December 1965, but abandoned this idea. Cardinal Shehan let it be known that he had signed the letter before reading the new text of Schema 13. This probably explains the 483 *non placet* regarding the chapter on peace (4 December) and the 251 unfavourable to the whole schema (5 December).

We have a right to ask whether this American bomb was well-advised, for precisely at that time and for long after, American policy was the subject of much controversy because of Vietnam.

The final vote took place on 7 December. If we compare the 75 unfavourable votes cast then with the 249 and 251 adverse votes which the schema had received at the previous vote in the general congregation, and if the background of the whole debate on this schema is taken into account, we can only suppose that the American bishops and their supporters passed over their difficulties in the end. They had little understanding of Chapter V, but when a decision had to be taken, they voted loyally and collegially out of respect for the majority, the Pope and the historical solemnity of the hour.

The small group of what has been called the anti-Council bloc — they may be identified with the Coetus Internationalis Patrum — maintained its stubborn opposition to the end.

As already noted above,[18] the origin of the second section of Chapter V cannot be separated from the first. This is clearly shown by the Council's speeches, which dealt with the two together. Some of the ideas about war in the schema text gave rise to criticism. As for the consolidation of peace and the international community, unanimity seems to have been so total that no one mentioned it except to approve the text. In general it may be said that the greatest difficulties were caused by the problem of defence in relation to nuclear weapons. The subordination of international policy to the demands of military policy is a problem that was beyond the scope of the Council. They therefore tried not to raise it, and limited themselves to a compromise satisfactory to all.

The impossibility of clearly distinguishing these two sections of the chapter is also due to the fact that they changed places at the last minute. This is explained by pastoral considerations and a decision taken regarding the concept of peace. The pastoral preoccupation is evident. The aim was to show all men that the Church above all desires to see an end to the misery of war. This makes it possible to point to two phases in the construction of a community of nations. War must first be eliminated as an instrument of international policy. This would signify the end of the epoch dominated by Clausewitz's doctrine of war. The *ius ad bellum*, which formerly was generally admitted, is thus called in question.

It is one thing not to make use of war to settle conflicts between nations

---

[18] See above, pp. 98 f.

and another thing to create a system of international relations which would provide a peaceful means of settling such conflicts, which will persist as long as men are men. The world is not completely built once and for all. Changes are probable and even desirable. But it is essential that changes produced by the dynamism of progress and the activities of the nations, should not destroy the system of peace. Precise guidelines for the organization and administration of human society cannot be found in the text. Moral principles and, even more, a Christian view of human life, must penetrate world history and contribute to shape it in a more humane way. Only an international society in which the rules of law take the place of sheer force is adequate to the human person and humanity.

Criticism is easy. For some the Constitution says too much, for others too little. That was the criticism of the Council fathers and of those outside the Council. Nevertheless mankind can salute this constitution with joy and hope, because it makes a moral and intellectual contribution to the construction of a world which is a more human one for everyone everywhere. It is also an important fact in the history of the Church and of mankind that more than 2,000 bishops, who every day are brought face to face with the difficulties and anxieties of their own smaller provinces, were able to agree on a really world-wide conception of the great problems of our time. Furthermore, their words called upon Christians actively to encourage the creation of a new international law which is acknowledged to be indispensably necessary at the present time.[19] The Pastoral Constitution also calls war an "ancient servitude" from which divine providence demands us to free ourselves. The idea of the inevitability of war which we find in quite a lot of Christians, is therefore seen to be un-Christian.[20] Finally, the fathers expressed the wish for a universal organization in the Church for the purpose of stimulating the Catholic community to help the progress of poor regions and to establish social justice between the nations.[21]

A simple but very fruitful view of the activity of Christians in inter-

---

[19] A. Ottaviani, *Institutiones iuris publici ecclesiastici* (4th ed., 1958), Part I.

[20] Cf. L. J. Lebret, *op. cit.*, p. 277.

[21] On 11 January 1967 Paul VI established this post-conciliar commission by the motu proprio *Catholicam Christi Ecclesiam*. It is called "Iustitia et Pax". Although the description of the role of the commission says that it is to deal with problems of peace, "which above all include the problems of development", it is almost exclusively composed of specialists in development. This certainly derives from the conviction, which we find in *Populorum Progressio,* that development is the new name for peace. This identification is not a very well-chosen starting-point. It misconceives the more general character of peace, its object and distinctive method. It reduces the construction of a peaceful international society to the solution of a problem of an economic and social kind. Even a universally prosperous world would need appropriate structures to regulate the behaviour of prosperous nations.

This one-sided orientation of the commission is all the more unexpected as Article 83 of

national society is that "peace is never something achieved once and for all, but has perpetually to be constructed". That is a modern version of the Sermon on the Mount: "Blessed are the peace-makers", those who work incessantly to build peace in the world.

Commentary

Article 77. From the beginning, the fathers and Council theologians were faced with the problem of what literary genre or mode of expression was to be used. Some theorists were of the opinion that the choice was between a prophetic outlook and style and a pastoral perspective and style. The first would have had to concentrate on an inexorable statement of the absolute demands of evangelical love, however timeless and harsh that might seem, and even at the risk of repelling and discouraging many Christians. The second alternative would chiefly take into account concrete influence on the daily life of men and women who are not always saints, and would aim at a gradual education of their faith, starting on their real level. Put in this way, the alternative is not very accurate. The prophetical element has to be pastoral, for the word of God is directed to concrete human beings involved in particular situations; it always endeavours to help them to advance, and generally this can only be done step by step. Conversely, the pastoral element must be prophetic, that is to say, it must in its educative action never forget the ideal, to which it endeavours to lead those entrusted to it. The Council rightly refused the dilemma. Whatever judgment may be passed on it, it chose, as in duty bound, a direction which was both prophetical and pastoral. The line followed is, therefore, in principle the correct one. However, it is a matter for regret that the prophetical aspect of its pastoral message was insufficiently stressed and even sometimes forgotten.

With this proviso, we may say that the Council was no doubt right not to enter into casuistical questions which inevitably would simply have hard-

---

Gaudium et Spes ends with the words: "... unwearying efforts must be made to create agencies for the promotion of peace". Was it never considered in Rome that a policy of setting a good example might increase the effectiveness of these words? Nobody would have been surprised if the Church had taken the initiative in Rome or elsewhere in creating an institute for "peace research".

Another danger of the identification of peace with development is the risk of creating in the public mind a relation between the cost of armaments and the sums that would be released by disarmament for development. A realistic view must be taken of the ability of the nations to disarm in a limited space of time. Development must not depend on disarmament policy. Both disarmament and development must be pursued simultaneously. Neither presupposes the other. If they did, it would be a very discouraging prospect for developing countries. *Populorum Progressio* does not replace *Pacem in Terris;* it is its necessary complement.

ened the different parties in the Council. (The criticisms that were voiced, despite everything, on this account, came from commentators unacquainted with the most elementary rules of moral reflection.) It was sufficient for the Council to lay down clear guidelines of thought and action and trust to the reason, imagination and courage of those who took it seriously. The Church has too much respect for the human beings involved in temporal problems to wish to anticipate their decisions. The Church gives them light and help in their endeavours, and calls upon them emphatically (as happens several times in this section of the text), especially if they are Christians, actively to work at establishing peace in the world.

Article 78. Something must first be said about the nature of peace. Without actually quoting it, the Council refers to the famous Augustinian definition which has repeatedly figured in Catholic theology and official pronouncements: *Pax omnium rerum tranquillitas ordinis.*[1] Peace is understood here in Augustine's sense. For him, order is not a certain mechanical behaviour imposed by despotic power (which would be the worst disorder, as in the cynical "Order prevails in Warsaw"). It is an inner force of justice and love. It takes into account both the individual human person and the community, the whole of humanity and changes of all kinds in collective interpersonal life. Such order is in constant process of development and perpetually requires new forms for its realization. This definition is of permanent value. The deeper and quicker changes occur, as at the present time, the greater the need for stability and security. The concrete description of peace in the conciliar text is sure to gain the approval of all men of goodwill, including those in the uncommitted nations, and in the communist States. It can readily be interpreted as a declaration of the peaceful coexistence which must become a key principle of international morality, as soon as it has been subjected to the necessary clarification.

We have used the term international morality. It implies that international relations must be subjected to the norm of ethical values. According to theological teaching, this norm has two sources. The first is natural law, that is, the organic system of those requirements of moral and legal order which follow from the structure of human nature itself, if this nature is considered both in its stable characteristics and in its ontological history, in its concrete reality as the nature of a being who is both spiritual and corporeal, radically endowed with reason and will, essentially and existentially dependent on its Creator and linked at its deepest roots with the whole of humanity. This theory is often rejected because badly understood, but it is of great importance, not only because of its content but also as a basis for discussion with non-Christians. Is it not in fact the implicit foundation of the human

---

[1] *De Civitate Dei* XIX, 13, 1.

rights formulated in the Charter of the United Nations and in the general Declaration on Human Rights?

The second source of international morality or peace (for us the two terms are practically equivalent, as in *Pacem in Terris* and *Gaudium et Spes*) is the gospel itself, if we give this word its full New Testament meaning: Christ's message in its totality, of which he himself is the infinitely attractive and eternally present model. For the Christian, this is the primary source, for its definitive binding norm is the word of God. The Church's doctrine of peace is a theology of peace; the Church has to render present to the world the peace of Christ. What is this? It is first and foremost the inner peace of the God-man himself, fundamentally a participation in the peace of the living God, the total communication, infinite love and perfect harmony of the three divine persons. Christ gives us this peace, which is his, if we desire it. If we accept it freely, we come to share in the peace of God by being taken up, without any merit of ours, into his inner life, with resulting joy and profound development of our own being. This makes profound demands on all relationships between human beings, individual or collective (and therefore for the international domain). Their charter is the Sermon on the Mount which must be seen in the theological light of Christ's farewell discourses. The two commands of love of God and the neighbour (without exception, including the worst enemies) constitute their essential norms. The following words of our Lord form the "golden rule": "So whatever you wish that men would do to you, do so to them; for this is the law and the prophets" (Mt 7:12). This supplies all human activity with a concrete guide. Certainly we must distinguish between a collective (or inter-collective) and individual (or inter-personal) domain, but the fundamental demands remain the same; the only question is how they are to be applied or transposed without substantial alteration. Politics must be stamped with the pattern of the gospel, although they remain entirely what they are, namely a specific and essentially human activity with their own problems, requirements and solutions. Whatever is valid in our human striving for peace is assumed, clarified, illumined from within and enriched with inestimable values and possibilities. Anyone who has once understood this, must feel elevated and drawn by it to live seriously in the spirit of the two complementary beatitudes of meekness and peace. The teaching of the gospel contains a force of superabundant strength. Christians, who have to bring it into action, have unfortunately so far given it small scope. The Church of today needs to reflect earnestly on this and has fortunately begun to do so. It is a pity that the Council contented itself with a few all too brief, though noteworthy, observations.

We have deliberately left aside one basic gospel maxim, that of non-violence. Is it not self-evident, though too often forgotten, that renunciation of force is always both condition and consequence of charity and peace? Can it be doubted that for Christians non-violence, both collective and individual, is the norm? It is so in a much wider and more compelling way than in natural law, where the same principle exists. Can it be doubted, therefore, that legitimate defence (if there is such a thing — this is dealt with in the next paragraph) can only be an exception and can only be exercised under very strict conditions and with an attitude that excludes absolutely all revenge and hate? All Christians should be agreed on this minimal interpretation of Christ's will; it is not possible to reduce it to less. We must denounce as a scandal the levity with which Christians have failed to recognize this teaching of Christ, all too often centuries on end, and even in our own times. We may be grateful to men like Mahatma Gandhi[2] and Pastor Martin Luther King,[3] who by their teaching and example have forced us to rediscover the fire in the words of the gospel which we had damped down for fear it might consume us. A plain commitment to non-violence to the very limits of possibility is called for. The content of this principle must, however, be precisely understood. It must not be reduced to a particular scholastic opinion or a special technique, nor should it be limited to absolute non-violence. Every endeavour to find peaceful solutions to human conflicts, whether individual or international, every genuine initiative to maintain and promote peace, to improve the condition of the workers in order to remove or at any rate to lessen economic alienation, respect for national or racial minorities, progress in international and universal spirit, collaboration for the development of the Third World, every work of justice and love, every search for dialogue, anything that can make the world more fraternal and assist it to a more intensive and better existence in the political, economic or social sphere, all these activities deserve to a certain extent to be considered as applications of non-violence. We may be grateful to the Council for having given official recognition in the Church to non-violence, which many people had previously regarded with suspicion. It is a pity that it was given on too limited a scale, because the idea of non-violence is still too linked to the narrow views of some pacifist movements. An entirely fresh start would have been needed, and this was quite impossible. It would have been necessary to show what great demands this high ideal makes. Of course it is an obvious thing for the weakest, for children and the poor, the sick and old people, but it also demands a high degree of courage, patience and magnanimity. It must therefore certainly be held up before the eyes of Christians. The words of Matthew 5:46 ff. are addressed to all.

But is there not a duty to do even more? Does the gospel not oblige us to acknowledge absolute non-violence as a universal principle, and consequently

[2] For closer knowledge of Gandhi's thought, cf. above all his own writings, in particular *Autobiography: The Story of My Experiments with Truth; Non-violent Resistance*. Cf. *Non-Violence in Peace and War* (Texts of Gandhi on non-violence, ed. by Mahadev Desai), 2 vols. (1948–49).

[3] M. L. King, *Strength to Love* (1963).

to reject every recourse to legitimate defence even in the most tragic and generally recognized cases? This is an extremely difficult problem, for at first sight the interpretation of the gospel seems to point in this direction. It is surprising how often the question has been treated superficially, or even passed over in practice as though it did not exist. Though we cannot justify our opinion in detail here, we concur with Vatican II, with the unanimous tradition of Catholic doctrine since Augustine (who for his part reflects the view of the major part of the early Church) and with the great majority of theologians, in holding that Christ did emphatically propound his dynamic ideal of non-violence but did not mean it absolutely to forbid Christians any recourse to legitimate defence, especially when this appears absolutely necessary for the defence of the innocent. He was aware, of course, that God's witnesses under the old covenant interpreted the decalogue precept "Thou shalt not kill" as condemning murder but not resistance to unjust violence. Neither his words nor his behaviour prove that he rejected this interpretation or replaced it by a law that admits of absolutely no exception. The apostolic Church which made such efforts to be perfectly faithful to his teaching, indubitably accepted the right of legitimate defence, at least against common law crimes (e.g. Rom 13:1–7; 1 Pet 2:13f.). Love for our brethren must be active. In a humanity profoundly marked by sin, in which individual and collective crime is present on an immense scale, it can unfortunately be necessary to meet force with force in order to break force and so prevent to some extent the law of the jungle becoming the only law. Although the ideas of absolute pacifism contain some valid elements, they err by overlooking the grim reality which we are compelled to take into account for the sake of our brethren — individual crimes of all kinds, totalitarianisms, serious infringement of the rights of national or racial minorities, exploitation of man by man, wars of aggression.[4]

Two fundamental observations will not, however, be out of place. Firstly, the Christian can only personally resort to legitimate defence after he has attempted the impossible to limit himself to non-violent methods, after he has resisted every feeling of hatred and revenge, and if he only accepts with profound sorrow the obligation of risking the life of a human being who remains his brother even if he is the worst of criminals. If this attitude were practised more often, people would certainly be much more rarely exposed to such extreme necessity. Secondly, we must recognize unreservedly that there are personal vocations of a prophetic kind to absolute non-violence. Their authenticity is guaranteed by the intensity of their charity in daily life, their willingness for dialogue, their unassuming character, patience and unselfishness. Such men and women silently show their brethren the way which they too must strive to follow. They are linked in a common testimony of

---

[4] See René Coste, "Pacifism and Legitimate Defence", *Concilium* (May 1965), pp. 45–52.

charity with those who are called by God to live in dedicated celibacy. There can be no doubt that our age needs to hear such a call. The Council statements are more restricted in scope, but certainly provide the foundation for views of this kind.

Article 79. As Clausewitz says, war is "a real chameleon which changes its nature a little in every concrete instance".[5] The latest inventions of military technology do not necessarily cause the oldest to disappear. The spread of guerrilla warfare since the end of the Second World War shows that the dagger is not yet obsolete in the age of the atom bomb. Despite the particularly terrible effects of the atom bomb, it must not make us forget that there are or can be other chemical or bacteriological weapons of mass destruction. Wars of subversion or revolution have been raging for 50 years in every continent, organizing whole nations by a system of leaders, mythical propaganda, terror and brainwashing. Others threaten to break out sooner or later.

What is to be done when a war breaks out? "Necessity knows no law", Bethmann Hollweg, the German Imperial Chancellor, declared in the Reichstag on 4 August 1914, while the German army was invading Belgium in violation of Belgian neutrality, which had been solemnly guaranteed by the German Empire. Such a justification, which is nothing but an assertion that might is right, is unacceptable. We must hold fast with the Council to the principles of international natural law, which we might call principles of humane behaviour, and to three in particular: respect for human life (no human life can be sacrificed except when legitimate defence requires it), respect for the person (e.g. in particular the prohibition of torture),[6] the prohibition of all intrinsically bad actions. Actions which are inherently bad remain so whatever purpose they are intended to serve. The assumption that the end justifies the means, whatever they may be, is the negation of morality.[7] The Council rightly mentions in particular the crime of genocide which was strictly condemned by the Convention of January 1948. With Pius XII, we regard the punishment of major war criminals as desirable, at least if this punishment is undertaken according to the fundamental rules of proper judicial procedure.[8] With him, we are also of the opinion that the international tribunals of Nuremberg and Tokyo, despite their constitutional defects and despite the passionate controversies they provoked, represented a

[5] C. von Clausewitz, *Vom Kriege* (17th ed., 1966), E. T.: *On War* (1961).
[6] Pius XII on 3 October, 1963: *Discorsi e Radiomessaggi di Sua Santità Pio XII*, XV, pp. 343 f.; on 15 October 1954: *ibid.* XVI, pp. 213 f.
[7] "No higher authority is entitled to order an immoral act; there is no right, no duty, no permission to carry out an intrinsically immoral action, even if it is ordered, even if refusal to perform it involves the most serious personal consequences." (Pius XII on 3 October 1953; *op. cit.* XV, p. 346.)
[8] On 3 October 1953: *ibid.* XV, pp. 338 f.

positive, if imperfect, achievement. It would be regrettable if this were not continued some day.[9]

It goes without saying that belligerents must respect international agreements on warfare and its direct consequences. Those agreements are rightly concerned to limit savagery and barbarism. The Council refers to a few of them. Special mention should be made of the Geneva Convention of 12 August 1949 regarding the improvement of the lot of the wounded and sick in the armed forces in the field; the convention on the improvement of the lot of the wounded, sick and shipwrecked in the armed forces; the convention on the treatment of prisoners of war; the convention on the protection of civilians in times of war. Mention must also be made here at least of the Hague Convention of 1909 on the laws and customs of land warfare (particularly Article 23 which forbids generally barbaric and base methods of warfare), and also the Treaty of Washington of 6 February 1922 and the Geneva Protocol of 17 June 1925, the first of which expressly forbids poisonous and asphyxiatory gases, while the latter forbids bacteriological methods of warfare. Gratitude and honour are due to the humanitarian work of the International Red Cross. Its members surely stand in the front rank of those who effectively work to lighten human suffering. The Christian unhesitatingly believes that the Lord of the Last Judgment will reward them (Mt 25:31–46).

Some countries have a particular problem in regard to conscientious objection to military service, i.e. refusal of military service on serious grounds which are felt to be the dictates of conscience and are not inspired by egoism, comfort or anarchy, which have no claim to consideration. This refusal takes two forms, depending on its extent: absolute conscientious objection to military service, that is refusal to perform any military service whatsoever, because of a unconditional will to non-violence, and limited or partial conscientious objection, which is a limited refusal to take part in a particular war because it is regarded as unjust. Out of concern for effective charity in a world torn apart by force, Catholic doctrine directly recognizes the first form as based on an exceptional vocation of a prophetic kind. As regards the second form of conscientious objection, Catholic tradition not only regards it as permissible, but expressly forbids participation in an unjust war. "If subjects, rightly or wrongly, are convinced of the injustice of a war, they may not take part in it", wrote Vitoria.[10] For a long time actual appeal to this principle was very rare, although it was always affirmed in theory. Now, however, in some Catholic circles the opinion is held, and with good reason, that it may be applied in practice much more frequently. The example of Fr. Franz Reinisch is rightly famous. He was executed in Brandenburg on

[9] On 24 December 1947: *ibid*. IX, p. 396.
[10] *De iure belli* 22.

21 August 1942 for refusing to serve in the army of a government which he considered illegitimate. Both kinds of conscientious objection must be recognized on grounds of freedom of conscience, even by those who are convinced that they are objectively erroneous modes of action. Good faith must always be respected, if it is genuine and rests on high motives. This raises the concrete problem of knowing how good faith can be recognized, and what suitable peaceful work for the community of a genuine and arduous kind can be substituted for military service. States which have made legal provision for conscientious objectors generally establish two institutions, a court or commission to inquire seriously into the conscientious objector's decision, and a civilian service as substitute for the military service from which an objector is exempt. Vatican II emphatically endorses a general solution of this kind. It is to be hoped that its ruling will put an end in future to the reserves which many Catholic theologians and other persons still feel in regard to conscientious objection.

The objection might be made here that before speaking of humanizing warfare *(ius in bello)* the question ought first to be answered whether there is any such thing as a right to use collective weapons against another collectivity *(ius ad bellum)*. This objection is valid. It must be admitted that the conciliar exposition does not proceed logically, and should in fact have started with this question. What attitude is to be adopted to this essential problem? Fortunately, theologians have recently taken it up again seriously, after contenting themselves for centuries with comfortable clichés. Must the old theological doctrine of the just war be finally abandoned, as many people think? This was several times said at the Council, and perhaps is tacitly implied by the second paragraph of Article 80. At the risk of shocking many readers, we are of the opinion that it would not have been correct to have made such a gesture and that the criticisms of the doctrine of the just war spring from the fact that people have not taken the trouble to disentangle its essential elements from incidentals which must in fact be abandoned. Its real point, which must be retained, is what it teaches about collective resistance to attack. Two forms have to be taken into account, that of collective nonviolent or spiritual resistance (which in traditional teaching is unfortunately not dealt with sufficiently) and that of collective armed resistance. According to the traditional teaching, the latter is permitted only under the three following conditions: 1) when a manifest and extremely grave injustice is done which indubitably creates a situation of legitimate defence; 2) if all concretely feasible pacific solutions have failed, although they have been attempted in accordance with the norm of obligatory pacific settlement of international conflicts; 3) when the evil which arises from armed conflict is less serious than the injustice which provokes it — which also presupposes a well-founded probability of success. Two conditions are thus presupposed: the prime obligation is that of genuinely seeking a peaceful solution of every conflict; and the conviction that armed conflict can only be justified, if it is justified, in a situation of real international disorder. Two consequences follow from this: prohibition of active participation in a manifestly unjust war (as we have already seen) and the obligation of belligerents always to respect the elementary rules of humanity (which we have also referred to) and their duty never to continue fighting longer than necessary.[11] If the real meaning of this doctrine is expounded in this way, it retains its relevance (as will also be seen from the commentary on Article 80). It was laid down by Augustine on the basis of older teaching, developed by Aquinas, Vitoria, Suárez and Taparelli, and remained the view of the great majority of theologians, of contemporary Popes (Pius XII, John XXIII and Paul VI) and also of Vatican II whose pronouncements ultimately represent simply an elucidation of that doctrine for our time.[12]

That is the content of the key-sentence in the article, which we shall simply reproduce here so that each of its words, which were chosen with great care, may receive due attention: "As long as the danger of war remains and there is no competent and sufficiently powerful authority at the international level, governments cannot be denied the right to legitimate defence once every means of peaceful settlement has been exhausted." This text justifies our view. It may of course be objected that this doctrine ultimately solves nothing, because all belligerents maintain (sometimes even in good faith) that they are in a situation of legitimate defence. The only answer to this is that the false applications of a concept which is correct in itself, prove nothing against its correctness, just as mistakes in calculation are no reason for doubting mathematical principles. The concept of legitimate defence is correct and the theological doctrine, if interpreted accurately and conscientiously, offers objective criteria for ascertaining whether it is rightly applied or not. In a world marked by sin and where crime prevails, legitimate defence is unfortunately often a harsh necessity if worse evils are to be avoided.

It is nevertheless to be regretted that the Council did not emphasize more strongly the tragic character of such necessity. Collective armed resistance to an attack can only be a solution imposed for want of anything better in a

---

[11] R. Coste, "Faut-il abandonner la notion de guerre juste?", *Cahiers universitaires catholiques* (February 1965).

[12] R. Coste, *Le problème du droit de guerre dans la pensée de Pie XII* (1962); id., *Mars ou Jésus?* (1963.) Cf. F.-M. Stratmann, *Weltkirche und Weltfrieden. Katholische Gedanken zum Kriegs- und Friedensproblem* (1924); L. Sturzo, *La communauté internationale et le droit de guerre* (1931); R. Ragout, *La doctrine de la guerre juste de saint Augustin à nos jours, d'après les théologiens et les canonistes catholiques* (1934); F.-M. Stratmann, *Krieg und Christentum heute* (1950), E. T.: *War and Christianity Today* (1957); L.-L. McReavy, *Peace and War in Catholic Doctrine* (1963); J.-D. Tooke, *The Just War in Aquinas and Grotius* (1965).

situation of extreme despair. The Christian may only accept it, and then with the greatest sorrow, if he is convinced that love for his brethren absolutely forces it upon him. As long as there is still time, he is obliged to do everything within his power to prevent the occurrence of such a terrible eventuality. It is scandalous that in the past so many wars were accepted with such an easy conscience and even light-heartedly, by men who called themselves disciples of Christ. What a bad example was given to the world by Europe, the great majority of whose inhabitants were Christians, in unleashing two world wars, which were primarily European wars. The clergy must bear their share of responsibility. They had not done enough to educate men to peace, and often enough they had allowed themselves to be misled by nationalist ideas.

It is also to be regretted that the Council, though leaving no doubt about its opinion, did not directly condemn aggressive war in the same way as it did condemn total war in the next article. The initiation of violence surely incurs the heaviest responsibility. It is true that there can sometimes be doubts how a certain action is to be judged. This in fact explains the Church's caution in adopting a position on international conflicts. Nevertheless there are modes of action which are so abominable (such as the action of the Nazi government in starting the Second World War) that attentive observers rightly regard them as indubitable aggression. With Pius XII and the majority of present-day theologians, we must take into consideration here aggression committed against the fundamental personal rights of a great number of human beings, quite as much as an attack on the existence or independence of a State.[13] It is no exaggeration to say that aggressive war is the worst crime of our age against God and humanity.

Article 80. The Council now deals with total war, which is the characteristic form of war in our time. It is total when the belligerents seek completely to mobilize their entire resources, their whole economic, demographic and psychological potential, and when it involves at least a clash between powers which have the latest scientific weapons at their disposal. This could lead to mutual extermination, collective suicide. In a declaration made *in camera* before the military commission of the House of Representatives, the American Defence Secretary, R. McNamara, said at the beginning of 1963 that in his opinion 300 million human beings would be killed in the first phase of a nuclear world war (between the two nuclear great powers). The indescribable chaos that would ensue is unimaginable. With H. Kahn *(On Thermonuclear War)* we are forced to wonder whether the survivors will envy the lot of the dead.

Does this mean that a completely new phenomenon is present, as the Council indirectly states? Yes, if we judge by the characteristics just

[13] On 24 December 1948: *op. cit.* X, p. 322; on 17 November, 1949: *ibid.* XI, p. 281.

described. No, if our analysis goes deep enough. The nature of war does not alter under the particular form which it assumes in each age. That is why the traditional theological doctrine retains its validity.

The Council had to endorse the condemnation of total war so clearly expressed by recent Popes. It rightly refused to diverge from the principle of the inviolability of the civil population, which has been called in question by politicians and soldiers and even by public opinion and some theologians. Acceptance of the distinction between combatants and non-combatants means that only the former may legitimately be directly attacked, and this represents a great advance in civilization. To abandon the distinction would be a return to barbarism; it could only be justified by affirming a kind of total solidarity between the members of a nation similar to the conception of the tribe or clan in ancient times. But such a view is unacceptable, for it would completely merge the individual human being in society. The principle of this distinction is therefore to be maintained and a rational concrete solution found. It has also been incorporated in binding international agreements (Preamble of the Fourth Hague Convention of 1907, Convention on Defence of Civilian Personnel in Wartime, 12 August 1949, etc.). Its best expression is found in Article 6 of the draft of rules for limiting the dangers to the civilian population in time of war, drawn up by the International Committee of the Red Cross (Geneva, September 1956) which we must hope to see incorporated in positive law.

It would have been good if the madness of war had been actually called madness. In view of the possibility described by R. McNamara, it is not clear what value — not even the defence of the fundamental rights of tens of millions of human beings — could in any way be proportionate to such a collective catastrophe. Pius XII invoked the traditional doctrine: "It is not sufficient to have to defend oneself against some injustice or other to justify the employment of the violent method of war. If the calamity produced by war is out of all proportion to the damage inflicted by the injury suffered, there can be an obligation to accept the injustice." [14] Mere common sense surely demands this. Must we not agree with John XXIII: "It is hardly possible to imagine that in the atomic era war could be used as an instrument of justice"? [15] Theoretically, perhaps, a case can be imagined in which atomic weapons might be used with sufficient regard for the principle of the inviolability of the civil population, but it is surely obvious that even this case would mean embarking on an extremely dangerous course. There would clearly be the risk of continual escalation until the uttermost pitch had been reached, with its appalling consequences. Warfare of this kind against cities would surely amount to genocide. General Martin has rightly said, "War has

[14] On 18 October, 1953: *ibid.* XV, p. 422.
[15] *Pacem in Terris*, art. 127.

become meaningless".[16] Human as well as Christian conscience obliges us to reject such an insane eventuality. Rigorous moral reflection on the traditional theological doctrine leads precisely to this conclusion.

Can nothing be done? Are we simply to capitulate and passively to wait for circumstances to change in our favour? The Council did not answer this question but we cannot evade it. Theological tradition and very ancient human experience teach that there is another way, that of non-violent resistance. Gandhi, for example, practised it in South Africa and India, so did the Christians of the first centuries in the imperial persecutions, and so did many Christians and non-Christians under the dictatorships of our time. Governments are too one-sidedly concerned with armaments. The most effective force of resistance is that of intelligent men and women who are accustomed to reflect on their actions and to direct them according to the dictates of their conscience. It is fighters of this kind who need to be trained at the present time as fighters for peace. They alone can win the true victories — those of the mind.

Article 81. The Council could not avoid the problem of the nuclear deterrent, which presents moral reflection with one of the most difficult problems of the age. Oversimplified solutions must at all costs be avoided here. What is in question is a military theory based on the certainty of terrible destruction if atomic weapons are used, since in the present state of science there is very little defence against them. The theory maintains that an enemy can be effectively prevented from beginning a war, and consequently peace can be preserved, through the possession of a minimum atomic armament, which, however, must be proportionately greater the more terrible the possible enemy. Now in fact nuclear weapons exist. As long as humanity is deeply divided, and as long as no honest agreement has been reached about the aims of constructive collaboration, the possessors of such weapons cannot simply bury them in the desert or sink them in the depths of the sea, because

---

[16] "L'Armée de l'air dans le contexte nucléaire", *Revue de défense nationale* (1964), p. 1501. Cf. on atomic war: H. Gollwitzer, *Die Christen und die Atomwaffen* (1957); D. Dubarle and others, *L'atome pour ou contre l'homme* (1958); H. Gollwitzer and others, *Christlicher Glaube und atomare Waffen* (1959); R. Fleischmann, N. Monzel and others, *Kann der atomare Verteidigungskrieg ein gerechter Krieg sein?* (1960); R. Fleischmann, F.-M. Stratmann and others, *Atomare Kampfmittel und christliche Ethik* (1960); W.-J. Dagle, ed., *Morality and Modern Warfare* (1960); H. Kahn, *On Thermonuclear Warfare* (1960); P. Ramsey, *War and the Christian Conscience* (1961); D. G. Brennan, ed., *Arms Control, Disarmament and National Security* (1961); U. Allers and W. O'Brien, *Christian Ethics and Nuclear Warfare* (1961); D. Dubarle, *La civilisation et l'atome* (1961); R. Aron, *Paix et guerre entre les nations* (1962), E. T.: *Peace and War;* Beaufré (Général), *Introduction à la stratégie* (1963), E. T.: *Introduction to Strategy* (1965); K. Jaspers, *Die Atombombe und die Zukunft des Menschen* (1960); Beaufré (Général), *Dissuasion et stratégie* (1963), E. T.: *Deterrence and Strategy* (1965); H. Kahn, *On Escalation: Metaphors and Scenarios* (1965).

otherwise they might one day become the victims of blackmail by a treacherous enemy who had retained such weapons. Is not fear the beginning of wisdom? Such is in outline the theoretical argument.

What is to be thought of it? The Council could not express a simple condemnation, as some wished, but it gave an answer which is both firm and discriminating. It must be admitted that the considerations we have just briefly summarized are imposed to some extent by the absurd situation in which we are placed by the nuclear arms race, and that the mere fact that a country possesses such weapons and is even improving their quality and power, does not necessarily imply the will to use them. Serious objections must nevertheless be brought against such a policy. The Council states them and they are entirely cogent. We should like to add an additional objection which appears to be particularly important. On elementary psychological grounds we cannot share the view that, despite their awareness of the monstrous danger, those responsible will always maintain their sang-froid even in times of extreme international tension, especially when they themselves are really involved in this diabolical game, which would mean a nuclear duel right from the very start. Consequently political leaders must be emphatically invited to use the breathing-space which still remains — perhaps only a few years more — to do everything possible to lead mankind out of the tragic blind-alley which it has unwisely entered through the nuclear arms race. The Council's language here is really appropriate to the gravity of the drama. This is perhaps the best part of the whole section.

Article 82. After analysing various aspects of the problem of war in our time, the Council now deals with how it is to be avoided.

The goal to be aimed at is a final ban on war. "Never another war. Peace must guide the destiny of nations and of all mankind." [17] This appeal of Paul VI to the United Nations awakened a deep echo in public opinion. Will this dream of so many men and women for so many generations, so poetically expressed by the prophet Isaiah, ever be fulfilled? Optimists and pessimists have long argued about it. We will not say that either is right, but only that it is possible of achievement if mankind wills it, yet it is very far from certain. At all events it is good to do everything possible to achieve it and to work to the utmost to establish peace. Erasmus's moving appeal is more topical than ever: "I call on all who glory in the name of Christian, to collaborate with all their might in a common effort against war, and to show how important in a State is the union of all against the tyranny of the powerful. Let each put forward his suggestions for peace and let perpetual concord unite those who, by nature and by Christ, are united by so many ties." [18]

[17] On 4 October 1965: *AAS* 57 (1965), p. 881.
[18] *Querela pacis* LXXIV.

For this purpose the Council, with recent popes, especially Pius XII,[19] John XXIII[20] and Paul VI,[21] rightly calls for the establishment of a genuine supranational world organization. It is needed to deal with the great problems arising on the threshold of the planetary age (underdevelopment, rapid growth of world population, peaceful use of atomic energy, space travel, etc.), and is quite especially necessary for the establishment of peace. As long as it does not exist, the outbreak of a savage war in any part of the world, and its incalculable spread, is to be feared at any moment. In a case of conflict, only a supranational world organization could lay down the law to States, because it would be superior to them and would be able to inspire sufficient respect if it had appropriate power at its command. But is it not utopian to strive for such an organization? We must give the same answer as before. We must at least attempt to move in this direction, which is indubitably the right one, even if we have to stop half-way. Until it is realized, the United Nations — to which a sentence of praise is devoted in the conciliar text — have an important part to play despite the weakness of the means at their disposal.

As regards disarmament, the Council is content to repeat the traditional teaching of the popes since Pius XII, the balance and wisdom of which is hidden under apparently commonplace phrases. The general principle is that one-sided measures of disarmament would give an unscrupulous opponent considerable advantages. In some circumstances, however, exceptions may reasonably suggest themselves. That, for instance, is the view of the French "Movement against atomic armaments" (MCAA). This demands unilateral nuclear disarmament for France by way of example, in the hope that such action would be followed by most countries in the world, thus creating a political force with which even the great powers would have to reckon. This view is not necessarily convincing but deserves special attention. We must also recall the profound remark of John XXIII about complete disarmament which includes even the soul.[22] Such moral disarmament, as it might be called, is in our view even more important than material disarmament. It is the foundation of the latter and alone makes it effective. Unfortunately the Council did not attempt to give new impetus in this important question which has been in the forefront of international relations for the last forty years. If it had, it would have done political and military experts a great service.

---

[19] On 24 December 1944: *op. cit.* VI, p. 245; on 6 April 1951: *ibid.* XIII, pp. 33 f.; on 24 December 1951: *ibid.* XIII, p. 427; on 6 December 1953: *ibid.* XV, p. 484.

[20] *Pacem in Terris,* arts. 137 f.

[21] On 4 October 1965: *AAS* 57 (1965), p. 880.

[22] *Pacem in Terris,* art. 113.

The next section contains important statements which deserve to be pondered by all governments. The Council is aware of the complexity of the problems which weigh on all governments. They escape the attention of armchair politicians and are not taken into account even by the intellectual who sits in sovereign judgment in the quiet of his study. Nobody is entitled to throw the first stone at governments. It is better, as the Council does, to place a high ideal before their eyes: "To go forward perseveringly and to follow through courageously on this work of building peace with vigour. It is a work of supreme love for mankind" (one of the finest formulas of Chapter V).

Next, an appeal is made to all men of goodwill. It would be a serious error to think that the building up of peace depends only on politicians (even if their prestige is very impressive and they themselves are tempted to regard themselves as demi-gods). The establishment of peace depends just as little on military commanders or great financiers or, on the ecclesiastical plane, on the Pope and the bishops. Certainly each of them has an important task, and we have the duty, like the Council, of showing special gratitude to those governments which we know are striving to the uttermost for greater fraternity in human society. But we must also be deeply convinced that its realization also depends on each of us. Whoever we may be, however modest our social position, we have a concrete task. Every just and fraternal action, every effort at mutual help and solidarity, even though it is known to very few people, contributes to building peace. It unites with all the actions of a similar kind by people whom we do not know at all. When taken together, an astonishing total can result. Through many individual actions, greater friendship between human beings necessarily arises and therefore more peace. There is also civil, economic and social peace inside the various countries of the world. General peace is the global result of these different categories in all the details of their actual realization. More than ever before, everything affects the life of mankind (mutual dependence, unification of the world, socialization). An assassination, a revolution, a rebellion, has repercussions throughout the world. In a certain respect, at least indirectly, the same applies to the most modest events. In the spiritual as well as in the material universe, everything is interdependent. Whenever some unfortunate is helped, for example, this benefits the whole of humanity whose suffering member he is. The Christian remembers our Lord's words, that every service we do to the poor and unfortunate is ultimately done to him.

With good reason, the Council stresses the indispensable change of heart which is a condition of the building of peace. Here the Council is speaking a language which recalls great thinkers like Husserl, Teilhard de Chardin, Einstein, Jaspers, Heidegger and Oppenheimer. With Husserl we might speak of conversion; we use the term "change of heart". A change of mind presupposes a new grasp of essentials, and for this we may point to the statements of the Pastoral Constitution as a whole. Even more necessary, however, is a change of heart. We must discover, as Gandhi said, that "love is the most powerful force in the world". In many contexts Teilhard de Chardin spoke of the tremendous dynamism of love which can develop when it is lived intensively. "Love was always carefully kept well away from the realist and positivist systems of the world. One day, however, people will probably have to make up their minds to see it as the fundamental energy of life, or, if it is preferred, the only natural environment in which the ascending movement of evolution can continue. Without love, we have before us in fact the prospect of levelling and enslavement, the lot of the termites and the worm. With and in love our innermost self is deepened and human beings are brought closer together in life. And in it there also lies a free imaginative ascent to all untravelled ways."[23]

Article 83. The analysis of the causes of war in this section is exact, and one can only agree with it, but it is too brief. War is becoming more and more a kind of madness, yet every day people allow themselves to be seduced by it. "Why in some cases are leaders and nations deaf to the voice of moderation, why do they almost lose the power of imagining the dangers and sufferings? This is the deeper problem of the science of war."[1] As Tolstoy wrote, "A workman can no more move a mountain entirely on his own than one single human being can force half a million to die. What are the real causes then?" Closer investigation, taking into account the convergent results of the various branches of the human sciences, is indispensable. But who would claim that it has already been undertaken?

Article 84. This article contains a warm-hearted plea on behalf of international organizations. It expresses good wishes for the work accomplished by those that already exist, encouragement for the tasks which still lie ahead or must be pursued more intensively, and a call to create new institutions both on a world-wide and on a regional basis, especially the organization of development aid for the Third World. The Council is obviously thinking of the United Nations and the specialized institutions linked with it (we list them with their initials, centres and dates of foundation): International Labour Organization (ILO, Geneva 1919); Food and Agriculture Organization (FAO, Rome 1945); International Bank for Reconstruction and Development (IBRD, also known as the World Bank, Washington 1945); International Monetary Fund (IMF, Washington 1945); World Health Organization (WHO, Geneva 1948); International Finance Corporation (IFC, Washington 1956); International Development Association (IDA, Washington 1960); General Agreement for Tariffs and Trade (GATT, Geneva 1948); Universal

---

[23] *L'Avenir de l'Homme* (1959), p. 75.
[1] G. Bouthoul, *Sauver la guerre* (1961), p. 82, E.T.: *War* (1963).

Postal Union (UPU, Berne 1874); International Telecommunication Union (ITU, Geneva 1947); International Civil Aviation Organization (ICAO, Montreal 1947); World Meteorological Organization (OMM, Geneva 1951); Inter-Governmental Maritime Consultative Organization (IMCO, London 1959); United Nations Organization for Education, Science and Culture (UNESCO, Paris 1946); International Atomic Energy Commission (AIEA, Vienna 1957). The regional institutions (e.g. European institutions so strongly encouraged by Pius XII and Paul VI) are no less necessary. The law of large-scale operations means that the development of our industrial society demands large human and material resources and therefore large geographical units.

Article 85. For obvious reasons, the drama of underdevelopment intensely preoccupied the Second Vatican Council. Some experts consider that it is in fact the chief problem of mankind at the present day. John XXIII wrote, "The most important problem of our age is perhaps that of the relations between economically developed countries and countries in the course of development."[2] The Secretary-General of the United Nations, U Thant, wrote in his annual report in 1962: "Poverty, epidemics, hunger and illiteracy are not only an insult to human dignity ... but threaten the stability of governments, increase tensions and threaten international peace ... The present division of the world into rich and poor countries is of greater import and ultimately more explosive than the division of the world by ideologies." The phenomenon has to be seen as a whole. When analysed, it displays a structure with numerous features: the shameless wealth of a tiny minority side by side with dreadful want among the urban and rural masses, starvation of whole nations, illiteracy, the lack of trained personnel to undertake modernization, excessive growth of population in relation to the growth of economic resources, etc. The most terrible of all is hunger (undernourishment and poor diet). The FAO in its third investigation of world nutrition, based on the statistics of 83 nations representing 95% of the world's population, states that the percentage of undernourished human beings is certainly higher than 50% of mankind as a whole.[3]

The wound is so deep that it cannot be healed by the underdeveloped countries themselves. They urgently need massive assistance from developed countries, which will have to be generous on grounds of universal solidarity and fraternity based on the essential unity of mankind. As the Council declares, that assistance must include two fundamental elements: a contribution of material goods (economic aid) and a contribution of personal activity (technical aid). Economic aid consists of the provision of capital (financial aid) and the delivery of material and food (e.g. delivery of completely equipped

---

[2] *Mater et Magistra*, art. 157.

[3] FAO (1963), *Étude de base*, n. 11 (1963).

factories) either as loans (necessarily at a low rate of interest) or as gifts (which are essential because of the poverty of the underdeveloped countries). Technical aid consists in sending specialists (engineers, technicians, doctors, teachers, scholars, administrators) to help in the difficult enterprise of getting development started, and to train cadres. Without them the machines would not be put to use and the mass of the population would still remain in want and ignorance, while the capital would only serve the luxury of a few privileged people.

Article 86. The experience of the last ten years makes it possible to lay down some useful rules, and they are briefly listed in this article.

Section (b): what is development? The best definition known to us is that of Fr. Lebret, "The series of transitions of a particular population and all the partial populations of which it is composed, from a less humane phase to a more humane phase, at the quickest possible speed while taking into account the solidarity of all populations."[4] To this the observation of Fr. Houang may be added: "The real problem of development is not a purely technical and economic matter; in reality it is a question of developing everything that is included in the capacity of men."[5] Lebret also says, "In itself, development is 'integral' like that of a living being. As with a developing living being, everything must grow harmoniously and simultaneously. The only genuine development is 'integral harmonized development', that of every human being and of all human beings, of all territorial units and of all social levels."[6]

We must therefore agree with the Council that, in principle, development is primarily a matter for the underdeveloped peoples themselves. If they have to be helped (and that is the case, as we have just seen), then it is essentially in order that they may become capable of taking development into their own hands with courage and determination. That is the primary task incumbent on their political leaders. If they wish to fulfil it properly, they must develop a rigorous ethics of government and personally conform to it. They must draw up, normally with the help of foreign experts, a comprehensive plan of development for their country as a whole, set it in motion, undertake to guide and control its realization. They must pursue a dynamic and humane policy on population. They must simultaneously give impetus and example, serve as leaders and give encouragement. They must show they have a realistic sense of mutual dependence especially in regard to neighbouring countries, and not be afraid of forming larger economic and even perhaps political units with them.

---

[4] "La vocation des peuples au développement", 46ᵉ *Semaine sociale de France* (1959), p. 148.
[5] *Ibid.*, p. 162.
[6] *Ibid.*, p. 148.

The Council repeats that the Third World must receive massive aid from the developed countries. Its distress and difficulties are so enormous that they cannot be remedied or solved without collaboration on a world basis, and this must be embodied in institutions with comprehensive powers. The whole of mankind is concerned. Courageous initiatives are indispensable. It is impossible to be satisfied with customary methods.[7] It is to be regretted that the Council's suggestions in this regard are very timid. Certainly the Council rightly stresses the reform of international trade, but in our view it should have outlined a more definite programme. Why, for example, did it not take up Pope Paul's Bombay appeal for the creation of a world fund in favour of the underdeveloped countries?[8] The best solution for financing development would be a world tax. When it is realized that humanity expends each year more than 120,000 million dollars on armaments, it is easy to see that if military expenditure were reduced yearly, it would be possible to find the 40,000 million dollars which are required effectively to combat underdevelopment and its tragic consequences. Egotism and mutual fear are certainly still too strong to make such a solution possible straight away. At least awareness of it must be intensified even now and attitudes encouraged which can contribute to the well-being of humanity. It ought to be possible for our fellowmen to understand that fraternal help of this kind, however much it may cost, would be infinitely more reasonable than to continue the senseless race for the possession of increasingly terrifying weapons which may lead to the destruction of hundreds of millions of people. Without wanting to succumb to naive optimism, we should like to believe in the possibility of such understanding. The Council would have gained greater respect if it had spoken more decisively and urgently.

Article 87. The problem of the increasingly rapid growth of world population has become one of the gravest of our time. Whereas world population at the beginning of the Christian era numbered 250 million people (the figure is very conjectural) and about the year 1650 amounted to some 500 million, it rose by 1800 to 900 million, by 1850 to 1,150 million, by 1900 to 1,600 million and by 1950 to 2,500 million. In 1961 the figure of 3,000 million was reached. Demographers regard it as not at all unlikely that by the year

---

[7] Cf. the ten-point programme: R. Coste, *Morale internationale*, pp. 552 ff. On development cf. G. Myrdal, *International Economy: Problems and Prospects* (1956); L.-J. Lebret, *Suicide ou survie de l'Occident?* (1958); J. de Castro, *Géopolitique de la faim* (1959); A. Hirschman, *The Strategy of Economic Development* (1959); T. L. Smith, *Fundamentals of Population* (1960); F. Perroux, *L'économie du XXᵉ siècle* (1961); X. Zolatas, *The Problem of the International Monetary Liquidity* (1961); F. Van Mechelen, *Dynamiek van over- en onderbevolking* (1963); F. Elbialy, *La société financière internationale et le développement capitaliste des pays sous-développés* (1963); G. de Lacharrière, *Commerce extérieur et sous-développement* (1964).

[8] On 4 December, 1964: *AAS* 57 (1965), p. 135.

2,000 the world population will be 6,000 million. Even leaving out of account the fantastic problems created by the simultaneous presence of so many human beings on the earth, this demographic growth immediately involves direct and terrible consequences in conjunction with underdevelopment. "How can one not be profoundly disturbed to realize that according to demographic estimates, the population of the less developed countries is increasing between 1962 and 1970 by about 300 million? This increase is equivalent to the total present-day population of the United States, France and England. It means that the total income of the less developed parts of the world must increase by nearly 40,000 million dollars (the total present income of these regions amounts to about 180,000 million dollars) merely to maintain the income perhead at its present level."[9]

The Council became intensely conscious of this problem. But why could it contribute nothing really new in comparison with the earlier statements of Pius XII, John XXIII and Paul VI? There was general surprise and disappointment at this. This reaction was due to the fact that people are not sufficiently aware of the demands made by fidelity to the gospel and the truth committed to the Church's keeping. The Church only has a right to offer new solutions when it is convinced of their validity, and this presupposes a thorough investigation of the question under all its aspects (cf. the Commentary on Part II, Chapter I, and the Excursus on *Humanae Vitae*).

Articles 88–89. After speaking to all men of goodwill, Christians and non-Christians, the Council now specifically addresses Christians. They must personally take part in building peace, like everyone else and, it might be said, even more than anyone else. Have they not heard that all men are brothers, children of the one Father in heaven, all redeemed by one and the same Christ? Did the latter not teach that the command to love the neighbour is inseparably bound up with that to love God? Did he not reveal that no act of devotion is lost, because even if it is not recognized by the person to whom it is directly addressed, it nevertheless serves to build up God's kingdom and the Mystical Body? Did he not identify himself with those in need? To serve them is to serve him; to be indifferent to their fate is to reject him. Any spirituality of evasion would be in tragic contradiction to the message of the gospel. Non-Christians expect from us deeds not words, and they are right. The parables of the Good Samaritan and of the beggar Lazarus must be a perpetual reminder; they are relevant on the collective, not merely on the individual plane. As biblical basis for the duty of development aid, John XXIII quoted the Letters of John: "By this we know love, that he laid down his life for us; and we ought to lay down our lives for the brethren. But if

---

[9] S. M. Fine, "La croissance économique dans les pays moins développés", *L'Observateur de l'O.C.D.E.* (August 1963), p. 20.

any one has this world's goods and sees his brother in need yet closes his heart against him, how does God's love abide in him?"[10] The poor of the 20th century are not only individuals but whole nations, in fact three-quarters of mankind. The Christian, less than any other can remain indifferent to their need. "If one has really understood and experienced in one's own flesh just how the alienated human being suffers, it is just not possible to do nothing. And how can one without shame cling to one's wealth and culture, well-being and privileges, when Christ is still mutilated or enslaved in three-quarters of humanity?"[11] By adopting an attitude of this kind one bears genuine witness to the peace of Christ, that is to say, ultimately to Christ himself, whom non-Christians learn to discover through our fraternal attitude and the radiance of faith. The Council did not pursue this line of thought, but it is an essential aspect of the biblical spirituality of peace.

Article 90, § 1 (Abbott, §§ 1 and 2). This expresses the meaning and special purpose of international Catholic organizations. It might be considered that they need even further development, a better structure, closer co-ordination. Unfortunately they all too frequently lack the necessary funds. Too often work in the Church is fragmentary.

§ 2 (Abbott, § 3). After John XXIII and Paul VI, the Council very strongly emphasizes the Christian duty of dialogue. In an endeavour to create a more fraternal world, Christians must loyally co-operate with all men of goodwill, whatever their philosophic or religious attitude. Christians would be false to their own mission if they wanted to shut themselves off in a ghetto. Of course, dialogue often raises difficult problems, whether it is undertaken with those who fully share our humanist ideal (the one which, for example, lies at the basis of the UNO declaration of human rights) or, even more, when it is entered on with governments, political parties and other organizations which infringe or combat some of the essential rights of the human person (e.g. freedom of thought, of conscience, religion or opinion). In the second case, clear judgment and prudence are particularly necessary. But if the appropriate prudence is used, there need be no fear of taking the first steps and then of going on as far as the attitude of the partner in dicussion permits.

§ 3 (Abbott, § 4). It is very welcome to see that the Council wished some agency of the universal Church to be set up to promote aid for developing countries. This is a matter of great importance. But why was no similar wish expressed for the creation of a secretariat for peace (under this or some other title)? Such an agency, which has been suggested by many people, could

---

[10] 1 Jn 3:16 f., *Mater et Magistra*, art. 159.
[11] R. Prideau, "Séduction communiste et réflexion chrétienne", E. Mounier, *Œuvres* III, p. 624.

at least promote more precise inquiries into peace, calling on the collaboration of bishops, theologians and specialists of all the various sciences from all over the world. It would be of great service to the Holy See, the bishops and all who are endeavouring to build peace. Perhaps it could even set itself higher aims. The wish for its establishment which we share with so many others, may still be fulfilled.

This concludes Chapter V. With due moderation we have put forward some criticisms and pointed out some gaps. We could also draw attention to evident faults of presentation, which means that the composition of the chapter is not logical enough in detail and some elements are not where one would expect to find them. It is also the case that the chapter adds very little that is new to the official doctrine of the Church, as we have pointed out on occasion. Are we then to echo the disappointment or critical severity of some commentators? There can be no question of this. On the contrary, we think that the Council's statements are of eminently positive importance. The Council has found clear and balanced answers to the problems which it raised. However difficult, it did not evade them, not even, for example, the question of the nuclear deterrent. The critics of this chapter show that they either have a superficial or one-sided acquaintance with these problems, or that they are not clearly aware of what the function of a Council is. An outstanding theologian who had specialized in international problems would probably have written a text of greater objective validity in depth of thought and literary expression, but he would only have propounded his own view. Here, however, because of the mode of preparation involving the collaboration of specialists from all over the world, and consideration of the numerous opinions expressed by the Council fathers, we have a document which in fact expresses the consensus of the Catholic episcopate. Even if it adds little that is new to the teaching of recent popes, that fact itself is of great importance. The continuity of doctrine must be emphasized. The same fundamental line of thought and the same spirit persists from Pius XII who took over the important themes from his predecessors and whose teaching retains its full importance, whatever some may say about it, [12] through John XXIII whose two great encyclicals attracted so much attention, down to Paul VI whose teaching on international problems is already so substantial, and so to Vatican II. The Christian has surely a right to regard this as a sign of the special assistance of the Holy Spirit. If he does not find everything he seeks, why should he complain? Does that fact not summon him to pursue further thought on his own initiative? Progress is in his hands. Catholic thought on international problems has woken again after

---

[12] Cf. R. Coste, *Le problème du droit de guerre dans la pensée de Pie XII;* this presents the teaching of Pius XII on international affairs as a whole. Cf. P. Duclos, *Le Vatican et la seconde guerre mondiale* (1955); G. Herberichs, *Théorie de la paix selon Pie XII* (1964).

sleeping — with few exceptions[13] — far too long. The task in front of it is limitless.

See Excursus on the Problems of Part II, Chapter V, Section 2, on *Populorum Progressio,* on Article 90: The Commission "Iustitia et Pax", and on the "Church of Love" *(Ecclesia Caritatis).*

---

[13] For further inquiry into international problems (including all those dealt with in Chapter V), cf. R. Coste, *Morale internationale* (1965); id., *Dynamique de la paix* (1965); cf. J. T. Delos, *La société internationale et les principes du droit public* (1929); J. Eppstein, *The Catholic Tradition of the Law of Nations* (1935); G. Gonella, *Presupposti di un ordine internazionale nella dottrina cattolica* (1944); Union internationale d'études sociales, *Code de morale internationale* (1948); A. Ottaviani, *Institutiones iuris publici ecclesiastici* (4th ed., 1958); R. Bosc, *La société internationale et l'Église* (1961); J. Comblin, *Théologie de la paix,* 2 vols. (1960–63); R. Bosc, *Sociologie de la paix* (1965).

Conclusion

by
Charles Moeller

Text 3, which derived from the Zurich text, already had a conclusion. The first paragraph was devoted to the Holy Spirit; the Church, it pointed out, must come more and more to resemble the Lord "respondendo signis Spiritui Sancto". Then a long paragraph dealt with the endeavours which have already been made by the separated brethren. This was followed by a paragraph on believers in other religions, unbelievers and men of goodwill. Finally, an appeal was made even to those who reject or persecute the Church.

The paraenetic and pastoral style was not repeated in Texts 4, 5 and 6, but the general structure of the concluding part remained the same. It seeks to place the stress "super positionem principalem et vocationem hominis". In other words, the basis is anthropological. If there is anything which is proving increasingly important for the post-conciliar period, it is the need to elaborate a Christian doctrine of man.

The conclusion has three parts. The necessity of acting, the necessary "colloquium" and Christian hope "in mundo construendo et ad Deum dirigendo". This structure and the essential ideas were maintained in the last three versions. Only 20 amendments were proposed.

Article 91. The report on Text 4 states: "Inculcatur necessitas *operose agendi* ad mundum ita aedificandum, ut *dignitati* hominis eiusque integrae vocationi respondeat. Doctrinam generalem ad particulares regiones et specialia adiuncta *ulterius determinare* et applicare oportet, ducentibus Episcopis eorumque coetibus."

§ 1. Text 5 replaces the phrase "principia et normae" which was not very conducive to dialogue, by "ex thesauris doctrinae Ecclesiae proponuntur". This alteration prepares another in the second paragraph, where an attempt is made to offer some elements of a theological epistemology with reference to this schema. Text 5 replaced "diversis quidem rationibus" by "sive non explicite eum agnoscunt". Instead of "instaurent" it put "appetant". To "fraternitatem" it added the words "altius fundatam". The reason given is important: "Ita conclusio convenit prooemio: uni voci *fraternitatis* sensus tribuitur qui integrae vocationi, et ita etiam ordini gratiae correspondet".

§ 2. Text 5 has "propositio haec" for "non agitur tantum de doctrina" in the same sense as the epistemology to which we have referred. Text 5 had added a remark which was intended to state that the schema was not complete. It spoke of "quaedam imperfectio qua laborat". It seemed rather difficult to leave this sentence as it stood in a "constitution", even a pastoral constitution. Text 6 hit on a better version: "Immo, licet doctrinam . . . erit." A negative formula was turned into a positive one.

The Council hoped that its doctrine, since it expounds for the faithful and for other men their full human destiny, may contribute to building a world more in harmony with the dignity of man, inspired by a deeper brotherhood and a more generous love, capable of meeting the needs of the present time.

The Council recognized that in view of the complexity of the questions dealt with, it could only offer a few general considerations. It even expressly states that this doctrine will have to be "further pursued and amplified", but is confident that it will be deepened and wisely applied by the pastors of the various Churches. This point corresponds to the decision of the World Council of Churches at Geneva in 1966 that it is not possible to work out a "theology of *the* revolution", although it is possible to reflect theologically on certain special situations occurring in the world.

Article 92. The *relatio* on Text 4 says: "Ad fructuosum laborem requiritur *colloquium* cum omnibus, cuius fundamentum invenitur in universali fraternitate humana, et magis adhuc christiana, inter universos homines. Ecclesia sit *'domus colloquii'*. Consideratio applicatur successive fratribus seiunctis, deinde credentibus in Deum, denique etiam non-credentibus. Indicabuntur conditiones ad colloquium requisitae. Finaliter insistitur super dialogum inter ipsos catholicos."

§ 1. Text 5 rewrote the first paragraph and replaced the term "colloquium" by "dialogus". The new version gives the theological basis of this dialogue: the mission of the Church to all nations and cultures. Text 6 reads "signum" instead of "symbolum", which seemed too vague; "signum" also serves as an allusion to Vatican I.

§ 2. The first words in Text 5 ("Quod autem requirit") explained the connection with what had gone before. The word "imprimis" was added for the sake of greater clarity. In comparison with Text 4, this paragraph is practically new, at least in style. This was not pointed out in the conciliar edition of Text 5. The central new idea is mutual respect in the Church and recognition for all legitimate differences. It is also pointed out that what unites the faithful is stronger than what separates them. This is an important theme: unity is not uniformity, and the Church is resplendent in its manifold variety "circumdata varietate".

§ 3 (Abbott, §§ 3 and 4). In Text 5 "eorumque communitates" was added at the wish of the observers, in order to show that not merely individuals but also their communities are referred to. Text 5 speaks "etiam a multis in

Christum non credentibus", for "etiam qui in Deum credunt, non verum in Christum, hoc loco respiciendi videntur". Furthermore, Text 5 read "et in formis huic praeclaro fini efficaciter appetendo magis magisque aptatis", in order to meet another wish of the observers. Text 6 amended "appetendo" to "assequendo" and finally, Text 5, at the wish of one Council father read "in Christo Jesu, in familiam filiorum Dei vocatur".

§ 4 (Abbott, § 5). In Text 5 "alacriter" and "fideliter" were introduced. They avoided speaking of man's further development separately, so as not to give the impression that two different goals are in question.

§ 5 (Abbott, §§ 6 and 7). Text 5 indicates the prudence necessary for dialogue. In the second sentence the text was amended to bring it more into harmony with biblical vocabulary. In the last sentence the Text 5 version mentioned with "vera pace" the divine elements of this peace. Text 6 adds "possumus et debemus" and makes the sentence positive.

The Church has the task of bringing the light of the gospel to the whole world in order to unite men in the Holy Spirit. It is the "sign" of the true brotherhood which makes honest dialogue possible. For this purpose mutual respect and mutual regard are necessary within the Church. Emphasis has been laid on the need for dialogue between clergy and laity in the one People of God. In this context it is recalled that the common elements are stronger than the divisive. One can only hope that both wishes will be fulfilled. Dialogue in our own house is certainly the most difficult kind at present.

The text then speaks of the ecumenical aspect of this dialogue. Much of Text 3 has been incorporated. An allusion is made to the basic idea in the general assembly of the World Council of Churches at New Delhi; unity is awaited by many non-Christians; we are all the nearer the "praesagium unitatis" the more efforts are effectively made to achieve unity. Finally, mention is also made of ecumenical action. 1966 may be said to have envisaged a prospective ecumenism. This answers questions of doctrine and service which are put *by the world* to all Christian denominations equally. An important change has taken place here. Retrospective ecumenism has not lost its importance but has changed its sign, so to speak, and now consists in achieving harmony with parallel endeavours to bear witness and to serve the world. The key to the younger generation's impatience for intercommunion is to be found in an ardent desire to share in the deepest possible "communio" in order to bear common witness and serve side by side.

The Council next turns to believers in the non-Christian religions. Reference is made to the Declaration on the Relationship of the Church to the Non-Christian Religions and to the Secretariat for Non-Christians. Finally, the text mentions those who do not profess any religious belief. It is stressed that since they are children of the same Father, dialogue can and must be pursued with them. Reference is made to the Secretariat for Non-Believers.

These last three paragraphs point beyond the texts to existing agencies or to those which are to be established. This openness gives the Pastoral Constitution its true dimensions.

Article 93. The *relatio* to Text 4 declares: "Ecclesia in hoc opere et colloquio praebet lumen Verbi et roborem Spiritus Sancti; a. v. christiani dare debent testimonium Veritati et divulgare mysterium amoris Patris, cum firma *spe* in consummatione finali." This last article is thus placed in the perspective of eschatological hope.

The text "nihil . . . inserviant" was phrased in this way in Text 5 to replace a very colourless and banal passage. The expression "de quo Ei, qui omnes iudicabit ultimo die" was used to give the conclusion a more biblical and ecumenical tone. The expression "Christum fratrem" was used to achieve a more biblical style. Text 5 and above all Text 6 avoided even more clearly the concept of a "mundus perennis" by saying "in patria quae gloria Domini effulget".

The urgent need for collaboration between Christians in the building of the world is stated. Its ground is their faith and their vocation to love one another. Emphasis is laid on the danger of a merely verbal Christianity, of "mystification" as some would say. God the Father wills us to see in everyone a brother and to love him "verbo et opere". By bearing witness to the truth like this, we all share in the mystery of heavenly love. In this way Christians will spread hope, which is a gift of the Holy Spirit. The eschatological aspect is presented in the last section on peace and blessedness in that home country which is radiant with the splendour of the Lord.

The quotation from Ephesians 3:20 concludes this Pastoral Constitution *Gaudium et Spes,* which has endeavoured always and everywhere to proclaim the risen Jesus Christ, known in the Holy Spirit, and to do so with an Easter voice.

The conclusion thus once more recovers an ecumenical aspect which was largely lacking in versions 4, 5 and 6.

Two problems have proved crucial in the post-conciliar period. The witness and the service of those who believe in Christ are called in question by the world. In order to give an answer, unity must be achieved in regard to theological inquiry and learning, so that by ecumenical co-operation it may be co-ordinated within an international and interdisciplinary framework. We must become one in action and in service. We must become one in prayer. *Ut unum sint.*[1]

---

[1] An outline of this prospective ecumenism appeared in the *Unam Sanctam* volume devoted to *Gaudium et Spes.* Cf. also C. Moeller, "Ecumenismo e storia della salvezza", *Humanitas* (January — February 1967), pp. 296–8. On the theme of hope, cf. J. Moltmann, *Theologie der Hoffnung* (1964), E. T.: *Theology of Hope* (1967).

Excursus on the Problems of Part II, Chapter V, Section 2

by

Oswald von Nell-Breuning

In section 2 of Chapter V, "Building up the International Community" (arts. 83–90), discussions on international and certainly on supranational institutions take second place to measures of so-called development aid, and of economic aid in particular. Institutions of that kind occupied a prominent place in *Pacem in Terris*, and especially the task of creating an authority competent and equipped to safeguard the common good of the whole of humanity and to reach solutions binding on all in the problems which concern mankind as a whole. The very title of Article 85 contains an express restriction: "at the economic level". Moreover, in Article 87 the pressure of overpopulation from which many countries suffer appears as a consequence of the asynchronic growth of population and social product, and is treated as such. It is true that *Pacem in Terris* mentions economic measures first among the "hinc atque illinc sociata multiformiter opera" of development aid, but it also includes the whole social and political domain, cultural life ("ingenii cultum"), public health and sport (*Pacem in Terris*, art. 98; cf. also art. 140). It is all the more striking, therefore, that the Council restricted itself almost entirely to economic development aid. The reason is that the Council regarded the glaring inequality of economic position between rich and poor countries as an injustice threatening world peace (art. 83).[1] Consequently, measures aimed at balance in this domain appear as an important contribution to the promotion of peace, which is dealt with in the first section of Chapter V. Obviously, however, the contrast between poor and rich preoccupied the Council, for it was visibly present, as it were, day after day in the Council fathers from poor and rich countries. It constantly disturbed the Council fathers and recalled their attention again and again to the distress, but also to the beatitude, of poverty (cf. art. 72).

We cannot claim that the Council succeeded in saying the last word on these problems. Here, too, the pressure of time under which the Council

---

[1] Cf. the comments on the attitude of the Council to imbalances and inequalities above, pp. 292 f.

worked, particularly towards the end, probably played a decisive part. Very much more time would have been needed to work out a complete conception of development aid instead of a few guidelines particularly concerning economic aid. It goes without saying that the Council did not fail to point out the cultural, social and political framework into which all economic measures must be fitted if they are to be fruitful. An extremely important idea has certainly not been adequately expressed. It is true that the Council pointed out that it was not sufficient to give material aid but that hand in hand with it guidance must be given on how to use the aid correctly. But that is not everything, and perhaps not even the essential. The enormous lead which the advanced countries have over the so-called developing countries is really based on the fact that not only in the economic sphere but far beyond its borders, we proceed in a "rational" way, whereas those countries proceed in a "traditional" way. The economic distress of backward countries cannot be relieved by material gifts alone, nor by reshaping commercial relations and the like into a form which is more to their advantage. What is decisive is the intellectual changeover of the developing countries from traditionalism to rationality. This, however, is not merely an extremely difficult task; it also involves terrible danger. In this respect, development aid is first and foremost a cultural problem, and one of social education. It is only secondarily an economic task.

The Scientific Advisory Council of the German Federal Ministry of Economic Affairs, which is a specialist body primarily concerned with the economic aspect of the matter, expressed its reserves in a statement published on 23 January 1960. "Rapid introduction of technology or a one-sided encouragement of certain economic sectors, without sufficient care being taken for equal development of the other sectors of social and economic life, would not only be economically meaningless but would also inevitably produce dangerous social and cultural tensions. The success of economic aid will largely depend on whether the peoples who in many respects are still living in a world of non-rational views will find their way to rational economic and technical thought. Rational procedure, however, must be presented only as an objective requirement, not as a higher ethical value."[2]

In the chapter on economic life, the Council touched on the problem as it were at one point. The customs by which help in need is provided among primitive peoples should neither be retained without change nor abandoned without replacement, but must be transformed into rational forms (art. 69). The problem, however, is quite general, and even if under different forms, is

---

[2] *Der Wissenschaftliche Beirat beim Bundeswirtschaftsministerium*, V: *Gutachten vom Januar 1961 bis März 1961* (1961), here, *Gutachten vom 30. Januar 1960:* "Probleme einer rationellen Wirtschaftshilfe an die Entwicklungsländer", I, 7, p. 62; cf. on this the author's "Die ethische Begründung der Entwicklungshilfe", in: J. Höffner, ed., *Jahrbuch des Instituts für christliche Sozialwissenschaften* III (1962), pp. 333–45.

no less important in nations of very ancient high civilizations, for example India, than it is among primitive peoples. Passing reference to this is found in Article 86, but not much more.

A further extremely important question on the frontier of economics and ethics was not dealt with by the Council. Is economic development aid unselfish beneficence, or business, or a combination of both? Or, to put it another way, are economic measures of development aid useful only to the recipients or are they profitable to the donors as well? The question has its importance for determining the grounds of the duty of giving development aid. A duty which involves perceptible and final sacrifices is more difficult to justify and its limits have to be drawn more narrowly than one whose fulfilment sooner or later brings in a profit. No one will contest statements of the kind that "if an economic order is to be created which is genuine and universal, there must be an abolition of excessive desire for profit" as well as a number of other undesirable things (art. 85), but they do not take us very far. It is only a partial truth that some so-called direct investments in developing countries bring a handsome profit for the investors and at the same time are extremely useful for the developing countries themselves. The decisive question is whether it is to be expected that the economic help taken as a whole will prove to be economically profitable to the advanced countries which are providing the aid, or, if not immediately, will at least prove so in the long run. "A clear answer to this question lies in the interest of the country giving the aid and of the country receiving it. If the answer is affirmative, the recipient country is spared the humiliation of feeling it is receiving alms, and the country giving the help must avoid the mistake of playing the role of a noble and selfless benefactor, which would destroy its credibility in the eyes of the recipients."[3]

The Council regarded economic development aid as obligatory for the sake of the common good of the whole of humanity, and in particular for the sake of world-wide economic well-being. It is therefore plausible to assume that countries giving economic aid will have a share in this common advantage. The Council was in no position to decide, and it must therefore remain an open question, whether this advantage (as the German Federal Scientific Economic Advisory Council is inclined to assume) equals or even exceeds the sacrifices made for development aid. But certainly that Advisory Council's recommendation that countries giving aid should avoid the mistake of playing the role of a noble and unselfish benefactor, is quite in accordance with the mind of the Council.[4]

---

[3] *Gutachten* as above, I, 2, p. 60.
[4] This recommendation is to a certain extent out of date, since at least some of the developing countries are claiming development aid as compensation due to them for their exploitation by the colonial powers.

To whom are the Council's admonitions addressed? As long as the Council still dealt with the international community in general, i.e. before it turned specifically to economic development aid, it directly addressed the "community of nations". Since the world government called for in *Pacem in Terris* does not yet exist, it expressed the quite general admonition to that community to give itself the organization it needs in order to be equipped to deal with the tasks that face it (art. 84). Explicit appeal is made to existing institutions and organizations of every kind, world-wide and regional. The conciliar expressions would suggest in particular FAO (food), WHO (health), UNESCO (education), ILO (employment). Specifically economic agencies do not appear in this list. On the other hand special mention is made of agencies dealing with refugees and migrants (art. 84). The Council regarded all these as promising attempts and bases on which to work, and expressed encouragement and good wishes for them.

When the Council turned to the special circle of problems of economic development aid (art. 85), it did not address particular institutions such as GATT, IMF or IBRD, for example, but directly formulated the objective problems. It is then evident from the nature of the case who has to deal with them.

The Council then noted that in order to advance, developing countries need assistance in human and material resources. This division suggested by the Council corresponds exactly with that given by the German Scientific Advisory Council already quoted. Technical assistance comes first: advice and practical guidance from the appropriate experts from the highest level of science and administration, down to simple artisanal and domestic skills; secondly, better international division of labour to be achieved by the advanced industrial countries opening their markets to developing countries on favourable conditions ("trade not aid"); and thirdly, capital assistance in various forms — gifts, loans, partnerships, direct investment (art. 85). This presupposes two things — goodwill and the renunciation of selfish intentions and ambitious aims of an economic, political or ideological kind.

In Article 86 the Council lists the following as being under the obligation of performing a specific set of duties:

a) The developing countries themselves. They are not to depend solely on outside help, but in the first place must make use of their own resources. The Council sets before them as the goal of their endeavours, the complete human fulfilment of their citizens.

b) Advanced industrial nations. They are said to have a very heavy obligation to help the developing nations to achieve that fulfilment. Consequently they themselves must make all the necessary adjustments in order to prepare themselves materially and psychologically for this task.

c) The "international community" has to co-ordinate and stimulate the necessary measures. While observing the principle of subsidiarity, it must organize international economic relations with a view to justice. This is the field of operation of agencies such as GATT, IMF and IBRD. The Council does not mention them, in fact it explicitly refers only to organizations which have still to be created ("let suitable organizations be established").

d) There is no corresponding reference under (d), which is concerned in a very similar way to the German Scientific Advisory Council, with the changeover from traditionalism to rationality though of course the Council views this in a different light.

It is impossible to deal with development aid without discussing the gravest of all problems for some of the developing countries, the population problem, or, rather, the pressure of overpopulation. The Council devotes a separate article to it (87). It rightly points out in the first paragraph that this is a world problem which must be attacked by world-wide increase of production. Then the Council speaks in rather vague terms about the competence of governments in the matter, but in very definite terms about the limits of that competence. The right to marriage and procreation is inalienable. Married people alone must decide the size of their family; the State has no authority here. The parents' decision presupposes a rightly-formed conscience. A correspondingly high religious or at least ethical level of education has therefore to be aimed at. The necessary scientific information should not be withheld from parents, but should be made available to them. Catholic specialists should make their contribution to research.

The Council also assigns a special duty to Christians in regard to economic development aid as such (art. 88). In the person of the poor of the developing countries, Christ himself cries out for the loving help of his disciples. There must not be any scandal of rich Christian countries living in superfluity while others lack necessities. The Council gives special recognition to the volunteers, mostly young people, who go out to developing countries to work for them. Collections of donations is praised, with the noteworthy remark: "As was the ancient custom in the Church, they should meet this obligation even out of the substance of their goods and not only out of what is superfluous." In Article 69, mention had already been made of the obligation to help the poor "not merely out of their superfluous goods".[5] Here a further step is taken — though no obligation is laid down — and it is said "even out of the substance of their goods". In the individual case that may certainly be eminently pleasing to God, but if practised as a rule for all, it would not promote development aid but frustrate it. Development aid is not a problem of distribution but (as was aptly said shortly before in connection with the pressure of overpopulation) it is chiefly a problem of production. Consequently the advanced countries must not weaken their capacity for economic production. On the contrary, they must strengthen and

[5] Cf. above, p. 307.

continually increase it. The individual, whether Christian or non-Christian, can give away even of his "substance", out of noble generosity and a spirit of sacrifice. But advanced industrial nations cannot. There is no need to warn them of this mistake, for, after all, there is not the slightest danger of their committing it.

According to the wish of the Council, organized collections are to be made on a diocesan, national and world-wide scale, but without compulsion on the faithful. With good reason, the Council recalls that those who want to volunteer for work in developing countries should be given proper training. Idealism alone is not enough. Idealism and proper training together can accomplish great things.[6]

---

[6] On this cf. the present writer's "Arm und reich. Zum bischöflichen Werk 'Misereor'", *Stimmen der Zeit* 167 (1960–61), pp. 401–10; "Armutsidee und Entwicklungshilfe", *ibid.* 176 (1965), pp. 331–42.

Excursus on Populorum Progressio

by

Oswald von Nell-Breuning

Mater et Magistra described development aid as aid for economic development. *Pacem in Terris,* at least by implication, also included general cultural development. The Council took into account not only the predominantly distributive aspect but also the political and productive aspect (transition from "ancient methods of farming in favour of modern techniques", art. 87). The encyclical *Populorum Progressio,* published at Easter 1967, goes much further. Its aim is nothing more or less than the progress or ascent of all nations to a culture which is richly diversified regionally, ethnically and nationally, but which is nevertheless a culture comprising the whole of humanity (art. 14). In the sense of a Christian humanism (Maritain; cf. art. 42), the Pope's aim is a total culture animated by a Christian spirit. But since he is not addressing his encyclical only to Christians but to all men of goodwill, this Christian element scarcely figures in details. At all events the indispensable condition is economic advance. Backward nations, however, can only purchase this at the immense cost of fundamental change in mental attitude from a mode of thought determined by tradition, to a strictly rational kind of thought and action. Furthermore, the transformation must be accomplished with unparalleled rapidity. Is it not too great a burden for these nations? Do they not run the risk of losing their very best possession, their entire inheritance of cultural, ethical and religious tradition, and, as a consequence, of falling victim to cultural, ethical and religious nihilism? What can the advanced nations, and Christians in particular, do in order to help them to withstand this crisis? The encyclical views this problem more in the light of a clash between two cultures, between the native culture of the developing countries and that of the advanced industrial countries pressing on them from outside (art. 10), particularly in the person of those who, after studying abroad, return to their underdeveloped home country (art. 68).

By far the most space is devoted in *Populorum Progressio* to economic distress and to means of overcoming it. Distributive measures still clearly predominate. Development policy here clearly retains the character of development "aid", i.e. of alms from rich nations to poor ones (though inculcated as strictly obligatory). Only here and there are there rudiments of a breakthrough to a genuine strategy of development, e.g. when the Pope supports the fight against illiteracy (art. 35) and especially when he supports nations taking their destinies into their own hands (art. 65). When the encyclical urges common planning, i.e. mutual agreement about measures of aid (arts. 33 ff., 50), what it has in mind is the measures taken by those giving the aid, not, or at least not so much, the strategy of the development itself. To elaborate a complete concept of development strategy is no doubt not the business of a Church pronouncement, but the Church can claim the right to point out this duty to those whose business it is, and imprint it on their conscience. It is a merit of *Populorum Progressio* that it extends the policy of development, which at first was limited to economic aid, into a comprehensive cultural policy of development (arts. 14, 42). Moreover, it gave a powerful new impulse at a moment when development was in danger of succumbing to indifference and fatigue in many circles.

The fact that *Populorum Progressio* does not go any further in the matter of birth control than the pronouncements of John XXIII and *Gaudium et Spes* is not surprising. A doctrinal decision by the Pope in such a fundamental matter was not to be expected in a document of such a practical character as this.

Excursus on Article 90:
The Commission "Iustitia et Pax"

by
Stefan Swieżawski

1. After several months of intensive work, a team of priests and lay people appointed after the Council by the Holy See completed the preparations for a plan to form the new central agencies in the Church provided for in the Decree on the Apostolate of the Laity (art. 26) and the Pastoral Constitution (art. 90). Paul VI made use of their work, created the two bodies and determined their form by a motu proprio of 6 January 1967. The first is the "Concilium de laicis". Its task is to promote and organize the apostolic activity of the laity. It was closely linked with the other advisory body entitled "Commissio studiosorum: iustitia et pax". The close link between the two is not due only to the fact that both are under the same direction (president: Maurice Cardinal Roy; vicepresident: Archbishop Alberto Castelli). There is a deeper connection, because one aim of the Iustitia et Pax Commission is to establish guidelines for the activity of the laity at the present day. Easter 1967 was a decisive date for Iustitia et Pax; the Pope proclaimed the commission's Magna Carta: *Populorum Progressio*.

2. Iustitia et Pax is a brains trust or advisory organ. Its aim is to stimulate studies, formulate programmes for education and the formation of public opinion, and encourage specific activities. Since the reason for its existence is to promote deeper understanding and to spread as widely as possible the ideas and principles of development contained in *Populorum Progressio*, Iustitia et Pax occupies a mediating position between this encyclical and the People of God as well as the world generally. Its work is a sort of catechesis of *Populorum Progressio*. The demands of international justice and development (here understood in the widest sense as unlimited development) are closely connected with the work of peace, for "development is the new name for peace" (Paul VI) and can only be effectively realized on the basis of a well-thought out fundamentally reformed education based on the authentic demands of the gospel.

The studies which the commission encourages[1] must be pursued in con-

---

[1] Documentation and bibliography of development; world reaction to *Populorum Progressio*; deeper knowledge of the present social, economic and cultural position, with projects for the future; special inquiries in all matters concerning development.

junction with lasting and determined educational efforts[2] and schemes for concrete activity.[3] Iustitia et Pax is doing its utmost to realize this programme on three planes: in the Church, with its rich variety of institutions, secondly through ecumenical relations in the widest sense (Christians, believing non-Christians, non-believers), thirdly in non-denominational international institutions.

3. Iustitia et Pax has devoted itself to the enormous task of development and has an important part to play in the dialogue between Church and world. The aims it has been set are binding not only on the laity but on the whole Church. For this reason, its 14 members and 14 consultors include priests and laity. The Church of the poor is not represented on the commission in proportion to its real numbers, nor are all important social classes, all geographically important parts of the earth or all professions concerned with comprehensive development. Nevertheless the range of professions represented is marked by a clearly perceptible world-wide tendency. At all events, the presence of economists and specialists for social and international questions, of scientists, theologians and philosophers contributes to enrich and deepen its meetings and discussions.

4. The projects undertaken by Iustitia et Pax are the result of the initiative of the commission itself and of its various members and consultors. Two full meetings, each lasting a week, have taken place in Rome (April and October 1967). They resulted in reports of discussions and revised working documents. Decisions were taken, studies promoted, enterprises planned and permanent committees established. A secretariat in Rome with Mgr. Joseph Grémillion as secretary is developing constantly increasing activity, especially by founding national and regional commissions for justice, development and peace. Ecumenical contacts have increasingly to be cultivated at the present time, as a matter of primary importance. Several Iustitia et Pax commissions have already been established by the bishops in various parts of the world. The commissions for Western Europe and North America met in Brussels in December 1967. The local commissions and the individual members and consultors of the papal commission make all kinds of efforts to make Iustitia et Pax and its functions better known — local meetings, books, articles, lectures, studies, seminars, etc. All these enterprises have an ecumenical character.

---

[2] Redirection of all forms of education and training towards deepening and broadening the attitude of mind and conscience, in order to recognize the dignity of the human person in every human being, to spread world-wide international justice, to safeguard the rights of small groups despite racialism, nationalism and egotism of every kind, to create really human relationships which spring from the powers of wonder, understanding, contemplation and personal judgment (Gaudium et Spes).

[3] For example the campaign in favour of a tax of 1% of the national income for the benefit of developing countries; collaboration in view of juster solutions in international trade; various ecumenical obligations, in the United Nations, etc.

Excursus on the "Church of Love"
(Ecclesia Caritatis)

by
Richard Völkl

All the documents of Vatican II contain statements about *caritas* and its importance for the various expressions of the Church's life; only the more important aspects and passages can be dealt with here.[1] Everything the Church can and must do is based on what it is. Its action as *ecclesia caritatis* follows from the fact that it is a community of love established by the love of the triune God. This interconnection of being and doing, of indicative and imperative, which characterizes the biblical ethos in particular, must always be remembered in regard to all the demands of love and service. The way the Church's action is rooted in what it is, can be seen, for example, in the following statements of the Dogmatic Constitution on the Church: Love is the first and most necessary gift of God, who in his saving action has revealed that he himself is love; this gift makes it possible for all believers to fulfil their duty of expressing love of God and their neighbour in their whole life in Church and world (art. 42). The People of God as such is holy, and must therefore strive for sanctification and perfect love (art. 40); the law of the "communion of love" *(communio caritatis)* is the new commandment, which does not demand only love "for one another" but includes a mission to the world (art. 9). By sharing in Christ's prophetic office in particular, the People of God must bear witness "especially by means of a life of faith and charity" (art. 12). The Church is the beloved bride of Christ and must therefore be obedient to him in love and fidelity; the body of Christ whose members live and grow in service and love (arts. 6f.). The Church is the incipient, already present kingdom of Christ, which is mani-

[1] All the relevant passages are studied in: R. Völkl, "Kirche und 'caritas' nach den Dokumenten des Zweiten Vatikanischen Konzils", *Caritas* 67 (1966), pp. 73–96, 123–45. On what follows, R. Völkl, "Ecclesia caritatis. Zur Dogmatischen Konstitution über die Kirche", *Caritas* 66 (1965), pp. 113–26. The *ecclesia caritatis* is to be aimed at for the sake of renewal of the Church and the world: Paul VI's speech at the opening of the second session: *Herder Korrespondenz* 18 (1963–64), p. 80; cf. pp. 76–83.

fested and spreads by imitating the service of its Lord (arts. 3, 5, 36); it is a community filled and guided by the Holy Spirit who distributes manifold gifts and unites all its members in love and mutual service (arts. 4, 7).

Yet the Church is not simply a "mystical" reality. It is also a visible reality, a "societas", a visible community of love with a hierarchical structure. An order of love must prevail in it; it has to fulfil its function of love and service in the world with human means but without seeking human power (arts. 8, 13; cf. art. 32). It is Church for the world, "sacrament, or sign of intimate union with God and of the unity of all mankind" (art. 1; also arts. 9, 48, 59). It fulfils this specific service as an eschatological, pilgrim Church, still bearing the figure of this world yet linked by mutual love with the Church in heaven (arts. 48–51). It is "foreign" to the world and must therefore "seek what is above"; yet its longing for eschatological fulfilment does not cause it to flee the world, because the very love which makes it aspire to be "with Christ" imposes the duty of service in the world and for the world (arts. 6, 48). It can only perform this, however, if it is and remains "other" than the "world", and only if, precisely for the sake of its function in the world, it is guided by the spirit of poverty and love.[2] These few points indicate how the Church's action is grounded in its being. Moreover, the being of each member of the Church is differentiated by the different gift he has received. Consequently each in accordance with his gifts and graces has to practise faith and hope and charity and thus manifest the love of God to all by temporal service (art. 41).[3]

In the performance of this service, the love of God and the neighbour, as the New Testament understands them, form an inseparable unity. According to *Gaudium et Spes* (art. 24; cf. art. 38), "love for God and neighbour is the first and greatest commandment". Here, therefore, the statement that the second commandment of love of the neighbour is "like" to the first in importance (Mt 22:39), is taken really seriously. Furthermore, with the New Testament it is emphasized that in practical Christian life the will of God is fulfilled, that is, the love of God is realized above all by practising love of the neighbour (cf. Rom 13: 8–10; Gal 5:14; 6:2; Jas 2:8). In most passages, *caritas* appears in the comprehensive theological sense as the fundamental attitude and function of the People of God, of the body of Christ and of all

---

[2] "Spirit of poverty and love" as opposed to "spirit of the world": Paul VI's encyclical *Ecclesiam Suam* (arts. 48–52, 54–58); cf. R. Völkl, "'Die Wege der Kirche' und die christliche Liebe. Zur Enzyklika Papst Pauls VI. 'Ecclesiam suam'", *Caritas* 65 (1964), pp. 255–62; F. Wulf, "Vom Geist der Armut", *Glaube und Leben* 38 (1965), pp. 135–46.

[3] On what follows: R. Völkl, *Dienende Kirche — Kirche der Liebe* (1968), with bibliography; H. M. Féret, "Brotherly Love in the Church as the Sign of the Kingdom", *Concilium* 9, no. 3 (1967), pp. 9–19; cf. W. Beinert, "Die geistige Gestalt des Zweiten Vatikanischen Konzils", *Anzeiger für die katholische Geistlichkeit* 75 (1966), pp. 195–204, 253–64; cf. H. U. von Balthasar, *Sponsa Verbi* (1961).

its members; it is presented as the "ecclesiological virtue" and at the same time as essentially witness for the world. Another series of statements also explicitly brings out the right and obligation of the Church to engage in independent, planned, organized and co-ordinated social and charitable activity (*Apostolicam Actuositatem*, art. 8; *Gaudium et Spes*, art. 42; *Dignitatis Humanae*, art. 4).[4] This claim does not exclude the collaboration of Catholics in non-Catholic social organizations or the co-operation of Church institutions with them. In fact, *caritas* must itself assume institutional form for the sake of such collaboration. A wish for it is expressed several times (*Apostolicam Actuositatem*, arts. 8, 27; *Gaudium et Spes*, arts. 88, 90; *Unitatis Redintegratio*, art. 12). Above all, however, the visible Church must become visibly the *ecclesia caritatis* by its "works".

Because the apostolate has to be carried out personally and socially, *caritas* must be attested by personal action and also in social, institutionalized and organized forms. That is "even indispensable" (*Apostolicam Actuositatem*, arts. 15 f.; 18 f.; 23) in the world of today, to achieve efficiency and not least in order to make possible the kind of co-operation mentioned above. Thus an individualistic and angelist conception of *caritas*, inclined to regard its organization as a falling away from the spirit of love or as a kind of secularization, is clearly rejected: "For the spirit of charity does not forbid but rather requires that charitable activity be exercised in a provident and orderly manner (providum ordinatumque actionis socialis et caritativae exercitium)" (*Gaudium et Spes*, art. 88). Once again this is in complete agreement with the New Testament, which regards *agape-caritas* as the greatest virtue and the fundamental function of the congregation (e.g. 1 Cor 13; cf. 12–14), while at the same time it calls for and describes its realization in organized forms (especially 2 Cor 8 f.; cf., for example, Acts 6:1–7; 1 Tim 5:9–16). In what follows, therefore, *caritas* as a fundamental attitude and *Caritas* as the work of the Church will be envisaged together.

All Church offices are ministries, services. Consequently those who hold them, in particular the bishops in unity with the Pope and with one another "in the bond of unity, love and peace", serve the Church, their particular Churches and the comprehensive "community of love". The whole performance of their *diaconia* has as its purpose the building up of this community of faith, hope and love. In their care for the Church and the Churches, as expressed for example from the earliest days in Councils and synods and

---

[4] P. Nordhues, *Gedanken über Konzil und Caritas* (1966); R. Völkl, "Der caritative Auftrag der Kirche", *Caritas* 67 (1966), pp. 1–9; K. Rahner, "Praktische Theologie und kirchliche Sozialarbeit", *Schriften zur Theologie* VIII (1967), pp. 667–88; B. Dreher, "Caritative Kirche in der sozialen Welt", *Caritas* 69 (1968), pp. 1–9; N. Greinacher, "Zur Funktion der kirchlichen Sozialhilfe in unserer heutigen Gesellschaft", *ibid.*, pp. 10–20; A. Stehlin, "Caritasdienst gestern, heute und morgen", *ibid.*, pp. 63–71; cf. W. Dirks, "Caritas im Geiste des Konzils", *Jahrbuch der Caritaswissenschaft* (1967), pp. 9–29.

practical help to neighbouring and needy Churches, they bear witness to and strengthen unity in love (*Lumen Gentium*, arts. 8, 13, 22, 18–24). For present needs a call is made for advisory bodies to be created on all levels, from the parish to the international plane, in order to support and co-ordinate the Church's apostolic activity, including that "in the sphere of charitable and social work" (*Apostolicam Actuositatem*, art. 26; cf. below: "Development aid").

In his diocese the bishop "by teaching, by sanctifying and by ruling ... so feeds the family of God that the new commandment of charity may be fulfilled by all" (*Lumen Gentium*, art. 32).[5] In the accomplishment of his threefold ministry, he must perfectly exercise the office of pastoral love (*caritas pastoralis*) as a father and brother to his priests and the laity by word and example, in short by every aspect of his care and service, and also by "all the works of charity (*omnibus operibus caritatis*)". In particular he must come to the help of the poor and weak, with due regard for the social conditions in which they live (*Lumen Gentium*, arts. 27, 41; cf. arts. 26, 30, 37; *Christus Dominus*, arts. 13, 16). This purpose again necessitates the organized assistance of those associations and undertakings which experience shows to be indispensable in a diocese. Under the guidance of the bishop, therefore, undertakings and associations concerned with charitable works and social questions should be encouraged and co-ordinated. And those endeavours and associations should be cultivated and adapted to the needs of the present day, which "pursue social aims or perform works of piety and charity", especially for believers who cannot be sufficiently provided for by the ordinary pastoral services of parish priests (*Christus Dominus*, arts. 17 f., 23, 3).

The service performed by the clergy and religious orders also has as its goal the *ecclesia caritatis*. Priests are linked by sacrament and mission with their bishop and with one another in fraternal *caritas*, especially those priests who live and work in the same parish (*Christus Dominus*, arts. 28, 30; *Presbyterorum Ordinis*, arts. 7 f.). They should therefore help one another in a variety of ways, even in their material needs, by supporting institutions which can prevent distress or come to the help of priests in need (*Presbyterorum Ordinis*, arts. 8, 21; *Lumen Gentium*, art. 28). In view of the number and variety of functions at the present time, the difficulties of priestly life and the temptation to apathy, it is particularly important for the priest to find direction in his spiritual life as well as in his pastoral work.

---

[5] Y. Congar, *L'Épiscopat et l'Église universelle* (1962); P. V. Dias, *Vielfalt der Kirche in der Vielfalt der Jünger, Zeugen und Diener* (1968); B. Lambert, ed., *La nouvelle image de l'Église* (1967); R. Völkl, "Bischofsamt und 'caritas' in den Dokumenten des Zweiten Vatikanischen Konzils", *Oberrheinisches Pastoralblatt* 67 (1966), pp. 352–56; cf. H. Küng, *The Church* (1967), pp. 388–480 ("Ecclesiastical Office as Ministry").

He should view this "pastoral love", *caritas pastoralis,* which has been frequently mentioned, as such a unifying direction (*Presbyterorum Ordinis,* arts. 14, 22). That is the ultimate aim of the spiritual and intellectual formation of future priests. They have particularly to learn to understand and affirm the renunciations connected with their services as "signs and stimulus of pastoral love" (*Presbyterorum Ordinis,* art. 16; *Optatam Totius,* arts. 8–11, 16, 19; Encyclical of Paul VI "On Priestly Celibacy", e.g. arts. 24 f., 30, 32, 50, 56, 76). The parish priest in particular in carrying out his threefold office must receive, announce and transmit *caritas* and practise it by unselfish service, so that his parish may be built up in accordance with the demands of the new commandment of love and become increasingly united in love (*Presbyterorum Ordinis,* arts. 6, 9, 13, 15). The congregation must not only be "rooted in faith, hope and love" (*Christus Dominus,* art. 30), but must "bear witness by love" (*Christus Dominus,* art. 30). The parish priest has therefore not only the task of educating the faithful to a frame of mind of love, but also to "the various works of brotherly love", "works of charity and mercy" which are an outstanding testimony to Christian life (*Presbyterorum Ordinis,* art. 6; *Apostolicam Actuositatem,* art. 31).

In this sense too, "pastoral care and works of charity" must form a unity. In particular the celebration of the Eucharist and all liturgical and sacramental life must be fruitful for the congregation itself and for the world (*Sacrosanctum Concilium,* arts. 9 f., 47 f., 59, 105, 110).[6] In this sense, the parish will be "an obvious example of the apostolate on the community level" (*Apostolicam Actuositatem,* art. 10) if the parish priest fulfils his duties in this respect. In a spirit of poverty he has to care for the poor and sick and to support works of charity; he must be particularly devoted to the poor and sick with a paternal love, and in the administration of Church property he must take due account of works of charity (*Presbyterorum Ordinis,* arts. 6, 17, 20; *Christus Dominus,* art. 30; cf. art. 28). To fulfil his mission of charity he will get the laity to collaborate in the various associations and activities (*Apostolicam Actuositatem,* art. 25; *Lumen Gentium,* art. 37). They will in fact generally be the actual specialists engaged in them, but the priest's training and refresher courses must make him familiar with welfare and charitable work for they belong to the "matters which have a special bearing on the sacred ministry" (*Optatam Totius,* art. 19; cf. arts. 21 f.). Finally, the official activity of a priest in organized charitable work is to be regarded as "priestly service" (cf. *Christus Dominus,* art. 29; *Presbyterorum Ordinis,* art. 8).

[6] E. Tewes, "Die Caritas in der pastoralen Neuordnung nach dem Konzil", *Caritas* 68 (1967), pp. 109–117; A. Fischer, "Seelsorge und Caritas im Dialog", *ibid.* 65 (1964), pp. 318–22; P. Nordhues, "Liturgie und Caritas", *ibid.* 66 (1965), pp. 127–36; id., "Kirche — Priester — Gegenwart", *Theologie und Glaube* 55 (1965), pp. 162–70; cf. *Lebendige Seelsorge* 17 (1966), pp. 97—125.

Deacons serve "the People of God in the ministry of the liturgy, of the word and of charity, in communion with the bishop and his group of priests"; they fulfil "duties of charity and administration". The "exercise of social or charitable works" by deacons is stressed particularly in missionary territories, but since they are collaborators of the bishops and priests, they share in principle in their social and charitable activity, though this is not always explicitly stated. Such activity is one of the functions absolutely and vitally necessary for the Church which demand and justify the restoration of an independent diaconate (*Lumen Gentium*, art. 29; *Ad Gentes*, art. 16; cf. art. 15; see also Paul VI's motu proprio of 18 June 1967, arts. 10, 22, 9 and 11, 25, 36).[7] But even the deacon who later becomes a priest should be trained in this activity and, at the bishop's discretion, should work as an ordained deacon for a suitable length of time, among other things on welfare and charitable activities (*Optatam Totius*, art. 12; cf. arts. 19, 21).

Members of religious orders and institutes follow the evangelical counsels and, by a renunciation which goes beyond what is obligatory, obey those admonitions to imitate Christ's love and abnegation in the narrower sense, which in principle apply to all Christians. The purpose of the self-denial involved is perfect love of God and the neighbour for Christ and his Church, not primarily or solely their own "perfection" (*Lumen Gentium*, arts. 42–47; *Perfectae Caritatis*, arts. 1, 6, 12). This applies not only to members of institutes of "active" but also of "contemplative" life. Both must achieve and bear witness to perfect "caritas", though in different ways. Moreover, the life of religious orders bears the stamp of brotherly love and so influences the world by its example (*Ad Gentes*, art. 40; *Perfectae Caritatis*, arts. 14 f., 24). The Council's instructions on the "appropriate renewal of the religious life" also constantly admonish religious to link "apostolic love", "practical virtue", and therefore social and charitable activity, with devotion to God and his worship, with imitation of Christ and contemplation, in short with that inner renewal which is the ultimately decisive factor. According to the character of their particular community, they must devote themselves more intensively to the external works of the apostolate "and for the sake of this service adapt themselves to the world of the present day" (*Perfectae Caritatis*, arts. 2 f., 5, 9; cf. arts. 16–18; *Christus Dominus*, art. 33).[8] Members of secular institutes in particular, while maintaining their secular character, must strive for perfect love of God and fulfilment of their apostolic purpose (*Perfectae Caritatis*,

---

[7] K. Rahner, "Die Lehre des Zweiten Vatikanischen Konzils über den Diakonat", *Schriften zur Theologie* VIII (1967), pp. 541–52. Information on these questions is available from the "Internationales Informationszentrum für Fragen des Diakonats" (Freiburg i. Br.), and from the reports published there: *Diakonia*; cf. J. Hornef, "Römische Ausführungsbestimmungen zu den Diakonatsbeschlüssen des Konzils", *Klerusblatt* 48 (1968), pp. 127–9.

[8] Cf. *Herder Korrespondenz* 20 (1966), pp. 465–8; D. Wiederkehr, ed., *Die Situation des Bruderberufs heute* (1968).

art. 11). In many clerical and lay institutes, however, "apostolic and charitable activity is an actual part of the life of the order. It has been entrusted to them by the Church as their holy service and work of love and is exercised in the Church's name." This activity too must spring from close union with Christ; it is a service of Christ in his members and consequently an expression of love of God and the neighbour (*Perfectae Caritatis*, art. 8).

The Council also praises the work of religious orders done in a spirit of poverty for the poor, and the welfare and charitable activities they engage in in a spirit of love, for example in education and nursing. These activities, too, require planned and organized collaboration, inspired by a spirit of love, between the religious orders themselves and with other organizations in the Church (*Perfectae Caritatis*, arts. 10, 13; *Lumen Gentium*, art. 46; *Christus Dominus*, art. 35; cf. *Ad Gentes*).

The laity "are in their own way made sharers in the priestly, prophetic and kingly functions of Christ", and "carry out their own part in the mission of the whole Christian people in the Church and in the world". But by reason of their secular character, they have the specific function of announcing the Church as present and active in the world and of making Christ known above all by a life of faith, hope and love (*Lumen Gentium*, art. 31; cf. Chapter IV). They fulfil this task in a personal and social apostolate of word and deed, by their whole conduct in a life bearing the stamp of charity; by collaboration with the clergy inspired by that fraternal love within the congregation which is itself a sign of Christ's disciples in contrast to the world. They repeatedly receive in their liturgical sacramental life, especially in the celebration of the Eucharist, that love of God and men which is the "soul of the whole apostolate" (*Apostolicam Actuositatem*, arts. 3 f., 6, 13, 15 f.; *Lumen Gentium*, arts. 33, 37).

Special importance attaches in the world of today to Christian marriage and family. In contrast to various false ideas of love, it bears witness as a community of personal, human love, as a sacramental community and as an image of the love between Christ and the Church (*Gaudium et Spes*, arts. 47–52; *Lumen Gentium*, arts. 35, 41). Its mission to be "the first and vital cell of society" will be chiefly fulfilled by showing itself, by the mutual affection of its members and their common prayer, to be "the domestic sanctuary of the Church", which promotes "justice and good works for the service of all the brethren in need". Among the works of the family apostolate, mention is made, for example, of the adoption of abandoned children, the support of other families and care for old people (*Apostolicam Actuositatem*, art. 11). The children of the family itself must be educated by word and example to genuine love of God and the neighbour, but families, in particular younger ones, must be induced through the organization of lay groups and associations to fulfil their social and apostolic duties (*Apostolicam Actuositatem*, art. 30; *Gaudium et Spes*, art. 52;

Gravissimum Educationis, art. 3). All the laity have the specific task of filling the world with Christ's spirit so that it may reach its goal "in justice, love and peace" (*Lumen Gentium,* art. 36). It is precisely the laity's business to contribute to the best of their ability to the creation of a healthy social order, to establish justice and equity and the principles of Christian social doctrine generally. Consequently it must be emphasized "that the new command of love is the basic law of human perfection and hence of the world's transformation" (*Gaudium et Spes,* art. 38). Again and again the conciliar documents emphasize the duty of justice *and* love. The Christian laity in particular must practise justice and love and thus serve the common good, perfect the work of justice under the impulse of love and in this sense act "socially" (*Gaudium et Spes,* arts. 26, 30, 69, 72). The Christian who neglects his earthly duties thereby neglects his duties to God and the neighbour and therefore ultimately does not fulfil the commandment of love.

Repeated reference is consequently made in the passages on work and professional life, and on the laity's obligations in the whole social domain of cultural, economic and political life, to the importance of charity (*Lumen Gentium,* art. 41; *Gaudium et Spes,* arts. 43, 57, 67, 69, 75; *Inter Mirifica,* art. 8). The corresponding activity could be called social and charitable in the wide sense, but the conciliar documents also speak of a planned, organized and co-ordinated "social and charitable" action (*Apostolicam Actuositatem,* art. 26; *Christus Dominus,* art. 17; *Ad Gentes,* art. 16; *Gaudium et Spes,* art. 88; *Dignitatis Humanae,* art. 4). In particular, according to the only specific statement on charitable activity, the *actio caritativa* itself is an *actio socialis* (*Apostolicam Actuositatem,* art. 8; cf. art. 7): charitable activity itself is and remains an essential witness borne by the Church of Christ before the world. But precisely in the world of today the traditional forms of care for the poor are no longer sufficient. To put it briefly, the Church has above all to give personal and psychological help, which is often allied to pastoral care; it has to act as a partner, providing objective and specialist help, "help to self-help". Nor should it offer as a charitable gift what is already due in justice. The practice of *caritas* in organized form must take into account the psychological and social situation of those who are to be helped (*Apostolicam Actuositatem,* art. 18). This *caritas* must be exercised in "social" works (cf. *Ad Gentes,* art. 16: "caritatem exercentes in operibus socialibus seu caritativis"); thus not only justice is social (cf. *Gaudium et Spes,* arts. 26, 29–31, 72); charity itself must become "social".[9]

By adapting itself in this way to the world of today, it will better contribute to the transformation of the world of which the Council speaks, and

[9] R. Völkl, "Zum 'sozial-caritativen' Handeln der Kirche", *Jahrbuch für Christliche Sozialwissenschaften* (1968), pp. 9–22; id., "Kirchliche Caritas in der heutigen Welt", *Handbuch der Pastoraltheologie* II/2 (1966), pp. 403–23; cf. pp. 389–402.

also to the collaboration between Church and non-Church social organizations, especially on the international level, the desire for which is repeatedly expressed. Once again lay people in particular are to "hold in high esteem and, according to their ability, aid the works of charity and projects for social assistance whether public or private, including international programmes" of assistance, and in so doing "co-operate with all men of goodwill" (*Apostolicam Actuositatem*, art. 8). For this, however, in our pluralist society with its multifarious kinds of assistance, there is a need for organized charitable work on all levels, that is, parochial, inter-parochial, diocesan and inter-diocesan, national and international (cf. *Apostolicam Actuositatem*, art. 26).

On the basis of its universal mission, the *ecclesia caritatis* must carry out its service on a world-wide scale, promote as far as it can the community of nations and in particular strive for the unity of the Church by its missionary and ecumenical activity. As regards the fostering of world peace and the promotion of a community of nations, the Church, without seeking earthly power, endeavours to serve the human family by its attempt repeatedly mentioned in this context to promote justice and love and the "union of minds and hearts" of faith and charity (*Gaudium et Spes*, arts. 42, 76; cf. arts. 77–90). Certainly peace is the work of justice, but it is also the fruit of that love which goes beyond what justice exacts; it is an image and effect of the peace of Christ who conquered hatred and gave men the spirit of love.

In collaboration with all men of goodwill, therefore, it is a matter of overcoming self-seeking and of assisting in establishing peace in justice and love. This once again is a task which specifically belongs to the laity (*Gaudium et Spes*, arts. 77 f.; *Apostolicam Actuositatem*, art. 14).[10] In order to create a fraternal community of the nations, the Church must be present in international society and promote human collaboration. "It must achieve such a presence both through its public institutions and through the sincere collaboration of all Christians motivated solely by the desire to be of service to all (*Gaudium et Spes*, art. 89). "In view of the progress of social institutions" this calls, on the international level in particular, for careful planning, strict organization and co-ordination of Church initiatives and enterprises, especially in the social and charitable domain (*Apostolicam Actuositatem*, art. 19; cf. above art. 26). Furthermore, co-operation with non-Church organizations is needed. The Church recognizes, supports and promotes their efforts, except when they are incompatible with its own mission. Finally, the co-operation of the faithful in these institutions is encouraged (*Apostolicam Actuositatem*, art. 14; *Gaudium et Spes*, arts. 84, 88–90; *Ad Gentes*, art. 12).

[10] L. Berg, "Das Ethos der Enzyklika Pacem in terris", *Jahrbuch des Instituts für Christliche Sozialwissenschaften* VII/VIII (1966), pp. 81–104; cf. R. Völkl, "Mater et Magistra", *Caritas* 62 (1961), pp. 293–302; id., "Friede und Liebe. Zur Enzyklika Johannes' XXIII. 'Pacem in terris'", *ibid.* 64 (1963), pp. 137–48.

The works of international assistance carried out by the Church itself, however, are a realization of the universal love which is incumbent on it in view of world-wide distress. "The spirit of poverty and of charity", which is the "glory and authentication of the Church of Christ", must mark its work of assistance especially in the form of development aid, "Caritas Internationalis", the "Misereor" and "Adveniat" programmes. The same spirit, however, demands their planning and organization (cf. *Gaudium et Spes*, art. 88). The "agency of the universal Church" proposed by the Council, to stimulate the Catholic community to foster progress in needy regions and to promote social justice on the international plane, and justice and Christian love for the poor everywhere (*Gaudium et Spes*, art. 90), has since been created in the form of the papal Iustitia et Pax Commission. The problems of comprehensive development aid are, however, dealt with above all in the encyclical *Populorum Progressio*. This presents development aid as a duty of solidarity, social justice and universal love (art. 44).[11] The encyclical also recognizes the work of "Caritas Internationalis" which it terms *institutum nostrum*, and the aid achieved by Catholics under the guidance of their bishops (art. 46). But it also calls for new, opportune, world-wide planned and co-ordinated projects inspired by brotherly love (e.g. arts. 50, 71).

All these efforts of the Church are of course primarily aimed at lessening and abolishing the various kinds of poverty by suitable specialist assistance. But they are also intended to foster personal dignity and the common good of the human family, to create a fraternal community and, not least, they are meant as a missionary attestation of service and love (*Gaudium et Spes*, arts. 26, 88, 90; *Apostolicam Actuositatem*, arts. 8, 14; *Ad Gentes*, arts. 10 to 12, 19). In this activity, though not of course exclusively on the international level, the *ecclesia caritatis* is manifested as the Church of the poor. Guided by the spirit of poverty in the gospel sense, it directs all its members and works to practise justice and love for the poor and to serve Christ in them (*Lumen Gentium*, arts. 8, 42). In fact it identifies itself with the poor, for "the joys and the hopes, the griefs and the anxieties of the men of this age, especially those who are poor or in any way afflicted, these too are the joys and hopes, the griefs and the anxieties of the followers of Christ" (*Gaudium et Spes*, art. 1).[12] In giving assistance, the Church does not restrict itself to the

---

[11] R. Völkl, "Die Sorge der Kirche um den Menschen und die Menschheit nach der Enzyklika 'Populorum Progressio' Papst Pauls VI.", *Caritas* 68 (1967), pp. 118–30; "first in order": address of Pope Paul VI to the representatives of Caritas Internationalis 10 September 1965: *Caritas* 66 (1965), pp. 293–95; C. Böhle, "Sozialarbeit in Entwicklungsländern", *Jahrbuch der Caritaswissenschaft* (1968), pp. 66–74; on the "employment agency for social work abroad", see *Caritas* 68, no. 5 (1967).

[12] Y. Congar, *Power and Poverty in the Church* (1964); id., "The Place of Poverty in Christian Life in an Affluent Society", *Concilium* 5, no. 2 (1966), pp. 28–39; O. von Veghel, *Die Kirche der Armen in der Sicht des Zweiten Vatikanischen Konzils* (1965);

traditional forms of beneficence but performs "social and charitable" aid in the above-mentioned sense. The Council appeals to a very old tradition of the Church by asking, "since there are so many people in this world afflicted with hunger", the whole People of God to give "out of the substance of their goods and not only out of what is superfluous" in order to lessen the distress of our time (*Gaudium et Spes,* arts. 69, 88). Since, however, "a man is more precious for what he is than for what he has" (*Gaudium et Spes,* art. 35), the Church offers psychological and religious helps in its total care for salvation (*Gaudium et Spes,* arts. 4, 10f., 41–43). From its belief in divine love it derives confidence that "the way of love lies open to all men and that the effort to establish a universal brotherhood is not a hopeless one" (*Gaudium et Spes,* art. 38).

The Church, which has its origin in the *caritas* of God and therefore can be said to be *natura sua caritativa,* is missionary by its very nature *(natura sua missionaria).* That means that in accordance with God's universal salvific will, it is sent to announce and convey to all men and nations the love of the triune God "so that by hearing the message of salvation the whole world may believe, by believing it may hope, and by hoping it may love" (*Dei Verbum,* art. 1; *Ad Gentes,* arts. 2, 10).[13] At the same time in its missionary activity inspired by the spirit of love, it speaks as it were the languages of all, understands them all and, in accomplishing God's prevenient love and in fulfilment of the universal commandment of charity, it is ready for dialogue with all and therefore with non-Christians (*Ad Gentes,* arts. 4, 12; *Gaudium et Spes,* arts. 21, 28). It recognizes human values and what is truly good in all its partners in discussion, in particular their religious life, justice and love. It is prepared for missionary adaptation and admonishes the faithful to seek for discussion and collaboration with all, prudently and charitably. Love must not, however, make it indifferent to truth, but imposes the duty of announcing saving truth, of awakening a desire for revealed truth and love, and of bearing witness to this by its whole life. But the spirit of love forbids any judgment of human beings and any compulsion to conversion (*Gaudium et Spes,* arts. 16, 19, 92f.; *Ad Gentes,* arts. 11, 19, 22; *Dignitatis Humanae,* arts. 11f., 14; *Nostra Aetate,* arts. 2–4). The Church shows itself once again in this way to be *ecclesia caritatis,* and so the "spirit of love" must also be

---

Herder Korrespondenz 19 (1964–5), pp. 420–5; *Caritas* 43 (1965), pp. 6–10 (Paul VI on the "Church of the poor"); P. Gauthier, *Tröstet mein Volk. Das Konzil und "die Kirche der Armen"* (1966); W. Adlhoch, "Die Caritas in einer 'Kirche der Armen'", *Caritas* 67 (1966), pp. 281–95; I. Gobry, *Die Armut des Christen in der Welt* (1968).

[13] R. Dulucq, " La charité en mission" in *Mission et charité* (1966), pp. 23–28; G. Blond, "Pour aider à comprendre à lire le décret sur l'activité missionnaire de l'Église", *ibid.* (1967), pp. 115–69; cf. *Herder Korrespondenz* 19 (1964–5), pp. 691 f.; J. Schütte, ed., *Mission nach dem Konzil* (1967).

operative in its missionary work and "missionary aid" (cf. *Ad Gentes*, Chapters II, VI), "in right order" (*Ad Gentes*, art. 28; cf. Chapter V). The Council therefore repeatedly demands that the relevant undertakings and organizations should be planned, organized and co-ordinated by the hierarchy, that social and charitable service should be carried out through collaboration between priests, deacons, religious and, not least, laity, while an order of love and justice is built up by the laity. Here, too, the Church is not seeking earthly power and dominion, but is accomplishing its selfless ministry of love specifically through its missionaries and their collaborators. It is striving for the young congregations and particular Churches increasingly to become communities of faith and charity and thereby signs of the presence of God in the world (*Ad Gentes*, arts. 12, 14–16, 19, 24 f., 28 f., 36, 38).

The Church called by God "to the unity of faith, hope and love" finally strives for the restoration of the unity of all Christians by an "ecumenism in the spirit of love".[14] It therefore turns to the separated Christian brethren and Churches, acknowledging their faith, hope and love, their work for the realization of justice and love of the neighbour, and recognizes that it is closely linked with them in this way. Existing differences, sometimes very grave, are not passed over in silence. Precisely because of them the Council asks for a dialogue to be pursued with love of truth and mutual love, with the aim of achieving unity in truth and love (*Gaudium et Spes*, art. 92; *Unitatis Redintegratio*, arts. 2 f., 11, 14, 18 f., 23). Even if this goal is beyond human powers, all, and not least the members of the hierarchy, must seek this dialogue and promote unity, under the guidance of love inspired by the Holy Spirit, in mutual toleration and forgiveness (*Unitatis Redintegratio*, arts. 7, 24; *Christus Dominus*, art. 16). Together with the separated brethren, all believers must bear witness by a profoundly Christian life in the service of God and the love of the neighbour, helping to remove the scandal of division as far as possible *(Ad Gentes*, arts. 29, 36). That can and must be achieved, particularly by collaboration in the social and charitable domain, and in those countries in which social and technical development has still advanced little. This common social and charitable endeavour bears witness to love of Christ and Christian brotherly love, even if it still seems premature to preach the gospel; to a certain extent the one Church is already visible and operative as the "ecclesia caritatis" and a ministering Church (*Unitatis Redintegratio*, arts. 6, 12; *Apostolicam Actuositatem*, art. 27; *Ad Gentes*, art. 6; *Gaudium et Spes*, arts. 88, 90). Precisely by this collaboration "all believers in Christ" are able to learn easily how they can understand each other better and esteem each other more, and how the road to unity of Christians may be made smooth (*Unitatis Redintegratio*, art. 12).

---

[14] R. Völkl, "Ökumenismus im Geiste der Liebe. Zum 'Dekret über den Ökumenismus'", *Caritas* 66 (1965), pp. 153–9; cf. H. and W. Goddijn, *Sichtbare Kirche, Ökumene und Pastoral* (1967).

The Second Vatican Council was characterized by Pope Paul VI as *actus caritatis*, an act of threefold *caritas* towards God, the Church and mankind.[15] The conciliar documents clearly show that the Church understands itself as *ecclesia caritatis*, and *caritas* as the vital expression of all its members. They also make it plain that it must practise the "spirit of love" in the world of today by its planned, organized and co-ordinated *Caritas*, its social and charitable institutions and undertakings. Consequently, with the encyclical *Ecclesiam Suam* (art. 52), it is to be desired and hoped that the hour of charity has not ended with the Council, but that *caritas* will occupy its due place, "the first in the scale of religious and moral values, not only in theoretical estimation but also in the practical realization of Christian life. That applies to love of God who has given his love to us as well as to the love which we, for our part, must give in return to our neighbour, that is to say, to all men."

[15] Love for God, the Church and mankind. Speech of Pope Paul VI at the opening of the Fourth Session: *Caritas* 66 (1965), pp. 296–300 (main section); cf. *Herder Korrespondenz* 19 (1964–5), pp. 627–31.

Excursus on Humanae Vitae

by

Leonhard M. Weber

The encyclical *Humanae Vitae* of 25 July 1968 gives Pope Paul's answer to the problem of the regulation of births *(de propagatione humanae prolis recte ordinanda)*. It constitutes the papal decision foreshadowed in *Gaudium et Spes* (art. 51, n. 14; Abbott, n. 173).

1. The contents of the encyclical fall into three parts, introduced by the affirmation that the Church cannot ignore questions concerning the transmission of life which are raised by the evolution of society. In the first part the changes which have taken place are said to be important and of many kinds. It asks whether new points of view, which it does not go into more closely, make it advisable to re-examine the moral norms in force until now. It points out the duty and competence of the magisterium in this matter (art. 4) and, in contrast to certain suggestions made by the commission of experts (art. 5), the second part of the encyclical teaches that in the light of a correct and comprehensive view of man, each and every marital act *(quilibet matrimonii usus)* must remain in itself ordered to the transmission of life *(ad vitam humanam procreandam per se destinatus permaneat:* art. 11). This doctrine, already set forth on a number of occasions by the magisterium, is said to follow from the twofold meaning inherent in every marital act: that of union and of procreation. The inseparable connection between these two aspects is stated to be posited by God; man may not annul it *sua sponte,* on his own initiative (art. 12). The encyclical deduces that any interruption of the generative process once begun, especially by abortion (even on therapeutic grounds), must be totally rejected; similarly the direct sterilization of men and women, whether permanent or temporary; likewise any action performed in anticipation of marital intercourse, during it or after it, in the course of its natural consequences, with the purpose of preventing procreation, or which is performed as a means to this end. The encyclical describes a marital act which is deliberately rendered infertile as *intrinsice inhonestum.* It is therefore an error to think that such an action can be morally approved

in a married life which in principle is directed towards fertility (art. 14). In cases of organic illness *(morbus corporis)*, the Church does not regard necessary therapeutic treatment as illicit, even if it prevents procreation, provided the prevention is not what, for whatever motive, is directly intended (art. 15). In virtue of their prerogative as rational beings, married people for grave reasons and with respect for the order established by God, may use the infertile periods (art. 16). The encyclical fears that very grave effects will ensue if artificial birth control prevails (art. 17). The third part of the encyclical contains pastoral directions, and in successive sections it addresses governments, scientists, married people, the family apostolate, doctors and nurses, priests and bishops. It looks to Catholic scientists to establish a sufficiently secure basis for a regulation of births in conformity with nature, and thus to prove that there can be no contradiction between the divine laws pertaining to the transmission of life and those which promote true married love (art. 24).

2. Public reaction to the encyclical was intense, whether in rejection, agreement, gratitude, admiration or criticism. Anyone who had attentively noted the Pope's previous pronouncements and the endeavours of the World Congress for the Lay Apostolate in this matter could have foreseen the reception the encyclical was likely to meet with. Nevertheless, comparison of *Humanae Vitae* with Pius XI's encyclical on marriage, *Casti Connubii*, indicates a certain development of doctrine. *Humanae Vitae* endeavours to regard marriage from an integrally human point of view (art. 7) and deals expressly with the mutual perfecting of the partners (art. 8), whereas in *Casti Connubii* this was only referred to with an allusion to the *Catechismus Romanus*. Furthermore, in *Humanae Vitae* the distinction between the primary and secondary ends of marriage is avoided in favour of marital love and the intrinsic connection between loving union and fertility, although the primary end and marital rights still form the background of the argument (cf. arts. 4, 8). Responsible parenthood *(conscia paternitas)* is treated comprehensively as a duty (art. 10), and moral conscience is affirmed as the guide of moral action (arts. 1, 10). Reference to the biblical account of the sin of Onan is avoided, in accordance with present-day exegesis of this text. In style, the encyclical is kind and persuasive; its main section is severe but reserved, without harsh words, threats or condemnations. No explicit mention is made of mortal sin (but cf. arts. 14, 19, 25, 29). In comparison with *Gaudium et Spes*, *Humanae Vitae* is perceptibly narrower. This is evident in the choice of quotations and its mode of expression; it prefers to speak in terms of nature rather than of person. On the other hand the encyclical confirms the content of *Gaudium et Spes* as set forth by the Council *summa auctoritate* (art. 7), and supplements it with essential aspects, particularly social ones, on the lines of *Populorum Progressio*. But the very much more complex criteria of marital fertility and birth control presented in *Gaudium et Spes*,

and the mention which it makes of the danger to marriage when the intimacy of married life is broken off (1 Cor 7:5), are passed over in *Humanae Vitae* by reference to the biological laws which are part of the human person (art. 10). It is true that on 25 November 1965 Pope Paul VI suggested to the conciliar commission a number of *modi* which were not all incorporated in *Gaudium et Spes* because it was considered they would contradict the fundamental structure of the text. Consequently many Catholics and also prominent non-Catholics are pleased that this line of thought, which they share, is not passed over in silence by the encyclical (arts. 18, 23, 25). *Gaudium et Spes* would, of course, have left room for a different answer from the Pope and would have provided the preamble to it.

3. As a result of *Humanae Vitae,* specialist theology has the duty of receiving and acknowledging this doctrinal decision in an ecclesiastical spirit and with full respect for the Pope and the papal primacy. But it also has the duty of asking how it is to be understood and what perspectives and tendencies lie behind it, especially as the papal pronouncement is intended to be an adequate reply not only to the expectation of the faithful but also to that of world opinion (art. 5). Since the moral problem of birth control is at most indirectly connected with the deposit of faith, the papal decision has to be justified and explained without recourse to revelation within the framework of human knowledge. Hence the encyclical appeals to the *constans doctrina* of the Church (arts. 11 f.) and to the divinely-willed and inseparable connection between loving union and fertility in the unity of the conjugal act (art. 12). It is not said why this connection is inseparable and why man must not intervene and control precisely in this matter. The Pope even considers that people at the present time are particularly capable of seeing for themselves the profoundly reasonable character of this doctrine. The encyclical takes the doctrine to be established simply by the physiological facts of the marital act; perhaps also by a metaphysics of procreation which is not actually explicitly mentioned but the traditional influence of which is still felt (cf. art. 13). Nevertheless, the encyclical does not appear to be entirely sure of the grounds of its argument. It states that in order not to abandon to human caprice the mission of transmitting life, infrangible limits must necessarily be set to man's possible power to dispose over his own body and its functions. And these laws, it is said, can only be determined by respecting the integrity of the human organism and its functions (art. 17). And when the Pope calls for obedience from priests, he does so less for the reasons stated than on account of the enlightenment of the Holy Spirit which is bestowed on the pastors of the Church for the exposition of the truth (art. 28). Consequently the theological problem arises: What exactly does it mean when the Pope makes a decision which is binding, though not infallible (cf. *Gaudium et Spes,* art. 51: sons of the Church may not undertake methods of regulating procreation condemned by the magisterium in its unfolding of the

divine law), when that decision takes no account of recent theological inquiry, or of any of the opposing arguments put forward by the papal commission of experts, and simply inculcates once again the doctrinal pronouncements of Pius XI and Pius XII, practically on the sole basis of an ethics of the single action as such and of a static concept of natural law? Moreover, it does so in the light of a particular conception of the Church seen from the hierarchical point of view, without collegial collaboration of the bishops and without the testimony of the People of God which also shares in Christ's prophetical office. Does this not retrospectively impose on the Council's renewed consciousness of the Church and its pluralism, a restrictive interpretation in the sense of ecclesiastical integralism? Has a door been bolted or opened on endeavours within the Church to achieve a correct understanding of the *magisterium ordinarium?* After all, it was the doctrinal statements of recent Popes (which, according to Roman theology, are binding for salvation), which decided Paul VI to renew in essentials the previous teaching, and to do so independently of whether the rational argumentation adduced is thought cogent or not (cf. art. 28).

4. An urgent task of pastoral application is set by the encyclical, for it has not produced unity among the faithful (cf. art. 28) but emotional tension and division. Even among enthusiastic defenders of the encyclical there are some who are chiefly gratified by the Pope's candour, his stand against moral decline, economic exploitation, manipulation of human beings by themselves and others. They maintain that the Pope will never be able to allow the "pill", because of its consequences. But they think that as long as there is no sufficiently certain method of birth control except by intervention, the instructions given by the encyclical are to be regarded as prescribing the end to be aimed at. This interpretation may be correct as regards the personal endeavour of married couples on whom the Church's pronouncements now impose the obligation of practising responsible parenthood (cf. arts. 18–22, 25–29). The objective doctrinal statement of the encyclical, however, expresses a precept to be fulfilled, and therefore admits of no exceptions: *intrinsice inhonestum* (art. 14). Therapeutic means may of course be employed to regulate the female cycle (art. 15); it is not certain whether this is meant to extend more widely to hard cases. Nevertheless, Christians of independent mind will reject a casuistical interpretation, and it is certainly in accordance with the spirit of the encyclical not to accept any subterfuges or expedients.

One can only accept or reject the papal decision on birth control, and perhaps take comfort in the idea that this encyclical is not the last word on the matter. But the Church's pastoral care will have to take account of those members of the faithful who know about the views of the papal commission of experts and who are more accustomed to a concrete empirical mode of thought than to the formal principles of the encyclical, which may be entirely inaccessible to their minds. It will also have to consider pastorally committed married people who, honestly and responsibly, and in accordance with *Gaudium et Spes,* have found a way which is practicable for them, whose experience does not confirm that the consequences are as described in the encyclical (art. 17), and who therefore think that they cannot agree with this indiscriminate condemnation. Some bishops who are aware of this have kept a respectful but free discussion open in the diocesan Catholic press. For ultimately it is not a question of the revealed deposit of faith, or of an apostolic tradition, and not even of an unambiguous *doctrina constans* in the history of tradition. The "Letter of the German Bishops to All who are Entrusted by the Church with Proclaiming the Faith" (22 September 1967) actually envisages the case of a believer who in the face of a non-infallible doctrinal pronouncement may privately be of the opinion that he already possesses the Church's future and better insight, and consequently thinks he may diverge in his private theory and practice from the present teaching of the Church's magisterium. This appears to be the actual position, as far as *Humanae Vitae* is concerned, not only in the case of individuals but in that of whole groups of people. And to judge by the pattern of opinion within the Church, it can hardly be expected that these groups will gradually come to accept the encyclical. Of course there are also groups of people moving in the opposite direction who, with unheard-of confidence in their mission, object to this passage in the bishops' letter. These events must be regarded as a consequence of "authentic" doctrinal pronouncements having been treated in practice as infallible, while the *consensus* or *non-consensus fidelium* rarely found open expression. Of course this consensus, as Church witness, is not constituted by a manipulated unanimity of the faithful.

5. Long-term forecasts are scarcely possible at present, for most of the bishops' conferences have not yet published their decisions. Probably no absolutely uniform solution can be found, except at the risk of the emigration of a large number of the faithful (perhaps even of schisms) or of failure to observe the Pauline maxim, ". . . whatever does not proceed from faith is sin" (Rom 14:23). For reasons of this kind the bishops of Western Germany discussed the new situation at a special conference (29–30 August 1968). A communiqué and a pastoral statement affirmed the competence of the Church's magisterium in regard to the moral order of married life, and at the same time called for religious obedience to the encyclical (in accordance with *Lumen Gentium,* art. 25) and for correct proclamation and exposition of its teaching. They also promised thorough study of the problems raised, continued exploratory discussion and, with reference to their doctrinal letter of the previous year, respect for responsible conscientious decisions (even on the part of pastors in regard to married people). The Belgian bishops appear to have emphasized personal conscientious conviction even more clearly (30 August 1968). If this is not a mere form of words, its theological meaning is that the doctrinal decision of *Humanae Vitae* is not fully comprehensive, and that in addition to

this qualified but nevertheless limited pronouncement there are also other sources forming the conscience. In a collegial spirit, the German bishops intend to pursue discussions with the Pope and the episcopate of other countries. Some of the faithful place their hopes in this. They think that the juridically systematic understanding of the Church's magisterium should not exclude that personal, courageous initiative which was familiar to the early Church (Gal 2:11). They have in mind a mode of discovering truth through the collaboration of the whole Church, which also includes each individual according to his measure of grace. The answer sought would then be less the conclusion of a long line of theological development than a new start produced by the Spirit. The encyclical, written with a profound sense of responsibility, and necessary and salutary not only as a supplement to *Populorum Progressio* but also for a correct assessment of the *magisterium ordinarium*, will probably prove to be a turning point, at a fateful moment for humanity, for a powerful movement of faith in the Church. The Church for its part carefully respects the dignity of conscience and its free decision (*Gaudium et Spes,* art. 41).

INDEX OF NAMES